An Unpatriotic History of the Second World War

An Unpatriotic History of the Second World War

James Heartfield

Winchester, UK
Washington, USA

First published by Zero Books, 2012
Zero Books is an imprint of John Hunt Publishing Ltd., Laurel House, Station Approach, Alresford, Hants, SO24 9JH, UK
office1@jhpbooks.net
www.johnhuntpublishing.com

For distributor details and how to order please visit the 'Ordering' section on our website.

Text copyright: James Heartfield 2011

ISBN: 978 1 78099 378 2

A CIP catalogue record for this book is available from the British Library.

All pictures from the collection of Murray McDonald unless otherwise stated
Cover image: 'The Procession of the Victims', by John Olday, first published by the Freedom Press, 1943

Design: Stuart Davies

Printed and bound by CPI Group (UK) Ltd, Croydon, CR0 4YY

We operate a distinctive and ethical publishing philosophy in all areas of our business, from our global network of authors to production and worldwide distribution.

CONTENTS

The myth of the Good War

At the conclusion of the First World War, militarism was widely condemned by the intelligentsia, deeply unpopular among working class leaders - a scepticism that entrenched pacifism and socialist anti-militarism in the 1920s and 30s.

In September 1934, US Senator Gerald Nye opened a hearing into the munitions industry in the First World War – the 'merchants of death' – saying: 'when the Senate investigation is over, we shall see that war and preparation for war is not a matter of national honour and national defence, but a matter of profit for the few.' Neutrality Acts in 1935, 1936 and 1937 forbad US citizens from trading arms with belligerents, and from lending to them. In Britain, in 1933 the sons and daughters of the British ruling class at the Oxford Union voted 'That this House will in no circumstances fight for its King and Country'. In July 1935 Dick Sheppard chaired a meeting of 7000 pledge signatories in the Albert Hall – soon 100,000 took the pledge against war. Both the German and Soviet Republics were born out of popular dismay at the losses in the war.

By contrast to the First World War, the Second is seen in retrospect as the Good War. The ideology of the Good War was manufactured from the outset, by radicals who wanted to steer the conduct of the war towards their preferred ends - anti-Fascism, social reform and popular accountability. The entry of the Soviet Union into the war and the mobilisation of partisan armies in Europe reinforced the myth of the Good War. The opening of the death camps identified the Nazi regime with atrocities that allied propagandists never dared allege. Post-war accommodation of popular aspirations like the G.I. Bill and the Home Owners' Loan Corporation in America; or mines nationalisation and the NHS in Britain cemented the perception of a social transformation allied with the People's War. As time passed, the myth of the Good War became even more intense, as all political traditions, East and West derived their popular authority from interpretations of the war.

The People's Democracies of Eastern Europe depended on the

Popular War Against Fascism as their founding myth. British socialists derived their ideology from the 'social revolution' of the war. French and Italian Communists vied with Gaullists and Christian Democrats over ownership of the resistance struggle. All of the permanent members of the UN Security Council derived their status from the allied victory. The Israeli state gave an organisational form to the supposed centrality of the Holocaust to the European disaster. US troops stationed in Germany and Japan were policing the post-war settlement, as were the Soviet Troops in Eastern Europe. All relied on the Good War ideology to justify their status, and continued to manufacture ever more black and white versions of it. Successive war-time anniversaries have become a battleground of interpretation for just that reason.

For all that, the Good War is a myth.

The phrase, 'people's war' was coined by Woodrow Wilson, when he said 'This is a people's war, not a statesmen's.' But Wilson was not talking about the Second World War, he was talking about the First World War, which most people since have come to understand was a General's and a Banker's war.

It was much more common to talk about the Second World War as a People's War. In the Hollywood melodrama of Britain's war, Mrs Miniver, the rector of a bombed church is given this speech

This is not only the war of soldiers in uniform, it is a war of the people – of all people – and it must be fought not only on the battlefield, but in the ... heart of every man, woman and child who loves freedom. This is the people's war. This is our war.

The phrase had been taken up by the Chinese Communists fighting against Japan and was later taken up by many radicals seeking to invest the Second World War with a popular purpose, like the Indian Communists who called their newspaper *The People's War* (though many Indians disagreed). It was true in a sense that whole populations were drawn into the war in a way that they had not been in any previous conflict, and indeed that popular identification with the war aims of the participants was far more important. Still the death toll of more than 60 million, 2.5 per cent of the world's population, suggests that this was a war *against* the people.

The elites that fought the Second World War had enriched themselves at the expense of their own peoples, but still they needed more. They had run out of ideas about how to grow, and their countries were at a standstill. They silenced their critics at home and left their democratic chambers as empty shells. More and more it seemed to those elites as if the barriers they faced were those raised by other countries, and the solutions to their problems were to be found abroad. They denounced each other's trade barriers while raising their own. They demanded territory and resources in far-flung places, and prepared to take or defend them by force. They drove their own people even harder to build the weapons to fight. And they dreamt of seizing the industries of their neighbours. Patriotism turned to hatred for 'the enemy', as it silenced dissent at home.

Russia's entry into the war gave the allies a much needed opportunity to re-brand their war as a 'People's War' against Fascism. Though the Communist Party newspaper the *Daily Worker* had been banned in December 1940, the British took advantage of the change to recruit more radicals into the war effort.

The war when it came was the greatest descent into barbarism ever. Sixty million soldiers and civilians were killed outright, and millions more were starved to death. Under military orders tens of millions were put in the line of fire, dragooned from one end of the world to another in miserable and often terrifying ways. People were enslaved in their millions too, put to work in factories, mines and plantations at gunpoint. Millions more were told where they had to work by officials who fined or imprisoned them if they would not. Almost all the participants put their citizens on rations, sharply cutting back the amount of goods given over to the people, feeding instead their voracious war engines.

At the end of the war eastern and southern Europe was left in the hands of military dictators. Even in Western Europe where ordinary people had fought to free themselves they were disarmed and put under military rule. In the east Vietnam, Korea and Indonesia were invaded a second time and put under European rule. The defeated powers, Germany and Japan faced military occupation and the destruction of their industries. The rest of the world gloated as their 'guilty' people suffered hunger and repression. Not a new beginning, but long years of bitter austerity, not freedom and democracy, but Cold War paranoia and authoritarianism followed the brief victory celebrations.

This is the history of the Second World War that they will not tell you. Instead we have an official, sanitised version, where the Allies fought for freedom and plenty. All the race-hatred, imperial land-grabbing and repression that took place, they tell us, was on the part of the defeated Axis powers, and so ended with the allied victory.

In the defeated, Axis countries, historians have had to confront the myths of their own war propaganda. Though some might prefer to re-write history and reinstate the case for German, Italian or Japanese militarism, most have faced up to the barbarities of those wartime regimes. But the victors, their victory sanctifying the outcome as the best possible, have not had to think about what was done in their name. Retrospectively, it seems that any atrocity is acceptable if it meant bringing a halt to the enemy's worse crimes.

Too often the history of the Second World War is reduced to one defining atrocity: the extermination of six million Jews at the hands of the German authorities. There is no doubt that this was an act of unparalleled barbarism. But sadly the massacre of defenceless citizens was not unique, but common to all the participants. What is more, racial purification and racial oppression were means that the Nazis copied from authorities in America and the British Empire. That the architects of the Final Solution were executed, while those of the Bengal Famine, the massacre at Katyn and the bombings of Dresden and Hiroshima were decorated, was Victor's Justice. That history still remembers the one, and turns away from the other, is Victor's History.

The custodians of Victor's History tell us that it is wrong to compare the atrocities done by the Axis with those of the Allies. 'Moral equivalence', they say, must not be allowed. That is the deadly logic of warfare – 'my country, right or wrong'. But equivalence is what morality means: equivalence between all people, no matter which country they come from; that they should be judged by their deeds, not by the colours of their flags.

Strip away the national and racial labels. Look beneath the fog of war. The Second World War was a class war. It was a war where the governing elite lorded over those who worked in factories and fields.

4

'A bayonet is a weapon with a worker at either end' runs the old slogan. The American financier Jay Gould's answer to the challenge of industrial labour was 'I can hire one half of the working class to kill the other half'. In 1939 the capitalist elite had run out of answers, and lived in fear of the great mass of working people that made their millions. Their solution was to get one half of the working class to kill the other half. The elite said 'obey us, or join the enemy'. This is what came to be known afterwards as 'the People's War', a war that saw sixty million of the people slaughtered, and the rest put under martial law, while Generals became Kings and arms manufacturers became as rich as Croesus.

I am grateful to Ian Abley, Floyd Codlin, Phil Cunliffe, Neil Davenport, Paul Ennis, Freedom Press, Tariq Goddard, Trevor Greenfield, Stuart Davies, Solomon Hughes, Patrick Hughes, Mick Hume, Eve Kay, Brendan O'Neill, Peter Ramsay, Josephine Berry Slater, and James Woudhuysen for encouragement and comments on earlier versions of the text and for help with research.

PART ONE

THE MEANING OF THE WAR

Chapter One

The War in the Factories

The labour question was not an afterthought in the Second World War. It was the greatest question of all. The victors in the national struggle were those who best mobilised their domestic workers and so best equipped their armies. The net impact of the war on the working class was that more of them worked much harder, and got paid less. Even in the biggest and most successful wartime economy, the US, personal consumption fell from 72 per cent of output in 1938 to 51 per cent in 1945.

At the same time, the numbers in work grew by ten million and hours increased by a quarter. All of that excess production was going somewhere: it was going to fight the war. The sheer waste is beyond our wildest dreams. But the waste was not hurting everyone. Business, especially US business, was reborn through the war effort. Like business across the globe, they needed new markets for the great amount of goods they made. The war fixed that.

Destructive as it was, the war laid the basis for new industry. Plant created in Detroit and Dagenham, the Urals and Silesia during the war would lay the basis for the post-war boom. 'A nazi public utility like Volkswagen, or private utility like Daimler-Benz, laid down plant and equipment in the 1930s (and early 1940s) that would form the basis for post-war growth', says Mark Mazower.[1] Even in Soviet Russia 55 per cent of the national income was given over to war production that would be the basis of industrialisation after.[2]

Before one shot could be fired in the Second World War the bullets and the rifles, the uniforms, the trains and lorries to carry the soldiers, the steel to supply the munitions factories, the coal to furnace the steel, the oil to power the engines all had to be made, dug and drilled by another army, the industrial workforce. In the decade from 1935 to 1945 the warring nations turned their factories into engines of destruction. Between 1933 and 1936 US armaments spending rose from $628 million to $1161 million,[3] by 1942 government awarded $100 billion to US business in military contracts.[4] Between them, the Allied and Axis powers built

49,799,000 guns, rifles and pistols, 1,881,600 tanks and 8,820,000 ships between 1942 and 1944.[5] The growth in output was phenomenal. Aircraft production was more than twenty times greater in 1944 than in 1935.

AIRCRAFT PRODUCTION [6]

	1935	1939	1941	1943	1944
Germany	3183	8295	11 776	24 807	39 807
Italy	1000	2000	2400	1600	0
Japan	952	4467	5088	16 693	28 180
United Kingdom	1140	7940	23 672	26 263	26 641
USA	459	2195	26 277	85 898	96 318
USSR	3578	10 832	15 735	34 900	40 300

To get this much out of industry, factories had to be placed under military discipline - not just in the Fascist countries, but in the democracies, too.

The war changed the balance between labour and capital. Most think that it shifted the balance in labour's favour. The real lesson of the Second World War was that it crushed the independent organisations of the working class. In the Axis countries they were taken apart, before being re-made as company unions by the occupying powers. In the Allied countries, unions lost their independence and became recruiting sergeants for the war effort.

In 1935 the Nazi regime began a compulsory system of workbooks. One copy was held by the employer, another by the labour exchange. Workers were barred from leaving named key sectors, like aircraft and metal production.[7] The September 1937 Nazi Party Rally of Labour announced rearmament and public works schemes under a four-year plan, and the following year Goering's decree for Securing Labour for Tasks of Special State Importance effectively conscripted labour. Within a year 1.9 million workers had been subject to compulsory work orders.[8] Japan passed a General Mobilisation Law in 1938. Japanese civilians were barred from leaving work without the say-so of the local office of the National Employment Agency, under the Employee Turnover Prevention Ordinance (1940), and given work books from March 1941.[9]

In January 1940 the British Cabinet agreed to Ernest Bevin's proposals for a Register of Protected Establishments, and in March for a Register of Employment Order. Men up to the age of 46 had to be registered by 1941. Most agreed to reassignment after a talking to at the Labour Exchange, but one million directions had been issued by 1945, 80 000 to women. Under the Essential Work Order, workers were forbidden from leaving their jobs without permission - thirty thousand orders were made, covering six million workers. In 1943 12,500 people were found guilty of breaking a Control of Employment Order. In this way Bevin boosted the armaments industry so that it ate up 37 per cent of the workforce - up from 30 per cent in a year.[10] These were the people who sweated to make Vickers-Armstrong, ICI and Hawker-Siddeley into world class businesses.

Under New Zealand's National Service Emergency Act of 1942 it was an offence to leave or be 'absent from work without a reasonable excuse' in 'essential industries'.[11] Australia's government wanted to direct labour but did not dare to overturn the rights of its States. In America the War Manpower Commission's Chief Paul McNutt drew up a Worker Draft Bill that would have let him send labour to the North American Aviation Plant in Texas, and other war industries.[12] In the event, America's business lobby won the government over to the idea that they could recruit labour. In fact they signed up 17 million new workers between 1940 and 1944.[13] But as in Australia, the American authorities still kept butting in to regiment the factories - still they kept employers sweet with war contracts worth billions.

In June 1941 Soviet authorities assumed the right to direct labour to war industries, and over the next six months a number of decrees put first munitions and then all workers under military discipline. Leaving work was punishable by between five and eight years imprisonment, and a labour draft was in place for men aged between 16 and 55, women between 16 and 50.[14] In the war one million were tried and convicted of absenteeism – 300 000 sent to the Gulag by military tribunals. Penalties were harshest in munitions but still 200 000 were convicted of leaving each year. One tenth of steel workers would quit each year.[15]

In 1941, Roosevelt helped war profiteers by banning strikes and taking away labour legislation protections in the armaments industry.[16] As a sop, he set up a War Labor Board that could hear worker's complaints on 12 January 1942. In 1935 he had made a dispute procedure, the National Labour Relations Board, which barred wildcat strikes. In Britain Order 1305 banned strikes.[17] In New Zealand Emergency Regulations of October 1939 banned strikes and inciting strikes.[18] In Nazi Germany a law on the National Organisation of Labour imposed the fuehrer-principle on the "shop community", with workers cast as "followers", while a Court of Honour heard labour disputes.[19] By 1944 some 87,000 Germans had been jailed for breaking workplace rules, and in 1943 5,336 of them were put to death.[20] The model was Mussolini's Italy, where workers and bosses were put in the same corporations, and 'strikes, protest demonstrations and even verbal criticism of the government were illegal'.[21] The battle between labour and capital that had raged between the wars was settled when governments all over came down firmly on the side of industry.

Once they had clocked-off workers were not free from extra duties for the war effort. Before the war started, and unemployment

'Give 'em both barrels', by Jean Carlu for the US Office of Emergency Management

was high, governments had experimented with different kinds of Labour Service to keep people busy. The Civilian Conservation Corps (1935) took a quarter of a million Americans off the unemployment register and put them to work clearing forests and building dams. In Germany, the Nazis forced everyone to do the Labour Service that had been set up for those out of work. In wartime this kind of compulsory volunteering became the norm. Herbert Morrison made six million Britons Fire Guards, who had to put in one night a week.[22]

Under the discipline of war, hours spent working for the boss were ratcheted up. Roosevelt twisted arms to get rid of American workers' overtime payments.[23] 'Let us work and work harder' was defence Commissioner Knudsen's blunt slogan.[24] In France the average working week went up from 35 hours in 1940 to 46.2 hours in March 1944 [25] and decree laws increased hours in the armament industries to 60 a week.[26] 'Resentment of the working classes at the 40 per cent levy imposed by the Government on overtime pay' was 'serious'.[27] French cabinet minister Paul Reynaud told the Chamber of Deputies that 'to conquer the enemy we must first conquer ourselves' – meaning conquer organised labour.[28] In New Zealand workers lost overtime and holiday entitlements, and hours were put up to 48 on the farms and 54 in defence factories.[29] In Germany, defence workers were put on a seventy-hour week,[30] and a ceiling was put on wages in 1938.[31] British men worked 47.7 hours a week in 1938, rising to 52.9 in 1943,[32] but in a Factory Inspectorate survey of war plants, the sixty-hour week was the norm for men and women.[33] Japanese authorities extended the working day to 11 or 12 hours in heavy industry.[34] In the USSR, three hours overtime was made mandatory (two hours for 12-16 year olds), and holidays cancelled. The working week for public employees went up from 48 hours in June 1940 to 55 in June 1941.[35]

The BBC's Music While You Work helped output, but in 1943 Roy Christison was arrested by the FBI for cutting the cable to the loudspeaker that played swing music at his shipyard though his workmates backed the protest.[36] Reichmusicführer Baldur von Blodheim published rules for the playing of Jazz, that said 'preference is to be given to brisk compositions as opposed to slow ones (the so-called blues); however, the pace must not exceed a certain degree of allegro commensurate with the Aryan sense for discipline and moderation'.[37]

A sign that people were working harder was the rise in workplace injuries. In Germany from 1933 to 1940 accidents and illnesses at work rose from 929 000 cases to 2 253 000, occupational diseases from 11 000 cases to 23 000 and fatalities from 217 to 525 (outstripping the growth in employment from 13.5 to 20.8 million).[38] So, too, in the US, 'long hours in hastily constructed industrial plants increased the rate of industrial accidents'.[39]

Putting workers under army-like orders could happen because of the sacrifices made by the army. Civilians knew that if they stepped out of line, there was harsher work waiting for them in the army. The US Army was 11.4 million strong at its highest, the German 9.5 million, the Japanese 7.7 million, the British five million, the Italian 3.8 million and the Soviet 12.2 million.[40]

Slave labourers at Dachau concentration camp

As well as moral pressure, bans on strikes, greater hours, telling people where to go, business also got the benefit of forced labour in civilian production. Most extensive was German forced labour from occupied Europe. Six million were sent from Holland (500 000), France, Poland (1,000,000), Czechoslovakia, Yugoslavia Ukraine and Russia to slave in factories and offices in the Third Reich. Along with allied prisoners of war and German Jews, there were 7 128 000 forced workers in 1944.[41] The conditions for these slave workers were terrible, and for some, just the beginning of the end. The Japanese drafted thousands of young workers into industry under the General Mobilization Law.

The Allies used forced labour, too. Forty-eight thousand men aged 18 to 25 were sent down Britain's mines between 1943 and 1948. Twenty-one thousand seventeen year-olds forced to dig. They were called the 'Bevin Boys' after Labour Minister Ernest Bevin. One in every ten that were called up for National Service in the Army were sent to the mines – after their ID numbers were 'pulled out of Ernie Bevin's hat'. More than a third appealed, and a few were jailed for refusing.[42] Conscientious Objectors, if they managed to convince a board of their sincerity, would then be forced to work in mines or on the land. Worse than the Bevin Boys's deal, though, was that of the forced workers in the Empire, which we look at later. The Soviet Union's forced labour prisons, the Gulags, had 3.5 million inmates at the outbreak of war, though the number fell back as it went on.[43] One in five of the Gulag population died during the war as rations were cut back, while output demanded of them was pushed up by eighty per cent. One million prisoners served in 'penal battalions'[44] The NKVD secret police offered 250 000 prisoners to industries for work, so that 'few industries and enterprises were without slave contingents'.[45]

Prisoners of war were used as forced labour by everyone, despite the Geneva Convention. The Japanese made British and American captives into labour details - most infamously at Tamarkan; Germans enslaved Russian prisoners of war; Italian POWs worked Scottish farms; US Serviceman Kurt Vonnegut was put on a detail clearing bodies from the cellars of the firebombed city of Dresden, while the captured Italian partisan Primo Levi avoided the gas chambers by working as a chemist's assistant at Buna. And after the war, the Allies made defeated Germans slaves. British and American forces gave the French 55 000 and 800 000 prisoners respectively. Britain took 400 000 German prisoners back home to work. America had some 600 000 at work in Europe and America.[46]

A new division of labour

Business recruited a whole new labour force during the war. The people working the lathes, hammering the rivets, directing the traffic, ploughing the farms were not the same people they had been. Apart from skilled workers in protected trades, the male core of the working class was sent to war. Others - women, minorities, young people, migrant labour - were recruited to fill the gaps. These new workers were easier to handle at first and worked harder to prove themselves.

Roosevelt put ten million men into the American Army, and six million more women into the workforce. In 1940 one quarter of all workers were women, by 1945 more than a third were women (a share not repeated until 1960). Two fifths of workers in the airframe industry were women, and the United Auto Workers had 250 000 women members, the United Electrical Workers 300 000.

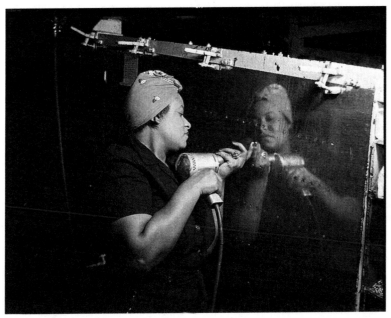

Working a hand drill at Vultee-Nashville, Tennessee, on an A-31 Vengeance dive bomber, February 1943

Between 1942 and 1945 the number of black Americans in work tripled. The number working in industry grew one and a half times to 1 250 000 (300 000 of them women). The number of black people working as civil servants grew from 60 000 to 200 000. The great migration of black Americans from the rural South to Northern cities changed America. One million six hundred thousand, black and white, moved north - but then people were moving everywhere. Between 1940 and 1947 more than a fifth of the country, 25 million people, moved county, and four and a half million moved from the farm to the city for good.[47]

Britain was the first country ever to introduce conscription for women, and they were given the choice of war work instead. Those who refused could be fined up to five pounds a day, or imprisoned. [48] Two million more women were put to work in the war, a growth of 40 per cent. In 1941 the Ministry of Labour worked out that four fifths of all single women aged 14 to 49 were at work or in the services. Among wives and widows, two fifths were working, but only thirteen per cent of those with children under 14 did. [49] Over 300 000 worked in the explosive and chemical industry, more than half their workforce, a million and a half in engineering and metal industries, 100 000 on the railways, thousands more on farms as part of the Women's Land Army. [50]

Germany did not put many more women to work, even when war production minister Albert Speer begged the Fuhrer to in 1942, but in 1943 new laws called for the registration of all women aged 17 to 45. These laws came too late to make a difference. Instead, Germany made up its shortfall of factory hands by bringing in six million foreign labourers from occupied Europe.[51] From 1943 on Speer changed the policy of bringing war workers in, by putting them to work making goods for the German war effort - but in France, the Netherlands, Czechoslovakia and Poland. This had the advantage that factories in France were less likely to be bombed.

Speer's economic plan for Europe was a late flowering of the Grossdeutsche Reich that shows us one more way that the working class was re-made through the war. As well as a new division of labour at home, the war created a new international division of labour, too. This international division of labour was less driven by free trade than it was by forced seizure. Germany did not only wring labour from its occupied states. It took grain from Greece and Poland, oil from Rumania and the Caucasus, manufactured goods from France, Holland and Norway. The one-way traffic made a mockery of the Fascist Internationalism that Norway's pro-Nazi figurehead Vikdun Quisling dreamt about. In that way the work of yet millions more beyond Germany's pre-war borders were made to serve the German industry. In the Japanese Co-Prosperity Sphere four million Koreans and ten million Javanese were drafted into work by the Japanese authorities on plantations and some 200 000 were relocated for special projects like the Thai Burma Railroad. A further 365 000 Koreans were seconded by the Japanese Army for military and civilian work, while 200 000 were prostituted as 'Comfort Women'. [52]

The Allies made a much deeper international division of labour too, firstly by the lend-lease programme that made America the 'Arsenal of Democracy'. Lend-lease extended free credit to Britain and other allies, without worrying too much about the terms of repayment. It was a brilliant way of getting American industry back to work, just when it was sliding back into recession. America's surplus output would be sent off to Europe, and the higher cause of war would put off the awkward point when the goods had to be paid for. This is the beginning of the system that made Ford, Chrysler, Douglas, IBM and Pan Am into world-beating businesses after the war.

Labour's reaction

In the ten years from 1935 to 1945 the working classes across the world were pushed harder and in greater numbers to produce much more. Those changes would not have been possible without a shift in the terms between workers and bosses - not just on a plant by plant basis, but country-wide, and world-wide. That shift happened worldwide. But its terms were not the same country by country. The difference between the national terms of the deal between capital and labour are the key to the broader differences between the fascist countries and the democracies.

The NSDAP in Germany, like Mussolini's Fascist party had come to power on a programme of crushing bolshevism - which was a code for crushing the labour movement (its more militant activists being Communists). In March 1933 the Dutch anarchist Marinus van der Lubbe – not knowing that he had been set up by the NDSAP to do it – burned down the parliament building. One hundred thousand Communists, Social Democrats and trade unionists were put in new concentration camps, and 600 killed. On May Day 1933 the leaders of the Trade Unions marched behind the Swastika, hoping to curry favour with the Nazis. On the 2nd of May union offices were occupied by brown shirts, the premises and assets seized by emergency decree.[53] The working class were made to kneel before the Fuhrer or get sent to the camps, and their own unions were broken up.

Nazi Robert Ley led a substitute Labour Front that, being based on workplace subscriptions like the unions it replaced, was much bigger than the Nazis' old union faction the NSBO. Indeed the Labour Front quickly became one of the weightiest bodies in the Nazi state, with a lot of room to manoeuvre. The Nazis thought that they were different from the other right-wing parties because they were carrying the German worker with them, not just taking a whip to him. The masses did support the war, most of all in the early years of victory, and they joined in the big rallies. But there was a gap between rulers and ruled that, ironically, made the fascist state the less efficient at war-time mobilisation.[54]

Before Germany's Labour Front, Italy had its own Fascist Unions, and Labour Minister Alfredo Rocco said that 'the organisation of the unions must be a means of disciplining the unions'. Under Mussolini 'strikes, protest demonstrations and even verbal criticism of government policies were illegal'. For the first years after the disso-lution of the free unions, workers were resentful of the Fascist unions put in their place. During the 1930s, though, membership of the state-sponsored unions grew (and were even a focus for real discontent). But years of austerity cost Italy's leaders what little loyalty they had.[55]

In Japan there was strife in the workplace between the wars, but union membership was only 6.8 per cent of the workforce. The Sanpo (short for Sangyo Hokokukai) movement that wanted respect for workers' industrial contribution to the nation very quickly took the union's place covering 70 per cent of the workforce, or 5.5 million members at its height in 1942. Started by some right-wing union leaders and intellectuals, Sanpo was pushed onto employers first by the Aichi Prefecture Police Department, and then later the Labor

Ministry. Sanpo set up workplace committees to talk through problems. Very quickly Sanpo turned into a semi-official body that dealt mostly with absenteeism, productivity and efficiency. The workers' keenness at the start turned to distrust.[56]

In Britain, the deal between labour and government was different from the German one. Instead of just coercion, the government and the bosses got the leaders of the trade unions onside. The trade union officials' support for the war was strong. Engineers' Union (AEU) president Jack Tanner - who had fought bitter battles with employers in the first world war - was thrilled:

This is an engineer's war … It is a machine war with a vengeance. Whether it is in the anti-aircraft defences or the machines on land and sea, or in the sky, it is the engineer who stands behind them all.[57]

Seats on Joint Production Committees lured trade unionists to give their all for the war effort. These were set up to plan ways of boosting output, and after Germany invaded the Soviet Union in 1941, British Communists got behind them. A deal between the AEU and the Engineering Employers Federation brokered by Ernest Bevin in March 1942 founded JPCs in the Royal Ordinance Factories, and that month 180 JPCs answered an AEU survey. 'Once the political conviction of the workers has been won', Walter Swanson told the Engineering Allied Trades Shop Stewards Committee, 'they will display an initiative, drive and energy to increase production never witnessed in this country before'.[58]

Before the Japanese attack on Pearl Harbour (7 December 1941) the Roosevelt government was tilting towards the use of force to control Labour. When the United Auto Workers struck out Allis-Chalmers in early 1941 the Office of Production Management (OPM) and Navy Secretary Frank Knox ordered the men back to work, and police in armoured cars opened fire on picket lines. Then in June a strike at North American Aviation prompted President Roosevelt to open the plant by force, using 3500 federal troops to quell this national emergency.[59] The government's despotic moves were tough for the Confederation of Industrial Organisations (CIO) to take. Though its membership was more militant that the rival, craft-based

American Federation of Labour, its leaders had tried hard to win influence in Roosevelt's New Deal administration, supporting the National Labor Relations Board. After Pearl Harbour, the CIO got patriotic and offered a 'No Strike' pledge. Leader Philip Murray told the CIO convention two weeks later: 'I say to the government of the United States of America, the national CIO is here with its heart, its mind, its body ... prepared to make whatever sacrifices are necessary.'[60] British Brigadier General George Cockerill told the *New York Times* that in England and America it was 'an enormous asset that men whom labour trusts should now be lending their aid in invoking a ready response to longer hours, fewer, if any, holidays, and unaccustomed restrictions'. [61]

The no-strike pledge worked - at least for the first two years of the war - and strikes were down. Roosevelt used the no-strike pledge to take away overtime and weekend work payments. In April 1942 Roosevelt summoned CIO and AFL leaders to a 'War Cabinet' and told them they would have voluntary wage stabilization. He told a meeting of Shipyard Owners, government officials and union officers in May 'the full percentage wage increase for which your contracts call, and to which by the letter of the law you are entitled, is irreconcilable with the national policy to control the cost of living'.[62] To make the wage freeze work for the union leaders, if not their members, Roosevelt introduced a 'Maintenance of Membership' Clause, preventing workers from moving unions to get a better deal. Unions collaborated in the wartime recruitment, and the combined membership of the AFL and CIO rose from 8 944 000 in 1940 to 14 796 000 in 1944.[63] The War Production Board set up 1700 labour-management production committees at the prompting of the (CIO) on the understanding that they were 'solely to increase morale and boost production'.[64]

Chapter Two

Rationing

As well as working more people harder for longer, business and government worked together to hold down their wages - so boosting industry's operating profits.

Holding down wages was not easy because putting so many more people to work ought to have pushed wages up. In fact, in cash terms, weekly wages did go up. But on closer inspection we find that hourly wages tended to go down. People were working for much longer hours, sometimes giving up their time for free, often losing out on overtime payments. What increases there were in wages did not keep pace with the increase in output.

Also, the increase in cash wages did not buy more consumer goods. Governments intervened in the economy to grow the armaments and industrial firms not those that made consumer goods. People had more cash, but less to spend it on. Price rises swallowed up the bigger wage packets, and government war bonds soaked up the growth in savings. As they regimented the workplace to increase productivity, governments regimented social life, too, to keep consumer spending down, the better to boost investment in industry.

In Germany and Italy, the fascist governments drove wages down early on - by more than a quarter in Germany between 1933 and 1935, and by half in Italy, between 1927 and 1932.[1] In the first year of Nazi rule, Krupp A.G.'s wage bill fell by two million RM while the workforce grew by 7762, I.G. Farben got a third more workers with just a 1.5 per cent bigger wage bill.[2] After that, wages rose in Germany until the outbreak of the war, when living standards were cut again.[3] Even then, though weekly earnings rose by a quarter between 1932 and 1938, hourly rates were marginally down over the same period.[4] So it was in Britain between 1938 and 1943, where people had more cash in their pockets 'not because their rates were relatively better, but because they were putting in more hours'.[5] Americans, too, were earning their extra wages by working more - by 1945 their hours were up by a quarter on 1938. Japanese industrial pay was cut by a fifth under the Wage Control Ordinances of 1939 and 1940.[6] Italians' wages came to a standstill under the Fascists, so that by 1941 they were just 113 per cent of what they had been in 1913.[7] By the end of the war, under the Allies, consumption was only three quarters of what it had been in 1938, and the number of calories Italians had a day had fallen to 1747.[8] In Vichy and Occupied France real wages went down as wage controls proved much more effective than price controls.[9]

In America, a bigger wage bill was not matched by more goods in the shops, so business just put up prices to claw the money back. Around munitions plants housing was in short supply, transport was overcrowded and shop windows empty. The Department of Labor worked out that the 80 per cent rise in cash wages between 1941 and 1945 was only a twenty per cent rise when inflation and shortages were taken into account. A Union of Autoworkers local official Jess Ferrazza explained that though 'workers were drawing fairly good salaries... there were not too many things that it could be spent on'.[10] *Fortune* reported from Pittsburgh 'to the workers it's a Tantalus situation: the luscious fruits of prosperity above their heads - receding as they try to pick them'.[11] Though they ate well enough, their clothes and household goods were shabbier as real incomes stagnated.[12] In Britain, too, more cash wages chased fewer goods to push prices up by half as much again between 1939 and 1941.[13] In Germany, living costs were pushed up by a law allowing cartels to fix prices in 1935,[14] and by 1941 household spending was down by a fifth from its already low point in 1938.[15]

John Maynard Keynes' pamphlet *How to Win the War* set out the argument that the working class consumption would have to be cut back just as the greater demand for war workers would ordinarily push their wages up. Keynes' friend Josiah Stamp explained 'the war can only be paid for by annexing a large part of the increased purchasing power of the wage earning class and also encroaching on the pre-war standard of living'.[16] Trade Union representatives 'will be unable to escape the conclusion that sacrifices will have to be made by the British working class', editorialised *The Economist*.[17] In *The Times*, Keynes wrote that 'the workers must not make a greater immediate demand on the national resources than hitherto', adding: 'the community may have to ask of them a reduction'.[18] 'You have got to suffer the reduction one way or another' Keynes wrote to the Labour Party leaders – and they chose rationing because it would seem to mean an 'equality of sacrifice' on the part of all social classes – though of course, wealthy people easily ate 'off the ration', at restaurants, that Chamberlain had exempted.[19]

'In the restaurants of the great hotels the privileged few could, and did, chomp and guzzle their way towards the armistice without forfeiting a single coupon', explains John Carey. Protestors rallied outside the Savoy with banners that read 'Ration the Rich' and 'Our children must not starve'. On the night of 14 September 1940 a group of Stepney workers and their families pushed their way into the Savoy's bomb shelter as the air-raid warning rang out – so that they could shelter beside the Duke and Duchess of Kent, and demanded their fair share of the tea and toast served up on silver trays. The following night the police were waiting to make sure that the action did not happen again.[20] 'If you are asked to lessen your consumption of bacon and sugar, remember that you are making available space in ships which can be used for iron ore or machine tools', Chamberlain said to a crowd at the Mansion House on 9 January 1940.[21]

The link between austerity measures under Fascism and in the democracies was noticed. In January 1941, radical journalist Claud Cockburn wrote in his newsletter *The Week*:

> The German government – like the British government – has of course been making the most strenuous efforts to prevent the rise of working class earnings ('in the national interest') partly by an actual restriction of the possibilities of consumption, partly by a direct attack on earnings.

Cockburn, like Keynes, understood that they were trying to stop what had happened in the last war, that war workers had held out for better pay to match the longer hours.

> Both the British and German governments, in their attempt to prevent a rise in working class wages, or in any way to defend their policies, are forced, naturally enough, to accuse the leadership of those who resist of "Fifth Columnism" – just as in

the last war the engineers on the Clyde and the German navy mutineers at Hamburg ... were accused of being "agents of the enemy" by their respective governments.[22]

The police seized the following issue of *The Week* – the newsletter had been banned by order of the government.

Governments grabbed worker's unspent cash for the war effort - handing it straight back to industry as payment on war contracts. In 1942 Americans were strong-armed to putting one tenth of their wages into war bonds, and in 1943 were taxed at source for the first time, a five per cent victory tax.[23] Britons, too, felt the moral squeeze to put their money into National Savings at War Weapons Week (1941) Warship Weeks (1941 and 1942) Wings for Victory Weeks (two in 1943) and Salute the Soldier Week (1944). And like their American comrades, seven million manual workers had their first taste of Income Tax, when Pay As You Earn deductions were begun.[24] In Germany, where a War Bond issue had fallen flat in 1938, government raided the Sparkassen savings banks where people kept their spare cash for eight billion Reichsmarks in 1940 and 12.8 billion in 1941.[25]

The greatest cut in working class income came through rationing. Food and clothing was rationed in Germany in the first two weeks of the war.[26] In Britain meat, eggs, milk, butter and sugar were rationed from January 1940, canned meat, fish and vegetables from November 1941, followed by dried fruit and grains in January 1942, canned fruit and vegetables the following month, condensed milk and breakfast cereal in April, syrup in July, biscuits in August and Oatflakes and rolled oats by the end of 1942.[27] German rations were a healthy 2570 calories for German civilians in 1939, but a cut in 1942 was found by scientists to lead to a loss of body fat in factory workers.[28] It was under the Allies that German workers fared worst: their rations were cut to 1100 calories in the American and British Zones.[29] When the Nazis cut German civilian rations, they starved the Ostarbeiter in German factories, and in 1940 rations for occupied Poles stood at 938 calories, while Jews rations were cut from 503 to 369.[30] Italians' food was rationed from 1941. In Japan the rice ration of 0.736 pints was slowly adulterated with husks, and the standard calorie allowance cut from 2400 in 1941 to 1800 in 1945.[31] Soviet citizens household consumption had already been cut back to fund rearmament between 1937 and 1940. They saw their calorific intake fall from 3370 per head in 1940 to 2555 in 1942 after rationing was brought in, in July 1941.[32] Food for workers was kept down so that more could be given over to building up industry.

The rationing schemes in Britain and Germany were envied by US administrators, like Harry Hopkins, who warned Americans 'You Will be Mobilized':

Through forced savings and taxes, our spending will be limited and priorities far more widespread that at present will determine the kinds of food, clothing, housing and businesses which we will have, and will affect every detail of our daily lives. We should not be permitted to ride on a train, make a long distance telephone call, or send a telegram without evidence that these are necessary.[33]

To hold working class living standards down, authorities in Britain and Germany ordered their lives outside the factory as well as in. The German Strength through Joy clubs laid on theatre and exhibition visits, concerts, sport and hiking groups, dances, films and adult education courses. Strength through Joy's supported tourism was widely admired, though professional rather than working class members generally bagged the cruises. Its assets included two ocean liners and a car dealership, though delivery on instalments for the new people's car - Volkswagen - never materialised.[34]

In Britain, the Entertainments National Service Association gave dinner-hour shows for factory workers. Shakespearean actors did pit-village shows for the Council for the Encouragement of Music and the Arts. Soon every hour of the day was planned, with CEMA-funded exhibitions by the Artists International Association, or a well-earned local authority Holiday at Home. Like the Strength through Joy clubs, people remember the comradeship at the workplace concerts and lectures with happiness. Still, these cultural offerings were laid on to cut the costs of out-of-work pastimes and keep the men and women happy at their benches and desks -

working to win the war, and enrich their employers.

Propaganda put 'guns before butter' - in the infamous words of Hitler's propaganda minister Joseph Goebbels, parodied by John Heartfield in a 1935 poster. In Italy a pompous Mussolini had told the Chamber of Deputies in 1934 that 'we are approaching a period in which mankind will find its equilibrium on a lower standard of life'.[35] The Japanese press lauded the Aichi Watch Company's new 'family wage system' as 'livelihood, family-oriented wages' as distinct from the 'western, selfish, individualistic, skill-based wages'.[36] 'Consumer goods production was reduced', says the Soviet war historian G. Deborin. 'The motto was: "Everything for the front, everything for victory!"'[37]

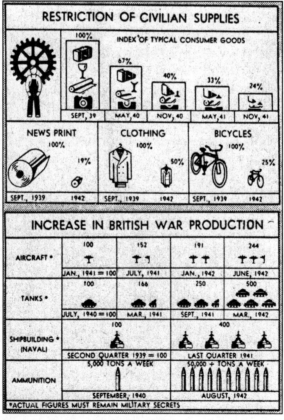

A Ministry of Information poster telling the American public how Britons were going hungry to feed the arms industry

John Heartfield, 'Hurray, the butter is gone!' 1935 © The Heartfield Community of Heirs/VG Bild-Kunst, Bonn and DACS, London 2012.

Cutting back on household goods changed the balance of industry. Businesses and factories that were making goods for home use were changed over to munitions, guns, uniforms, tanks and aeroplanes.

In America Walter Reuther of the Union of Auto Workers put forward a plan to convert car plants to war work. Though Auto Executives smarted at being told what to do by the Socialist leader, by 1943 'about 66 per cent of all pre-war machine production had been converted to aircraft production'.[38] Between 1938 and 1944 the output of Germany's consumer goods industry fell from 31 per cent of all output to just 22 per cent.[39] In Britain, output of beef and veal fell by a sixth, eggs by a half and pigmeat by two-thirds[40] Soviet workers in civilian goods and services were cut by 60 per cent.[41] In Leningrad toy factories were turned over to grenades, musical instrument shops to anti-tank mines, in Moscow bicycle factories tried their hand at flame throwers while typewriter manufacturers made automatic rifles.[42]

In the summer of 1942, economist Simon Kuznets at the War Production Board wrote a paper warning that US military buying had gone too far. One reckoning was that if all army and navy orders were met then civilian consumption would have to fall to 60 per cent of its level *in 1932* – in the depth of the recession. Vice President Henry Wallace wondered whether 'the public could be brought to accept such a reduction'.[43]

Workers' wages were held down even though the factories were full. That made sure a greater share of the national wealth went to the war, and to business.

Chapter Three

Military Industrial Complex

'In the councils of government, we must guard against the acquisition of unwarranted influence, whether sought or unsought, by the military-industrial complex' Dwight D Eisenhower, Farewell Address, 17 January 1961

As national rivalry heated up in the 1930s governments spent more on arms. In the depths of recession arms spending had a striking outcome. The economic writer Paul Einzig explained in 1934

> Until comparatively recently it was considered the supreme task of mankind, in the sphere of economics to produce more so as to be able to improve the standard of living of consumers. Any raw material and labour spend on armament was considered a dead loss because it reduced the volume of goods available for consumption.

But

> It is no longer production that has to make desperate efforts to keep up with consumption; it is consumption that is lagging far behind productive capacity, and even behind actual production.

Einzig's argument takes a strange turn:

> In such circumstances disarmament means the reduction of the world's capacity and willingness to consume, while rearmament means an increase of that capacity. All rearmament does is to absorb part of the surplus products which would otherwise be unsaleable in our present economic system.

Moreover

> So long as the problem of adjusting the world's capacity of

consumption and the world's capacity of production to each other is left unsolved, any demand for goods, no matter how artificial and unproductive, is calculated, on balance to benefit trade.[1]

For sure, the trade of the big armaments companies benefited from the sabre-rattling – and even governments were glad to see some industry get up off its feet, even if it was down to government spending. The man whose name is most often linked to this road out of recession, John Maynard Keynes, himself granted that 'cynics ... conclude that nothing except a war can bring a major slump to its conclusion'.[2] The Economist reported the 'stimulating effect of armament orders in Europe, America and Japan, and that there are many cases where the "rearmament industries" are the only ones that are doing well'. Like many, the *Economist* was most alarmed by Germany's rearmament, though accepting that 'the case of Germany differs from that of other countries only in degree'. The *Economist* rightly saw this military Keynesianism as 'sinister because nations will obviously be' reluctant to agree to cut back on arms spending 'if it should emerge that they are the only cause of renewed activity in a world in a state of depression'. These militaristic interests, worried the *Economist* 'depend for their existence on the maintenance of political unrest', having been born out of 'political tension'.[3]

The second Four Year Plan of 1936 in Germany saw 'the economic regime of the bourgeoisie placed in rigid symbiosis with the Nazi Party, the Gestapo [**Ge**heime **Sta**ats**po**lizei] and the State bureaucracy' as Goering's Air Ministry took control of industry.[4] That was the judgement of Alfred Sohn-Rethel, who worked as an analyst at the big business association, the Mitteleuropäischer Wirtschaftstag, before fleeing to Britain in 1936. Economic historian Adam Tooze says that what emerged was 'an alliance between Hitler's regime and the leading elements of German industrial capitalism' – 'it seemed that the Communists and Social Democrats had a point' Tooze adds: 'The Nazi regime was a "Dictatorship of the Bosses".'[5] In December 1939 Hitler made his Fuehrerforderung, or Fuehrer's challenge of an eight-fold increase in ammunition output – taking that up to 70 per cent of all arms spending by 1940. The businesses that met the targets were the Vereinigte Stahlwerke, Krupp, Kloeckner and the Reichswerke Hermann Goering – a massive combine of steel manufacturers pulled together by government fiat.[6]

Air Ministry orders boosted the aircraft makers Arado, Heinkel Dornier, Focke-Wulf, Bayerische Flugzeugwerke (Messerschmitt) and greatest of all Junkers. From 1933 to 1935 the air workforce grew from 4000 to 54,000. To make sure of their control of the largest firm, Dr Hugo Junkers was arrested on 17 October 1933 on made up treason charges, and held till he signed over his holdings to the Reich.[7] The Air Ministry also boosted I.G. Farben with a contract to build a plant at Leuna to make 200,000 tons of air fuel each year.

Economic Minister Walther Funk promised German industrialists, fearful of nationalisation that 'nothing could be more false than to claim, as some do abroad, that Germany plans to introduce a system of economic controls and state capitalism excluding private initiative'[8] But collaboration came with a price. Hermann Roechling, an industrialist who became minister of war industries warned his fellow steel barons that 'to justify the existence of the private economy we must achieve extraordinary results'.[9] In truth, the ownership of German industry stayed in private hands, and the profits fell to the capitalists, but the demand was artificial, coming from the state.

With $475 million invested in German industry, American capitalists participated in the Nazi-policed exploitation of German workers. IBM's German subsidiary paid $4.5 million in dividends to its US parent company, as its profits doubled to four million Reich Marks (RM) in 1939 as it helped keep tabs on the Jews by mechanising the census. Fordwerke's assets mushroomed from RM 25.8 million to RM 60.4 million between 1934 and 1939. In the same year General Motors subsidiary Opel earned RM 35 million. Coca-Cola's German subsidiary increased sales from 243 000 cases in 1934 to 4.5 million in 1939 - an alternative to beer for German workers who were being driven to 'work harder [and] faster' according to manager Max Keith.[10] Woolworths, Singer, and ITT (whose subsidiary Conrad Lorenz made radios for the Luftwaffe) were also investors. British companies with a share in the Nazi war machine included Anglo-Persian – later BP – and Royal Dutch Shell (which invested in German oil companies), and Dunlop.[11]

Lend Lease – Military Keynesianism

'Lend lease' was a scheme thought up by Roosevelt to supply Britain, and later Russia and China, with war supplies. 'Give us the tools, and we will finish the job', Winston Churchill said after Dunkirk. Roosevelt's cornpone explanation was that you do not sell your neighbour the hose when he needs to water the lawn, but lend it to him. Roosevelt had succeeded in persuading Congress to vote first one billion, then three billion dollars for defence after the German offensive of 1940.[12] Of course there was no likelihood that Britain would be giving back the $3 billion worth of supplies next week. 'These orders are an important factor in United States economic activity in general, and in developing the aircraft industry in particular,' Roosevelt said, adding 'they mean prosperity as well as security'.[13] Absorbing America's excess capacity was an essential means of raising her out of the persisting recession that had seen unemployment climbing back up to ten million in 1937.[14] US exports to Britain rose from $505 million in 1939 to $5.2 billion in 1944.[15]

In the United States war mobilisation was signalled by an extensive command economy, run by the Supply and Priorities Board, the War Production Board, the War Manpower Commission, the National War Labour Board and a score of similar authorities. Doctor Win-the-War replaces Doctor New Deal, said Roosevelt.[16] But in fact the alphabet soup of war agencies was less important than the armed services' own buyers, who chose which companies to go to.[17]

Gabriel Kolko set out just what rearmament did for America;

> All the problems that American capitalism could not solve before 1941 were seemingly swept away in the rush to rearm and do combat with the Axis. Resources which were unimaginable in 1937 were freely available just a few years later, and most of the Congressional political constraints of the preceding decades of national politics disappeared. The grave problem of insufficient demand and an oversupply of capital and labour within a year turned into shortages.[18]

In the US the production of raw steel increased by 20 per cent between 1940 and 1945, that of Rayon and acetate yarn by 55 per cent, fuel oils by 44 per cent and wheat flour by 27 per cent. Only 560 locomotives were made in 1940, 3213 in 1945.[19] Overall, output in 1944 was nearly twice output in 1940 (while consumption only increased 15 per cent). The growth of capacity was possible in the first place because of the under-utilisation of plant and workforce in the preceding period. Unemployment fell by 7.45 million.

In Britain, between 1932 and 1938 state spending on arms rose from £100m to £800m, which the Economist was by that time calling 'the greatest public works programme ever'.[20] Keynes himself wrote that arms spending could boost recovery in the depressed areas in the north of England, Scotland and Wales ('Special Areas') – and targeting the growth there would also be cheaper as wages would be lower: 'To organise output in the Special Areas is a means of obtaining rearmament without inflation.'[21]

In 1940 Keynes was asked by propaganda minister Duff Cooper to give a radio talk on the evils of Nazi economic strategist Walther Funk's plan. Keynes protested that the plan was 'excellent and just what we ourselves ought to be thinking of doing'. [22] Keynes had a lot of time for the command economy, and in the preface to the 1936 German edition of his book *The General Theory* had written:

> the theory of output as a whole, which is what the following book purports to provide, is more easily adapted to the conditions of a totalitarian state, than is the theory of the production and distribution of a given output under conditions of free competition and a large measure of laissez-faire.

In both America and Britain, the war led to the introduction of payroll taxes, which also demanded much better statistics, from which the industrial census was born – something that Keynes lobbied hard for in the UK.

After the Arcadia conference between Churchill and Roosevelt in December 1941, 'the free market was abandoned in order to achieve maximum efficiency in reorganizing trade'.[23] Under the Combined Food Board and the Combined Shipping Adjustments Board, distribution and shipping was planned across a great span of the world, taking in the British Empire, America, the Soviet Union, Latin America, the French Colonies and the Middle East. The main players were the War Shipping Administration in America and the War

Transport Board in Britain. 'The navy took over the organisation of all British shipping in a remarkable feat of economic planning' says Richard Overy. [24] Germany's New Order in Europe saw Belgian and Dutch arms manufacturers export to Germany, while Danish farmers exported butter and beef. Neutral countries like Switzerland (arms) and Sweden (iron ore) also fed the German economy. The German Reich seized labourers from the occupied countries, and later Albert Speer dreamed of 'a rationalisation of production which treated the whole of north Western Europe as a single economic unit'. Having rubbished the idea of working with the collaborating regimes in Europe 'by 1943 many Axis sympathisers were keener "Europeans" than their counterparts'. [25]

In the Soviet Union industry was not run along market lines – but if anything even more chaotically organised. Widespread problems of inertia, waste and misreporting of resources sapped the Soviet state. War, though, gave the Soviet leadership the vision it needed to pull the country behind it – and to rein in the bureaucracy. On 30 June 1941 a State Defence Committee (GKO) to deal with 'the rapid mobilization of all forces of the peoples of the Soviet Union' was set up. The team of Stalin, Molotov, Beria, Maelnkov and Voroshilov overrode the Politburo, and Central Committee. Other state bodies like Sovnarkom (Council of People's Commissars) and Gosplan (the State Planning Commission) found their powers enhanced, stemming from those of the GKO.

Japanese industry was less regulated than most – apart from the simple influence of government purchasing, as the Tojo government exercised its control over society largely through the military and street committees. At the end of 1943, though, industry was effectively taken over. [26]

The war led to a shift from small to big business in the US. Before the war around 70 per cent of all output came from small and medium sized businesses, but in the war, that slipped back to just 30 per cent, while big business grabbed the rest. [27] Meanwhile in Japan, the Home Minister told the liason conference of 29 July 1941 that 'the rich have become richer because of the China incident, while small and medium businessmen are in difficulties because they went to the front'. [28] In Germany corporations with a value over 5 million Reichsmarks represented 55.8 per cent of all capital in 1928, 74.6 per cent in 1938. Labour Front spokesman Robert Ley told the small traders who had been the backbone of the NSDAP that 'the independent artisan who cannot compete against the factory or trust has no right to exist in the Third Reich', adding: 'He can become an industrial worker'.[29]

Costs Plus

In America 'the federal government … guaranteed profits by allowing corporations to charge it productions costs plus a fixed profit.'[30] The same system was used in Britain, as aircraft engineer Fred Westacott set out. 'Employers had a bonanza, not only in the power' that the Essential Works Order 'gave them over their workforce, but also in the no-risk profits they could now make'. 'The government' he wrote, 'introduced an incredible "cost-plus" system, whereby firms were guaranteed profits amounting to a percentage of total costs'. The link between employers' profits and the performance of the goods they had made was broken – 'a bonus for inefficiency!'[31] White farmers in Rhodesia, too, 'used the conflict to demand guaranteed prices' for crops farmed with conscripted labour.[32]

Germany, too, took up the 'costs plus' system of fixed prices. Later, Albert Speer fixed the 'costs plus' system to one that worked out what profits were due in keeping with the amount of capital used. This change was supposed to stop profiteering, but since the prices were fiat prices, set by government contractors, not market prices, the effect was the same. The link between profit and productivity was broken, and industrialists' profits became a rent on the state.[33]

Great public procurement and the Costs Plus system were wide open to all kinds of fraud. A Truman-led war watchdog committee found that the aeroplane firm Curtiss Wright 'was producing and causing the Government to accept defective and substandard material, by the falsification of tests, by destruction of records, by forging inspection reports'.[34] The Anaconda Wire and Cable Co. faked inspection tags for wire cable going to the USSR under lend-lease – about half of which turned out to be defective. The Carnegie-Illinois Steel Company sold 'steel' which was closer to cast iron, and was discovered when the USS Schenectady broke in two, just hours after its delivery to the US Maritime Commission on 17 January 1943. War contracts were so generous to manufacturers that they were valuable in themselves, and a 1942 Congress report found that up to 74 per cent of the cost of the commission was being skimmed by brokers.[35]

War Profiteers

During the four war years 1942-1945 the 2230 largest American firms reported earnings of $14.4 billion after taxes, up by 41 per cent on the previous four.[36] After tax profits in the US went up from $6.4 billion in 1940 to nearly $11 billion in 1944.[37] In the third quarter of 1943, according to a Department of Commerce report, corporation profits were 'the highest for any quarter in American history and 16 per cent above the same quarter in 1942'.[38] The Civil Appropriations accounts for 1942-3 show that one quarter of firms working on war contracts made profits up to 15 per cent, just over a third made profits of between 15 and 30 per cent, and another third made profits over 30 per cent on cost.[39] By the end of the war, US corporations had made profits of 52 billion dollars after taxation, increased the productive power of their plant by one half and accumulated capital reserves of 85 billion dollars.[40]

Roosevelt's government bent over backwards to help big business. In 1940 tax legislation was passed that said that war-related plant that was five years old was written off ('amortised'), spurring new dealer Harold Ickes to say that 'it seems intolerable to me to allow private people to use public funds to make a guaranteed profit for themselves'.[41] War Secretary Henry Stimson explained 'If you are going to prepare for war in a capitalist country you have to let business make money out of the process or business won't work'.[42]

In December 1938 the British aircraft manufacturer Hawker Siddeley announced a record dividend, leading the Treasury to demand the Inland Revenue publish figures on war profiteering. They found that the Society of British Aircraft Producers were making an average profit of ten per cent – and 20 per cent on their own privately invested capital – and were set to get even higher returns in the following year. The Air Minister called for an immediate excess profits duty, but the Treasury said no for fear of a 'shock to business confidence'.[43] Later the SBAC did agree to return one third of excess profits to the Treasury, but still 'got its golden years of profit'.[44] One investor whose portfolio did well in the war years was John Maynard Keynes. Between 1938 and his death in 1946 his assets rose in value from £181,244 to £479,529.[45]

In 1937 a Nazi economic journalist wrote that 'most companies have enjoyed huge profits during the last few years on account of the measures taken by the national socialist government'. 'Profits have been high', he added, 'because wages and salaries have remained stationary'. In fact the share of the national income falling to big business had grown from 19 in 1932 to 28 per cent in 1937.[46] In 1940 the Reich price commissioner Gauleiter Josef Wagner protested at excessive profiteering, and the following year permissible profit rates were cut back by 20 per cent.[47] But as late as 1944 Hitler vetoed further tax increases, even though the war was eating up 60 per cent of all output, a staggering 99.4 billion Reichmarks.[48]

After the war Japan's premier Yoshida Shigeru struggled to defend 'the leaders of Japan's business world' against charges 'that the nation's capitalists had lured the politicians into an imperialistic and aggressive war in pursuit of personal profits'.[49]

Chapter Four

Dig for Victory

A terrible crisis in agriculture took place in the 1920s, preceding and pre-empting the wider crisis that followed the Wall Street Crash of 1929. Agriculture world-wide was ruined by overproduction, leading to falling prices before governments took control of the process and rationalised production by consolidating small farms into larger ones, forcing more bankrupt farmers off the land. The social ramifications were international.

In the mid-western United States, farmers responded to falling prices by over farming their land, creating the ruinous 'dust-bowl'. In the South former slaves who had survived a generation working the land as truck farmers, paying their rent in produce rather than cash, were also ruined. The dispossession of the black truck farmers inaugurated the single greatest internal migration since the push west, as three million moved north between 1930 and 1960 swelling the depressed inner cities. In Germany farm prices fell while other prices rose. Inflation ate up the small farmer's savings and drove them, ruined and embittered into the hands of Adolf Hitler's National Social Democratic and Workers' Party, the NSDAP or the Nazis. Hitler's appeal to blood and soil was framed to appeal to the farmers, who were flattered in right-wing ideology as the backbone of the nation. Hitler solved the farming problem by effectively nationalising land ownership, and reducing the once independent peasants to state employees, working to feed the nation. In Soviet Russia, Stalin imposed a brutal policy of forced collectivisation on the 'Kulak' peasantry.

The agricultural crisis of the 1920s arose out of a reconfiguration of the balance between town and country. With investment directed largely at heavy machinery and incomes depressed, the market for foodstuffs was held down. The agricultural crisis led to a consolidation of many smaller farms into fewer larger ones, often with the state taking a key role in organising agriculture, and a development even more pronounced with the outbreak of war. Larger farms meant more mechanisation and a divergence between farm labourers and farm-owners. The countryside was becoming more like the town with the emergence of modern agribusiness. World war raised the importance of food security for European nations, and self-sufficiency informed the war effort as allotments were dug and in Britain a 'land army' of women recruited to farm the countryside.

Just as agriculture was being turned into an industry, the culture of capitalism was greener in its outlook. The further people were from nature, the stronger the cult of nature became. Cultivating a sense of the natural rooted-ness was how elites tried to overcome the fear of change and disorder.

Nature was a powerful motif of Hitler's political appeal, and in 1926 he wrote about the dangers of threatening the natural order, warning of 'the harder fate is that which strikes the man who thinks he can overcome Nature, but in the last analysis only mocks her': 'Distress, misfortune, and disease are her answer.'[1] Nature represented an order that belied the pretensions of social reform for the early Fascist orator:

> At this point someone or other may laugh, but this planet once moved through the ether for millions of years without human beings and if can do so again some day if men forget that they owe their existence, not to the ideas of a few crazy ideologists, but to the knowledge and ruthless application of Nature's stern and rigid laws.[2]

The English conservationist and founder of the Soil Association, Eve Balfour gave voice to a similar idea of restoring the natural balance, though for her it was framed in the struggle *against* Fascism. In 1942, she warned against the belief in man's 'conquest of nature', saying that, 'This is at present of the same order as the Nazi conquest of Europe.' And just 'as Europe is in revolt against the tyrant, so is nature in revolt against the conquest of man.'[3] US President Roosevelt, too, worried about upsetting the natural order, and put many reforms in place for conservation. For him:

> A nation that destroys its soils destroys itself. Forests are the lungs of our land, purifying the air and giving fresh strength to our people.[4]

Mussolini thought that Italian youth should be taught 'a love for the woods, fount of spiritual and physical wholesomeness which will remove adolescent Fascists from corrupt and enfeebling suburbs'.[5]

Hitler's idea of 'living space' was 'a term the geographer Friedrich Ratzel borrowed from ecological theory'. Indeed modern-day environmentalists have been disturbed to see how many of their ideas were pioneered by the Nazis. In particular the Reich Nature Preservation Law of 1935 protected what it called 'Natural Monuments'. Section 19 of the law said that 'prior to conducting any project which might lead to alterations in the free landscape' permission had to be sought from nature protection authorities. It also put in place special 'Reich Nature Protection Areas', that were needed for 'curtailing unattractive, unplanned economic development'. In 1938, and then again after the War, the British Government, too brought in 'Green Belts' to rein in urban sprawl under a Town and Country Planning Act. The editors of the Journal *Natur und Heimat* wrote that 'the foundation of the Reich Nature Protection Law states clearly that nature protection is an essential part of the worldview of National Socialism'. Hans Klose, director of the Reich Nature Protection Office argued for the extension of nature protection laws into occupied Poland, and planned a huge national park in the Białowieża Forest, an area occupied by Polish and Jewish villagers.[6]

In Britain, the Army Bureau of Current Affairs drew on an idea of bucolic England to show what the country was defending, in posters by Frank Newbould, like this from 1942:

But even then the country was one of the most urbanised in the world, so villages like this were not really 'your Britain' for most.

For Hitler, the broad ideology of nature also connected with the more immediate importance of land for farming and controlling the population. The ideal was of a 'Folk which no longer needs to shunt off its rising rural generations into the big cities as factory workers, but which instead can settle them as free peasants on their own soil.'[7] Predictably, the land hunger was tied to territorial conquest for this anti-Versailles patriot: 'An additional 500000 square kilometres in Europe can provide new homesteads for millions of German peasants'.[8] The impoverished small farmers were key to the NSDAP's election strategy, as the Reich Minister of Food and Agriculture Walther Darré sought to win them from the traditional conservative farmer's party:

> Send your former leaders to the devil. What have they ever done for you? Suffering and hunger, hunger and suffering.[9]

Winning those broken farmers over to the party was a vital counter-weight to the left's urban vote. In the event, the Nazi government's rearmament and industrialisation policies led to a fall in the agricultural workforce, of around ten per cent, or more than a million farm labourers by 1939.[10] Tariffs brought in under the preceding Bruning administration to guarantee the incomes of the Prussian Junker landlords were carried on under the Nazis.[11]

In the United States action over falling farm prices was undertaken by the Agricultural Adjustment Administration and Roosevelt's Agriculture Secretary, Henry Wallace, a moderate Republican farmer who embraced the New Deal. Wallace's policy was to subsidise farmers by buying up surpluses – the 'ever-normal granary' – and paying them to stop planting cotton. Travelling round the country he won over farmers' to the government payment scheme.[12] But the payments were biased to larger farmers, and the small farmers, most of all the black 'truck' farmers, who paid their rent in kind, lost out. Southern blacks dubbed Roosevelt's National Relief Agency 'Negroes Ruined Again'.[13] It was the main cause of the greatest internal migration in the country's history as millions of black Americans moved from the southern farm states to northern cities – where many were drawn into the growing war industries. As land was retired from production, Roosevelt supported 'reforestation, which must be jointly a State and Federal concern',[14] and the expansion of the national parks system in an executive order of 1933.

Germany, Britain and America all shrunk the amount of land under the plough in the recession, only to greatly grow it again during the war. War upset the international division of labour where developed nations – notably Britain – traded made goods for grain and other foodstuff. The war of the Atlantic disrupted trade and made for greater 'food security' biases, or autarky. Much more land was dug over, so that nearly ¾ of Britain was made farmland. As well as enlarging farmland, the British authorities promoted small allotments, with a slogan 'Dig for Victory' encouraging home grown vegetables. The allotments turned out to be very popular with an urban population that missed its links to the land.

Walther Darré's Farm Inheritance Law stopped farmers from selling their land, which also meant they could not raise credit on it. Because farmers could no longer pay labourers, the state sent 'Landjahrmadchen' – landgirls – and 'volunteers' from the National Labour Service to help with the harvest.[15] As rearmament picked up, the arrested rural development fell short of what was needed, and shortages appeared. As farmers struggled to put food on the German table, Hitler looked east to meet the need for fodder for livestock and dray horses. The schemes to replant eastern Germans on Polish land managed only to wreck the Polish economy, while leaving the relocated in a miserable state. To meet the shortfall at home, Goering announced loans of one billion reichsmarks to the farmers, making them more and more into state functionaries.[16]

In the US, wartime production represented the victory of big agri-business over the small farmer. Under Public Law 480 agribusiness was paid to overproduce and the surpluses were dumped in the third world. Europe, too, adopted a generalised 'food security' programme that saw farmers become dependents on the European Economic Community, their surpluses bought up at 'cost plus' prices.

Chapter Five

Trade War

'War is the trade of governments'[1]

When the US stock market collapsed it plunged America, and those countries that depended on American lending into recession. With domestic buying dampened, foreign sales were fought for. 'The contraction in the demand for goods caused intensified national competition', explained British socialist Fenner Brockway.[2] Quite quickly governments raised up tariffs against foreign imports to protect their own markets. US Senator Reed Smoot and Representative Willis C. Hawley, both Republicans, pushed the Smoot-Hawley tariff amendment in 1930, raising the highest import controls seen in America since 1828. 'So again tariffs began to mount', wrote Fenner Brockway: 'Under the pressure of this demand Britain, the historic Free Trade country, became Protectionist.'[3] In 1932 the British parliament passed the Import Duties Act, imposing a tariff of ten per cent. That year the Dominion Conference in Ottawa, Canada, agreed the system of 'Imperial Preference' that gave Britain and its colonies access to each other's markets, and raised import controls against the rest of the world.

In October 1932, Earl Lytton's report for the League of Nations condemned Japan's intervention in China, prompting the Japanese to leave the League. The state of Manchukuo set up with Japanese backing in China, brought an end to the 'Open Door' policy under which the Great Powers agreed to open up China to 'free trade'. In the first half of 1938 global trade fell by 20 per cent, straining international cooperation yet further.[4] In 1940, Britain yielded to Japanese demands that the Burma Road, that supplied China's nationalists, be closed. Later, on 1 August 1941, Japan's Foreign Minister Matsuoka Yosuke would announce a Greater East Asian Co-Prosperity Sphere, under the slogan 'Asia for the Asians'.

Hitler's banker Hjalmar Schacht stopped payment on Germany's overseas debts: money borrowed to pay off its reparations from the First World War, the lion's share from Americans. Service on the debts was 600 million Reichsmarks a year. Roosevelt called Schacht a 'bastard'.[5] Borrowing from the US and Britain paid for imports from those countries, which were wound down. In September 1934, Schacht brought in the 'New Plan', that held all imports down to the level justified by means of payment. Through trade agreements Germany set up trading bloc with Hungary, Romania, Yugoslavia and some South American countries, 25 countries by 1938. [6] It was called 'autarky', economic self-sufficiency, and 'amounted to a selective policy of disengagement directed above all against the United States, the British Empire and, to a lesser degree, France', according to economic historian Adam Tooze, or as Secretary of State Cordell Hull called it, 'an act of aggression against the entire American system of trade treaties'.[7]

The fact that Nazi protectionism had reduced the German share of US exports from 8.4 to 3.4 billion between 1933 and 1938, as those to Britain rose helped Roosevelt to decide which side to support, argues Jacques Pauwels.[8]

To the British Treasury, the export trade was the 'fourth arm of defence'. [9] 'Our foreign trade is suffering from German' competition, protested one Churchill-sponsored pamphlet, before adding the complaint that 'it is not competition, it is simply brute force, compelling the creditor to order in Germany if he wants to see his money back'.[10]

The Reichsbank reported to Hitler in January 1939 that 'Gold or Foreign exchange reserves of the Reichsbank are no more in existence' – exports were just not enough to meet the demands of rearmament, despite Goering's call for a renewed overseas sales drive in November 1938.[11]

Following Germany's occupation of the Sudetenland in March 1939, US President Roosevelt put a 25 per cent tariff on German goods – twisting the knife hard.[12] Economic planner Carl Krauch thought that the time when Germany 'would solely have the possibility of determining the timing and scale of the political transformation in Europe whilst avoiding the power group led by England' had passed: 'The economic war against the anti-Comintern powers [i.e. the Axis] that has already secretly begun under the leadership of England, France and the United States has now been openly declared and with time it will take on ever more severe forms'.[13]

Third Reich propaganda attacked Wall Street Jewry – the financier turned political advisor Bernard Baruch, mostly – and its supposed spokesman Roosevelt for trying to shut Germany out of export markets.[14]

In the 1930s the fruits of Japan's rapid industrialisation were felt, just as America and the British Empire were struggling with the depression. 'The flooding of Japanese goods into foreign markets after 1931 brought frantic outcries in the West', recalled to Princeton's William Lockwood. Though she had secured Chinese markets through colonisation 'almost everywhere else, after 1932, tariffs were raised or quotas established against Japanese goods'.[15]

Germany was by 1940 the world leader in aluminium production – 300,000 tons a year – making the US struggle to outproduce them, with plans for 450,000 tons a year by 1942. In turn Germany planned to boost output to one million tons, in new plant centred on Norway under the Nazi magnate Heinrich Koppenberg.[16]

Before long, the trading war would turn into armed competition. The American slogan of the day, carrying more than a little menace, was 'if goods can't cross borders, soldiers will'.[17] Just as trade war led to a shooting war, war itself was a matter of controlling trade.

At the start of the war, Britain stamped all trade with Germany – including food – 'contraband'. Neutral ships were stopped and their cargoes searched. The Soviet government protested that the policy 'gravely endangers the lives of the peaceful population' and that it is 'not permissible to deprive the peaceful population of foodstuffs, fuel and clothing, and thus subject children, women and aged people and invalids to every hardship and starvation by proclaiming the goods of popular consumption contraband'. 'When practically the whole population is either in the colours or engaged in some form of war work' answered British jurist J. L. Brierly 'it is practically impossible to have any assurance at all that food which is allowed to pass will be consumed by non-combatants'.[18] Churchill gloated that Hitler would have 'to hold down a whole continent of sullen, starving peoples'.[19] In the first two months of the war, the Allies seized half a million tons of 'contraband' on ships destined for Germany.

As Richard Overy explains, the German reaction was punitive: 'During 1940 a thousand ships were sunk totalling 4 million tons, a quarter of British merchant shipping'. 'In the first four months of 1941 almost 2 million tons of shipping were destroyed, over half in the North Atlantic'. 'British trade was slowly being bled white: 68 million tons were imported in 1938, 21 million tons in 1941'.[20]

At the same time 'The opportunity is being taken to replace Germany in markets into which she has crept by methods often closely related to the unscrupulous and unfair practices now exhibited in the more deathly struggle'.[21] According to *The Economist:* 'There is now widespread recognition of the necessity to use the weapon of export and import competition against Germany in these markets that are still open to her and to us'. Seeing the war as an extension of market competition, they counselled denying raw materials Germany needed by buying over the odds, and undercutting German exports: 'Export industries are not an alternative to munitions industries, they are munitions industries'.[22]

The economic stranglehold that the combatants put on each other did not limit their war-like ambitions, but provoked them even further: 'Given the isolation imposed on the European continent by the British blockade, only the Ukraine could provide Western Europe with the millions of tons of grain it needed to sustain its animal population,' writes economic historian Adam Tooze.[23]

War for Oil

In November 1922 at the Lausanne conference America had come out against Britain and France for trying to carve up Middle East oil between them. 'In view of the American contributions to the common victory over the Central powers no discrimination can be rightfully made against us in a territory won by that victory'.[24] Still, at that time, Britain and France had the military might to uphold their monopoly, and the US had to put up with it, in what was known as the 'Red Line' agreement. Oil executive Sir E. Mackay Edgar, boasted to the Times that the agreement would give Britain the dollars it so badly needed:

To the tune of many millions of pounds a year, America, before very long will have to purchase from British companies and to pay for in dollar currency, in increasing proportions, the oil she cannot do without and is no longer able to furnish from her own store. I estimate that ... Americans in ten years will be under the necessity of importing 500 million barrels of oil yearly at 2 dols. a barrel ... and that means an annual payment of 1,000,000,000 most, if not all of which will find its way into British pockets.

With numbers like these, Edgar could be forgiven for thinking that 'the British position is impregnable'.[25]

On 17 May 1920 the American senate read a report that showed how Britain monopolised oil:

- By debarring foreigners and foreign nationals from owning or operating oil-producing properties in the British Isles, Colonies and Protectorates.
- By direct participation in ownership and control of petroleum properties.
- By arrangement to prevent British oil companies from selling their properties to foreign-owned or controlled companies.
- By Orders in Council that prohibit the transfer of shares in British oil companies to other than British subjects or nationals.

The report charged that 'British monopolies have already been established in the United Kingdom, Persia, India and many other countries'.[26] America pushed Britain to accept Standard Oil's exploitation of the Persian oil fields as well as exploiting new fields in Venezuela, as well as domestic sources in California, Oklahoma and West Texas.[27]

It was not only America that suffered from the British stranglehold on oil. In Germany Carl Bosch's managed to synthesize methane from coal in 1923 and his I.G. Farben conglomerate embarked on a 330 million Reichsmark investment in the oil substitute at their Leuna plant. Slow progress was fatally undermined when international markets were glutted by American developments in 1930.[28] The German-Romanian trade treaty of 23 March 1939 guaranteed Germany's oil and grain supplies for the short term – and alarmed London and Paris. Guaranteeing Romania against Hungarian threats Germany dictated terms.[29] Later in the war, the Wehrmacht headed south to try to grab the Caucasus oil-fields. The main challenge to German industry, said the Berlin Institute for Business Cycle Research in 1936 was access to raw materials.[30] Germany's oil problems arose out of the Versailles settlement, its loss of colonial possessions and the enlargement of its rivals' territorial reach.

Becoming an industrial power, Japan was more dependent on the supply of raw materials. It relied on 'iron ore, rubber, tin, coal and above all petroleum from British Malaya, the Philippines, French Indochina and Indonesia'.[31] One quarter of Japan's oil imports came from Indonesia, and more than half from America.[32]

In July 1941, the United States, which was already restricting oil supplies to Japan, looked at a total embargo over their seizure of Indonesia from Holland, but Roosevelt dissuaded his cabinet, and explained to the public:

Whether they had at that time aggressive purposes to enlarge their empire southward, they didn't have any oil of their own up north. Now, if we cut off the oil supply, they would probably have gone down to the Dutch East Indies a year ago, and you would have had war.[33]

Despite the President's insight, Dean Acheson, working at the State Department remembered that 'I knew little, as we tightened the economic blockade of Japan, of the tension it was producing there': 'It was a life and death struggle for them'. Looking at the American boycott, General Tojo told the Privy Council that the United States 'has not shown any sign of concession from its past position' and 'it is now clear that Japan's claims cannot be attained through diplomatic measures'.[34] Within the week Japan attacked Pearl Harbor.

For America, war would transform her international position as much as the new oilfields had at home. Giving evidence to a US State Department Advisory Committee in April 1943, Isaiah Bowman looked forward to helping Arabs to make the most of their oil:

There is Bahrain Island in the Gulf of Persia, with a few hundred square miles and 90,000 people. Some millions of gallons of oil are exported from Bahrain every year. Suppose, starting our plans of trusteeship, we try to use this oil for the benefit of the people through promotion of education and self-government. These people are raisers of goats and fishers of pearls who have no understanding whatsoever of the modern oil industry in their country, which some westerner created when he came along and bored a hole. How, therefore, are we to relate these millions of gallons of oil to the 90,000 raisers of goats in terms of our trustee principles?[35]

William Bullitt, Under-Secretary of the Navy put it more simply 'To acquire petroleum reserves outside our boundaries has become ... a vital interest of the United States' in a June 1943 memorandum to President Roosevelt.[36]

War for Rubber

In 1922 Sir John Stevenson brought in the plan to restrict the British Empire's rubber output. Falling demand was hurting prices, but as Stevenson explained 'quite frankly, I did not embark on this proposition with any regard for the Rubber Growers' Association' but rather because 'I am deeply interested in the development of the British Empire'. Later the Stevenson plan was expanded into an international agreement – first and foremost with the Dutch whose East Indies plantations were almost the only other source at that time – which ran from 1934 to 1943, when the Japanese overran Malaya and Indonesia.[37] In his novel *Life of the Automobile*, Ilya Ehrenburg imagines Churchill congratulating Stevenson – 'you will go down in history' only to add the qualification: 'rubber history'. The rubber agreement damaged Ceylon's industry that had been overtapped and needed new planting – banned under the agreement. After Britain got the Dutch to stymie American attempts to buy into the Indonesian industry, Harvey S. Firestone demanded that 'America must grow its own rubber'. Congress put aside $500 000 to finance a survey of rubber producing countries, and in time Liberia and Brazil were made into American rubber colonies. The extraordinary conditions on Firestone's loan, that gave him control over the country's budget, land and trade were undertaken to avoid it being colonised by another European power.[38] During the war, the restrictions on output were thrown into reverse as the industry was subsumed into the war effort. In Ceylon in March 1942, 'the British Ministry of Supply became the sole purchaser of rubber' and local prices were determined by a Rubber Commissioner: 'he fixed a price that was likely to secure as large an output as possible'. After years of under-investment, growers were told to take up 'slaughter tapping'.[39] The United States was looking at other raw materials to feed its industrial needs. In 1940 Fortune wrote about tin reserves in Malaya and the Dutch East Indies, where European empires were a barrier, thinking them 'a purely materialistic case for playing a strong imperialist game in South-eastern Asia' – ambitions that would be realised with the eventual defeat of Japan.[40]

Business as usual

Even though commercial competition had given way to military rivalry, cynical capitalists carried on trading with the enemy where ever they could, and even enjoyed the connivance of their governments.

Throughout the war Britain and America traded with the Fascist – though neutral – government in Spain, supplying her with much needed oil, even though Spain in turn supplied Germany with wolfram, or tungsten, which was used in precision engineering and armaments, as well as other minerals. When US Secretary of State Cordell Hull questioned the wisdom of sending oil to Spain, Prime Minister Churchill threatened to go public to defend the deal. Eventually, the US used its purse to buy up Spanish Wolfram to deny it to Hitler, so boosting Franco's dictatorship.[41]

The Allies traded, too, with neutral Sweden and Switzerland, though both were in turn supplying Germany with iron ore and machine tools respectively. Between 1940 and 1943 Sweden sent ten million tons of iron ore a year to Germany.

Chapter Six

Imperialist War

In 1936 the British Empire covered 13,300,000 million square miles with 500 million people living under its writ, a bit less than a quarter of the world's surface, and around a quarter of the world's population. Of those 500 million, 430 million were colonial subjects in the Empire, 50 million in Britain, and 20 million in the white dominions (Canada, New Zealand and Australia).[1]

Around that time the French Empire covered 5,020,000 square miles of territory, home to 110,631,000 – 41.5 million of whom were in France itself. Holland had possessions in South America and Indonesia – but both of these Empires would be torn apart by war – as indeed was much of the British Empire.

'England's Shame', as Nazi propagandists saw it

By the end of 1940 Germany's New Order had engulfed Austria, the Czech Republic, Poland, Norway, Denmark, Holland and northern France – 'almost 1,000,000 square miles of territory and 225,000,000 white people' in January 1941, reported *Flight*.[2] That year the Third Reich added the Ukraine, Estonia, Lithuania, Latvia, Greece, and

Serbia – though the last two were rebellious throughout. Italy had colonies in Eritrea, Somaliland and Libya – and invaded Abyssinia in 1935.[3]

The United States held the Philippines, Samoa (under mandate), Hawaii, Guam, the Panama Canal Zone and Puerto Rico. Without holding territory, America gathered client states in Latin America and the Pacific. US influence was decisive in Cuba, where Batista ruled; Haiti and Panama were both subject to military intervention, Bolivia and Argentina the US sought to protect its investments in oil and its access to tin, rubber and other goods, by shoring up relations with local leaders, through loans and trade agreements: 'the whole western hemisphere under the control of the United States means the possession of war material resources unequalled in the world', wrote one radical commentator.[4]

In 1931 Japan held the Sakhalin Islands, the Korean peninsula, Formosa (modern-day Taiwan) and effectively ruled over the 'Manchuko' regime in Manchurian China. By 1942 Japan's New Order had swallowed Indo-China (modern-day Vietnam), the Dutch East Indies (Indonesia), Burma, Hong Kong, Singapore, Malaya and the Philippines.

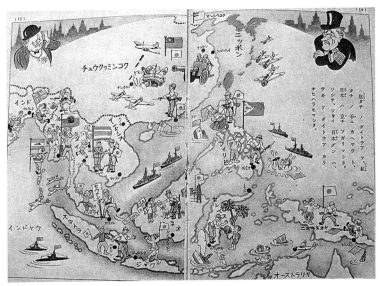

Japanese propagandists picture Roosevelt and Churchill looking on while the 'Co-Prosperity Sphere' is built

As a non-capitalist power, the Soviet Union did not have the same drive to exploit other lands through capital investment, yet its strategic defensiveness made it just as rapacious in its demand for territory and the extinction of rival powers at its borders. Under the Hitler-Stalin pact the Soviet Union seized the baltic states of Latvia, Lithuania and Estonia, as it conquered eastern Poland in the early years of the war. Russian domination within the Union of Soviet Socialist Republics, and the internal subjugation of the peasantry under forced collectivisation undermined the loyalty of Ukrainians and Chechens.

The struggle over Empire was the cause of the Second World War. Those countries that tried to enlarge their empires clashed with those who were trying to defend their own. As we shall see, the balance among the great powers had shifted greatly – and that was true of the shifting importance of their Empires. In 1913 Britain controlled 60 per cent of the world's foreign investments, down to 50 per cent in 1936. Over those same years, France's foreign investment dropped from a quarter to a tenth of the world share. Germany's share went from 15 per cent to minus 6 per cent – that is, she was in debt, and heavily so. America's overseas investments rose from minus 12 per cent to fully one quarter of the world's total.[5]

At the end of the First World War defeated Germany was dismembered, losing territory in the east and on the Rhine. The 'restoration' of Greater Germany, and the taking of territories where ethnic Germans lived in eastern Europe was a goal that drove extreme nationalism – though pointedly Hitler's own 1926 manifesto *Mein Kampf* rejected restoration of the pre-1914 borders of Germany as too limiting.[6] The invasion of western Europe was not in the first place an attempt to build an Empire but to eliminate its continental European rivals – France most of all. Once occupied, though, western Europe was plundered for cash reserves, food, manufactures and labour.

It was through conquest of the east that Hitler saw Germany's future. He had written in 1926 that 'our aim in foreign policy' is 'to secure for the German people the land and soil to which they are entitled on this earth'. More, 'if we speak of soil in Europe today, we can primarily have in mind only Russia and her vassal border states'.[7] With the invasion of the Soviet Union that longstanding aim was made real. Germany's demand for grain and oil had been met until then by trade agreements with the Soviet Union. The Hitler-Stalin pact of 1939 included an agreement to exchange Russian raw materials for German technology. Hitler met with Goering, Rosenberg, Bormann and Keitel in his Rastenburg Headquarters on 16 July 1941 and set out a goal of Europeanising the Steppe – marshes would be drained, motorways built, plantations and German towns founded, peopled with two or three million migrants 'from Germany, Scandinavia the Western countries and America', he predicted.[8]

Hitler's ambitions for colonising the east were not odd, but mainstream thinking at the time. The models he drew from were those of Britain and America. 'I, as a man of Germanic blood, would, in spite of everything, rather see India under English rule than any other', he wrote.[9] His plan for the east was 'to Germanise this country by the immigration of Germans and to look upon the natives as Redskins'.[10]

On 5 May 1936, as the Italian troops marched into Addis Ababa Benito Mussolini boasted that 'Italy finally has its own Empire: a fascist empire, a peaceful empire, an empire of civilisation and humanity' – though ironically as a radical young socialist he had been imprisoned for protesting against Prime Minister Giolitti's seizure of Libya in 1911.[11] Italian goals were two-fold: the seizure of Ethiopia in the face of the League of Nations' criticism was an assertion of prestige; and Mussolini saw Libya as a territory to be settled by Italian farmers. In Libya, governor Giuseppe Volpi launched military campaigns that left 6,500 Arabs dead. His successor Pietro Badoglio faced down resistance led by Omar al Mukhtàr – who was hung in September 1931, while thousands were held in concentration camps.[12]

'The British Empire and Commonwealth is a religion to him' Canadian Prime Minister Mackenzie King said of Winston Churchill, during the war.[13] The Secretary of State for India, Leo Amery made Britain's war aims clear:

After all, smashing Hitler is only a means to the essential end of preserving the British Empire and all it stands for in the world. It will be no consolation to suggest that Hitler should be replaced by Stalin, Chiang Kai-Shek or even an American President if we cease to exercise our power and influence in the world.[14]

Though later assessments re-wrote Britain's war aims as those of spreading democracy, the historian A.J.P. Taylor understood that 'The archives now reveal that Great Britain was fighting the Second World War in order to recover the British Empire and even (as with Libya) to add to it.'[15] After the First World War, in January 1919 British Chief of Staff Henry Wilson reported to the Cabinet that the only policy was to 'get our troops out of Europe and Russia and concentrate all our strength in our coming storm centres, England, Ireland, Egypt, India'[16] One third of the British training manual on air power was given over to 'control of semi-civilised tribes within our jurisdiction' - drawn from the RAF's air-bombing of Iraq, Somaliland and Waziristan in the 1920s.[17] On 3 October 1939 Chamberlain warned that Britain was 'mobilising all the might of the British Empire for the effective prosecution of the war'.[18] Even a Communist like Jürgen Kaczynski – writing propaganda for Churchill under the pseudonym James Turner – got the Empire bug, warning that Germany 'wants to steal our colonies'.[19] H.V. Hodson at the Ministry of Information launched an 'Empire Crusade' late in 1940 that boasted 'the Nazis have started the old futile game of building a slave Empire', but 'The British Empire is exactly the opposite' – in full page advertisements in the Mirror and Times newspapers. Polls showed that the man in the street was wholly unmoved by this appeal, and it was shelved.[20]

Prince Konoe Fumimaro, three times Prime Minister of Japan set up an important think-tank, the Shōwa Research Association that trailed the two main strategy initiatives, the Greater East Asia Co Prosperity Sphere (his foreign minister Matsuoka Yōsuke came up with the phrase) and the New East Asian Order. Konoe had written an essay around the time of the Versailles Conference after the First World War, 'Reject the Anglo-American Peace'. There he attacked the League of Nations as 'the ideology of sustaining the status quo' and called for 'the eradication of economic imperialism and the unbiased, equal treatment of the yellow race'.[21]

The sentiments behind the Japanese slogan 'Asia for the Asiatics' were sincere, but the practicalities of advancing Japan's offshore possessions – most pointedly in China and Korea – soon made a mockery of them. War time Foreign Minister Tōgō set out the case for a more practical application of the policy on 5 November 1941: 'Basically the conclusion of the China War and the establishment of the Greater East Asia Co-Prosperity Sphere signify as a pre-requisite the Empire's own survival, while acting as a cornerstone of East Asia's stability.'[22]

As the most rapidly growing economy, America wanted to break into the colonies through its 'Open Door' free trade policy, and was especially concerned to secure raw materials in the colonised areas.[23] In the course of the war the United States raised the standard of the liberation of Europe from German rule, and, as we shall see, put a great deal of pressure on her allies' colonial rule. Still, America was by no means a consistent opponent of imperialism. Roosevelt, shortly after signing the Atlantic Charter:

> there seems no reason why the principle of trusteeship in private affairs should not be extended to the international field. Trusteeship is based on the principle of unselfish service. For a time at least there are many minor children among the peoples of the world who need trustees in their relations with other nations and peoples.[24]

At the 'Informal Political Agenda Group' (forerunner of the International Organisation Group) at the State Department in spring 1944 Stanley Hornbeck proposed amending the 'general colonial declaration' of the United Nations to drop the contentious words 'national independence'. Said Hornbeck 'there are many people in the islands of the Pacific who will never be capable of self-government'.[25] America's 'Open Door' policy was to take down imperial barriers to US trade. Through the course of the war, America moved step by step towards the position of the World's policeman. Her rhetorical objections to colonial rule fell away as she took on responsibility for stabilising world order.

An example of the arms-length policy of client states the US worked can be seen in Brazil. President Vargas ran a dictatorship that banned strikes, and unauthorised labour meetings. In 1939 the regime banned Jews, non-whites and the children of working class families from its military colleges. Vargas had leaned in the direction of Nazi Germany, until the US flooded the country with Lend Lease aid of $366 million just as Germany sunk the ship the Cairu cementing the country's support for the Allies. Still US Generals had a secret plan to invade – the 'Operation Plan of Northeast Brazil Theater' – just in case. Vargas' support for the democracies did not stop his police chief Corialano de Gòis (known as 'Gòistapo') gunning down student demonstrators in November 1943 or planning to eliminate oppositionists.[26] In Liberia, the Firestone Rubber Company and the American government collaborated on a scheme where all of the country's national debt was bought up by a US-based banking subsidiary, on conditions that the country's budget was overseen by US officials. Also the Firestone Company had unimpeded rights to any plantation land it wanted up to 100 acres, a twentieth of the country's territory, wholly exempt from local laws and taxes.[27]

As the Second World War was fought over Empires, success or failure in war depended on the exploitation of Empires to feed the rival military industrial complexes.

In June 1941, the Wehrmacht was committed to living off the land in its eastern conquests – a goal that was underlined by making sure that no food was sent to them from the Reich, so clearing supply lines for military needs. By the autumn of 1943 as much as half of French industrial output was being taken by Germany.[28] In Greece German businessmen were seconded to the Economics Staff of the Wehrmacht High Command from firms such as Krupp and I.G. Farben, seizing the entire output of Greek mines of pyrites, iron ore, chrome, nickel, magnesite, manganese, bauxite and gold.[29] Between 1940 and 1944 the occupied lands' contribution to German steel needs grew from 3 per cent to 27 per cent.[30] From the east, German troops hoped to take 4 millions of tons of grain from the Ukraine, and seized control of the bulk of Russia's industry, depriving Stalin of 65 per cent of coal production, 65 per cent of iron and 60 per cent of steel and aluminium.[31] In truth, though, the German Empire in the east, like the Italian Empire in Libya, was still-born. The migration of Germans to Poland was disappointing – only 4,500 of a planned-for 40,000 applied. So too did Mussolini's plans for the settlement of North Africa fail to materialise, with the flow of emigration actually slowing down.[32]

Ashley Clarke the head of the Far Eastern Department at the Foreign Office wrote 'I know that some American critics think that the British Empire exists in order to keep the holders of rubber, tin and oil shares in immense comfort in the West End of London; and I don't deny that we derive economic advantages from our system.'[33] Historian Lizzie Collingham writes that 'the war intensified the exploitative nature of colonialism' in the British Empire. In 1940 Britain passed a Colonial Development and Welfare Act, but 'first and foremost, colonial economic and industrial development during the war facilitated Britain's exploitation of its empire's resources'.[34] The puppet administration in India was told to hand over rice to supply the British army in the Middle East, and to feed plantation workers on Ceylon, Britain's main supply of rubber after Malaya was invaded.[35] Throughout the war India was made to lend the British what Churchill called 'a million pounds a day' so that by the end they had extended credit of £1,300,000,000 – money they could not afford. With bad grace, the Prime Minister moaned throughout about 'Indian money lenders'.[36]

From Nigeria Britain extracted 400,000 tons of palm oil kernels a year that Food Minister Lord Woolton needed to meet the fat ration back home; and cocoa that was sold to the US for chocolate rations, raising £2,700,068 for the British reserves. The colonial West African Produce Board set prices low so that African farmers subsidised Britain. Elsewhere the white farmers of Kenya and Rhodesia were given higher prices so that they could take advantage of the £1.5 million that the British Army was spending each year on meat, maize, vegetables, bacon and dairy goods.[37] By contrast, Holland had rested on her Empire in Indonesia for fully one seventh of her national income[38] – a stream of gold dammed by the Japanese occupation in 1942.

Forced Labour

'Humans are the Empire's capital and in the new Reich we cannot do without the labour of seven million Czechs' wrote Deputy Reich Protector Karl Frank in 1940.[39] As well as the workers in the occupied territories, more and more were dragged in to work as slave labour in Germany. By August 1944 there were 7,615,970 foreign workers on the employment rolls in the 'Greater German Reich' – 1.9 million were prisoners of war, and 5.7 million civilians press-ganged by the Plenipotentiary for Labour Deployment Fritz Sauckel from 1942. There were a quarter of a million Belgians, 1.3 million French, 590,000 Italians, 1.7 million Poles and 2.8 million Soviet citizens (mostly Ukrainians). In no real sense were these volunteers, having been sent by occupying forces or collaborationist authorities (in France under the Service Travail Obligatoire) under duress, and in the case of eastern workers, housed in barracks and kept apart from ordinary Germans.[40]

Like the Nazi authorities, the Allies were more brutal to subject peoples. On 1 August 1942 the British colony of Rhodesia passed a Compulsory Native Labour Act to force Xhosa people to work on settlers' farms and as labourers at the large air force bases. [41] Indigenous chiefs selected the unhappy victims, or if not, the Native Commissioner would have to 'hunt the natives in the reserves until the required numbers were obtained'.[42] In Tanzania the British authorities brought 6000 hectares of Ceara Rubber plantations, abandoned when the colony passed from German hands after the First World War back into production. 'Conscription for periods of twelve months was introduced in Central Province, mainly targeting the Gogo' writes William Clarence Smith:

> Many died, especially in the early months, when conditions were particularly poor. Although workers' compounds were guarded, others managed to desert.[43]

Even as the British army 'liberated' Burma, officials impressed labour to build military supply roads under the 'Defence of Burma' rules, starving the countryside of farmers.[44]

In Brazil 55 000 people were drafted as 'Rubber Soldiers' to work in the Amazon under a deal between US President Roosevelt and the dictator, Getúlio Vargas to fill America's rubber shortage.[45] John Foster Dulles explained that the five-year rubber agreement signed on 3 March 1942 laid claim to all exports. Frustrated at the poor output of the rubber slaves, the US 'furnished barracks' and 'even sent troupes of entertainers to brighten their lives'. Many thousands died from Malaria and other diseases but America secured rubber supplies of around 29,000 tons a year.[46] In Liberia, too, the Firestone Rubber Company bought labourers from tribal chiefs and paid the indentured men in kind, or with what overseer Arthur Hayman called 'coolie wages', so that by 1945 output was up to 20,000 tons from 4,800 tons in 1939.[47]

Also the Japanese seized 700 000 Koreans and 40 000 Chinese, many to work in the mines.[48] Thousands of Malays, Chinese and Burmese, as well as British Prisoners of War were forced to work, too, building the Burma-Thailand Railway.[49] Tens of thousands of women, mostly Korean, were forced into prostitution as 'comfort women' to the Japanese Army.[50]

Malthus' law

Raiding the colonies to feed the war, the protagonists risked starving them. To the colonisers, though, it did not seem that it was the exploitation of the colonies that led to starvation, but the excess of 'useless mouths' there, expecting to be fed. These were the prejudices of the economist, the Reverend Thomas Malthus.

In peace, Japan had traded manufactures for raw materials and basic goods in East Asia. But to fight the war, her industries had been given over to armaments, so that she had nothing to trade. Just as military might united the Greater East Asia Co-Prosperity Sphere territorially, conversion to war industries made Japan an exploiter, not a partner.

Finance Minister Kaga Okinori told the imperial conference on the 5 November 1941 that

The Southern Regions to be occupied have been importing considerably large amounts of various commodities [from Japan]. When we occupy the areas, importation of these items will stop. If the local economies were to be maintained effectively, we should be supplying these commodities. However we do not have the necessary capabilities. For a considerably long period we cannot afford to pay attention to the economic well-being of the local people. We cannot but adopt so called exploitative policies.[51]

Matushita Masahisa of Rikkyō University was blunt at the secret

Navy Symposium of 7 October 1940, saying that the 'co-prosperity sphere' was deceptive because Japan would exploit the sphere's resources, but had nothing to reciprocate with. It would be a 'co-poverty sphere'.[52] The Finance Minister underlined the point. In the Southern Areas 'it will not be possible for us to be concerned with the livelihood of the peoples in these areas'.[53]

At a Cabinet meeting on 10 November 1943, Prime Minister Churchill said Indians had brought famine on themselves because they were 'breeding like rabbits' and so would have to pay the price of their own improvidence.[54] Churchill's prejudices were backed up by his chief scientific advisor Frederick Lindemann, Lord Cherwell, in a letter the following day: 'This shortage of food is likely to be endemic in a country where the population is always increased until only bare subsistence is possible.' Cherwell carried on to turn the truth on its head, moaning as if it was Britain that was subsidising India, not the other way around:

> After the war India can spend her huge hoards of sterling on buying food and thus increase the population still more, but so long as the war lasts her high birth rate may impose a heavy strain on this country [i.e. Britain] which does not view with Asiatic detachment the pressure of a growing population on limited supplies of food.[55]

The principle that the Japanese Finance Minister Kaga and the British scientific adviser Cherwell rested on was the economist Thomas Malthus' theory of 'overpopulation', according to which shortages arose from an excess of mouths over resources. Malthus' theory had been used in the past to show that famines in Ireland and India were bound to happen, and not the outcome of colonial seizures. The Nazi authorities in the east, though, made the most ruthless appeal to Malthus' theory. On 2 May 1941 the State Secretaries representing the Ministerial Agencies met General Thomas to draft plans for the occupation. They concluded:

1 The war can only be continued if the entire Wehrmacht is fed from Russia in the third year of the war
2 If we take what we need out of the country, there can be no

doubt that many millions will die of starvation

Reich Minister for Food Herbert Backe outlined the 'Hunger Plan', which was agreed by Hitler and Goering in February of 1941. According to the plan, some 30 million Russians would be made surplus – useless mouths – who would be starved to death once all grain was diverted, so that it flowed from Ukrainian and Russian farms, to German, rather than Russian towns. Himmler's speech to the SS Gruppenfuehrer on the coming race war used these same sums: 'through military actions and the food problems 20 to 30 million Slavs and Jews will die'.[56]

The Malthusian calculations proved all-too accurate. 2,800,000 Russian Prisoners of War starved in German camps, and countless more Russian Ukrainian and Byelorussian civilians followed them. [57] In Greece a quarter of a million died in the 1941-43 famine under German rule. [58] Even Holland lost 10 000 to famine in the later years of the war. In Bengal as many as 3.5 million died as British authorities redirected Indian grain to Ceylon and elsewhere, wrecking the supply system to stymie a feared Japanese invasion. On the Burma Railway 14,000 British Prisoners of War died of malnutrition and disease – and ten or twenty times more Burmese, Indians, Malays and Chinese died alongside them.[59] In Vietnam, where both French and Japanese troops commandeered food while the allies bombed supply lines, between one and two million starved to death in 1945. Starvation, it should be said, was not just an unpredictable by-product of wartime disruption. Colonial rulers planned to redirect resources from their starving subjects to feed the engines of war.

Chapter Seven

Militarisation of Everyday Life

War was not only fought on the battlefield. The spirit of militarism moved its way through the whole of society. The elevation of the warrior-caste put in place new ideals of authority and obedience. 'Never in the field of human conflict was so much owed by so many to so few,' Churchill told the House of Commons about the 'battle of Britain' on 20 August 1940. It was a statement of the masses debt to the elite. By defending British airspace, the aristocrats of the Royal Air Force had saved Britain from invasion. As it happens, the Battle of Britain was less important than was claimed at the time. Nor, indeed, was it true that the Battle of Britain pilots came mostly from Public Schools. Today historians accept that there was little real danger that Hitler would invade, but the myth of the civilians' debt to the military was important all the same.[1]

Militarism seeped into the lives of ordinary people across the world long before the war began, and when it did the War on the Home Front was every bit as important as the battlefield. As we have seen the organisation of war industries, the regimentation of war workers, farming and rationing all re-made civilian life along military lines.

Both the German and Italian governing regimes had their origins in militias, drawn from ex-servicemen, the squeezed middle classes and the unemployed. There were right wing militias, too, in France – Croix de Feu and Action Française – and in Britain Moseley's black-shirts (which were suppressed during the war). In coming to power, Hitler (and to a lesser extent Mussolini) had to rein in his brown-shirted Sturmabteilung, or SA, whose leaders were attacked in the 'Night of the Long Knives', 30 June 1934, and their supporters largely inducted into the army. ('Hitler has shown his honest deter-mination to change from a revolutionary to a sober constructive policy', reported the *Times* in London: 'Although having come to power by force this power is now used to destroy all radicalism based on force', 2 July 1934.) The other Nazi militia, the Schutzstaffel, or SS, carried out the attack. It was split in two parts of which one part enforced order at home, while a second, the Waffen SS was integrated into the army as an 'elite' force. The Hitler Youth, starting from a membership of just 100 000 in 1932 grew quickly, and from 1936 was renamed the State Youth, by which time membership was effectively compulsory (and actually so from 1938):[2] 'the entire German youth within the Reich territory is organized in the Hitler Youth' (Hitler Youth Statute, 1 December 1936).[3] In Italy, membership of the Partito Nazionale Fascista climbed from 2.6 million members in 1939 to 4.77 million in 1942.[4]

In Soviet Russia 'Uniforms were introduced for diplomats, then for the legal profession and for transport workers.' A friend of Ilya Ehrenburg's joked that 'there would soon be uniforms for poets, with one, two or three lyres on the epaulets according to rank'.[5]

Not just the dictatorships, but also the democracies saw people's energies directed energies into volunteering and uniforms. Men and women worked in the ATS, the Land Army, and the Civilian Conservation Corps in the US. 53 000 British Boy Scouts took on National Service work in 1940, taking part in the cross channel evacuation at Dunkirk.[6] George Orwell told Americans that 'In a very little while we will all be in uniform or doing some kind of compulsory labour, and probably eating communally.'[7]

Communities were drawn into volunteering campaigns like the Winter Relief Fund in Germany – those who did not contribute

Pots and pans were collected to make Spitfires – but this is the closest they came to flying

might be beaten up – or the collection of scrap metal. Japanese families were organised into street committees, to keep an eye on one other. Lord Beaverbrook led a campaign to unite personal sacrifice with the war effort: 'we will turn your pots and pans into Spitfires, Hurricanes, Wellingtons and Bleinheims'.[8] The alleged aluminium shortage, though, was denied by scrap merchants.[9] Iron railings were also taken down, to emphasize that the wealthy too were making sacrifices, though these were never put to war use but still sat in a secret warehouse in Durham as late as the 1970s, as presumably did the pots and pans.[10]

The intensive mobilisation of society was underscored by a constant haranguing from the Ministry of Information in Britain to 'Turn that light out', 'Make do and mend', and demands such as 'Is your journey really necessary?', and 'Keep mum'. US propaganda warned that 'loose lips sink ships', and enjoined Americans to think of Europeans under the jackboot before themselves. The word 'propaganda' got its negative connotation from the widespread use of it in Nazi Germany and posters there promoted militarism, the Fuhrer, motherhood and the rural life, alongside vicious caricatures of enemies real and imagined, international bolshevism and the Jewish conspiracy. Mass rallies sustained the German war effort, in the purpose built auditoria of Nuremburg and elsewhere. Americans had their mass rallies, too, for war bonds, where the heroes of Iwo Jima were paraded.

Air raid precautions were a real enough problem – but they were also an opportunity for drawing the public into exercises of civil defence that would break down the divide between military and civilian. In 1938, while the crisis in the Sudetan Land was underway Londoners dug trenches in the parks, and put on gas-masks. Before the war, opinion was divided between those who wanted to prevent war and those who wanted to prepare for it. They coalesced on the need for air raid precautions –Europeans had no experience of air warfare, and the prospect terrified them.

Where they took on the cause of the war as their own, workers in many countries sacrificed a great deal for victory. Loyalty did not come all at once, but built up, over the course of the war. Workers, like everyone else, were cheered when their side won, angry when they were attacked.

The 'blitzkrieg' motorised invasion of the old enemy France thrilled many Germans. It was a victory that cost them very little. Britons, sceptical about the Phoney War between 1939 and 1941 were gripped by the drama of Dunkirk when the British Expeditionary Force were saved by 'a flotilla of small ships' - in the words of J.B. Priestley's radio broadcast. The myth that civilian volunteers had rescued the army was not true - those ships that did take part were commandeered. Still the Ministry of Information understood that the divide between the armed services and the population had been broken down - in spirit if not in fact. Americans, not won over to Roosevelt's pro-British policy, were stung into action by the Japanese attack on Pearl Harbor. The wider fight stirred patriotism on the shop floor. From New Orleans the Office of War Information got this telegram: 'Please rush gruesome photos of dead America soldiers for plant promotion Third War Loan'.[11]

Civil Liberties

In 1933, the NSDAP terrorised their left-wing opponents, throwing thousands into makeshift camps. By the end of July the camps were made official and the inmates counted: 26,700. After, the number fell off till it was just 5000 in 1936. Then in 1937 it started to rise again as a new wave of repression was launched, and the following year it climbed to 24,000. 'Professional criminals', vagabonds, prostitutes, Gypsies and the unemployed had been rounded up. In November 1938 – the November Pogrom, also known as 'Kristallnacht' – 35,000 Jews were thrown into the camps. On the eve of the war there were 22,000 detainees, half political, half 'anti-social'.[12] With the eclipse of the SA, the SS directed policing operations and ran the concentration camps. On top of the SS, was the new Gestapo, **Ge**heime **Sta**atspolizei, or Secret State Police under SS leader Himmler. Outside of the law, the Gestapo were greatly helped by the existing police forces, taking over their files of subversive communists and socialists.[13] The collaboration of the ordinary police meant that just a handful of Gestapo officers were needed to dominate German towns and cities.

In Japan, the Peace Preservation Law was passed in 1928 to curb labour unrest and the left.

Peace Preservation Law Violations

	1928	1930	1933	1935	1940	1941	1942	1943
Arrested	3426	6124	14,822	1785	817	1212	698	159
Prosecuted	525	461	1285	113	229	236	339	52

Most of these were leftists, though towards the last years of the war they were outnumbered by religious opponents of the war.[14]

When it came to attacking civil liberties, the Fascist powers set standards of depravity that were unique in the west, only matched by Stalin in the east. It would be wrong to see Fascism and Democracy as all much of a muchness. There were clear differences. But it would be wrong too to see the Allied States as free societies. They were governed by profoundly authoritarian rulers, under the rules of an 'emergency' that lasted for six years. The populace had not been crushed as it had in Italy and Germany, but it was, nonetheless browbeaten and anxious after years of depression, war-mongering, and 'strong leaders'. There were important differences. But just as the onset of war cemented the brand of 'democracy' as unique selling point for the allies, in contrast to the fascist states, war also drained the democracy of its real substance, leaving it as little more than a label. Both Allies and Axis governments tended to rule through emergency powers, and even in Britain and America, democratic consultation tended to boil down to a discussion amongst elites and experts, with the common people reduced to onlookers.

Speaking for the Emergency Powers (Defence) Act of 1939 Sir Samuel Hoare said that its powers were 'very wide, very drastic and very comprehensive'. The British Act was followed by Australia's draconian National Security Bill, with Premier John Curtin saying 'we are at a stage in our history when the struggle for survival as a nation overrides every other consideration'.[15]

George Orwell, a reluctant supporter of the war effort told American readers of the Partisan Review that 'a foolish law was passed some time back making it a punishable offence to say anything "likely to cause alarm and despondency".' [16] This was regulation 39a and on 17 July it was reported that a man had been sent to prison for telling a woman in a fish shop that Britain had no chance of winning the war. That month Prime Minister Churchill refused to lift the regulation, saying that the government wanted to 'curb, as it is their duty to do, propaganda of a defeatist nature'.[17] Churchill used the regulations to suppress communist literature:

> This kind of propaganda ought not to be allowed, as it is directly contrary to the will of Parliament and hampers the maintenance of resistance to the enemy. I do not see why if Mosley is confined subversives and Communists should not be equally confined. The law and the regulations ought to be enforced against those who hamper our war effort from the extreme Right or the extreme Left.[18]

The Cabinet set up a Suspicious Political Activities Committee under Philip Cunliffe-Lister, Lord Swinton, to 'counteract fifth column activities', but would not tell Parliament anything about its work because it was 'not in the public interest'.[19]

Defence Regulation 18b gave the authorities the right to detain people without trial. This regulation was used to imprison 1,800 people – mostly members of the British Union of Fascists. Though it was used against the far right, regulation 18b was also used against leftists and labour militants. Sheffield shop steward John Mason was detained in 1940 for 'impeding the war effort' – despite a number of protests in his defence. In 1941, asked why it was right to imprison trade unionists, the Home Secretary said that it was since the man concerned had been 'involved in attempts to slow down war production'.[20] On 12 August 1940 Co-op store manager Alfred Comrie was interviewed at Hucknall Police station, about his political activities, and warned that under Regulation 18b he was 'compelled to answer'. The police wanted to know about Communist Party membership, and about his wife Mary's involvement in the MP George Lansbury's peace campaign.

On 4 May 1941 George Johnson Armstrong, a 39-year old merchant seaman from Newcastle was tried as a spy in a secret court before Justice Lewis at the Old Bailey. In fact Armstrong was guilty of jumping ship in Boston, where he spoke to anti-war meetings organised by the American Socialist Party. Far from being a Nazi spy, Armstrong was a supporter of the Independent Labour Party. His appeal disallowed, Armstrong was hung in Wandsworth Prison

on 10 July 1941, again, in secret.[21]

Four anarchists, opponents of the war, Marie Louise Berneri (pictured), Vernon Richards, John Hewetson and Philip Sansom were tried at the Old Bailey, and the last three were found guilty on 26 April and jailed. They had been selling the anti-war paper *War Commentary*.[22] In June 1940, six members of the Peace Pledge Union, (Alexander Wood, Maurice Rowntree, Stuart Morris, John Barclay, Ronald Smith and Sidney Todd) had been convicted of encouraging disaffection amongst troops, but not imprisoned.

As well as acting against Fascists, Socialist and Anarchists, the British state fought against Irish Republicans seeking to free their country from the military occupation of its six northern counties, where most Catholics had no vote. In 1939 a Prevention of Violence (Temporary Provisions) Act was brought in to detain without trial alleged IRA volunteers who threatened to wage war against Britain. Among those imprisoned were the future playwright Brendan Behan, and over the next year 167 were excluded from the UK.[23] On 7 February 1940 two IRA men Peter Barnes and James McCormick were tried and hung at Winson Green Prison for a bomb planted in Coventry in 1939 – though it was admitted they were not the bombers they were convicted for taking part in the conspiracy. All over Ireland flags hung at half-mast, and the boy Ruairí Ó Brádaigh, who would become the IRA chief of staff and president of Sinn Fein, knelt to pray. In 1942 the IRA launched a series of attacks on the Six Counties of Northern Ireland in Belfast in April, and then in Armagh in September. The British Cabinet thought about bringing in 'internment camps' to detain Irish suspects, and IRA men were interned in the Peel Camp on the Isle of Wight alongside members of the British Union of Fascists.[24]

Some of the left thought that there was nothing wrong with the state holding political prisoners – as long as they were fascists. Labour members of parliament, and even the Communist Willie Gallacher were angry when Oswald Mosley was released from prison in 1943. It was a mistake they had made before. In 1934 left wingers supported the introduction of the Public Order Act on the grounds that it was the best measure for sending Fascists to jail. In the event, of course, the police were happier jailing left-wingers than right-wingers, and many were arrested under the Act. The same thing had happened in Germany. Laws that Socialists had put on the statute books to jail Nazis were instead used by the right to jail them.[25]

In Germany ten thousand Jehovah's Witnesses were sent to concentration camps, and 2500 of them killed because of their unwillingness to support the war or give allegiance to the Nazi state. Church men were imprisoned for their opposition to the Nazis, like the pacifist Dietrich Bonhoeffer who was executed in April 1945 after a closed trial, and Lutheran Pastor Martin Niemöller – who, as he says in his celebrated poem, watched while the Communists and the trade unionists were taken away, and even sanctioned some anti-Jewish laws, but in time spoke out against Nazi control of the church and was sent to Sachsenhausen and then Dachau concentration camp.

As we have seen Britain's conscientious objectors were made to do war work in the mines and elsewhere. In America, pacifist churches agreed with the government the terms of the Selective Service Act of 1940 that let conscientious objectors do Civilian Public Service instead of going into the army. In practice, though, this meant that they were sent to work camps, that the churches oversaw, but were mostly prison camps, where inmates were poorly fed. By 1943 many pacifists were refusing to work and leaving the camps to risk jail instead: 'one out of six inmates in federal prison during World War II were objectors to war'.[26] At the Lewisburg and Danbury jails, objectors went on strike, refusing to clear their cells or do prison work. On 12 January 1944 peace activist Bayard Rustin was jailed for three years for his refusal to go to a CPS camp, where he protested against segregation and was further persecuted for his homosexuality.

Concentration camps were first used by the British to house rebellious Boers. But the Nazi concentration camps and the Soviet Gulag system are generally understood to have been the most barbaric. In the German concentration camps Jews, Poles, Gypsies and leftists were detained alongside homosexuals, and other so-called deviants. From 1941, there were selective killings of inmates, and in 1943 a full-blown policy of extermination aimed first and foremost at Jews was put into action. The Soviets 'Gulag' system, was called *Glavnoye upravlyeniye ispravityel'no-trudovih lagyeryey i koloniy* or Chief Administration of Corrective Labour Camps and Colonies. It was born out of the Soviet leadership's paranoid relation to its citizens, especially after the suppression of the Soviets (workers' councils) and the purges of the Bolshevik party itself for oppositionists. As we have seen, millions were detained in the Second World War, and many died.

Internment without trial was also practised by both Britain and America. Britain jailed 27,000 'enemy aliens' – Germans, Austrians and Italians – by June 1940. Foreign nationals were examined before a tribunal to assess their danger to the war effort. Despite the supposed political complexion of the conflict, the National Council for Civil Liberties showed that often the tribunals marked down leftists as a particular danger.[27] Many Jewish and political refugees from Germany were swept up in the internment, including writer Sebastian Haffner, montagist John Heartfield, the general secretary of the International league for the Rights of Man Carl von Ossietsky, and the Marxist Alfred Sohn-Rethel, who was painted there by Kurt Schwitters.

There was opposition to the policy, and Eleanor Rathbone protested in parliament at the 'mass of evidence pouring in upon all of us of the widespread misery and fear suffered by the refugees'. Lord Swinton, speaking after the war was unrepentant: 'As for the scum, quite rightly we put a lot of them inside at the critical time, but a great many of them did not matter very much'.[28]

In America President Roosevelt signed Executive Order 9066 on 19 February 1942 aimed at Japanese Americans, mostly farmers, who lived on the West Coast. The Order created an 'exclusion zone' that extended around 250 miles inland from the Pacific, taking in the whole of California, where Japanese Americans were made to relocate to camps, after selling up their farms at firesale prices. One hundred and ten thousand Japanese Americans were detained up until 1944, in a breach of their rights under Article 1, Section 9 of the US constitution. The internees lost land and goods valued at around $400 million, and traded their small farms for cold and windy tar-paper shacks. Lobbying for the measure Austin E. Anson of the Shipper-Grower Association of Salinas said:

> We're charged with wanting to get rid of the Japs for selfish reasons. We might as well be honest. We do.[29]

Quite apart from the selfish commercial interests of their neighbours, the Japanese Americans were caught in the racial hysteria of wider American culture.

If the belligerent powers of World War II were indifferent to the rights of their citizens at home, they were brutal in their treatment of subject peoples in their colonies.

Censorship

Censorship was of course rife in the armed services, with letters routinely read by censors in all nations. But as more and more of society was organised on military lines, then censorship spread. As well as controlling the output of official information, governments influenced the output of the privately owned presses, either by having them taken over, or by applying pressure or outright bans.

Germany had introduced state control of the radio in 1932 under von Papen, but Goebbels went much further, controlling what was broadcast and who worked there. Ownership of radios went up from four to 16 million between 1933 and 1941. Collective listening was encouraged and 'Radio Wardens' made sure it happened. On coming to power the NSDAP closed as many as 200 Socialist-affiliated newspapers, and 35 Communist ones. The Nazis' Eher Verlag Press bought up Jewish-owned publishers' like Ullstein's at knock-down prices under the 'Aryanisation' measure. The regional catholic press passed into Eher Verlag's hands, as did the respected *Frankfurter Zeitung*. In time, Eher Verlag owned 82.5 per cent of the German press.[30]

German universities were purged and mass book burning was organised with students throwing works by Karl Marx, Rene Descartes and Thomas Mann onto the flames.

In Occupied Europe listening to Allied radio broadcasts was banned, and conservative newspapers often willingly collaborated with the Nazi authorities, like Norway's *Aftenposten* (on 7 May 1945, *Aftenposten* carried a eulogy to Hitler, written by Knut Hamsen: 'We, his closest supporters, now bow our heads at his death.')

In Italy, the Fascist movement had put pressure on the conservative editor of *Il Giornale d'Italia* to give up his position since 1924, when he was assaulted in his home. The following year, Luigi Albertini was persuaded to stand down as editor of *Il Corriere della Sera*, being replaced eventually by Aldo Borelli, who followed the fascist line. By 1928 every working journalist had to be a registered fascist. Radical papers like the Socialist *Avanti!* And the Communist *L'Unità* were shut down – *L'Unità* going underground from 1927, *Avanti!* publishing from Switzerland.[31]

In Japan a Provisional Law for Control of Speech, Publications, Assembly, and Association said that all meetings and speeches had to have prior approval from officials before they went ahead. The prior approval system was imposed on newspapers and magazines, too. The law contained harsh punishments for spreading of 'false reports or rumours' and 'information that confuses public sentiment'.[32]

Offices were set up in Britain during the war to censor post and telegraph messages going overseas.[33] In the 'Fifth Column' scare of 1940 suspicious busybodies informed on their neighbours, sending police officers off to raid their houses:

Members of the Left Book Club and workers in adult education seem to have attracted at least as much attention as the followers of Sir Oswald Mosley. Up and down the country, police officers returned in triumph to base with such works as Lord Addison's *A Policy for Agriculture*, the Duchess of Atholl's *A Searchlight on Spain*, Leonard Woolf's *Barbarians at the Gate*, Ellen Wilkinson's *The Town that was Murdered*, G. E. R. Gedye's *Fallen Bastions* and even John Stuart Mill's *The Principles of Political Economy*.[34]

Regulations were in place to suppress articles and newspapers, but generally the government preferred to talk privately to editors and proprietors. In cabinet Meetings in October 1940, the British Cabinet discussed coverage in the News Chronicle, Sunday Pictorial and Daily Mirror, which they felt were mischievous. Sir Archibald Sinclair, Secretary of State for Air, was asked to 'use his influence with the proprietors'. Plans to suppress the Mirror under regulation 2D for 'spreading a spirit of defeatism' were made, but not in the end acted on.[35]

As we have seen, the Peace Pledge Union was harassed by the authorities, and its publications seized. The authorities also went after the publishers of Peace News, who then refused to print it. [36] In November 1940 a booklet by the Union, 'The Conquest of Violence' was held to be so seditious that the Director of Public Prosecutions told them that it would be an offence to possess it. Sellers of the Communist Party newspaper, the Daily Worker were often moved on or threatened with arrest in 1940, and in January 1941 the cabinet agreed to suppress the Daily Worker – as well as Claud Cockburn's newssheet, The Week – under regulation 2D. On 21 January the party's offices and printworks were raided and the paper closed down. Herbert Morrison explained to the House of Commons that these two publications had

By every device of distortion and misrepresentation sought to make out that our people have nothing to gain by victory, that the hardships and sufferings of warfare are unnecessary and imposed upon them by a callous Government carrying on a selfish contest in the interests of a privileged class.[37]

Following the German invasion of the Soviet Union in 1941, the British Cabinet looked closely at the changing policy of the Communist Party of Great Britain and was particularly impressed by the organisation's newfound dedication to boosting war production. Even so, it was not until a year later that the *Daily Worker* was allowed to begin publishing again, which it did on 7 September 1942, though now as a demonstratively patriotic paper.

Chapter Eight

Caesarism

The true Fascist should see himself as 'the rightful descendant of Caesar,' said Benito Mussolini.[1] The Italian parliament was stripped of its authority, while political power went to the 'Fascist Council' and 'Il Duce'.

In Germany, military circles never accepted the defeat in 1919, but blamed the politicians: 'the German army was stabbed in the back' said President Hindenberg.[2] With the upheavals after the war, the elite wanted authoritarianism. Under the Weimar Constitution 'If public security and order are seriously disturbed or endangered within the Reich, the President of the Reich may take measures necessary for their restoration, intervening if need be with the assistance of the armed forces.' Article, 48 was drawn up under the guidance of the 'liberal' sociologist Max Weber, as a needed stop-gap against the left.[3]

A crock of Schmitt

The theory of 'decisionism' was developed by the German jurist and Nazi collaborator Carl Schmitt, who argued that all judgements were acts that made the law more than they followed it. The theory is not without meaning – it is true that in the end judgements are a kind of leap that one cannot second guess or reduce to the arguments that lead up to them. But Schmitt's error was to make a fetish of the decision and overstate the departure from the legal, (or political) argumentation that precedes it. With the destruction of the political process in Nazi Germany, decisionism made the law, which, as the exiled German jurist Franz Neumann explained really meant that there was no law in the meaningful sense of the word. The will of the Fuhrer was the law, and that will was capricious.[4]

The formalisation of the leadership principle, the abolition of the distinction between the National Socialist party and the state (party property was exempt from taxation), the suspension of citizenship rights, the loss of the distinction between the private realm and the public, retrospective legislation and the practice of judicial preemption of yet-to-be-passed laws all added up to a suspension of ordinary legal norms. Mysticism, charismatic leadership - 'decisionism', and intuition all took precedence over rational norms in law and government - often in ways that seem like they were inimical to the creation of a secure business environment. Franz Neumann argued that corporate capitalism made abstract law problematic: 'In a monopolistically organized system the general law cannot be supreme', because the state is acting against one corporation, not adjudicating between many interests.[5] But it was of course unlikely that the suspension of general law would work in the interests of the masses. In the German Reichstag and the Italian Senate, the Nazis staged political demonstrations, and manhandled deputies that refused to join in the salutes. Debate gave way to the leadership state. Philosopher Martin Heidegger dismissed the 'Idle chatter' and 'publicness' of 'the They', while the Nazi Lawyers group simply rubbished reason as 'Jewish'.[6]

In the Soviet Union the jurist Evgeny Pashukanis fought a losing battle resisting the demand that the law be made an instrument of 'class justice'. It was premature to say that the interests of the Socialist state and the individual were identical argued Pashukanis, saying that the Soviet courts should observe civil rights. Jurists like Yudin and Andrey Vyshinsky scoffed at such legal niceties as harshly as SS Deputy Reinhard Heydrich did in Germany. In a series of 'show trials' led by Vyshinsky opponents and others were denounced for fantastic plots against the state, on the basis of forced confessions. In 1937 Pashukanis himself was convicted as a 'Trotskyite saboteur' and executed.[7]

Though more extreme in the German and Soviet cases, such features were hardly unknown elsewhere. In Britain, as war was engaged to defend democracy, the elected Members of Parliament abandoned contestation in favour of coalition, once Neville Chamberlain handed the key to Number Ten Downing Street to Winston Churchill. The main political parties, Conservative, Labour and Liberal also undertook not to challenge each other's constituency seats in by-elections, so that there would be no ordinary political contest in the country. The MP Kenneth Pickthorn voiced the House of Commons' own disquiet, saying 'to some of us, it seems that the real danger in which our general liberties are involved at present is precisely that the Executive controls some 99/100ths of this House'. Bob Boothby, Churchill's energetic champion in the House of Commons let the truth slip saying 'it is a complete fallacy to suggest that any real power is exercised by Members of this House over the Executive'.[8] Just as Britain's law-making chamber lost importance, the character of its rules changed. Lawyers Ewing and Gearty point out 'the degree to which emergency rather than ordinary law was the normal state of affairs' between 1914-1945.[9]

One leader was setting out his stall in March 1933:

> We must move as a trained and loyal army willing to sacrifice for the good of a common discipline, because without such discipline no progress is made, no leadership becomes effective. We are I know all ready to submit our lives and property to such discipline because it makes possible a leadership which aims at a larger good. This I propose to offer pledging that the larger purposes that will bind upon us all a sacred obligation with unity of duty hitherto evoked only in a time of armed strife. With this pledge taken, I assume unhesitatingly the leadership of this great army of our people dedicated to a disciplined attack on common problems.

The speaker, as historian Niall Ferguson points out, is not Adolf Hitler, but Franklin Roosevelt.[10]

Today Roosevelt is often reckoned one of the great radical architects of the modern democratic movement. But in the early days of his administration observers saw a fascistic flavour in the New Deal. The Independent Labour Party leader Fenner Brockway wrote about his visit to America in 1934, which he subtitled 'A Study of the Fascist tendencies in America'. Brockway felt he saw 'exactly the same kind of hero worship poured out by exactly the same kind of Governmental propaganda as extols Adolf Hitler in Germany'. More, Brockway found a readiness to 'resort to violence' and 'tendencies towards racialism' as well as 'demagogy and theatricalism' that all seemed to cast Roosevelt in a Fascistic light.[11] Brockway's instincts were not so odd on the left. In 1937, another radical commentator wrote that 'In the election of Roosevelt was not revealed so much the will of the masses to activity, rather the instinctive recognition of their present impotence, which seeks after the strong man.'[12] Certainly Roosevelt demanded from congress 'a broad Executive power to wage war against the emergency', [13] and tried to pack the Supreme Court when it voted down his National Industrial Relations Act.

The US Round Table of Economic Experts argued in 1940 that: 'If this war leads Europe to adopt the totalitarian economic system in which government directs production and foreign trade, the United States might move more in the same direction for reason of self-defence.'[14] Back in 1934, Fenner Brockway already thought that 'America has already gone far towards the industrial autocracy which is the essence of the Fascist economic structure'.[15] Labour Secretary Francis Perkins told George Rawick that at the first meeting of the Roosevelt Cabinet in March 1933, 'Bernard Baruch, and Baruch's friend General Hugh Johnson, who was to become the head of the National Recovery Administration, came in with a copy of a book by Gentile, the Italian Fascist theoretician, for each member of the Cabinet, and we all read it with great care'.[16]

With America's involvement in the War, 'Dr New Deal' became 'Dr Win-the-War'. Indeed the New Deal had rather run out of steam, and the war invested Roosevelt's programme with a new sense of urgency. Dean Acheson at the US State Department saw that war gave the government a new mission: 'The indecisions, hesitations, and doubts of the past year, the pretenses and fumblings, were gone.' Instead, 'Argument over, the country and the capital turned to what Americans like and do best, action.'[17]

Roosevelt's demotic appeal was a high-risk strategy, that suspended the usual democratic debate, but did not get rid of rivalry altogether. Instead challenges were mounted in the same register. In 1942, after General Douglas MacArthur fought a powerful public relations campaign (rather better in fact than his defence of the US position in the Far East) a Republican lawyer Joseph Savage led a grass-roots appeal to draft him for the Presidency. The 'American Caesar' was a more attractive dictator for many on the right who resented Roosevelt's social welfare programmes. Father Charles Coughlin charged that MacArthur had been betrayed in the Far East. George van Horn Moseley wrote to MacArthur that subversives were terrified of the General , and that the American people, outraged by the 'mongrelization' of the country at the hands of blacks, immigrants, New Dealers and Jews would overthrow the government and make him dictator. A poll for Fortune put his popularity at 57.3 per cent, and Senator La Follette proposed a congressional resolution bringing in a national MacArthur day.[18] Carefully, Roosevelt set about managing this rival for the post of American dictator.

General de Gaulle, leader of the 'Free French' was no democrat, but looked forward to his country being free of the 'decadent' Third Republic and what he saw as its 'corrupt' system of party politics. Time and again Resistance leaders drawn by the General's appeal, were repulsed by his dictatorial instincts and the right-wingers around him. Even his best agent Jean Moulin asked 'is he really a democrat? I don't know.'[19] Pressed by Resistance leader Christian Pineau to promise a democratic France after the war, de Gaulle could only re-emphasise his own personal authority: 'tell those brave people that I will not betray them'.[20]

'The defence of capitalism is,' John Hobson explained in 1938 'bound up in every country with the enfeeblement of the public franchise and representative government'.[21]

Prestige

The ground for the Second World War was prepared by the relentless growth of the capitalist powers – their commercial rivalry and the way that bled into military and territorial competition, too. But war was more than mere rational calculation of material interests. It was fought too for something altogether less easy to get a hold of, and that is the ethereal resource of *prestige*. Prestige, a power's standing in the eyes of other powers was as real as the stockpiles of missiles and shells, and the troops' positions on the ground. To be taken seriously as a power by other powers was what it meant. Over the years 1939 to 1941 all the major powers went to war, to defend their honour, as well as their export markets.

In 1935, as the Führer-Principal of Freiburg University Heidegger lectured on the "collapse of German idealism": 'It was not German idealism that collapsed; rather the age was no longer strong enough to stand up to the greatness, breadth and originality of that spiritual world, i.e. truly to realise it'.[22]

Mussolini protested against German invasions in the first year of the war, fearing that they would expose Italy to danger. But seeing Hitler's prestige grow he complained 'It's humiliating to remain with folded arms while others make history.' The economic gains of alliance with Germany were not so great, but still he felt the need for a sacrifice of Italian blood. 'It doesn't matter much who wins' he told his Foreign Minister Ciano: 'To make a people great it is necessary to send them into battle, even if you have to kick them in the pants.' 'I speak to him of his diminished prestige and of the none-too-brilliant role of playing second fiddle', goaded Ciano. The dictator told his Army Chief of Staff Pietro Badoglio on 5 June that 'I only need to have a few thousand dead so that I can sit at the peace conference as a man who has fought'.[23]

In 1938 Hitler's demands on Czechoslovakia were at first resisted, and then accommodated by Neville Chamberlain. Looking on, Mussolini understood what the brinkmanship meant: 'There will not be war, but this is the end of British prestige'.[24] Unable to dictate terms, Britain's fundamental weakness was exposed, and that would lead Chamberlain, and his successors to ever-more hysterical reactions. When Hitler put pressure on Poland for a road bridge to Danzig, Chamberlain told Parliament on 31 March 1939 that 'in the event of any action which clearly threatened Polish independence and which the Polish government accordingly considered it vital to resist with their national forces, His Majesty's Government would feel themselves bound at once to lend all support in their power'. Chamberlain's promise to Poland shocked former Prime Minister David Lloyd George, who thought that the British Army General Staff 'ought to be confined to a lunatic asylum' for agreeing it. Basil Liddell Hart thought Chamberlain's tough-talking would 'make war inevitable':

It incited Hitler to demonstrate the futility of such a guarantee to a country out of reach from the West, whilst making the stiff-necked Poles even less inclined to consider any concession to him, and at the same time making it impossible for him to draw back without "losing face".

In 1938 First Lord of the Admiralty Duff Cooper had resigned over

Chamberlain's weak stance at Munich. But in 1939 he was shocked by Chamberlain's overreaction the other way: 'Never before in our history have we left in the hands of one of the smaller powers the decision whether or not Britain goes to war'.[25] Chamberlain's *amour propre* was wounded at Munich, which led him to make an empty threat against Germany in 1939. On 3 September 1939, Chamberlain declared war on Germany, not in truth for the Poles, who were, after all, abandoned at the end of the war to the Soviet Union, but to defend Britain's prestige. After the declaration of war, Chamberlain was adamant that there could be no peace with Germany while Hitler was in power. According to his Private Secretary, there was 'an element of damaged vanity'. Hitler had 'made a dupe of Chamberlain'.[26]

In the course of the war, when Roosevelt put pressure on Churchill over the British Empire, the President mocked the Prime Minister's 'warped ... idea of sovereignty'. Demanding that all dependent territories be open to oversight from a future United Nations, Roosevelt said that he had no objection to the form of Sovereignty: 'Winston you can keep your old rag flying any place you want'. Indignant, Churchill demanded to know what Roosevelt meant by calling the Union Jack, 'an old rag'. Roosevelt, confident in the fact of power more than mere tokens, replied that it was no great insult since all flags were made of rags.[27] For Churchill, though, the prestige of the British flag was worth every life sacrificed before it.

Hysteria

In their personal style of leadership, Churchill, Roosevelt and Hitler were all remarkably similar. All three were known for manipulating their advisors, setting them in competition with each other. They often created different government bodies to do the same job, under rival heads, to see which would come up with the best solution. Hitler and Roosevelt in particular often sketched out the general direction of their administrations in a broad sweep and let others fill in the detail. On the other hand both Churchill and Hitler were guilty of micro-managing the battlefield, often with more confidence than sense. All three had a demotic, even hysterical side. Hitler 'excelled at creating a sense of perpetual movement and accomplishment to compensate for his specious legitimacy and incongruous social program'.[28] Both Hitler and Churchill tended to burn their bridges behind them, tying their respective nations to quixotic strategies that promised ruin or redemption. Hitler's overreaching territorial expansions were each funded by the preceding, as each new venture tended to forestall any doubts about what had happened before. Before the invasion of Poland, Hitler told his senior military commanders at the Reich Chancellery 'we must burn our boats'. On the eve of the invasion of Poland Mussolini asked Ribbentrop what it was that he wanted, the 'Corridor or Danzig':'Neither. Not now,' he said, gazing at me with his cold metallic eyes. 'We want war!'[29]

War was what the Nazi leadership needed to make Germany great both in the eyes of the German people, and her rivals abroad. Such were the deranged realities of nationalism that only blood sacrifice could redeem the country. War, too, would tie the German people into a pact with the Nazi leadership that they could not escape. Fighting on was the Nazis insurance against being overthrown in favour of a peace party. In 1943 Hitler told the situation conference:

> Don't fool yourself. There is no turning back. We can only move forward. We have burned our bridges.[30]

This kind of fatalism would prove disastrous for the German people – and many others – cutting off any option of pulling out of the war short of annihilation.

In his own way Churchill did something similar by telling the armed services on 9 February 1941 that they should forget about the costs and expect whatever they needed: 'ask and it shall be given'. In effect he bankrupted the exchequer and threw himself on the mercy of the United States. As the leader of the war party in Britain, Churchill had little choice but to lock the country into as ambitious a war strategy as he could, since any climb-down would have been the wreck of his career.

The thrill of war led to all kinds of magical thinking. In July 1941, the Soviet People's Commissariat of Armaments demanded a six fold increase in 37mm gun ouput in a week: 'the fascist horde has swept down on us; to discuss a lesser plan is impermissible.'[31]

Roosevelt, too, was guilty of being more mouth than trousers at a key moment in the war. At the Casablanca conference in January 1943, with Stalin demanding that his allies in the West open a Second Front Roosevelt disappointed him. To outmanouevre Stalin, Roosevelt sprung a new war aim on his allies: 'unconditional surrender' of the Axis powers. He was talking tough to hide the fact that America and Britain were not ready to cross the Channel onto mainland Europe. It was the unconditional surrender demand that Hitler was replying to when he said 'we have burned our bridges'. It was Roosevelt that had burned everybody's bridges. 'The politicians may believe that they decide events yet it is the war' explained Paul Mattick, 'that moves the movers, controls the controllers':

> How under such circumstances can Hitler be trusted? He can no longer trust himself. He ceases to understand what he is doing. And this he shares with all his enemies.[32]

At war with their own people

According to Hitler, the German people deserved to 'disappear' if they could not preserve themselves.[33]At the Prime Minister's country residence Chequers in August 1940, Free French leader De Gaulle was surprised to find Churchill disappointed that the German bombers had not attacked: 'So they won't come!' 'Are you in such a hurry to see your towns smashed to bits' De Gaulle asked Churchill. 'The bombing of Oxford, Coventry, Canterbury will cause such a wave of indignation in the United States that they will come into the war'.[34]

Chapter Nine

Race War

War, especially world war, was war waged in the name of nations, between nations. The elites that sent their people to war claimed authority over them in the name of the national community. Nationalism was the sentiment that undergirded the struggle. But national pride quickly shaded into racial hatred. As the exiled German sociologist Hans Speier explained 'In modern war, in which mass opinions count ... the enemy has to be wholly identified with the principle of evil, so that one can mobilise the power of right for one's own side.'[1] Racial hatred was what made people fight wars. All the participants in the Second World War tried to galvanise race hatred to promote their war aims.

The concept of a unification of all German-speaking peoples was a goal of foreign policy under Gustav Stresemann (in office from 1923 to 1929). It was especially pertinent since the country had lost six million of its citizens and 13 per cent of its territory in the Versailles peace. Stresemann's idea of the Volksgemeinschaft was carried over into National Socialist ideology.[2] This was a challenge to the peace settlement of 1919, but it was not so exceptional. Winston Churchill, too, posed the idea of the Union of English Speaking Peoples – in effect a union of Britain and America, as an alliance that would manage the changing power relations of the modern world. But the racial idea of Germany also meant the identification of the non-German other, the Slav and the Jew.

The extermination of European Jewry stands out as the defining moment of the Second World War, and of the barbarism of the Nazi regime that carried out this 'final solution' to the Jewish question. Anti-Semitism was not an incidental feature of Nazi policy, but right at its centre. In 1935 Hitler proclaimed the Reich Citizenship Law and the Law for the Defence of German Blood and German Honour, known as the race laws. Under this law German bloodedness (*Deutsch-blütigkeit*) was protected against admixture with that of Jews, gypsies, Negroes, Mongolians and any others who were 'not akin to German bloods'.[3] On this framework racial minorities, first and foremost Jews and then gypsies, had their marriages dissolved, were incrementally excluded from the professions, denied their civil liberties, made to wear special armbands, herded into ghettos and eventually deported to concentration camps. The historian Michael Burleigh has a point when he chooses the title *The Racial State* for his 1993 book about the Nazi regime. In planning the final solution of the Jewish question at the Wannsee Conference of 20 January 1942, setting troops to slaughter Jews, and then making camps given over to the extermination of Jews, the Nazi authorities took racial ideology to its terrible summit.

The Ideology of Anti-Semitism

Nazi anti-Semitism was ideological – which is to say that it was a fantastic inversion of reality. No doubt there were some cynical uses of anti-Semitism, but Nazis seem really to have believed that Jews were destroying Germany. 'The Jew' in Nazi thinking was a mythical projection of the limitations of the German middle classes. In the figure of the Jew, the Nazis combined everything that they felt threatened the position of the German middle class. To them the Jew represented international capital and local money lenders strangling honest Germans, debasing the coinage. Jews were imagined to be the barrier to the small businessman by competing unfairly with him. The Jews represented the threat from the east, for a middle class imagining itself swamped by migrants. The Jew was disease and corruption, the danger to social hygiene. The Jew was the morass of 'party politics', the incessant, sapping waste of clever lawyers endlessly debating in the Reichstag. And the Jew was political agitators, agents of a Bolshevik conspiracy.

The figure of the Jew in the ideology of anti-Semitism was a fantastic mirage that showed up everything that was lacking in the position of the German middle class: stability, a position, customers, credit, sure money, good health, loyal employees, a working political system that you could forget about. The Nazi party connected all those dots with its magical solution of a National Revolution that would free the Reich of Jews.

The ideology worked because it tied the fortunes of the benighted middle classes closely to that of the nation and the state. Anti-Semitism corresponded to certain Nazi policies, such as the political solution to the problem of inflation; the reassertion of Germany's independence and standing in the world; the claim for the return of the lands of the German people in the east; the assertion of Germany's position at the top of the racial hierarchy of nations; and the struggle against the radical leaders of the working class, socialist and communist. So far, the ideology of anti-Semitism served the Nazis well.

Franz Neumann understood at the outset that 'anti-Semitism provides a justification for eastern expansion':

> The theory of German racial superiority and Jewish racial inferiority permits the complete enslavement of the eastern Jews...It actually establishes a hierarchy of races - giving no rights to Jews, a few to Poles, a few more to the Ukrainians and full rights to the Germans.[4]

Ruling through military commanders (Gauleiters) the Nazis had no interest in extending rights to the subjected. Instead they ruled by dividing populations against each other. Some, like the Ukrainians, Croats and Hungarians were granted a specious authority over the more despised, particularly Jews. 'The anti-Semitic bacilli exist naturally everywhere in Europe', thought Goebbels, 'we must merely make them virulent'.[5]

But in the agonies of the Second World War, the impossibility of the position of German imperialism was writ large. The ambition for 'living space' in the east had tempted Germany into an overwhelming storm of conflicts. Defeats at the hands of Soviet and partisan forces made a mockery of the Nazi claim to be supermen. Embattled, the position of the Nazi elite became increasingly hysterical. The ideology of anti-Semitism had helped to get them into the mess they were in, but it was the only way for them to understand it, too. The more impossible the German position became, the more extreme the fantastic inversion of reality became. Where the battlefields of the eastern front offered up only defeats, the imaginary struggle against the Jew offered the staged spectacle of total victory over the enemy. The final solution to the Jewish problem was a mirage. The very ambition for a 'final solution' showed the magical thinking at work. Here was a desire to transcend all worldly problems and escape into fantastic solutions. The more impossible the German position was, the more extreme the ideological inversion of the problem.

Race thinking

Though the Nazi government in Germany took racial thinking much further than anyone had thought possible, those prejudices were hardly unique to the Nazis.

'I think one man is just as good as another as long as he is not a nigger or a Chinaman', the future US President Truman wrote early in his career, 'He' (his uncle Will):

> does hate Chinese and Japs. So do I. It is race prejudice I guess. But I am strongly of the opinion that Negroes ought to be in Africa, yellow men in Asia and white men in Europe and America.[6]

On July 21 1946 Truman used the diary to vent his anger at the former treasury secretary, Henry Morgenthau, who had sought his intervention on behalf of a ship of Jewish refugees who had been denied entry by Britain to what was then Palestine. "He'd no business, whatever to call me," Truman wrote. "The Jews have no sense of proportion nor do they have any judgment on world affairs."

In the same entry Truman goes on to say:

> The Jews, I find are very, very selfish. They care not how many Estonians, Latvians, Finns, Poles, Yugoslavs or Greeks get murdered or mistreated as D[isplaced] P[ersons] as long as the Jews get special treatment. Yet when they have power, physical, financial or political neither Hitler nor Stalin has anything on them for cruelty or mistreatment to the underdog.[7]

Truman's predecessor, though known for the executive order that guaranteed Black Servicemen their civil rights, could also give voice to casual prejudice. Roosevelt discussed the high birth rate in Puerto Rico with his advisor Charles Taussig:

"I guess the only solution is to use the methods which Hitler used effectively." He said that it is all very simple and painless – you have people pass through a narrow passage and then there is the brrrr of an electrical apparatus. They stay there for twenty seconds and from then on they are sterile.[8]

All the same, Roosevelt was often taken aback by his ally Churchill's choice of words. Frederick Eggleston, Australian Minister, in his diary records that Roosevelt 'said that he had numerous discussions with Winston about China ...and he continually referred to the Chinese as "Chinks" and "Chinamen"'[9] Churchill was steeped in racial prejudice and talked about the Soviet Union as a 'world wide communistic state under Jewish domination', 'the international Soviet of the Russian and Polish Jew', or just 'these Semitic conspirators'.[10] British Minister Harold Macmillan complained in 1943 that Henry Morgenthau 'He had a frightful little Jew – the worst type – Dr White with him' who had an 'insulting attitude to the British.'[11] The casual prejudices of the time seem surprising, but they were endemic.

Prejudice is not the same as the systematic racial laws that Hitler introduced in Germany. Still, the prejudices that the Allies shared were also linked to policy. Both Britain and America were societies that had white supremacy woven into their fabric.

The British Empire was built on white supremacy, and subjected its 430 million colonial subjects to a rigorous colour bar, where English colonial officers and white settlers led a privileged existence on the backs of the black and Asian servants. After the abolition of slavery in the British Empire in 1830, many kinds of coerced labour, 'apprenticeship' and indenture persisted, and native people were denied civil and political rights. So ingrained was the inequality that brutality, imprisonment and even casual killings were endemic, as were famines, and even the wholesale slaughter of those natives who stood up to their colonial masters. The fear – and hatred – that Britons felt towards their colonial subjects early in the twentieth century was well expressed by Bertrand Russell:

the sinister threat of colored Labor in the background. There is a very real danger that ... European civilisation as we know it will perish as completely as it perished when Rome fell before the Barbarians.[12]

Not surprisingly, German 'liberals' followed the lead offered by Britain. Max Weber saw imperialism and race supremacy as part and parcel with political growth: 'Only a politically mature people is a "master race" ... only master races are called upon to intervene in the course of global developments.'[13]

The United States of America had its own internal racial conflict. The reconstruction of the southern states after the Civil War rolled back the brief gains that former slaves had made, creating a harsh racial segregation known as the Jim Crow laws that held 12 million black Americans in thrall.

America's race conflicts were further rocked by the wave of immigration from southern and eastern Europe between 1890 and 1910. In 1910 Congress was sent a report from a special commission had been studying almost every imaginable aspect of immigration that 'showed that a majority of the children in the schools of 37 of our leading cities had foreign-born fathers.'[14] The anti-immigration uproar revived the Ku Klux Klan whose numbers grew to four million in 1924. Madison Grant's 1908 book *The Passing of the Great Race* celebrated the contribution of the 'Nordic Race' to America, as it warned of the dangers of the new immigration. The principle targets of this new campaign were Mediterranean, Jewish and Slav, more than they were black. In 1920 president Warren G Harding was initiated into the Klan in a ceremony at the White House.[15] In 1924 the Johnson-Reed immigration act, which imposed quotas based upon the 1890 census of the ideal proportions of 'Nordic' races and Southern and Eastern European immigrants (around two per cent).

The rise of Scientific Racism
Racial thinking was not only turned on black subject peoples, but also on the urban 'residuum', too. The Socialist intellectual Harold Laski worried that Britain was 'fostering the weaker part of mankind until its numbers have become a positive danger to mankind'. The scientists Francis Galton thought that a breeding programme and forcible sterilisation of the unfit elements would 'improve the racial qualities of future generations'.[16]

Galton's fantasies were soon given force as Eugenics movements sprang up in Britain, America, Germany and elsewhere. Enthusiasts of the Eugenics movement included intellectuals like Julian Huxley and the Webbs, scientists like Galton, and political leaders like Winston Churchill and Theodore Roosevelt.

Roosevelt set up a national Heredity Commission to investigate the genetic heritage of the country, and with the goal of 'encouraging the increase of families of good blood, and of discouraging the vicious elements in the cross-bred American civilization'.[17] The Commission members were drawn from the American Breeders Association. The Carnegie Institute and the Rockefeller Foundation were keen promoters of Eugenic projects. Indiana was the first state to bring in a eugenics law that permitted the sterilisation of incompetents, followed by Washington and California in 1909. Eventually some 65,000 people were sterilised in 33 states in programmes that carried on into the 1970s. [18] Sweden and Switzerland had sterilisation laws. In 1913 the British Parliament passed a law that said that 'defectives … in whose case it is desirable in the interests of the whole community that they should be deprived of the opportunity of producing children' could be detained.[19]

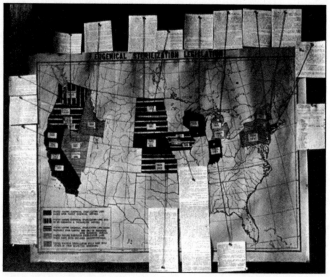

A poster from a 1921 eugenics conference displays which US states had by then implemented sterilization legislation.[20]

International Eugenics Conferences were held in 1912 in London, at the American Museum of Natural History in New York in 1921 and 1932. First Lord of the Admiralty Winston Churchill and Lord Balfour were at the London Conference. Churchill concluded that 100 000 'mental degenerates' should be sterilised.[21] The US State Department sent invitations out for the conference in New York. In 1934 a conference was called by the International Federation of Eugenic Organisations in Zurich, which served to put a rubber stamp on the Nazis Eugenic laws.

The US government-sponsored Eugenic movement gave heart to German eugenicists, many of whom went on to frame the Nazis own extermination laws, like Ernst Rüdin. In 1934 Adolf Hitler wrote to Leon Whitney of the American Eugenics Society, and to Madison Grant – saying that *The Passing of the Great Race* 'was his bible'.[22] That same year Whitney's Society enjoyed a boost in interest because of Hitler's plans to sterilize 400,000 Germans. William H. Peter, Secretary of the American Public Health Authority went to Germany to see how the programme was coming along, and judged that the Nazi government were working in a 'legally and scientifically fair way'. Germany was, said Peter, the 'first modern nation to have reached a goal toward which other nations are just looking, or approaching at a snail's pace'.[23]

Race on the American domestic front

The Second World War greatly accelerated change in race relations in many different directions. Black Americans had suffered hardship in the great depression because of the collapse of truck farming in the southern states. The rapid growth of the war industries boosted employment, much of it in northern cities, leading to the great internal migration northwards of black America.

Employers and white supremacist politicians favoured the American Federation of Labor over the Congress of Industrial Organisations because it turned a blind eye to segregation, while the CIO ruled against it – in keeping with their recruiting policies. State authorities broke up CIO recruitment. In Savannah, 1942, CIO organiser Lucy Mason was attacked by white workers in the AF of L for recruiting blacks. The police intervened on the side of the attackers, proclaiming their support for the AF of L. In spring 1944

International Woodworkers of America (a CIO affiliate) organiser John Hawkins was arrested in Bolton, Mississipi and told 'if we would organise the white men that would be alright, but they were not going to stand to see the negroes organised.'[24]

Blacks did organise – most pointedly in the threatened March on Washington organised by A. Philip Randolph of the Railway Porters Union and Bayard Rustin. Rather than see this happen, Roosevelt signed Executive Order 8802 that banned discrimination in the war industries. Some black Americans were moved by the anti-Fascist element in the war, and started the Double V campaign, for victory over Fascism abroad and over racism at home. Bayard Rustin talked to black Americans who voiced 'outright joy at a Japanese military victory', because 'thousands of negroes look upon successes of any coloured people anywhere as their success'. One student told Rustin 'it is now a question of breaking down white domination over the whole world or nowhere.'[25]

Eleanor Roosevelt spoke up for some modest race reform stirring deep fears amongst whites. Rumours of black servants ganging together in 'Eleanor Clubs' had spread alleging that the servants slogan was 'A white woman in every kitchen by 1943'. [26] Other rumours alleged that blacks were buying up ice-picks for a mass insurrection during the black-out. In 1942 Georgia Governor Eugene Talmadge summed up the color bar: 'We love the negro in his place, but his place is at the back door.'[27]

The 'Collective Guilt' of the Germans

In Britain the Ministry of Information's Propaganda Committee struggled with the question of how to present the war. In the early stages of the war, they were still under the influence of the policy of 'appeasement' and wanted to find some good in the enemy. One Ministry of Information pamphlet went so far as to say that 'National-socialism began as an honourable experiment' and 'its leaders started with many fine ideals and the German people had every right to expect that they would be realised.'[28] More plausibly, the historian D. A. Routh wrote a paper for the Ministry that made an important distinction between Nazi rulers and German people. 'The tragedy of Germany is the tragedy of a great people', wrote Routh, who have fallen 'into the hands of violent and ambitious rulers'. Routh saw the overthrow of national-socialism offering a future for the German people.

Soon, though, the British Cabinet sought to have the tenor of British propaganda made harsher, and the distinction between Nazi rulers and German people ignored. Director General of the BBC Sir John Reith told the Cabinet that 'You are fighting the German people – 80 million of them'. Reith said 'the Ministry should now begin to stir up people's more primitive instincts'.[29] Foremost in Reith's mind were the defeats in Norway and Dunkirk. Two weeks after that withdrawal, the British Cabinet discussed a proposal for an 'Anger Campaign' because the public were 'harbouring little sense of real personal animus against the average German man or woman'. A number of themes were to be worked unattributed into the media, such as 'the recurring madness of the German empire', 'German lust for world domination', 'they do not change', 'blows are all they understand' and 'inferiority complex – root of German aggression'. For the 'sophisticated and educated classes', there would be more finely tuned prejudices like 'the fundamental "rottenness" of the German character', backed up with quotes from Neitzsche and Treitschke.[30]

Sir Robert Vansittart, Chief Diplomatic Advisor to the British Government, gave a series of radio broadcasts in 1940, published the following year as *The Black Record: Germans Past and Present*. Pointedly, the veteran diplomat saw the German failing as intrinsic to them as a race:

> Hitler is no accident. He is the natural and continuous product of a breed which from the dawn of history has been predatory and bellicose

Vansittart warned that 'we must all drop the habit of making allowances for the Germans'.[31] It was a theme that inspired the entertainer Noel Coward. Coward mocked what he saw as the naivety of those who saw good in the German people, in his ironic song, 'Don't let's be beastly to the Germans'. Coward was working for British intelligence at the time, but the song was banned by the BBC, perhaps because it was too arch. [32]

Author J.B. Priestley wrote a wall poster for the Ministry of Information that was more direct:

The Secret Beast

...

They are Europe's secret beasts, roused to senseless fury. It is all Europe's mission to cower them and cage them today as all Europe had to do before.

The Hun is at the gate. He will rage and destroy. He will slaughter the men and the women. But in the end he will run from the men as he has always run in the past.

Out then and kill ... the extermination of the wild animal let loose on Europe is the plain business of Europe's citizens.

Perceptively Ian McLaine suggests that the Anger Campaign was put together by the British Cabinet 'to stir up their own "primitive instincts" as profoundly as those of the people at large'.[33]

One might have thought that anti-German hatred was not so hard to come by in Russia, after the brutal means the Wehrmacht used there. As we shall see, though, there were in fact a lot of disaffected Soviet citizens who allied themselves with Germany, especially in the early stages of the invasion. Anti-German propaganda was closely tied to the rediscovery of Russian national sentiment on the part of the Soviet elite. For the official ideology of Marxist materialism, though, galvanising anti-German feeling meant correcting the generally Germanophile outlook of the intellectual founding fathers Karl Marx and Frederick Engels.

Ilya Ehrenburg, novelist and wartime journalist working with the Red Army explains that before the war 'every Soviet schoolboy had been taught that the cultural standards of this nation or that was expressed in mileage of railways, numbers of cars, the existence of a technically advanced industry, the spread of education and of social hygiene'. That was the Marxist ABC, and 'on all these counts Germany was among the leading nations'. It was a view hard to square with his wartime role. Instead he wrote a notorious article 'The Justification of Hatred' in August 1942:

This war is unlike former wars. For the first time our people face not men but cruel and vile monsters, savages equipped with every technically perfected weapon, scum acting according to rule and quoting science, who have turned the massacre of babies into the last word of State wisdom.

Ehrenburg goes on to dehumanise the enemy

We are fighting not men but automata in human likeness. Our hatred of them is the stronger because outwardly they appear to be men... because they are disguised as human beings, as civilised Europeans.[34]

In the same year E. P. Kandel and I. I. Preis at the Moscow Marx-Engels-Lenin Institute published a booklet *Marx and Engels on Reactionary Prussianism* which aimed to show, like Vansittart's Black Record, that 'Hitlerism has resurrected all that was most execrable and vile in the history of Germany'. Kandel and Preis, also want to show that their anti-Prussian campaign was in the spirit of Marx and Engels who 'in their day mercilessly exposed all the specific traits of Prussianism and the aggressive, predatory ambitions of the Prussian Junkers and barons'. The way they tell it, modern German history is just one long succession of Prussian and Junker misdeeds, whether it is 1843, 1869, 1914 or 1933 or 1942.[35]

Georg Lukacs' book *The Destruction of Reason,* was based upon his lectures to the German Communist Party's anti-fascist school in Moscow in 1945.[36] In a chapter on Germany's Historical Development, Lukacs writes 'our concern in these studies is therefore briefly to outline the socio-ideological features which made up the disgracefully swift and disgracefully long-term triumph of fascism'. Like Kandel and Preis, Lukacs constructs an exceptional history for Germany, in which the Prussian Junker landlords are a reactionary influence. Worse still, Lukacs thought, 'the masses were far more quickly and intensively influenced by chauvinistic propaganda in Germany than in other countries'.[37] Couched in Marxist language, Lukacs, Kandel and Preis were all manufacturing a story of the German people's exceptionally barbaric character, much like Sir Robert Vansittart's Black Record. Most of all they were abandoning the Marxist and internationalist view that 'working people have no country'. The hopes that Marx, Lenin ... and even Stalin had once invested in the German working class were forgotten.

The view of the Germans as intrinsically flawed not only helped to dehumanise the enemy during the conflict, it also helped to justify the political domination of Germany after the war. Churchill argued, that perhaps after 'a generation of self-sacrifice, toil and education, something might be done with the German people'.[38] By contrast, the radical Marxist Oskar Hippe, who worked underground against the Nazis saw an attempt to spread the blame as a way of avoiding the actual guilt of those responsible. 'The collective guilt of international capitalism with Hitler's fascism can only be emphasized' he wrote 'when these self-same international capitalists spread the lie of the collective guilt of the German people'.[39]

Race in the international conflict

At Versailles in 1919 the Japanese delegation were bitterly disappointed that their resolution barring discrimination against foreign nationals 'on account of their race or nationality' was voted down by the American and European delegates. Harold Nicolson of the British delegation protested that it implied the 'equality of the yellow man with the white man', and even 'might imply the terrific theory of the white man with the black'.[40] Later in 1924 the Tokyo government was aggrieved that American immigration laws discriminated against Japanese.[41]

The Japanese victory over Britain in Singapore, and the overthrow of the white administrations in Burma, Malaya and Indonesia caused real fear in the British and American elite. Margery Perham at the Colonial Office was forced to admit that 'Japan's attack in the Pacific has produced a very practical revolution in race relationships', because 'An Asiatic people has for the moment successfully challenged the ascendancy of three great white imperial powers' – Britain, France and Holland.[42] At the American Security Sub Committee in 1943 Captain H.L. Pence made it clear that 'Every step should be taken to assure the absolute dominance of the position of the white rule in the Pacific.'[43] In May 1945, Robert S. Ward, US Foreign Service Officer in Chungking warned that Japan had exposed the peoples of the east to 'a virus that may yet poison the whole soul of Asia and ultimately commit the world to racial war that would destroy the white man and decimate the Asiatic'. [44]

America's need to contain the Japanese virus led directly to the choice of target for America's only use of the atomic bombs in wartime, on Hiroshima and Nagasaki.[45] As President Truman explained on 11 August 1945:

> The only language they seem to understand is the one we have been using to bombard them. When you have to deal with a beast you have to treat him as a beast. It is most regrettable but nevertheless true.[46]

Life Magazine carried this photograph of Natalie Nickerson and the Skull that her sweetheart had sent her from New Guinea, with the motto 'A Good Jap - a Dead One' May 22, 1944, pages 34-35.

Through race, the warmongers dehumanised the enemy. As Truman called the Japanese 'beasts', the Nazi high command called the Slavs to the east 'untermenschen'. That way they could withhold the usual rights that were due to enemy prisoners. 'We are talking about a war of extermination' Hitler told his Generals on 30 March 1941: 'We must disavow the standpoint of soldierly camaraderie.'[47] In the first weeks of the Barbarossa campaign as many as 600,000 Russian prisoners were summarily executed, and over the course of the war over three million Soviet soldiers died in captivity.[48]

Wherever occupying forces overran other peoples the victory might be understood in words of race. Japan's war in the Far East was underscored by a violent race prejudice against the Chinese. At the Chinese nationalist capital Nanking in 1937 the Japanese tenth vented their frustration by slaughtering more than a quarter of a million civilians. Lieutenant Colonel Tanaka Ryuichi explained to a journalist:

> Frankly speaking, you and I have diametrically different views of the Chinese. You may be dealing with them as human beings, but I regard them as swine. We can do anything to such creatures.[49]

One regimental commander explained that in China: 'Our policy has been to burn every enemy house along the way as we advance'. The army called it an 'extermination policy'.[50]

Later, as Japan's forces progressed through East Asia, anti-Chinese racism was a constant theme – that even found some echo in the petty prejudices of Malays and Indians against the small traders that lived among them. On taking Singapore, on 15 February 1942, Japanese troops took thousands of Chinese to the beach to be killed. The slaughter was known as the Sook Ching massacre, the Chinese translation of the Japanese *Kakyōshukusei*, or 'purging of Chinese'.

The dread of coloured troops

The use of coloured troops was a politically explosive issue for European and American authorities. It was a big taboo to arm coloured troops and to put them into battle against white soldiers, still more so to give them authority over white civilians. Those without rights had often earned them in the past by taking up military service. However, the needs of war did draw millions of coloured troops into battle – most often under white commanders.

The use of Moroccan troops in the French occupation of the Rhineland after the First World War had given rise to a great outrage – 'Black Shame on the Rhine' reported newspapers across Europe, mostly sympathetic to the German burgers' dread of 'misce-genation'. In 1937 the Gestapo ordered that any 'bastard' offspring of the French African troops and Rheinisch womanhood should be sterilised. [51] Even the Spanish Communist hero of the civil war, Dolores Ibarruri – known as La Pasionara played the race card when she protested on Radio Seville of 'Peasant girls violated by legionaries, mercenaries, and Moors, who have been tempted from their African villages by the promise of a "good time," bear witness to this "patriotism" of the fascist murderers.'[52]

Still, the allied armies relied on colonial troops, however unwilling they were to acknowledge it. Two hundred and twenty thousand British Commonwealth troops were killed in the North Africa campaign. Of the British Commonwealth troops that survived, tens of thousands of Indian Army soldiers were sent to fight on in the east against Japan. Most of the British and other white colonial troops were sent on to fight in Italy. On July 1st 1945 the troops of the Indian Army numbered over 2,250,000 commanded by 37,187 British officers and 13,355 Indian officers.[53] The regular British Army stood at 2,900,000.

De Gaulle's 'Free French' drawn from the colonies relied heavily on black troops, too. Harold Macmillan watched a military parade in Tunis, on 20 May 1943, and wrote snootily in his diary

First came the French – Zouaves, Tirailleurs, Moroccan and Algerian native troops and Foreign Legion. The procession was led by a detachment of Spahis, making a brave show with their white horses, red cloaks, red leather saddles and drawn swords. ... The great majority of the French were of course natives.[54]

Among the native troops that fought so hard for France were the Tirailleurs Sénégalais who fought on in Corsica, Elba and Toulon. But the French commanders were embarrassed to have France liberated by colonial soldiers, and even more so to have them invade Germany. The three regiments of the Tirailleurs Sénégalais were moved back to more temperate areas on the grounds that they were not constitutionally suited to the winter fighting. Later the regiments were re-categorised as European, or 'blanchiment' (whitened) as the army documents put it.[55]

Black Americans served in the forces, but these were still segregated at the start of the war. Black servicemen were usually allotted to work details, and struggled to be allowed to take part in the fighting. One remarkable experiment – encouraged by the First Lady Eleanor Roosevelt – was the training of a wholly black squadron of airmen, the Tuskegee 332nd Fighter Group. General Henry Arnold protested that 'Negro pilots cannot be used in our present Air Corps units since this would result in Negro officers serving over white enlisted men creating an impossible social situation.'[56] Under white officers, the Tuskegee Airmen took part in 1,578 missions, and 150 of them lost their lives serving their country. The US Army was eventually integrated by President Truman's Executive Order 9981 in 1948.

When the balance of power tipped in Abyssinia Italian settlers appealed to British troops to save them from the Ethiopians who were fighting on the Allied side. Settler put out signs for airmen to read: 'come and save us from the Abyssinians'. British armoured cars

were sent to another settlement where 'they had to fight through the tribesmen, pack the cars with white women and farmers, and fight their way out again', according to war correspondent Alan Moorehead. He says that in many places 'empire troops and Italians were fighting side by side against the angry natives'. Moorehead's driver asked who 'the hell are we fighting anyway – the Wops or them niggers?' It was a question he could not answer.[57]

Where non-European troops took part in the seizure of white civilians, race anxiety was intense. Pornographic propaganda dwelt on Japanese molestation of white women: 'The Jap Beast and his plot to rape the world' (1942) 'Jap Blood Cult: Rape! Torture! Kill!'

Moroccan Troops in the French Expeditionary Force in Italy were held to have raped thousands of Italian women – and after the war the French government paid compensation after the matter was debated in the Italian parliament. In 1953 a Federal German government sponsored project, Documentation of the Expulsion of the Germans from East Central Europe published several volumes of testimony of atrocities, much of it of the rape of German women at the hands of Soviet troops. Not content with recording rape, the editors wrote that 'these rapes were the expression of a manner of behaviour and mentality, which for European sensibilities is inconceivable and repulsive'. Rape is tragically a feature of war. What was pointed in the German documentation project was that the threat of rape was highly racialised. Frau Anitta Graesser remembered that the Russians were all 'Asians' who 'rode camels, wore high spiked, white fur hats'.[58] One victim interviewed by historian Anthony Beevor for the BBC Timewatch Programme, broadcast in May 2002 remembered that she had been set upon by 'hordes of Mongols with slitty eyes'.

In 1944, the commander of the Nord Army Group issued the following Order of the Day:

Ilya Ehrenburg [the Soviet propaganda officer for the Red Army] is urging the Asiatic peoples to drink the blood of German women. Ilya Ehrenburg insists that Asiatics should enjoy our women. "Take the flaxen-haired women they are your prey", he says.

Ehrenburg denied any such order was given, and though Soviet troops were disciplined for acts of rape against German women, the troops used in the occupation of Germany were not drawn from the Mongolian People's Republic. The head of the Federal German Documentation project, though, former Nazi Theodor Scheider would have been familiar with this propaganda theme.

Chapter Ten

A Soldier's Life

Waste was the overwhelming condition of the soldier's life. Their lives were wasted. Around 25 million soldiers were killed. Of those between 9 and 10 million were troops of the Soviet Union and 5,300,000 German soldiers. Between three and four million Chinese and 2,120,000 Japanese troops were killed. 217,600 French soldiers, a quarter of a million Polish soldiers, 300,000 Rumanian soldiers, 301,400 Italians soldiers, 383,800 British soldiers, 416,800 American soldiers, and 446,000 Yugoslav soldiers were killed. Tens of thousands of British Empire troops, other European troops, and other colonial troops were killed. In the First World War Eric Bogle wrote the Green Fields of France, about the Irish volunteer 'Willie MacBride': 'Well I hope you died quick and I hope you died clean/ or Willie MacBride was it slow and obscene?' Many of the soldiers of the Second World War died quickly, if not exactly cleanly because of the greater reach of mechanised warfare, but many, too died slowly, in horrific circumstances, from wounds, infections and starvation. The main theatres of War, in Russia and China were scenes of awful routs as armies collapsed in the face of overwhelming odds, alternating with gruelling deadlocks that tested the troops to destruction. Every one of these 25 million soldiers killed was some mother's son, or daughter.

Not just their lives, but their time was wasted. Wasted waiting, or wasted in futile expenditure of energy – drill (square bashing), marching, 'exercises', PT, digging holes, filling holes, filling sandbags, peeling potatoes, painting stones white. While their sisters and brothers were thrown into a frenzy of productive work on the farm and in the factory, the soldiers' efforts were wasted on destructive activities. Louis Kreizman was called up in 1940 and spent the rest of the war drilling, and making sea-defences on the South coast of England. In 1945 he was sent to Alexandria, and then on to Palestine – but after a month he was sent back because he was Jewish, and not to be trusted against the Irgun guerrillas. 'It was the biggest waste of time', was this soldier's take on the Second World

War.

The soldiers of the Second World War were not for the most part volunteers, but conscripts. In Germany the Wehrmacht had been kept down to around 100,000 strong under the terms of the Versailles peace, until Hitler announced a new conscription drive in 1935, which grew the Wehrmacht by 300,000 a year, until at its height it was 12.5 million strong, and 'overwhelmingly an army of conscripts'.[1] In 1939 the British government brought in the Military Training Act, and later that year, when Chamberlain declared war, the National Service Act. By 1942 all men between the ages of 18 and 51 were liable to be conscripted, and all women between 20 and 30 years, with the exception of those in 'reserved occupations'. Article 132 of the Russian Constitution of 1936 declared military service a duty, and a 1939 law brought in conscription. The United States Congress agreed peacetime conscription in September 1940. Initially there was a ceiling of 900,000 draftees. By the end of the war the armed forces were 16 million strong, of whom ten million were draftees.[2] Conscription had been brought in in Japan in 1873 and from the 1905 war the army had become predominantly a conscript army. There was opposition to conscription. In Canada there were protests and even riots against it after a plebiscite supported by English-speaking Canadians, but opposed by French speakers brought it in. In the main, conscription was not unpopular however, though it is still the case that the individual conscripts had not chosen to fight, but were made to by their governments.

Conscription was just the beginning of a life where orders, duty and obligation took the place of choice, agreement and freedom. The Soldiers life was to be ordered about. Orders were its currency. The 'G.I' in the US Army stood for General Infantryman, or General Issue. Orders were often mysterious, wrong, or just pointless. Commanding officers were often in the grip of error, or larger schemes that just could not be foreseen, and often just using up the troops surplus energy to keep them from running amok. Disobeying orders – even those that made no sense – was not easy: you could be on charges for it, or you might just have missed the bigger picture and end up in all kinds of trouble.

Military discipline was harsh. In the winter of 1939-40 the Soviet leadership issued orders to shoot stragglers and deserters and appointed special troops to do it, the *Zagradotryady* or blocking detachments. In 1940 a number of tribunals sentenced officers to death for cowardice, by NKVD firing squad. These were panic measures in the early years of defeat, and a High Command memorandum warned that 'the highest form of punishment is being overused'. The blocking units were also disbanded later as ineffective, though the punishments carried on.[3] The German military authorities had some 17,000 soldiers executed for desertion. Typically 65 per cent of all those found guilty were executed, and the others imprisoned for on average seven years. A Special Wartime Military Penal Code, and a Wartime Criminal Code of Procedure speeded up punishment by limiting the accuseds' rights to representation and appeal. In total 21,000 US servicemen were court martialled for desertion (Nineteen thousand US soldiers deserted in France and Germany, and were known as 'the lost division'), and imprisoned for around 17 years on average, or life in certain cases. Only 162 death sentences were imposed and only one carried out – Private Eddie Slovik's on 31 January 1945. During the battle for Normandy, four British officers and 7,018 other ranks were court martialled for desertion. In all 100,000 British troops deserted. The British parliament abolished the death penalty for desertion in 1930, and the average sentence was between three and five years' imprisonment. During the war, 142 US servicemen and 40 British were executed, most often for murder or rape.[4]

Despite the risks, though, there were many times that men mutinied against their officers throughout the war.

To make them follow orders without asking why, armies had training. Sergeant Myles Babcock of the 37th US Infantry Division kept a diary of his own time training troops, where he wrote

> The psychological effect of lessons in hand-to-hand killing proved brutalising. Lack of feminine companionship encouraged vulgarity, almost completely stilled courtesy. The individual citizens poured into the crucible of hate, brutality, and organised murder undergo a subtle change. ...
>
> He embodies myriad vices, virtues and traits including profanity, vulgarity, chronic complaining, scepticism, irritability, brutality, disrespect for the rights of colleagues, disrespect and

envy of civilians, loneliness, hatred of monotony, a type of fatalism, despair, animalism, stamina, a Spartan reaction to pain, and a burning hope that destiny dictates a return to the states.[5]

Red Army training officers dealt with Tank Fright by making recruits lie in a trench while Soviet tanks were driven over their heads, which they called 'ironing'.[6]

A US army medical officer gives his account of training in a report of 1941:

The men in a successfully trained army or navy are stamped into a mould. Their barrack-talk becomes typical, for soldiers are taught in a harsh and brutal school. They cannot, they must not, be mollycoddled, and the education befits nature, induces sexual aggression and makes them the stern, dynamic type we associate with the men of the armed forces.[7]

This is how it looked to General Infantryman James Jones, who wrote in his diary:

Living in herds like steers or fish, where men (suddenly missing deeply the wives or girlfriends they had left so adventurously two weeks before) literally could not find the privacy to masturbate even in the latrines. Being laughed at, insulted, upbraided, held up to ridicule and fed like pigs in a trough with absolutely no recourse or rights to uphold their treasured individuality before any parent, lover, teacher, or tribune. Harassed to rise at five in the morning, harassed to be in bed at nine-thirty at might.[8]

Much of the cultural life of the army is a running commentary on the daftness of orders. Bill Mauldin's cartoons, Joseph Heller's novel Catch 22, 'It's That Man Again', with 'Colonel Chinstrap,' on BBC radio - just as Bilko, M.A.S.H. were for later wars, and Jaroslav Hasek's novel the Good Soldier Schwejk was for the Great War. Low's cartoons of Colonel Blimp mocked the unthinking, irrational officer who bellows incomprehensible or just plain foolish orders at his wincing troops. When the filmmakers Powell and Pressburger began production of the film of Colonel Blimp Churchill wanted it suppressed 'on the perfectly precise point of "undermining the discipline of the army".' The War Cabinet disagreed, though Churchill put it on the record that he 'did not agree with this surrender'. The Colonel Blimp film, like Low's cartoons were not mutinous, but a much-needed letting off of steam for the troops. The Air Ministry pointed out to the Ministry of Information that since Colonel Blimp 'has broken all previous box-office records' it would be wise not 'to maintain our illegal ban' on its export.[9]

As well as orders, armies worked on the chain of command. Non-commissioned officers might have risen through the ranks to become sergeants or corporals. Commissioned officers though were recruited separately, from the upper and middle classes and were trained separately, too. The officer class were often seen as toffs by their men, and their authority was institutional rather than charismatic for the most part, backed up by bullying NCOs, Courts Martial or in the last instance, the officer's pistol. An intelligence officer's reading of captured Italian mail in the North Africa campaign led to the conclusion that 'the men did not usually believe in the war or care how it went so long as they personally did not get hurt: the officers as a rule were astonishingly Fascist'.[10]

The Officer-general ranks relation was just the mirror image of the class relations of ruling and working classes in society. So much so in fact, that other ranks were often surprised to see that the bonds of class between officers were stronger than those of nation. When His Majesty's Ship Zola arrived in Halifax, Canada, from North Africa, with British troops and German prisoners on board, the German officers complained that they could not be expected to carry their own bags ashore, and the British officers agreed: 'so the British Tommies were ordered to take the German luggage ashore', 'angry to the point of mutiny with their own officers'.[11]

After the fall of Singapore the Japanese captured 90,000 Allied troops and their officers. The Japanese relied on Allied officers to command their men in Prisoners of War Camps in Thailand. The men were put to work building bridges and railways and British officers, who were not only excused work but also received officers' pay based on Imperial Japanese Army rates, directed the troops. Lieutenant Colonel Philip Toosey – the model for Colonel Nicholson in the novel and later film The Bridge over the River Kwai – kept his men in order. Toosey told one soldier, accused of stealing:

> If you ever step out of line I'll starve you to death and you know I have the power to do it because I've got control of the food. Now you are going to be beaten up by two regimental sergeant majors behind this hut and if you dare do anything about it or report me after the war, all I can tell you is that you will suffer more than I will.[12]

Toosey kept up good relations with the Japanese officers, and intervened to save the life of camp commandant Risaburo Saito in the war crimes tribunal held after the war. Allied commanders in the Japanese camps were at one point ordered to work alongside their men and protested at the indignity, but the Japanese later relented thinking the officers were more use in command. The troops had mixed feelings about their commanders putting them to work building bridges for the Japanese. Some were glad that men like Toosey put themselves between the guards and the prisoners as a buffer. Others recoiled at being ordered around by British officers they called 'Jap-happy bastards'.[13]

Political Education

More than any previous conflict the military authorities in the Second World War sought to indoctrinate the troops under their command. As well as the military drill, weapons training and lectures on military objectives, the military put in place political education for the troops. The Soviet Army had the most developed system of 'Political Officers', the 'Politruk', with one attached to each brigade. The Politruk 'is the central figure for all educational work among soldiers', according to army orders.[14] The Political Officers' authority stemmed from the campaign during the Civil War of 1917-19 to put the military officers under the political control of the Communist Party of the Soviet Union. When the Soviet army was professionalised in 1942 the political officers lost their authority to challenge military decisions and took more of a back seat, though regular circulars and army newspapers motivated the war throughout. On 6 June 1941, just before the German invasion of the

USSR, Hitler signed the 'Comissar Order' that all political officers captured were to be shot. Quite a few Red Army soldiers would have agreed, like the conscript who wrote 'the first person I will kill will be Politruk Zaitsev'.[15]

The British Army Bureau of Current Affairs organised lectures on war aims and political goals, distributing ABCA pamphlets that were published fortnightly, with titles such as The Enemy in the East, The Mind of a Nazi, The Beveridge Report, Cripps on India, South African Survey and How Russia Fights. The ABCA was distrusted by military officers who, with some justification, believed that it promoted the Labour Party view of the People's War and the case for social reform afterwards.

The Wehrmacht had accepted its political integration into the Nazi system with the personal oath to Hitler and the adoption of Nazi symbols on its uniforms.[16] In the Wehrmacht, the SS had a specific role in political education, as well as one of disciplining the army, and it was closely controlled by the Nazi authorities. Theodor Eicke's SS Death's Head Unit that ran the concentration camps for political prisoners in the late 1930s worked one week in the month on guard duties, and gave over the other three to training, including political indoctrination in obedience to the Fuehrer and Nazi ideals.[17]

Prisoners

By 1944 only 1,050,000 of 5,000,000 Soviet Prisoners of War in German hands survived. Of between two and three million German Prisoners of War in Russian hands more than one million died. Of the 132,000 British and American Prisoners of War taken by the Japanese Army 27 per cent died in captivity. Just 26,304 Japanese army and 12,362 navy personnel were taken prisoner. Of the five million Germans taken prisoner by the Americans 56,000 died.[18]

The artist Terry Frost was held as a prisoner in a German Prisoner of War Camp. He told the story that there was an unspoken agreement in the camp that when a prisoner's birthday came, the other inmates would do their best to recreate an ordinary day back in civilian life. If he wanted to catch the bus to work, then twenty or so prisoners would trot along beside him around the camp, as if they were his fellow passengers. Then they might sit down as if at imaginary desks if he was a clerk, and then later perhaps act out going to the pub. Soviet prisoners of war captured by the Germans on the eastern front faced much worse conditions that were a death sentence for most, as they were often denied food altogether and subject to summary executions. In the Pacific War Allies operated an unofficial policy of taking no prisoners, meaning that hundreds of thousands were killed outright.

The main difference between the different troops was due to the relative wealth of their states. Troops in the less developed world had less equipment, those in the developed world, more: 'of all the world's armies, the American army gets the best equipment,'[19] Bill Maudlin has happy to record. This was not a small thing. The US, German, British, Japanese and French military was capital-intensive (the American most of all); the Russian and Chinese armies, the partisans of East Europe and Asia, the colonial troops under European command were mostly labour-intensive. An editorial in the Soviet newspaper Pravda tried to put the best possible gloss on a bad situation:

> Military thought in the capitalist world has got into a blind alley. The dashing "theories" about a lightning war, or about small, select armies of technicians, or about air war which can replace all other military operations; all of these arise from the bourgeoisie's deathly fear of proletarian revolution. In its mechanical way, the imperialist bourgeoisie overrates equipment and underrates man.[20]

There was from time to time a problem of military leaders looking for a technical fix when they were in a hole. But overall the Soviet Army's labour intensive warfare was a terrible weakness that accounts for the shocking imbalance in war dead. One Soviet soldier explained that waves of men were sent against the German troops, often with only one rifle between twenty. When the man with the gun fell, he explained, the nearest man picked it up, and the charge went on.[21] By contrast US servicemen were valuable resources, which were used much more sparingly. 'Americans decided to confine the war on their side as far as possible to machines', wrote historian Jon Halliday.[22] Douglas MacArthur developed the tactic of

'Island Hopping' – leaving Japanese positions dug in to Pacific Islands left behind as the front advanced to 'whither on the vine' as the US advanced on Japan. It was a policy to save the cost in US servicemen's lives, while the proxy armies of Chinese and Russian troops that fought on the Allied side were more expendable.[23]

The other marked difference in the experience of war was in the extent to which the laws of war were observed in different campaigns. For the most part the Wehrmacht observed its obligations under the Geneva Convention of 1929 on the Western Front, as did the Allies in turn. That meant that surrendered Prisoners of War were not executed or deliberately starved, and had access to the International Red Cross. On the eastern front, the Wehrmacht was told that it was not bound by the Convention, and prisoners were routinely executed and starved. The Soviet treatment of German prisoners was unpredictable. Many were held though summary execution often took place. In the Pacific War the Japanese authorities followed the letter of the Geneva Convention but in practice often broke it. In the war against China, the Japanese fought did not observe the convention. The Allies, in their drive to re-take the Pacific did not in practice honour the Geneva Convention, but fought a war without mercy or restraint.

War could be ennobling. Hundreds of thousands, even millions of men and women, acted heroically, fighting against terrible odds. Those people became better, more confident, and braver, with a greater sense of comradeship and loyalty to their friends. But war could just as easily be deeply degrading. Ordinary soldiers were brutalised by their commanding officers and their own comrades. From the enemy they could expect anything, from respect to depraved cruelty. Troops killed other soldiers, and slaughtered civilians, drawn themselves into terrible depravity. The German auxiliary Einsatzgruppe in occupied Russia were set to work slaughtering Jews. On 9 August 1941 Einsatzgruppe C 'transformed the public hanging of two Jews into a festive spectacle that was followed by the execution of more than 400 Jewish men'.[24] US troops in the Pacific War tortured and mutilated the bodies of Japanese troops in a war without pity.

Chapter Eleven

Love and War

The lives of women and men were changed greatly by the war, which brought many more women into the workforce, and many men into the services. Family life was turned upside down as the division of domestic labour was changed. There was a strong move towards socialised child care. People were moved around all over the world, breaking up traditional domestic life, and bringing the young especially, into contact with people and experiences that they would never have seen. Despite the conservative motives of the war leaders, sexual relations were revolutionised, with a great acceleration of sex outside of marriage, marriage for love, divorce and, pointedly, towards a much greater prevalence of homosexuality.

Many of these changes could be called a breakdown in the traditional family, though marriage survived and prospered on a reformed basis. The greater prospects for promiscuity and for homosexuality were of course unintended effects of the war drive, and the military-industrial establishment reacted with often vicious attempts to regulate sexuality, and to repress promiscuity, heterosexual and homosexual.

In the 1930s, before the war, governments had promoted traditional family policies, with a heavy emphasis on hearth and home.

The US Economy Act of 1932 was typical of recession laws that aimed to give men priority over women in work, and as far as possible to drive women out of the workforce and back into the home. The law barred the Federal Government from hiring two people from the same family. Twenty six American states brought in laws stopping women from 'taking men's jobs'.[1]

In Nazi Germany, the government went much further promoting a 'healthy' role for mothers, and according to Hitler, there was 'nothing nobler for a woman than to be the mother of the sons and daughters of the people'.[2] There were 'medals for motherhood', bronze for five children, silver for six and gold for seven. This natalist policy of promoting Aryan families was the other side of the attempts to sterilise those alleged to be incompetent or asocial, and the growing movement to drive Jews from the Reich. There were tax breaks for children – 15 per cent of income tax for each child, and those in the Marriage Loan Programme got 25 per cent taken off the principal for each child born.[3]

In Italy, too, 'the Fascist family is the essential object of Fascist policy', the journal *Critica Fascista* editorialised. In the domestic hearth there must be 'no fusion between the sexes', but instead 'the woman should return to being queen and *signora*'. A tax on bachelors had been introduced in 1926 and in 1931 beauty contests were banned as 'demeaning'.[4]

The Fascist Roberto Bompiani explained that

The healthier the family is, the more precious its contribution to the State and to the nation... healthy unions deliver healthy and strong offspring, therefore they meliorate the society and the race. Unhealthy unions however are harmful for the community propagating and disseminating the bad. They undermine the race, deteriorating it physically and morally. Therefore the State needs to intervene.[5]

The Nazi women's organisation, the Frauenschaft, issued ten commandments for choosing a partner:

Remember you are a German!
Remain pure in mind and spirit!
Keep your body pure!
If hereditarily fit, remain pure and simple!
Marry only for love!
Being a German, choose only a spouse of similar or related blood!
When choosing a partner inquire after his or her forebears!
Health is essential to outward beauty as well!
Seek a companion in marriage, not a playmate!
Hope for as many children as possible![6]

There was a boom in marriages in the Third Reich, but the natalist policy was not as successful. The birthrate did not rise as high as the postwar bump enjoyed under the supposedly decadent Weimar

Republic, and in 1936 senior Nazis worried about 500,000 good German women seeking abortions.[7]

Industrial mobilisation was having its impact upon family life. Five million German women moved back into work in the 1930s, rising to fourteen and a half million during the war. In offices and factories German women could earn as much as seventy per cent of a man's wages, or just fifty per cent in agriculture.[8] There was no sense in which the growth of women's work and wages were supposed to lead to equality – after all, women's places in university were cut back from 20,000 in 1933 to just 5500 in 1939 – these were unintended effects of the war industry drive. In the US the number of women in work grew by 60 per cent between 1940 and 1945 and of them, three quarters were married.[9] At Boeing's vast Seattle plant that made Flying Fortresses 24 hours a day more than half of those that made up the workforce were women.[10] In Britain women were directed into work under the February 1942 Employment of Women Order, which had exceptions for women with domestic responsibilities, but was tightened up further in 1943. As many as seven and a quarter million women were in full time work in Britain, and with those in part time work they made up half the female population. Thousands of women were charged for refusing war work under the Defence of the Realm Regulation 5a, like pacifist Constance Bolan, who was sent to prison in January 1941 for refusing hospital work.[11]

The Saturday Evening Post ran Norman Rockwell's painting of a buxom Rosie the Riveter. The 1942 song of the same name ran 'She's making history, working for victory', and in 1944 Paramount made a film of Rosie. The writers gave Rosie a boyfriend: 'Charlie, he's a marine/Rosie is protecting Charlie/Working overtime on the riveting machine'. It was sentiment that one German munitions worker shared: 'Earlier I buttered bread for him, now I paint grenades and think this is for him'.[12]

In Britain the BBC appealed 'Today we are calling all women. Every woman in the country is needed to pull her weight to the utmost'. In November 1941 'War Work Week' saw floats and demonstrations around the country with slogans like 'Be a welder!' and 'Don't be a shirker, join the women workers'.

The Ministry of Information turned the image of women's fecundity on its head, as this factory worker gives birth to tanks and

WOMEN OF BRITAIN
COME INTO
THE FACTORIES

ASK AT ANY EMPLOYMENT EXCHANGE FOR ADVICE AND FULL DETAILS

bombers

In real life, the women in the workforce had to fight against outright prejudice from their male overseers, who struggled to see things from the women's point of view. There was an unofficial strike 'at the Ford Willow Run Plant when women workers refused to wear a company-prescribed suit, a blue cover-all thing with three buttons on the back and a drop seat'. The women started to turn up without the suit and were disciplined, 'the rest of the women struck and that was the end of the suit'.[13] In Britain, the new women workers were viewed with suspicion by men who feared that their skills would be 'diluted'. One machinist complained 'Here's one woman doing it – they'll be getting other women in and then we'll be out of jobs and sent into the army'.[14]

One of the most extraordinary state interventions in family life was the policy of 'evacuation'. On 16 November 1937 the House of

Commons heard MP Oliver Simmonds claim that 'if the Government do not evacuate the people from those areas in an orderly manner, the people will evacuate themselves in a disorderly manner'.[15]

The idea had been argued out in the Committee on Imperial Defence, and led the Government to worry about 'a large exodus from London' and that 'unless the Government took firm control chaos and confusion were bound to ensue'.[16] The Committee was convinced that 'a disorderly general flight' would happen and the issue was 'how control of the population was to be exercised'.[17] The outcome of these fears would be the policy of evacuation. The proposal was to move children from bombing target urban areas to the countryside.

LEAVE THIS TO US SONNY—YOU OUGHT TO BE OUT OF LONDON

MINISTRY OF HEALTH EVACUATION SCHEME

In the first three days of official evacuation, 1.5 million people were moved-827,000 children of school-age; 524,000 mothers and young children (under 5); 13,000 pregnant women; 7,000 disabled persons and over 103,000 teachers and other 'helpers'. Local authorites were tasked with billeting the evacuees with families in the towns and villages. Quite soon most of the adult evacuees had moved back home, as did many of the children later on. Some stayed, though, and their experiences were mixed. Some took to country living with generous and loving foster parents. Others were treated as skivvies, poorly fed and clothed. Complaints about the unruly manners of the evacuees mounted up and it became plain that dealing with the burden and distraction of childcare was the main point of the programme. Back in 1937 when Parliament debated the issue, Somerset Maxwell explained that:

Members have made a mistake in assuming that you have to evacuate the whole of the East End of London or that you have to evacuate nobody. I think only certain people will have to be evacuated. You cannot evacuate the whole of the people in the East End of London. Most of them will be there because they are doing important jobs, and they must remain. But others will have to be evacuated.[18]

Getting rid of children was seen as the best way of concentrating the city-dwellers' minds on 'getting the job done'. Within less than a year, most of the children had been brought back home.

Nurseries were thin on the ground for British women and they protested, blocking streets with prams carrying slogans like 'We Want War Work – We Want Nurseries'.[19] Other tasks were taken away from housewives, like cooking a midday meal, as munitions workers ate at works canteens (Churchill insisted that the UK's be called 'British Restaurants', because 'canteen' was too socialistic), though the New Statesman reported on the troubles wives had working the fifty or more hours a week expected and keeping house.[20]

For American women the tug of war between work in the factory and work in the home meant it was hard to keep to the clock. The US Government targeted women's absenteeism as a challenge to their authority and the 'war effort'. According to historian John Costello the 'high rate of female absenteeism became a major issue at the peak of the war production drive in 1943' and women were accused of 'throwing a monkey wrench in the war effort' and of being a 'boon and ally to the Axis'.[21]

The great movement of young men and women into new lives in the services, and into work had a marked impact on their love lives. In the weeks after the attack on Pearl Harbor there was a twenty per cent leap in the marriage rate in the US, so that more than a thousand couples were tying the knot each day – and by the autumn, the birthrate rose too.[22] Women and men thinking that they might not live so long married more freely. They made love more freely, too, under the excuse that it might be their last night. The war was a flux of people that gave lots of opportunities to get along, in more fleeting relations, in camps and at dances, on weekend passes, or in the 'blackout' (to rob bombers of targets).

In Germany, the Federation of German Girls (Bund Deutscher Mädel, or 'BDM') had quite a reputation for sex – as did The Hitler Youth - with girls losing their virginity and getting pregnant. By 1939 there were one and a half million in the BDM, almost as many as in the Hitler Youth. The Reich Labour Service also made new chances for men and women to get together. According to an interviewee of Researcher Dagmar Herzog the Labour Service had a 'very sexual climate' and (in a statement that seems bizarre out of context) 'in general the Nazis were in favour of fun'.[23]

In exile, the German Marxist Herbert Marcuse got work with the Office of Security Services of the FBI, where he was set to work analysing German society. It was there that he developed the theory that the Nazis grip on German society was made stronger by an 'emancipation of sexuality' – he was talking about the official propaganda's promotion of good breeding, what he saw as a quasi-sexual climax in the drama of Nazi rallies, and the cult of youth. All of these things added up to a breakdown in sexual taboos, and 'the abolition of sexual taboos tends to make this realm of satisfaction a public domain ... the individual recognizes his private satisfaction as a patriotic service to the regime, and he receives his reward for performing it'.[24]

There is some evidence that the Nazis did some things that broke down sexual taboos. The SS Journal *Das Schwarze Korps* mocked 'eager clerical moralists' and their ideas of 'original sin' and 'the denominational morality' that sees in the body something to be despised, and wants to interpret what are natural processes as sinful drives'.[25] There was something about the cult of youth, of fecundity and of the body beautiful that did lead to a greater emphasis on sexuality. It is not easy though to argue the case that young lust was at work in Germany alone.

Mass culture in America, too, was erotically charged. In 1944 *thirty-thousand* bobby-soxers rioted before a Frank Sinatra concert (the singer had been graded 4F, rejected for service by the draft board, and was booed when he went to entertain the troops the following year.)[26] Chuck Berry played for the black troops at the United Services Organisation, and remembered it as a time when a young man could meet a lot of girls.[27] German girls had the BDM, and from September 1944 American girls had *Seventeen*, which told its half million new readers 'you are the bosses of the business'.[28]

The war leaders had set a great mass of youthful enthusiasm in train, and with it came many more opportunities for people to meet up and get together. War brought with it the makings of a sexual revolution, and the drill sergeants, chaplains and women's leaders across the world struggled to damp it down.

In 1944 US Postmaster General Frank C Walker banned the magazine Esquire from the mails, withholding the girly magazine from eager troops. 'Such pictures are objectionable to all persons of refinement and good taste' thought the US Army Chaplain General.[29] Banning the 'Cheesecake' pin-up pictures of girls in bikinis, though, was impossible, as American G.I.s made them good luck charms on every plane and tank.

All armies carried on vigorous campaigns to warn their troops of the dangers of sex. Lectures, leaflets and films about the dangers of Venereal Disease were how the military authorities sought to frighten their troops away from fraternising with local women. Posters showed women as death – the skull behind the veil – the lascivious come-on leading to the grave. In the North Africa campaign, it was drummed into troops that Arab women were diseased whores, and that any contact would leave them scarred by exotic maladies. Women were also portrayed as gossips, if not outright enemy agents, who would trick men into revealing military secrets.

Saboteuse

Women were blamed for the spread of venereal disease. In Queensland Australia, fears over fraternisation between troops and local women led to a parliamentary enquiry and the founding of the 'Lock Ward' in hospitals, where promiscuous women could be held against their will. In this way Australia's medical authorities claimed that 'the greatest difficulty of all, the control of the irresponsible promiscuous girl, is provided for'.[30] In the autumn of 1941 the Icelandic Surgeon General bemoaned that 'Reykjavik has become a training centre for harlots', under the 'Situation' – the siting of Allied troops on the island. Outraged by young women's friendships with the soldiers, the Icelandic government issued the 'Situation Report' that put the blame largely on 'Icelandic women' for whom 'the difference between a whore and an honourable woman is far from clear'. 'Situation Laws' followed the 'Situation Report' and young women were subject to surveillance by welfare and school committees, while those straying could be sent to private homes or reformatories for up to three years'.[31]

The Nazi authorities inherited strict laws against prostitution, but lobbied by the military, they moved towards the legalisation of licensed prostitution in state-regulated brothels. On 9 September 1939 the Reich Ministry of the Interior ordered the strict supervision of prostitutes. All sado-masochistic sex toys were banned, but the police in Berlin and other cities did oversee brothels. The German authorities were driven to regulate commercial sex in part because they were in a panic over homosexuality. Himmler gave a speech in favour of licensed brothels in 1937 in which he said 'one cannot prevent the entire youth from drifting toward homosexuality if at the same time one blocks out the alternative'.[32]

Nazi campaigns against homosexuality date back to the 'Night of the Long Knives' when Hitler sanctioned the killing of Ernest Rohm and other leading 'Brownshirts' of the SA. To explain why he had turned on his own radical supporters, Hitler highlighted Rohm's homosexuality, calling the SA leaders 'a small group of individuals joined by a common predisposition' in the Reichstag on 13 July 1934. Successive waves of repression against homosexuals followed. In 1936 there were extensive police raids in Hamburg, called for by Himmler. In April and May 1937 a number of Catholic priests were tried, accused of 'unnatural sexual relations' and abuse of children –

and attacked in the press. 100,000 Germans were charged with homosexual offences under the Nazis. Around 10,000 were sent to the concentration camps, where they were made to wear the pink triangle. In 1941 Hitler issued the warning that

> Any member of the SS or the Gestapo who engages in indecent behaviour with another man or permits himself to be abused by him for indecent purposes will, regardless of age, be condemned to death and executed.[34]

Italian homosexuals, too, were persecuted. In 1939 the Questore of Catania, Molina, railed against a 'homosexual plague', a 'wave of degeneration' sweeping over Catania. Determined 'to stop, or at least to contain, such grave sexual aberrations which offend morality, damage health and limit the improvement of the race', Molina had fifty-six men arrested as 'pederasts' and confined in the Tremiti islands. Elsewhere another 250 were seized in the same dragnet.[35]

American troops did not face execution for homosexuality. They did though face fierce repression by a terrified Military Command. Draft boards were told to weed out gay men to keep them out of the services, but many men evaded the question, and many more were only introduced to homosexuality in the forces. Homosexual servicemen who opened up to sympathetic-sounding army psychiatrists found themselves confined in special wards. For those who were discovered, though, the punishment was much more aggressive. Officers who uncovered the many gay circles in the US military jailed the miscreants in 'pink stockades'. Woodie Wilson, who edited the 'Myrtle Beach Bitch' was seized by MPs charged with misusing government property, but taken to a stockade 'surrounded by barbed wire'.[36]

At Noumea, New Caledonia, scores of gay servicemen were caged in individual wooden cells in a 'pink stockade'. The men were taken to eat and paraded in front of thousands of jeering soldiers. Woodie Wilson was singled out for fraternising with men inside the stockade, so he was boarded into his bed at night. David Barrett, who was at the Noumea stockade looked back: 'it wasn't a concentration camp, but psychologically it was. We weren't going into ovens, we ate, but the rest of it was all there.'[37]

Men were interrogated, and made to name the names of other men they had had sex with, who were interrogated in turn. There were raids of 'rings' in Moffet Field California, the Eighth Naval District near New Orleans and Myrtle Beach. Forty seven men were arrested and thrown out of the army after raids in New Orleans, April 1944. More than thirty were rounded up and discharged from a South Pacific base – perhaps the same men that Frank Jacober saw behind barbed wire. Twenty-one officers and 201 soldiers stationed in Australia were discharged as homosexuals.[38]

British troops were also hounded by MPs who broke up gay clubs they went to in Cairo and Algiers. King's Regulations barred homosexuals from the services. A British Army study warned that the homosexual was likely to be rebellious – 'he must lead, cannot be led' – and also, this being the war against fascism, fascistic: homosexuals had 'Fascist leanings and were facile exponents of power politics'.[39]

Tens of thousands of US servicemen were given a dishonourable discharge, called a Blue Discharge after the colour of the paper, after spending months in psychiatric cells or 'queer compounds'. The Blue Discharge was a disaster because it denied them the many benefits that ex-servicemen got, like housing and college loans, as well as excluding many from jobs where employers expected to see service records.

War time had turned sexual relations on their heads, pushing men and women into all kinds of relations that defied tradition. When the war was over, the authorities struggled to put the Genie back in the Bottle. One of the greatest challenges they faced was to recreate the patriarchal family after the war.

A Mrs Gould of the Women's Advisory Committee to the American War Manpower Administration went with Eleanor Roosevelt to look at the British war effort. 'One hears much discussion of what will happen after the war and much speculation as to whether women will be willing to go back to their old place when the need for them is over'. Herbert Morrison had said that 'you can't help wondering if they are going to be a bit hoity-toity after the war'.[40]

After the war there were a great many lay-offs of women

workers, and in many cities there were protests. House Beautiful lectured its readers: 'He's head man again' and 'your part is to fit his home to him, understanding why he wants it this way, forgetting your own preferences'. Marynia Farnham and Ferdinand Lundberg, a psychologist and economist respectively, wrote that career women were symbolically castrating their husbands in their book *Modern Women: The Lost Sex* (1947).[41]

Chapter Twelve

Power Politics

At its heart the Second World War was a war among the Great Powers, the ranking and strategic play of which was always much more decisive than the propagandistic claims they made. The Great Powers were always battling, sometimes openly, sometimes keeping it under wraps. The slump made the struggle between them sharper. Overall, the framework that had been set at the end of the First World War no longer fitted the real balance of power. The Versailles Treaty of 1919 was victor's justice, giving everything to Britain and France, and punishing Germany with territorial losses

The First World War ended with the defeat of Germany, Austria-Hungary, Bulgaria and the Ottoman Empire at the hands of Britain, France, Belgium, Italy, Japan and the United States of America. The settlement of the First World War at the Paris Peace Conference in 1919 was punitive, exacting economic reparations – to total £6 600 000 000 – against Germany, and taking territory away from Germany on its border with France (the Ruhr was occupied, and the disputed Alsace-Lorraine passed back into French hands), and in the east Germany lost Posen and Upper Silesia to Poland, the port of Memel to Lithuania, Danzig became a free city – all in all 25 000 square miles of territory and seven million inhabitants. Austria-Hungary was broken up, with the new state of Czechoslovakia taking much of old Austria and the Kingdom of Hungary, which also lost land to Yugoslavia. The Ottoman Empire collapsed, losing its Arab provinces to France and Britain (that ran them as 'mandated territories') and its European territory to Greece (though Ataturk won some of it back). In 1920 Lenin told the Second Congress of the Communist International that 'for Germany and a whole number of the defeated nations the Versailles treaty has created conditions which make economic existence physically impossible, deprive them of their rights and humiliate them'.[1]

The Versailles Treaty laid the basis for a new 'League of Nations', and the dream of 'collective security' – the policing of world disputes by the powers, in harmony. The Versailles Treaty suffered all the faults of any attempt to make a given moment in the struggle for power into a permanently fixed settlement with an institutional form. The hard carapace of Versailles would strain and crack as the organism it contained grew and changed. Taking Germany's lowest ebb as its starting point, the settlement was quickly contradicted by that country's industrial expansion, that strained against the exacting conditions of territory and reparations lost to her rivals. Successive attempts were made to adjust the terms to make them more workable. In 1924 US banker Charles Dawes' plan underwrote German reparations with American and British loans – helping along an economic recovery in Europe. At the end of 1925 the borders between Germany, Belgium and France were stabilised under a treaty signed at in Switzerland, (but not those to the east, to Poland's dismay); after Locarno the Allied forces left the Rhine, and Germany was admitted to the League of Nations.

USA	USSR	Germany	UK	France	Japan	Italy
28.7	17.6	13.2	9.2	4.5	3.8	2.9

Source: Paul Kennedy, The Rise and Fall of the Great Powers, London, Fontana 1988, p 426

These percentage shares in world manufacturing output in 1938 illustrate the disproportion between economic strength on the one hand, and territorial and political influence on the other. Germany, America and Japan were all constrained by an international system where Britain was the hegemonic power. For Britain and France, however, the problem was that they were punching above their weight.

Have and Have Not Powers

The fashion of the day was to talk of the 'have' and 'have-not' powers (or satisfied and dissatisfied): 'sympathy for the poor "Have-Not" Powers deprived of colonies' was a theme raised at the 'National Peace Council's well-intentioned conference on Peace and the Colonial Problem'. 'Have not' powers were not only those that lost the First World War. Japan and Italy were on the winning side, but their energy needs and territorial ambitions were not guaranteed by colonies, as France and Britain's were. In a sense,

America, too, was a dissatisfied power. Though America had, by 1900, already eclipsed Britain as the pre-eminent economic power, it had no colonies outside of the Pacific. America clashed with Britain, as it did with all the European Empires over access to colonial markets. The satisfied powers had a natural interest in the status quo, and could readily counsel peaceful coexistence and collective security in the knowledge that any disturbance to the existing order was likely to cost them. France's position was the most brittle, as its territorial extent was far greater than its economic dynamic justified, but Britain, while having more room to manoeuvre, had the most to lose.

E. H. Carr, who was at Versailles with the British delegation, wrote that 'the war-mongering of the dissatisfied Powers was the "natural, cynical reaction" to the sentimental and dishonest platitudinising of the satisfied Powers on the common interest in peace'.[2] On the other hand, Rajani Palme Dutt, who sat on Lenin's Comintern scorned the claims of the 'have-not' powers: 'it is impossible to fail to be reminded of the child who, on being shown the picture of the Christians Being Thrown to the Lions, was full of sympathy for "the lion who had not got a Christian"'.[3] The 'have not' powers challenged collective security with Japan's invasion of Manchuria in 1931 and with Italy's of Abyssinia in 1935.

It has been said that the 'have not' powers ought to have tried to meet their needs through trade, not by grabbing empires.[4] But to have traded peacefully with the armed Empires of Britain, France, Holland, and the emerging sea power of the United States would have been always to trade at a loss. When Japan became a commercial challenge to the United States, the US used military force to limit its success. French and British support for nations in East Europe was meant to hem Germany in. Only by overcoming the national divisions among societies could there ever have been free and equal relations between all producers. As long as world society was divided into hostile states, warfare would be the outcome. Towards the end of the decade the international treaties had one main purpose, the regulation of military might.

Collaboration and Conflict
Across the world, governments' military ambitions were held back

by their people. The First World War cost 17 million lives, and anti-war sentiment was strong. The powers were exhausted, and unstable. Elites cooperated with each other because they were weak, and banding together to face down the popular challenge from the left. US loans helped stabilise Germany's Social Democratic government, suggesting to the Bolshevik leader Trotsky that 'American capitalism is seeking the position of world domination; it wants to establish an American imperialist autocracy over our planet'. And since the Social Democratic parties were winning out in this stabilised capitalist order, Trotsky thought 'European Social Democracy is becoming before our eyes, the political agency of American capitalism'.[5] US lending to Europe and Germany helped American capitalists to share in the profits made by the Military Industrial Complex there, as General Motors and IBM teamed up with their European counterparts. German industrialists extended the collaboration eastwards, investing in the otherwise ideologically hostile Soviet Union with trade deals that brought much-needed technology to the embattled regime there. Collaboration between the powers, though, was only the prelude to conflict.

Isolationism

From the heightened moral stands set down in the course of the war, 'isolationism' in America, and 'appeasement' in Britain were damaging charges. After the event the accusatory label of 'isolationism' was stuck on every critic of the war, of whatever motive, and taken to mean that the so-labelled were closet Fascists, like the anti-Semitic campaign Father Charles Coughlin. The America First committee was supported by nationalists – some of whom, like Charles Lindbergh, were racists (though hardly more so than the architects of the American war effort, Roosevelt, Truman, Patton or MacArthur). Other America First supporters were Republican Congressman Gerald Nye (whose Congressional Committee blamed arms manufacturers for stoking the last war), socialists like Norman Thomas and even anti-Fascists like writer Sinclair Lewis. On the whole America First framed its case in simply patriotic terms, and got support from a war-fearing public. It called for the defence of America and opposed involvement in the European war, including the 'lend lease' bill.

Putting America First, rather than waging war, was a fair approximation of the interests of capitalist America in 1940. Indeed in February 1940, after the German invasion of Poland, Roosevelt sent his Under Secretary of State on a tour of the west European capitals on a mission to 'bring France and Britain to terms with Germany'.[6] But the Chief Executive had already worked out that he needed to push American interests more aggressively in the rest of the world. The ideological struggle against isolationism at home was the argument that Roosevelt needed to win to get the country behind the war, which is why 'isolationism' is to this day such a poisonous charge. In truth both policies made sense at different points in time: standing back from the war in 1939 and then joining it in 1941 meant that America got the most out of the changing world order, with the least cost in American lives.

Appeasement

The British government's policy of appeasement from 1935 to 1939, under Prime Ministers Stanley Baldwin and Neville Chamberlain, is probably even more reviled today than that of isolationism in America. Under the pseudonym 'Cato', Michael Foot, Frank Owen and Peter Howard, published a pamphlet *The Guilty Men* in 1940 that accused the country's leaders – including Chamberlain, Baldwin, Lord Halifax and Samuel Hoare – of appeasing Hitler. Another journalist, the radical Claud Cockburn struck a chord when he wrote about the 'Cliveden Set' – upper class supporters of Germany and appeasement that included Nancy Astor and Times editor Geoffrey Dawson – in his newssheet *The Week*. Since then, the historian Andrew Roberts has claimed that appeasement was a sensible policy that let Britain re-arm in time to take on Hitler. It is true that the real difference between the appeasement policy of Chamberlain and the war policy of Churchill are tactical differences over how best to promote the British Empire. As the world's foremost military power, with nowhere to go but down, Britain was bound to hope for stability, and dread war, which could only mean change, which is to say, change for the worse. By the same token Britain had most to lose, so at the point that its status was at risk, it would fight tooth and nail to hang on to power. 'Appeasement' was a rational course for an ageing and over-extended imperial power to adopt. Still, there is a point to the radical critique of appeasement. Elite caution over waging war went further than pragmatism, arising from sympathy for Hitler and Mussolini. In November 1937, Lord Halifax personally told Hitler how much the British government appreciated that Germany was 'a bulwark of the West against Bolshevism'.[7] 'In the case of Hitler, as in the case of Mussolini, the greedy, the Tories... all heralded his rise to power with enthusiasm', wrote US Under Secretary of State Sumner Welles.[8]

Even after German tanks crossed into Poland, Britain waged war in words as much as in deeds. It was called the 'phoney war'. Historian Klaus Hildebrand writes that 'beneath the façade of the "phoney war", the policy of appeasement was basically continued'.[9] In the British war cabinet on 27 May 1940 Churchill said that 'if Herr Hitler was prepared to make peace on the terms of the restoration of the German colonies and the overlordship of central Europe' that was something he could accept.[10] As with isolationism in America, the difference between appeasement and war was not one of core principles but two different policies, pursuing by the same national egotism, as the conditions changed.

'Germany is not striving to smash Britain'

Just as the British elite were willing to share the world so too was Hitler. Hitler told Chamberlain that 'Britain and Germany were the two pillars upon which the European social order would rest'.[11] In May 1940, with the invasion of France underway, Field Marshal von Runstedt was astonished to be told by Hitler that he did not want to defeat Britain.

> speaking with admiration of the British Empire, of the necessity for its existence, and of the civilization that Britain had brought into the world. He remarked with a shrug of his shoulders that the creation of its Empire had been achieved by means that were often harsh, but "where there is planing, there are shavings flying." He compared the British Empire with the Catholic Church – saying that they were both essential elements of stability in the world. He said that all he wanted from Britain was that she should acknowledge Germany's position on the

Continent. The return of Germany's lost colonies would be desirable but not essential, and he would even offer to support Britain with troops if she should be involved in any difficulties anywhere. …He concluded by saying that it was his aim to make peace with Britain on a basis that she would regard as compatible with her honour to accept.[12]

Hitler's desire to avoid all-out war with Britain seemed to be confirmed by his unwillingness to break the British Expeditionary Force on its retreat from Dunkirk. According to Runstedt's aide Blumentritt, Hitler 'showed little interest in the plans' for the invasion of England, 'and made no effort to speed up the preparations'.[13] In August 1940 Hitler said

Germany is not striving to smash Britain because the beneficiary will not be us, but Japan in the east, Russia in India, Italy in the Mediterranean and America in World Trade. That is why peace is perfectly possible with Britain – but not so long as Churchill is Prime Minister.[14]

Indeed Britain and Germany continued to avoid direct engagement on each other's territory until 1944, when Britain invaded the continent, on the way to the German frontier. Before then, British and German forces carried on their war in other people's countries. First, both brought invasion forces to Norway, Britain aiming to use the country as a gateway to Finland, to fight the Russians there. Then the British Expeditionary Force sought to use the defence of France as a means to check German expansion. After Dunkirk, the German and British troops faced each other on the sands of North Africa and the Middle East where the peoples of Algeria, Egypt, Tunisia, Libya and Iraq were only peripherally involved. Apart from the Desert War, German and British forces fought indirectly, Germany attacking shipping in the Atlantic, Britain and Germany attacking each other's civilian populations with bombing campaigns. The cost of direct invasion was simply too high for both sides in 1940. Only when Germany started to lose control of Europe in 1944 did Churchill succumb to Russian and American demands for an invasion.

The Failure of the Axis

The Axis was based on a common struggle against the socialist working class movement. The Axis was in the first place between the two fascist powers Germany and Italy. At its height it took in other reactionary regimes in Europe, and Japan. Hitler's personal affinity with the Italian 'Duce' Mussolini was central. 'Without Mussolini's friendship', Hitler said, 'I would be alone in the world'. Hitler offered a division of labour to Mussolini: 'our interests are in the North, yours in the South'.[15] Italy's ambitions in the Mediterranean were to displace France, and even Britain, in North Africa. Seeing Germany's success in Western Europe, Mussolini felt compelled to push into Albania and then Greece. But Germany was driven to defend its fascist ally as both the North African and Balkan campaigns faltered. Rommel's advance force took on the 8th Army after the Italians lost ground. Germany occupied Greece in April 1941 after the Greek Army pushed Italy back, exposing Mussolini's pretensions of equality with Germany.

Germany's other Axis partners were Romania, Hungary, the Baltic states and Finland. In Croatia, Ante Pavelić's Ustase fought a war of racial domination over the Serbs. In occupied Europe Germany's 'anti-Bolshevik' alliance was supported by collaborationist reactionaries like Anton Mussert in Holland, Vikdun Quisling in Norway and, most importantly, by first Pétain, and then Laval in France. These local fascist and reactionary leaders, though, had weak support – and were further weakened by the unpopularity of the German occupation forces. In the east the Axis had some support from Ukranians, Caucasians and Balts. In November 1941 the Foreign Ministers of Germany, Italy and Japan met to renew the 1936 Anti-Comintern Pact in Berlin (the Comintern was the international organisation of the Communist Parties led by the USSR). They were joined by eight new signatories: Bulgaria, Croatia, Denmark, Finland, Hungary, Romania, Slovakia and Spain.

The Axis though struggled to reconcile the nationalist ambitions of its lesser lights with the overwhelming dominance of Nazi Germany. Hitler's partners discovered that the dictator had no real common cause to offer other than subordination to Germany. The other European signatories of the Anti-Comintern Pact hoped for a declaration on Europe from Hitler to rival the Anglo-American

'Atlantic Charter' (see below). When the German Foreign Ministry asked Hitler to outline the post-war order, he refused to be drawn. 'No such preparations for peace are necessary', he said – he would dictate terms when the hour came. Mussolini despaired that the Germans 'have no political sense'.[16] But that was the problem at the heart of Fascism – it was the end of politics, the fantastic ambition to cut the Gordian knot. Under the pressures that came as the fascist ascendancy first peaked, and then lost ground in the east and in North Africa, the Axis cracked. One by one Germany's allies concluded that they had more to lose than gain by the association. Spain, too weakened by the Civil War to commit to Hitler's war, returned to the British sphere of influence. Finland signalled its willingness to work with the Allies, and, most decisively, the Fascist Grand Council, with the backing of King Victor Emmanuel, forced Mussolini out of office and belatedly joined the Allies, only to suffer the indignity of a German occupation.

Only the alliance with Japan lasted – and that because it had no real content beyond platitudes. Pointedly there had been neither military nor economic cooperation with Japan, the partnership being wholly opportunistic.

Germany's Soviet Policy

Treaty of Non-Aggression, between Germany and the Soviet Union, better known as the Nazi-Soviet pact, or Molotov-Ribbentrop pact, was signed in Moscow on 23 August 1939. The words 'Non-Aggression' were grotesque: the secret protocols of the Pact set out the joint invasion and division of Poland between the signatories, which began when German troops crossed the border on 1 September 1939. With the Nazi-Soviet Pact, Germany used the USSR as a proxy, to help fight its war against the Poles. The Pact was followed by the German–Soviet Commercial Agreement of February 11, 1940 that boosted trade between the USSR and the Reich, with Germany importing much-needed oil, minerals and grain, in exchange for engineering goods.

There was a basis for economic cooperation between Germany and the Soviet Union – the two sides had often traded Soviet raw materials (grain and oil) for German technology. Politically the Nazi-Soviet pact was opportunistic on both sides, though there were precedents. At Rapallo in 1922 the two pariah states of Versailles broke out of their isolation from the Western states collaborating in military manoeuvres and trade. As we have seen, however, Nazi Germany's plans for the east were to be won by force, not cooperation. 'First we'll pump oil out of Russia', German officers told Ilya Ehrenburg in 1940, 'then blood'.[17] In 1939, Hitler needed the Soviet leadership's help in carving up Poland, but once that had been achieved their usefulness was all but exhausted. With victory over France and Holland in the West, Hitler baulked at the likely cost of invading Britain, and turned his attentions instead to the east. In the early hours of 22 June 1941 Germany broke the Pact, invading the Soviet Union – a turnaround that sent Stalin into shock. The uplift after the victory over France was intoxicating, but the Nazi state was incapable of standing still and Hitler needed yet another mobilisation to keep up the pace. Ironically, given what followed, Hitler most likely chose to invade the USSR as the easier option.

The USSR: turning in the wind

'Until the revolution takes place in all lands, including the richest and the most highly civilised ones, our victory will be only a half victory, perhaps still less.'[18]

The origins of the Soviet state in revolution committed to overturning not just the Russian order, but also the imperialist system overall, made it a pariah among the powers. But after Lenin's death, Stalin beat his rival Trotsky to the leadership of the new state, and promptly overturned Lenin's policy, saying that 'in the new period ... the old formula ... becomes incorrect and must inevitably be replaced by another formula, one that affirms the possibility of the victory of socialism in one country.'[19] Gustav Hilger, official in the German Embassy in Moscow traced the big shifts in USSR to the failure of the Hamburg Communists' uprising of October 1923:

> it gave Stalin occasion to develop his theory "Socialism in a single country". In Moscow's relations with Germany it resulted in a determined return to the Rapallo policy of friendship with the bourgeois government in Berlin.[20]

In fact Stalin's shift to Socialism in one country was widely under-

stood by the other powers to be a great concession, an accommodation to the 'System of States' that was rewarded by the USSR's
admittance to the League of Nations – which Lenin had rubbished as
a 'thieves' kitchen' but the more supplicant Stalin called the 'friends
of peace'.[21] From that point on, Stalin's strategy was to make peace
with whichever powers would stabilise the Soviet Union's borders
and help her get hold of the technology she needed. Under Stalin,
Soviet Russia became an opportunist state, cynically wooing any and
all of the Great Powers. Even with the Nazi victory, Stalin saw no
problem. In September 1933, as the German Communists were being
rounded up and jailed, Foreign Minister Molotov wrote

> We of course sympathise with the sufferings of our German
> comrades, but we Marxists are the last who can be reproached
> with allowing our feelings to dictate our policy. The whole world
> knows that we can and do maintain good relations with the
> capitalist states of any brand, including the fascist.[22]

All the same, Germany's military intervention in the Spanish Civil
War made the Soviet leaders fearful of Nazi ambitions. In 1937
Commissar for Foreign Affairs Maxim Litvinov tried to interest
France and Britain in an 'antifascist alliance', but was rebuffed.
Having rejected the Trotskyist policy of promoting the overthrow of
the imperialist powers, Stalin sought alliance with these wherever he
could. After Neville Chamberlain went to Munich to woo the
German Chancellor, Stalin switched strategy and sought out his own
alliance with Hitler. After the 'Non-Aggression Pact' ended with
invasion, Stalin struck up a new alliance with Churchill against
Hitler. On 12 July 1941 the Anglo-Soviet agreement was signed
under which 'the two Governments mutually undertake to render
each other assistance of all kinds in this war'.[23]

Asia for the Asians – under Japanese leadership

To the editor of *Pacific Affairs,* and advisor to Chiang Kai-Shek Owen
Lattimore, Japan was an exponent of 'cut-rate imperialism'. She
played off Chinese warlords against each other and then 'when
disorder resulted, the Japanese came forward as loyal supporters of
the international system of "law and order," strengthening their

military forces on the spot and appealing to the common interests of Britain and America' in stability.[24] In many ways Japan acted like a conventional imperialist power. Korea was under Japanese influence from the end of the nineteenth century and then direct rule from 1910. After defeating Russia in 1905, Japan seized the Manchuria railway concession, which became the foothold of its Chinese outpost. As the Algerian colony was to the socialist Prosper Merimée, the South Manchuria Railway was a platform for social programmes of improvement – hospitals were built in Mukden, Ch'ang-Ch'un and Darien. 'Many leftists came to Manchuria to work for the SMR, feeling a sense of mission could be exercised there which was impossible at home'.[25] Nearly a quarter of a million Japanese civilians settled in Manchuria, with 100,000 soldiers to back them up and in 1932, a Japan-backed state of Manchukuo was set up under the Emperor Pu Yi.

Japanese meddling in China was extensive, and not always unwelcome to local warlords, like the supporters of the North China Autonomy Movement of Autumn 1935. Pointedly, the nationalist Kuomintang, led by Chiang Kai-Shek since Sun Yat-sen's death, left the Manchuria settlement alone. But Tu Chung-yuan, a refugee from Manchukuo in Beijing made the case against Japan in the journal *Shenghuo Zhoukan* and through the North East National Salvation Society.[26] Japan met more and more resistance from nationalist China, becoming bogged down in a bitter war culminating in the massacres at Nanking. US criticisms of the rising Pacific rival were getting louder – with evidence of atrocities supplied by the many American missions in China. But British policy was to accommodate Japanese expansion and draw Tokyo in as an ally in lordship over subject races. 'The attitude of the United States' the British Foreign Secretary was complained 'was not very helpful' as America adopted a more aggressive stance to Japan.[27] Alliance with Germany and Italy did not come till 27 September 1940 and did little good to Japan. There was no aid or consultation between Japan and the other Axis powers.

The thing that changed Japan's fortunes was the fragility of the European Empires in the Far East. Britain ruled Burma, Malaya, Singapore; France ruled indo-China (modern-day Vietnam) and Holland ruled the Dutch East Indies (modern day Indonesia). It was the stalemate in China that led Japan's political and military leaders to turn from a northern (i.e. Chinese) to a Southward Advance Doctrine on 7 August 1936, which is to say one aimed at the European colonies. As Saburō Ienaga says, 'they plunged the country into war with America and England in the hope of cutting the Gordian knot in China.'[28] Japan entered French Indo-China with the support of the Vichy-loyal administrators – but still that was the excuse that America used to impose a crippling oil embargo with the help of the British, Chinese and Dutch (all together, the 'ABCD' group). Japan's war began with the attack on the US base in Pearl Harbour and the destruction of the US Navy's fleet, with the intention of forcing America to the negotiating table. The Imperial Conference of 6 September 1941 heard this report:

> Although America's total defeat is judged utterly impossible, it is not inconceivable that a shift in American public opinion due to our victories in Southeast Asia or to England's surrender might bring the war to an end.[29]

Those were the kind of tactics that the Japanese had learned from studying Clausewitz and other western military theorists, but they did not anticipate that it was an age of total war, or that America's intense feelings of racial insult would override any rational calculation of national interest.

After the Imperial Navy's dramatic victory at Pearl Harbour, the Imperial Army shocked the world by seizing Burma, Malaya and then Singapore, Indonesia and the Philippines. Her victories were carried on the wings of native resentment at white rule, and she found willing collaborators among national-minded subjects of British and Dutch rule. The appeal of Asia for the Asians was compelling.

In time, Japan's appeal to locals palled, as the Co-Prosperity Sphere failed to prosper, and the Kempeitai military police imposed a brutal order. From the outset Japan had faced resistance from Chinese nationalists in China, and ethnic Chinese supporters of the Malayan People's Anti-Japanese Army. Increasingly, the Japanese faced resistance from the same national leaders that they had raised up to fight against the Europeans, like Aung San in Burma. In June

1942 a fierce naval battle at the Midway Atoll – the midway between the two continents either side of the Pacific Ocean, Admiral Chester Nimitz decisively defeated Japan's navy, and a tortuous campaign to overturn her island gains was begun. On land, though, it was not until the battle of Imphal in July 1944 that the Japanese Army began to lose the war.

America's rise to Globalism

Over the course of the Second World War America tore down the walls of the European Empires to become not just the dominant industrial power, but the 'world's policeman', too. Domestic opposition stopped America from taking its seat on the League of Nations in 1920 (though President Woodrow Wilson was its architect). In San Francisco, on 25 April 1945 the United Nations was founded under American leadership. America took its place on the 5-strong permanent Security Council and New York became the UN's permanent headquarters. 'The American flag flies over more than 300 overseas outposts,' the *Chicago Daily Tribune* reported in 1955:

> Camps and barracks and bases cover 12 American possessions or territories held in trust. The foreign bases are in 63 foreign nations or islands.[30]

A conference at Bretton Woods, New Hampshire put in place America's policy of an 'Open Door' for trade (the General Agreement on Tariffs and Trade), and an International Monetary Fund with the dollar as a 'world currency'.

America's ascendance was made in the teeth of popular hostility to 'foreign entanglements', by a President who had promised 'Your boys are not going to be sent into any foreign wars', in Boston on 30 October 1940.[31]

America's victory over the old Empires of Europe, and against its Japanese rival in the Pacific were won first and foremost by her industrial might. When Roosevelt said that America would become the 'arsenal of democracy' what he meant was that US arms would be exported to allies who did the lions' share of the fighting.

According to Stephen Ambrose:

The United States had taken Britain's place and played her nineteenth century role of avoiding huge battles on the Continent paying others to do the fighting, and thereby being the only nation at the conclusion strong enough to assume a predominant position.[32]

America fought the first part of the war, through proxies: the Nationalist Chinese, the Soviets, and the British Army

After the German invasion of the Soviet Union, President Roosevelt invited Soviet Ambassador Konstantin Ousmansky to draw up a list of Russia's needs to fight the war. In September 1941 Roosevelt included the USSR in the lend-lease agreement and all-in-all provided military goods to the value of $10 billion[33] - equal to one fifth of all Soviet output in 1943. Britain and America risked ships and men to send more supplies by the Arctic ports at Murmansk and Archangel.[34] Some Soviet troops fought against the Wehrmacht wearing US-made uniforms, others driving American jeeps, loaded with ammunition from the production lines of Chicago. 'With our country not yet fully engaged in hostilities', recalled O.S.S. officer H Stuart Hughes, 'the overriding, the agonizing concern in Washington was to keep the Soviet Union fighting'.[35]

Missouri Senator, and future president Harry S. Truman, who as head of the the US Senate Special Committee to Investigate the National Defense Program planned the war effort outlined a cold calculus: 'If we see that Germany is winning we ought to help Russia, and if Russia is winning, we ought to help Germany, and that way let them kill as many as possible.'[36]

Truman's cynicism was not a personal bugbear, but a thought through US strategy. A report of the Joint Army and Navy Board read:

The maintenance of an active front in Russia offers by far the best opportunity for a successful land offensive against Germany, because only Russia possesses adequate manpower, situated in favourable proximity to the centre of German military power.[37]

Thirteen million six hundred thousand German soldiers were killed or wounded in the Second World War. Of those ten million were casualties on the eastern front. Nine million Soviet soldiers and nineteen million civilians were killed outright.[38]

The weakness of the American position was that, relying on the Soviet Union to do all the fighting, it would be difficult to deny them a share in the spoils. Roosevelt explained to his son that letting the Russians do all the work, America still had to snatch the victory:

> Just figure it's a football game. Say we're the reserves sitting on the bench. At the moment the Russians are the first team, together with the Chinese and to a lesser extent, the British. Before the game is so advanced that our blockers are tired, we've got to be able to get in there for the touchdown.[39]

With the collapse of Germany's Eastern Empire, the American position became more and more precarious. At the Teheran Conference in November 1943, Roosevelt watched the Soviet army advance within sixty miles of the Polish border, and concluded it was time to act:

> The Americans and the British must occupy a maximum part of Europe ... we must reach Berlin. Then let the Soviets occupy the territory east of the city. But Berlin must be taken by the United States.[40]

America's war against Britain

Back in 1926, Bolshevik leader Leon Trotsky had deduced from the shifting balance of power that 'the victory of the US over Europe, that is, first and foremost over England, is inevitable'.[41] Four years later, US Generals, led by Douglas MacArthur, drew up plans to invade Canada, 'War Plan Red' and other British colonies in the hemisphere.[42] In the event there was no open war between them, but still a massive shift in power so that the British Empire gave up its dominant position in the world to the US. As Keynes' biographer Robert Skidelsky puts it 'America's main war aim, after the defeat of Germany and Japan, was the liquidation of the British Empire.'[43] The struggle between the 'First Power on Earth' and the World's Policeman was hidden from view in their common struggle against the Axis powers.

In 1939 Britain's Empire was hopelessly over-extended, and broke. By the end of 1940, it would have been wholly 'out of gold and dollars'. 'Britain's broke', said British Ambassador to the US, the Marquis of Lothian; Lord Keynes counted the days till the 'cupboard was stripped bare'. Robert Skidelsky writes that Churchill was 'determined to fight the war regardless of cost' which was indeed the meaning of his speech of 9 February 1941.[44] Keynes admitted to the US Treasury Secretary Henry Morgenthau that Britain had acted with a 'wartime imprudence that has no parallel in history'.[45] In fact fighting the war *was Churchill's answer* to the bankruptcy of the British Empire (just as invading Europe was Hitler's answer). Churchill's only strategy was to draw the US into financing the British Empire, which meant drawing the US into a wartime alliance. The Prime Minister went out of his way to charm Roosevelt's envoy Averell Harriman, as he did the President, and invited him to take part in War Cabinet meetings. Churchill told Harriman that 'he would have to risk the loss of Singapore should the Japanese attack', because 'in that event, he felt certain, the United States would enter the war and that would change everything'.[46]

The American decision to fund Britain's war effort was pragmatic. Henry Morgenthau said on 23 July 1940 'the longer we keep them going, that much longer we stay out of the war'.[47] Averell Harriman recalled that Roosevelt supported the British for the same reason he supported the Russians - so that when America went in 'it might not be necessary to send large ground forces into battle'.[48] US backing, of course, was not free. Remembering that Britain had defaulted on loans in 1933, arms were at first given on a 'cash and carry' basis. The administration held back Lend Lease aid until Britain had exhausted all of her funds. Keynes wrote that Morgenthau was determined to 'impose his will on us, at stripping us of our liquid assets'. Britain's goal was 'the retention by us of enough assets to leave us capable of independent action' – in which he was fighting a rear-guard action against Morgenthau and his secretly Soviet sympathising assistant Harry Dexter White.[49]

Cordell Hull wanted the Lend Lease agreement with the British to say that it should 'provide against discrimination in either the United States or the United Kingdom against the importation of any product originating in the other country' – or, an end to the 'Imperial Preference', the tariff against US exports to the British Empire. According to a contemporary report:

> The United States will propose that Britain jettison or drastically modify her system of empire trade preference controls as one condition of further financial aid from this country. This suggestion, it became known today, is one of several that will be made to British envoys in conferences due to begin this week over what monetary help this country may be willing to extend England now that lend-lease has shut down. (*New York Times* 3 September 1945)

This demand started a huge row between Hull, Dean Acheson at the US State Department and John Maynard Keynes, Churchill's negotiator. The Secretary of State for India L.S. Amery said he would prefer the 'New Order of Hitler' to the 'Free Trade' of Cordell Hull.[50] The British Cabinet, was, in Foreign Secretary Anthony Eden's words 'unwilling to barter Empire preference in exchange for ... planes, tanks, guns, goods, et cetera'.[51] Having taken the British to the brink, Roosevelt reined in his own side and let the issue be heavily qualified in the Atlantic Charter of 14 August 1941 which promised only 'enjoyment by all States, great or small, victor or vanquished, of access, on equal terms, to the trade and to the raw materials of the world which are needed for their economic prosperity'. Cordell Hull was dismayed, but the Americans had served notice on Empire preference.

As well as tightening the fiscal noose, America took advantage of its as yet undeclared war to take over as much of the British supply networks as it could, patrolling the North Atlantic, and, on Harriman's suggestion, substituting the long haul flights to the Middle East with a service by Pan American.[52]

The 'liquidation of the British Empire'

In their joint manifesto of August 1941, the Atlantic Charter, Roosevelt and Churchill promised the 'right of all peoples to choose the form of government under which they will live'. At the Memorial Day Address, secretary of State Sumner Welles drew out the anti-colonial logic of the Atlantic Charter:

> Our victory must bring in its train the liberation of all peoples. Discrimination between peoples because of their race, creed or color must be abolished. The age of imperialism is ended ... The principles of the Atlantic Charter must be guaranteed to the world as a whole – in all oceans and in all continents.[53]

Churchill did not think that right applied to the subject peoples under the British Empire. The Atlantic Charter 'was directed to the nations of Europe whom we hoped to free from Nazi tyranny, and was not intended to deal with the internal affairs of the British Empire, or with relations between the United States and, for example, the Philippines,' Churchill told the Cabinet, 4 Sept 1941.[54] But American officials used the claim to squeeze Britain.

More painfully, the row spilled out into the public. In an Open Letter to the People of England, the editors, *Life Magazine* wrote 'One thing we are sure we are not fighting for is to hold the British Empire together'.[55]

Winston Churchill exploded, writing in the *Times*:

> Let me make this clear, in case there should be any mistake about it in any quarter. We mean to hold our own. I have not become the King's First Minister in order to preside over the liquidation of the British Empire.[56]

In response to the American pressure, the British Colonial Office opened a campaign to embarrass the Americans about their own race relations. 'The Americans' wrote Margery Perham in the *Times*, 'do not expect us to accept all their criticism or to believe ... that they have solved all their own difficult race problems'.[57]

In the House of Lords, Listowel said 'we need a supplement to the Atlantic Charter', which 'might be called the British Colonial Charter, and it would add to our list of war aims the achievement of those conditions of life which are sought by the peoples of our dependencies.'[58] – the idea was later taken up by Lord Hailey in a 'Colonial Charter', trying to make the positive case for colonialism. *Life* magazine carried an interview with General Smuts, saying that the new Commonwealth was 'the widest system of organized human freedom which has ever existed in human history'.[59] Winston Churchill put the question of 'Empire' or 'Commonwealth' more cynically 'British Empire or British Commonwealth of Nations – we keep trade labels to suit all tastes'.[60]

Privately British civil servants were scathing about the US's anti-colonial stance:

> Independence is a political catchword which has no real meaning apart from economics. The Americans are quite ready to make their dependencies politically 'independent' while economically bound hand and foot to them and see no inconsistency in this.[61]

In 1944, Sydney Caine at the Colonial Office wrote 'The Americans are not really interested only in the welfare of Colonial peoples but also in the exploitation of natural resources in colonial territories'.[62]

Roosevelt floated the idea of trusteeship bases at the Teheran conference. Suspecting that this might include British colonies, Churchill was adamant he would give no ground, even going so far as to threaten his allies. Churchill told Stalin and Roosevelt that 'war would result if these trusteeship schemes veiled a threat to the British Empire':

> as far as Britain was concerned they do not desire to acquire any new territory or bases, but intended to hold on to what they had. He said that nothing would be taken away from England without

a war. He mentioned specifically Singapore and Hong Kong.[63]

At Yalta, Assistant Secretary of State Alger Hiss kept pushing the question of 'trusteeship', which would have meant international oversight, the implication being that this would apply to British colonies. Churchill again lost his temper:

> I absolutely disagree. I will not have one scrap of British territory flung into that area. After we have done our best to fight in this war and have done no crime to anyone I will have no suggestion that the British Empire is to be put into the dock and examined by everybody to see whether it is up to their standard. No one will induce as long as I am Prime Minister to let any representative of Great Britain got to a conference where we will be placed in the dock and asked to justify our right to live in a world we have tried to save.[64]

With the war approaching its end, though, American sympathies for colonial freedom dried up. US officials of the Truman administration were less willing to give ground they had fought for, or to give credence to nationalist movements. They were more sympathetic, too, to Britain's rule, relying on British military and diplomatic resources to help them govern their new world order. There was a role for Britain as junior partner.

The Free French

After Marshal Pétain's policy of collaboration with the German occupation of northern France, the country was effectively extinguished as a power – but for the determination of the youthful minister Charles de Gaulle to keep it alive by setting up a government in exile in London. De Gaulle was no great democrat, and had been very close to the reactionary Pétain. He grew up in a house that did not celebrate Bastille Day but did take the far right paper *Action Française*. When he summed up his 'certain idea of France', de Gaulle took the phrase from the far right leader Maurice Barrès.[65] De Gaulle stood for the imperialist wing of the French ruling class, and though he shared Pétain's contempt for democracy could not stomach the loss of national prestige collaboration entailed. De Gaulle's relation to the popular resistance, especially its far left wing was difficult: 'I shall give orders'. He sought to build his 'Free France' by 'trying to win over the territories in France's Empire'.[66] Rebuffed by the Vichy-supporting North African colonialists, de Gaulle won support from the governors of Chad (Felix Éboué), Gabon and Tahiti. Apart from Éboué these endorsements came from European officials lording over natives.

While Churchill sponsored Charles de Gaulle's 'Free French' forces, Roosevelt was hostile to the recreation of French imperialism after the war.[67] 'France's role as a great power is finished for good', US leader Wendell Willkie told Ilya Ehrenburg, 'it's not in our interests to restore her to her former position'.[68] Lord Halifax, reported Roosevelt's views on French Indo-China: The 'poor Indo-Chinese had nothing done for them during a hundred years of French, responsibility, no education, no welfare.' Roosevelt's 'idea was that the Indo-Chinese who were not yet ready for elective institutions of their own, should be placed under some United Nations trustee-ship, whose duty would be to educate them on towards the ability to govern themselves.'[69]

After de Gaulle made a landmark speech at Brazzaville, setting out the position of the Free French, Ralph Bunche of the Office of Strategic Studies drew up a critical report: 'Brazzaville clung tenaciously to conventional French policy of integration and assimilation of the colonial territories and their people' and 'rule out any idea of autonomy, and possibility of evolution outside of the French bloc of the empire'.[70]

The anti-imperialist tenor of US criticisms of France in America would have been more credible if Washington was not at the same time making overtures to Pétain's Vichy administration. America sent an ambassador to Vichy, Admiral William Leahy, who persuaded Roosevelt that Pétain could be a force for good. In May 1941 Roosevelt announced food shipments to France.[71] Earlier that year Roosevelt's envoy to French North Africa Robert Murphy had advised supplying those colonies and an agreement to do so was signed with Maxime Weygand, Vichy's Delegate General. When Allied troops took the French colony of Madagascar in May 1942 they had not told the Free French – and they left the Vichy administrator in place.[72] On 30 May 1942 in Washington, Vichy diplomats were invited to the Memorial Day ceremony – where enthusiastic participants, thinking they must be of the Free French, complemented them on the heroic defence of Bir-Hakeim in Eastern Libya against overwhelming German and Italian forces.[73]

Hostile to de Gaulle, America tried to promote other leaders. First General Henri Giraud was talked up, and later the defecting Vichy Admiral Darlan, though an enthusiast of Pétain's 'National Revolution' and an anti-Semite, became Washington's champion. Darlan brought Algiers over to the Allies but both the Free French and the Resistance leaders were appalled. Roosevelt fielded the criticism:

> I did the right thing to support Darlan – I saved American lives ... If Darlan gives me Algiers, long live Darlan! If Laval [Hitler's French puppet] gives me Paris, long live Laval! ... When we get to France we will have the power of an occupying force ... by right of occupation the Americans will remain in France until free elections are organised.

De Gaulle's representative said the French would no more back an American occupation than they did a German one, and Roosevelt snapped back: 'I will speak to the French people on the radio and they will do what I wish'.[74]

Even Churchill, who gave refuge to de Gaulle's Free French was at times eager to rein him in, in the hope of promoting 'a collusive conspiracy in the Vichy government'. Cabinet Secretary John Colville worried that de Gaulle's agitations in Africa 'are rather an embarrassment in our relations with Vichy'.[75]

Just as America was reluctant to see regime change in Vichy and North Africa, it had outlawed it in the Western Hemisphere under the Havana Convention of 1940 – an enlargement of the Monroe Doctrine that guaranteed stability to British, Dutch and French colonies. When the Free French asked if they could try to overthrow the Vichy-loyalist administration in French Guiana, Cordell Hull replied that 'any overt insurrectionary movement in French Guiana ...would in the opinion of this government be unfortunate'.[76] US support for Vichy officialdom came to a head over the small colony of St Pierre and Miquelon, two small islands off the Newfoundland

Coast settled by 6000 French. The US had agreed that the Vichy Commander Admiral Robert should keep authority in 1940. Robert was unpopular, and pedantically enforced the anti-Jewish statutes, even though no Jews lived on the islands. On Christmas Eve 1941, the Free French Admiral Muselier landed three boats and arrested Robert. Instead of welcoming the fall of this Vichy administration, Cordell Hull condemned the 'so-called Free French' for their 'arbitrary action contrary to the agreement of all parties' and even threatened to invade.[77]

The Second Front and 'Unconditional Surrender'

Stalin demanded to know when the Allies would open a Second Front in Western Europe, to take the pressure off the Soviet Union, a theme 'initiated at the very beginning of our correspondence' – 18 July 1941, that is – wrote Churchill, and 'to recur throughout our subsequent relations with monotonous regularity'[78] In May 1942 Roosevelt and Churchill committed themselves to opening a second front in Europe that year. But Churchill postponed it in August 1942, in favour of an invasion of North Africa.[79] The challenge of the 'Second Front' showed up the cynicism at the heart of the allied strategy of letting Russians and Germans slaughter each other, while America and Britain waited to take the prize.

The Second Front demand had an impact on domestic politics. Communists, who had up till 1941 been isolated by the Hitler-Stalin pact, could now out-Jingo the establishment. 'Time does not wait', said the American Communist Party's May Day Call: 'America must strike now'. 'Single-handed the Soviet Union has engaged the full might of Hitler', they said.[80] Fearing the British Communist Party would win support on the back of Russian victories, the Ministry of Information set up its own Anglo-Soviet Friendship societies to 'steal the thunder of the left'.[81] The Second Front campaigns could have embarrassed the allies, but they were also useful: Here was a bottom-up campaign to support the war effort. Second Front campaigns could be steered towards getting workers to sweat harder for their embattled Russian brothers and sisters.

At the Casablanca Conference in January of 1943, Churchill and Roosevelt decided that there would be no Second Front that year. Not only were the American and British armies staying in North

Africa, but Roosevelt's compromise with the Vichy administration there raised doubts about how seriously they were willing to fight Fascism. It was then that Roosevelt sprung his announcement that the Allies would seek 'unconditional surrender'. Churchill, who said he had not been consulted, and 'would not myself have used those words', nonetheless grasped their meaning:

> It must be remembered that at that moment no one had the right to proclaim that Victory was assured. Therefore, Defiance was the note.

But the note of defiance rang hollow while Russia still took the weight of the German war effort. Roosevelt's speechwriter Robert Sherwood wrote that the timing of the 'unconditional surrender' demand was down to the uproar over the compromise with Vichy in North Africa, and 'the liberal fears that this might indicate a willingness to make similar deals with a Goering in Germany or a Matsuoka in Japan.'[82] 'Unconditional Surrender' was reaffirmed in the Moscow Conference of October 1943, which also vowed that German would be tried as war criminals, in a 'Statement of Atrocities'.

At Tcheran, on 28 November 1943 Stalin

> questioned the advisability of the unconditional surrender principle with no definition of the exact terms which would be imposed upon Germany. He felt that to leave the principle of unconditional surrender unclarified merely served to unite the German people, whereas to draw up specific terms, no matter how harsh, and tell the German people that this was what they would have to accept, would, in his opinion, hasten the day of German capitulation.[83]

The truth was that Roosevelt's 'unconditional surrender' demand made sure that the peoples of Germany, Russia and the lands between would be locked into a war of total destruction, leaving America to dictate terms afterwards. The fear of prosecution for war crimes before Vyshinsky-style show trials was used by the Nazi leadership to block off any attempt by the German elite and military to pull out of the war. A negotiated peace in 1944 would have saved tens of millions of lives and as the Nazis knew, would have meant the end of their regime. Both the Nazis and the Allies, though, were bound together in a war to the bitter end.

The Limits of US Anti Imperialism

As we have seen, American officials put tremendous pressure on the European colonies to open their doors, and even put colonialism on notice. According to historian William Louis, at the United Nations conference in San Francisco, 1945 the 'Americans had raised expectations that they might unfurl an anti-imperialist banner' but 'when it came to the test, the United States sided with the colonial powers'.[84] Harold Stassen, American Delegation to the San Francisco Conference, May 18, 1945 signaled the change in US thinking with a bit of word play:

> Independence... was a concept developed out of the past era of nationalism. We should be more interested in inter-dependence than in independence and for this reason it might be fortunate to avoid the term "independence".[85]

An Egyptian motion that the United Nations give dependent peoples a share in government, and take oversight to send inspectors to trust areas and even set a date for self-government was voted down. Under Secretary of State Edward Stettinus warned his colleagues that 'when perhaps the inevitable struggle came between Russia and ourselves, the question would be who are our friends' and asked 'would we have the support of Great Britain if we had undermined her position?'[86] At San Francisco, Stettinus assured the French delegation that the United States had never 'even by implication' questioned French sovereignty in Indochina. And later Dean Acheson declared brazenly that the US had 'no thought of opposing the reestablishment of French control' over Indochina.[87] Then later, at the Potsdam Conference in July 1945, the US supported the return of Italy as the trustee power in Somalia and Libya.

Sumner Welles, whose Memorial Day speech promised an end to the age of imperialism had already showed his true colours talking to the US Advisory Committee on Post War Foreign Policy in

October 1942: 'the Negroes are in the lowest rank of human beings', he said, and in Africa 'we are not confronted by any such desire [to independence] on the part of native populations'.[88] Independence was kicked into the long grass 'in the case of the Congo and many other areas, it will certainly take more than a hundred years ... in the case of Portuguese Timor it would certainly take a thousand years'.[89]

The change in US policy from rhetorically anti-imperialist, to explicitly pro-imperialist was pointed. For Dean Acheson it was the point he learned from the English that Americans' idea of 'the sovereign equality of states' was a 'grand fallacy' and that diplomacy was indeed 'an instrument of power'.[90] The change in outward rhetoric was helped by the change in personnel. Sumner Welles was replaced by Cordell Hull who had made no promises of ending colonialism, only of opening the door to US trade. Hull claimed that 'at no time did we press Britain, France or The Netherlands for an immediate grant of self-government to their colonies'.[91] Yet more decisive was President Roosevelt's death and the inauguration of President Truman. That change replaced a man at least verbally committed to the freedom of peoples with one who would fight against national liberation movements in the name of anti-Communism.

Spheres of Influence

After beating Germany, General Patton had told Secretary of State James Patterson 'if you wanted Moscow, I could give it to you' adding that 'we must either finish the job now' or be forced to do it later.[92] But in truth, discipline in the US army was rapidly falling apart as troops could not see why they were still in Europe after Hitler had been defeated,[93] and were in no position to take Eastern Europe. Neither Britain nor the US had the means to prevent the Soviet army from conquering Eastern Europe, having relied upon them to fight Germany there. At the Foreign Office, Sir William Strang thought that it was 'better that Russia should dominate Eastern Europe than that Germany should dominate Western Europe'.[94] Some Western strategists were carried away by the promises of the US-Soviet alliance. J. K. Galbraith thought 'Russia should be permitted to absorb Poland, the Balkans and the whole of Eastern Europe in order to spread the benefits of Communism.' Vice

President Henry Wallace 'saw in the march of history a coming together of the Soviet experiment in Russia with the New Deal programmes of the United States.'[95]

On the whole, though, the surrender of Eastern Europe to Soviet domination was pragmatic. When Fitzroy Maclean questioned the wisdom of backing Communist insurgents in the Balkans, Churchill challenged him: 'Are you going to live there?' No, replied Maclean. Churchill replied: 'Neither am I, so had we not better leave the Jugoslavs themselves to work out what sort of system they are going to have?'[96] In 1943, Roosevelt told Cardinal Spellman that Russian domination of Europe was inevitable.[97] Years later Secretary of state Henry Kissinger formalised the realistic policy of 'détente', saying 'we cannot gear our foreign policy to the transformation of other societies' and 'peace between nations is also a high moral objective'.[98]

At the Teheran Conference, Roosevelt tried to interest Stalin in a common role as one of the 'Four Policemen' (i.e America, Russia, Britain and China) keeping order in the world.[99] In Moscow, on 9 October 1944, Churchill met with Stalin and talked about setting down 'spheres of influence' that would divide East and West Europe.

I said, "Let's settle our affairs in the Balkans. Your armies are in Rumania and Bulgaria. We have interests, missions and agents there. Don't let us get at cross-purposes in small ways. So far as Britain and Russia are concerned, how would it do for you to have 90 per cent predominance in Rumania, for us to have 90 per cent of the say in Greece and go 50-50 about Yugoslavia?" ... I wrote on a half sheet of paper:

Rumania: Russia 90 per cent – The others 10 per cent
Greece: Great Britain 90 per cent – Russia 10 per cent
Yugoslavia: 50-50 per cent
Hungary: 50-50 per cent
Bulgaria: Russia 75 per cent – The others 25 per cent.

I pushed this across to Stalin, who had by then heard the translation. There was a slight pause. Then he took his pencil and made a large tick upon it, and passed it back to us. It was all settled in no more time than it takes to sit down

Averell Harriman, who made efforts to show that he was not present at this meeting, advised Churchill not to tie America's hands, and the eventual carve-up would find America occupying Britain's percentages. Though Cordell Hull had disparaged the 'spheres of influence' policy in wartime, afterwards it was the basis of US policy. The State Department said no to the Sovietisation of the east but lived with it anyway.[100]

To the Yugoslav Communist Milovan Djilas, Stalin explained:

whoever occupies a territory also imposes on it his own social system. Everyone imposes his own system as far as his army can reach.[101]

Years later, East Europeans would look back on Roosevelt and Churchill's acquiescence to Stalinist dictatorship as a grotesque betrayal – and so it was. The war that started with the conquest of Poland ended with the conquest of Poland, and much more besides. But reliance on military dictators to stabilise the world order was not restricted to the east. The Allies banked on Fascist dictatorships in Spain, Portugal and Greece, colonial rule over much of the Third World, and the military occupation of the former Axis powers. After the war, America had enough 'Marshall Aid' to fan the sparks of capitalist restoration in the North Western corner of Europe, but not to extend it Eastwards. It would be wrong to credit Stalin's theory of social systems imposed by occupation with any great insight (later on, this would be called 'tankie' communism). His military-administrative clique just filled the vacuum left between the collapse of the German Empire and the limits of *Pax Americana*. Without the promise of aid and growth to bolster loyalty, the Powers relied upon Stalin's henchmen to impose order in that part of the world, as they did upon Franco's and Salazar's in theirs'. Later, of course, American policy projection would become more pointedly 'anti-Communist', and Presidents would protest at the Soviet presence in East Europe, as though they had not underwritten the Red Army's progress.

PART TWO
THE COURSE OF THE WAR

Chapter Thirteen

A Time of Reaction

'Business interests in every one of the democracies of Western Europe and the New World welcomed Hitlerism as a barrier to the expansion of Communism.' Sumner Welles, 1944[1]

After the First World War, governments staggered and some fell. In October 1917 Kerensky's provisional government in Russia was overthrown by the RSDLP 'Bolsheviks'. In Hungary, too, a Soviet government was set up, and in Germany, socialist revolution was only just diverted by the reformist government. In Ireland, having threatened a rising in 1916, Sinn Fein set up a provisional republic three years later. A wave of industrial militancy spread across Europe, from the Clydeside to Milan. Nor was this disorder restricted to Europe. In China nationalists challenged the mandatory powers, and the warlords. The African National Congress demanded political rights, and the Congress Party called for independence for India. With the support of the working class, the left challenged the power of the existing order. In this great upsurge there were many disagreements and contests between Socialists, Communists and anarchists, nationalists and constitutional reformers. And there was hesitation. The strike wave of 1919 did not know where to go. The Soviet government struggled with civil war and famine. The German socialists swung between reform and revolution. American loans were helping to stabilise Europe. The powers-that-be proved more resilient than the rebels hoped.

Post war stabilisation had the effect of tying the Socialist parties closer to the state. In power, their authoritarian instincts and social conservatism were on display. Before the 'Anschluss' uniting Austria and Germany, in Red Vienna 'Marxist councillors offered a "social contract" with parents ... offering assistance in return for their commitment to responsible parenting', but where this was lacking 'social workers were on hand to remove children to the municipal child observation centres'.[2] In Belgium, Workers Party leader Henrik de Man's 'Plan of Works' caused a stir across the Socialist Parties for its strident economic nationalism, and later de Man would embrace Nazism as 'the German form of socialism'.[3] In France the 'Popular Front' government enjoyed the support of the Communists for its denunciations of the top '200 families' while the Socialist president assured critics that the economy remained capitalistic.[4] Austerity, not prosperity, though was what the Socialists had to offer - 'more apartments were obtained by Nazi Aryanization policies in the Austrian capital in three years than had been built by the Social Democrats in the 1920s'.[5]

Then there was the reaction against the left. The counter-revolutionary White Army reduced Russia to bloodshed and famine. In the spring of 1918 the Whites gained the support of a force of British, American, Japanese, Czechs and Slovaks invading from Siberia in the east, Murmansk and Archangel in the West. At the War Office Churchill demanded a full-scale invasion to overthrow the 'tyrannic government of these Jew Commisars'.[6] In Hungary, Admiral Horthy's reaction successfully overthrew the short-lived Soviet Republic. 'Horthy's courts and officer gangs killed thousands of people in "reprisals" and interned, imprisoned and maimed tens of thousands', according to Victor Serge.[7] In Germany the 'Socialist' Ebert set the paramilitary Freikorps on his Communist rivals, and had Rosa Luxemburg and Karl Liebknicht killed along with hundreds of supporters of the Spartakusbund in January 1919.[8] In Ireland, auxiliaries known as the 'Black-and-Tans' were recruited to back up the Royal Irish Constabulary against nationalist rebels. 'When we begin to act we must act like a sledgehammer, so as to cause bewilderment and consternation among the people of southern Ireland,' said Churchill.[9] In the USA in 1919 anticommunist hysteria was whipped up and followed by the Palmer Raids against socialists, and the election of Warren G Harding on a platform of 'normalcy'. Anti-socialist repression in America was directed at newer migrants from Southern and Eastern Europe. In 1920 Anarchists Nicolo Sacco and Bartolomeo Vanzetti were framed for a robbery in Boston (they were eventually sent to the electric chair on 23 August 1927).

While the left-wing of the workers' movement was met with violence, tentative feelers were put out to the moderates. Social Democrats held office at local and national level in Germany, and in

Britain, first in McDonald's Labour-Liberal alliance government of 1923. US loans underwrote a moderate Social Democracy in Europe. 'In the autumn of 1923 everyone thought that Germany was on the eve of civil war', recalled Ilya Ehrenburg, 'but nothing happened ... the workers were worn out'. Instead 'the days of the Dawes plan were approaching, of Stresemann's shrewd diplomacy, of sudden plenty after years of unremitting want'.[10] In Ireland the Treaty negotiated between David Lloyd George and Michael Collins in 1922, divided Ireland between the 26 Counties in the South and a six-county northern Ireland that remained under British rule. Liam Lynch and Liam Mellowes on the anti-Treaty side, and Collins himself on the pro-Treaty side died in the ensuing civil war between the Republicans.

Though the White Army had been defeated, the cost to Soviet Russia was too great to survive in the absence of a European revolution. The working class, always a minority, had come close to extinction, leaving the Soviets (workers' councils) an empty shell, until their suspension in 1919. Bolshevik party activists were consumed with bureaucratic tasks. The Bolsheviks had managed to stabilise the economy by permitting a controlled market in grain (the 'New Economic Policy') though with destabilising consequences. In the debate over how to proceed, the advocates of 'Socialism in one country' won - though this meant not socialism, but an unstable and dictatorial regime based on Russia's backward technological base. Under Joseph Stalin, the regime took the final step of destroying democracy within the party in 1924, purges of old party members soon followed, leading to the executions of Zinoviev, Bukharin, Kamenev and in 1940, after years in exile, Trotsky. The ascendance of the new leadership did not mean a restoration of the market though, in fact when peasant-proprietors threatened the regime, Stalin 'collectivised' agriculture, at a terrible human cost. The majority of communists in the West continued to believe that the Soviet Union was building socialism, an illusion that would cost them dear.

In Italy in the First World War Samuel Hoare, for the British Secret Service, bribed a maverick Socialist Benito Mussolini to use his group and its newspaper to support the war effort. Mussolini's damascene conversion to the cause of war took him from far left to far right, and soon he was organising ex-servicemen to attack militant workers. Henry Channon, to whom Hoare had opened up wrote in his diary 'so English government funds did much to create the Fascist revolution', adding: 'this is very secret'.[11] In 1921 his Fascists won 36 seats drawing support from agricultural workers, students and small proprietors. In 1922 Mussolini led a 'March on Rome' (though he personally travelled by train) and – taking advantage of a power vacuum – made himself 'Il Duce', dictator of Italy. In Germany there were many small parties of the far right, but it was the National Social Democratic Workers Party (NSDAP), which took advantage of the decline of the mainstream Conservative parties, and offered a more brutal challenge to the left in its city redoubts. On the 8th and 9th of November 1923, Adolf Hitler attempted a Putsch in Munich, and after a hiatus of indecision the army used force to restore the Bavarian Government.

Far right parties sprung up all over Europe. Hungary's National Defence Association, grounded in the struggle against the 1919 Soviet was one of the first, Romania's Iron Guard was founded in 1927, and Anton Pavelić's anti-Marxist and anti-Serbian Ustaša began in January 1932 – all three went on to found governments that would be a part of the Axis. Even in Britain, though, Winston Churchill mobilised middle class volunteers in the Organisation for the Maintenance of Supplies to defeat the General Strike of 1926. In Shanghai, Chiang Kai-Shek ordered a brutal purge of leftists from the Nationalist Kuomintang movement that left 12,000 dead in April 1927.

In 1932, 25 000 army veterans and their families camped out in Washington asking for payment on their Service Certificates – they called themselves the 'Bonus Expeditionary Force' (BEF). Saying that there was 'incipient revolution in the air', General Douglas MacArthur, the army Chief of Staff, ordered Major George S. Patton to gather infantry, tanks and cavalry around the Washington monument: 'we are going to break the back of the BEF'. Despite orders from President Hoover not to pursue the men across the Anacostia River, MacArthur did and routed their camp. William Hushka and Eric Carlson were killed and two babies died from the effects of adamsite gas. 'It was a great victory', said Secretary of War, Hurley.[12]

Hitler mobilised the middle classes against the KPD and militant labour, but depended upon the backing of industrialists and the establishment to put him in office. Despite the belief that Hitler's NSDAP enjoyed popular support, he came to power in 1933 two years after the party's vote had peaked in the 1931 elections. Panicked that the Nazis influence might be waning, those backers gave him what he wanted. Between 1933 and 1939 225 000 people, Communists and Socialists, mostly, were convicted of political offences by Nazi courts, with nearly twice as many again imprisoned without trial.[13] Ordinary Germans protested vehemently at the euthansia programme against the mentally ill and disabled, and succeeded in stopping the policy. When their Jewish husbands were imprisoned, German women massed in Berlin in protests over three days, and won the release of 6000 men.[14]

The class character of Fascism

Hermann Rausching was a farmers' leader who 'joined the [Nazi] party in the summer of 1931'. Rausching remembered that 'just as the mass of the lower-middle class suddenly became interested in politics and crowded into Nazism, so sections of the educated felt compelled to play their part in public life' – because of the failure of the mainstream parties.[15]

Left-wing activist Daniel Guerin wrote in 1936 that Fascism was buoyed by the squeezed middle classes, both in the towns and in the country (Fascism and Big Business, New York Monad Press, 1973 (orig. 1936), pp 41-62). In Italy, Fascists appealed to the broken peasants: 'You see, the socialists have promised you everything and given you nothing; they prevented you from even becoming independent farmers'. On the other hand 'the fasci have installed hundreds of families on their own land which they can farm all year round'. In his manifesto Mein Kampf Hitler feels the middle class pain: 'For people of modest situation who have risen above that social level, it is unendurable to fall back even momentarily.'[16]

Students, in particular played a big part in the German Nazi party's breakthrough: 'student organisations fell into the hands of the Nazis long before the government institutions did', writes Victor Farias. In the winter term of 1930-31 Nazis were elected in the common rooms of the Berlin Technical University, Breslau University, Erlangen, Giessen, Greiffenswald, Jena, Liepzig and

Rostock. At the Conference of German Students that year, the Nazis won an outright majority and took the union presidency. So, too, did schoolteachers play their part. Of the 700,000 NSDAP leaders, more than a fifth, 160,000 were teachers, mostly from elementary schools.[17]

The unhappy middle classes made up the foot soldiers of the Nazi movement – and they were much needed as a counter-weight to the working class supporters of the Socialist and Communist parties. But the big push that made the German NSDAP into a governing party was the support of big business, in the shape of the 'Circle of Friends of the Economy' got together by Wilhelm Keppler. The Keppler Circle met Hitler on 18 May 1932. Among those present were Dr Karl Fuetefsich of the chemical giant I.G. Farben, Karl Lindemann of the Norddeutsch Kreditbank, a Bremen-China trading firm and a Salzberg cement works, Herbert Goering, August Rostberg, who was in a Potash syndicate, Rudolf Bringel of Siemens, Emil Helfferich (Hamburg-America Line), Otto Heuer (Heidelberger Portland Zementwerke AG), Graf von Bismark and many other industrialists, CEOs and bankers.[18]

Earlier, on 27 January of that year, Hitler spoke to the Industrial Club in Dusseldorf. Warning them that without the work the Nazi party was doing 'already today there would be no more bourgeoisie alive in Germany', Hitler promised that 'we have formed the inexorable decision to destroy Marxism in Germany down to its very last root'. More, with his middle class followers, Hitler had the means to make good his promise. 'Where is the organisation which can boast as ours can, that at need, it can summon 400,000 men into the street who are schooled to blind obedience and are ready to execute any order?'[19]

Scandalised, scholars from Max Horkheimer to Daniel Goldhagen have tried to cover up the middle class foundations of the Nazi Party and its business-backers. Instead they have tried to turn the truth on its head and claim that the Nazis were the working class, and their victims cultured property-owners.

In Austria, Engelbert Dollfuss led the ruling Christian Social Party. The rival Social Democratic Party had deep roots in local and regional government, especially in cities, most notably 'Red' Vienna. Taking advantage of a constitutional crisis to claim dictatorial powers, Dollfuss had created his own Fascist movement, the Fatherland Front in 1934. Using the paramilitary Home Guard to attack the Social Democrats, Dollfuss launched a war against the left. When the Social Democrats fought back, Dollfuss sent in troops, who blasted Karl-Marx-Hof housing estate with howitzer cannons. Many hundreds were killed, more wounded, more than a thousand arrested, nine Social Democrat leaders executed, and the party was outlawed.

In Britain the ruling elite were similarly embattled, facing down challenges from the working class and demands for greater democracy. Looking across to Europe many establishment figures identified readily with the fascist struggle against the left. In 1927 after a visit to Mussolini, Churchill, then Chancellor of the Exchequer said 'Had I been Italian, I am sure that I would have been with you ... in opposition to the bestial appetites and passions of Leninism'.[20] It was Churchill, wrote his cousin Claire Sheridan, 'who is talked of as the likely leader of a Fascisti party in England'. [21] Churchill said of Adolf Hitler's book *Mein Kampf* that 'the story of that struggle cannot be read without admiration'.[22] Churchill's views of Communism were close to Hitler's. As Home Secretary Churchill used troops to kill two revolutionaries in the 'siege of Sidney Street' in January 1911 he used troops to break up strikes at Newport Docks in May 1910, at Tonypandy 9 November 1910, and at Liverpool docks in August 1911, when he anchored the warship Antrim in the Mersey. During the 1926 General Strike Churchill established military control of the country, including a government newspaper, the *British Gazette*. Churchill's sympathised with the fascist cause and in 1937 Brigadier Packenham Walsh reported 'Winston says at heart he is for Franco'.[23] Asked about anti-Jewish laws in 1938, Churchill thought 'it was a hindrance and an irritation, but probably not an obstacle to a working agreement'.[24] Britain's Prime Minister in the First World War, David Lloyd George also saw value in Hitler's National Socialist revolution. 'In a very short time, perhaps in a year or two, the Conservative elements in this country will be looking to Germany as a bulwark against Communism in Europe', Lloyd George had told the House of Commons in 1934. 'Do not let us be in a hurry to condemn Germany' he said, 'we shall be welcoming Germany as our friend'.[25]

In Britain itself, though, the fascist movement failed. Maverick rightwingers like Noel Pemberton Billing and Archibald Ramsay won seats in Parliament, but failed to build up much of a movement. Oswald Mosley, the sixth Baronet of Ancoats, had been a Labour MP before setting up first the 'New Party', and then the British Union of Fascists, which gathered a following among lesser establishment figures and the unemployed. Employers' associations showed little interest, though, fearing 'countervailing industrial disruption by the Left'. Instead they put their hopes in the National Government formed when Labour Party leader Ramsay Macdonald led a cross-party coalition that isolated the left.[26] Having lost the chance of influencing government, the British Labour Party and its backers the trade union leaders dedicated themselves to proving their commitment to the nation. In Britain Trade Union leaders like Walter Citrine and Ernest Bevin did such good job of isolating the more radical militants and Communists (and Churchill was always on hand to put some stick about) that the establishment had little need of a fascist militia to beat them on the streets. Though Bevin's loyal and respectable Labour movement was kept at arm's length by the National Government in the 1930s, it would turn out to be the factor that gave Churchill's government the advantage over Hitler in the 1940s. 'I have to ask you,' Bevin told trade union delegates in May 1940, 'virtually to place yourselves at the disposal of the state'.[27] It was Bevin's sacrifice of labour's interests to the greater good that made the 'People's War against Fascism' a plausible ideological appeal.

On 27 February 1939 Neville Chamberlain recognised the 'nationalist' government of Francisco Franco, installed after three years of military rebellion against the centre-left government elected in 1936. Spain joined the list of dictatorships created to frustrate popular power:

Admiral Horthy's created in Hungary in 1919,
Mussolini's from 1922,
General Pilsudski's in Poland and Salazar's in Portugal from 1926,
King Alexander's dictatorship in Yugoslavia from 1929,
King Carol II's in Romania from 1930
Hitler's from 1933,

General Metaxas' in Greece, (formed to break a general strike) in
1935.

What the democracies and the dictatorships had in common was that
they had channelled popular aspirations into nationalist and
militarist movements. Even where voting was not suspended, the
political process was more and more focussed on the assertion of
national status through military strength. Nationalism displaced
socialism as the voters were asked to identify not with class but
country. The claims of the working classes to a greater share of the
national wealth, and a greater say in the governing of the land were
subdued in the name of a supposedly greater glory, the nation. Next
to the nation, it was claimed, the demands of organised labour were
merely sectional. Party politics, where left and right fought out their
quarrels in constituent assemblies, was seen as a divisive distraction
from national greatness, that would dissipate that power.
Nationalism was an ideology that overrode the movement towards
socialism, but it was one that set in train yet more dangerous aspirations in Italy, Japan and Germany. Having cranked up their
supporters to expect great victories for the nation, elites would be
expected to deliver on those promises. In Britain heightened national
identification made Prime Minister Neville Chamberlain's policy of
appeasing Germany unpopular.

Chapter Fourteen

Blitzkrieg – The German Invasion of Europe

In the 1930s military strategists General Charles de Gaulle of France, Mikhail Tukhachevsky in the Soviet Union and J.F.C. Fuller[1] and Basil Liddell Hart in Britain developed a theory of motorised warfare that argued for a much greater emphasis on tanks, with motorised support breaking through enemy lines, in contrast to the slow attrition of trench warfare. After the war it was often claimed that German General Heinz Guderian had used De Gaulle and Liddell Hart's doctrine to plan the invasion of Germany's European neighbours. Guderian wrote about the doctrine in his book *Achtung Panzer* (1937). In a later work Guderian described the theory

> I became convinced that tanks working on their own or in conjunction with infantry could never achieve decisive importance. My historical studies; the exercises carried out in England and our own experience with mock-ups had persuaded me that the tanks would never be able to produce their full effect until weapons on whose support they must inevitably rely were brought up to their standard of speed and of cross-country performance. In such formation of all arms, the tanks must play primary role, the other weapons being subordinated to the requirements of the armor. It would be wrong to include tanks in infantry divisions: what was needed were armored divisions which would include all the supporting arms needed to fight with full effect.[2]

Armoured, or Panzer Divisions were set up in the German army and, backed up by aerial bombardment of enemy positions, played a decisive role in the invasion of western Poland, between 1 and 19 September 1939; and again in the invasion of both Holland and Belgium between 10 and 15 May 1940; and of France between 13 and 26 May, when the tank divisions famously by-passed the supposedly impregnable underground fortresses of the French 'Maginot Line'.

The style of warfare became known as Blitzkrieg, or 'lightning strike'. On one level the way that the internal combustion engine changed warfare is uncontroversial. On another, just how important motorised warfare was to German military strategy has been questioned since. Military historican Victor Madej points out that 'Germany accomplished what it did with an army that was about 75 per cent horse-drawn'. The United States Strategic Bombing Survey undertaken after the war found that Germany's motor industry had not been integrated into the country's military to any great extent.[3]

Whatever the operational importance of motorisation, the idea of the Blitzkrieg mystified the real nature of the invasion of western Europe. Blitzkrieg summons up a vision of Germany's overwhelming industrial-military might, before which an unprepared Europe was powerless. That is an account that seems to help explain how 'the military conquest of large parts of Europe had taken place with relative, surprising ease'. 'In the first two years of the World War, the well-greased German military machine seemed almost unconquerable', according to the Danish resister and historian Jørgen Hæstrup.[4] But it was not the well-greased military machine, or the Panzer-driven blitzkrieg that was the real reason for Germany's initial successes.

The German occupation of central and western Europe succeeded in 1939-40 because it was not just an invasion from the outside, but one that found an echo in the countries invaded. There were outright collaborators in France, and some in Holland and Norway too; and among the governing classes in Holland and Austria, there was so much shared ideology with the National Socialist revolution, that they found it difficult to object to occupation. As well as a German occupation, the invasion supported the ascendance of reactionary politicians in France, Belgium, Holland and Norway, and to the east in Austria, Slovakia, Croatia, Bosnia, and the Ukraine. For many of the occupied countries, the German invasion was a continuation of the wave of reaction that swept over much of the rest of Europe. 'A merciless civil war was added to the war between the occupiers and occupied', as resistance historian Henri Michel put it.[5] Put another way, the National Socialist revolution in Europe was 'the same revolution', said Goebbels, 'which we have accomplished on a smaller scale in Germany'.[6] Germany ran France with the aid of just

6000 military and civil police, and Norway with 806 administrative personnel, while the Dutch police were the bulwark of the occupation of the Netherlands.[7]

Things were different to the east. In Poland, by contrast, there would be no room at all for local collaborators. 'Certain high-ranking Polish aristocrats and well-known intellectuals offered their services', says resistance historian Henri Michel, but were snubbed by Hitler, for whom Poland 'ceased to exist'.[8] The further east the Reich extended, the more uncompromising its rule was, but in western Europe, Nazi authority rested on indigenous reactionary movements as well as military might.

Austria

Austria's incorporation into the German Reich in 1938 was not achieved by invasion, but the threat of invasion persuaded Austrian Chancellor Kurt von Shuschnigg to resign and accept the 'anschluss' – or 'link up' between the two German speaking states. Already in an agreement with Berlin in July 1936 Schuschnigg had given up many of his nation's rights, notably to an independent foreign policy, and the appointment of the Austrian Nazi Arthur Seyss-Inquart to the ministry of the interior. Hitler's claim to Austria was put in terms of the rights of ten million Germans artificially cut off from the Reich by the settlement at Versailles, which forbade union. In 1939 Cordell Hull at the US State Department made it clear that 'the Government of the United States recognizes that Austria has ceased to exist as an independent state and has been incorporated in the the German Reich'. British Ambassador Sir Nevile Henderson had made it clear too 'the German government that England would make no objection if Hitler seized Austria'.[9]

Austrian resistance to the Anschluss was unlikely – not just because the ethnic German population wanted union with Germany – but also because Schuschnigg, and his predecessor Engelbert Dollfuss had prepared the way with a National Socialist-style revolution of their own. As his own dictatorship so closely paralleled Hitler's Dollfuss struggled to make the case for Austria's distinctiveness. Still the Austrian dictator insisted that he was a follower of Mussolini's model, and likened Hitler's National Socialism more to Stalin's rule in the Soviet Union – a pedantic difference that eluded many. The contest between these rival German fascisms was always unequal and despite being outlawed, the Austrian Nazi Party inaugurated its own terror campaign, culminating in the assassination of Dollfuss on 25 July 1934. Dollfuss' successor Schuschnigg struggled to insist on his country's independence, but the force that could have stood up to Hitler in 1938 had been already destroyed by the Austrian Fascist movement in 1934. Anschluss went ahead with astonishing success, but then it was only a matter of putting the icing on a cake that had already been baked. Incorporation of Austria into the Reich caused few difficulties. In November of 1938 after the Nazi diplomat Ernst vom Rath was assassinated assassinated by Herschel Grynszpan, Germany erupted in a government-organised campaign of attacks on Jews' houses and businesses, known as 'Kristallnacht' (the night of broken glass). The campaign was particularly enthusiastically taken up in the Austrian capital, Vienna. Most of Vienna's 94 synagogues and prayer-houses were partially or totally destroyed. People were made to scrub the pavements whilst being jeered by their Austrians neighbours.

The Netherlands Union

Overrun in five days, the Netherlands lost 2192 soldiers and sailors, and 2559 civilians. As terrible as those deaths were, the relatively lesser total showed both that the Dutch had invested their hopes not in military preparedness, but on a policy of non-alignment, and also that the Germans saw the Dutch (like the Norwegians and the Danes) as 'sister Germanic peoples' in a Greater German Reich. Queen Wilhelmina left for London on 13 May 1940, followed by her Ministers, who left civil servants instructions to carry on their offices under the occupation as best they could. Before long, though, the political vacuum was filled with the founding of the Netherlands Union.

Hendrik Colijn, leader of the main opposition party and a former Prime Minister called together representatives of all the Dutch political parties (except the Communists) to found the Nederlandse Unie 'in a grave hour in the history of our fatherland, in order to gather together all Dutch people for resolute work for the preservation and strengthening of fatherland and community'.[10] The Netherlands Union promised to work in a 'loyal relationship' with the German Reichskommisar telling its supporters to back the new Nazi Labour Service, and to contribute to the new 'Winter Aid'. Its political themes echoed those of the Fascist movement in Germany, calling for 'a strong Dutch people closely linked with the overseas colonies ... under the leadership of a rigorous and enterprising authority'; society, thought the NU, should be an 'organic structure'. The Union was 'against Communism' and willing to cooperate 'gladly in anti-Communist propaganda' with the Reichskommisar – the one element of German NSDAP policy that was missing from the Dutch NU was its anti-Semitism.[11]

Very quickly the Netherlands Union grew from 250 000 members in the first two weeks, to 800 000 in February 1941 and published its own paper Die Unie. Colijn, though, had misjudged the occupation authorities, which were not interested in allowing any independent expression of Netherlands' patriotism, and wanted instead to see the much smaller National Socialist Movement of Anton Mussert act as a figurehead leader. The Union tried to prove its worth and issued an instruction to its members on 10 January 1941 saying that 'a loyal attitude to the occupation authorities is a precondition and that members must keep to this'. Later that year the NU started to purge itself of Jewish members.[12] No amount of crawling to the Reichskommisar helped – on the same day as its instruction of loyalty was issued, the NU offices were occupied by the Gestapo and its leaders briefly arrested. Later that year Colijn was arrested again, and this time interned in Ilmenau Camp near Erfurt in Germany, possibly as a potential go-between to talk to the Allies, but instead he died on 16 December 1944.

The Netherlands Union failed to become a Dutch Vichy, not for want of trying, but because the occupation authorities did not think they needed it. Dutch business, though, boomed under the occupation, as manufacturers made armaments and other goods to feed the German war effort. Between January and September 1942 the Netherlands Armaments Inspectorate recorded 154 big guns made, 2155 gun parts, 1126 machine-guns, 150,000 machine gun parts, and large amounts of ammunition. The value of exports to Germany grew from 159.2 million guilder in 1938, to 313.1 million in 1940, 497.1 in 1941 ... peaking at 523.3 million in 1943. At the same time the value of German exports to Holland rose from 308 million in 1938 to a peak of 500 million in 1941, whereafter it declined again to pre-war levels. The Dutch Economic Secretary General Dr Hans Max Hirschfeld attacked violent acts by the resistance because they put 'unreasonable extra pressure on the fabric of the political and economic order'.[13]

To the North, in Norway, Vikdun Quisling was 'a believer in the germanic racial community'.[14] Forty-five thousand joined Quisling's Nasjonal Samling Party – one in seventy of all Norwegians. To the South in Belgium, de Clercq and his Flemish movement painted French influence as 'oppression' and identified with German ascendance. In Wallonia there was Degrelle and his 'Rexists', also there were other parties of the right La Rocque and his French Social Party, Doriot and his French Popular Party.

In Czechoslovakia Hitler relied on the sizeable German minority to justify the 1938 occupation. The following year Germany made Bohemia and Moravia a 'Protectorate', taking control of foreign policy and matters of state, while leaving domestic affairs to a local regime. Germany also gave the authoritarian leader of Slovakia, Father Tiszo, rights of succession, gaining greater mastery over both states.

France's National Revolution

On 10 May 1940 the French Army had twice as many wheeled vehicles and 4,638 tanks to the German 4,060.[15] On the Western Front, where France had followed Britain's ultimatum, 'the phoney war continues' wrote German Colonel von Vormann in his diary on 6 September:

> So far not a shot has been fired on the Western front. On both sides there are just huge loudspeakers barking at each other, with each side trying to make it clear to the other how impossible their behaviour is and how stupid their governments are.[16]

On 17 May 1940, the French armies were 'broken on the Meuse', said Sir John Hammerton.[17] In fact French resistance melted away, and General Rommel was surprised to see that commanders surrendered before battle had been engaged.[18] Pierre Mendès France, a Minister in the government of Leon Blum and later part of de Gaulle's Free

French, said that the Generals 'tackled the war unenthusiastically': 'This attitude of preferring Hitler to Leon Blum was an attitude that had become very popular in Bourgeois circles and this was a world to which many of the soldiers belonged'.[19] Mendès France was talking about the great reservoir of reactionary feeling among the well-to-do. They nursed a lingering resentment at the way that Blum's government let the working classes carry on protesting and striking, and looked jealously at Hitler's repressive measures. To these people 'France was in decay thanks to the Front Populaire and the côterie of corrupt politicians, Freemasons and Jews', wrote Arthur Koestler, who was imprisoned as an enemy alien. The leaders of this reactionary outlook 'in the ministries and on the General Staff' were 'scared by the bogy of a social revolution, they regarded Hitler as their saviour'.[20] Indeed with the German army bearing down on the capital, the French cabinet's greatest fears were summed up in the false report from General Weygand on 13 June that the Communists had seized Paris and installed their leader Jacques Duclos in the Elysée Palace. Four days later Marshal Pétain announced that he had formed a new government and was seeking an armistice: 'With a heavy heart, I tell you today that it is necessary to stop the fighting'.[21]

Dunkirk

On 26 May the British Expeditionary Force was evacuated from Dunkirk. A humiliating defeat was turned around by government propaganda that the British had courageously fought a rear-guard action against overwhelming odds. The truth was that the combined British, French, Belgian and Dutch forces of 3.7 million were much greater than the German force of 2.7 million. In spite of the tales of heroism, the British Parliament heard in secret session that officers had pushed in front of their men to escape from the beach. In disgust many soldiers had thrown their equipment from the trains carrying them back from the coast, and others had asked their families to meet them, with civilian clothes to change into.[22] In fact the British troops were saved by Hitler, who held back while they departed. He told his staff that he wanted a 'reasonable peace agreement' with Britain immediately so that he would be 'finally free' for his 'great and real task: the confrontation with

Bolshevism'.[23]

Collaboration was not just a pragmatic policy for Pétain's government. His Foreign Minister Paul Baudouin made it clear in July 1940 that this was a positive chance to fix the problems that he felt had beset France:

> The total revolution of France has been prepared by twenty years of uncertainty, discontent, disgust and latent insurrection ... The war has burst open the abscess ... This possibility of doing something new thrills men of every walk of life.[24]

The point was reiterated by Pétain in a broadcast of 30 October: 'in the framework of the active construction of the New European order, I enter today on the path of collaboration.'[25] Far from being a reluctant victim of occupation, the French government used the new balance of power to press on with a 'National Revolution' whose themes were 'Travail, famille, patrie' – work, family, country – to replace the now too radical ideals of 'liberté, égalité, fraternité'. Pétain suspended civil and political rights, put the workforce under military discipline, instituted 'national education' and organised a youth movement, the Compagnons to act as the vanguard of the National Revolution. Ominously, the 'Institute of Jewish Questions' hosted 'Jews and France – a morphological exhibition'.[26]

On 3 July 1940 the Royal Navy attacked the French fleet at Mers El Kebir, off Algeria, killing 1,297. Four days later Pétain's minister Pierre Laval contacted the German Generals Huntzinger and Walther Warlimont at the Armistice Commission at Wiesbaden 'to discuss the possibility of change the armistice clauses to allow military collaboration', and so the terms were discussed 'which are now known as collaboration'.[27]

The Limits Of The National Socialist Revolution In Europe

In Britain, the cynics at the *Economist* wondered out loud that

> The odd thing about the extent to which this prospectus of the "new order" coincides with the plan of reformers of both Right and of Left in democratic communities. The union of Europe has been under discussion for two decades. Now it is an

accomplished fact.

With more than a suggestion that they saw the merits of the national socialist revolution in Europe, the *Economist* went on to say that 'the lesson of the New Order' is that 'the age of free enterprise has given place to the age of security'. Europe's business leaders, mused the *Economist's* editors, seemed to prefer the New Order:

> The extent …to which the Nazis have found willing collaborators is not altogether surprising. Industrialists have, of course, been driven into collaboration by the need for raw materials, but there is no doubt that many of them would have been ready for it without this compulsion. It is after all only extending to the whole of Europe the practice of monopoly which has been the goal of the average businessman and his associates.

According to the businessman's in-house journal, big business was itself welcoming Hitler's new Order in Europe:

> The heavy industry of France, Belgium and Holland were already inextricably bound up with German industry and one of the reasons why there was so little resistance is that the Nazis are not altering economic relations so much as abolishing the economic frontiers which, until 1940, hindered the unlimited cartelisation and merging from which many industrialists were perfectly prepared.[28]

In April 1941, with Poland, the Czech lands and western Europe under occupation an over-indulgent George Kennan at the US Consulate in Berlin wrote that Germany's leaders did not want to 'see other people suffer under German rule' but that they were 'most anxious that their new subjects should be happy in their care' - indeed that they were making 'important compromises' to see that happen.[29]

Certainly, Belgian business leaders profited by the decisive victory over organised labour that came with the occupation. They took heart from the end of trade union consultation (*commission paritaires*) and boasted that the disappearance of labour unions and the elimination of the commission paritaires prepare the way for a rapprochement between owners and workers by the establishment of a relation that does away with the class struggle.[30]

The unification of Europe, though, foundered on the German exploitation of Europe. Some Danish farmers, Belgian and Dutch industrialists, and the French haute bourgeoisie prospered, but the people did not. If there was a question mark over whether the occupation was soft or hard it is because different classes of people did better or worse. The main cost of the occupation fell on the working class, who had their rations cut and their sons taken away under Fritz Sauckel's detention of workers for the Reich.

In August 1941 Goering gathered a meeting of those in charge of the Occupied territories, and attacked them for what he saw as the kid treatment of their subject peoples: 'I see people there are stuffed full of food [sic] while our people are starving'. The field marshal scorned the military commanders and Reich commissars complaining 'I have reports of what you are planning to deliver in front of me' and that 'it seems like nothing at all'. Goering revised the amounts upwards – doubling France's grain requisition to 1.2 million tons, and pushing Norway's fish target up to half a million tons. Total European grain deliveries rose from two million tons to more than five million in 1942-3 (helped by a bumper harvest). Goering gave a special Harvest Thanksgiving speech, boasting that the Reich had beaten Churchill's blockade.[31]

'As far as I am concerned I propose to loot' Goering said to the Reich Commissars of the occupied territories and military commanders of 6 August 1942, 'and on a large scale'. Still, the looting would be dressed up as buying: 'I shall despatch to Belgium, Holland and France a number of special purchasers who will be authorised to buy up practically everything they find in the high class shops and stores; all this I shall put in the show windows so that the German people can have it'. 'It must all be done in one swoop – out with the stocks and over to us'.[32]

Austria's National Bank yielded up 345 million Reichsmarks in gold and foreign exchange reserves, and in the country as a whole, Germany grabbed a foreign exchange boost of 782 million

Reichsmarks. This pirate raid pushed Hungary's dependence on Greater Germany's exports from 26 to 44 per cent. Just as handy was the shift in the share of Yugoslavia's exports going to Germany from 32 to 43 per cent. These new facts on the ground helped Germany get better trade treaties with its neighbours.[33]

While collaborators dreamed of a united Europe of Fascist states, Germany was only interested in exploiting the occupied powers, appropriating in 1943 40-50 per cent of French industrial output, for example.[34] Looking on from Chicago, the Marxist Paul Mattick pointed out the limits of European unification under German domination: 'the interests of the diverse ruling classes in the various European nations prevents a European unification by agreement'. 'The defeat of a nation' after all, wrote Mattick, 'is the defeat of its ruling class', adding, with cold detachment '"defeat" is just another name for the concentration of capital in fewer hands'.[35]

Chapter Fifteen

Morale Bombing – a war against the working class

With the declaration of war US President Roosevelt sent a letter to the governments of Germany, Poland, Italy, France and England:

> I am addressing this urgent appeal to every government which may be engaged in hostilities publicly to affirm its determination that its armed forces shall in no event, and under no circumstances, undertake the bombardment from the air of civilian populations or of unfortified cities.[1]

On 14 May 1940 during the invasion of Holland, Germany sent an ultimatum threatening the destruction of Rotterdam if there was no surrender. Before the Dutch could agree, the bombardment went ahead with fifty Heinkel Bombers. Nine hundred people were killed and the city centre burned, fuelled by oil from a margarine factory.[2]

The British Cabinet seized on the opportunity of the Rotterdam bombing to break the injunction against attack civilian targets in Germany. Permanent Under-Secretary Cadogan wrote in his diary 'Cabinet this morning decided to start bombing Ruhr', adding 'Now the total war begins'.[3]

On 24 May 1940 Hitler announced that the Luftwaffe would give 'an annihilating reprisal for English attacks on the Ruhr' – but no attack was ordered. In June, the RAF bombed Genoa and Milan in Italy, and Muster, Wertheim and Dusseldorf – where they returned for a second raid just as people were coming out of their shelters. German secret service opinion polls reported 'strong hatred against England' and 'calls time and time again for revenge'. Instead Hitler made a speech calling for peace with Britain – 'I see no reason that should compel us to continue this war'. Hitler appealed as one imperialist to another, that he did not want to attack Britain: 'A great world empire will be destroyed, a world empire which it was never my intention to destroy or damage'. Of course, the Chancellor expected a free hand to attack civilians in Poland and Holland – but his anxiety about all-out war with Britain was real. Churchill, though, owed his position to the war policy and could not pull back without losing his one last chance of leading the country. When the Luftwaffe dropped copies of Hitler's 'final appeal' for peace on English towns, the RAF replied by bombing civilian targets in Wismar, Bremen, Hamburg, Pinneberg, Paderborn, Hagen, Bochum, Schwerin, Wilhelmscaven and Kassel in July.[4]

'It has now been decided that the primary objective of your operations should now be focussed on the morale of the enemy civilian population and, in particular, of industrial workers,' said Chief of Air Staff Charles Portal, September 1941.[5] The following February Arthur Harris of Bomber Command carried Portal's policy through. Harris's doctrine was that aerial bombardment would break enemy morale, right back to the attacks in Iraq in the 1920s, when he recommended 'one 250-pound or 500-pound bomb in each village that speaks out of turn', adding: 'the only thing the Arab understands is the heavy hand'.[6]

On 7 May 1942 the Cabinet in London told Bomber Command to destroy fifty-eight of Germany's largest urban centres, with the euphemistic goal of 'dehousing' 22 million people.[7] On 28 July 1942 'Bomber' Harris made a threatening broadcast to Germany

We are going to scourge the Third Reich from end to end ... we are bombing Germany city by city and ever more terribly, in order to make it impossible for you to go on with the war. That is our objective. We shall pursue it remorselessly

Harris went on

I will speak to you frankly about whether we bomb single military targets or whole cities. Obviously we prefer to hit factories, shipyards and railways. It damages Hitler's war machine most. But those people who work in these plants live close to them. Therefore, we hit your houses and you.[8]

Indeed, Harris explained that the aim of the Combined Bomber Offensive should be unambiguously stated as 'the destruction of German cities, the killing of German workers and the disruption of civilised community life throughout Germany'. Harris made it clear that it was not his aim to destroy old people, women and children, because, being unproductive citizens they were a drain on Germany's 'means and capacity to wage war'. Rather, the target was 'any civilian who produces more than enough to maintain himself', that is the working class.[9]

Annihilating the German working class from the air was what the British did in the place of waging a real war on the ground. Aerial bombardment was a substitute for sending in the troops. Under pressure from Stalin over the lack of a Second Front, Churchill said he 'hoped to shatter almost every dwelling in almost every German city'. 'That would not be bad', Stalin said back.[10]

Charles Portal hoped to drop 1.25 million tons of bombs on Germany between 1943 and 1944. 'Twenty five million Germans would be rendered homeless, 900,000 would be killed and one million seriously injured'. In the event Portal overreached himself: Britain dropped only 675,000 tons of bombs on Germany throughout the war. By 1943 100,000 civilians were killed.[11]

Russian troops prepare to burn the bodies of the Dresden dead

At the Casablanca Conference in January 1943 a joint strategy for bombing Germany was agreed between Britain and America with the goal of smashing industry and 'undermining the morale of the German people to the point where their capacity for armed resistance is fatally weakened'. In 1945 the bombing campaign was ramped up taking 1,023 lives every day, nearly ten times as many as in 1944. By the end of the war half a million people had been killed by the Allied raids on Germany.[12]

Over the night of 13 and 14th February 1945 the RAF and the USAAF launched attacks on two German cities Darmstadt and Dresden. In Darmstadt the 877 tons of bombs set a firestorm. More would have escaped after the raid had ended, but just south of the Darmstadt rail station a munitions truck was set on fire and its shells kept on firing into the air, making people think the raid was still on. The cellar-shelters offered protection from bomb debris, but when the firestorm overtook them, people were trapped inside, suffocated and scorched. One tenth of all the people of Darmstadt, 12,300 people died that night.[13]

The same tonnage was dropped on Dresden around ten in the evening on the 13th in a fan that covered three quarters of the old town, again setting a firestorm which sent a plume of smoke into the sky a mile high. But this time Bomber Command planned a second strike, which followed three hours later, as people were struggling out of their shelters. Lancaster bombers dropped 1,800 tons of explosives on Dresden starting just after one in the morning of the 14th. They used the same fan formation, with its point starting at the old town but this time spreading into the suburbs to catch those fleeing the first raid. Tens of thousands had fled from the first raid in the 'Great Garden' park and the banks of the Elbe, and also by the main railway station. These refuges were targets in the second raid. Forty thousand people were killed in Dresden.[14]

Arthur 'Bomber' Harris gathered photos of the wreckage of German cities in blue scrapbooks, copies of which he sent to Churchill, Buckingham Palace, and Marshall Stalin.[15] 'Often in life, there is no clear choice between absolute right and absolute wrong' said Archbishop Cyril Garbett of York, wringing his hands:

> Frequently the choice has to be made between the lesser of two evils, and it is a lesser evil to bomb a war-loving Germany than to sacrifice the lives of our fellow countrymen who long for

peace, and to delay delivering millions now held in slavery.[16]

The United States Air Force had its own survey of the impact of strategic bombing, with a vast team of statisticians, planners and economists poring over aerial photographs and interviewing leading Nazi industrialists. The survey was led by John K. Galbraith, who summed up his findings later on:

> Attacks on factories that made such seemingly crucial components as ball bearings, and even attacks on aircraft plants, were sadly useless. With plant and machinery relocation and more determined management, fighter aircraft production actually increased in early 1944 after major bombing.[17]

German morale was actually boosted by the great bombing raids on cities and even by the losses to the Red Army - all of which let the Nazis pose as defenders of the nation.[18] The Strategic Bombing Survey was heavily doctored by the US Air Force to hide its findings and its author blocked from a number of teaching jobs.

Just as Britain and America bombed Germany, Germany bombed Britain.

'The Londoner, proud Cockney, became a warrior' during the Blitz. '"London can take it" became the common man's cry'. At least that is what popular historian Arthur Mee wrote about the Blitz. But 'We can take it' was not an innocent remark, it is a line from a Ministry of Information film, *London Can Take It.* An American reporter Quentin Reynolds wrote the script: 'I can assure you, there is no panic, no fear, no despair in London Town ... London can take it'.

Curiously, Reynolds tried out this line first in Germany, not London, when he was a reporter there for *Colliers* Weekly Magazine between 1933 and 1940. 'Trained to take it' was first an article about *German* preparedness for a *British* bombing campaign.

In the Ministry of Information, public attitudes were polled in expectation of a collapse in morale. Among the elite the view that Britain would lose the war was widespread, and many had already relocated to Canada and America, where senior civil servants were advised to send their families. But among the public, the expected collapse in morale did not happen. When it did not, the government and the Ministry of Information reacted the other way, reading great fortitude into the doughty Cockneys. 'We can take it!' was the formulation of that response, an act of ventriloquism, where the establishment assumed the right to speak for the people.

As a slogan, 'We can take it' evoked pride. But it also heaped shame on anyone who raised doubts. 'The trouble with you people is – you can't take it', Ernest Bevin told Communist shop stewards in Coventry on 14 November 1940, scornfully. Coventry was the most intensively bombed of all British cities.

Put in the mouths of Londoners, 'we can take it' rings hollow – they did not have any choice in the matter. And though the Ministry of Information was impressed by the lack of panic, tens of thousands of people tramped off into the Kent countryside during the first raids, without any real direction. On 3 March 1943, 173 people were killed in a panic crush on the steps of the Bethnal Green underground station, though no bombs fell on East London that night. Nina Masel, reporting for the Mass Observation project described the bombings of 7 September 1940 as 'unplanned hysteria':

The press versions of life going on normally in the East End are grotesque. There was no bread, no milk, no electricity, no gas, no telephones ... The press version of people's smiling jollity and fun are a gross exaggeration.

Pointedly, 29 890 Londoners could not 'take it', but were killed outright, with a further 50 000 seriously injured; 116 000 houses were destroyed outright, and 288 000 badly damaged. A third of the Port of London Authority's warehouses were destroyed. The considerable industrial workforce in Finsbury never recovered from the bombing of its factories and workshops and the City of London lost 40 per cent of its industrial workers – part of the reason that today both are non-industrial districts. Between 1938 and 1947 London's population fell by 20 per cent to 3 245 000. The London boroughs most hit by the blitz suffered the greatest population loss: Bermondsey, Finsbury and Southwark each lost 38 per cent of their population, Poplar, Shoreditch and the City lost about 45 per cent and Stepney lost over half. London did not 'take it' but was substantially depopulated and destroyed by the blitz, to be re-invented as the Greater London conurbation after the war.

In the east aerial bombardment was yet more destructive. The bombing of Moscow began on 21 July 1941. Half a million Muscovites were killed – ten times the number killed in the London Blitz.[19]

In 1943, when the war reached its turning point and Germans began to understand that they would lose, Hitler became ever more

preoccupied with 'secret weapons' that were being developed. At Peenmünde in an underground factory, rocket scientist Werner Von Braun developed the V2 rocket, leading Hitler to proclaim that 'this is the decisive weapon of the war' and 'a technical breakthrough which would change the face of the future'.[20] Hitler was deluded. The V2 rocket terrorised and killed scores of Londoners, but it could not change the course of the war. Ten thousand slave labourers died making the V2, twice the number that died from the V2 bombings. The same resources could have made a much more decisive 24,000

V2 rocketeer Werner von Braun in 1964, at NASA

fighter aircraft.[21] Like the Allies, Hitler used aerial bombardment as a substitute for real victories on the ground. The great human sacrifice went on for the simple reason that there was no victory at hand. After the war, Von Braun and his engineers were seized by an advance US Commando Squad, and he went on to help develop the American Space Program.

Chapter Sixteen

Collapse of the Soviet Empire

In 1928, Stalin's 'Soviet' state, having beaten off the political challenge of the left opposition, steadied its rule by the forced collectivisation of agriculture. The policy underwrote industrialisation as peasants were forced into the towns to work in factories, but for the country it was a disaster. Productivity fell so much that more than a quarter of the capital stock of the farms was lost between 1928 and 1933. By 1932, the Soviet Union was starving, and five million died over the next two years. Collectivisation shored up the urban based officialdom that ran the country, but weakened the Soviet state's grip on the countryside – especially the grain rich Ukraine, that was officially a Soviet Republic to the south west of Russia. To the north on the western border with the USSR stood the Versailles-created state of Poland, that, under its military leader Marshall Pilsudski, had invaded the Ukraine in 1920.[1]

Under Stalin the Soviet leadership had lost confidence in its revolution, and hoped to hang onto power by alliance with those it once called imperialist states. Above all, the USSR needed advanced technology to develop, and sought it from Germany under the terms of the commercial agreement of February 1940. As we have seen, alliance with Germany led to the Molotov-Ribbentrop non-aggression pact, that agreed the division of Poland between them.

The Soviet betrayal and destruction of Poland in 1940 was profound – and only laid the basis for Germany's invasion of the Soviet Union in June 1941. German troops entered Poland on 1 September 1939, absorbing West Prussia, Upper Silesia and other districts into the Greater German Reich. Seventeen days later the Soviet army invaded the east (at German prompting) and divided that territory between the Ukraine and Byelorussia, handing Vilnius over to Lithuania. For the Comintern Dolores Ibárurri dismissed the 'state artificially created by the Treaty of Versailles' as 'a republic of concentration camps'. To the Spanish firebrand-cum-Stalin-apologist 'Social Democracy weeps for the loss of Poland, because imperialism has lost a point of support against the Soviet Union, against the fatherland of the proletariat'.[2] The Soviets deported two million Poles eastwards to Arctic Russia, Siberia and Kazakhstan, many of whom died in the upheaval. In the Spring of 1940 15,000 Polish officers, professionals and reservists – identified by the Soviets as potential leaders of a resistance – were taken prisoner. Later they were killed in Katyń, near Smolensk, in Byelorussia – clubbed to death like cattle.[3] Under the non-aggression pact, Hitler blessed Stalin's use of military force against the Versailles-created Baltic States. The Soviet Union first imposed 'mutual assistance pacts'[4] and then later annexed Lithuania and Estonia in June and Latvia in August on 1940 – while Germany invaded Western Europe, without condemnation from Moscow. The reach of Moscow's western expansion, though, was dependent on German sponsorship, as became apparent in the 'Winter War' with Finland.

Over the winter of 1939-1940 the Soviets pressed their rights under the non-aggression pact and invaded Finland. Unlike its authoritarian Baltic neighbours, the Finnish government was popular and the nation put up a successful resistance. One hundred thousand Soviets were killed, against 23,000 Finns, and on 13 March a Peace Treaty was signed respecting Finland's borders.[5] Watching the Finns struggle, the German leadership changed their minds about the USSR, thinking that victory would be easier than they had feared.

The German decision to turn east to invade the Soviet Union was opportunistic, and borne of weakness. The decision to abandon Sea Lion was taken on 12 October 1940, and Hitler signed Directive number 21 authorising operation Barbarossa on 18 December. The Fourth, Twelfth and Eighteenth Divisions were moved from the Atlantic coast to Poznan in Poland.[6] General Franz Halder wrote in his diary on 28 January 1941: 'Barbarossa: purpose not clear. We do not hurt the English.'[7] But that was the point. Barbarossa was an evasion of the challenge of taking on the British Empire – on the assumption, which turned out to be wrong, that the USSR would quickly crumble. The westward progress of the blitzkrieg had faltered. Berlin needed a new campaign to bind the German people to the war policy.

Moscow got many warnings of the coming war – from the spy Leopold Trepper (who was monitoring troop movements with the help of French railworkers), from the spy Richard Sorge and from Marshal Golikov. Each report was marked in the margins 'Double Agent', or 'British Source'.[8] On 14 June 1941 the Tass News Agency in Moscow made the announcement that

> according to Soviet information, Germany complies with the terms of the Soviet-German nonaggression pact as scrupulously as does the Soviet Union, in light of which, in the opinion of the Soviet Union, rumours about Germany's intentions to annul the pact and to launch an attack on the Soviet Union are completely baseless.[9]

A week later, the Soviet Union, wholly unprepared, was invaded by an overwhelming force of German military firepower. When he was later asked about the wisdom of this announcement, Molotov defended it as a part of the 'game of diplomacy', an attempt to win a concession from the other side – but that only shows how far the Soviet leadership's reliance upon its allies amongst hostile and predatory powers, and its indifference to the fate of its people, had gone. By midday on the day of the invasion, 22 June 1941, the Soviet Air Force lost 1,200 aircraft, 900 of them on the ground, around a seventh of its total.[10] An invasion force of 153 divisions, 600,000 vehicles, 3,580 tanks, 7,184 artillery pieces, 600,000 horses and 2740 planes poured eastward along a front that stretched 930 miles.[11] Stalin himself disappeared from sight, and refused to address the people over the radio. 'I can't,' he said. 'Let Molotov speak.'[12] The dictator fled Moscow to a dacha in Kuntsevo. Stalin feared that he would be blamed, and overthrown, perhaps to be executed, as so many of his rivals had been. But he underestimated just how successful the purges had been. There was no other candidate left. When he did emerge to rally the Soviet people on 3 July 1941, the architect of the disaster was their only plausible leader.

But the Soviet Union's misery was only beginning. The second stage of the invasion operation Typhoon was launched on 30 September 1941. In October 1941 Stalin offered Germany the Baltic States, Moldavia and much of Byelorussia and the Ukraine for an end to the war.[13] By December, though, the German advance had taken as much as that and more, a territory of 500 000 square miles, moving the border 1000 miles to the east to take in all of the Ukraine and some of western Russia. One third of all Soviet citizens fell under the occupation. By December 1941 the Wehrmacht was closing in on Moscow and Leningrad, having taken Lvov, Kharkov, Kiev, Odessa, Smolensk and scores of other cities and towns. 3,350,00 Soviet troops were captured by the end of 1941 – of whom 2 million were starved to death by the end of 1942.[14]

The success of the German campaign was premised on superior equipment, but just as importantly the disaffection of the peasantry, and of national minorities under Soviet rule.

In the summer of 1941 Germans offered Ukrainians on the west bank of the Deieper a generous payment of one in three sheaves – which was more than they were accustomed to under the Soviets.[15] German troops were greeted as liberators when they marched into Lwow, Riga and Hrubieszów – where locals offered the traditional gifts of bread and salt.[16] Germans recruited legions of Soviet citizens – Vlasov's Russian Liberation Army, as well as Balts, Georgians, Turkistanis and Caucasus Muslims. Even Finland joined the German campaign against the Soviets, in what was known as the 'Continuation War'. In time these allies would pay a heavy price for their choice.

In 1941 Ukrainian nationalists under hetman Taras Bulba-Borovets fought alongside Germany. General Andrei Vlasov had been awarded the Order of Lenin in 1940 and fought hard in the defence of Moscow. But when he was captured on 12 July 1942 he offered to lead an anti-Stalin Russian Liberation Army, saying he was sick of the Red Army's dictatorial waste of its own soldiers. In December 1942 Vlasov put out the 'Smolensk Declaration' against the Soviet system – to abolish collective farms and the state run economy, and for civil rights. The Declaration was drafted to flatter the Nazis, trying to fit Russian interests together with Fascist ideology:

Stalin's allies, the British and American Capitalists – have betrayed the Russian people. They aim to make use of Bolshevism in order to take over the natural riches of our country. These plutocrats not only save their own skins at the cost of millions of Russian lives, but they are signatories to secret pacts biased in their favour.

Germany, meanwhile, is not waging a war against the Russian people and their Motherland, but only against Bolshevism. Germany does not wish to encroach on the living space of the Russian people or on their national and political liberties. Adolf Hitler's National Socialist Germany aims to organise a 'New Europe' without Bolsheviks and Capitalists, in which every nation is guaranteed an honourable place.[17]

Hitler, though, did indeed want to encroach on the living space of the Russian people, and was opposed to the Vlasov project as he was of most alliances with anti-Stalinist Slavs. All the same his generals in the east went ahead anyway. Later, much of Vlasov's army was redeployed to the West.[18]

Germans recruited two Ukrainian divisions, a Turkestan division and an SS division from Galicia. There were more than 150 000 Latvians, Lithuanians and Estonians fighting alongside the Wehrmacht. In 1942 the Germans crossed into the Cossack homelands – and were welcomed as liberators with songs and garlands. In 1943 a Cossack division was raised and by 1944 a quarter of a million Cossacks were fighting for the Axis.[19] Around a million Red Army soldiers fought for Germany as the Soviet system collapsed under the pressure of invasion.

Having lost the support of much of the people, the Soviet state was on the verge of collapse. In September 1941 the civilian ministries were ordered to evacuate. Anyone who stumbled into the NKVD headquarters would have heard nothing but telephones ringing unanswered while papers fluttered around the offices. It was rumoured that Stalin himself had left.

Under pressure, the Soviet Union starved. One third of Soviet Citizens fell under the German occupation – but its losses in food were much higher, as agricultural and food-processing output fell by three fifths.[20] In Leningrad around one million died from hunger and hunger-related illnesses – about 40 per cent of the city's people. In Kalinin (today called Tver) typhus numbers multiplied 88 times till seven per cent of the population were infected. Between 1940 and 1942 the death rate rose from 18 to 24 per thousand.[21]

In an extraordinary desperate defence, the Soviet leadership ordered its industrial base to be relocated to the east. Factories were taken apart and moved from Leningrad, Moscow and Kiev eastwards to the Urals, Siberia and the Far East. In 1940 37 per cent of industrial workers were in the east – but by 1942 that had risen to 70 per cent. In 1943, output had fallen to just 38 per cent of its 1940 level.[22]

Suspect populations were also moved east, to prevent them from collaborating. In 1941 400,000 Volga Germans were deported to Siberia and Central Asia – many to work in NKVD camps. Between 1943 and 1944 one million Crimean Tartars, Chechens and other Caucasus people were relocated to Kazakhstan, an operation that took up more than 100,000 Soviet troops.[23] By December 1941 it was assumed across the world that the Soviet Union's days were numbered.

In Berlin, at the Theatre Hall of the Ministry of Propaganda on 10 October 1941, press chief Otto Dietrich showed off a great map of the Soviet Front before the foreign press corps. The German press headlined CAMPAIGN AGAINST THE EAST DECIDED! A week before Hitler had boasted to a rally of the Winter Relief of winning the 'greatest battle in the history of the world' and that the Soviets were defeated 'and would never rise again'.[24]

Chapter Seventeen

The Arab Revolt

Between the fall of France and the invasion of Europe, the major conflict between Britain and Germany was in North Africa. Italians, the Free and Vichy French and even the Russians all fought in the Middle East between 1940 and 1943. But despite the to-and-fro between these different actors, the more substantial conflict was that between the occupying European powers and the Muslim peoples that they ruled over. First Italy, and then, with some reluctance, Germany played on Arab grievances to undermine Britain, and attacked the British Empire where they knew it was weak. Arabs and Persians saw European powers divided, and one by one, beaten by their rivals – all of which emboldened them to challenge their European overlords. Britain, in particular, dismissed the Arab revolts as Nazi manipulation. War gave the Allies a cover to clamp down on Arab demands for self-government, repressing nationalists, and tightening up control over government and resources.

Hitler's cynical Directive No 30 claimed 'The Arab Freedom Movement is, in the Middle East, our natural ally against England'.[1] German sympathies for the Arabs were of course limited. News reports of the surrender of France in 1940 carried shots of Moroccans and other Africans, horsing around, and grinning shyly at the camera, amongst the Prisoners of War: 'The prisoners came from every nation – so-called defenders of a great nation', said the voice-over, adding that it was 'a shame for the white race' and that 'these are the black brothers of the French race'.[2] Hitler gave little material help to the Arab nationalists fighting against Britain and France, for the all-too practical reason that his Italian allies were themselves carving out an empire over the Arabs of North Africa, and did not need any talk of Arab freedom. Still, many Arab nationalists were impressed by Hitler's lightning victory over the French and the British at Dunkirk since these were the two nations that had dominated the Arabs. There was some admiration, too, for the anti-Jewish policy, since the Arabs of Palestine were seen by many in the Middle East to be suffering under a British administration that favoured the Jewish population, boosted as it was by Zionist-inspired migration. The Allies willingness to paint any opposition to their rule over the Arabs as Nazi-inspired, however, is far from the truth. Arab's willingness to fight against Britain and France sprang from their own conditions more than it did from Nazi propaganda.

The Franco-German armistice of 22 June 1940 signed at Rethondes left French colonies in the hands of the Vichy government. On 3 July 1940, Britain turned on its ally to attack the French fleet at Mers el Kebir by Oran, Algiers as well as bombing the Richlieu at Dakar. 'For God's sake stop firing' Admiral Gensoul pleaded at Mers el Kebir: 'You're murdering us!' More than a thousand French sailors died in the attack. Churchill announced the destruction of the French fleet in the House of Commons: 'I leave the judgment of our action, with confidence, to Parliament.' US Liaison Officer General Raymond Lee watched as 'the decorum of parliament vanished': 'All were on their feet, shouting, cheering and waving order papers and handkerchiefs like mad'.[3]

By the autumn of 1940 'a fragile modus vivendi was established between London and Vichy' wrote Howard Sachar, 'both sides tacitly recognising the existing divided status of the French empire and agreed to refrain from military efforts to alter it'. 'General Wavell, the British area commander in Cairo, feared Axis influence in the Middle East much less than disorders among the native populations', explained Sachar. 'As Wavell saw it, anything that challenged Vichy authority in the Levant would similarly undermine British influence in neighbouring countries'.[4]

The armistice did severely limit British authority in the Mediterranean as the North African coast between Gibraltar and Alexandria passed into Axis hands, under German and Italian armistice commissions, with the Italian army well-placed in Libya to threaten Wavell's isolated Nile Army.

On 10 June 1940 Italy declared war on Britain. At that time General Wavell, G.O.C. Middle East commanded 36,000 troops in Egypt, 28,000 in Palestine and 22,000 in Kenya, Aden, British Somaliland and Cyprus. Both the Egyptian and Iraqi native governments resisted British demands to join the war on the allies' side. Churchill remembered:

I wished to arms the Jews at Tel Aviv, who with proper weapons would have made a good fight against all comers. Here I encountered every kind of resistance.[5]

Unable to win his colonial officials and army leaders over to arming the Jews, Churchill depended on white troops to fight this war to 'defend Egypt' and Palestine, berating General Ismay for not calling on the 'Union Brigade of 6,000 white South Africans', and the New Zealanders and Australians who had already been training in Palestine for six months. 'Let me have a return of the white settlers of military age in Kenya', he wrote, asking 'are we to believe they have not formed any local units for the defence of their own province?'[6] Churchill was increasingly critical of Wavell for wasting forces in internal security duties in Egypt and Palestine.[7]

Egypt

Egypt's native leaders wanted to avoid being drawn into the war between Italy and Britain, and withdrew Egyptian troops from the borders when the Italians were close by, to avoid clashes. When Prime Minister Ali Mahir told the Egyptian parliament of this plan, he was cheered. With Egyptian help, the Italians kept a one-hundred strong delegation under Count Serafino Mazzolini while the war was underway. The British tried to push the Egyptians into having these Italian officers in Cairo jailed. 'One met with interminable delays,' moaned the British Commander of Forces in Egypt, Henry Maitland Wilson, 'and at times faced with releases on the order of a minister without reference or consultation'.[8] The former Prime Minister Ismail Sidai said the 'Italian offensive is not an act of aggression directed at Egypt, but another belligerent on the territory of a third occupied power'.[9]

Under the timid leadership of General Graziani, Italy's attack on British mandated territories ran out of steam. Wavell's successful counter-attacks in December 1940, and Graziani's flight sent Mussolini and Ciano into despair, coming as they did on top of a successful repulsion of the Italian invasion of Greece. 'If we lose Africa, we lose the war', General Ugo Cavallero had said – and that was before he was made Badoglio's replacement as Commander in Chief of the Italian army. Still Wavell pressed on, and took Benghazi from the Italians, destroying five of Graziani's seven divisions and taking 38 000 prisoners.

Before Wavell's successes German generals were looking again at North Africa. Reversals in the Battle of Britain and in the north Atlantic underscored the unlikelihood of a successful invasion of Britain. As a frontal assault on Britain looked less attractive, so an attack on Britain's overextended Empire appealed more. Once again, Arabs would suffer Europeans fighting out their differences in Arab lands. In a Memo of 26 September 1940 Admiral Erich Raeder outlined the case for taking on Britain in the North Africa:

> Gibraltar must be taken. The Suez Canal must be taken. It is doubtful whether the Italians can accomplish this alone.[10]

By February it was clear that the Italians would need help not just to take Suez, but help to stay in the war at all. Sending Rommel's army to North Africa was not only a substitute for taking on Britain directly; it was also a desperate attempt to shore up the Axis.

Later, in 1942, with the Axis again at the Egyptian border (this time led by Erwin Rommel) Prime Minister Hussein Sirri to broke off relations with Vichy France when asked to by the British. In the poorer districts crowds massed shouting 'Come on, Rommel'.[11] King Farouk's loyalists were angered and rioted against the government. The British Ambassador Sir Miles Lampson – ignoring Farouk's hand in the riots – took him to task for not putting a *more* pro-British government in office, and telling him to appoint the Wafdist Mustapha Nahas Pasha. Stung, Farouk stalled for time. Lampson set a deadline of 6.00pm on 4 February for Farouk to change the government, which the king let slide. At 9.00 British troops, backed up with tanks invaded the palace, and Lampson handed Farouk a letter of abdication. 'Will you give me another chance, Sir Miles?' asked a shaken Farouk. 'Of course', replied Lampson, 'if you send for Nahas' – which he did.[12]

Henri Curiel, Jew and Communist, wanted to rally opposition to a Nazi takeover. He explained to his comrades that such was the record of British rule that 'we won't be believed if we claim that Hitler's Germany is worse than Britain':

No one will follow us if we advocate an alliance, even a temporary one, with the British in order to rid ourselves of the Nazis. We can say the Nazis are as bad as the British, but no more. And that implies refusal of any collaboration with the British Embassy.[13]

The British did try to organise a Brothers of Freedom group to rally Egyptian opposition to the Nazis, though it sank without trace. Just before the battle of El Alamein, the British rounded up Egyptian nationalists, and radicals, including Henri Curiel, who was jailed alongside the supposedly Fascist Egyptians. His view was that most of them were just patriots who would have sided with the devil to 'kick Britain out of Egypt'. Talking to his fellow prisoners Curiel thought that 'no "diplomacy" regarding the British could possibly be accepted under any conditions by a true Egyptian patriot'.[14] Curiel went on to help organise the protests in 1946 that forced the British to quit Egypt after the war.

Iraq revolt

Freed from Turkish rule at the end of the First World War, Iraq had been handed over into the quasi-colonial status of a mandated territory, under British control. The mandate system allowed that Iraq could become a sovereign state if Britain proposed it to the League of Nations. Britain's condition was a Treaty that would set down Iraq's ongoing ties and debts to Britain. Under the treaty, Iraq agreed to pay Britain back £588,000 for public works undertaken, to keep 'gazetted' officials, British advisers to senior Iraqi ministers paid by Iraq, but still 'servants of His Britannic Majesty', Britain kept two air bases and 47.5 per cent of the Iraqi Petroleum Company. The League of Nations agreed Iraqi 'independence' under these terms in 1932.[15] Rashid 'Ali al-Gaylani was made Prime Minister in March 1940 – pro-British at first, he was pushed to a more pro-German line by the 'Golden Square' of Army officers, Colonels Salah-al-Din al Sabbagh, Kamil Shabib, Fahmi Said and Mahmud Salman.

Rashid 'Ali protested at British plans to site Indian troops in Basra, and made contacts with Germany. By the end of 1940 Britain had decided that 'Ali was a threat, and told the ambassador to use all his influence on the Regent Crown Prince Abd al-Ilāh of Iraq to get rid of him – which he did in January 1941. But on 1 April Rashid 'Ali's military friends besieged Baghdad, and the Crown Prince fled. The army put Faysal II on the throne, and Rashid 'Ali back in government. 'Ali told the British that Iraq would take no more troops, but on 29 April three more troopships arrived and the new ambassador Sir Kinahan Cornwallis declared war on 1 May.

On 4 May 1941, Churchill wrote to General Wavell:

A commitment in Iraq was inevitable. We had to establish a base at Basra, and control that port to safeguard Persian oil ... it is essential to do all in our power to save Habbaniya and control the pipe-line to the Mediterranean.[16]

The explanation for the Iraq Revolt was straight-forward as far as the British Chiefs of Staff could see: 'Rashid 'Ali has all along been hand-in-glove with Axis Powers'.[17] Much easier to blame Iraqi disaffection on the Axis than face up to the unpopularity of British rule. Iraqi premier Rashid 'Ali's hostility to the Allies was 'a blow to our prestige throughout the Arab world'.[18] To show that Rashid 'Ali was indeed an agent of the Axis, the British forged a secret document, supposedly an agreement between the Prime Minister and the Italian Ambassador signed on 25 April 1941 in Baghdad. The imaginary deal was to stop the pipeline travelling to Haifa and reopen the one to Tripoli (closed since the Italians joined the war), as well as nationalising the Iraqi oil fields under German and Italian control.[19]

In the event the Rashid 'Ali uprising 'aroused instant and widespread enthusiasm throughout the Arab world' according to the historian Howard Sachar, who also wrote that 'more serious by far than the advance of Rommel's army in the western desert was evidence that the barely repressed native enmities of a generation now appeared to be closing in on Britain's precarious foothold in the Arab world.'[20] Among the Arab leaders voicing their support for the rising were King Farouk, political leaders like Hashim al-Atasi in Syria, Riad al-Sulh of Lebanon, and religious leaders like Hassan Mahmud Amin Husseini, of the Lebanese Shi'ites, and Muhammed Tewfiq Khalid, the Sunni Mufti of Lebanon. There were demonstrations in support of the rising in all major cities of the Levant and Trans-jordan, and committees were set up to collect money and medicines to help the Iraqis. Bedouin tribes attacked British camps and oil workers.

Churchill credited the defeat of the revolt to the Indian division sent to Basra, and the promise of Indian reinforcements. Also RAF squadrons and Wellington bombers sent from Sha'iba attacked Iraqi troops at Habbaniya. After the first day the War Office reported that 'Iraqi morale was higher than expected and showed no signs of cracking'.[21] Iraqi artillery destroyed 22 British planes at the Sha'iba airfield. Iraq lost 32 planes in RAF attacks on bases at Baghdad, Baquba and al-Mussayib. A column of Iraqis coming from Falluja to support their countrymen were destroyed by forty British aircraft, a scene described by one British pilot:

> The road was a solid sheet of flame for about 250 yards with ammunition exploding and armoured cars and lorries burning fiercely. The charred and battered remnants of this convoy which littered the road between Falluja and the Canal Turn remained for several weeks afterwards as evidence of the enemy's defeat.[22]

The British took Habbaniya on 7 May 1941. General Wavell tried to warn the Chiefs of Staff about 'the limits of military action in Iraq ... without a favourable political situation'. But Churchill was blunt that 'there can be no question of negotiation' with the Iraqi leadership and telling Wavell that he should imitate the German blitzkrieg: 'you should exploit the situation to the utmost, not hesitating to try to break into Baghdad'. Against Wavell's fears for political unrest, Churchill assured 'You do not need to bother too much about the long future in Iraq'. Wavell took the hint and reported back 'we try to liquidate this tiresome Iraq business quickly'.[23]

Some of the leaders fled to Iran, Rashid Ali and the Mufti to Istanbul, six were tried by court martial on 4 May 1941, and three, Yanis Sabani, Colonel Mahmud Salman and Colonel Fahmi Said were hung;[24] others were rounded up in August of 1941 and were interned in Rhodesia for the duration of the war.

Looking back, Cornwallis wrote

The Rashid 'Ali uprising in May 1941, during the course of which not only the Iraqi army but the majority of the population of Iraq demonstrated dislike for the British, came as a great shock to Britishers in Iraq.[25]

The invasion of Syria

France's rule over the Levant was far from liberal. In July 1938 France suspended the constitution of Syria, closing its national assembly and dismissing its Arab representatives. On 21 September 1939 High Commissioner Puaux did the same in Lebanon. As the Levant passed over into Vichy hands, not much changed for its Arab peoples.

During the Iraq Revolt, the Vichy Admiral Darlan offered French airfields in Syria to the Luftwaffe to give air support to Rashid 'Ali. In the event, the German air force flew few flights, being tied up in the east. But the challenge led the British and Free French to engineer an invasion of Syria. De Gaulle overstated the support that he could expect from the French colonial officers and troops in Syria, who were mostly loyal to the Vichy's High Representative, Dentz. Wavell told Churchill that 'progress at first being by propaganda, leaflets and display of force', in the invasion of Syria. 'If resistance was encountered, the utmost force would be used'.[26]

When the invasion by Indian troops under British command sidestepped de Gaulle, the General was outraged at the usurping of *French* rights in Syria.[27] The Free French leader General Catroux said 'I am entering Syria with my forces in the name of France. Honour forbids that the people of the Levant, remaining faithful to France in spite of her defeat, be placed under the odious heel of Germany.'[28]

At the time, though, many fought with the Germans against the Allied invasion, like the French trained Fawzi al-Qawuqji, a veteran of the revolt in Palestine in 1936, who had taken up arms against the Vichy-Syrian authorities earning himself a death-sentence which he avoided by fleeing to Iraq to take part in the Rashid 'Ali revolt. It was in Iraq that the British set up a special flying column to attack al-Qawuqji and his men, called Mercol.[29] German General Rudolf Rahn got al Qawuqji pardoned so that he could fight against the Allies.[30]

When de Gaulle arrived at forts that had been allocated to the Free French, he found British flags flying over them. A wired game of words followed, where Syria's "independence" was an empty claim, but the "rights" of France and England over her territory were hotly contested. Churchill pleaded with de Gaulle not to name Catroux as High Commissioner, for the trouble it would cause the alliance. De Gaulle complained to a friend:

> Our partners wanted to create the impression that, if the Syrians and Lebanese received independence, they would owe it to England, and so place themselves in the position of the arbiters between us and the Levant states.

To Churchill, de Gaulle wrote

> I shall appoint Catroux Delegué-General and Plenipotentiary. We shall proclaim and respect the independence of the Levant States on condition of a treaty with them enshrining the rights and special interests of France.[31]

In Cairo, on 21 July, de Gaulle told the British Secretary of State for the Middle East Oliver Lyttleton that within three days the French Forces would no longer consider themselves under British command, raising the spectre of fighting between the allies. Lyttleton eventually gave way recognising France's historic rights in the Levant and a promise of 'non-interference' in these on Britain's part.[32] 'We must make clear to both the French and the Syrians and the Lebanese that we have no desire to see French interests in the Levant overthrown', wrote British Minister Harold Macmillan.[33] At the Druze town of Soueida in late July, Lyttleton had to stand down a brigade of English troops who were about to start fighting their French rivals over which European flag should fly there.

The rights of the Syrians, of course, were wholly secondary. At the end of July de Gaulle toured Beirut and Damascus trying to set up local government amongst Arabs, but the results were patchy and 'left Arab nationalists discontented'.[34] As soon became clear, the 'Free French' expected to inherit the rights of the mandatory power in full. The virtual France that De Gaulle was trying to create out of its colonies could never regain the prestige that defeated and occupied Vichy France had lost, unless its full imperial rights were honoured. France had tried to divide the Levant against itself, dividing the Lebanon, with its substantial Christian share of the population, from Syria; and France's *mission civilisatrice* was quite an investment in the education and training of a civil and military elite that, it was hoped, would be loyal.

Catroux's replacement as Delegué-General in Syria and the Lebanon, Jean Helleu, repeated the formula that independence could only happen in the framework of a treaty with France that set out her pre-eminence. The Syrians answered by electing a pointedly nationalist assembly on 16 August 1943. Worse still, on 21 September, the Lebanese snubbed Helleu's preferred leader Emile Eddé in favour of a Constitutional Bloc that united Christian and Muslim behind the banner of Lebanese independence. With Lebanese President Bishara Al-Khuri rejecting negotiations, Helleu had the French marines round up him and his ministers at 4.00 am, on 11 November 1943: 'the president's son, his face streaming blood, staggered into my room saying his father had been taken from his bed by Senegalese soldiers', wrote Churchill's Free French liaison officer Edward Spears.[35] The Lebanese ministers interned at the Rechayya fortress, Helleu suspended the constitution and made Eddé puppet ruler of a French police state. To Helleu's horror, the two ministers who escaped the dawn raid effectively rallied cross-community support for a free Lebanese government in the forests, while Eddé was boycotted by everyone.

De Gaulle could not believe that the Lebanese actions were their own, assuming that they were being influenced by Edward Spears, as part of a British attempt to push the French out of the Levant – a view seemingly confirmed by British protests at the suppression of Lebanese representatives. But Britain would not, he thought, let conflict with Arab nationalists come into the open: 'I am convinced that London is bluffing', he said, 'for the English have every reason to hope that disorders will not occur in the Lebanon or Syria'. De Gaulle was right to think that London feared an Arab revolt, but wrong to think that they would rely on France to prevent it. Already Churchill had told General Wilson to draw up plans for a *British military occupation of the Lebanon*.[36] With protests and riots threatening further instability, the French released al-Khuri who again asserted independence. On 27 November 1943, the Syrian constituent assembly, having followed events closely, themselves abrogated France's rights as a mandatory power. This time France chose not to provoke further moves by reacting.

The following year, as France's claim to pre-eminence in the Levant rang yet more hollow, De Gaulle sent French and Senegalese troops, which stirred up a general strike starting on 19 May 1944, a suspension of all negotiations between the Levant representatives and the French, and rioting across Beirut and Damascus. On 28 May, the fighting got worse as insurgents attacked French military installations, and French cars and homes were attacked. Rioters in Damascus were chased by French troops into the parliament, Syrian police headquarters, the Bank of Syria and other public buildings. General Oliva-Roget ordered these 'centres of insurrection' to be bombarded. Some 40 civilians were killed and 1400 injured. With France on the verge of losing control, the allies' response, on 31 May 1944, was to give the go-ahead to a second British invasion of Syria in three years. Exasperated, de Gaulle made it clear that if French troops were fired on by British troops in the Lebanon, they would fire back to defend their military rule against the establishment of a British military rule over the Syrians. Crowds in Beirut 'hissed and booed' the French troops as they were escorted out of town, and shouted 'down with de Gaulle' and 'down with France'.[37]

The crowds cheered the British troops that escorted the French, though they might have been less happy if they had seen what the Syrian Prime Minister Quwatli had to offer the British to get them to clear out the French. In the letters from Quwatli to Britain's Terence Shone, the Prime Minister swears 'to grant Britain concessions for oil exploration in Syria and a preferential political, economic and financial status in the country; to adopt a foreign policy compatible with Britain's; and to allow Britain a role in establishing the Syrian army.'[38]

The Persian Campaign

At the outbreak of the Second World War, an Iranian government official complained to the German intelligence officer Bernhard Schulze-Holthus that the British act like 'white lords who look on us as colonials and treat us with unbearable arrogance'.[39]

'There is in fact no possibility of any British action in the West', Churchill had written to Stalin on 4 Sept. 1941 'before the winter sets in'. But Churchill saw the appeal of opening 'the fullest communication with Russia through Persia': 'We welcomed the opportunity of joining hands with the Russians and proposed to them a joint campaign' to invade Persia (present-day Iran).[40]

The British used the danger of a German fifth column in Iran 'as a pretext for the eventual occupation of Iran and are deliberately exaggerating its potency' said Lewis Dreyfus in a cable to the US State Department 19 August 1941).[41]

The Foreign Office's Eastern Department asked

Would it not be best, when we are in a position to talk strongly to the Iranians, to come out into the open and say frankly that we must look after the oilfields for the duration of the war, and (if we and the Russians feel equal to the task) take special steps to ensure that the railway functions in accordance with our requirements (the Soviet Government making similar demands)?[42]

But on 25 August the British Foreign Office issued a statement that since the Iranian government 'are not prepared to give adequate satisfaction to the recommendations', to expel German engineers, 'His Majesty's Government and the Soviet Government must have recourse to other measures to safeguard their essential interests', that is, an invasion.

As well as a chance to bond with Stalin along the lines of the pact to divide Poland between the Marshall and Hitler, Churchill had other reasons to invade Iran; 'The Persian oil fields were a prime war factor'.[43] The Foreign Secretary Anthony Eden thought 'all depends upon our ability to concentrate a sufficient force in Iraq to protect the Iranian oil fields', and warned that 'the Shah is fully conscious of the value of the oilfields'. Churchill feared that 'the Persian troops around and about the Ahwaz oil fields' might 'seize all the Anglo-Persian Oil Company employees and hold them as hostages' or worse the 'danger of the oil wells being destroyed rather than they should fall into our possession'.[44]

The British landed at the Abadan refinery at dawn on August 25, having assembled the 8th Indian Infantry division under General Harvey, the 9th Armoured Brigade under General Slim, one Indian regiment of tanks, four British battalions and one regiment of British artillery. 'At Abadan there was considerable opposition', wrote Sir

John Hammerton: 'For seven hours hand-to-hand fighting continued between the Persian soldiers and Indian troops'.[45] According to the Shah Mohammad Reza Pahlavi 'the Royal Air Force bombed military targets such as Ahvaz, Bandar-Shapur and Korramshahr, taking pains however to avoid petroleum plants'. [46] H.M.S. Shoreham sank an Iranian frigate off Abadan, while the Soviet Air Force bombarded Tabriz, Ghazvin, Bandar-Pahlavi, Rasht and Fezajeh. 'Some parts of the country will take some time to disarm', worried British Ambassador Reader Bullard.[47]

'A brief and fruitful exercise of overwhelming force against a weak and ancient state', boasted Churchill, though 'the deep and delicate questions about oil, Communism and the post-war future of Persian lay in the background'. Churchill warned Stalin that 'there are in Persia signs of serious disorder among tribesmen, and of breakdown' of authority.[48] More difficult was the hostility of the King Rezā Shāh, who denied British and Russian authority. Under threat of a column of Russian troops marching on Teheran, Rezā Shāh abdicated ('do you think I can receive orders from some little English captain?' he asked his son[49]), and was sent into exile, in

Mauritius, and then later South Africa, where he died in 1944.

In fact Churchill knew that Stalin was overstretched, fighting the German invasion in the west, and hoped to grab Persia from his ally: 'If you wish to withdraw the five or six Russian divisions for use on the battle front we will take over the whole responsibility of keeping order'[50] – it was a pious hope: Stalin hung onto the northern provinces he occupied till 1946, trying to peel off a separated Azerbaijani state.

Rezā Shāh had built up the country's communications, with 10,000 miles of road repaired and built under his rule, along with the Trans-Iranian railway, but his critics complained that 'these developments had been built along purely national lines: the chief network of communications centred about Teheran and was hardly linked with Russia, while by deliberate act the communications were neglected'. Under Anglo-Soviet rule these shortcomings were mended 'the Russian and Persian systems were linked by a railway between Tabriz and Kazvin' as also there was an 'extension of the Indian railway from Quetta across Baluchistan to Duzdab. [51] Rezā Shāh's son was put on the throne in his place.

Under the Tripartite Treaty Alliance of 29 January 1942 the Russians and British swore to respect the national territorial integrity, sovereignty and independence of Iran' – as long as they had use of Iranian labour and the Iranian roads and rail. But they trampled over Iran's sovereignty, too, throwing one sovereign out of office, as well as freely censoring the press.[52] Churchill wrote bullishly 'we hope it will not be necessary in the present phase at any rate to have an Anglo-Russian occupation of Tehran, but the Persian government will have to give us loyal and faithful help and show all proper alacrity if they want to avoid it'.[53]

Ambassador Reader Bullard made few efforts to hide 'the low opinion that I have formed of the Iranians'. Even Churchill was moved to complain that 'Sir Reader Bullard has a contempt which *however natural* is detrimental to his efficiency and our interests'.[54]

As all of Iran's trains and roads were given over to stocking Russia with Allied aid, the trade of rice and beans from India was stopped. The economy was 'weakened by Russian and British requisitioners who took what they wanted and paid little attention to our needs', wrote Reza Shah's son.[55] 'Allied expenditure in Persia put money in circulation which increased the competition for scarce goods', and at the same time 'Allied requisitioning of lorries and railway goods wagons prevented the transport of food and other items, thus forcing up prices'. On top of that, the 'wheat and rice from the northern provinces had normally helped feed the rest of the country' but 'now the Russians refused to allow them to be shipped south, diverting them instead to their own uses'. Famine, and inflation, swept the country and 'increased the cost of living nearly 400 per cent'.[56] On 8 December, 1942, students parading in Tehran drew large crowds, and then again the following day, leading a march on the parliament building. They were fired upon with machine guns, and a strike closed city shops the next day. All told 20 were killed, 700 wounded, 150 arrested, and 150 stores sacked and burned.[57] The police action was overseen by one H. Norman Schwarzkopf, the New Jersey State Police superintendent sent over to organise the gendarmerie (his son, of the same name, was Commander of Coalition Forces in the invasion of Iraq, Desert Storm, in 1991).

Ambassador Reader Bullard wrote about a capital city whose streets were forbidden to the natives, while foreigners walked freely: 'The whole population except favoured persons such as foreign diplomats, is shut up indoors to be registered for the issue of ration coupons for bread.' The ration coupons were 'allocated by the allies'.[58] Bullard outlined the harsh cut in bread planned: 'it is hoped to reduce the daily consumption of wheat in Tehran from about 250 tons to 200 tons'. Luckily, there was special provision for the English: 'the Ministry of Foreign Affairs set aside one bakery for the diplomatic corps'.[59]

The rioting in Tehran led Bullard to wonder whether there was any point to letting the Iranians have any say in the running of their country: 'I admit that the problem of the press and the Parliament in a country like this, where the people are irresponsible and almost to a man corrupt, is beyond me, and I do not see how the country can escape the choice between anarchy and despotism'.[60] The new Shah remembered that after the riots 'the British brought their troops back into the city ostensibly to quell the disturbances' but in fact they 'intimidated Parliament into meeting their demands' to inflate the currency.[61]

The Desert War

In Western Europe, neither Britain nor Germany were willing to cross the channel – bombing each other's cities, and attacking ships; the Axis and the Allies' respective armies did not meet on their own soil, but in North Africa. Italy's bid for African Empire ended in ruins. Germany's overtures to Arab nationalists added to the Empire's troubles. Once the British Army had regained control over the Middle East, they could face the threat of Rommel's Desert Army. Europeans would vent their hatreds in other people's countries.

Britain had assembled an army of 630 000 British and colonial troops under Auchinleck, outnumbering Rommel's men by three to two. Auchinleck had 900 tanks to Rommel's 560 but were still being out-foxed. Pressed to take on the German, Auchinleck in February of 1942 threw the War Cabinet into despair when he said he needed four months to get ready. In the end he was told to strike before 15 July or be relieved of command, which he did. But still Rommel fought back, taking Tobruk after intense fighting on 20 June. The next day, wrote Ribbentrop's press officer,

> Rommel entered the city of Tobruk at the head of his combat group. He found a pile of ruins. Hardly a house remained intact. … the harbour installations and the streets had been transformed into a maze of rubble.[62]

Thirty three thousand prisoners were taken, among whom were fully one third of all of South Africa's armed forces.[63]

Once Italy entered the war in 1940, trade in the Mediterranean was called to a halt by attacks on shipping, which undermined Middle Eastern economies. A Middle East Supply Council under E.M.H. Lloyd struggled with shortages of tea, coffee, spices, sugar and grain. In June 1941 Lebanon's rich cereal harvest was broken up by the Allied invasion of Syria, so that by the winter the Middle East was without grain and close to famine. There were riots in Damascus. Allied authorities ordered all grain be sold to a control board for distribution, closing – in some cases burning – local mills. The Allies taxed the Middle East heavily and put a freeze on wages and salaries, just as prices were rocketing.

Cost of Living Index

	1939	1945
Egypt	100	293
Palestine	100	254
Levant states	100	620
Iraq	100	390
Iran	100	699

Operation Torch and the restoration of Allied Authority in North Africa

In October and November of 1942 the British Eighth Army – now under the command of General Bernard Montgomery – and Rommel's Afrika Korps fought their decisive battle at El Alamein. At the same time American and British forces landed to the west, catching the Axis forces in a pincer movement. The Axis surrendered on 14 May 1943, with 275,000 taken prisoner. For nearly three years the Axis and the Allies had been avoiding a direct confrontation over their own territory, by hitting at each other in North Africa, but the surrender brought that phase of the war to an end. In September 1945 Sir Edward Grigg, Minister Resident in the Middle East summed up the British position:

the Middle East is no less vital to Britain than Central and South America to the United States, or than the eastern and western glacis of the Russian land mass to the Soviet Union ... It was not for nothing that we sent to Egypt in 1940, when this island was in imminent jeopardy of invasion, the only armoured division of which we stood possessed. It was no mere accident that the whole face of the war began to change after our victory, two years later, at Alamein.[64]

In North Africa the restoration of allied authority turned out to be something rather less than liberation.

In Tunisia the nationalist Neo-Destour party's leader Habib Bourguiba had been imprisoned by the French after disturbances in 1938. From prison, though, he had the foresight to counsel the younger Destour party activists against the overtures from the Italian (and later German) authorities that took over. André Gide who was in Tunis condemned the high altitude bombing of the country by the Allies, which rarely damaged German positions but killed thousands of civilians: 'What sense to these idiotic destructions make?'[65] Released from prison by the Germans, Bourguiba would not back their rule. When the Allied forces' 'reconquest of Tunisia' began on 7 May 1943, the Destour gave them a cool reception. When Bourguiba, 'called on the Tunisians to join up with the fighting French, the latter rather had it in mind to liquidate the Neo-Destour'. The French 'Resident General' Mast arrested around 10,000 Tunisians accusing them of collaborating with the Germans, or having betrayed and mistreated the French Colonists. The Comité Français de Libération Nationale made successive rulings claiming ever-greater French authority over Tunisia.[66]

Libya was divided when Britain established a Military Administration in Tripolitania and Cyrenaica, while the Free French made its own Military Administration in Fazzan 'after the country's final conquest by the allies in 1943'.[67] The United States took over the airbase at Mellaha east of Tripoli, that they renamed Wheelus Field after an American officer killed in Iran, and spent $100 million developing – the beginning of a network of Mediterranean bases that served the US throughout the Cold War. Libyan exiles in Egypt led by Sayyid Idris had rallied to the allied cause in the hope that they would get their independence, though the British authorities wanted instead to give them self-government under British advisers, as the commander of the Eighth Army, General Bernard Montgomery made clear in his statement of 11 November 1942.[68] Five infantry battalions of volunteers drawn from the 14,000 exiles in Egypt joined the Allies, though they were used only as 'base troops', not in action, and as a local gendarmerie. Later Britain played off the Sennusi supporters of Sayyid Idris of Cyrenaica against the Tripolitanians to frustrate calls for a free and undivided Libya. The Libyan cities of Tobruk, Benghazi and Tripoli, over which Italy, Germany and Britain fought throughout the desert war were thoroughly destroyed and the country was left with a deadly legacy of mines that took thousands of lives in the decades after the war had ended.[69]

Restoring France's North African Empire

On 8 November 1942 Anglo-American forces commanded by

General Eisenhower landed at Casablanca, Oran and Algiers. On 14 November 1942, Admiral Darlan, on leave in Algiers, defected from the Vichy regime, made himself French High Commissioner of North and West Africa with American support.

De Gaulle made Algiers the capital of his Comité Français de Libération Nationale – but soon clashed with the Americans. However, the Americans' strategy of peeling off Vichy loyalists like Darlan as allies was frustrated when Bonnier de la Chapelle assassinated the Admiral in the St George Hotel on the outskirts of Algiers. Charged with murder, de la Chappelle was sure that 'they will not shoot me – I have saved France'; but he was shot the following morning.[70] Roosevelt's choice as Darlan's replacement was another Pétain supporter, General Giraud, who wanted to hang on to the Vichy era anti-Jewish laws.[71] Roosevelt's distrust of the Free French was unabated, and even in spite of Churchill's pleas, the American government gave only limited credence to de Gaulle's committee in a statement of 24 August 1943 which

> does not constitute the recognition of a government of France or of the French Empire by the Government of the United States. It does constitute the recognition of the French Committee of National Liberation as functioning within specific limitations during the war.[72]

The Comité was committed to France's liberation, but its views on the French colonies were in marked contrast.

Some 47,000 Moroccans had served in the French Army in 1939 and 1940, and on 10 December 1943 Moroccans started their own Independence party Hizb al-Istiqlal. Gabriel Puaux, France's Resident General in Morocco, having switched sides from Vichy to de Gaulle, accused Istiqlal of fomenting a 'pro-German' insurrection. Puaux demanded the exclusion of two Istiqlal sympathising ministers from the government and had four of the party's leaders, including Ahmad Balfrej and Muhammad al-Yazidi arrested. 'Bloody riots broke out in Rabat, Salé and, particularly, in Fez'.[73] 1800 arrests were made, and more than a thousand convictions followed. Civil servants and Viziers whose loyalty to France was in doubt were dismissed and schools and universities were closed.

Puaux did start a series of Reform Commissions, but Istiqlal organised a successful boycott. The Resident General had the advantage that the Moroccan Communist Party had denounced the riots as 'untimely', but in the end this only isolated them from popular support, and later they fell in behind Istiqlal's agitation. Early in 1945 great crowds mobbed the Sultan in Marrakech shouting 'Long live the King! Long live the country! Long live independence!' Still, the French faced down the demand for independence for years to come.

Under the Vichy regime militants of the Algerian People's Party had been jailed in March 1941. On 12 February 1943 Ferhat Abbas published the 'Manifesto of the Algerian People', which called for self-government within the French Empire. General Catroux ordered Abbas arrested. The French released the PPA leader Messali in April, and on 12 December 1943 de Gaulle announced reforms that would have given only 63,000 Algerians voting rights alongside the French colonists – an offer which left the Algerian nationalists cold. When Frenchmen celebrated Victory in Europe on 8 May 1945 Algerians also took to the streets. In Sétif they carried the Tricoleur alongside the Algerian flag – and the French police opened fire. Troops were brought in and the demonstration turned into a massacre. In nearby Kherrata a Foreign Legion began an 'Arab hunt':

The people were massacred without warning and without pity... The Kherrata gorges filled up with corpses. People were thrown dead or alive into deep crevasses.[74]

The 'Arab hunt' went on into June, and left tens of thousands dead.

British and Commonwealth losses in the North Africa Campaign are reckoned at 220 000. German losses are listed as more than 100 000 killed or missing, Italians, 22 000, Americans, around 18 500. Not everyone lost out, though. Tony Cliff wrote at the time that 'during the war the capitalists and especially the big foreign companies active in the east made tremendous profits' – boosted by military spending. Cliff cited these examples:

the big Egyptian sugar company (a French company) ended the year 1941 with 266,000 pounds; 1942 with 1,350,000 pounds. The

National Weaving Factories paid 11 per cent dividends in 1938 and 22 per cent in 1942. Misr Weaving Factories in Mahallah paid 7 per cent dividends in 1938 and 28 per cent in 1943. Misr Weaving Factory in the village Dawar paid 12 per cent in 1941 and 20 per cent in 1943. The Marconi Broadcasting Company paid 7 per cent in 1935 and 25 per cent in 1940. Egyptian Hotel Companies paid 10 per cent in 1938 and 25 per cent in 1941. The number of millionaires in Egypt before the war was fifty, and in 1943, four hundred.[75]

Chapter Eighteen

Collapse of the European Empires in East Asia

Between the two world wars, Japan often played host to Pan Asian conferences. Chinese nationalist leader Sun Yat-Sen gave a speech in Kobe in 1924 contrasting Asia's Kingly Way with Europe's Forceful Way – though he did charge his hosts with following the European Forceful Way, pointing to the claims on China Japan made at the Versailles conference.[1]

When Japan did send troops into mainland China to face down nationalist protests, the established military power in the region, Britain, was for the most part sympathetic. Leo Amery, who would be Secretary of State for India in the Second World War, said in 1933: 'I see no reason ... why we should go against Japan in this matter'. 'Japan needs markets' Amery thought, and asked, stretching the meaning of Christ's words, 'who is there among us to cast the first stone and to say that Japan ought not to have acted with the object of creating peace and order in Manchuria and defending herself against the continual aggression of Chinese nationalism?' Immediately identifying with the goals of imperial domination Amery said 'Our whole policy in India, our whole policy in Egypt, stand condemned if we condemn Japan.' At that time Churchill saw the same parallels: 'China was in the same state that India would fall into if the guiding hand of Britain was withdrawn', and he certainly was not going to 'wantonly throw away our old and valued friendship with Japan' by protesting against the incursion, but rather thought that 'it was in the interests of the whole world that law and order should be established in the northern part of China'.[2] Britain identified with Japanese conquests in China, but it was a different matter when they threatened the British Empire.

In December 1941 and early 1942 the Japanese swept through Hong Kong, Malaya, the Philippines, Burma, Indonesia, the Solomon Islands and New Guinea. The Japanese encouraged the formation of youth groups, student groups and other associations – often with a paramilitary flavour. While Dutch and English were banned,

Burmese, Malay and Tagalog were encouraged.[3]

'Japanese Inspired Fifth Columns'

Just before the war, Japan sent around a thousand intelligence agents disguised as diplomats, journalists and businessmen all across Southeast Asia, among them Major Fujiwara Iwaichi and Colonel Suzuki Keiji. These two led the intelligence groups 'Fujiwara Kikan' (Fujiwara Agency) and Minami Kikan (Southern Agency) respectively. The Fujiwara Kikan brought together nationalists in Thailand and Malaya with the Japanese, while the Minami Kikan did the same in Burma. In the Dutch East Indies, Lieutenant Yanagawa Munenari helped organise the Army of Defenders of the Homeland – Sukarela Tentara Pembela Tanah Air, or Peta, for short. The policy had been developed by Research Bureau of the South Manchuria Railway – one of many political think tanks working between the wars.[4] The Imperial General Headquarters Continental Directive of June 1942 instructed the Southern Army: 'in important parts of the Southern Theatre, in order to facilitate the execution of new duties, we will train necessary armed groups'. British India Command Dispatches referred to 'JIFs': Japanese-Inspired Fifth Columns to belittle their native support.[5]

Burma

Kokubu Shōzō an ex-navy man who had lived in Burma for 19 years (he published a two-volume history of the country in 1944) kept up his interest in the navy, as did the South Seas Association of Konishi Takehiko. Another policy group, the National Policy Research Institute's Nationality Question Committee wrote up a report 'Measures to be taken towards the people of East Asia – Measures for Burma', which proposed that 'the purpose is to free Burma, as part of the Greater East Asia Co-Prosperity Sphere, from the fetters of British Imperialism as soon as possible'.[6] On the 15th of November 1941 the Prime Minister, Foreign Minister, Army and Navy Ministers and Chiefs of Staff at the Imperial General Headquarters Government Liaison Conference decided that 'the independence of Burma will be promoted and this will be used to stimulate the independence of India'. Five days later, at the same conference, the same political and military leaders qualified themselves, saying that they needed to 'lead and encourage the native peoples to have a deep appreciation and trust for the imperial army and to avoid any action that may stimulate unduly or induce an early independence movement'.[7]

Still, Britain's promises to Burma were a lot less attractive: 'At the moment, Burma's great value to the democratic powers lies in its unequaled position as a base from which to launch a flank attack upon the Japanese in Thailand and Malaysia', reported the *Far Eastern Survey*: 'Moreover, Rangoon has the advantage of ample supplies of aviation petrol refined in the great Syriam works of the Burma Oil Company.' Burmese Premier U Saw was refused independence, and said 'discussions with Prime Minister Churchill have not fulfilled the high hopes of my countrymen'. The rules of diplomacy were tossed aside and U Saw was arrested, accused of aiding Japan, and exiled to Uganda for the rest of the war.[8]

Already, in 1940, the intelligence officer Suzuki had identified Aung San, a leader of the radical nationalist youth movement, the Thakins, or Dobama Asiayone ('We Burmans Association'). Aung San had been at the Indian National Congress that year and formed his own Burma Revolutionary Party (actually a faction working within the Thakins). Suzuki was worried that the Burmese nationalists would make links with the USSR or China. Suzuki also made secret links with politician Ba Maw who at that time was a part of the British administration. After Suzuki helped him hide from British search parties Aung San agreed to bring fellow Thakins to a Japanese Naval Training Camp at Samah on Hainan Island. 'The Thirty' learned military strategy, drill, and to use machine guns, grenades howitzers.[9] More recruitment grew the team to 200.

Iida Shōjirō, General in charge of the 25th Army that crossed through Thailand into Burma announced on 22 January 1942 'the aim of the Burmese advance of the Japanese Army is to sweep aside British power which has been exploiting you and oppressing you for a hundred years and to liberate all Burmese people and support your aspirations for independence'. Suzuki's Burmese recruits – reformed as the Burma Independence Army in December 1941 took part in the invasion, going ahead of the Japanese troops, until their numbers were swelled to 12,000 by enthusiastic villagers. It was in fact a revolution against British rule, under the cover of the Japanese invasion. Put to the test the Governor's rule failed, as the British settlers' servants fled. Dorman-Smith learned to his amazement that without someone to carry away the shit – 'that lowest of all human beings, who holds in his hands the difference between health and disease, cleanliness and filth' – the colonists were helpless. With all authority ebbing away, the Governor looked for help but found that after half a century under British rule 'there were no representatives of labour I can call into consultation', 'there are no responsible trade unions'.[10] The Allies further damaged their support amongst Burmese by bringing in a Chinese army from the Kuomintang under US Commander Joe Stilwell – raising fears that China's historic claim on northern Burma would be revived.

'The BIA became the effective government away from the Japanese gaze',[11] and provisional committees were set up. Suzuki overstepped his brief by setting up a local Burmese administration led by Tun Oke, who had been one of the Thirty. The BIA continued to grow, till it was 200 000 strong. Thakin rule in the villages was a source of great pride to Burmese, but the Karen and other minorities who had been favoured by the British (to stymie majority rule) were persecuted, less by the Japanese than the BIA.

Clashes between the BIA and the Japanese Kempeitai led the Southern Army HQ to disband the Minami Kikan. A more pliable Ba Maw was made head of the Burmese government, and Aung San was told to disband the BIA in favour of a more regular and slimmed down Burmese Defence Army, which he did early in 1942. The Defence Army was supposed to be just 2-5000, and Japanese trained, but in rivalry with Ba Maw's administration, Aung San recruited more and more people to the BDA so that it too blossomed and by April 1943 it was 55,000 strong. In 1943 Japan declared independence for Burma and the Philippines – as the Japanese advance was faltering.[12] But on the ground, Aung San's supporters were already bristling at the casual brutality of the Japanese. Aung San opened secret negotiations with Britain in preparation for a second liberation struggle. Looking back General Iida regretted that 'Burmese independence was only used as a means for carrying out Japan's war', and that Japan had only replaced Britain as the imperial power.[13]

Meanwhile, the British High Command needed to show that it

would soon be back in charge in Burma. To this end the 'Chindits' – the 77th Indian Brigade under Brigadier General Orde Wingate launched a series of raids aggrandised as the 'Chindit War'. Wingate planned to get behind Japanese lines using air drops for supplies. In February 1943 the Chindits pressed into Burma to sabotage two railway lines. One was cut, but it did not take long to repair. Wingate's forces were scattered and had to make their own way back to India in small bands, the journeys taking many months. By any tactical assessment the raid would be called a failure, but it was lauded in the British presses, desperate for some good news, and to shore up Britain's standing in the east. A second Chindit expedition to infiltrate with gliders ended when Wingate was killed crashing his into the side of a mountain on 25 March 1944.[14]

Malaysia and Singapore

Guy Wint, who served with the British forces in Asia, bemoaned the 'local Malay population, giving a lead to other colonial communities of the empire, regarded it as politic to transfer their loyalties as quickly as possible to the Japanese'. [15] Major Fujiwara Iwaichi made links with the Malay Youth League, and the local leader Tani Yutaka, called Harimau, the son of a Japanese shop keeper. Anti-Chinese campaigns were popular with the Malays, who resented the traders settled among them. Quickly, the Japanese troops passed through the Malaya peninsula down towards the 'Fortress' Singapore.

Churchill had already written off Singapore, but committed his forces of occupation to a scorched earth policy of destruction, as he made clear in a telegraph to General Wavell on 20 January 1942:

> I want to make it absolutely clear that I expect every inch of ground to be defended, every scrap of material or defences to be blown to pieces to prevent capture by the enemy and no question of surrender to be entertained until after protracted fighting among the ruins of Singapore City.[16]

Bridges, roads, rubber factories and plantations were burned and blown up ahead of the Japanese advance. London was angry that Dorman-Smith had let so much of Burmese industry fall into Japanese hands.[17] In British eyes these were British possessions,

THEIR USE WAS DENIED TO THE INVADER
As far as the swift advance of the Japanese would allow, factories, mines, and other industrial plants were destroyed in the enemy's path. Left, a blazing rubber factory near Kuala Lumpur. Right, a fine steel bridge in the same region is prepared by Indian sappers to receive the explosive charges that will bring its spans crashing down.
Photos, British Official: Crown Copyright

though of course they had been built up with native labour, and paid for through native taxation and industry. The scorched earth policy and the war would cause the region hardship for years to come, and in India, it would set off a disaster.

On 10 February 1942 Churchill sent another telegram to Wavell, even more rabid than the last:

> There must at this stage be no thought of saving the troops or sparing the population. The battle must be fought to the bitter end and at all costs ... Commanders and senior officers should die with their troops. The honour of the British Empire and the British Army was at stake.[18]

Churchill's commitment to Singapore was qualified. He had already told Averell Harriman that he would have given up the colony if that was the cost of America's entry into the war.[19] After the attack on Pearl Harbour America's support was no longer an issue, so Churchill demanded that troops fight to the bitter end, whatever the cost in civilian lives, to save, not Singapore, but the honour of the Empire. However, the speed of the Japanese advance on Singapore unnerved the British commanders, whose resistance collapsed. The Japanese sent pictures of Lieutenant General Arthur Percival's surrender around the world. The defeat was all the more disgraceful since General Yamashita's attack was an audacious bluff – his forces were 30,000 and out of ammunition, while 85,000 British and Commonwealth troops surrendered. Percival agreed to station 1000

British troops in the town centre to keep order while the Japanese took over. Elsewhere it was the Allied troops own discipline that broke down, as they looted and rioted, turned their guns on their officers and fought over the few places on boats out. British reports blamed the Australian troops for the 'bestial' behaviour and breakdown in order. Australian General Gordon Bennett who escaped to Sydney defended himself against charges of desertion, in a number of trials, so that his name became slang for an unlikely escape.[20]

The British troops abandoned their allies among Malays and Chinese, forcing them off the boats leaving Singapore. 'I will never help the British again' vowed local Kuomintang leader Lim Bo Seng. Under the light of the invasion the British Empire's white supremacy was thrown into relief.[21] The officials in charge of the evacuation of Burma got the white Europeans out before the other for the darker races, Indians, Anglo-Indians and Burmese. The non-whites were held back in transit camps while transport for the whites was sorted out. The two races were marched along separate routes, a 'white road' and a 'black road' – though the Europeans did have Naga tribesmen to act as coolies. Without supplies, medicine or much in the way of transport, thousands of the less favoured died of hunger and disease. Jawaharlal Nehru of the Indian National Congress went to meet the refugees as they finally arrived in Assam, and told the world about the colour bar operating in the British evacuation.[22]

According to F.C. Jones of the Royal Institute of International Affairs:

> The Japanese ensured that the old order of Western political domination could never return. But they did more than this. They attacked not only Western rule in Asia, but the whole Occidental way of life.[23]

In the ruins of Singapore, the Japanese army set about sorting through the Chinese that the British had left behind. They were screened and thousands were killed in the 'cleansing' of the Sook Ching, between 18 February and 4 March 1942. At the post war trials of the Japanese the numbers killed were put at 5000, though

Singapore's Chinese leaders put the number far higher – as high as 50,000. The Japanese military saw the Chinese in East Asia as hostile – but they did not see everyone that way.

The Indian National Army

Of the surrendered Commonwealth troops most, 50,000, were from the British-Indian Army. On 17 February they were corralled into the Farrer Park Race Course, expecting the worst. An Indian officer translated Major Fujiwara's address, which opened with the words 'Beloved Indian soldiers!' As Fujiwara promised to back Indian independence, the troops broke out into wild cheers.

> We hope you will join the Indian National Army. The Japanese Army will not treat you as prisoners, but as friends. We will recognise your struggle for freedom and give you all-out assistance.[24]

On that day more than half of those Indian troops – 42,000 of them according to one count – who had until then been under British command, joined the Indian National Army.

The Indian National Army had been formed by Captain Mohan Singh on 1 January 1942. Taken prisoner at Alor Star in December 1941, Singh was made the officer commanding by a wounded Lieutenant Colonel Fitzpatrick. Singh agreed to help the Japanese restore order after Indians and Malays had attacked Chinese shops, for which he came to the attention of Major Fujiwara. Fujiwara introduced him to Lt. General Yamashita of the 25th Army, and they agreed to form an Indian Army fighting against the British, alongside the Japanese. Two companies of the Indian National Army, under Captain Allah Ditta, joined the battle to take Singapore. With the recruitment of the surrendered British-Indian army at Singapore, the Indian National Army had become a real force. The large expatriate Indian communities in East Asia sent delegates to a conference in Tokyo on 28 March 1942, led by the exiled nationalist and Japanophile Resh Behari Bose, which announced the formation of an Indian Independence League. 'Without the liberation of India', Prime Minister Hideki Tōjō told the Japanese Diet, 'there can be no real mutual prosperity in Greater East Asia'. Another conference in

June gathered enthusiastic support from the Indian diaspora in East Asia. Chairman Rash Behari Bose warned 'the octopus grip of the Anglo-Saxon imperialism in the east must be destroyed, root and branch'.[25] As we shall see, in India proper, the Indian National Congress was harshly suppressed by the British, and though its leaders were unhappy with the pro-Japanese INA and IIL they were in no position to stop it.

Over time, the Indian National Army under Mohan Singh began to feel that it was being used. Singh and other officers were overheard complaining, and the Japanese arrested them. Without Singh at its head, the INA more or less collapsed. But the army got a second lease of life with the arrival of the radical Congress leader Subhas Chandra Bose in Tokyo on 2 May 1943. Bose had been elected the chairman of the Indian National Congress in 1938, but broke with Gandhi calling for a more confrontational policy. Bose left India to escape his trial for sedition set for 26 January 1941. In Europe he sought help from the Axis leaders, though both Ribbentrop and Ciano refused to back an Indian nationalist challenge to the British Empire (Goebbels on the other hand, helped Bose set up the Azad Hind Radio). Seeing the damage Japan was doing to the British Empire in the east, Bose argued hard with his German sponsors to be allowed to leave. In June 1943 he talked a now sceptical Tōjō around once again to the appeal of an Indian independence movement.

Arriving in Singapore on 2 July 1943, Bose was garlanded by the Indian diaspora, who gathered up their small funds of money, family gold and jewellery into a great fund for the re-born INA. Taking over from Rash Behari Bose's Indian Independence League, Subhas Chandra Bose announced a Provisional Indian Government – Azad Hind – founded on 4 July. Bose had got Tōjō's promise that Japan would give 'unconditional help to the Indian Independence movement' – which cause he pledged himself to once more in the Japanese Diet on 16 June 1943. 'We shall have to be awake and alive, on our guard, not only against the enemy British imperialism' Bose told a journalist, but also 'against imperialistically inclined Japanese bureaucrats'.[26] Among Bose's troops were a women's regiment, 1000-strong, led by Dr Lakshmi Swaminathan, and named after the Rani of Jhansi. Under the slogans 'To Delhi!' and 'Jai Hind', Subhas Chandra Bose rallied the INA. His hope was that once the INA attacked British positions on Indian soil 'a revolution will break out not only among the civil population at home, but among the Indian Army which is now standing under the British flag'.[27] Nor were these hopes fanciful as Britain's dicta-torship over India began to sway and captured troops deserted to the INA. Ian Stephens, editor of the Calcutta Statesman thought that all Bose would have to do was to parachute into Bengal and 90 per cent of the population would rise up and follow him.[28] On 29 December 1943, the Japanese handed over offices on the Andaman Islands in the Bay of Bengal that they had captured the previous March to the Provisional Government, so that Bose could rule over liberated Indian territory.

Subhas Chandra Bose

The Indian National Army went on to fight in the pivotal battle of the war in the Far East, at Imphal in 1944, alongside the Japanese Army, with the aim of capturing territory in north-eastern India, and in June of that year the Shah Nawaz Regiment did get to the South of Kohima, crossing the border into Assam on 6 April 1944, though they were forced back shortly afterwards. Tensions between the Japanese and the INA ran high as Shah Nawaz thought that he was being denied a full combat role. No doubt that was true, but there were also commanders who believed in the INA's mission, like Lt. General Masakazu Kawabe, who looked on the approaching defeat with despair.

> So long as there remains any step to take we must persevere. The fate of both Japan and India depends on this operation. I said to myself that I would commit double suicide with Bose.[29]

At Imphal the INA casualties were 20,000 of a force of 40,000, and 1500 were captured. Tōjō ordered the retreat on 8 July 1944, and the course of the Indian National Army in the field was from that point on one of retreat. Later, though, the INA would play a pivotal role in the political struggle for India's freedom.

The Philippines

As an American dependency, and one that had been promised self-government, the Philippines were less open to Japanese appeals to revolt. But nor was the recently-elected ruling council that committed to becoming part of America's Pacific War.

When President Manuel Quezon made US General Douglas MacArthur Field Marshall and founder of the Philippine Army, he was giving a nod to the country's sponsor: thirty-five years before MacArthur's father had been Governor General. The outgoing Governor General Frank Murphy warned that under General Douglas MacArthur the country was being 'militarised' and with the US sanctions making war likely, the Japanese saw the Philippines as a dagger to their throats.[30] In 1941, Roosevelt had the Philippine Army once more placed under formal US command, though MacArthur had an independence that grated Washington. In the event, MacArthur's battle plan to confront any Japanese invasion force on the beach were hopelessly out-dated, and the Japanese destroyed the entire US air force in the Philippines as they lay idle at Clark Air Base and the Cavite Naval Base south of Manila. 'I just don't know how MacArthur happened to let his planes get caught on the ground', said General George C. Marshall.[31]

Roosevelt promised back-up, cabling to Quezon that 'Every vessel available is bearing ... the strength that will eventually crush the enemy,' but those promises were empty. 'ROOSEVELT REASSURES THE GALLANT FILIPINOS' headlined the *New York Times*. The US – British Joint Basic War Plan 'Rainbow Five', adopted by Roosevelt's Army-Navy Joint Board set out the goals of concentrating all resources against Germany and Italy ('Europe First'). 'Strategy in the Far East will be defensive' because 'the United States does not intend to add to its present military strength' there.[32] As the truth sank in that there was no help coming President Quezon tried to pull out of the war: 'We must try to save ourselves and to hell with America', he told Carlos Romulo: 'the fight between the United State and Japan is not our fight'. MacArthur cabled the State Department that 'the temper of the Filipinos is one of almost violent resentment against the United States'. War Secretary Henry Stimson, Army Chief George Marshall and Roosevelt looked over Quezon's plea for neutrality and refused it on the grounds – finally admitted – that the

Philippines was not an independent country but a *possession* of the United States. Marshall said that the key question was moral: 'it was a part of the necessary tragedy of war that this moral issue must be met by a command to other men to die'. MacArthur was told to prepare his forces to hold out as long 'as humanly possible'.[33]

The United States Armed Forces in the Far East retreated along the Bataan Peninsula. They left Manila after destroying ten million gallons of gasoline and tons of food that they did not have the means to take with them. Their equipment was poor, without helmets, and with canvas shoes – 'there was no Philippine army to speak of' Eisenhower, then MacArthur's second-in-command, admitted on the eve of the war. Food stocks in Bataan were twenty days' worth of rice and forty of meat and fish. All the troops were put on half rations. Filipino and American troops (of whom there were 20,000) in the US Army Force Far East (USAFFE) forces were used to being treated differently – the Americans were paid $30 a month, a Filipino $7. In Bataan, the American troops were mostly held in reserve while the Filipinos were on the front line. On capture, the differences in nutrition told: of 50,000 interned by the Japanese more than half, 26,000 died, while of 9000 Americans one sixth died. According to MacArthur's press releases the USAFFE was 'greatly outnumbered', but in fact there were 50,000 Japanese troops on Bataan and 70,000 USAFFE.[34] Hiding in the underground tunnels in the Island of Corrigedor MacArthur was called 'Dugout Doug' by his troops.

As defeat loomed, MacArthur left, issuing the statement, 'I shall return'. The Office of War Information wanted it to read 'We shall return', but MacArthur got his way and it became a key slogan in Pacific War propaganda, and in the MacArthur cult. Quezon awarded MacArthur an honorarium of half a million dollars and a promise of his old job back after the war.[35] In Sydney MacArthur received a telegram from the officer he left in charge, Major-General Jonathan Wainwright, 'tell Quezon and MacArthur we have done our best', asking permission to surrender. MacArthur cabled back that he should prepare an attack with the last of his starving men. To Washington MacArthur cabled 'it is of course possible that with my departure the vigor of application of conservation may have been relaxed'.[36]

The Japanese had no trouble finding willing collaborators among the Filipino elite. With Attorney General José Laurel at its head, the new government was 'led by the capital's pre-war elite – the General's friends and Quezon's colleagues'. At first MacArthur was outraged saying that on return 'it shall be my firm purpose to run to ground every disloyal Filipino who has debased his country's cause'. Over time, though, Quezon nagged and pleaded with MacArthur to sympathise with the collaborators who were 'virtually prisoners of the enemy'. While Harold Ickes kept up the pressure for punitive action, MacArthur changed his tune insisting that there was 'no prima facie case of treason' where a man had accepted duties under the Japanese.[37]

Indonesia

In Indonesia, nationalists formed Freedom Committees in many towns in Java and Sumatra, and offered to help the Japanese armed forces.[38] The Imperial Navy occupying Indonesia and its outer Islands, with allies in the Imperial General Headquarters and in the 25th Army in Sumatra, were banking on a 'permanent possession of part or all of Indonesia'.[39] On the other hand, there were only 10,000 troops occupying the whole of Indonesia so Imperial army had little choice but to rely on locally recruited supporters, like Peta.

The Failure of the Co-Prosperity Sphere

At the point that Japan took over the co-prosperity sphere, its domestic economy was given over to war production, bringing a halt to its role as supplier of manufactured consumer goods to the region.[40] Militarism used up industrial foundations of cooperation. In June 1943, Lieutenant General Inada Masazumi, Deputy Chief of the Southern Army toured South East Asia and concluded that the Japanese Army would be crippled by manpower shortages if locals were not recruited.[41] Without resources to trade the Japanese leant more and more on violence to control the native populations and force them to toil. In the Philippines the 'death march' of prisoners from Bataan fed national hostility to the Japanese invader.

Some 14,000 allied prisoners of war died building the Burma railway as slaves of the Japanese. Ten or twenty times that number of Burmese, Indians, Chinese and Malays died.[42] The 'Co-Prosperity

Sphere' was already waging war against the Chinese and subjugating the Koreans. Despite their ongoing war against each other, the Kuomintang and the more radical Communists under Mao were costing the Japanese dear. In Malaya and the Philippines People's Armies were organising against the occupation, as they would shortly in Korea and Vietnam. Under the pressure of economic failure it began to clash with the self-same national forces that they had used to take on the British Empire – most pointedly in Burma.

Chapter Nineteen

Quit India

On 3 September 1939 Governor General the Marquess of Linlithgow declared war on Germany for India, without asking any of the elected Indian representatives.

The younger Congress leaders, most importantly Jawaharlal Nehru had close ties to the British Labour Party, and believed in the war against Fascism. On 14 September 1939 they put out a call to

the British Government to declare in unequivocal terms what their war aims are in regard to democracy and imperialism and the new order that is envisaged, in particular how these aims are going to apply to India ... Do they include the elimination of imperialism and the treatment of India as a free nation ...?

Nehru's plea was 'that India should play her full part and throw all her resources into the struggle for a new order'.[1]

The British declined, and Congress withdrew from elected government.

Gandhi cautioned Nehru that it was less important to fight in the war than he thought, drawing on a story from the Mahabhatra:

The warring nations are destroying themselves with such fury and ferocity that the end will be mutual exhaustion ... And out of this holocaust must arise a new order for which the exploited millions have so long thirsted.[2]

In February 1940, the Marquess of Zetland, Secretary for State for India said to the British Cabinet that they might think of making the colony self-governing after the war. Churchill was adamantly against, saying that they should aim to keep the colony quiet for the duration. He did not agree with those who wanted 'to promote unity among Hindu and Muslim communities', whose 'immediate result would be that the united communities would join in showing us the door'. He saw 'the Hindu-Muslim feud as the bulwark of British rule in India'.[3] The policy of divide and rule was well-established. In 1905 Viceroy Lord Curzon had tried to divide Bengal into two parts, one mostly Muslim, the other mostly Hindu, saying 'one of our main objects is to split up and thereby weaken a solid body of opponents to our rule'. At Curzon's invitation, the All-India Muslim League was founded as a sectarian rival to the all-Indian Congress Party in 1906.[4] After the war, these divisions would lead to disaster.

In 1941 the Congress began a series of speeches against the Empire that led to the arrest of many of its leaders, including Nehru, sentenced to four years in November. Soon after, though, Viceroy Linlithgow released the Congress leaders.

Cripps crept into the crypt...

In March 1942 Richard Stafford Cripps, the independent Socialist MP was sent to negotiate terms with Congress, offering everything but self-government. Cripps mission was from the outset not serious, but a ploy by Churchill to avoid pressure from critics in his own cabinet and from President Roosevelt for a more liberal policy in India. Churchill told Leo Amery, the Secretary of State for India that 'it was just because Cripps was of the left that it would be much easier for him to carry through what is essentially a pro-Muslim and reasonably Conservative policy'. Having stayed at Cripps' country house, Filkins, when he was in England in 1938, Nehru was optimistic about what the mission held out, but on that score he was naïve. Cripps included the fatal clause 'the option that any province not wishing to accede to the new Constitution stand out'. That was a green light to the Muslim League to threaten to divide India and secede as the independent Muslim state of Pakistan (meaning nation of the pure). More, Cripps was told by the War Cabinet in a telegram on 6 April that the special powers of the Viceroy must be preserved. Gandhi understood that the opt-out clause meant the end of India – the Congress leaders were keen students of Britain's colonial history and knew well how the partition of Ireland had wrecked the movement for freedom there. 'I would advise you to take the next plane home', Gandhi told Cripps. The offer was 'a post-dated cheque' he told journalists (one of whom made the quote stronger by adding 'on a failing bank'). Cripps knew, said Gandhi, that the proposal contemplated the splitting up of India into three parts'

Churchill was thrilled that the mission had failed, as he had always planned, and danced a jig around the Cabinet room. Cripps had done the right thing, and better still for Churchill, he put the blame onto Gandhi for the failure of the mission.[5]

Bertolt Brecht following the story thought it would be a good play:

The red lord, India's friend, arrives. Then the old clichés of Colonel Blimp issue from his mouth. And the Red Lord returns to London town, insulted because the 'disunified' Indians refuse to take anything from so friendly a hand.[6]

In parliament, the pacifist James Maxton broke through the wall of silence surrounding the issue:

If the Indian people as a mass have no intention of fighting in this war, they will not do it. Surely if you have learned anything in this war, you have learned that. ...You could not get Malaya to fight. You could not get Burma to fight. ... Do not delude yourselves that you can trick 400,000,000 people on to the battle-field.[7]

Quit India

After the false promise of the Cripps Mission Congress girded itself for an all-out struggle against British rule. Gandhi told The Harijan of 26 April 1942

Whatever the consequences, therefore, to India, her real safety and of Britain's too, lie in orderly and timely British withdrawal from India. All talk of treaties with princes and obligations towards minorities are a British creation designed for the preservation of the British rule and British interest.[8]

On 14 July Congress passed a resolution calling on Britain to withdraw from India, reaffirmed at a further Congress in Bombay on 8 August - 'Quit India!', as it was contracted in the protests that followed.

The British Cabinet leapt on the chance to finally attack the

Congress movement head on. The Congress leaders, Gandhi, Nehru and scores of others were thrown in jail in August 1942, and Gandhi would not be released until 6 May 1944. While Indian troops were still being taken out of the country, white British troops were being sent in – by May 1943 105 battalions were taken up with the crackdown. One of the British soldiers, Clive Branson, was convinced that the British had provoked the rebellion for the 'long-sought opportunity to smash the nationalist movement'. Protests followed the jailing of the Gandhi and Nehru. Leo Amery accused the Congress leaders of sabotaging the war effort in a BBC broadcast – but then the War Cabinet had agreed back in 1940 that 'if conflict with Congress should arise, it should appear as an outcome of war necessity, rather than as a political quarrel unrelated to the war'. The British response was barbaric. Protestors were gunned down in the street. A contemporary report put the numbers killed at 940 – but later estimates put the numbers killed over all at as many as ten times that. In Bihar hundreds were killed when planes strafed protestors. On 9 August 1942 the fighting cost the lives of scores of Indians and nine British officers. In retaliation there were hundreds of arrests and beatings, and nine prisoners were taken in Chimur and six at Ashti, and sentenced to death. In the first wave 60,222 protestors were arrested and 18,000 jailed under the Defence of India Rules. The total eventually jailed rose as high as 90,000. In an orgy of sadistic brutality the British forces got an Emergency Whipping Act passed into law.[9]

The British government had some excellent advice on how to deal with Congress. In 1938 Adolf Hitler told Lord Halifax (himself a former Viceroy of India):

> Shoot Gandhi, and if this doesn't suffice to reduce them to submission, shoot a dozen leading members of Congress; and if that doesn't suffice, shoot 200 and so on until order is established.[10]

Gunning down the protestors was in the end what the British did, though having already jailed the Congress leaders, they were saved summary execution. Still, Britain's jails were harsh. Gandhi's wife Kasturba died in prison in Pune in his arms. Nehru's brother in law

Pandit Ranjit died in jail, as did Gandhi's Secretary Mahadev Desai and scores of others.

In Parliament the Independent Labour MP for Camlachie Campbell Stephen spoke out

> What is the position in India to-day? Thousands of the most trusted and loved leaders of the Indian people are in gaol. They are under detention, in concentration camps, shut up, and along with the imprisonment of thousands of leaders, the people are under a reign of terror. ..there are the flogging and machine-gunning of people in case of rioting, and collective fines are being imposed. Where is this happening? ... Exactly what you condemn in Norway under the Hitler régime is what the British Government are doing in India.[11]

Starving India

The British Prime Minister made no secret of his feelings: 'I hate Indians,' he told Leo Amery: 'They are a beastly people with a beastly religion.'[12] Churchill's hostility to natives was ingrained, but in the case of India it was well-honed on the resentment of a parasitic imperial power.

The historic relation between the occupying power Britain and the colony was skewed so that India's trade was always disadvantaged, through onerous taxation and discriminatory trade controls. India was forced to trade low value basics for much higher value produced goods. Throughout the history of the Raj, income flowed from India to Britain, and the colony was forever in Britain's debt. Churchill reckoned that one third of the British population were sustained by profits made in India. With the war, the Cabinet made sure that as much of the Indian economy could be given over to war production as possible. Said Viceroy Linlithgow:

> My whole conception is that of India humming from end to end with activity in munitions and supply production and at the same time with the bustle of men training for active service of one sort or another, the first operation largely paying for cost of the second.[13]

The British-Indian Army put nearly as many men into the field as the British, more than two million by the end of the war, with recruitment running at its high point at 50,000 a day. Those troops were the backbone of the British war effort in Iran and Iraq, as well as playing a major part in North Africa and the re-conquest of the east. Under the agreement those men who were not directly defending India were paid for by the British government, with credits to be paid for after the war ended. All in all India was the greatest single contributor to the British war effort after Britain herself, giving up £2 billion in goods and services. Indian manufacturers made munitions and supplies for the troops, while her farmers gave up grain to feed the rest of the Empire.

Historians like Niall Ferguson have resisted the comparison between Britain's occupation of India and Nazi rule in the east, but it was current at the time. Leo Amery referred to Churchill's 'Hitler-like' policy for India. 'The Russian space is our India', said Hitler. 'Like the English, we shall rule this Empire with a handful of men.' His favourite film was the 1935 Hollywood production Lives of the Bengal Lancers.[14]

Over time the impact on the Indian economy was severe. Like the Japanese 'Co-Prosperity Sphere' the imperial power was demanding more in basic goods, just as it was redirecting its own production away from manufactured goods towards armaments. Rice, cotton and manufactures were leaving, but nothing was coming in. On top of that, the British authorities' purchasing on credit was bidding up the prices of the dwindling stock of goods – a dangerous spiral of inflation. The Congress resolution of 8 August 1942 launching the Quit India campaign carried the complaint that Britain was 'degrading and enfeebling India'. It was a warning of what was to come.

At the same time as denuding India of goods, the British exchequer was accumulating debts to India that reversed the historic relation, and laid bare the true dependence of the metropolitan power on its colonial hinterland. Churchill's anger against those he called 'Baboos' and 'money lenders' got worse as the war went on. Late in 1942 Churchill demanded that the Indians be presented with a counter-claim for the cost of defending India against the growing debt. The two questions of Indian loyalty and the Indian claim on future income were bound together in his mind: 'Are we to incur hundreds of millions of debt for defending India only to be kicked out by the Indians afterwards?'[15]

Rice Denial

Though Churchill was drawing up the bill, the British had no intention of defending India. That was what Field Marshall and later Viceroy Archibald Wavell told Roosevelt's envoy Louis Johnson. [16] From the Japanese advance they had learned that their colonial subjects had no loyalty to the Crown, and apart from the Chinese, would take the opportunity of an invasion to rid themselves of the British Empire. When General Claude Auchinleck asked for tanks for the Indian Army the Prime Minister asked 'but General, how do you know that they wouldn't turn and fire the wrong way'.[17]

With the progress of the Japanese Army towards the borders of Bengal – alongside the battalions of the Indian National Army led by Subhas Chandra Bose – the British were panic-stricken at the fear that Bengali saboteurs and provocateurs – the 'Fifth Column in India' – could 'gravely impair the efficiency of Indian defence'.[18] And so it was, at that crucial moment in the war, that the British forces attacked, not the Japanese, but their own colonial subjects, the people of Bengal.

The policy they adopted was 'Rice Denial'. This was the same scorched earth policy that Churchill had demanded of Dorman-Smith in Burma and of Wavell in Singapore, except that this time they would follow it through. The authorities planned first to impose the policy across Bengal, but then re-thought and restricted it to a strip twenty-five miles in from the coast – which meant that the brunt was borne largely by Hindus, and much less so by Muslims.

The essence of the policy was that rice stores in the countryside would be seized or destroyed. The pretext was that they were being denied to the invading Japanese forces, but in fact it was the disloyal Bengali civilians who were being punished. If resources could not burned or blown up 'dumping in the sea will suffice'. As well as destroying rice, troops and police were sent to destroy the boats that, in that low-lying delta were the only transport. Wavell was not sure, but Amery cabled him on 27 March 1942 'it is essential that destruction should be ruthless and should achieve without fail total denial of such resources as would assist enemy operation'. Wavell, who had been humiliated by Churchill for letting the Japanese take Singapore was not going to fail a second time. More than 40,000 boats, two thirds of the total registered, were wrecked. Nearly ten thousand bicycles were taken from the Bengali town of Midnapore.

British historians talk about the Bengal Famine today as if it was a natural thing, and as if it was wholly unrelated either to the war or to the British campaign against Congress. It 'began with a cyclone and the loss of imports from Japanese-occupied Burma, not with an order from Churchill to starve Bengalis'.[19] There was a cyclone, and there was a loss of imports from Burma, but the cause of the famine was an order from Churchill to starve the Bengalis, the order was called the Rice Denial policy.

The truth was that Bengal was already at the point of collapse before the Rice Denial policy was put in place. As the British war effort sucked resources out of India, the country was close to starvation. While the Bengalis were being robbed of their rice, many different authorities were buying up what few stores were left in the country. The Civil Supplies Department was buying rice for the war effort, as were the Bengal Chamber of Commerce, the railways, the Government of India and the army. Prices doubled in days, and carried on rising. All the time government agents were buying up rice to store it in warehouses. In 1942 Bengal was made to export 185,000 tons of rice to Ceylon, the British Army in North Africa, and Britain itself, to make up the shortfall created by the loss of Burma. Ceylon was particularly important because after the loss of Malaya, it was the Empire's only source of rubber. Linlithgow told Chief Minister Hug in January of 1943 that he 'simply must produce some rice out of Bengal for Ceylon even if Bengal itself went hungry'. Over and again the War Cabinet had been warned of the impending famine – by Sir Jeremy Raisman in August 1942, by Lord Linlithgow from the beginning of 1943. Linlithgow was desperate by March, but Churchill was adamant that 'they must learn to look after themselves as we have done'.[20] Churchill was advised by Lord Cherwell, who, as we have seen, applied Malthusian logic to the question of Indian hunger: 'In my view the Indians have got themselves into a mess very largely through their own fault'.[21]

The impending famine, though, had nothing to do with India's population, which far from being a drain on resources was the source of the surplus that was paying for Britain's war effort. It was Britain's requisitioning – and its wanton destruction – of the Indians' food and resources that caused the famine. That plunder was not incidental to the war, it was caused by the war; and the destruction was the policy that Britain pursued to crush those they feared would become India's Fifth Column, the population of West Bengal. Already in 1942 Sir John Herbert was ordering the removal of 'excess rice from the three districts within 24 hours', while others reported thousands of tons of rice being destroyed.

Rice Denial was a policy closely tied up with the plan to crush resistance in India. In September 1942 police occupied Midnapore District to smash pro-Congress protestors. The District Magistrate ordered that relief should be withheld until the 'disaffected villages' give 'an undertaking that they will take no further part in any subversive movement'. Police burned down huts and destroyed rice in those villages. When distribution centres were set up, villagers complained that police followed them home and smashed pots and trampled on the cooked food. The following January hundreds of soldiers and police occupied the village of Masuria, beating men and raping 46 women. 'The war has to be won and the Congress rebellion kept under', explained Sir John Herbert.[22]

Once the famine took hold around three and a half million Bengalis died. As the death toll mounted, the authorities went from denial, to bluster, to eventually demanding control over the relief effort.

According to the authorities the answer to the Bengal Famine was that the government needed to take control of the rice and distribute it. But Indians fiercely resisted the British-backed authorities' attempts to requisition rice for famine relief. They set up their own Relief Committees like those run by Shyama Prasad Mukherjee, who called on cultivators not to sell to government agents, saying 'the bureaucracy has taken away the food for the army and for exports'.[23]

Subhas Chandra Bose, with the support of the Burman leader Ba Maw, offered to give Bengal Burmese rice – that was only days away across the border – through the Red Cross. Indeed Bose's supporters in India were already active in Mukherjee's Relief Committees distributing rice which the British were trying to grab for themselves.[24] The British authorities dismissed Bose's offer out of hand, preferring to see India starve than British rule exposed.

Chapter Twenty

The Revolt Against the War

As each of the belligerent powers pushed their people to work harder for victory, a growing revolt against the war effort began to build up. This was the hidden class war that was being fought beneath the official war between the Axis and Allied powers. These were the grounds on which all of the elites that were fighting each other were secretly united, in their hostility to their own peoples. In the factories, on the streets and amongst the troops, a revolt against the war was slowly emerging. Opposition to the war effort often started because of the onerous 'sacrifices' forced upon the ordinary people by elites. But because of the militarisation of society, any industrial dispute or protest was taken to be a direct attack on the 'war effort', the military and the government. Strikers had to take on troops in their factories, youth groups and gangs were met by troops on the street. Whether people meant to or not, they were often treated as if they were in revolt against the war itself, because they had spoken out against one aspect of it.

The most difficult place for any grass roots opposition to the war to take root was in Nazi Germany. The whole point of the regime was to crush popular, radical opposition. It was the country that had gone the furthest in ordering society on military lines. But even there, the working class could make itself felt.

Historian Tim Mason made the point that even in the extreme conditions of repression in the Third Reich, the German working class carried on a number of strikes that were recorded by the Information Office of the Labour Front, and successive acts of sabotage and unofficial go-slows worried officials in the early years of the war.[1] 'Unpopular measures' Hitler told Speer, 'might lead to riots'[2]

In April 1942 Goebbels pored over reports that morale was not good, and that a speech of Hitler's had aroused doubts: 'The German people are asking, in surprise, why he had to be granted new plenary powers and what reasons might have caused him to castigate and criticize domestic conditions thus publicly'. Goebbels worried that the speech had 'spread a feeling of insecurity' and that 'the people now want especially to know what the Fuehrer now intends to do to improve the conditions he criticized'.

> There is also some scepticism about the military situation. Above all, since the Fuehrer spoke of a second winter campaign in the east, people believe that he, too, is not convinced that the war against the Soviet Union can be finished this summer.[3]

Goebbels consoled himself with the thought that Waechter had planned 'a great anti-Soviet Exhibition in the Berlin Lustgarten' which 'promised to be an event of the first magnitude and to show the justification for our war against the Soviet Union'. He had some qualms and added that 'of course I am going to see that nothing is included that might in any way be an advertisement for Bolshevism'. In the event the exhibition was the target of an arson attack by Herbert Baum's communist underground group.

Baum had organised a circle of oppositionists, and had been detained as they handed out anti-Nazi leaflets. For that he was made to work for the Berlin Elmo-Werke factory in a special part of the plant they put aside for Jewish forced labour. It was among them that Baum organised a larger group of around 100 who were behind the attack on the Lustgarten anti-Soviet exhibition. A few days after the attack, on 22 May 1942, Baum was arrested. Baum killed himself before he could be tortured and twenty of his comrades were executed.

In Dusseldorf a Committee to Struggle against Fascism had support mainly from foreign labourers and others in Nuremburg set up a Committee of the Red Flag.[4] In Cologne an extensive Popular Front Committee drew in hundreds of German and foreign workers headed by Engelbert Brinker, who was tortured and killed by the Gestapo in 1944. But his committee sowed the seeds of resistance, and the authorities struggled to keep down a rising tide of opposition in the early months of 1945.

Small groups of leftists carried on secret meetings in workplaces – like Oskar Hippe's friends in the International Communist Party – writing leaflets and trying to sabotage the war effort.[5] Leopold Trepper organised a Soviet Spy ring in Nazi Germany and occupied

Europe that sent military secrets and reports of troop movements back to Moscow, before he was arrested in November of 1942 (he escaped and survived, only to be imprisoned by the Soviets, as Hippe was by the East Germans). Harro Schulze-Boysen and Arvid Harnach organised an underground group that infiltrated a number of government and military offices. The group made contact with Trepper and put up posters across Berlin 'Nazi Paradise = War, Famine, Lies, Gestapo? How Much Longer'. He was arrested and hanged in August 1942.[6]

In 1943 workers outside the capital were being ordered back to Berlin for 'Catastrophe Work', while restaurants were closed to give up their employees to the war effort on 2 February of that year.[7] The atomisation of the German working class, both at the hands of the Nazis, and then later under the allied attacks, meant that the marked discontent felt by many individuals was not organised.

Many youth groups with an anti-authoritarian flavour came together in the war:

In Essen they were called the Farhtenstenze (Travelling Dudes), in Oberhausen and Dusseldorf the Kittelbach Pirates, in Cologne they were the Navajos. But all saw themselves as Edelweiss Pirates (named after an edelweiss flower badge many wore).[8]

The groups sang anti-Nazi songs and fought with the official Hitler Youth. Three thousand names of alleged Edelweiss Pirates were on the Gestapo files in Cologne.

In October 1944, with the allied forces close to the western borders of Germany, Edelweiss Pirates and other oppositionists rioted in Cologne, which had been largely evacuated. Gestapo and other officials were attacked. The Nazi leadership ordered a terrible clampdown with gunbattles in the street, that ended with the arrests of 200 and dozens hanged in the streets – including six teenagers of the Edelweiss Pirates, one of them Barthel Schink.[9]

Political Opposition to the War in the Allied Countries

There was in America a strong anti-war tradition that was rooted in the labour movement and the left. The Independent Labour League proclaimed in 1939 that 'this second world war is neither more nor less than the continuation of the first'. 'It represents the same imperialist conflict ... THIS WAR IS NOT OUR WAR'.[10] Those wise owls in the more patriotic left, who thought that Roosevelt and Churchill were in fact friends of the oppressed were given to mocking these socialist anti-war campaigners as 'dupes of Hitler'. On the other hand Irving Howe wrote that the war was not 'a holy crusade for "democracy" but rather an imperialist war; that is a war for profits, for economic domination.' To him 'The babble about the four freedoms was just... talk.' It was 'Talk to prod us into war and into blood and into death. Talk to make us give up the greatest right a workingman has: his right to strike.'[11]

Most active amongst anti-war campaigners was A. J. Muste, whose Fellowship of Reconciliation struggled to get the message across throughout the conflict. To Muste the war was

a conflict between two powers for survival and domination. One set of powers, which includes Britain and the United States, and perhaps "Free France", controls some seventy per cent of the earth's resources and thirty million square miles of territory. The imperialistic status quo thus to their advantage was achieved by a series of wars including the last one. All they ask now is to be left in peace, and if so they are disposed to make their rule fair but firm.

The other set of powers, controlling 15 per cent of the earth's resources, though, were going to challenge them. Muste predicted that an Allied victory would yield 'a new American empire' and that 'we shall be the next nation to seek world domination – in other words to do what we condemn Hitler for doing'.[12] Muste and the fellowship of reconciliation organised and supported conscientious objectors. Among New York's intellectuals Dwight McDonald and Irving Howe started the anti-war journal *Politics*.[13]

On 27 October 1941 six members of the Socialist Workers Party in America were brought to trial accused of undermining the government under a clause in the Aliens Registration Act (the 'Smith Act') passed the previous year. Twenty three were sentenced to terms between a year and sixteen months. James Cannon, the party's leader and one of the charged wrote:

The Roosevelt regime claims to oppose fascism but it collaborates, when expedient, with the fascists. It claims to be defending the four freedoms while trying to deny these freedoms to its political opponents. We Trotskyists, however, are defending democratic rights here at home against Roosevelt's assault upon them. We are fighting for the freedom he hypocritically pretends to be safeguarding.[14]

Harold Laski of the Labour Party's Executive Committee wrote a pamphlet *Is This An Imperialist War?* which conceded that 'a large number of Labour Parties contain members' for whom 'the present war is simply, like the last, another "imperialist war"'. [15] In spring 1940 Labour leaders Clement Attlee and Ellen Wilkinson were barracked at regional conferences in South Wales, the East Midlands and Stirling for arguing the case for war. By March of that year ninety Constituency Labour Parties had passed anti-war resolutions to the annual conference that was to take place in June, though the war drums silenced that opposition by the summer.[16]

In the British Parliament, the James Maxton of the Independent Labour Party objected when Churchill announced that the position of Leader of the Opposition had been 'put in abeyance' as all the major parties had joined in coalition: 'there is an attempt being made to put opposition into abeyance'.[17] Throughout the war Maxton tried to challenge the government, though he was mostly shouted down. Maxton's allies in the small but vociferous Independent Labour Party felt isolated by the rush to war on the left, but still they kept up the argument. In a pamphlet *Socialism can beat Fascism*, Fenner Brockway and John McNair wrote in 1940

We want an end to the war, not by a victory for Fascism, not by a victory for Imperialism, not by a victory for Capitalism on either side, but by a victory of the peoples across the frontiers over Fascism, Imperialism, Capitalism. (p 10)

Brockway branded the British war effort imperialist and argued that 'dictatorship is also growing in Britain':

No socialist, indeed no sincere democrat can identify himself with imperialism against Nazism, or can be satisfied with an end of the war which would destroy the Nazi form of dictatorship only.[18]

The communist parties had a strong core of working class leaders. Their allegiance to the nominally 'communist' military dictatorship in Russia played havoc with the development of their political stance, imposing some abrupt reversals. It is common to dismiss the parties' opposition to the Allied war effort in the first year of the war as just an opportunist adaptation to the Hitler-Stalin pact. But when CP USA leader William Foster wrote in *The Communist* of July 1941 that 'the present war represents a violent redivision of the world among the imperialist power', he was right. In those early years the Communist Party of Great Britain organised a Peoples' Convention with large numbers of working class delegates sceptical about the direction of the war. As evidence of the British government's nervousness at such opposition, *The Daily Worker* was banned.

Class War in occupied Europe

The Fascist regime in Italy, despite its many years of repression aimed at the left and organised labour, was hit by labour unrest at the height of the war, beginning with a rash of strikes early in March 1943. Communists and other radical groups helped to organise a small wave of strikes in Turin, beginning with a walkout at Mirafiori plant that was followed by a strike of the 800 workers at the Rasettie factory on the Corso Cirié on 5 March. On Monday, 8 March yet more joined the protests, either coming out of work, or by organising go-slows and working to rule. 100, 000 joined the disputes in the Piedmont region, and on 24 March in Milan around 130 000 workers came out in support. Mussolini demanded that strikers be shot, but on the ground the Fascisti avoided face to face attacks – 300 were arrested in Milan and 150 in Turin, but most were quickly released again. Mussolini said that the Fascist movement had been put back twenty years – within four months he was to be deposed.[19] There was little hope for the anti-Fascist opposition from the Allies, though. Eden, in a letter to Cordell Hull that January argued that the view of His Majesty's Government was that they should 'aim at such disorder in Italy as would necessitate a German occupation'. And 'the best means of achieving this aim is to intensify all forms of military operations against Italy'.[20]

Eden's hopes came true, and northern Italy was occupied by the Germans and made the puppet state of the Italian Social Republic, or 'Salo Republic'. In Turin 50,000 Fiat workers went on strike in November 1943, demanding better pay and rations. On 1 March 1944 200,000 went on strike in Milan and Genoa, again centred on the Fiat plants. Strikers were deported to Germany, and later when the occupiers began seizing plant, too, there were more strikes in June 1944. The strike leaders were allied to the Communist Party, the Justice and Liberty group and the Committees for National Liberation.[21]

In occupied Western Europe the weight of the occupation was harsh, and open hostility was beginning to grow. French miners in the Nord Pas De Calais were loaded with increased targets to meet Nazi demands for industry, after British coal imports were stopped in June 1940. At the same time employers thought to take advantage of the way that the Nazi occupation had tipped the balance of power in their favour, by forcing down miners' pay. On 27 May 1941 miners at the Dahomey colliery stopped work. Within the week one hundred thousand miners were on strike. Other industries came out in support: engineering, railways, ceramics and textile workers came out in support – and open defiance of the Nazi occupation. Miners met secretly in woods to avoid the Nazis (earlier in the year a miners' delegation sent to negotiate a settlement to a local strike had been arrested). With the men at risk of arrest while picketing, their wives and daughters took their place, so that the Nazi authorities had to put them under curfew for the hour around the beginning and end of each shift. Vichy officials were so intimidated by the strikers militant challenge, that they avoided posting Nazi proclamations. Losing a grip on the situation the Nazi authorities could only cut rations and starve the men back to work. Emergency courts heard cases against the strikers and against the women pickets and around 400 were deported to Germany – around half of whom never came back.[22]

Pressure on the French authorities to send workers to Germany stoked anger. In the Gnome-Rhône works in Vichy-ruled Lyon 700 workers were chosen to be sent north in October 1942. Only 15 turned up and so the other 685 were dismissed. In reply all 3000 employees struck, and very quickly other workforces came out too as the strike spread throughout Lyon and to the towns of St Etienne, Grenoble, Annecy and Chamberry. There were further strikes in November 1943 again in Nord Pas De Calais and Lyon, with seventy thousand demanding better rations – though pointedly the strikes were concentrated in German interests. Finally, in June 1944, as the invasion was underway, scores of strikes broke out, concentrated in Paris and on the railways.[23]

In Amsterdam, on 17 and 18 February 1941 strikes were organised in shipyards to protest against plans to deport Dutch workers to Germany, and against Nazi attacks on the Jewish quarter. On 25 February, a general strike was called that shook the occupying authorities. In April and May of 1943 a wave of strikes across Holland against the internment of ex-soldiers broke out, starting in the town of Hengelo, spreading through the mining district of Limburg, the Philips works in Eindhoven and many other places. Important to German technology the Philips works were not working normally for ten days. That summer, in August 1943, a strike wave overtook Denmark.[24] In Norway around 25,000 trade unionists had struck in September 1941 – but the German authorities executed two union activists Viggo Hansteen and Rolf Wickstrøm , damping down industrial militancy. Still, when the Quisling government tried to dragoon teachers into a Fascist Teachers Union the following year, most of the 14,000 refused and a thousand were deported to forced labour in the north.[25]

Workers' protests against wartime conditions were by no means restricted to the Axis powers. The Allies, too, were pushing their own working people to the limit to arm their troops, and those workers began to fight back in earnest.

Class War in America

The conflict was starkest in the 'Arsenal of Democracy' itself. There strikes fell back after America joined the war, thanks to the No Strike Agreement that the unions signed. At first employers felt sure that they could crack down on workers 'because of the war', explained Flint union official Jack Palmer.[26] But in 1943 the number of strikes started to climb again with around two million joining in.

The union officers' 'no strike pledge' brought them close relations with the government, but won nothing for their members, who quite quickly bridled at the limits. Local Union of Auto Workers president Jess Ferrazza 'used to think I had accomplished something if one of the plants had not gone on strike because this thing kept popping up all over'. Ferrazza felt 'like a fireman with a water bucket running around trying to put fires out'. The unions were so hand-in-glove with the government contractors that Colonel George Strong, the Air Corps procurement officer blamed younger workers 'who aren't subject to control by either management or by the union' and 'who care nothing about unionism' for the strikes.[27] Trade unionists were losing faith with the War Labor Board calling it the 'graveyard of grievances'.

With goods shoddy and in poor supply, workers' extra wages did not go far. Still, the great increase in employment gave them a strong sense of solidarity. Grace Lee remembered an 'exhilarating', 'transcending time': 'People had been torn from their traditional moorings to fight in the armed services or to work in the defence plants.'[28] These turbulent times gave workers heart, which they needed if they were to break the 'no strike' pledge that their repre-

Striking Milwaukee munitions workers tear-gassed by state troopers

sentatives had made. According to Norm Bully, of General Motors' Buick plant in Flint 'When we found that there was no other solution except a wildcat strike, we found ourselves striking not only against the corporation, but against practically the government' and against 'our own union and its pledge'. According to labour historian Martin Glaberman 'military officers in uniform were present in all the war production plants during the war and they regularly intervened in strikes and potential strikes'.[29]

There was one union that did not sign up to the 'No Strike' agreement, the Mechanics Educational Society of America (MESA). The MESA was founded in 1932 by an English immigrant Matthew Smith who had been active in the Amalgamated Engineering Union. The MESA had around 64 000 members, hardly any full-time officials, and organised a number of strikes. The Detroit Press were outraged to hear that Smith had never bothered to become a citizen: 'I'm an internationalist, a citizen of the human race', he said. Called to account before a US Senate Committee, Smith was asked 'no matter what happens to the country, your membership come first'? 'I come from a country that had 91 wars in 100 years' said Smith: 'I am getting a bit cynical about them'. 'My members', said Smith 'don't know how to work for the four, five or six freedoms,' parodying Roosevelt's 'Five Freedoms' speech: 'They work for cash.' In revenge at the MESA's strike policy, the National Labour Relations Board gave over representation rights to their more compliant rivals in the Congress of Industrial Organisations – to which the MESA replied with an industry-wide strike in 1944.[30] The strike spread to 48 plants, and the Under Secretary of War Robert Patterson wired Smith:

> Your strikes . . . represent no honest grievance. . . . You are striking our fighting men from the rear. The War Department insists these strikes be stopped at once.

Smith said no, until President Roosevelt ordered the army to take over eight of the plants.[31]

In time, the militancy of the MESA spread to the CIO-affiliated United Autoworkers. M. F. Macauley, Manufacturing Control Manager at the Packard Motor Company, told a senate committee that he could not do 'time and motion' studies: 'the stewards of the plant objected every time' and 'some foremen ... were walked out of the plant'. In the same hearing one Colonel Anthony explained that 'only a very small proportion of the strikes appear in the newspapers' and according to Senator Ferguson the official record 'doesn't give us any true picture of the number of strikes in the war plants here in Detroit'.[32]

Year	Strikes	Workers taking part	Days lost	Per cent of employed
1941	4288	2362620	23047556	8.4
1942	2968	839961	4182557	2.8
1943	3752	1981279	13500529	6.9
1944	4956	2115637	8721079	7
1945	4750	3467000	38025000	12.2

Source: Glabermann, Wartime Strikes, 1980, p 36

In 1943, America's mines were shut down by a run of strikes. United Mine Workers leader John L. Lewis had signed up for the no-strike deal, but his members were hurting. The UMW's own survey showed that food prices had gone up 124 per cent between 1939 and 1943 even though wages were frozen. 'Mine workers are hungry', said Lewis: 'They are asking for food'. Accidents, he said were rising, 64,000 in 1941, 75,000 in 1942 and 100,000 in 1943. 'That's a lot of meat,' he said 'a lot of human meat to grind up in one year'.[33] A strike of anthracite miners began on 30 December 1942, without the Union's backing. On 15 January the National War Labour Board ordered the strike end, but the miners extended it. President Roosevelt, speaking as 'Commander in Chief' ordered the miners back to work, so they extended the strike again, until Lewis promised to fight for a big wage demand and they went back to work on 22 January.

'The government of the United States', said the New York Herald Tribune, 'has got to do something about John L. Lewis': 'It is not easy to exaggerate Lewis's challenge not only to the nation's prosecution of the war but to the basic conception of American democracy' (13 March 1943). On 26 March Lewis was summoned before the Truman Senate War Investigating Committee, but scoffed at those representatives who wanted his members to go hungry while leaving war profiteers alone.

The government tried to shunt the row off to one side in the War Labour Board on 22 April, while the President blustered that the wage and price freeze had to hold (even though prices were in truth out of control and the Office of Price Administration had just agreed a 23 cents a ton increase with the western Pennsylvania soft coal operators). Ordered to work on by the WLB, miners in Pennsylvania and Alabama started to walk out. Lewis joked that if there was no contract, then miners would surely not trespass on mine property. The mines were shut down on 1 May – and a panic-stricken Roosevelt ordered the mines taken over by the government. It was still the old management, but the flag flew over the mines and Secretary of State for the Interior Harold Ickes said the miners were working for the government and had to go back to work. Lewis tried to calm things down by offering a truce and told the men to go back, which they did, after another day's protest. Roosevelt gave a radio broadcast charging the miners with making 'a gamble with the lives of American soldiers and sailors'.[34]

On 1 June, the miners were out again: 530,000 of them, and the owners tried to settle, meeting demands for better pay and terms. But the War Labor Board ordered the men back to work and struck down the agreement. Meanwhile Congress passed the Smith-Connally War Labor Disputes Act which gave the War Labor Board statutory powers and outlawed strikes. In Detroit, the United Auto Workers' conference delegates snubbed their leaders and voted solidarity with the miners, and also that the Smith-Connally Act 'made a mockery out of avowed claims that this is a war for democracy'.[35] In reply, the miners came out again. The coalfields were in chaos. Lewis could not get the miners back to work, even when he tried. In despair, Ickes handed control of the mines back to the owners in October. On 20 November the War Labor Board accepted the pay rise that the miners and the coal owners agreed, breaking the wage freeze.

On 30 November 1943 railway workers voted by 97.7 per cent to strike. Again Roosevelt ordered the army in, and they seized the railways, though only after Secretary of War Stimson promised that he would not interfere with their profits. The Army Chief of Staff

George Marshall gave a news conference that called the railway strike 'the damnedest crime that was ever committed against America', and the White House Press Secretary made it clear that the President was 'thinking along the same lines'. [36] In fact in the first six months of the Smith Connally Act there were 1,919 strikes, of which only 34 were legal. That Christmas, 100,000 steelworkers joined the strike wave.

Truman, writing in 1946, remembered bitterly 'John Lewis called two strikes in War Time to satisfy his ego. Two strikes which were worse than bullets in the back of our soldiers. The railworkers did exactly the same thing.'[37] Soldiers, though, did not necessarily agree. An editorial in the *Army Newspaper* of 15 January 1944 complained about the 'way certain periodicals reaching soldiers have begun to campaign against labor':

> Soldiers generally are concerned about this unfair carping. Most of them are working men. It is estimated that nearly a million are trade union members ... In these days the working people need a few dollars more to cover the ever-rising cost of living.[38]

Race war in America

Over four nights from 3-7 June 1943 sailors on shore at Los Angeles, massing into crowds of as many as 1000-strong carried on a sustained attack on young Mexicans. Their target was the 'Zoot Suit'. Young Mexicans took to wearing the zoot suit, with its baggy pants coming to a peg leg, high waist, padded shoulders and long drapes. The cultural code was not so hard to work out. The suit might have its origins in Campesino-wear of the previous century, but most pointedly it was a contrast to the neat uniforms of the services, and an ostentatious use of cloth in an age of austerity. Zoot suiters' ostentatious 'loafing' was contrasted with hard-working and responsibly saving America. A letter to *Time* set out the way that the zoot suit offended:

> To a soldier who has been taken from his home and put into the army, the sight of loafers of any race, creed, religion or colour of hair, loafing around in ridiculous clothes that cost $75 to $85 per suit is enough to make them see red.[39]

The rioting white sailors understood the meaning of the zoot suit, too. They tore them from the backs of the young Mexicans they caught, and set them on fire, or pissed on them. Stripped and beaten, the young men's pictures were in the papers, surrounded by jubilant rioters, or sometimes by sympathetic crowds.

Hatred of the zoot-suiters was not just a spasm on the part of the sailors; they were backed-up by the authorities. On 9 June Councilman Norris Nelson put the resolution to 'prohibit the wearing of Zoot Suits with reet pleats within the city of Los Angeles'. In the event it was thought that the laws on rioting would do the job.[40] Days later the *Los Angeles Times* reported that 'the federal government stepped into the local zoot-suit picture by obtaining an injunction against a down-town store restraining sale of the zooters' "uniform"' (13 June 1943). Later the War Production Board decided that no more would be made.[41]

Official anger had been building against the young Mexicans. The previous year, after José Días was killed in a gang fight near the Sleepy Lagoon, the police took the opportunity for a great dragnet, arresting 600. Seventeen were tried for the murder on the strained argument that having crashed a party together they were engaged in a joint enterprise. The boys were refused a change of clothes before the trial so they would be seen by jurors in their zoot suits. Lieutenant Edward Duran Ayres of the Sheriff's office gave expert testimony that 'the Indian' has 'utter disregard for human life' – as could be seen in the history of Aztec human sacrifice. Three of the accused were found guilty of first degree murder, nine of second degree murder, five of lesser charges.

A Zoot-suiter is frisked by a policeman

A Sleepy Lagoon Defence Committee fronted by Orson Wells, Rita Hayworth and Anthony Quinn garnered support from the Longshoremen's Union, the National Maritime Union, the Amalgamated Clothing Workers' Union and the Screen Artists Guild. Though the Communist Party, which did a lot of the leg-work for the Defence Committee, opposed the persecution of the zoot-suiters, they balked at the evident cultural rejection of the popular war effort. Communist LaRue McCormick blamed the rise in juvenile delinquency on Mexican 'Fifth Columnists', known as 'Synarquista' – a religious movement of the far right, marginal in Mexico and non-existent in America. Even the Sleepy Lagoon Committee swore to fight 'against the Sinarchists and Falangists' who they thought were promoting 'delinquency'.[42]

The zoot suit was taken up by America's black hipsters, who understood its meaning well. Malcolm Little – who would later make his fame as Malcolm X of the Nation of Islam – was called before the draft board on 1 June 1943: 'The day I went down there, I costumed like an actor. With my wild zoot suit I wore the yellow knob-toe shoes, and I frizzled my hair up into a reddish bush of conk.'[43] It was a performance that earned him the 4F rating he wanted.

Many black leaders saw the war as a way of proving their respectability, and even working themes of racial justice into the case for war. The Double V campaign called for a victory against Fascism abroad and Jim Crow at home. But alongside that response, other black Americans were dismissive of the war effort, and contrasted the War for Democracy abroad with their condition at home cynically, not optimistically.[44]

The innovators of Be Bop Jazz managed to avoid the war altogether. Lester Young did time in military prison for brewing illicit liquor, but Charlie Parker, Dizzy Gillespie and Thelonius Monk worked across America indifferent to the whole event – except that restrictions on gasoline, shellack, and lighting along the west coast interfered with their touring and recording. Charlie Parker's biographer and sometime manager, Ross Russell, wrote that for them 'World War II was a grotesque show staged by sick old men who had succeeded in turning America into a huge prison camp.' There were black stars who worked for the war effort, like Paul Robeson and boxing champion Joe Louis. The cultural life black Americans made for themselves in the burgeoning centres of Detroit and Harlem was divided on the war.

Blacks migrated northwards, many to Detroit, to get jobs in the war industries. Life reported that 'the tremendous migration of white and Negro war workers from the south since 1940' had created problems. 'Detroit's abominable housing situation', the article went on, 'condemns thousands to living in slums, tents and trailers'.[45] Tensions between the two races grew as a special housing project for blacks, named after Sojourner Truth, was opened. White war workers – and police – barred the way. The following year black Detroiters clashed with whites on the bridge to Belle Isle, Detroit's beach and leisure centre. Angered at the challenge, whites toured black districts in cars threatening violence and attacking people. Blacks fought back, but the police joined in containing the blacks. Looting broke out in Detroit. Thirty four people were killed of whom 25 were black, and around 1000 were wounded. The police killed 15, most of whom were accused of looting, but some of firing on police.[46] 'Police brutality', the *Michigan Chronicle* reported, 'reached a new high in Negro sections of the city during the race riot' (26 June 1943). *The Age* wrote that 'the most horrible Nazi atrocity stories are no worse than these home front outrages' (26 June 1943).

'Tyranny and atrocities in America': Japan's *Global Knowledge* reports
Detroit race riots, June 1943

Just over a month later, on 1 August 1943, at 7 pm, patrolman James Collins was at the Braddock Hotel on West 126th Street where Marjorie Polite was arguing with the staff over money. Robert Bandy, on leave from the Army's 703rd Police Battalion took issue with Collins, and the two came to blows – at which point Collins shot Bandy dead. Before long 3000 people gathered outside the 28th Precinct Headquarters demanding justice for Robert Bandy.

At that time Harlem was, in poet Claude McKay's words, 'the Negro capital of the world' – 397 city blocks of northern Manhattan, south to north between 110th and 155th Streets, east to west between Third and Amsterdam Avenues, it was eighty per cent black. The rioting that followed was intense. Mayor Fiorello LaGuardia was thought of as more liberal than the Detroit City authorities, and had watched the trouble their closely. He sent 6600 city police and civil guards into Harlem, while a further 8000 State Guardsmen and 1500 civilian volunteers surrounded the perimeter. Still the police killed six people all black, 185 were injured and 550 arrested – overwhelmingly they were black.[47] In Harlem at that time many bought the pamphlet by 'Native Son' (the radical activist and scholar CLR James) that scoffed at the call for blacks to fight for democracy: 'I have no democracy and the democracy I haven't got, Hitler didn't take from me'.[48]

Class war in Britain

In Britain, as in France and America, miners were pushing back. In the first year of the war 62,318 miners left the pits, joining up, or taking on other war work. To get back in charge the Essential Work (Coalmining) Order said that 30,000 ex-miners and others were ordered down the mines by 17 March 1942. By May of that year 2681 workers over all – mostly miners – were prosecuted for refusing Essential Work Orders and 220 were imprisoned. Over the six years to the end of 1942 more than 5000 people were killed in the coal mines and 700,000 injured. When the miners' case was debated in parliament on 11 June 1942, Aneurin Bevan, a supporter of the government admitted that 'there is not the slightest difference between it' – the government's forced mine labour scheme – 'and the economic apparatus of Nazi Germany'. Bevan said 'This is economic fascism in all its elements,' and went on, over protests from the more moderate socialists:

> if industry is managed by the State and the unions become a part of State apparatus and the industry remains in private hands, then they make themselves partly responsible for administering it, and that is Fascism. That is exactly what happens in Germany. It is the Fascist labour front, and the nominees of the trade unions become gauleiters.[49]

Cartoonist David Low's view of the unofficial miners' strike

As it turned out, Bevan had not understated the miners' hostility to their subjugation. The Minister of Mines said that during the three weeks ending 23 May 1942 'there were 86 strikes involving 58,000 wage earners' and 141,688 shifts were lost.[50]

On 9 January 1942 miners at Betteshanger Colliery in Kent struck over rates. The Ministry of Labour decided to charge 1,050 miners for breaking Order 1305. Three local union officials were imprisoned. Branch Secretary William Powell got two months' hard labour; Branch president Tudor Davies and Isaac Methuen, both of whom were local councillors in Deal got one month's hard labour. More than a thousand miners were fined. Still, the Betteshanger miners struck on and other pits came out to back them. By the end of the month the miners won their better rates and the Home Office ordered the officials released. Only nine of the fines were ever paid. 'During WW2 the Union leadership proved a valuable asset in the state's war effort in trying to suppress strikes and stoppages within the coal industry', says NUM activist David Douglass, 'although this largely failed and widespread unofficial strike action and strikes by branches and lodges increased as the war entered its last year'.[51] In

1944, miners struck again, demanding higher pay. They came out on unofficial strike in South Wales, Kent, Lancashire, Yorkshire, Durham, and Scotland, 180,000 in all. Labour Minister Ernest Bevin said it was worse than if Hitler had bombed Sheffield and all the communications lines had been cut, but miners said their sons and brothers in the army backed them.[52]

Kent miners on the way to the courts, photograph by D.H. Calcraft

In November 1939 the London North Committee of the Amalgamated Engineering Union voted to oppose the imperialist war. In the spring of 1941 the Swift Scale factory in Park Royal, West London voted to strike after a union convenor was dismissed, 'until such a time as we secure the reinstatement of our convenor Brother Leslie'. The strikers ignored the dispute procedure under Order 1305 and seven of them were prosecuted on Ernest Bevin's orders.[53]

One of the first major disputes in Britain in the war was in 1941among Engineering Apprentices in Glasgow, Coventry, Lancashire and London over pay. They marched from workplace to workplace to build wildcat strikes. In September 1943 apprentices took part in a large engineers' strike at Vickers Armstrong in Barrow, where pay had been held down for years. The picket line was a mass protest of more than a thousand. Strikers were backed by local people, and the Irish Nationalist and St Mary's Clubs. When the

National Arbitration Council ruled for the employers, the strikers stayed out. When the Amalgamated Engineering Union sent the veteran Communist George Crane to talk the men around, they threatened to throw him down the stairs. The Union was alarmed that the Barrow strikers were backed by the Huddersfield District Committee, and did their best to damp it down.[54]

In 1944 Bevin's scheme for filling vacancies in the mines drafting one-in-ten apprentices by ballot provoked widespread anger. Over Christmas 1943, an unofficial Tyneside Apprentices Guild was set up to fight the plans. The Guild addressed a leaflet to the miners, 'we also will resist', it read, and 'We need your support in our struggles against the BEVIN BALLOT SCHEME'. The first boy chosen under the scheme on Tyneside, Martin, was backed by the Guild that threatened strikes from 14 March 1944 and his call up was cancelled. The Tyneside Apprentice Guild organised mass meetings and lobbied parliament, and on 28 March called a strike. More than six thousand backed them on Tyneside, 4,800 on the Clyde and more in Huddersfield. The Government, the press, Engineering Union and the Communist Party all attacked the strike leaders as 'Trotskyists' and the boys as dupes, and Guild leader Bill Davy was arrested – as were some of their left wing supporters (see below). In North Africa, the Eighth Army Signals Corp voted to back the apprentices and their right to strike.[55] The number of strikes climbed to a record 2,194 stoppages with 3,700,000 days lost in 1944.[56]

There were strikes throughout the British Empire, as native people resisted the pressure to yield up ever greater tribute to Mars. In Fiji in March 1943 sugar cane farmers – who in the peculiar racial set up in that colony are the descendants of Indian indentured servants – demanded an increase in the value of their cane in line with the price of sugar from the Colonial Sugar Refining Company. Their organisations, the Kisan Sangh, the Maha Sangh and the Rewa Cane Grower's Union organised strikes across the colony. The British authorities promoted racial divisions between the Indian farmers and the indigenous Fijians who had been largely excluded from commercial farming. As an escape from village life, military service was valued by Fijians, but Indians were indifferent, or hostile to the allied cause. Strike leaders A.D. Patel and Sami Rudranada were ordered to stay within five miles of their homes and to report to police daily. In the legislative assembly, Fijian leaders Ratu Sukuna and Edward Cakobau attacked the Indians for their poor contribution to the war. Eventually, the farmers gave in, after about a half of the crop was spoiled. The British got their revenge with the Native Land Trust Ordinance and the Fijian Affairs Ordinance both of 1944. These laws entrenched the racial animosities that would curse the colony for years afterwards, giving Fijians a titular monopoly over the land and the constitution that was in fact exercised on their behalf by the governor.[57]

In the British colony of South Africa, General Smuts had done all he could to feed the British war machine, recruiting black Africans to meet the demand for gold, coal, iron, chemicals, explosives and munitions so that their numbers swelled to quarter of a million in industry. Unlike their white counterparts, the black union members had no negotiating rights. Even in industry, where they could earn the most, black workers' wages were just a quarter of whites'. These new black recruits joined an unprecedented wave of strikes – 304 between 1939 and 1945, involving 58,000 black and Indian workers and 6000 white South Africans. Black workers had to cope with the pass laws that forced them to live in segregated areas. In 1944 blacks in the Alexandra township who worked in Johannesburg began a bus boycott to protest against fare rises that meant they had to walk eighteen miles a day. The campaign won, and helped build the campaign against the pass laws. Also James Mpanza led a movement to build a shanty town by Orlando, west of Johannesberg, which became known as Soweto.[58]

In 1942 the colonial officer J. A. Pitout was sent to settle a strike by Africans building Kumalo Airport under the forced labour scheme:

He was faced by an enormous and surly crowd of insolent and angry Africans. The other Europeans addressed them saying that they must be patriotic and do all they could to help the war effort.

Pitout gathered that this appeal to patriotism was not working and had the interpreter tell them that 'the Europeans were fighting a war and that in Logenbula's time fellows like them would be assegaied and thrown to the vultures.' The men were forced back to work.[59]

Even in India, where the repression had arrested the push for independence, workers fought back against the combination of a forced production drive and suppression of living standards:[60]

	Strikes	Workers striking	Real earnings, 1939 = 100	Prices, 1939 = 100
1941	359	291,054	103.7	107
1942	694	772,653	89	145
1943	716	525,088	67	268
1944	658	555,015	75.1	269
1945	820	747,530	74.9	269
1946	1629	1,961,948	73.2	285

The French Empire saw resistance, too. Indochinese nationalists had been fighting a sustained campaign against France leading to an uprising in 1930. In elections on 30 April 1939 the French administration's new war taxes were tested. Though the Communists of the Democratic Front supported the authorities they were opposed by a yet more radical Trotskyist group, La Lutte, who opposed the tax and the war, and against forced conscription. All the La Lutte candidates were elected.[61] When the French authority recognised the Vichy government, repression of the Indochinese radicals at the hands of the Sûreté became more severe.

Class war in Japan

In Japan the special laws against Labour disputes and the Sanpō company unions had an impact, but people were beginning to become cynical about the war effort. According to a Home Ministry Police Bureau report on the Sanpō in 1942

much of the general membership views the organisation merely as a group to facilitate rationing and therefore there are a good number of workers who ridicule the movement and are uncooperative.[62]

There were strikes at Osaka's Sumitomo Chemical Plant and also at Kanebō. As the war effort demanded more, the number of disputes tended to rise.[63] Also, the impact of reversals in the war tended to undermine morale leading to disorder at work.

Workers reacted to mobility laws with go-slows and unapproved absences. One Home Ministry Report found that young workers who had been made to work were given to not turning up, delinquency, moonlighting, deliberately shoddy work and even acts of group violence. In Uraga, where 9,423 youths were drafted into work there were violent protests when a boy was beaten by his dorm superior. Officials found that a many goods were ruined by acts of sabotage, sometimes as much as 60 per cent of output. Officials noted the destruction of 1422 units at Hitachi's Kameido plant, and destruction of equipment at the Hatshama Dock Company.[64]

Labour Disputes in Japan[65]

Year	No of disputes	Average no of participants
1940	271	121
1941	159	68
1942	174	54
1943	695	35
1944	550	34

By the end, there were no disputes as such, but absenteeism rocketed from 20 per cent just before the American air raids took hold, to 50 per cent in July 1945.[66]

MUTINIES

Civilians protesting against the war effort were taking some risks. But for soldiers it was an even greater hazard – they could be tried and executed for mutiny. Even so, there were mutinies and insubordination in all the armies fighting the Second World War.

The Greek Army in North Africa

In 1943 North Africa, and Cairo in particular was the point where British, Indian, Italian, German, Greek and American troops had been pushed to breaking point over the years of the desert war.

Late in 1943 British soldiers organised their own mock

parliament, building on the many talks put on by the Army Bureau of Current Affairs. The men were kicking their heels, and excited about the post-war plans they had heard were being talked about in London. Quite quickly the parliament veered to the left, under the influence of Private Henry Solomons, a Labour Party supporter who had been a union official in Stepney, and Sergeant Bardell who was a member of the Communist Party. Sessions drew as many as 500 men. Resolutions passed in favour of nationalising the banks made the army top brass and the government nervous. Brigadier J.L. Chrystal complained that the typical Army Bureau of Current Affairs talk would be 'The Future of the Empire' with 'some Yid gunner yapping about Freedom for India!' According to Chrystal there was 'nothing to be done except keep posting the bloody Reds to different places before they build up any more of their damned cells'. Private Solomons was moved out of Cairo, and the airman who moved the resolution to nationalise the banks, Leo Abse, was put under arrest and taken to Port Tewfik. The Forces' Parliament template was copied by airmen in the RAF base at Heliopolis. Goebbels broadcast that Cairo was under the rule of soldiers and airmen's Soviets. Of course the thing that stopped the Forces Parliament from getting out of hand was the leading role played by Communists, who were committed to the Anti-Fascist War. When the orders came to move on to Italy, Sergeant Bardell put up wall-newspapers headed 'On to Victory'. Not everyone was so enthusiastic – another Forces Parliamentarian and Independent Labour Party supporter Albert Gross scoffed at Bardell's patriotic fervour.[67]

Even with the efforts of the British Communists to rally the troops, the military authorities had good cause to be afraid. Cairo was a tinderbox, not just because of the British troops, but also because of Henri Curiel's Egyptian Communist group – who were talking to the British troops – the Egyptian nationalists and furthermore there were thousands of Greek troops in open rebellion against their Royalist officers. Greece's armed forces had pushed back an Italian invasion, only to be overwhelmed by the German invasion that followed. They were a force in exile with conservative nationalist officers integrated into the Allied Command. The fight against the German occupation fell to the more radical resistance movement ELAS while the government-in-exile dithered.

Across the Navy junior officers and men organised as 'Revolutionary Commissions' were challenging the exiled Navy chiefs, calling on them to join the fight with ELAS. Fleet Rear Admiral Alexandres surprised his own command by issuing an order that endorsed the rebels and became a general call to rebellion. Alexandres announced 'the unanimous wish of everyone in our Navy, from the Commander and the ship commanders to the last sailor, that our Government here cooperate effectively with' the 'resistance organizations fighting against the conqueror ...with the objective of joining forces for the continuation of our fight to free our Home Land.'

Ships of the exiled Greek Navy were harboured at Alexandria and on 4 April 1944 five crews mutinied. The destroyers Ierax and the Criti, the corvettes Sachtouris and Apostolis, the floating repair shop Hyphaistos, and in Port Said the submarine Papanicolis and the battleship Averof, all joined the mutiny. The mutiny spread to Malta, where three submarines, the submarine escort the Corinthia and the destroyers Spetses and Navarinon joined. Venizelos of the government in exile was told by Admiral Cunningham that he would lose his seat at the coming negotiations over Greece's future if he did not act, so he appointed Rear-Admiral Petros Voulgaris 'with the mission to crush the mutiny'.[68]

Two brigades of the exile Greek army, the First and the Fourth – veterans of the battle of El Alamein – joined the mutiny. The First Brigade was reluctant to support the move at first, because it was already scheduled to invade Italy on the 12th April – but when their loyalty was claimed by the Government in Exile, they joined the protests. The First Brigade, camped at Bourg el Arab, near Port Alexandria, was surrounded by the British Ninth Brigade, led by Colonel Paget who demanded that the Greeks give up their weapons. The Greeks replied:

We will keep our weapons: they are for the purpose of freeing our country. They were crowned in glory in Albania and Macedonia, in Crete and at El Alamein, and we will not relinquish them.[69]

The Greek Fourth Brigade was surrounded by British tanks at

Kassassin and disarmed. Another group were seized at Heliopolis. Some 280 Greek soldiers were held in an internment camp. On the 11 April 4,500 men of the First Brigade were surrounded by the Ghurkhas of the British-Indian Army. On the 14 April Churchill cabled to his Generals: 'before resorting to arms, the absence of food must certainly be allowed to take its effect in the camp and in the port.' The men were interned 'under the sky' – a euphemism for without food or water. On 23 April a joint British and Greek Government in Exile assault on the ships at Alexandria and Port Said left 12 dead and 30 wounded.[70]

The Greek community in Egypt held big demonstrations against the British internment policy in Cairo and Alexandria. The British responded by rounding up Greek trade union leaders, and disarming another Greek unit stationed in Cairo. The Greek mutineers were supported by Henri Curiel's Egyptian National Liberation Movement, by British Sergeant Sam Bardwell and an American sergeant Al Kuchler. Curiel and Bardwell helped to supply the starving Greek prisoners – at one point setting up a water pipe into the camps. The Greeks' sympathisers in Cairo helped to shelter escapees – of which there were many. The Manchester Guardian drew attention to what it saw as the danger that the 'Forces Parliament' would 'have a most mischievous effect' if it led to the war effort being 'weakened by mutinies'.[71]

Tens of thousands of Greek soldiers and sailors were held in British concentration camps in Libya and Abyssinia until after the war had ended.

Mutiny in the Eighth Army

One group of British troops of the Eighth Army, mostly of the Argyll Highlanders and Durham Light Infantry numbering around 1,500 were gathered in 155 Reinforcement and Transit Camp, outside Tripoli. Told that they were to be returned to their units, they were sent instead to Salerno, to fight with the Fifth Army in the invasion of Italy. Carried over in boats they were told that the landing was in difficulty and they were needed – when in fact the Salerno landing had, after some trouble, been successful. Not really needed, the men were left in another camp in Salerno, until they were told that they would be sent up the line to join the Fifth Army, and not returned to their units.

The men refused. They did not want to be separated from their comrades, the men they had fought with across North Africa. They were accused of Mutiny. Still they ignored the orders to move. After some days, they were warned again that they would face mutiny charges. This time, most of the men were persuaded to take orders. One hundred and ninety two of them refused. They were held behind barbed wire, before being taken back over the Mediterranean to face a secret Court Martial in the Tunisian town of Constantine. The three Sergeants amongst them were sentenced to death, the rest to seven years penal servitude. Later the sentences were reduced and most of the men allowed to fight in Italy – though they were stripped of all the medals they earned in the North Africa war, isolated from other soldiers, and used as 'cannon fodder'. Looking back, assistant prosecutor Lionel Daiches blamed the 'Montgomery Cult' – their loyalty to their commander, and to each other – for their insubordination. Archie Newmarch wrote to his parents from Wormwood Scrubs Prison:

> The British Army is built on pride, but where did it get me and the other 192 men: seven years of the best. Wasn't we proud of our units, our division, wasn't we proud of the men we fought with and where we fought and what we fought for: liberty, freedom, peace? If that is what they call pride, liberty, peace, then God help England.[72]

British troops in North Africa would organise strikes, Soldiers Councils and mutinies again at the end of the war, eager to get away from military rule and back to their civilian lives. Albert Meltzer, Duncan Hallas, Mick O Callaghan and 'Ginger' Foran took part in the strikes in Cairo.

Mutiny on the Cocos Islands

On 8 May 1942 men of the Ceylon Garrison Artillery on Horsburgh Island, part of the Cocos group in the Indian Ocean tried to seize hold of the island and signal the Japanese High Command to agree a surrender. The men were under the command of the English Captain George Gardiner and his Eurasian lieutenant Stephens. The leader of the mutiny, Gratien Fernando, was influenced by the radical left wing Lanka Sama Samaja Party, though he was not a member. Gardiner and Stephens abused the Ceylon Light Infantrymen under their command. Bombardier Fernando took issue with the way that 'the early British administration of Ceylon had changed the property laws so as to deny land title to Sinhalese and allow British settlers to flock into the country and grab land for planting'. His complaints were aimed at Lieutenant Stephens 'had benefited greatly by this theft'.[73] More than half the 56 men supported Fernando's plan to seize the island. In the court martial that followed Gunner R S Hamilton explained Fernando's motives: 'he was anti-British'. Hamilton said that Fernando wanted all the staff of Cable and Wireless on nearby Direction Island killed 'and then send a message to the Japs asking them to come and destroy this place'.[74] The men that took part in the attack were surprised and overwhelmed. On 4 August 1942 Fernando, Gunner Benny de Silva and Gunner Carlo Gander were executed in Welikada Prison for their part in the Cocos Islands Mutiny. Eight others, including state's witness Hamilton were sentenced to years of hard labour. Fernando's last words were 'Loyalty to a country under the heel of a white man is disloyalty'.[75]

The Port Chicago Mutiny

On the Sacramento River just before its entry into San Francisco Bay is Port Chicago, where the navy loaded ammunition onto boats headed for the Pacific. The loading was done by Navy men who were all black, while their officers were all white. Captain Nelson Goss said that the men 'insisted they had volunteered for combat duty and did definitely resent being assigned what they called laborer's work'. It was a common enough complaint, nearly all the 150 000 black seamen in the Navy did mess duty or were in labor battalions. Cynicism about the war set in. 'If the Japanese and the Americans got in trouble over in Okinawa or Iwo Jima or somewhere we knew about it, but we weren't concerned', one man said: 'I had no brothers over there; I had no close friends over there.'[76]

Senior officers set their juniors in competition to fill the holds, but the men complained that it was not safe. No safety regulations were posted because Captain Kinne did not believe black men would understand them. The Coast Guard was supposed to watch munitions being loaded, but they objected to the rolling and dropping of bombs, so the Navy got rid of the Coast Guard. At 9.30 pm 17 July 1944 men were loading 1000 bombs into hold no 3 of the ship *E. A. Bryan,* and 650-pound incendiary bombs into hold no 1 – with some difficulty as they were wedged tight in the boxcar. At 10.19 pm an explosion with a blast equivalent to five tons of TNT – similar in impact to the atomic bomb dropped on Hiroshima – exploded, tearing the base apart. Three hundred and twenty men were killed outright, and another 390 civilians and enlisted men were injured. Around two thirds were black. An enquiry failed to blame the Navy for avoiding safety precautions, or spurring the junior officers to race against each other's teams, but instead concluded that 'coloured enlisted personnel are neither temperamentally nor intellectually capable of handling high explosives'.[77]

On 31 July men from the fourth and eight divisions at Port Chicago were marched towards the loading bays, having been refused the customary 30 day survivors' leave. One man remembered:

I just said: No, I ain't going back on that damn thing. Why don't you get some whiteys to put them down there. I said, hell, I'm a gunneryman. They taught me how to fire guns; I'm supposed to be on a ship. Now they've got me working as a stevedore. And I'm not getting stevedore's pay.[78]

Ordered onto the pier, the men, led by Joe Small, refused, and 258 were imprisoned straight away tight in the hold of an airless barge while the officers worked out what to do. After three days the men were asked who wanted to obey orders. Fifty stood their ground and were charged with mutiny. The National Association for the Advancement of Colored People sent Thurgood Marshall to defend the men. On 24 October all fifty of the defendants were found guilty and sentenced to fifteen years in jail. The other 208 were given a bad conduct discharge and fined 3 month's pay.

The NAACP's campaign caused a lot of embarrassment, and even Eleanor Roosevelt pointed out the wrongness of the sentences. Desegregation of the Navy followed quickly on, and officers were given instructions, in the Guide to the Command of Negro Personnel (1945) not to call sailors 'nigger', 'boy', 'darkie' or 'coon'. After the war, the sentences were reduced and the men released, though their records still carried the mutiny charge.

German mutineers

Discipline in the German army was strict, and backed up by the political officers of the SS. Still there were moments when German troops resisted the orders they were given. On 16 August 1943, German troops of the 1st Gebirgs (Mountain) Division took part in the massacre of villagers at the Greek village of Komeno. Though they obeyed order, afterwards many registered their opposition to the massacre: 'most of the soldiers did not agree with this action... Many said openly that it was nothing but a disgrace to shoot unarmed civilians. ... The argument was so heated that I might almost speak of a mutiny'.[79] Wehrmacht officers reacted against atrocities committed by the special Einsatzgruppen against Jews in the east, and also against the slaughters carried out by Croatian and Romanian allies. These misgivings, though, were not so great that any counter action was taken.

There were though some German troops who did more to challenge the Nazis. German left-wingers organised underground groups in the Wehrmacht. A Communist cell working the army on the eastern front issued 'Front Letter No 3', that asked 'Comrades, who is not up to his neck in shit here in the Eastern Front?' The leaflet explained that 'it is a criminal war unleashed by Hitler and it is leading Germany to hell'.[80] The German Communist Party had a special section, Travail Allemand that agitated among soldiers based in France, printing the paper Soldat im Wesen (Soldier in the West). Groups were set up in the Navy Ministry, the Ste Germain-en-laye barracks to the west of Paris and in the Bordeaux submarine base. The group had some success getting Wehrmacht soldiers to avoid being sent to the eastern front by deserting to join the French Resistance 'Maquis' groups. Artur London, a Czech, led the group till he was seized and taken to Mauthausen concentration camp (London survived the war, only to be jailed again as a 'Trotskyite-Titoite-Zionist' by the Stalinist regime in Czechoslovakia during the Slánský trial of 1952). Still Travail Allemand carried on under Otto

Nibergall.[81]

Another group of leftists led by the German Trotskyist Martin Monat put out a bulletin called Arbeiter und Soldat (Worker and Soldier). They managed to organise a group of German soldiers and sailors in Brest – 27 of whom were arrested in October 1943. Ten were shot, along with their leader 22 year-old Robert Cruau.[82]

Robert Cruau

As a Marxist, Wolfgang Abendroth, a member of the breakaway 'Opposition' Communist Party, was jailed in 1937. But during the war he was dragooned into the Punishment Battalion 999 with other political subversives and common criminals. Sent to fight in the Balkans, Abendroth made links with both the Tito guerrillas and then later the Greek ELAS-EAM resistance movement, which he eventually joined, fighting against Germany. In North Africa, Abendroth was put in a second concentration camp, this time with the Greek Resistance fighters who mutinied against the Allies.

Wolfgang Abendroth

In September 1943 the 13th Waffen SS Battalion billeted in Villefranche-de-Rouergue mutinied. The battalion was made up of Bosnian Muslim and Croat recruits, under German SS officers, and had been talking to the Communist resistance. One hundred and fifty of the mutineers were killed, before the remainder were sent back to fight in the Balkans.[83]

On 20 July 1944 Lieutenant Colonel Claus von Stauffenberg of the Wehrmacht High Command planted a bomb that injured, but did not kill Hitler. Henning von Tresckow and other military leaders joined the plot, but the dictator's survival scared them into aborting the planned coup. Afterwards the July bomb plot was important to German nationalists who wanted to talk up respectable opposition to Hitler. In truth, von Stauffenberg was no democrat, but a militarist and an imperialist. Still 5000 were arrested in the clear up operation that followed, and some 200 executed (though not all those were involved).[84]

Two groups of the German army fought against the SS during the battle for Berlin, around Sophie Charlotte Platz and Kaiserdamm.[85]

In September 1944, two hundred and sixty five Japanese soldiers were so outraged that their officers had seized all food supplies for themselves that they surrendered as a group on the Island of Numfoor off the coast of West New Guinea.[86]

How the Communists saved the Allied War Effort

In the time of the Hitler-Stalin pact many Communists in Europe and America felt that they were out on a limb opposing the war when patriotism and anti-Fascism seemed to be coming together.

With the German invasion of the USSR the communist parties adopted a new position that the war was one between two camps, the fascist and the popular democratic. For those communists in occupied Europe the new policy was great release, meaning that they could at last relate to the opposition to occupation – and communists made a much-celebrated contribution to the partisan movement. Official communists were rewarded for their support for the war effort by the British government, too. The ban on the *Daily Worker* was lifted, as were bans on the Canadian and Indian parties (the latter rewarded for being more pro-British than Congress). In America and Britain, communists embraced the goal of increasing the output of armaments as their contribution to the war effort, on the Joint Production Committees in Britain. The communists proved their loyalty with some vicious attacks on those radicals who still held out against the war effort. Elsewhere in the British Empire, intelligence officers tried to get communists to work for the war effort, as they did in Iran and Malaya.

Though the communists had been won over to the war effort, there was still radical opposition to the war effort from the left, among Socialists, pacifists, Trotskyists, anarchists and others. These groups were mostly very small, since the militant workers they hoped to recruit were usually already in the official communist parties, or in the Socialist parties. Where the communists tended to have more supporters than principles, with the far left it was the other way around. Still, with the upsurge in working class protest against the war effort, there was an opening for the more radical, unofficial left and anti-war movement to get a wider hearing.

As we have seen, the anarchist publishers and distributors of War Commentary risked imprisonment, and sometimes were imprisoned for their agitation against the war. The British Cabinet debated the problem of Trotskyism in 1944, with a memorandum drawn up by the Home Secretary Herbert Morrison:

> The Trotskyists while hostile to "fascism," regard the war as a struggle between rival Imperialisms, as struggled which is being used by the capitalist class as an excuse more effectively to exploit and oppress the workers.

The Cabinet worried that the Trotskyists Roy Tearse, Heaton Lee and others were behind strikes among the Tyneside Apprentices, at the Rolls Royce aircraft works in Glasgow and at the Barnbow Ordinance Works. 'They have a closely knit core of energetic leaders and a membership which makes up in enthusiasm what it lacks in numbers.' The Cabinet report saw the Trotskyists success in the context of the suspension of normal political and trade union activity in the war: 'They are helped by the absence of competition' and 'the lack of normal political and trade union activity, and the sense of frustration ... produced by the absence of marked progress towards victory in the field or reconstruction at home.'[87] On 5 April 1944 Special Branch raided the homes of the Trotskyists Heaton Lee and Ann Keen in Tyneside, and Roy Tearse in Glasgow. Along with Jock Haston, who gave himself up, they were charged with conspiring to further an illegal dispute for the help they gave to the Tyneside Apprentices Guild and tried in secret. In Parliament Nye Bevan charged that they had been denied their rights, and there were calls of 'Gestapo'. After the four were jailed for sentences up to 12 months, protests by trade unionists up and down the country followed and on appeal the convictions were quashed.[88]

The problem for the left wing opponents of the war was that they were isolated by the strong left wing case for the war that was being made by the Socialists and Communists. For the most part these radical opponents of the war were internationalist in outlook, but were in no position to join up with others in other countries.

The greatest divide between those movements struggling against the war drive was the very one that was dividing the world. Opponents of the Allied War effort would find it pretty much impossible to explain their goals to the opponents of the Axis war effort. Such was the urgency of standing up to the Fascist domination of peoples and nations that few who dedicated themselves to that task would understand or sympathise with any who undermined the Allied campaign against Hitler. The European resistance would prove to be a great moral resource for the Allies, the 'People's War' transformed from words into a people's war. For all that, the popular resistance in Europe would prove to be the greatest challenge to the Allies' plans for the continent.

Chapter Twenty One

The European Resistance

German demands on West Europe, first in cash plundered, and then later in men and women taken to Germany on the orders of Nazi plenipotentiary-general for labour mobilization Fritz Saukel weighed heavily (manpower was the overwhelming problem of the German war economy from 1942, due to military losses in the east).[1] 'Like a gigantic pump, the German Reich sucked in Europe's resources and working population'.[2]

Occupation Costs paid to Germany, in billions of Reichsmarks, 1940-44[3]

France	35,520
Netherlands	8750
Belgium	5700
Denmark	2000
Italy (from September 1943)	10,000
Other	22,300
Total	84,000

In the east, the exactions were even more onerous. Resistance grew. A revolution was building in Europe against the Nazi occupation that was not in the hands of the Allied Chiefs of Staff.

The British Special Operations Executive had been set up by Churchill on 16 July 1940 with orders to 'set Europe ablaze!' Goebbels protested that the English 'intended from the very beginning to have other countries and peoples do their fighting for them'.[4]

But the SOE had a problem controlling not only the resistance, but its own officers, who were wont to 'go native' – to identify more closely with the resistance fighters they worked with than with Whitehall. SOE wrote a booklet *Principles of Training for Special Purposes* which set out rules for recruitment and training. 'Psychological testing was considered the first step, followed by loyalty checks on prospective volunteers' and 'elimination of egos and delusions of heroism were critical'. They wanted 'men who were apolitical, yet conscious of their role in establishing good Allied relations with potential future political leaders'.[5] As it turned out, SOE's fears had some basis. Officers James Klugmann and Basil Davidson clearly did identify with the insurgents to a point that enraged their superiors – though Klugmann, who rose to the rank of Major, had been recruited because his left-wing views made him a useful contact with Tito's partisans in Yugoslavia.[6]

After the war, the SOE's official historians would downplay the role of the resistance in defeating Fascism. It was of course true, as they claimed, that only a small minority of the peoples of the occupied territories took up arms. The European Resistance had many more supporters as the Axis cause began to falter, yet more when it collapsed. For those European states that were founded in the wake of the Allied invasion, the Resistance was a potent and necessary myth, that let them pretend they did not owe their independence to the Allies. Still, the Resistance was decisive in the defeat of the Axis. That they were a small minority is not so important: revolutionary change always begins with a minority, and gathers support through its leadership and courage. The post-war states did owe their existence to the Allies, but less for the defeat of the Axis forces, more for the taming of the popular resistance at the war's end.

France

According to the resistance historian Henri Michel 'from summer 1940 to autumn 1942 all resistance in Europe drew its support from Great Britain', 'gradually, however, clandestine resistance developed on a major scale and it was not prepared to accept orders so easily'. Furthermore, 'Churchill was himself somewhat alarmed by the growth of a force which he might not be able to control'.[7]

The Special Operations Executive (SOE) and De Gaulle struggled to control the Resistance, sending former prefect Jean Moulin to keep order. 'Centralisation and coordination will take place in London', read De Gaulle's instructions: 'All these operations will take place on the personal order of General De Gaulle'. De Gaulle thought the Resistance would be an intelligence gathering force, assisting the SOE, but already many different groups were at work and reluctant to be reined in. SOE recruited those leaders it could, like the Liberation-Nord group's Christian Pineau, as agents.[8]

To De Gaulle, the key was controlling the communists, for which he needed Moulin, who had been on the political left: 'It was Moulin more than any other who made it possible to bring the communists on board, as part of the Free French organisation, and thus to control them'. The machinery for controlling the communists was the Conseil National de la Resistance (CNR) that Moulin put in place, with representatives of all the main groups including the communist-led 'Francs Tireurs et Partisans', and it was agreed that 'in military terms the coordinating committee is under the orders of General de Gaulle within the framework of the Allied strategic plan'. 'Without the CNR, there would not have been *a* resistance but several resistances' de Gaulle explained: 'At the Liberation there would not have been a united people, but a divided country' and more alarming still 'we would not have stopped the communists from holding parts of the territory'.[9]

Though de Gaulle's fears of the Resistance escaping his control focussed on the threat posed by the communists, the Parti Communist Français (PCF) turned out to be his most loyal ally. Early on the leadership in France, influenced by Moscow decided on de Gaulle as the ideal leader for a 'United Front' of all the 'patriotic classes'. The party's paper *Humanité* wanted not only to rid France of the occupier, but also identified with 'the patriotic struggle which will restore France to its sovereignty and grandeur' – using de Gaulle's own code words for the restoration of the French Empire. British money was channelled from the SOE in London to de Gaulle and from de Gaulle to the PCF – no less than three million francs a month (or 100 times the amount given to the next largest resistance group Combat), and on top of this the Party got a further 2 million francs from de Gaulle's right-wing ally, the film producer Gilbert Renault's own funds. De Gaulle tacked to the left to flatter his new shock troops, saying 'national liberation cannot be separated from national insurrection' and even threatening to relocate the Free French operation to Moscow during one row with Whitehall. As it turned out the PCF, with its disciplined organisation and Moscow-oriented policy was something of a brake on the radical upsurge that the struggle against the occupation provoked. When the row with

America over Giraud broke out, the PCF argued that de Gaulle should compromise.[10]

The other resistance groups, not subordinate to Stalinist discipline could be more trouble for London. Combat, though its founders were of the French far right swung rapidly to the left, straining at Moulin's collar. Combat leader Henri Frenay explained 'liberation and revolution are two aspects of the same problem that are indissolubly linked in the minds of all our members', and 'a revolutionary army appoints its leaders and does not have them imposed'. Frenay accepted de Gaulle's military leadership, but as 'a revolutionary expression ... we retain our full independence'. On the other hand, Combat could be wildly opportunistic, and entered into its own talks with Vichy officers at one point, and then from February 1943, took 10 million francs a month from the American Office of Strategic Services (no doubt Washington was hedging its bets on Giraud and against de Gaulle). On another occasion the socialist Brossolette fell foul of Jean Moulin's jealous control of the Resistance when he helped set up a Resistance Coordinating Committee with Liberation Nord, communists and others in the occupied zone.[11]

Later, de Gaulle and Moulin's moves to order the resistance along lines pre-ordained in London fell apart. The terrible cost of German anti-partisan measures created a rapid turnover of leaders. Jean Moulin died during his interrogation by Gestapo head Klaus Barbie on 8 July 1943. The resistance became more spontaneous, as the 'Maquis' grew, swelled by those trying to avoid the Service du Travail Obligatoire – forced labour act – of 4 September 1942, and its even harsher version a year later.[12] There were around 13,000 *maquisards* across the country, and this new resistance organisation was not interested in waiting for instructions from either the SOE or de Gaulle. The group led by Georges Guingouin grew from around 100 to thousands operating in 25000 square kilometres around Eymoutiers.[13]

On 12th March 1944 a Maquis group of 465 seasoned fighters fought the Wehrmacht's 157th Alpen Division, which was supported by 12,000 Vichy police and infantry, holding the Glières Plateau for two weeks of heavy fighting.[14]

Albert Camus, wrote for the Resistance paper *Combat* on 23

August 1944 that 'a people who want to live free do not wait for someone to bring them their freedom': 'They take it.' To Camus it was clear that the Resistance was a revolution: 'we want the immediate realization of a true popular democracy' he wrote in *Combat*, adding 'we believe that any politics separated from the working class is futile, and that the future of France is the future of its working class'.[15] Camus' radicalism showed that the feeling that the Resistance would sweep away the old order spread much further than the official Communist Party presses.

Czech lands

One resistance movement that was closely under the influence of the Special Operations Executive in London was the Czech. Edvard Beneš the Czech Prime Minister set up a government in exile in London that cleaved closely to British strategy. Initially, resistance in the Czech lands was strong, with extensive acts of sabotage, and there were mass actions, like a boycott of the collaborationist press in September 1941. To shore up German rule a brutal overlord, Reinhard Heydrich was sent. Heydrich set about deporting Jews from the country.

The SOE and the government in London hatched a plan to assassinate Heydrich, which was carried out by two agents trained and parachuted in, Jan Kubiš and Jozef Gabčík. On 27 May 1942 the two ambushed Heydrich, shooting him with a Sten gun (he died from his wounds a week later). Though the attack was heroic and a great propaganda coup against one of the key architects of the Final Solution, it was a setback for the Czech resistance. German reprisals were savage, beginning with the destruction of Lidice and massacre of its male population, 19 June 1942, followed by the village of Ležáky on 24th June, and ending with the wrecking of the SOE-Czech network and the deaths of Kubiš and Gabčík.[16]

Italy

Italy's popular disaffection with Mussolini turned on the Fascists' failure to feed their people. The dictator had taken Italy into the war to galvanise the people around him, and for a while it worked, but doubts quickly emerged. By 1942, many Italians saw that they were only the junior partner, even subject to German whims. As the war ground on, the likelihood of being on the losing side was under-scored by Allied bombing raids and the push from North Africa into the Axis' own 'soft underbelly'. Italy's elite lost confidence in the wager they had made on Mussolini. The Italian people, long subdued by the Fasces, protested against hunger, and, as we have seen, struck out the industrial plants in the north.[17]

Fearful of mass disaffection, the Fascist Council, with the support of King Victor Emmanuel, deposed Benito Mussolini, on 24 July 1943. The Fascist Pietro Badoglio set up secret negotiations with the Allies to pull out of the German alliance. British representative Harold Macmillan was relieved: 'it would suit us much better not to be stimulators of a revolution, which we shall only have to suppress later'.[18] The Allies agreed that if Italy declared war against Germany it could become a co-belligerent, and so avoid a prolonged occupation after the war. Roosevelt and Churchill hoped for a clean handover of power, with the Italian authorities, newly cleansed of their Axis associations, fronting an Allied occupation.

The German forces in Italy by that time had been doing most of the fighting, and were well-entrenched. On 9 September the agreement was published, and the Italian government withdrew to Brindisi, while the Wehrmacht disarmed their already demoralised Italian allies, taking 647,000 prisoners. Late in September 1943 Field Marshall Kesselring fought the Allies to a standstill at Salerno, securing a German occupation of the country to the just north of Naples. Still, the German hold on Italy was tenuous, and two weeks after the surrender Rome was an 'open city', with the king and Badoglio having abandoned responsibility.

The Italian underground grabbed its chance and declared itself a Committee of National Liberation with Ivanoe Bonomi as head. The movement was not large – as few as 4000 in September 1943, growing to 10,000 in January 1944, 60,000 by July and 100,000 by October. Among them, around a third were factory workers, a fifth peasants, who fought alongside students, shop-workers, and clerks. Nearly a fifth were women.[19]

Their initial success was short-lived as the Germans reinvaded Rome on 23 September bringing in martial law. Though open liber-ation government was blocked, the CLN moved to create partisan groups to carry on the resistance, with some real success. Partisans helped Croatian Jews jailed on the camp on the Island of Rab to free themselves, so avoiding the German extermination camps.[20]

Liberation of detainees on the Island of Rab

The British response to the Badoglio government's surrender, and the attempts to liberate the north was to step up the bombing of Italian cities, in particular Turin and Milan – the centres of the labour opposition to Mussolini.[21]

In the summer of 1944 partisans succeeded in liberating at least 15 'partisan republics', like Carnia, Montefiorini, and Ossola, emboldened by the allied advance, and established Committees of National Liberation.[22] British General Alexander, the Allied Commander, told the *Times* that the partisans were holding down up to six of the 25 German divisions.[23]

Partisans of Florence take on the Wehrmacht

The Wehrmacht's war against the Italian partisans was brutal and unremitting. On 24 March 1944 in the Ardeatine caves 335 Italians were bound and shot on the orders of Luftwaffe Obersturmbannfuhrer Kurt Mälzer. The slaughter was a reprisal for the Gruppo d'Azione Patriotica's attack that killed 28 members of a German police battalion in the Via Rassella in Rome. There were other massacres, so-called reprisals for partisan attacks. More than 200 were killed in the Val di Chiana near Arezzo in June 1944, and later 771 were killed around Mazabotto on the outskirts of Bologna, 46 at Guardiastello south of Livorno. Between 1943 and 1945 44,720 anti-Fascists were killed in battle, 21,000 wounded and a further 9,980 were executed in reprisals.[24]

Greece

ELAS, the Greek People's Liberation Army was initiated by Aris Velouchtis, in the face of scepticism from his fellow Communist Party (EAM) members, as a way of organising the Greek klephtic brigands who were busy raiding rural towns, as a force against the German occupation late in 1941.[25] Joined by the liberal officer Stefanos Sarafis ELAS's successes were rapid, and the organisation founded liberated zones in the countryside, adding to the strikes against forced labour in the cities in 1943.[26]

ELAS grew from 12,500 in the summer of 1943 to 30,000 in the spring of 1944 to around 50,000 on the eve of liberation. They faced an occupation force of 300,000, made up of the German 5th Army, the Italian 11th Army (who surrendered in 1943) and the Bulgarian 2nd Army Corps. The Axis Commanding Officer Lieutenant General Alexander Löhr waged a brutal war. More than 1000 villages were burned down. More than a million Greeks had seen their homes robbed and destroyed. Their crops were burned and their churches desecrated. More than 20,000 civilians were killed or wounded, shot, hanged or beaten by the Axis forces. From the time they set up their General HQ in May 1943 ELAS recorded enemy casualties. ELAS killed 19,355 Axis troops, wounded 8,294 and took 5,181 prisoners.[27]

Axis strategy struggled with the tenacity of the mountain-based resistance. Mass sweeps were effective at first, but ELAS quickly recovered, and grew. The Wehrmacht and its allies followed a strategy of terrorising villages from which ELAS drew its strength, often taking local notables – doctors, lawyers – as hostages. In October 1943 General Karl Le Suire, responded to the killing of 78 soldiers of the 117 Jaeger Division by killing 696 Greeks from the town of Kalavryta and villages around. Kalavryta lost all its adult men. At the end of 1944 the Germans were using more local Greek battalions to take on ELAS.[28]

Despite the tenacity of the ELAS resistance, the Allies were alarmed that they had succeeded in liberating much of the country themselves. The British 'Minister Resident in the Mediterranean' Harold Macmillan was warned by the nationalist politician George Papandreou, that 'in our desire to attack the Germans we had aroused and armed most dangerous Communist forces in Greece itself' – though Stefanos Sarafis said that British arms supplies were not that great.[29] By September 1943, the Italian army was surrendering its arms and supplies to an ELAS force of 50,000, giving it absolute advantage over its smaller rival liberation forces.[30]

ELAS Partisans, photographed by Dmitri Kessel

Britain sent a youthful Captain Christopher Montague Woodhouse (later the fifth Baron Terrington and Conservative MP for Oxford) into Greece in the hopes of building up alternative 'national' bands, but he found that ELAS were in control, 'even motor roads were mended and used by EAM-ELAS'.[31] Indeed, according to historian Mark Mazower EAM-ELAS

> organised economic activity, reshaped the judicial and educational systems, and introduced social reforms for women. EAM officials handled relief for the victims of Axis raids and for guerrillas' dependents; they brought in a new system of local self-government, and even held national elections in March 1944.[32]

The ELAS-EAM fighters were painted as vicious brutes by their critics in Allied Head Quarters in Egypt, by the Greek Royalists, and by the Wehrmacht. Still, the liberated areas under EAM influence were remarkable for their self-sufficiency, and self-administration. Schools and children's groups were organised. Women, who fought alongside men in ELAS were also active in village organisation, and first got the vote in the EAM organised elections.

Still the British persevered in their attempts to build up the rival EDES militia – which regularly turned its guns on ELAS instead of the Germans, and in many instances, got support from the Wehrmacht as well. In October 1943 EDES forces made a surprised attack on ELAS troops in Roumeli, which was followed by an ELAS counter-offensive. Though relations were patched up afterwards, hostilities often broke out afterwards.[33]

Yugoslavia

The division of the Kingdom of Yugoslavia between Germany and Italy, left a rump Serbia ruled over by the quisling General Nedic and the pro-German Croat regime of Ante Pavelic with its Ustashe militia. The Ustashe slaughtered Serbs and Jews, killing 500 000. Two groups of Yugoslav partisans vied for leadership, the royalist 'Chetniks' under Draza Mihailovic, and the Communist-led group under Josip Broz Tito. Initially the British SOE favoured Mihailovic, with the King in exile in London, and the novelist Evelyn Waugh acting as contact officer. Waugh's high Tory prejudices (he reported back that Tito was in fact a woman, and even insisted on calling him 'Madam' when they met) helped to blind the SOE to the real conditions in Yugoslavia. On the ground, though, it was Tito who was fighting the war, while Mihailovic gave the struggle against

Communism the priority over that with Germany. At Uzice, the Chetniks joined in a German attack on the partisans. In 1943, the SOE sent nine missions to the Chetniks, trying to persuade them to fight the Germans, but without success.[34]

Ustashe militia man with Chetnik trophy

Tito's forces were the most remarkable of all the partisan armies, a quarter of a million in 1943, who inflicted extensive casualties on the German military. The partisans themselves lost 305,000 men and women.[35]

Tito clashed with the Soviet leadership, who reprimanded the Yugoslav partisans for ultra-leftism. The great strength of Tito's forces, though, was that they were committed to liberating themselves. 'If we ourselves do not do our best in the struggle against the invader, if we sit with folded arms, we cannot expect the Red Army to liberate us', said Tito's right-hand man Milovan Djilas. The Partisans 'Anti-Fascists Council of National Liberation' first met in Bihac on 26 November 1942, and would have named itself a government, but the Soviets objected that they could not, still hoping that the Royalists could be brought on side. Tito's Central Committee 'knew that the Soviets viewed our struggle, and our relations with the royal government, in the light of their relations with Great Britain'– in other words, the Soviets followed the British policy of demanding that the Royalist government's rights be observed.[36]

Between January and April 1943, the Partisans faced a sustained German offensive, 'Operation Weiss', or the Fourth Anti-Partisan Offensive, which rallied six German, three Italian and two Chetnik divisions. The campaign cost the Partisans 8000 men and women, but Tito survived by crossing the Neretva River into eastern Bosnia and scored the moral victory. Weiss was followed up with a Fifth Anti-Partisan Offensive in May and June 1943, but this time the German forces were pushed back after initial success, cementing the Yugoslav National Liberation Army's reputation. That December the Soviet government issued a communiqué supporting Tito's provisional government. The same month, in Teheran, the Allies together backed Tito's partisans and British support for Mihailovic was abandoned.[37]

In 1943 Churchill batted off criticism of the Titoists saying that 'the partisans and patriots in Yugoslavia and Albania were containing as many [German] divisions as the British and American armies together'. Hitler's SS liaison officer Obergruppenfuehrer Karl Wolff said that 'at least fifty divisions were engaged throughout the Balkans on occupation duty, primarily to check partisan activity' – which was indeed more than were deployed in North Africa.[38] British ambitions in the Balkans were damaged by their support for Mihailovic. The pressure for change built up in the SOE, and eventually, Churchill intervened sending the aristocratic Tory MP Fitzroy Maclean to Yugoslavia to support Tito.[39]

Allies' fear of the resistance movement

A sharp-eyed Dwight MacDonald saw that Allied policy had turned around, from making a big political appeal for support in the early years of the war, as the resistance grew 'everything is being done to de-politicize this war'. Rather the new official line was 'this is not a revolutionary war and must not be allowed to "get out of hand"'[40]

The British intelligence officer and Soviet spy Kim Philby saw that 'the resistance movements leant so heavily towards the Soviet Union, and the balance was only restored in France, Italy, and Greece by a massive Anglo-American military presence'.[41] Put simply, the reason that the Second Front was finally opened up was because of the fear that the people would liberate themselves. Nazi rule had been welcomed by western leaders in 1920 and 1933 when it helped stabilize capitalism. Even when Germany's territorial ambitions were too much for Churchill and Roosevelt to tolerate, they were still content to leave Fascist rule in place on the Continent – even seeking a *modus vivendi* with the authoritarian regimes in Spain, Portugal and Vichy France. On the other hand, they were prepared to use the partisan movements to destabilise Germany when it became a threat to American and British geopolitical ambitions. But now that Fascist rule threatened to provoke popular uprisings the Allies were finally persuaded to impose their own writ on Western Europe, rather than let power fall into the streets.

Chapter Twenty Two

Partisans of the East

In the east the Greater East Asian Co-Prosperity Sphere was proving to be a sham, and for many, a death-trap. Of all peoples who suffered, it was the Chinese, both in China and across East Asia who were the hate figures of the Japanese Imperial mission. While many Indians, Burmese, Malays, Indonesians and Filipinos had seen the chance of a positive change in the Japan's pan-Asian appeal, few Chinese could. When resistance to Japan's presence in East Asia grew it was led by the Chinese, though soon enough they would be joined by many of the nationalist movements that Fujiwara Iwaichi had helped to organise to fight the British Empire.

China

The Chinese nationalist movement was divided between the two wings of the Kuomintang, the Communists under Mao Zedong, based in Yunan since retreating from the cities to the countryside, and the Nationalists under Chiang Kai-Shek. The nationalists had fought in earnest since August 1937 when Chiang Kai-Shek sent his crack troops to challenge Japan in Shanghai, at a cost of 250,000 Chinese. Retreating into the interior, Chiang's forces inflicted a defeat on the Japanese at Tai'erzhuang that cost them 30,000 men.[1] In 1938, to try to halt the Japanese advance into China, Chiang Kai-Shek ordered the dykes on the Yellow River breached, flooding thousands of square kilometres of Henan, Anhui and Jengsu, killing more than 800,000, and cementing his reputation as a tyrant.

The clique at the head of the Kuomintang, Chiang, his wife, and finance minister HH Kung exploited the support of the US for personal gain. Their demands for aid were heard sympathetically at first, but over time it became clear to Washington that a lot of the money never got to China, and Henry Morgenthau listed the $460 million that was held in accounts in the US. Quite a lot of the money was financing lobbyists and promotions aimed at getting more money, so that the Kuomintang was having a greater impact in Washington than in China. The US Chiefs of Staff were convinced that Chiang was putting up only token resistance and wanted Commander Joe Stilwell to assume command of the Kuomintang Army – a proposal that was too much for Chiang to accept. After all, Stillwell had written that Chiang

> will only continue his policy and delay, while grabbing for loans and postwar aid, for the purpose of maintaining his present position, based on one-party government, a reactionary policy, or the suppression of democratic ideas with active aid of his gestapo.[2]

Chiang's nationalists were challenged by Mao's Communists. The Communist Party had recovered from its near destruction in Shanghai, and had hardened its core cadre through the 'long march' in inland China, and was recruiting nationally-minded youth, disappointed by the corruption under nationalist rule. By 1941 party membership had grown to 700,000.[3] That year, the Nationalists broke the truce between the two sides by attacking Ye Ting's New 4th Army at Maolin in Anhui. The action led Roosevelt to suspend a scheduled loan of $50 million.[4] Both nationalists and Communists were at different times suspected of withholding forces from the conflict with Japan in anticipation of their own war for predominance.[5] Still, it was in the end the Communists who earned the respect for taking the war to the enemy. A 1944 US mission to Yenan concluded that 'In Communist China there is ... the most cohesive, disciplined and aggressively anti-Japanese regime in China'.[6] By the end of the war Mao's army was 1.3 million strong, and the eventual victor of the Civil War that followed, where it had been just one sixtieth of Chiang's forces at the start.[7]

Korea

Japan's long term policy in Korea was to force peasants from the land, which it did by registering ownership under the Cadestral Survey (1911-1918) and buying up plots through the Japanese Oriental Development Company. These dispossessed had to work for Japanese industry in Korea, or in Japan (as two million did by 1945). Under Japan's forced industrialisation mining output grew five times between 1925 and 1940 while manufacturing doubled. All of Korea's exports were within the 'Yen block', nine tenths to Japan.[8]

Koreans had demanded equality since the March 1st Movement of 1919, when some two million took part in demonstrations across the country. That led to reforms which put the administration on a more civilian footing, but still the Japanese were in charge. In 1924 a Korean Workers and Peasants League (they became two separate organisations in 1927) gathered many supporters. In 1929 they fought a three-month long strike in Wŏnsan in 1929. In 1931, with the invasion of China on the pretext of the Manchuria incident, the Korean Workers League launched a strike that led to its suppression by the Japanese authorities.[9]

There were some partisan bands that fought the Japanese. The best known of these is the one led by the man who would become dictator of North Korea, Kim Il-sung. Like many Koreans who took up arms against Japan Kim Il-sung had been impressed by the Chinese Communist guerrillas. Having moved to Manchuria when young, he joined the North East Anti-Japanese Army in 1936, which was involved in a series of daring raids on Japanese posts between 1937 and 1940 on both sides of the Manchuria-Korean border. Kim led an attack on Pujŏn in 1937 that saw public buildings destroyed and Japanese police officers killed. Other leading Communist Partisans included Yi Hong-gwang (who was killed in 1935) and Ch'oe Hyŏn.[10]

Veteran nationalist leader and newspaper editor Yuh Woon-Hyung (Yŭ Un-hyŏng) organised an underground Korean Independence League from 10 August 1944, which called for the expulsion of the Japanese and carried out a number of actions. Yuh went on to found the Committee for the Preparation for Korean Independence in 1945.

Malaya

The Japanese forces found collaborators among the British-sponsored Malay leaders, like Tunku Abdul Rahman. Still, Japan's Total War Research Institute report of February 1942 showed just how little the Malays could expect. Welcoming the conservative influence of the Buddhist mainland, the Research Institute judged that the islands of the Malay Archipelago were underdeveloped, and would be 'permanent colonies' of Japan.[11] Abandoned by their local allies, the British authorities reached out to the radical Malayan Communist Party, who were keen to fight. On 19 December 1941the Special Operations Executive's Frederick Spencer Chapman began training Communists in guerrilla tactics – and even agreed that those who were at that time in jail for their subversive activities against the British Empire could be released to take part. According to Chapman, the Communists who were 'young, fit and full of enthusiasm were the best material we ever had at the school'. The first detachment of the Malayan Peoples Anti-Japanese Army was set up on 10 January 1942, at Serendah.[12]

Operating from jungle bases the Malayan Peoples Anti-Japanese Army, became a formidable guerrilla force, harassing Japanese troops, Kempetai, administrators and local collaborators. The British liaison officers, 'fascinated by the great seriousness of purpose and high intensity of life in the camps' were unhappy at the MPAJA's independence. The British had a spy in the Malayan Communist Party leadership named Lai Te, which gave them an advantage, though he also collaborated with the Japanese, calling his influence into question. In any event, the military leadership was effectively in the hands of the more resolute Chin Peng.

To spread their options, the British made links to other Chinese guerrillas who identified as Kuomintang, and tried to force the MPAJA to cooperate with them – though they were broken by the Kempetai in 1944. The British officers came to feel that they 'were vagrants, dependent on the guerrillas' charity' and kept as 'living exhibits of the decadent and degraded colonial planter class'.[13] Chin Peng had few illusions, though:

> the British and their Commonwealth allies retreated, scuttled and surrendered. They used us. They abandoned us. When they returned they expected our undivided loyalty.[14]

His determination that the MPAJA should rely on its own resources – but take whatever help it could – was the making of one of the most determined partisan groups fighting in the Pacific War.

Vietnam
Vietnam suffered a shocking famine as the French colonial officials

carried out Japanese orders that rice paddies be turned over to Jute, and much of what rice was grown was exported to Burma. Farmers who resisted were beaten or killed. As many as two million died in the hunger that followed. The Viet Minh Front was founded in 1941, and the demand that the rice stores be opened saw the Front's standing rise. The Vietnam Liberation Army was active from December 1944. On 9 March 1945 the Viet Minh sent a memo to the Free French leader in Indochina, Jean Sainteny, which looked forward to free elections with a universal franchise to found a Vietnamese government under a French governor, with independence to follow in five or ten years, after the colonial power had been compensated for its losses.[15] France's reply was a sharp rebuff. On 24 March Paris announced it wanted Indochina broken up into a French-run federation of five regions. That meant Vietnam would be divided between its provinces Tonkin, Annan and Cochin China.[16]

France's post-war plans were looking all the less plausible since the Japanese had, on 10 March, sent the Kempetai to arrest the Vichy administrator and his Sûreté agents, announcing that, with 'no intention of territorial conquest', it had decided to take over. Taking advantage of the Japanese promises 'to help the peoples of Indochina, hitherto toiling under the colonial yoke, to fulfil their ardent desire for independence', a National Party for the Independence of Vietnam, supported by followers of the Cao Dai religious sect called for demonstrations. But fearing the outcome, the Japanese banned them.[17]

By June 1945 the Viet Minh had created a liberated zone of six counties. At that time Ho Chi Minh had set up friendly relations with the US agents of the Office of Strategic Services, in particular one Robert Shapleen who remembered the future Viet Cong leader as 'an awfully sweet guy'.[18] Thirty thousand miners of the Hongai-Campha coal mines took control of their town. In the South demonstrators rallying behind the National Party for Independence demonstrated on 21 August 1945 calling 'Down with French Imperialism!' and 'Independence for Vietnam!'. But in July the Viet Minh were still pushing to work with the French and according to a report 'would have liked, at this juncture, to enter Hanoi side by side with the French delegate'. They had even ordered French tricolour flags for the occasion.[19] With the Japanese surrender in August the Viet Minh looked again at its strategy and 'decided to snatch power from the hands of the Japanese fascists before the arrival of the Allies'. Ho issued the call for a general uprising:

> Countrymen arise! Les us free ourselves by our own energies. Numerous oppressed peoples of the world are vying with one another in the ardent struggle for independence. We cannot lag behind ... Onward under the flag of the Vietminh.

Ho Chi Minh prefaced this call with the warning that 'we still have a hard fight ahead of us', and that 'the defeat of the Japanese does not render us automatically free and independent'.[20] On 17 August, with Jean Sainteny stranded in Kunming, the civil servants' union called a strike. In the hot monsoon rains tens of thousands of men in white shorts marched through Hanoi, and the custodian Consultative Assembly of Tonkin set up by the Japanese under the Emperor Bao Dai fled. The crowds grew with women and coolies joining the throng. Their banners were scarlet with the gold star of the Vietminh. On 14-15 August the Vietminh led a general uprising occupying Japanese positions.[21] Over the night of 19-20 August Vietnamese turned on French settlers, and ten or more were killed. By 25 August Bao Dai stood down, recognising the Democratic Republic and thereby granting the imprimatur of the Nguyễn Dynasty.

Burma

Towards the end of 1943 Thakin leader Aung San saw that the liberation that the Japanese had promised was a sham. His Burma defence Army began talks with the communist leader Thakin Soe, who had organised a resistance group in the Arakan countryside. Soe's modest Anti-Fascist People's Freedom League was all the same an inspiration to the disillusioned BDA. Aung San, while still leader of the BDA, gave sharply anti-Japanese speeches, and communicated to the British that he intended an uprising. Still smarting, Lieutenant Dorman-Smith and others in the Civil Affairs Bureau (Burma) were outraged that having helped kick the British out of Burma, Aung San was now offering to help beat the Japanese, and they had to be talked around by a more far-sighted Louis

Mountbatten to help arm Aung San. On 27 March 1945 the Burmese attacked Japanese positions. Over the next five months they killed 8,826 Japanese. The BDA proved a fearsome enemy, pinning down large numbers of Japanese, and escaping retaliation by fleeing to the countryside.

Indonesia

A Japanese Imperial Conference in May 1943 decided that 'Marai, Sumatra, Java, Borneo, and the Celebes are Japanese territory and a priority effort will be made to develop them as supply areas for major natural resources'.[22] The requisition of men and materials in Java was brutal. By November 1944 some 2.6 million were working as forced labourers. Farmers and labourers who were transported as labourers often died.[23] When Premier Tōjō promised that Burma and the Philippines would become independent, Sukarno was distraught asking why did the Japanese rip up railroads and round up labourers from Indonesia and send them to Burma, while ignoring loyal Indonesia?[24] As it happened, Indonesia was not that loyal.

In Java Japanese officers blamed opposition on lingering loyalty to the Dutch, rather than native resentment at their treatment. The Kempetai saw a 'full-scale anti-Japanese movement' which 'drew the entire island of Java into a vortex of strategems'. Kempetai commander Murase, frustrated at the slow pace of the courts-martial investigating rebels was 'thwarting Kempetai goals and paralyzing the army, thereby impeding the work of the military government'. Murase got the approval for a gloves-off strategy called 'Operation Hades'. Indefinite imprisonment and summary execution became the norm in Kempetai interrogations and some 300 Javanese lost their lives.[25]

Tensions between the Indonesian auxiliaries and their Japanese commanders were high, and a volunteer corps unit in Blitar mutinied in February 1945. In West Borneo, Japanese troops came under attack from Dyak tribesmen angered by the destruction of their forests for timber. On 16 August 1945 members of the Indonesian volunteer corps burned the Japanese flag and declared the first liberated zone in Indonesia.[26]

Philippines

Japanese administration in the Philippines was fronted by local collaborators, led by President Jose Laurel and the senior civil servant Jorge Vargas. The Filipino elite took MacArthur's advice to collaborate with the Japanese, and many of the wealthy landlords and merchants played key roles in the pro-Japanese administration. While paying lip-service to Filipino independence, and Jose Laurel's administration, the Commonwealth was dominated by the Japanese military and the Kempetai.

Disloyalty to the Japanese was punished severely, often with summary execution, and Kempetai commonly beat Filipinos. The Japanese censored newspapers, and made owners of printing presses, and even typewriters and radio receivers register with the authorities. On the other hand, the policy of promoting the Tagalog language in presses and the theatre was a popular move. The Japanese talked up opposition to American imperialism, just as they instituted their own. Farmers were encouraged to shift from sugar (which had been exported to America) to cotton, as a move to economic independence. As it turned out the imposition of an over-inflated Japanese-backed currency wrecked the economy and farmers mostly withheld their produce, so that the planned cotton targets were never met. What cotton was grown went into Japanese military uniforms. While the Japanese incorporated leading Filipino senators into the administration they banned political parties. In their stead the organised a conservative movement the Kalibapi, which was led by Benigno Aquino Sr (his son, of the same name, would play a decisive part in the struggle against the US-backed dictator Marcos).

There were many disparate resistance bands in the Philippines that were started by members of the United States Armed Forces in the Far East, both Americans and Filipino. For them, the resistance was carrying on the Philippine-American war effort, and giving force to General Douglas MacArthur's promise 'I will return'. As they made contact with MacArthur in Australia, though, they got the message back from him that their

Primary mission is to maintain your organisation and to secure maximum amount of information. Guerrilla activities should be postponed until ordered from here.[27]

MacArthur's opposition to independent action stymied the action of these bands. The exception was the Hukbo ng Bayan Laban sa Hapon, 'People's anti-Japanese Army', called the Hukbalahap, or just Huks. The Hukbalahap was set up by communists and socialists on 29 March 1942. To counter the Japanese-inspired Kalibapi the Hukbalahap organised Barrio United Defence Corps, community based self-government groups. The BUDCs elected their own officers (taking advantage of the democratic deficit in the Japanese-backed Philippine government) and organised local amenities, as well as hearing complaints in their own courts, and even officiating at marriages and baptisms. The BUDCs drew as many as half a million Filipinos into a parallel administration that was dedicated to liberation, while the guerrilla force itself grew to a strength of 100,000.[28] By 1944 Manila was, the Kempetai said, a place they feared, full of armed guerrillas who

> disguised as vegetable carriers would suddenly shoot at a sentry on duty in front of the military headquarters and then get away. Even Kempetai drinking coffee on the streets would be shot at, and in the evening Kempetai on their way to the cabarets would be met by assassins lying in waiting. Day or night, Manila was a city infested with assassins.[29]

The Hukbalahap raised such high hopes amongst the Filipino peasants that they often had to stop them from seizing landlords' holdings and rents. Though they took heart from Mao Tse-Tung's guerrilla tactics, they feared that land seizure would risk relations with the Allies and the United States in particular. The Hukbalahap had sent Casto Alejandrino and Fernando Sampo, two mayors to see MacArthur when he was still at Corrigedor, but got little encouragement. Still they held up the alliance, and when they led a force that seized the town of Nueva Ecija, they raised both the Philippine and US flags.[30]

The Japanese Empire turned out to have been built on sand. As quickly as the British Empire and the US Navy had melted away, so too the Japanese collapsed after them. It was not that the Japanese army was weak; on the contrary it continued to fight on fiercely, island by island, to defend the mainland. But just as for the British and Americans, it was the attitude of the local peoples that was decisive. The 'Co-Prosperity Sphere' had been conceived as an extension of the pre-war division of labour, with Japanese techno-logical goods exchanged for East Asian primary goods. But the needs of fighting the war turned Japanese industry to military work, so there was no exchange, just plunder. Japan's idealistic projection of 'Asia for the Asians' was undone by that basic inequality, and the promised political independence was withheld. Instead of freedom, the Japanese military had nothing to offer but brutality. Already predisposed to persecute the Chinese across East Asia, the Japanese failed to consolidate their initially promising base of support amongst other races. The exposure of the Co-Prosperity Sphere as just another western-style imperialism was its undoing. The great challenge for the region was whether the outcome of the war would be liberation or subjugation again.

Chapter Twenty Three

Collapse of the German Empire in the East

Early on in the German occupation of the USSR there had been some notable attempts to consolidate local support. Alfred Rosenberg, an early member of the NSDAP and a Baltic German pushed a policy of making a buffer zone of anti-Soviet states: Ukraine, Byelorussia, Finland and a federation of Balkan states. At first he had Hitler's blessing. Another German administrator, Wilhelm Kube tried to build ties with 'White Ruthenians' (Byelorussians) promoting local officials and education. The most suprising consolidation of local support was among the Baltic states, whose racial 'German-ness' and cultural ties with the Reich were emphasized, just as local police forces and municipal officials were integrated into the eastern regime.[1]

On the whole, though, German policy was viciously hostile to the people it ruled over. Rosenberg's eastern administration was a chaos, and he lost out to Goering, Himmler and Backe, who called for a wholly predatory rule. In the Ukraine Gauleiter Erich Koch had no interest in Rosenberg's plans to appeal to Ukranian national pride.

As a measure of the deleterious impact of the occupation, some 30 per cent of pre-war capital stock was destroyed, according to a Soviet government commission of September 1945, while in the occupied territories of Ukraine and Byelorussia, the figure was two thirds. Though peasants looked forward to an end to collectivisation when the Germans came, the collective farm system was kept in the occupied areas – the better to seize what grain they could, 'in the interests of the German war economy', said Goering on 27 July 1941.[2] The German embassy in Moscow had warned that the more mechanised collective farms would fail for lack of fuel, though, and German fantasies that the Ukraine would feed the Reich never materialised.[3]

Major-General Hans Leykauf summed up the insanity of the occupation policy:

if we shoot dead all the Jews, allow the prisoners of war to die, dish out famine to the majority of the urban population, and in the coming year a proportion of the rural population to hunger, the question remains unanswered: *who will actually produce the economic goods?*[4]

German failure to manage the economy quickly tipped into starvation and violent oppression, which in turn provoked a powerful backlash. The remarkable turnaround from German victories in 1940 and 1941 to getting bogged down and then routed by the partisan and Soviet armies can be explained without leaning on platitudes about Russian heroism (there was heroism, and cowardice, in the Wehrmacht and the Red Army alike). The watershed was the German occupation's own collapse, under the weight of its own shortcomings, which created the opening for Germany's opponents.

On the battlefield, the Red Army would inflict the most serious defeats on the Wehrmacht in the war. Eighty per cent of all German losses were in the east. The desert war in North Africa, and the Normandy landing were comparatively much less important. Still, as impressive as the Soviet victories were – all the more so seeing just how bad the Russian position was in 1941 – Germany's empire in the east was set to implode. The German army was over extended. Operation Barbarossa left Germans tending supply lines over a front 600 km wide and 1,500km deep.[5] That was a serious problem, but it was not the worst problem. Even with the technical challenges, the Wehrmacht was a formidable power. Under generals like Manstein and von Paulus the tank war was as deadly as ever.

The real failure was not the army but the administration of the population. Fixated on conquest and even extermination, the German empire was so hateful that it alienated the vast mass of the peoples of the east – so much so that it provoked ever greater opposition wherever it turned. SS Brigade-Fuhrer Otto Kumm said 'the effort to convert the masses to our ideology hinged upon how they were treated'. Kumm explained 'we could reduce a village and think that we had solved the problem in that area, only to realise that the problem had just increased in severity'. 'We could not convince our superiors in Berlin to agree', he said, to try to build local leadership. Even without the Red Army to contend with, the

German forces of occupation were set on an insanely destructive, and ultimately self-destructive course.

In the Ukraine, where Hitler had been lauded as a liberator, the Einsatzgruppen (Special Forces) attacked nationalists and intellectuals to crush any national sentiment even though that sentiment was largely anti-Soviet, and even pro-German. In September 1941 Erich Koch was put in charge of a commissariat over 50 million Ukrainians and others. 'Our job is to suck from the Ukraine all the goods we can get hold of' Koch explained to his staff: 'I am expecting from you the utmost severity towards the native population'.[6] Ukrainians were killed for being able to read, for withholding food, and flogged for not doffing their caps. Around 250 villages were razed in collective punishments. Ukrainians starved in their thousands. Ukrainians were also made to go to Germany to work in homes and factories, where they were kept in barracks behind barbed wire with 'Ost' armbands. Eighty per cent of all forced labour from the east was Ukrainian. And this was how the German empire treated its supporters.

Before General Zhukov's Soviet army turned the tide against the Wehrmacht, the German administration in the east had been consumed by a war with irregular partisan units. On 23 July 1941 Hitler had promised to 'spread the kind of terror' that would make the population 'lose all interest in subordination'. But the terrible atrocities and revenge attacks only made more partisans. On 18 August 1942 Hitler signed the High Command Directive No 46 calling for measures against 'partisan disorder in the east', which 'seriously threaten the provisioning of the front and the economic exploitation of the territories'. The Partisan bands, he said, should be 'virtually exterminated by the winter'. By the end of 1942 there were some 300,000 partisans – supposedly working with Moscow, but often on their own, fighting because they had little to live for under German rule. Partisans in Byelorussia and around Smolensk liberated large territories behind German lines. That winter, Hitler called for no restraint in the war against the Partisans 'more than ever one of to be or not to be'.[7]

Belgian SS volunteer Leon Degrelle said afterwards that 'Partisans were our greatest nightmare we as soldiers faced in the east':

> With the Red Army, we knew their tactics ... However the
> Partisans were dangerous because they did not wear uniforms
> and didn't operate as a disciplined, traditional military force.
> Instead the functioned as a random hit and run guerrilla unit,
> striking anywhere and everywhere without warning.

Partisans harried German troops destroying 65,000 vehicles and
12,000 bridges, driving the occupying forces into the state of terror
Hitler had promised the partisans.[8]

The German victories of 1940 and 1941 were built on the Soviet
Union's weaknesses. The Soviet state had brutalised the countryside
under 'collectivisation', most of all the Ukraine, and these areas fell
to the Wehrmacht because they had little loyalty to Moscow. But
after that the Wehrmacht faced the Soviet Union's strengths. The
Soviet state's core support was in the cities, where its rapid industrialisation gathered masses of Soviet citizens. One after the other, the
German army besieged Russia's main cities, Leningrad (from
September 1941 to January 1944, it is today called St Petersburg),
Moscow (in the winter of 1941-2) and Stalingrad (in the winter of
1942-3 – it was renamed Volgograd in 1961). In each case the Soviet
leadership succeeded in defending against extraordinary odds.
Already, as 1941 drew to a close, the German High Command knew
it was in trouble. In December 1941 Southern Command chief Gerd
von Runstedt retired to be replaced by the NSDAP stalwart Marshal
von Reichenau. General Field Marshall Walther von Brautchitsh
retired and Hitler made himself Commander in Chief. More chiefs
were replaced: Fedor von Bock and Wilhelm Ritter von Leeb were
both removed, along with some divisional chiefs. These were panic
measures. The failure to take Moscow in operation Typhoon
revealed the weakness of the German campaign.[9]

In a sense the Soviet leadership's determination to fight needs no
great explanation. As Arno Meyer said 'Unlike the political class of
France's Third Republic, which Berlin proposed to break without
utterly destroying it and its homeland, the Soviet elite was marked
for extinction and its country for conquest and dismemberment.'[10]
They really had nowhere else to go.

Historian Richard Overy explains how the Soviet Union's mobilisation made the difference:

no other state diverted so much of its population to work for the war effort; no other state demanded such a heavy and prolonged sacrifice from its people.

It was, he says, the most extreme case of 'total war'.[11] The Soviet Union could do this because it was neither a democracy nor a free market society, but one that worked on the basis of orders issued from above (euphemistically called 'planning' – though the demands were chaotic and without any evidence base). In times of peace, the 'command economy' was fundamentally weak because the 'plan' was unrealistic, and evaded by a truculent citizenry and defensive lower officials. But the war gave the Soviet people a sense of purpose even greater than the revolution of 1917. The rule of the Communist Central Committee gave way to the rule of the military council. Stalin reluctantly deferred to his generals on military matters. The role of the 'political officers' (who had been there to ensure the party's rule over the military) was downgraded and army rank honoured once again in epaulettes and gold braid.

On 16 December 1941 Hitler issued the *Halt Befehl* order that troops should not fall back, but stand and fight. In July 1942 Stalin issued Order 227, 'Not a Step Back!' that forbade retreats: 'each metre of Soviet territory must be stubbornly defended to the last drop of blood'. Special 'blocking units' were made up to stop deserters and push the infantry on into gunfire – though these proved ineffective and the job was given to the NKVD.[12]

Ideologically the Soviet leadership appealed less to the internationalism of Lenin, more to Great Russian chauvinism. Traditional military honours were revived, like the Tsarist 'Nevsky Order' (named after Alexander Nevsky, who drove back the Teutonic Knights in the Thirteenth Century). British Ambassador in Moscow Clerk Kerr reported to the Foreign Office that the portraits of the military heroes of the Napoleonic era were prominent – 'interesting as a further symbol of the throwback to the past which has been manifesting itself', while 'Marx and Engels looked allout in the cold in the corner they had been pushed into'.[13]

Toasting Red Army Commanders in May 1945, Stalin said Russia was 'the leading nation of all the nations belonging to the Soviet Union' – it had earned in war 'recognition as the guiding force of the

Soviet Union'.[14] In 1942 the Russian Orthodox Church – that had been roundly persecuted – was welcomed back and Metropolitan Sergei answered by blessing the war against the Germans.[15]

'Let holy hatred become our chief and only feeling,' wrote Pravda, the official government newspaper. 'If you can hold a weapon, even a spade or a pitchfork, attack the Germans with it,' Lieutenant Mikhail Alekseyev urged ordinary Russians. 'Kill a German and save the Motherland.'[16]

The defence of Stalingrad over 1942 and into 1943 was the propagandistic turning point of the war. The Stalingraders were driven to near extinction, but pressed to hang on. Marshall Zhukov's counter was a pincer movement that led to the encirclement of von Paulus' Sixth Army and the 4th Panzer Army – some 330,000 men. On 22 January 1943, the Sixth Army, against Hitler's express orders, surrendered, along with von Paulus.

The Red Army defended Stalingrad while the Allies refused to open a Second Front in west Europe, and the battle was fought primarily with Soviet-made tanks and guns, as the re-located war industries in the east were whipped into shape. In the second half of 1942 Soviet tank production outstripped Germany's.[17] Stalin buried the belief in Washington and London that the USSR would fall in a matter of weeks. Western propaganda even talked up the heroic defence of Stalingrad to give hope to their own people – and also gave succour to communists in the West.

Military success won the Soviet leadership something they had craved throughout the life of the USSR: western technological input for their industrialisation drive. That had been, after all, one of the central planks of collaboration with Germany since the agreement at Rapallo in 1922, and also of the Hitler-Stalin pact of 1939. After Stalingrad the promised lend lease aid began to arrive. Between 1942 and 1945 the share of US lend lease industrial goods in Soviet supplies grew from 23.1 per cent to 39.5 per cent. America and Britain gave the radios, telephones and cable that put the Red Army in touch with the Moscow leadership and around half of all military supplies, including jeeps, aircraft, tanks, ships and ammunition. Officially, lend lease was said to be of minor importance. 'US and British supply of arms were negligibly small', Soviet historian G. Deborin wrote, 'the Soviet Union defeated Hitler Germany with home-made arms and home-made equipment'. In private, though, Marshall Zhukov admitted that without aid 'the Soviet Union could not have continued the war'. Stalin, too, said that 'without the use of these machines, through lend-lease, we would lose the war', at the Teheran Conference, 1 December 1943. Military aid helped change the Soviet military industrial complex so that it became less labour-intensive, more capital-intensive, equipping 43 new tank corps and 22 new mechanized corps from 1942.[18]

So spectacular was the collapse of the German Empire in the east that the Red Army successes stacked up. In 1944 alone they won these ten victories:

- Relief of Leningrad (January)
- Encirclement of German troops in South West Ukraine (February)
- Destruction of German forces in Crimea (May)
- Defeat of the Finnish forces and restoration of the 1940 frontier (June)
- Liberation of Byelorussia (June)
- Entry of Soviet Forces into Poland (July)
- Occupation of Romania and Bulgaria (August)
- Occupation of Latvia and Estonia (September-November)
- Liberation of Belgrade (October)
- Expulsion of German troops from Finland and Norway (October)

The cost, though, was high. According to official statistics 8,668,400 Soviet troops and 27 million Soviet Citizens overall were killed.[19] Some 5,754,000 were taken as prisoners of war, of whom 4,700,000 died from disease and starvation, made worse by forced labour, or by execution.[20] These troops died to drive the Wehrmacht from their country, but also cemented Stalin's rule over the survivors. They died, too, as Roosevelt's proxy army, sacrificed to save the loss of America's armed forces in the defeat of its German rival.

The Soviet machine that would roll over Eastern Europe was armed and built with American industrial supplies. Its success and dominance over Poland, Middle Europe and the Balkans came as it filled the vacuum left by the internal collapse of the Third Reich's eastern Empire. Stalinism's expansion came thanks to the failure of western capitalism, both in its German and American exponents.

Chapter Twenty Four

The 'Final Solution'

Anti-Semitism was key to the ideology of the National Socialist Workers – Nazi – Party (NSDAP). The Jews were scapegoats in NSDAP thinking for the suffering of the ruined middle classes from which it drew its base. The spectral figure of 'The Jew' in Nazi appeals pulled together fear of big business ('plutocracy') especially banks ('money-lenders') but also Bolshevism, which was supposed to be a Jewish plot. Professional Jews were blamed for ruining Germans. The migrant Jewish poor from the east were seen as the very worst of the masses. Blaming the Jews was a way of saying that Germany's problems came from abroad, and the hand of Jewish financiers was seen in the onerous reparations imposed on Germany at Versailles.

Anti-Semitism was felt intensely by the Nazis and their followers in the rise to power. Wider German society – like much of Europe – had a casual anti-Semitism that was part and parcel of its nationalist outlook. By allying with the Conservatives to take state power, the Nazis became a far more potent threat. As they took power, the Nazi leadership tried to stoke anti-Semitic feeling, but Germans overall were unmoved by overt campaigns in the late 1930s, and many reacted against violent persecution.[1] With the Nazis' destruction of political opposition, though, there was no sustained protest against the reversal of Jewish emancipation.

Anti-Semitism served to explain and even order international relations. In their speeches, leading Nazis blamed Jewish financiers and leaders for Germany's diplomatic isolation, making great play of the roles and ethnic origins of Roosevelt's advisor Bernard Baruch, the English Minister Leslie Hore-Belisha, and the Russian Commissar Kaganovich. Later, of his allies, Hitler demanded anti-Jewish measures parallel to Germany's, as a test and proof of their commitment to the New Order in Europe (proof that many were all too keen to give).

Jews in Germany, Austria and the Bohemia Protectorate lost their civil rights, had their property seized, and were pushed to emigrate from the German Reich. The German Foreign Office seriously planned to deport Jews to the island of Madagascar, off the coast of Africa, in 1940, after the French Colony fell into their sphere of influence. It is tempting to read history backwards. Knowing what we do of the end point of the campaign against the Jews, it is easy to think that extermination was the plan all along. But it was not. In May 1940 Himmler wrote a memo on the expulsion of the Jews that ended 'however cruel and tragic each case may be, this method is still the mildest and the best, if one rejects the Bolshevik method of physical extermination of a people out of inner conviction as un-German and impossible'.[2] The Madagascar plan had been looked at before, by French, Polish and British officials (it was first thought up by the English anti-Semites Henry Beamish and Arnold Leese). Briefly popular with leading Nazis, the Madagascar plan was no kindness, but thought of as the most expedient way of ridding Germany of its Jewish population. The plan failed because Britain blocked the expulsion of German Jews – out of fear that they would come to Britain.[3]

German nationalism, like all nationalisms, has a powerfully irrational component, but with the prospect of defeat in the war, the irrational overwhelmed any thought-through pursuit of national interest. Unable to understand how Germany had failed to unite Europe behind its flag, Hitler descended into a morbid conspiracy theory to explain the alliance arraigned against him: 'international Jewry'. Defeating this fantasy enemy was a substitute for the real problems facing Germany. Once victory over their real enemies slipped from their grasp, the Nazis, who were incapable of considering the alternative course of a negotiated peace (a peace which would have meant the end of the NSDAP) and more and more fought a fantasy war against a fantasy enemy. The German philosopher Hegel said that the Crusaders' seizure of Jerusalem was a mistake that made the Christian ideal into a morbid reality.[4] Hitler's ideal was already depraved, but made real it was a descent into barbarism.

The war against the Jews was pitched from persecution to massacres with the invasion of Poland, and to outright extermination with the invasion of the USSR. The expansion of the Greater German Reich into the east had the unforeseen outcome that not less, but more Jews were under its rule. The policy up until that point had been to expel Jews, many of them eastwards. With the invasion of Poland, Germany began a complicated movement of peoples. Polish Jews were concentrated in ghettoes, notably in Warsaw and Lodz (which the Germans called Lemberg), and later these were also packed further with Jews from around Europe. Poles were moved east out of Prussia into the 'General Government' area – but later others were sent west as forced labourers in Germany. The Jews' homes and the Poles farms were to be cleared to make way for German settlers. These forced movements were brutal in the extreme.

The massacres began at the hands of the Einsatzgruppen der Sicherheitspolizei (special task forces of the security police). These were under SS Chief Reinhard von Heydrich, and were used by the Nazi leadership to take the brutal measures that they feared the Wehrmacht would shy away from.

With the invasion of Poland Einsatzgruppen attacked Poles but also singled out the country's sizeable Jewish population for special treatment. On October 26 1939 'General Government' governor Hans Frank ordered Jews to work for the occupation forces, digging defences and so on. On 13 November Frank issued the order that Jews were to wear the Star of David.[5] On 30 October 1939, Himmler ordered Jews removed from the German-annexed west, notably Danzig and Bromberg. Jews were sent east to Lodz, where around 170,000 Jews were sealed into the ghetto in spring of 1940. That autumn the Warsaw ghetto was also closed, after 400,000 Jews were pushed together. In the Autumn of 1941, the Nazi leadership ordered the expulsion of all Jews from Greater Germany eastwards, and tens of thousands were sent from Berlin, Prague, Vienna and other cities to the General Government district of Poland, primarily to Lodz, which was massively overcrowded; some were moved further east into Riga.[6]

Later the Einsatzgruppen played a murderous role in the suppression of the local population in the occupied territories of the Soviet Union. The atrocities mounted up – especially when the forward movement of Operation Barbarossa faltered in late 1941. At the end of June Einsatzgruppe B massacred 2000 Jews in Bialystok. Around Mid-October the same Goup B started to massacre

Belorussian Jews. Goup C, with Ukranian Auxiliaries in tow, slaughtered 3000 Jews in Zhitomir, on 19 September, Uman on 22 September, and those around Berdichev on 5 October, slaughters that took place after a gruelling struggle to take the Ukraine. The Germans took Kiev, at great cost, and were then caught in a timed bomb attack that blew up their HQ. In 'retaliation' Einsatzkommando 4a of Group C claimed to have killed 33,771 Jews of Kiev at Babi Yar, a ravine outside the city, where their bodies were thrown. More massacres followed at the Ukrainian cities of Dnepropretsk, Kharkhov and Rostov. In Odessa on 23 October, Einsatzgruppen D stood back while Rumanian troops took over the job of massacring Jews.[7]

The German rage against the Jews grew out of the task of conquering and controlling the territory. Though the Wehrmacht pushed the front line forward, the Special Forces were being used to hold the population in the rear. Where the front was, was important, but pushing east did not mean that the ground behind the line was German. With little to offer but violence, the occupation worked itself up into a storm of hatred. Jews were the target – they were the 'bacillus' that would have to removed. When the Einsatzgruppe leaders singled out the Jews for slaughter it had an exemplary effect on the population. Some joined in. Reactionary bands recruited from Baltic and Slav populations exorcised their own hatred of the Jews under the German umbrella – it was one of the few things that the German occupation had to offer them.[8] Others were cowed into submission, seeing the brutalisation and slaughter of the Jews. German treatment of the Jews got worse as the campaign in the USSR started to get bogged down. German victories came harder, and the job of holding territory in the face of Partisan warfare was greater. The slaughter of Jews was becoming a retreat from taking the war to the enemy – 'they found it easier to catch unarmed Jewish civilians than bolsheviks', suggests Arno Mayer.[9]

On 20 January 1942 at Wannsee, a conference of leading Nazi officials met to talk over the 'Jewish problem'. Governor Frank was clear: the Jews were of no use. 'We must annihilate the Jews wherever we encounter them and wherever possible, in order to maintain the overall mastery of the Reich here'.[10] The only ambiguity in the policy was that the labour ministry was determined to exploit the Jews by working them before killing them. Plainly the Nazi leadership had tipped over from a policy of dominating the east by repression into a hysterical programme of destruction. Adolf Hitler's speeches of early 1942 claimed that 'the war can only end with the extermination of the Aryan peoples or the disappearance of the Jews from Europe' (30 January) and then 'my prophecy will be fulfilled: this war will not destroy Aryan humanity, but will exterminate the Jew' (24 February).[11] In the Warsaw Ghetto Emmanuel Ringelbaum saw the link between the war and the extermination. Because the Germans 'are being defeated' and 'their cities are being destroyed' he wrote 'they are taking their revenge on the Jews'.[12]

The concentration camps were first built by the Nazis to house political prisoners. Jews were held in the 1938 persecution, though many were released after then. With military takeovers the concentration camp system grew. Mauthausen was built in Austria, and Auschwitz in Poland. In 1942 the camps were also turned to fill Germany's labour shortage, much of it met by captive Russian, Polish and Jewish prisoners. I G Farben, Krupp and Siemens built plants at Auschwitz, Siemens also built one at Ravensbruck. Walther Zella-Mehlis built a factory at Buchenwald. Other big name firms took workers from the camps. The numbers behind the wire grew from 100,000 in late 1942 to 710,000 in January 1945.

Exploitation, however, was not the main point of the camps, which were punitive, and deadly. Auschwitz and Majdanek were also labour camps, but Chelmno, Belzec, Sobibor and Treblinka served no other point than to exterminate people. On arrival at Auschwitz, prisoners were 'selected' for work, or for extermination, though to live on was only a stay of execution. In 1942 42,000 Jews were sent from France to Auschwitz, and in 1944 hundreds of thousands of Hungarian Jews were sent, pushing the population to 135,000 – and leading to ever greater exterminations. From Salonika, Greece, where the Wehrmacht had failed to extinguish the ELAS resistance, Jews were deported to Auschwitz between March and June 1943 – 48,974 Jews came from Northern Greece of whom 37,386 were immediately gassed. In all Greece lost 60,000 of its 70,000 Jews to the 'final solution'.[13]

Polish Jews were the first victims of the extermination camps Chelmno, Belzec, Sobibor and Treblinka. Jews were sent from all over Poland. In the first half of 1944 the Lodz ghetto was cleared and the last surviving residents sent to Chelmno and Auschwitz by July 14. In January 1943, the Warsaw ghetto inmates were rounded up and sent to the camps.

In Warsaw, Jews had been terrified and starved into submission, with the Jewish council agreeing to help the German authorities to select people for transportation. Jewish socialists, Zionists and Communists banded together as the Zydowska Organizacja Bojowa – the Jewish Resistance Organisation – or ZOB. On 18 January 1943, with the final clearance of the ghetto threatened, the ZOB attacked and killed SS men with what few arms it had gathered. One battle group was captured and taken to the carriage for deportation. All sixty refused to get on the train and were shot. The deportation was stopped. News of the Jews' resistance inspired the Polish Home Army, and the Polish Socialist Party, who rushed what arms they could. The ZOB took charge of the ghetto. On 19 April 1943 the Germans tried to take the ghetto, and a better armed, and more determined resistance killed more than a thousand of them. 'Poles, citizens, soldiers of freedom', the ZOB appealed: 'it is a fight for our freedom as well as yours; for our human dignity as well as yours'. Surrounded, they could not win, but German confidence was shattered, and the Poles inspired.[14]

On the 2 August 1943 prisoners at Treblinka set light to buildings and hundreds escaped, around forty survived. On 14th October 1943, prisoners the Sobibor death camp overpowered and killed guards, so that three hundred escaped to the woods, of whom 50 survived. On 7 October 1944, prisoners at Auschwitz blew up one of the crematoria used to burn the bodies of the gassed.

On March 27 1943 the Allies' Roosevelt, Anthony Eden, Cordell Hull, Sumner Welles, Lord Halifax and William Strang of the British Foreign Office met. 'Hull raised the question of the 60 or 70 thousand Jews that are in Bulgaria and are threatened with extermination unless we could get them out.' For the British, Anthony Eden replied that

the whole problem of the Jews in Europe is very difficult and that we should move very cautiously about offering to take all Jews out of a country like Bulgaria. If we do that then the Jews of the world will be wanting us to make similar offers in Poland and Germany. Hitler might well take us up on such an offer...[15]

Pointedly, the British Ministry of Information excluded atrocities against Jews from war propaganda: 'A certain amount of horror is needed but it must deal always with treatment of indisputably innocent people. . Not with Jews.' A white paper on German atrocities published in 1939 omitted atrocities against Jews, because of 'a reluctance to identify in any way with the Jewish plight or somehow connect the British war effort with the Jews'.[16] In the US, too, reports emerging of the Holocaust were suppressed by the State Department and even by the American Jewish Congress.[17] Stopping the persecution of the Jews never was an Allied war aim – at least not until after the war.[18]

In March 1944, fearing that Hungary was trying to break from the Axis, Hitler confronted Admiral Horthy, and demanded proof of his loyalty by action against his country's Jews. With the German military taking control of the country, half a million Hungarian Jews were sent to the camps - few survived.

Franz Neumann wrote in 1944 that 'so vast a crime as the extermination of the Eastern Jews' was an attempt to make the masses 'perpetrators and accessories in that crime and make it therefore impossible for them to leave the Nazi boat'.[19] The rage of extermination was an attempt to 'burn bridges'. It was also a fantasy war against a spectral enemy, one that raged all the more as actual victory slipped from Germany's grasp. In February 1945, as Soviet troops advanced Hitler admitted that he had failed to 'lance the Bolshevik abscess'. He had though, he claimed 'lanced the Jewish abscess' and dreamed that 'the world of the future will be eternally grateful to us'.[20] The act would indeed be remembered, with horror. It was the very nadir of the depravity of the Second World War.

Chapter Twenty Five

The Second Invasion of Europe

The argument over the 'Second Front' ran from 1940 to 1944 when in June American and British forces at last invaded Normandy beginning the western assault on German-occupied Europe.

The reason why the Second Front was delayed was that British and American military leaders feared what it would cost them. Their hostility to German domination of Europe was not principled, but pragmatic. Western leaders supported Hitler's rise to power in Germany, and the ascendance of reactionary and collaborationist regimes in Europe. They objected to German domination because it threatened their own global standing. So it was that the first four years of the war were fought to decide which colonial powers would hold sway in North Africa, the Middle East, and East Asia.

For much of the war, the US was content to fight the war through proxies. Nationalist and Communist Chinese were armed to fight Japan. When the Soviet Union showed that it could reverse German conquests in the east, US aid began to flow to Russia. Even Britain was, to US strategists, a proxy that could be relied upon to take the fight to the enemy – though the British, struggling to hang onto their Empire were also reluctant to commit their own forces to a direct assault on Europe.

By 1944 the policy of leaving Europe to German control was falling apart, because the German Empire in Europe was falling apart – in the east, where it was overextended, and in southern Europe where the Italians had pulled out of the Axis.

Why, after so many delays did the western Allies agree to invade Europe? Harry Hopkins told Roosevelt on 17 March 1943 'one of two things would happen – either Germany will go Communist or an out and out anarchic state would set in; that indeed the same kind of thing might happen in any of the countries in Europe and Italy as well'.[1]

The reactionary regimes that had succeeded in containing radical and popular movements in Europe from 1933 to 1942 were exhausted. Instead of keeping a lid on the revolutionary movement they were provoking ever greater opposition. Partisan resistance to German domination threatened open rebellion not just against the occupiers, but against the stability of the capitalist social system itself. Instability, and the rise of the armed resistance, was a potential nightmare for Western policy makers. They would have to invade Europe to save the established order from total collapse.

The invasion would bring the most intense fighting between the western Allies and the Axis forces that the war had seen. But at the same time, western policy was to contain the popular opposition to the collaborationist regimes from spinning out of control. The Allies would use overwhelming force to ensure that they could dictate the settlement in Europe, and stop the European peoples from seizing power for themselves. 'Liberation' was the propagandistic goal, but the Allies fought to make sure that the liberation was on their terms and to avoid the danger that the Europeans would liberate themselves.

Rajani Palme Dutt, the Anglo-Indian Communist anticipated the likely response to a breakdown in the Nazi regime:

> In such a situation of general disorder, with spreading civil war, and with the popular forces still poorly armed and only partially organized, a trained and disciplined army of one million in the field could do a great deal to take over from Hitler the task of holding down the peoples of Europe and strangling the socialist revolution – just as the British forces in 1918 took over directly from the waning German imperialist forces in the Baltic States.[2]

Fenner Brockway, the Independent Labour Party leader, too, saw the likely course of events:

> When the revolts against Nazism begin, British and American troops will probably be in occupation of parts of Europe; as the revolts develop, the occupation will extend. This occupation, if it is under capitalist direction, will allow the revolt to go sufficiently far to enable "safe" governments to assume control, **but no further.** After that the British and American forces would be used to maintain law and order, or in plain words **to prevent or undermine the socialist revolution.**[3]

Both the western Allies and the Soviet Union began to push forward, just as the partisan movements were on the verge of liberating their own territories. The American radical Dwight MacDonald explained the military thinking:

> The Allied High Command like the Red Army High Command, does not approve of cities spontaneously liberating themselves without waiting for the duly constituted military authorities. Most irregular, most irregular! [4]

In 1944, events began to move much more quickly. The governments of Finland and Rumania pulled out of the Axis. More importantly, partisan bands in Greece, Yugoslavia, the Ukraine, Italy and even France were directly challenging the German-backed authorities. The partisans took succour from Allied victories insofar as they hurt the enemy, but as they would quickly learn, 'liberation' at Allied hands led to the loss of their power.

Icelanders were the first to experience the benign dictatorship that the Allies had to offer. When the Allies occupied Iceland in 1940 they were challenged by trade unionists there (the sheer weight of Allied purchasing on the Island started an inflationary spiral). In 1941 the trade union Dagsbrun struck threatening the building of an airfield outside Reykjavik. Threatened by the use of troops the Icelanders prepared an English-language leaflet: 'You are called upon by your officers to murder us. Don't do it'. The British imprisoned five strike leaders, banned the Communist Party paper *The People's Will* and sent the MP and editor Einar Olgeirson to prison in Brixton.[5]

Sicily

The Allied invasion of Sicily came before Normandy. The US Navy's Lieutenant Commander Charles Haffenden, recruited American-based Sicilian Mafiosi, Vito Genovese, Charles 'Lucky' Luciano, Joseph Bonnano and Joseph Lanza. Mussolini's Sicilian prefect Cesare Mori had been intolerant of the bandit gang, but Haffenden saw them as useful power brokers. In July 1943 a US plane made contact with Don Calogero Vizzini the Sicilian Mafia leaderknown as Don Calo, flying a yellow pennant with the letter 'L' (for Luciano).

A few days later Don Calo led US tanks into the town of Villalba, again displaying Luciano's colours. Don Calo's men had seized the Axis commander Lieutenant-Colonel Salemi after telling his troops to make themselves scarce.[6]

The value of the Mafia to the Allied Military Government was that they were a militia who were neither for Mussolini, nor for the communist partisans. At the end of July 'Don Calo Vizzini was made mayor of the town', remembers one witness:

> Almost the entire population was assembled in the square. Speaking in poor Italian, this American lieutenant said "This is your master."

The townsfolk soon learned what Don Calo's rule meant. A meeting held by the Italian Communist Party in Villalba heard the firebrand Girolamo Li Causi say 'don't be fooled by these landowners...' at which Don Calo gave the signal and his men opened fire on the crowd gathered in the square, wounding fourteen. The American OSS officers were embarrassed enough to advise: 'give the incident as little publicity as possible'.[7]

Don Calo, Mafia chief installed by the Allies

Genovese, who had dealt in stolen gasoline ration tickets in America, worked as an 'interpreter' for many US officers, including the head of the Allied Military Government in Italy, Charles Polletti. Genovese used his position to raid the Army stores: 'that connivin' louse was sellin' American goods to his own Italian people' grumbled Luciano. Interviewed many years later, Poletti was strangely reticent: 'We had no problems at all with the Mafia', he said. 'Nobody ever heard of it.'[8] Harold Macmillan thought that Poletti was 'Tammany personified': 'He is the "boss" of Sicily, and just loves it.'[9]

Economically, the south had been bankrupted by the war, and only the Fascists' price and rationing system stopped runaway inflation, which broke out once the Allies landed. Unable to get a reasonable price, farmers withheld their grain and the cities starved. To restore order, the allies recreated Mussolini's police state.

In western Sicily the Allied authorities shut down flour mills and bakeries alleging criminal speculation in grain prices. On 19 October 1943, Allied troops fired on a demonstration against wage and price levels in Palermo leaving 14 dead. The exploitative 'collective contracts' between workers and employers that had been introduced by Mussolini were continued by Lt. Colonel Charles Poletti for AMGOT.[10]

The use of criminal gangs to put down militant workers was not restricted to Sicily. In 1948 the French police used gangsters of the Unione Corse to attack striking dockworkers in Marseille. 'The Unione Corse obliged by providing an army of strikebreaking longshoremen to unload the ships and a crew of assassins to gun down defiant union leaders.'[11] Like the Mafia, the Unione Corse had been involved in actions against the Axis in the war.

Greece

Throughout Greece's fierce war of resistance against first the Italians, and then German occupation, British Special Operations Executive Officers had tried to build up a right-wing alternative to the radical ELAS resistance movement, and its political arm EAM.

Eventually Britain used the Soviet Union's influence to rein in ELAS. Following preparatory discussions between Eden and the Soviet Ambassador to London in May, Stalin and Churchill agreed that Greece would be a part of the British sphere of influence at a conference in Moscow in October 1944. Between the two discussions a Soviet mission to Greece under Colonel Popov, had contacted the partisans to tell them of their agreement in July.[12] The British with American and Soviet support pushed the Communist leadership into accepting the installation of George Papandreou's puppet government of 'constitutional' (meaning unrepresentative in this case) politicians. Harold Macmillan told Papandreou that there would have to be some token action against the Germans to justify Allied support:

It was vital to have a National Army partly to play some part, however modest, in the war against Germany so long as it lasted, and partly to maintain internal order. It was only when a National army was created that he could proceed to disarm the guerrillas.[13]

At Caserta, EAM, Papandreou and the Allies agreed that all guerrilla bands would be disarmed, before the formation of a new Greek Army, with only Serafis dissenting. Meanwhile, the Allies recruited national Bands from the rapidly disintegrating collaborationist Greek forces to take on ELAS.

Even as they were using the Soviet leadership to get leverage over the Greek Resistance, the British were using the threat of Soviet invasion to scare the Germans into helping them deal with the Resistance. In December 1943, the British Middle East HQ sent Captain Don Stott to negotiate with Hitler's envoy in Greece, Hermann Neubacher of the Gestapo on the best way to defeat the partisans. 'This war should end in a common struggle by the allies and the German forces against Bolshevism,' Stott told them.[14] It was point of view that Neubacher understood well, having already said

that 'we are the sole obstacle in Greece to the revolutionary success of the Soviet policy against British interests in the Mediterranean.'[15] According to Albert Speer, German troops cut off on the Greek islands were given safe passage to the mainland on the understanding that they would be used to hold Salonika until the British took over.[16]

The conditions were prepared for the British Expeditionary Force under General Scobie to enter Greece. 'Do not hesitate to act as if you were in a conquered city where a local rebellion is in progress', read Churchill's orders of 5 December 1944.[17] At first, though, the EAM did not want to fight, but instead welcomed the British: 'perhaps because the order had been given from Moscow,

Captain Don Stott, who brokered the deal to take over the Nazis' anti-ELAS Security Battalions

EAM seemed ready to accept the situation fairly good-humouredly.'[18] Churchill was not satisfied, telling Scobie 'the clear objective is the defeat of the E.A.M.' - not the German or Italian armies, which had already been defeated. And making clear his desire to inflict a physical defeat, Churchill added 'the ending of the fighting is subsidiary to this'.[19] On the same day, in the House of Commons, an opposition amendment regretted that the King's speech of 29 November 'contains no assurance that H.M. Forces will not be used to disarm the friends of democracy in Greece and other parts of Europe, or to suppress popular movements which have variously assisted in the defeat of the enemy and upon whose success we must rely for future friendly cooperation in Europe'. Churchill replied that valorous action against the Germans did not entitle the popular movements to become masters of their countries, adding, guiltily: 'Democracy is no harlot to be picked up in the street by a man with a tommy-gun.'[20]

At British prompting, Papandreou ordered ELAS be disarmed and disbanded. A demonstration in Athens against the move were fired, on killing scores. Afterwards Harold Macmillan had tea with Papandreou, and noted in his diary that 'The Greek bourgeois class is determined to eliminate the Greek Communists and will fight to the last British soldier to do it.'[21] ELAS fighters struck back and, disastrously, took a number of hostages. A British-brokered peace agreement at Varkiza rubber-stamped the disarming and breaking up of the Resistance – as well as shifting the blame for the violence on the Communists.[22]

At the Caserta Conference Scobie had been granted authority over Greece's armed forces. With cynical clarity Regional Command in Athens was given to the Fascist Colonel Spiliotopolous. As the Germans withdrew, they handed over command of their local Security Battalions, anti-Resistance forces that had been characterised as 'enemy organisations' at Caserta, to the British. Scobie's orders to Spiliotopolous were 'when the Germans withdraw or surrender, you will instruct the Battalions to desert to their homes (and hide) or to surrender to our forces'. The Foreign Office told the BBC to stop all criticisms of Security Battalions, and a British liaison officer newly arrived was told 'all our best chaps are in the Battalions'. The Security Battalions' war against the Resistance was barely interrupted by the change of masters.[23]

Funeral procession for Greek resistance protestors killed by the British troops in Syntagma Square, photograph by Dmitri Kessel

The British held Athens, bombing working class districts from the air and freeing pro-Nazi collaborators to fire on demonstrators, only because the ELAS fighters were kept out of the city by the Communist Party leadership. Field Marshall Alexander complained of a 'stubborn core of resistance', Athenians held up banners reading 'the Germans are back'.[24] ELAS leader Stefanos Sarafis was imprisoned while Aris Velouchtis took to the hills to fight on.

All the while that the British were demanding ELAS be disarmed, the Security Battalions and General Grivas' pro-Nazi 'X' group were slaughtering resistance fighters. Their war against ELAS would carry on for another five years.

The Greek Civil War is often claimed as the opening salvo in the Cold War. For the Americans, who took over Britain's sponsorship of the Special Battalions' war against the former resistance fighters that was true. For Stalin, though, there was no question that his agreement with west that Greece should remain in their sphere of influence should hold: 'The Greek revolution should be stopped immediately', he told Milovan Djilas.[25] The brutality of the reaction left little room for constitutional politics, which played out as a

The Security Battalions counted their victories in the heads of the Resistance fighters that they collected

parlour game while war raged in the hillsides. Stefanos Sarafis, released from prison in 1948 was killed when a US officer crashed into his car in 1957. ELAS fighters were held in brutal torture camps into the 1960s for the crime of defending their country against the German occupation.[26]

Italy

Many Allied officers and troops were angry at the opportunistic way that the Badoglio government had been allowed to have Italy re-classified as a belligerent against Germany, when just moments before it had been part of the Axis. Their cynicism towards the Italian Fascist Council's anti-Fascist credentials was justified. But the Italian partisans had indeed taken up arms against the German occupation of northern Italy, at great cost. The Committees of National Liberation set up in Italian cities were a beacon to a people who had been suppressed and starved under Mussolini, and sacrificed to a pointless war.

In 1943 the Allied forces under General Alexander were pressing north against the Wehrmacht. In May Alexander told the Times that the Italian partisans were holding down six of the 25 German divisions in the country. On 6 June Alexander issued a proclamation calling on the partisans to be ready for an insurrection that summer. Emboldened, partisans declared liberated areas all over northern Italy. But as we have seen, the Allied push stopped, and the Wehrmacht and the SS exacted a terrible price from the partisans, who had been encouraged to show themselves. On 13 November Alexander broadcast to the partisans saying that the invasion would be delayed till the following year, and that they should 'save their munitions and matériel until further orders'. 'It was a grave setback for the resistance', remembered Roberto Battaglia, but to the Germans 'it was a tonic': 'they decided to make the most of the respite and deal the partisans a crushing blow'.[27] Special Operations Executive Officer Basil Davidson judged that the broadcast 'in effect was an invitation to the partisans to disband, and to the enemy to come up and finish them off while they were doing it'.[28]

Leaving the partisans to face the wrath of the Wehrmacht over the closing months of 1943 reduced the number of militants they would have to deal with later. But the Allies knew that they would have to take control if the partisans were not to get the credit for defeating the occupiers. In January 1945 British and American political advisors wrote that 'speed in getting ourselves established is the essential factor; without this there is a real danger of extreme Communist elements taking control regardless of the AMG or the Italian government.'[29]

When the Armistice was signed with Badoglio, Nye Bevan told the House of Commons that it ought to have been signed with the striking workers and peasants of Milan.[30] A survey of post-war Italy for Chatham House recalls 'by the time the war ended, these liberation committees and the parties that composed them, had come to occupy an important position'[31] But the Allies had no intention of handing power to the militant partisans in the North. The Allies closed down CLNs in Arezzo, Siena and Viareggio, only acquiescing to them where they were too strong to be challenged, as in Florence. 'Care will be taken', said US Captain Ellery Stone 'to prevent these committees setting themselves up as alternative government'.[32] Harold Macmillan, who talked to Stone in January 1945 about the danger of Italy going the way of Greece, noted in his diary:

Unless we are very careful we will get another EAM/ELAS situation in northern Italy. The operations of the SOE in arming nearly 100 000 so-called patriots will produce the same revolutionary situation, unless we can devise a system for taking them, immediately on the liberation of the territory, into either our, or the Italian Army. Then in return for pay and rations, we may be able to get hold of their weapons. The lesson of Greece is that nothing matters except "disarmament". The political questions are the excuse for retaining armed power.[33]

Italian industrialists who had long collaborated with the Fascist regime briefly lost control of their factories, like Fiat in Turin that was patrolled by armed partisans. Valerio, head of the Edison electrical company called for 'the immediate construction of a strong force for public order, composed of some 100,000 men, capable of overpowering an armed population'. Fiat Managing Director Valletta had been condemned as a collaborationist by the regional CLN, but when men were sent to seize him he was under the protection of an English Liaison Officer 'who presented a safe conduct pass for Valletta'. Rocco Piaggio hoped that the Allies would take over Italian industry to save it from the partisans.[34]

According to one witness in Emilia.

> Those weeks after the liberation were weeks of joy, but also of anxious and vain expectation that a substantial measure of social justice would be applied. The Allies blocked even the most modest initiative which seemed to prejudice the principle of private property. Their stay as occupiers was therefore more than welcome to the forces of conservatism.[35]

Italian Fascists like Prince Valerio Borghese were secured from partisan reprisals, too. Sentenced to hang by the CLN he was rescued by the celebrated CIA agent James Angleton, on orders from US Proconsul Ellery Stone, and whisked away in a US army uniform.[36] When Badoglio asked if he could put the veteran Fascist Dino Grandi into his cabinet, 'General Mason-Macfarlane at this moment pointed out that it would be necessary to make use of some men who in the past have been associated with Fascism, owing to the twenty years that have passed.'[37]

As they were trying to stabilise the Italian order, the Allies finally won out against the radical partisans with the help of the Italian Communist Party leader Palmiro Togliatti, who returned from Moscow in March 1944. The Soviet Union, irked at the western Allies' determination to keep her out of the administration of Italy, had recognised the Fascist Badoglio's government, to gain diplomatic leverage – and Togliatti had called on all anti-Fascists in a radio broadcast from Moscow to 'rally round the Badoglio government'.[38] At Togliatti's insistence the line was held, and the Committees of National Liberation too recognised Badoglio. Dogmatically Togliatti held that the stage of 'democratic revolution' must precede that of social revolution, and so counselled his supporters restrict their wider ambitions in favour of 'continuity of the state'.[39] Harold Macmillan noted of the Soviet delegates Bogolomov General Solodvinik, that 'their apparently cynical support of the King and Badoglio has temporarily strengthened the latter and somewhat baffled all but the more hard-bitten and disciplined members of the Communist Party in Italy.'[40] As the Allies policed the partisans on the streets, the PCI policed them ideologically, and instead of aiming for power, the CLNs were used as a springboard to win Togliatti a seat in a new cabinet set up by the Allies. Communist historian G. Manacorda described how the CLNs were used to pull back from factory-workers' attempts to take over the factories: 'a concrete case' he said, 'of the self-limitation of the revolution, a political intervention aimed at preventing the spontaneous movement of the working class from reaching towards socialist objectives'. The American OSS (forerunner of the CIA) had already worked out that 'it is doubtful whether Russia wished to convert Italy into a Communist state'.[41]

By 1947 the OSS had become the CIA and its assessment of the communist threat was no longer based on fact, but on the new Cold War ideology: 'It is of vital importance to prevent Italy from falling under Communist control.'[42] America's ambassador to Italy, Clare Booth Luce (wife to *Life* publisher Henry Luce) used Marshall Aid to bankroll the fledgling Christian Democratic Party. There was of course no *Communist* threat. But under the cover of fighting communism the US could justify interfering in the Italian political process for the next thirty years.

An Anglo-American Invasion of the Balkans?

The collapse of Germany's eastern empire brought a sudden change in the balance of forces between the main Allies, America, Britain and the Soviet Union – to Russia's advantage, and Britain's disadvantage.

At the Allied conference in Teheran in 1943 Churchill put the plan for an Anglo-American invasion of the Balkans, rather than an invasion of France. It was a 'scheme for a joint British, American and Russian occupation of the Balkans.' To Stalin, though, it seemed 'that the purpose of his new plan was to forestall a Russian occupation of the Balkan lands', says radical historian Isaac Deutscher.[43]

Churchill's plans were transparent. Germany was already in serious trouble in the east, largely because of the resistance put up by partisans in Yugoslavia, Greece, Byelorussia and the Ukraine, and the Soviet Army was driving Germany back. The Anglo-American drive into the Balkans would have been an action against the Soviet rivals, not the Germans. Roosevelt was not impressed by Churchill's arguments, and told his son Elliott after the first day of the Teheran Conference 'I see no reason for putting the lives of American soldiers in jeopardy in order to protect real or fancied British interests in the European continent'.[44]

Looking back, many are surprised that Roosevelt was so unmoved by the fear that the Soviet Union would dominate East Europe. General Mark Clark, commander of the Fifth US Army wrote afterwards that not backing Churchill's plan was 'one of the outstanding political mistakes of the war'.[45] But that is to read history backwards. The United States did not have the capacity to beat Germany in the east; still less so did Britain. US policy was set out at the Quebec Conference, august 1943, in a War Department Memorandum:

> Since Russia is the decisive factor in the war, she must be given every assistance and every effort must be made to obtain her friendship. Since without question she will dominate Europe on the defeat of the Axis, it is even more essential to develop and maintain the most friendly relations with Russia.[46]

The War Department's realism rested on a hope that the Soviets could be relied upon to act as a power in the region. The Americans understood that they were not in a position to rule in the east, so they looked forward to seeing a power installed that would cooperate with them. This was what Harold Macmillan meant when he said after the war 'some day, a generation or two on, we may be able to persuade the Russians that they are Europeans, not Asiatics'.[47] Averell Harriman, Roosevelt's envoy in Moscow thought of it as 'the job of getting the Soviet Government to play a decent role in international affairs', and wrote that 'it is our problem to strengthen the hand of those around Stalin who want to play the game along our lines'.[48] Certainly, the US State Department were pleased to note that Molotov 'clearly confessed Soviet assumption of the "White Man's Burden" in the Balkans'.[49] That was good news to the State Department, but not so great for the British, who had much to lose in the region. 'I do not believe that there is much that we can do but stand in the pavilion and cheer the Russians innings,' wrote a rather glum Harold Macmillan on 30 March 44.[50]

Deutscher underlines the importance of the Teheran decision: 'Europe had now been militarily divided in two'.[51] Instead of an Anglo-American invasion of the Balkans, Operation Overlord, the invasion of Western Europe through France was scheduled for May of 1944, and the Red Army was given free rein in the east. What was more, Stalin's allies granted him two important rights in the Balkans 'that he should be free to intervene against pro-Nazi and Fascist groups and to establish a democratic order in the countries neighbouring Russia' and also that the Governments of the East European states should be 'friendly to Russia'.[52]

Poland

Poland's resistance movement developed along different lines from those of western Europe. With the entire nation extinguished there were little prospects of collaboration. The greater part of Poland's military and political leadership were forced out of the country under threat of summary execution. Poland had been invaded not only by Germany, but also by the Soviet Union. The Polish émigrés were more conservative, established older men with military experience than other resistance organisations. From 1939 to 1944 the Polish government in exile was based in Paris, and then in London, where many of the men had fled, and led at first by seasoned military officer Władysław Sikorski.

Two Polish divisions fought during the invasion of France and after 1940 regrouped in Britain. The Polish Air Force of around 20,000 fought under RAF command, while the Polish Armed Forces added divisions to the British Army. In 1941 Stalin agreed to release Polish prisoners to form an army in the east to fight from Soviet territory, under Władysław Anders. In the Spring of 1942 Marshal Zhukov asked Anders to prepare a division for the front, but Anders said no, and that the whole army must fight together. Stalin sought to discipline the Poles by halving their food allocation. After some arguments, the Russians agree to let the Poles re-locate, and by September 1942 70,939 had left to re-form under the British Command, mostly in the Middle East. By 1944 there were around 190,000 Poles fighting alongside the British, with great courage and commitment. The Polish government in exile claimed that a further 300,000 were organised as the secret Home Army in Poland, keeping their powder dry until the call came for a general uprising.[53]

The Poles problems came as they were sacrificed to Great Power politics. The Soviet Union had a history of hostility to Polish independence, and the other Allies needed the Russians to fight the war in the east. In the summer of 1938 the Soviet leadership had dissolved the Polish Communist Party, and killed or jailed many of its leading militants. But in 1942, as a rival to the London government in exile, a new Polish Workers Party was formed. A radio station, Kosciuszko, broadcast that the Soviet Union was the 'only saviour of the Polish people' and that the London exiles were aiding Germany by preaching 'passivity'.[54]

Toward the end of 1942 it was clearer that the Red Army was in a position to push west towards Germany. The Polish Government in Exile had good reason to fear the coming 'liberation' as it remembered the Soviet invasions of 1920 and 1939. Sikorski told the Home Army officers in Poland that 'the essential aim of the ultimate insurrection was the forestalling of the Russians in the liberation of Poland by the assumption of political power by the resistance.' Publicly though, and mindful of its Allies concerns the Home Army should present 'a positive attitude towards the Soviet Union'.[55]

Trouble flared between Moscow and the London Poles, though, over the USSR's territorial ambitions. On 1 March 1943 the news agency Tass reported that Soviets would take Polish territory up to the Curzon line, taking back the territory they had lost in the settlement of the 1920 war – some 52,000 square miles, including the city of Lvov. 'Whilst Poland will want her original boundaries'

British minister Eden and US president Roosevelt agreed in secret talks, 'the Big Powers would have to decide what Poland would have'. In London Soviet ambassador Maisky told Eden that the Soviet government would not accept an unfriendly government in Poland, especially not the London Government in Exile.[56]

Knowing of these rifts in the Alliance the German government announced the discovery of the bodies of thousands of Polish officers in mass graves in Katyn, the Berlin Radio reporting 'the Bolsheviks had secretly perpetrated mass executions' (13 April 1943). Two days later the Polish General Kukiel asked for an investigation into German claims. It was the excuse that Stalin had been looking for. He telegrammed Churchill attacking the Sikorski government for repeating the 'infamous fascist slander against the USSR' – except that it was not slander. According to Stalin, this was 'indubitable evidence of contact and collusion between Hitler and the Sikorski Government', which brought relations between them to an end.[57]

London did try to mitigate Stalin's moves to isolate the London Poles but their reliance on the Red Army to take the east meant that they were not willing to push the matter. For the Americans Cordell Hull made it clear to Molotov that he would not intervene on the London Poles' behalf. At the Allied conference in Teheran at the end of November 1943 Churchill said that 'Poland might move westwards' – compensating the loss of territory to the Soviet Union with a gain at the expense of Germany. Stalin asked whether the changes could be made without talking to the Poles about it, and Churchill said yes. Roosevelt agreed, but asked that the decision be kept secret because of the presidential elections to be held in 1944.[58]

Churchill's support for the exile Poles was abandoned in favour of the Grand Alliance. The close personal relationship with General Sikorski, who lost his life in a plane crash off Gibraltar did not carry over into his dealings with the new leader Stanisław Mikołajczyk. His attempts to put the Poles' case to Moscow gave way to an attempt to get the Poles to accept the Russians' demands. So it was that the London Poles were strong-armed into accepting first that the Curzon Line would be the *de facto* boundary between the Soviet Union and Poland; and second that the Polish Government-in-exile should 'include among themselves none but persons fully deter-mined to cooperate with the Soviet Union'. These concessions were ignored by Moscow where the founding of a Polish Committee of National Liberation was announced on 22 January 1944.[59]

Troops of the Polish Home Army took part in the liberation of Vilno in July, and of Lvov. On both occasions the victory celebrations were followed by the arrest of the officers and the forcible induction of the troops into the Red Army. The 27th Volnyhian Division of around 25,000, retreating after a tough engagement with the Wehrmacht to Lublin, was surrounded and disarmed by the Soviets. Stalin instructed the Moscow Radio to refer not to the Home Army, but to 'White Poles', or 'bandits.[60]

Knowing that they faced a second invasion, the Polish Home Army planned the General Uprising, called 'Tempest' The Home Army Commanding Officer Bar-Komorowski knew that military help to the Soviets against the Germans would also mean 'creating maximum political difficulties for them'. General Okulici said that 'an effort was needed which would stir up the conscience of the world'.[61]

At the end of July Soviet troops had advanced to gather on the Vistula River overlooking Warsaw. On 29 July Soviet aircraft dropped leaflets calling the people to arms in the name of the Polish Committee of National Liberation.[62] The Home Guard launched its uprising on 1 August 1944, and the city was plunged into the most desperate war. The Home Army led the fighting, but it was joined by the pro-Soviet Polish People's Army (PPA) – 'we overcame whatever our differences were' remembered Krzystyna Kulpinska, a Home Army supporter.[63] The Moscow-based Polish Radio service on 3rd August proclaimed that 'The People's Army has taken to arms in Warsaw' and 'German blood is flowing in the streets'. From their point of view 'Soldiers of the Home Army have joined up with the action of the People's Army'. One Russian Captain Konstanty Kalugy who had been a prisoner of the Germans but escaped in the fighting sent a message to Stalin 'I have established personal contact with the commander of the Warsaw garrison, who is conducting the nation's heroic battle against the Hitlerite bandits'. The Moscow Radio promised that 'the Red Army is approaching Warsaw'.[64]

But the Red Army halted. Poles Janek Karniewicz and Michal Miecielica were with the Polish First Army of General Berling – a Soviet-organised force with the Red Army – on the east side of the

Vistula. 'We could hear the uprising' recalled Miecielica 'we could hear shells killing our people':

> It was clear to everyone, including the Russians, that the obvious military strategy was to proceed to Warsaw – only fourteen days into the Uprising.

'And for the Russians to cross the river once we had reached it,' adds Karniewicz.[65] In September, Berling did take four infantry battalions over the river, after begging permission from the Russians, and even held a shallow bridgehead on the West Bank, though he failed to contact the insurgents.[66] But the Russians did not cross the river. They were of course under no obligation to help the Home Army, though they had led all the Varsarvians, including their own Polish People's Army, to believe that they were going to carry on into Warsaw. While it was true that the Werhmacht had put up a strong defence in the first two weeks of the Uprising, they could have fought on after that.[67]

The paralysis of the Red Army on the Vistula was not down to a German counter-offensive but was a ploy to let the Germans do the work of pacifying Warsaw before the Soviets took control. Himmler's reaction to the uprising showed that he was motivated more by revenge than any real war aim. He said that Warsaw would be liquidated and the 'Poles themselves will cease to be a problem for our children and for all who will follow us' – except that it was the Red Army who followed, not Germany.[68]

Stalin's denunciations of the Home Army as 'Whites' or 'Black Hundreds' showed that they were the enemy as far as he was concerned. Asked by Mikołajczyk to make arms-drops to the insurgents on 9 August Stalin agreed, but then did not. When the Western Allies offered to drop supplies to beleaguered Warsaw, Vyshinsky explained to the US Ambassador on 18 August that they could but that the Soviets 'decidedly object to British or American aircraft, after dropping arms in the region of Warsaw landing on Soviet territory, since the Soviet Government do not wish to associate themselves either directly or indirectly with the adventure in Warsaw'.[69] There it was. The Soviet reason for not supplying the Uprising was that they were opposed to it. Without being able to land behind Soviet lines, Allied planes flying from Italy would not be able to reach Warsaw. The rising went on till October, costing 250,000 lives as the city centre was reduced to dust. A further 630,000 people were deported from the ruined city. The Home Army lost 15,000 dead, but the fighting also cost the Germans 10,000 dead, 9,000 wounded and 7,000 missing.[70]

A week after the surrender of the Home Army Stalin met Churchill along with Averell Harriman and Anthony Eden in Moscow. The Allies fell over themselves to exonerate Stalin's betrayal of the Poles, as Eden recorded up the discussion on 11 October 1944:

> Stalin was at great pains to assure the Prime Minister that failure to relieve Warsaw had not been due to any lack of effort by the Red Army. The failure had been due entirely to the enemy's strength and difficulties of terrain. Marshal Stalin could not admit this failure before the world... The Prime Minister accept this view absolutely and he assured Marshal Stalin that no serious persons in the UK had credited report that the failures had been deliberate ... Mr Harriman ... said the same was true of the people in America.[71]

Moscow's press campaign painted the Home Army as dangerous and deluded adventurers who had cost the people of Warsaw their lives. The attacks on the Polish resistance were repeated in the Western press, by the popular cartoonist David Low in the Daily Mirror, for example. The Russians did not enter Warsaw till mid-January of 1945.

In the meantime Churchill took Mikołajczyk to Moscow on 13 October 1944 to ask that the London Poles be included in the administration of the 'liberated lands', alongside the Polish Workers' Party. Mikołajczyk had been persuaded to promise 'a durable Polish-Soviet friendship based on an alliance aiming at close political and economic collaboration between the two countries' and even that 'the Polish armed forces in the Eastern Zone would come under Soviet Supreme Operational Command'. On the day that he arrived in Moscow with Churchill, the Soviet Union recognised the Soviet-sponsored Polish Committee of National Liberation (known as the

Lublin Committee). Stalin told the leader of the London Poles that he would have to talk the Committee of National Liberation, and that in any event, agreement could only be made on the basis of Mikołajczyk's acceptance of the Curzon line. To the Pole's dismay Churchill agreed saying that 'the sacrifices made by the Soviet Union' entitle it 'to a western frontier along the Curzon line'. Then Molotov told Mikołajczyk that Roosevelt had agreed as much at Teheran – which was the first that the Polish leader knew of the 'secret agreement'. Grasping at straws, Mikołajczyk asked Stalin for a guarantee of our independence. 'Who is it that threatens your independence? Is it perhaps the Soviet Union?' Stalin demanded brazenly, knowing Mikołajczyk would not risk losing what little influence he still had by telling the truth.[72]

At a reception for the Lublin Committee Stalin turned to one of its leaders, a radical who had been persecuted in pre-war Poland and asked 'how many years, comrade, have you spent in prisons?' 'Which prisons do you have in mind', the Pole asked, 'the Polish or the Soviet ones?' Stalin answered 'the quicker we forget about the Russian prisons the better it will be for both our nations'.[73]

Moscow trial of the Polish Home Army leaders

Under Soviet occupation, the resistant Poles organised an underground organisation. In March 1945 leaders Jan Stanislaw Jankowski, who had survived underground as the representative of the London Poles under the Nazis, and Home Army General Leopold Okulicki were invited to talks with the local Soviet Commander. The promise of 'safe conduct' turned out to be a lie, and they were taken to Moscow. In June they were tried along with fourteen other underground leaders, accused of anti-Soviet activity. The leaders were jailed for long terms, and many died in jail. The Soviet security forces rounded up Home Army fighters and other suspect nationalists who were kept in camps.[74]

Yugoslavia

Britain continued to nurse ambitions in Yugoslavia, and tried to get Tito's National Committee to enter into a coalition with the Royalists. The British said, Milovan Djilas, did not even hide their attempts to 'water down Tito's wine'. Worse still, British bombing raids on Split and Belgrade were hurting the Yugoslavs more than the Germans. On Easter Sunday 1944 the Allied airforce indiscriminately bombed Belgrade – 'blanket bombing' – such that 'not one military target was hit', but 'the devastation was no less and the despair even deeper, that that caused by the German attack on April 1941'. Djilas recalls that we 'believed that the Allies were carrying out such bombings in order to make postwar rehabilitation and administration harder for us Communists'.[75]

Tito's partisans were cautious, too about their Soviet allies. 'Our fears were especially aroused by the Warsaw uprising, as were our conflicted feelings about the sufferings of the Polish people under the noses of the indifferent Russian troops', said Djilas. The Soviet Union forced Red Army troops and also Bulgarians on Tito's partisans. It was important to Moscow that the Bulgarians, having only just switched sides, get an opportunity to prove their socialist credentials. More important, it was an attempt to water down the Yugoslav partisans' prestige. Djilas complained that the Soviets had no reason to 'boast of their decisive role in liberating this or that part of Yugoslavia', since the partisans had done almost all of the work.[76]

The Red Army troops could be brutal in its treatment of the Yugoslavs, which created resentments. At Čukarica the rape and murder of a pharmacist was followed by a funeral march of five thousand: a demonstration against the troops' actions. Later, the Soviet intelligence service recruited agents in the Yugoslav Communist Party. Of all the East European states in the Soviet Zone, the Yugoslavs had most independence, and were for a time subject to a propaganda campaign where they were labelled 'Trotskyists' and even 'Tito Fascists'.[77]

For all that, the development of Yugoslav society under the leadership of Tito's Communist Party was not that different from the course taken by the other Slav countries in the Soviet Zone. The society was administered by a military-bureaucratic elite, who took the place of the old ruling classes.

Stalinist Rule in Eastern Europe

In the spring of 1945 'Pan-Slavic Conference' was organised in Sofia on the initiative of the USSR. It was particularly important for the Bulgarian hosts who were seeking to minimise their participation in the Axis. The Bulgarian Exarch blessed the meeting (as he had once blessed the Bulgarian Axis army), though the 'only thing Slavic was the hackneyed phraseology of Russian imperialism', thought Milovan Djilas: 'In a fit of nationalist and Slavic intoxication, they all kissed the cross – members of the Bulgarian Central Committee, Soviet generals, the proud and the embarrassed Poles, and the meek and mild Czechs'. The appeal to pan-Slavic sentiment was Stalin's attempt to create a foundation for the Soviet Zone of East European states, and was a regional substitute for the Comintern which had been wound up in 1943.[79]

'In all of these countries governments were set up which nominally represented coalitions between several parties' explained Isaac Deutscher.

> But in each of these governments the Communists were in charge of at least two decisive departments: police and army. They used these departments to establish control first over their country as a whole, and then over their partners in the government, until they were able either to oust their partners or to compel them to cooperate.[79]

This was a way of working that anyone who had come up against the Stalinists' 'Popular Fronts' knew very well. Allies were sought to make the coalition look broad, but the important jobs like treasurer and press officer would be in the hands of loyal communists, and the committee would be manipulated behind closed doors.

In Government, though, Stalin's allies had much more to play for. One thing helped them to rebuild Eastern Europe on Soviet lines, and that was the collapse of almost all rival authority, civil and political. So much of the political class had been compromised by collaboration with Germany that there were few plausible challengers to the Moscow-allied Communist parties. The entrepreneurial class, too, had been tested to destruction first by the collapse of the German Empire, and then by the Soviet invasion. Two ethnic groups that had made a great contribution to trade, industry, and professional life, the Jews and the Germans, had been driven out of Eastern Europe, the first into the death camps, the second back to Germany after the war.

Czechoslovakia's President Eduard Benes, no Communist, described how

> The Germans simply took control of all main industries, main banks. If they did not nationalise them directly, they put them in the hands of big German concerns ... In this way they automatically prepared the economic and financial capital of our country for nationalisation. To return the property and the banks to the hands of Czech individuals, or to consolidate them without considerable state assistance and new financial guarantees, was simply impossible.[80]

So it was that the Czechoslovak state came to control three quarters of industry.

'De-Nazification,' Deutscher explains, made it easier for the Stalinists to take control.

> the Communists were assisted by the fact that each of those governments was under the obligation, stipulated in armistice terms to purge its civil service and its political institutions form those who had worked against Russia, from Nazis, Fascists, Militarists and so on.

> Those clauses, endorsed by the western allies, were enough to enable Stalin to initiate and direct, without flagrantly offending against inter-allied convention, a process by which the old ruling classes of eastern Europe were thrown into complete disarray, deprived of organisation and rendered completely impotent.[81]

'Anti-Fascism' became the ideological justification of the Stalinist regimes in Eastern Europe. To give that ideology a practical expression, those regimes launched a vicious campaign against German civilians. Germans had settled all across Eastern Europe since long before the war, and, with the loss of German territories under the Versailles peace, many more German communities were put under foreign rule. As the East European states were re-created, ethnic Germans were foreigners again, and now scapegoats for the Nazi occupation. A Czech politician explained the

> On May 17 the Germans were given smaller food rations ('the same basic food ration as the Jews received during the occupation' according to a government order of May 17). They had to wear special white armbands and were not allowed to use public means of communication ... In June all German schools were closed. Compulsory labour conscription was introduced ... Practically all movable and immovable property was taken away from the Germans ... The confiscation would make good wrongs committed on the Czech nation since the end of its independence in 1620. The Communist Party in particular emphasized the national movement and became the most nationalist party.[82]

Ilya Ehrenburg travelling through Eastern Europe thought that Fascism had poisoned the minds of the survivors. 'The weeds of racism and of nationalism had spread widely' he said: 'I saw Sudetan Germans wearing white armbands – a symbol of humiliation – and I felt how terrible it was to be repaying fascism in its own coin'.[83]

There were around 500,000 Germans in Yugoslavia, of whom around half left with the German Army. The remainder were 'encamped in two or three villages'. Their furniture was plundered and their young women made to work as maids by Communist Party officials, until the practice was outlawed. Moved into camps 'where hunger and disease raged, and prostitution with the guards flourished' the Germans were then moved across the border into Austria. Edvard Kardelj pointed out 'that we had thereby lost our most productive inhabitants'. In 1948 Djilas was travelling with Tito through Belje and noticed 'a long row of barracks with laundry hanging outside and poorly clad women and children milling around'. In the barracks the families lived separated by hanging blankets. A gamekeeper explained that they were 'Schwaben', the old-fashioned word for the German minority in Vojvodina. Their husbands worked, without pay: 'Slaves', said Djilas. There were around 30,000 of them, kept to meet labour shortages.[84]

Policies of persecution led inevitably to Germans leaving Eastern Europe. Seven million Germans were driven from Poland and the Soviet Union, three million from Czechoslovakia and thirteen million in all from the east. Some of this migration had already happened as Germans fled the oncoming Red Army. Others left under the persecution. At Potsdam in August 1945 the Allies agreed the 'orderly and humane' expulsions of Germans from Yugoslavia, Poland and Hungary.

France

In the planning of the invasion of France, the Allies saw no role for the Resistance. France was to come under the Allied Military Government of the Occupied Territories. For the Resistance, though, Overlord was universally welcomed as a blow against the occupiers, and they rallied to support it.

On the evening of D-Day, de Gaulle broadcast to France warning against any 'premature insurrection', fearful that the Resistance would take the initiative but they ignored him. When Overlord began, the entire French railway network was closed down by more than 1000 acts of sabotage – at a time when nine tenths of the German Army were transported by rail or horse. At the same time the miners of Toulouse struck, and declared the Republic from the Town Hall of the town of Annonay.[85]

Emboldened, Resistance fighters of the Francs Tireurs et Partisans under Jean-Jacques Chapou attacked German and Milice forces in the town of Tulle in Limoges. Fifty Germans were killed in the liberation. Shocked at the blow to German prestige the SS Panzer Division 'Das Reich' of 15,000 men took the town back. Twenty six maquisards and seventy Germans were killed in the fighting, but overwhelming force won out. The following day 3000 were brought out into the town square, and 99 were executed, hung from balconies and telegraph poles. Three hundred were taken away, and 149 of them deported to Dachau. Shortly afterwards the 'Das Reich'

Oradour-sur-Glane, photograph by Stuart Davies

division attacked Oradour-sur-Glane where 649 were killed.[86]

The savagery of the German reaction gave some weight to the demands of the Allies to stop the uprising. On 10 June General Koenig of the Free French set the message 'put maximum brake on all guerrilla action'. The aim though was not to save lives, but to stop the Resistance from liberating France before the Allies arrived.

On 8 June Colonel Marcel Descour, leader of a large Maquis group in the mountain plateau of Vercors ordered that the plateau be defended – making it the first liberated French territory. Four thousand fighters set up their own republic, with its own newspaper and courts. Soon, though, the Vercors liberated zone was surrounded. Political leader Eugène Chavant sent a desperate message to the Free French leadership in Algiers. 'If no aid we and population will consider Algiers criminal and cowardly'. The Germans, understanding who their real enemy was, sent 10,000 troops to attack. On 22 July 200 SS troops landed in gliders and the struggle to take back Vercors began. In the fighting German atrocities were shocking, with 326 maquisards slaughtered after being hunted down, and 130 civilians also killed.[87]

While they counselled caution militarily, the Free French had been very active recruiting civil servants to take over when the Vichy officials left. New local leaders, Commisaires de la République were appointed for every region, backed up by Comités Départmentaux de la Libération, to control the local Resistance groups. Though Roosevelt had cold-shouldered de Gaulle throughout the war, fearing that he was too close to the Communists, once the Allied troops were on French soil Generals Eisenhower and Montgomery realised they needed the Free French to rein in the Resistance. In thirty major cities there were insurrections that pitted Resistance fighters against the German occupiers.[88]

Initially Eisenhower had no plans to liberate Paris 'until a spontaneous rising in the capital forced his hand'.[89] US General Omar Bradley explained that the Allies were afraid the demands of the starving Parisians would derail the conquest of Europe

> Logistically, it could cause untold trouble, for behind its handsome façades there lived four million hungry Frenchmen. The diversion of so much tonnage to Paris would only strain further our already taut lines of supply. Food for the people of Paris meant less gasoline for the front.

Once again the Parisians were to be abandoned to the logic of war – except that they took matters into their own hands. Comités de Libération were formed in town halls across the capital and barricades put up in the north and east of the City. The Resistance had 20,000 fighters ranged against an equal number, though much more heavily armed, German army. On 20 August a group led by Léo Hamon entered the Hôtel de Ville and declared a provisional republic, and arrested the Vichy prefect. With revolution in the air, the Free French brokered an agreement to give the Germans 24 hours to leave the city. The Communist leader of the Resistance in Paris, Henri Rol-Tanguy saved the honour of the Allies and the Free French, by inviting them into the city as liberators: 'open the road to Paris for the victorious allied armies and welcome them here'.[90]

Not everything went well with the 'liberators'. General de Gaulle's Military Cabinet discusses the problem of sexual attacks after the Normandy landing:

> In the regions occupied by the Americans, women no longer dare to go to milk cows without being accompanied by a man. Even the presence of a man does not protect them. In the Manche a priest has been killed trying to protect two young girls attacked by American soldiers. These young girls were raped. In the Seine

Inférieur a woman was raped and killed after her husband had been assassinated.

Supreme Headquarters of the Allied Expeditionary Forces (SHAEF) stopped French newspapers reporting a number of rapes at the hands of US servicemen. In December 1944, a directive to all US Army and Air Force Commanders said that rapes and burglaries should be punished promptly and with 'appropriate severity'.[91]

In Paris, the surrender of German Commander von Cholitz – who had the foresight not to carry out Hitler's orders to raze Paris – was signed by von Cholitz, the US General Leclerc and the Resistance leaders Rol-Tanguy and Maurice Kriegel-Valmiront. De Gaulle, who arrived two hours later complained that Rol-Tanguy had been allowed to sign. The following day de Gaulle was urged to announce the re-establishment of the Republic, replied 'the Republic has never ceased to exist'. His provisional government was recognised by the Allies in October 1944.[92]

Within days of the liberation of Paris de Gaulle set about disarming the Resistance. After some protest the Resistance leaders in the Comité d'Action Militaire accepted the proposal that the resistance fighters be fused with the Army –l'amalgame – though in the process the officers of 1940 were allowed to keep their rank, whatever they had done during the occupation, while the Resistance men were carefully selected. The whole process put the traditional order back in charge. The activist workplace committees that had sprung up to organise factories were suspended after an agreement to include two communist ministers in de Gaulle's government, George Bidault and the communist FTP leader Charles Tillon. The self-organised police forces of the Milices Patriotiques that took over day-to-day organisation of localities between the fall of the occupation and the establishment of the new state were disarmed, and later disbanded. The communist leader Thorez, who had been amnestied by de Gaulle allowing him to return from Moscow, promised his support for 'one army, one police, one administration'. 'We want the revolution, tomorrow', he promised his supporters, and promised de Gaulle that 'meanwhile today we want the capitalist regime to function according to its own laws, which must be left intact'.[93]

De Gaulle's victory over the militant Resistance was helped along by the Parti Communist Français. Also, de Gaulle spoke clearly to that large constituency that feared the social change that the Resistance threatened. After all, many more people did not join the Resistance than did. De Gaulle's great advantage was that he could count on the support both of Vichy France, and also of the Resistance. De Gaulle's appeal to La France Profonde, the enduring France that lay beneath the hurly-burly of everyday political squabbles was quite similar to Petain's traditionalist outlook. Where Petain had promised order, he had in the end delivered more conflict. Only de Gaulle had the authority to rein in the runaway militancy of the Resistance, and for that *La France Profonde* was deeply grateful. De Gaulle faced down the left's ambitions for a Sovereign Constituent Assembly, and got the country to vote instead for an authoritarian presidency in a referendum on a new constitution. Even then, he balked at the prospect of ruling alongside the different political parties, and left the stage.

Conflict between the Allies and the Resistance happened in every country. In 1944, the allies opposed strikes planned by Central Dutch Resistance Council - this time to coincide with the invasion. In retrospect, British commander at Arnhem R.E. Urquhart admitted that an unwillingness to cooperate with the Resistance contributed to major setbacks in the winter of 1944-5.[94] In Belgium Max Nokin, an official of the Societé Generale de Belgique had written in 1942 that 'we would certainly compromise the success of our economic recovery if we turn to a regime of' economic and industrial liberty 'after the war'. Repression, though had provoked resistance, and the Belgian jurist René Marq described the mood of the final months of the occupation as one of 'virtual civil war'. The German Military Adminstrator's report of June 1944 noted that 'the national-conservative opposition movement is ... trying to unite all forces to preserve order, in hopes of providing a counterweight to the communist effort, which, because of the difficult economic situation is finding ever more support among the workers'. The Belgian Government-in-exile was hostile to the Front d'Indépendence which they feared was 'perhaps entirely communist'.[95] With the Allied invasion, the exile Government had the solution to the problem of a people in revolt. In November 1944 armed members of the wartime resistance were given two weeks to hand over their weapons. On 25 November there was a protest rally in Brussels. The police opened fire injuring 45 people.[96]

Spain

One fascist state that was not going to be invaded or overthrown in 1944 or 1945 was Spain's. Throughout the war, the Allies had sought to keep Spain out of the war, by flattering and bribing the Fascist dictator Francisco Franco. London's United Press news agency put out a report on Ambassador Sir Samuel Hoare's talks with the Spanish dictator: 'General Franco is striving desperately to reach quickest agreement with the Allies as it is virtually the last chance to save his personal regime.'[97]

It had already been explained to Franco's Foreign Minister that it was the Allies that represented the best guarantee of the continuation of the dictatorship. The Foreign Minister was frightened about the approaching defeat of Hitler by the Red Army, but British ambassador Sir Samuel Hoare assured him in Madrid in February 1943: 'the victory at the end of the war will be an Allied not a Russian victory, namely a victory in which the British Empire and the United States of America will exercise the greatest possible influence'. More, Britain and America have pledged themselves to 'keep garrisons in occupied areas as a safeguard against anarchy and chaos'.[98]

Allied troops on mainland Europe, Hoare was explaining, were the best guarantee of Franco's survival – and so it proved. Fascist Spain after the war was granted the status of a loyal ally in the 1953 Treaty of Madrid, under which the dictatorship was granted $500 million in aid up to 1962.

When Franco died in 1975 US President Nixon said 'General Franco was a loyal friend and ally of the United States. He earned worldwide respect for Spain through firmness and fairness'.

The Betrayal of the Cossacks

Many thousands of Russians who had fought on the side of the Wehrmacht under General Vlasov in the 'Russian Liberation Army' surrendered to British and American authorities at the end of the war. The prisoners were a headache for the western Allies who knew that their Soviet counterparts would not treat them as prisoners of war, but as traitors. The Russian authorities wanted them back because of the way that 'white' expatriates had organised against the Soviet Union in the past. On 24 June 1944 Patrick Dean, a legal advisor to the Foreign Office wrote that 'we are not concerned with the fact that they may be shot or otherwise harshly dealt with than they might under English law'. Anthony Eden told Molotov that 'the British Government wanted all the men to be placed under Soviet administration and discipline' on 16 October 1944. Edward Stettinus, when questioned, reiterated 'the policy adopted by the United States Government in this connection is that all claimants to Soviet nationality will be released to the Soviet Government irrespective of whether they wish to be so released'. Churchill noted 'we ought to get rid of them as soon as possible'. The Allied authorities had already decided that Stalin's brutal rule was what was needed to stabilise the east and the decision to hand him the Russian prisoners of war was just one part of that agreement.[99]

To the embarrassment of British officers holding the Russians, many attempted suicide rather than agree to be sent back. A British convoy got to Odessa in March 1945. As the men were taken down the gangplank they were met by the NKVD on the quayside. Lieutenant Lieven called out to the commanding officer: 'Sir, sir, they are murdering the prisoners!' Colonel Dashwood replied 'no, no, that's impossible'. But it was true. Afterwards, when there could be no doubt about Stalin's plans for the men, British officers dealt with around 30 000 Cossacks and Georgians who had surrendered, and were camped between Lienz and Oberdrauburg in Austria. Determined to hand the men over to the Soviets authorities, Colonel Bryar of the First Kensingtons issued orders that 'any attempts to resist will be dealt with firmly by shooting to kill'. At the end of May 1945 the officers were sent to Judenburg in the Soviet zone. British officers heard them being executed, each volley of fire being followed by a cheer. A day later the Argylls forced thousands of Cossacks onto waiting railway trucks. Fighting broke out and the British killed five and injured many more. Another camp was forced onto transport by the West Kents and Lancashire Fusiliers. In all 22,502 Cossacks and Caucasians were forced into Soviet hands.[100]

The Vlasov army had fought on the side of the Wehrmacht, and Vlasov himself deserved to be tried for treason, as he was in 1946, and hung, along with eleven other officers in his army. The ordinary soldiers, though, were victims of Allied realpolitik at the end of the war. The American and British authorities were glad to be rid of these awkward Russians, who they saw as just more strain on the post-war relief operation. To the Soviet authorities, they were scape-goats for the collapse in morale on the western front in 1940-41. Not just Vlasov's men, but all Soviet troops who had allowed themselves to be captured by the Germans were abused after the war. As many as a fifth of the 5.5 million Russians repatriated from the formerly occupied areas were met with 25-year sentences, or executed. Others got shorter sentences, or were exiled to Siberia, or sent as work conscripts to rebuild Donbas, Kuzbas and other ruined regions. On 17 September 1955, Khruschev amnestied the jailed repatriates.

Not everyone remembered Vlasov's Army unkindly. In May 1945 a Division of the Russian Liberation Army under Sergey Bunyachenko turned on their SS allies, and joined the Czechs to save the Prague uprising – which was dangerously short of guns. This last attempt to win favour with the Allies, though, did not work. The Czechs, getting ready to deal with the Russians were keen to get rid of Bunyachenko's men.[101]

The persistence of the nation state

Between 1935 and 1945 almost every continental European state had been invaded, overrun or over-thrown at least once. National ruling elites on mainland Europe were hopelessly compromised by collab-oration with Fascism, and dependent upon the United States - or the USSR - for their security. The compelling question is why did the nation-state, so easily overthrown in wartime, return in peacetime as the archetypal form of political organisation.

In 1943 the US State Department exhibited a disdain for national sovereignty while looking at proposals for an international Bill of Rights: 'a barrier to state supremacy and racial superiority which are inimical to individual rights'. But pragmatically they had to acknowledge that there was no international government to enforce individual rights.[102] The first reason for the re-establishment of nation-states in Europe was the limited character of US power. Eisenhower felt he was 'invading Italy on a shoestring', being heavily outnumbered by German and Italian troops. This, according to Stephen Ambrose, was the reason that the US recognised Marshall

Badoglio and King Victor Emmanuel's post-Mussolini government.[103] Though the US had the firepower to overthrow the collaborationist regimes, it lacked the resources to exercise continuing authority: 'Roosevelt privately confessed to Churchill that he doubted he could keep American troops in Europe for more than a year or so after the end of hostilities'.[104] According to economist and historian John Willoughby, American recognition of native German authorities was driven forwards by the collapse of military discipline in the post-war occupation.[105] All the same, the victorious Allies assumed the right to intervene in the internal affairs of the countries in their respective 'zones', or spheres of influence, as we shall see.

Though national elites were disgraced by their collaboration, the national idea was saved by the partisans: 'the legitimacy of post-war regimes and governments essentially rested on their resistance record', according to Eric Hobsbawm.[106] General de Gaulle's claim that 'eternal France' had never been defeated is essentially untrue. France had been defeated. More than that, its ruling elite had been craven in defeat, preferring Hitler to Blum.[107] But the efforts of the French resistance, and principally of the militant working class minority, saved France's honour. While the ruling class was indifferent to national sovereignty, Stalinism remained wedded to one country, even to the point of putting off socialism to a later date. The moral deficit of the European national ruling elites was a persistent problem, and one that predisposed them to transnational institutions after the war.

After the British Crown and lowland Presbyterians defeated and dispersed the Scottish highlanders, the new Scotland was built, strangely on an ersatz image of highland culture, with tartans and kilts. The Allied occupation of Europe was in the end the defeat of the popular resistance. But losing their real influence on the state, the Resistance became, like the Highlanders, an important mythical foundation for those newly 'liberated' European states. Their legitimacy was in question because of the way that the elites had collaborated with the German occupation of their countries. The Resistance lent a powerful and much-needed authority to the state, even as 'across Europe, former resistance leaders were being marginalized'[108] and the partisans were being disarmed and bullied into submission.

Chapter Twenty Six

A War of Extermination in the Pacific

After the Pacific battles of the Midway and Guadalcanal, Japan had lost the naval advantage it won at Pearl Harbour. The US Navy inflicted such losses on the Japanese fleet that its troops spread across the Pacific Islands could no longer be protected, and the war swung decisively against them. US forces could bring overwhelming power to bear on the Japanese, who were effectively tied down, and increasingly unsupported.

Once the tide of war had turned, the Japanese suffered catastrophic losses of men in a succession of battles on key Pacific islands that would gradually bring the war to the Japanese mainland. The extent of the Japanese losses was so great because very few were taken prisoner. The low numbers of Japanese prisoners taken – just 38,666 prisoners compared to one and a half million dead. The official explanation for the low numbers captured has always been that the fanatical Bushido code forbade troops from surrendering. It was true that the Japanese military leaders instilled in their men the message that they should not surrender – but that is not the reason for the low number of Japanese prisoners taken. The reason so few Japanese prisoners were taken was that the Allies, primarily the US, but also the British and Australian troops took no prisoners.[1] There were no logistical arrangements made for the holding of Japanese prisoner because there was no expectation that prisoners would be taken. In every engagement after the Allies started to win the number of prisoners taken was insignificant.

> The Marine battle cry on Tarawa was, "Kill the Jap bastards! Take no prisoners." The 41st Division under MacArthur ... bragged that "The 41st didn't take prisoners."[2]

According to historian Barak Kushner 'One reason behind the small numbers of Japanese soldiers captured by US forces may have been the fact that US soldiers slaughtered wounded or surrendering Japanese soldiers'.[3] As much as the Bushido code stopped Japanese from surrendering, their experience where they were at the mercy of the Allied Forces was such that few would have wanted to surrender anyway. Allied troops regularly beat, tortured and killed captured Japanese. One academic who had been with the army in Okinawa and Peleliu remembered GIs taking Japanese body parts and gold teeth, and urinating on the dead, as well as shooting defenceless old women.[4] Edgar Jones, who was War Correspondent of the *Atlantic Monthly*, wrote in February 1946

> We shot prisoners in cold blood, wiped out hospitals, strafed lifeboats, killed or mistreated enemy civilians, finished off the enemy wounded, tossed the dying into a hole with the dead, and in the Pacific, boiled the flesh off enemy skulls to make table ornaments for sweethearts, or carved their bones into letter openers.[5]

In December of 1944, Lance Corporal Viliame Lomasalato of the Fiji Military Forces Third Battalion was awarded the Military Cross after having eaten a Japanese soldier in the fighting at Bougainville in the spring.[6] At Bougainville an Australian Colonel protested 'But sir, they are wounded and want to surrender', to his commanding officer of Japanese troops. 'You heard me Colonel' replied the Major General 'I want no prisoners – shoot them all'. They were shot.[7]

The Bushido code was useful for papering over the Allies' no surrender policy. At times the code itself was made into an excuse for killing defeated troops. Bill Crooks of the Australian Imperial Force recalled that 'We knew their bushido banzai code was to take no prisoners in battle and never surrender. So we killed them'.[8] If the Japanese soldiers fought 'fanatically' that was at least in part because they knew they would be shown little mercy if they allowed themselves to be captured. As historians Mark Roehrs and William Renzi

US troops took the head of a Japanese soldier as a mascot

write 'for the man actually on the front line, the war was one of racial extinction'.[9]

In the US invasion of Saipan, an island in the Marianas group 100 miles North of Guam on 15 June 1944 where 30,000 Japanese troops were garrisoned cost the Americans 3,100 men. The Japanese dead were 27,000 troops killed and 22,000 Japanese civilians. On the Island of Peleliu, off the Philippines, all but 200 of the 11,000 Japanese defenders of the Island were killed. In the October 1944 'Battle of Bull Run' for the Gulf of Leyte – the greatest naval battle ever - the US lost 2800 men, the Japanese over 10,000. Overall, the battle for Luzon in the Philippines cost the Japanese 192,000 men for 8000 American deaths. At Mindano a further 50,000 Japanese were killed for the loss of 2500 Americans. On 19 February 30,000 US Marines

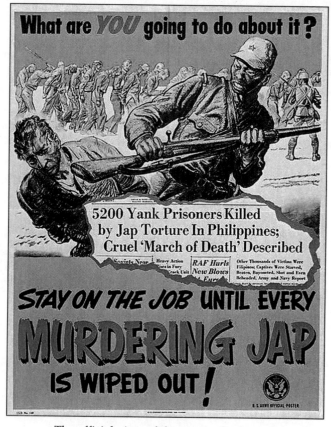

The official view of the war in the far east

landed on Iwo Jima and killed all but 212 of the 22,000 Japanese at a cost of 6,800 Americans. On 1 April 1945 an Allied invasion force of 100,000 landed on the Japanese island of Okinawa, which was defended by the Japanese 32nd Army under Lt. General Ushijima Mitsuru. The battle cost the Americans 7400 men, and the Japanese lost 127,000 troops (out of 130,000), and also 75,000 Japanese civilians were killed. A marine unit hearing voices from a cave on Okinawa demanded that those inside come out. When they did not the marines cleared the cave with a flamethrower. Inside they found 85 school girls who had been mobilised as nurses. Japanese battle deaths in the Second World War were 1.5 million – compared to American casualties (dead and injured) in the Pacific of 296,148, and Commonwealth (British, Australian and Indian) of 185,000. Responsibility for all these deaths lay first and foremost with the commanding officers – those Japanese who would not negotiate a surrender and those Allied Commanders who encouraged their men to take no prisoners.[10]

The reason that American troops were so willing to slaughter and abuse the Japanese was the sustained public relations campaign organised by the Office of War Information, with the support of Henry Luce's press empire, to dehumanise the Japanese as monkeys and termites, described above in chapter nine. According to polls taken in July 1945, 52 per cent of the American public believed that the Japanese people were incurably 'warlike and want to make themselves as powerful as possible'. Asked who was the 'most cruel at heart' 51 per cent picked Japanese, 13 per cent the Germans.[11]

The war of extermination was brought to mainland Japan with the capture of the Marianas Islands, a launch-point close enough for B52 bombers to fly from. General Curtis LeMay took over Bomber Command XXI in January 1945. LeMay worked out that by stripping out all the guns (on the assumption that Japanese anti-aircraft guns were not powerful enough to hit highflying B52s) the planes could make the distance to bomb Tokyo and other cities. A team of Harvard Scientists under Louis Fieser worked with DuPont and Standard Oil to develop a new incendiary by mixing Napthaline and Palmitate with gasoline – Napalm. The War Department got a team of artists and RKO pictures to build a mock-up of Tokyo and another of Berlin at the Dunway Proving grounds in Utah.[12] The experiment was a huge success, so LeMay went from test trial to trial run. On 9 March 1945 three hundred and thirty four B52 bombers specially stripped down so that they could carry the most Napalm set out for Tokyo. The raid went on for three hours. In the resulting firestorm some 150,000 citizens were killed and the authorities recorded 267,161 building were burned down – a quarter of all the buildings in the Tokyo City area. These fire raids were considered a great success and were repeated throughout the summer. Modern day estimates of the total killed in the fire raids are around two million. After the war LeMay was George Wallace's running mate as Vice Presidential candidate for the American Independent Party, and demanded that President Kennedy should bomb atomic missile sites on Cuba.[13]

On 6 August 1945 and the second on 9 August 1945 US bombers dropped atomic bombs, 'Little Boy' and 'Fat Man' on Hiroshima and Nagasaki in Japan – the only ever use of nuclear weapons in war. The atomic bomb had been created by a team of scientists working on the Manhattan Project under Major General Leslie Groves of the US Army Corps of Engineers, and project leader Robert Oppenheimer. The bombings killed 90,000–166,000 people in Hiroshima, either directly or soon after from injuries or radiation sickness, and 60,000–80,000 in Nagasaki. The targets had been chosen for suitability for testing, and left off the list of cities in the fire raids, so that the effects of the atomic bombardment could be isolated.

Shortly after the Hiroshima and Nagasaki bombardment Emperor Hirohito surrendered, and it has often been claimed as a justification for the use of atomic power that it prevented the high personnel costs of an invasion of mainland Japan.

However, America's own Strategic Bombing Survey reported that Japan had been on the point of surrender anyway:

> Based on a detailed investigation of all the facts and supported by the testimony of the surviving Japanese leaders involved, it is the Survey's opinion that certainly prior to 31 December 1945, and in all probability prior to 1 November 1945, Japan would have surrendered even if the atomic bombs had not been dropped, even if Russia had not entered the war, and even if no invasion had been planned or contemplated.[14]

Historian Gar Alperovitz looked at hundreds of pages of US National Security Agency intercepts of secret enemy wartime communications that showed that US intelligence knew top Japanese army officers were willing to surrender more than three months before the Hiroshima bomb was dropped. Eisenhower, the wartime Supreme Allied Commander in Europe who went on to become US president, later admitted that 'the Japanese were ready to surrender and we didn't have to hit them with that awful thing'. [15] The fire raids of 1945 and the atomic bombardment of that August brought Japan's civilian deaths up to three million – deaths that the Allies were prepared to countenance because they no longer thought of the Japanese as humans, but as lice or vermin to be exterminated.

Chapter Twenty Seven

The Second Invasion of East Asia

The Allied war against Japan in the Far East was at the same time a re-invasion by British (though mostly Indian) and America forces that would reverse the humiliation of the White Race. Japan was driven out of East Asia, but British and American troops took over. 'For most people in the Asia-Pacific, the Second World War was not a titanic struggle between democracy and fascism', writes Walden Bello, 'but a conflict between imperial powers seeking domination over them.'[1] In the conflict, though, many of the Asian nationalist movements that had been encouraged or provoked by Japan would struggle to shape their own future, while the Allies struggled to keep them down and divided.

Japan's Co-Prosperity Sphere was short-lived, and failed because it redirected resources to warfare that might perhaps have been the basis for real cooperation. As it expanded it had made a propagandistic appeal to Asian self-government. On the eve of defeat the Japanese again raised the issue of national independence, most pointedly in Indonesia and Korea. It was a kind of 'scorched earth' policy – for the invading Allies taking over territories with a real expectation of independence was a further challenge to their authority (on top of the humiliation that the Japanese had visited on them in 1942). Late grants of independence on the part of the Japanese made a logistical headache for the Allies, who, as they were advancing on Japan, would also have to cope with claims to self-government in their rear. Allied efforts would be split between pacification of the conquered territory and pushing on to Japan.

For the people of the region, the experience of Japanese occupation was confusingly mixed. On the one hand domination by the Kempetai, hunger and being forced into labour battalions was misery equal to any that Germany visited on Europe. For the Chinese in particular, but also the Koreans, Japan was a vicious and brutal master. There were though many national elites who enjoyed their first experience of self-government under Japan, and the Japanese occupation in the end dislocated Empires, rather than founding a new one.

Burmese leader Ba Maw summed up the paradox:

> The case of Japan is indeed tragic. Looking at it historicaly, no nation has done so much to liberate Asia from white domination ... Had her Asian instincts been true, had she only been faithful to the concept of Asia for the Asians that she herself had proclaimed from the very beginning of the war, Japan's fate would have been very different. No military defeat could then have robbed her of the trust and gratitude of half of Asia or even more...
>
> Even now, as things actually are, nothing can ever obliterate the role Japan has played in bringing liberation to countless colonial peoples. The phenomenal Japanese victories in the Pacific and Southeast Asia which really marked the beginning of the end of all imperialism and colonialism, the national armies Japan helped to create during the war which in their turn created a new spirit and will in a large part of Asia, the independent states she set up in several Southeast Asian countries as well as her recognition of the provisional governemt of Free India at a time when not a single other belligerent power permitted even the talk of independence within its own dominations, and finally a demonstration by the entire Japanese people of the invincibility of the Asia spirit when they rose out of the ashes to a new greatness, these will outlive all the passing wartime strains and passions and betrayals in the final summing up of history.[2]

In 1944, though, the Japanese yoke weighed heavily on the peoples of East Asia, who were summoning the strength to throw it off.

Malaysia

In October 1944 the leaders of the Communist Party of Malaya met near Serendah, north of Kuala Lumpur to work out their plans for when the Allied forces came. They were told that there forces would be organised as two – one an open army that 'would work with the British, and, in effect, function as a British force'. The other would be a secret army held in readiness to fight the British. The Anti-Japanese Army would become a National Liberation Army, the Anti-

Japanese League a National Liberation League. Commander Chin Peng remembered what 'amounted to a rousing call to revolution', and that 'our spirits soared'.[3]

The challenge of how to cope with the British came sooner rather than later, because of the collapse of the Japanese forces after Emperor Hirohito's radio broadcast surrender on 19 August 1945. Straight away the Malayan People's Anti-Japanese Army was contacted by Japanese commanders wanting to help them fight the restoration of British colonialism: 'if you choose to fight on, you can rely on our support'. Whole battalions and many weapons were offered, and in the event some 400 men did shift over from the Japanese to the Anti-Japanese Army, but this late flowering of Pan-Asian solidarity was de-railed by the Communist Party of Malaya's leadership.[4]

Instead of taking on the British, party chairman Lai Te (sometimes Lai Teck) announced an eight point plan that began 'support Russia, China, Britain and America in a new organisation for world security'. The plan called for an end to the 'fascist Japanese political structure' a 'democratic government' and 'freedom of speech' as well as various social progammes. But as Chin Peng understood, it made no reference to national self-determination and 'amounted to nothing more than a vapid move to appease the British'. Perhaps it was because Lai Te, despite posing as a representative of the Comintern was in truth a British spy, only uncovered in 1947, that he managed to trick the Malayan partisans into backing Britain. On the other hand, Lai Te's eight-point plan was pretty much in keeping with Soviet policy of collaborating with the Allies at the time. In any event, the clash between Britain and the Malayan freedom fighters was put on hold.[5]

'The first troops of reoccupation came ashore at a Penang Island beachhead on 3 September', and Chin Peng despaired that 'we are letting them back unimpeded to reclaim a territory they have plundered for so long'. From the outset, the British authorities were hostile, blaming the communists for outbreaks of ethnic hostility between Chinese and Malays. South East Asia Command told the British Liaison Officer Davis that when the Allied troops land the Malayan Peoples Anti-Japanese Army 'should avoid all towns and other districts where the Japanese are present' so as 'to avoid clashes and unnecessary bloodshed'. Davis objected on 19 August 1945 that orders for the MPAJA 'to remain in the hills while the Allies leisurely take over the administration from the Japs will not be reasonable'. Davis' telegram was passed on to Sir Edward Gent (who would later be appointed High Commissioner in Malaya) by the Special Operations Executive Colonel Sheridan with the comment 'our experience is that in cases of this kind the L. O. in course of time becomes rather imbued with the views of the resistance movement to which they are attached'. In other words, Davis had 'gone native'.[6]

As the British troops came ashore on 5 September 1945 a British Military Administration was set up. To appease the populace an advisory council was appointed and three members of the Communist Party of Malaya were invited – among 61 other notables. The pre-war Societies and Banishment Ordinances had not been repealed, so the communists were officially still illegal, despite having been the core of the liberation army. New military liaison officers were brought in, 'many of them old Malaya hands' – policemen, planters and game wardens.[7]

Quite soon the British Military Administration made itself felt. A decision to declare the Japanese occupation currency valueless wrecked the economy. Workers lost their savings at a stroke, food supplies dwindled and prices rocketed. The Administration stopped food movements, making things worse. Following Lai Te's orders, the MPAJA agreed to disband by December 1, and military parades were held up and down the country where arms were handed in. At the same time, Singapore workers were protesting at the austerity measures. Seven thousand Dockworkers struck on 21 October, calling both for higher wages, but also for an end to the shipment of arms to Dutch troops fighting the Indonesian nationalists. The Military Administration used British troops and demobilised Japanese soldiers to break the strike. Two days later the Singapore Bus company employees struck, and on 25 October 20,000 members of the Singapore General Labour Union crammed into the Happy World amusement park to protest against strike-breaking, and also in favour of the Indonesian and Vietnamese freedom fighters.[8]

On mainland Malaya there were a number of hunger marches. On 21 October 1945 troops were called out to put down large demonstrations in Perak State, at Sungei Siput, Ipoh and Batu Gajah. Ten demonstrators were shot dead in Sungei Siput and three more at Ipoh. The Military Administration banned left wing newspapers and arrested leading communists. Though the MPAJA were officially disbanded there were hand grenade attacks on British troops.[9]

Even while these conflicts were taking place the Malayan People's Anti-Japanese Army was being hailed as a part of the Allied victory celebrations. In January 1946 three commanders of the MPAJA were awarded the Burma Star by Lord Mountbatten in person in Singapore. Six months later the MPAJA marched as a contingent on the 8 June victory parade in London, and then later, Chin Peng was awarded the Order of the British Empire. In between the same men organised a general strike demanding the release of the communist Soon Kwong, which they won.[10]

The cat-and-mouse game with the militants of the MPAJA was motivated by Britain's need to raise dollars to meet its post-war debts. Malaya's rubber was one resource that could be guaranteed to

The British campaign against the Malaysian partisans exposed in the Daily Worker

raise funds as they sweated the colonies. Britain's Secretary of State for War – who had been reckoned the country's leading Marxist economist before the war – John Strachey explained in a Cabinet report: 'We emphasise and rightly, the most indispensable character of Malaya to us as a dollar earner.' – so much so that by 1952 export earnings per capita were amongst the highest in the world.[11]

Where other colonies might be written off, they would fight to keep Malaya. As the colony encouraged rubber planters to sweat their plantations native resentment grew. Attacks on the planters were met with vicious retribution. 'Joint Malayan Interests', a business pressure group, warned the Colonial Office against 'soft-hearted doctrinaires with the emphasis on self-government', and that 'until the fight against banditry has been won there can be no question of any further moves towards self-government'.[12] The underground army of the MPAJA was sparked back into life, leading to the most protracted insurgency in the Empire, where British troops were encouraged to show their kills by collecting the heads of their victims.

Burma

In Arakan Thakin Soe led the Burmese Communist Party in an insurgency against the Japanese from 1944. Their manifesto 'Drive Away the Fascist Japanese Marauders' protested at the forced labour that cost so many Burmese their lives. The manifesto also denounced the British Governor Sir Reginald Dorman-Smith and his plans to bring back British capitalism to Burma. Britain's South East Asia Command was wary of the rebels, and tried to persuade them not to rise up before the Allied invasion. The Burmese Communist Party, though, were only a regional force. The real prize was the defection of the Burmese National Army (BNA), which joined with the Burmese Communist Party to form the Anti-Fascist People's Freedom League.[13]

In 1945 the leader of the Burmese National Army made contact with British commanders and signalled his intention to take up arms against Japan. Lord Louis Mountbatten, Supreme Allied Commander of the South East Asia Command met with his senior officers in Kandy on 27 March 1945, where he set out the policy towards Burma and Aung San's Burma National Army. Outwardly the policy was to help Burma gain complete self-government. Seeing that Aung San would fight against the Japanese he hoped that the Burma National Army would be 'seen as national heroes with the British instead of against them'. The former colonial administrators of Burma though were deeply hostile to Aung San's BNA and to them Mountbatten said that those who had fought against Britain would have to stand trial according to the law obtaining in 1941. The threat was real since the British had prepared charges against Aung San for the murder of Abdul Raschid, a tyrannical village headman.[14]

Captain Takahashi tried to convince Aung San to stick with Japan, and asked him what kind of deal he had made with Britain. Aung San replied that 'our ideal is total independence', but that he would settle for a self-governing Dominion: 'If the British refuse to grant us one or the other, then we will fight them too'. On 16 May 1945 Aung San met Lieutenant General William Slim, commander of the Burma Corps of the British Army, who said that he could only expect to be a subordinate commander under British orders. Slim challenged Aung San 'you only came to us because you see we are winning'. Aung San replied 'it wouldn't be much good coming to you if you weren't, would it?' Though Slim and Mountbatten were impressed with the BNA commander, the Civil Affairs Officers – Sir Reginald Dorman-Smith in particular – still nursed the ambition to arrest Aung San for murder, and outlaw the Thakin Party.[15]

As the British moved into Burma tensions were high. Officers of the King's Own Yorkshire Light Infantry summarily executed 27 Burmese civilians claiming that they had collaborated with the Japanese in the 1942 retreat. Fearing an open rebellion against British rule, the new governor passed a Bill that let him keep the murder charge against Aung San and other supposed crimes committed by Burmese against Britain in 1942 on file, at his own discretion. Aung San's confidence was based on a pertinent assessment of the enduring weakness of the British position East of Suez. In a pamphlet titled 'Why We Should Not Continue to Revolt', the Anti-Fascist People's Freedom League judged that 'English vested interests' were still too weak to grab back what they had lost in Burma, and that the needs of domestic investment in the British economy would take priority. Astute as this assessment was, it only saw economic motives in British action, but not the fury with which the colonial power would defend its spiritual investment into Britain's prestige.[16]

As the Japanese fled, Rangoon was under an uneasy peace, with the Burma National Army renamed the Burma Defence Army, taking part in the victory parade on 15 June, while all the time the Civil Affairs Bureau was planning to disarm them. The British statement of intent on Burma's future was vague about the timescale of the move towards Dominion Status. On 20 June Governor Dorman-Smith arrived on the Rangoon River and held a party for all his old Burmese collaborators on board the HMS Cumberland. Civil rights for ordinary Burmese were not forthcoming.[17]

The new British Prime Minister Clement Attlee thought that Dorman-Smith had 'lost his grip' and replaced him as Governor with Sir Henry Knight.[18] In January 1947 Aung San went to London to sign the deal that would agree Burmese independence. He would not see that day, though, as on the morning of 19 July 1947 four assassins armed with tommy-guns stormed a cabinet meeting and killed all but three of the ministers there. The killers were sent by U Saw, who had been Burmese Prime Minister under Dorman-Smith, and the British government said that it was an internal matter. In the House of Commons, though, Labour MP Tom Driberg spoke out: 'the moral guilt of the assassinations attaches less to the brutal gunmen in Rangoon than to the Conservative gentlemen here who incited U Saw to treachery and sabotage'. Driberg meant the 'Friends of the Burmese Hill People', a group set up by Dorman-Smith to undermine Burma's independence, by promoting separatism and disorder. In 1997 filmmaker Rob Lemkin uncovered the files that showed U Saw's links with British intelligence and pointed to their hands in the assassination of Aung San.[19] Despite Britain's efforts to destabilise the country, Burma won its independence, declined invitations to join the Commonwealth and the South East Asia Treaty Organisation, preferring to ally itself with the Bandung Conference of independent nations.

Philippines

'People of the Philippines, I have returned!' General MacArthur on landing, 20 October 1944.

MacArthur immediately set about taking on the Huk guerrillas, to whom he wrote

> The United States Army does not recognise any political aims or ambitions, and it is the position that in time of war, the only political activity which is legal is political activity aimed at the maintenance of the loyalty of the masses to the established and legal existing government.[20]

G-3 Section in MacArthur's General Staff noted in January 1945 that it was 'necessary to take the wind out of the sails out of this organisation'. The Huks, thought G-3 were 'a distinct and potential threat to the Commonwealth government and future peace of the Philippines'. G-3 wrote revealingly that 'We have a measure of responsibility to the real patriots'; they meant the Filipinos who had been in the US Army Force Far East (USAFFE), who 'resolutely and with self-effacing loyalty have served our purposes'.[21]

Noting that the Huks had grown in confidence, and were surreptitiously meeting peasant demands for land reform by expropriating landlords under the guise of attacking collaborators, Gabriel Kolko argues that 'By the beginning of 1945 all that stood between the Huks and a total transformation of the agrarian economy was the United States military, led by MacArthur'.[22] It was true that when the US entered central Luzon in January and February 1944 they found that the Huks already had local government up and running in the towns of Nueva Ecija, Tarlac, Bulacan, Pampanga and Laguna. There were Hukbalahap-backed mayors: Casto Alejandrino in Pampanga, Juan Feleo in Nueva Ecija and Jesus Lava in Laguna. MacArthur expelled Alejandrino and Feleo from office – he replaced the peasant-leader Feleo with Juan O. Chioco a wealthy landowner, on the grounds that the province of Nueva Ecija was the 'breadbasket of Central Luzon', and could not be allowed to fall into the hands of a 'non-constitutional faction'.[23] In fact MacArthur's intelligence staff overstated the threat the Hukbalahap intended. While they had built up a solid following in the absence of any kind of established government – whether Commonwealth, American Military or Japanese – they were committed to the restoration of the Commonwealth, and promised loyalty to the US governor. On 15 June 1945 acting Commander-in-

Chief of the Hukbalahap Mariano Balgos protested that

> There are misconceptions emanating from those same elements who would not only cut the Hukbalahap off from America, but also separate us from the Filipino people. The Huk is not anti-Commonwealth government. We recognise President Osmeña as the legal president of the Commonwealth and the Commonwealth constitution as the legal constitution of the Philippines. We are opposed to civil war and shall fight for the orderly democratic progress of the Philippines.

What was more 'we are not seeking to conscript capital or socialise industry'.[24] These protestations of loyalty would count for little with General MacArthur, who had already decided that the Filipinos must not be allowed to liberate themselves, but wait patiently for his return and follow his instructions.

As he was hostile to the guerrillas who had fought against Japan after he ran away, so he was hostile too to the exiled president Sergio Osmeña (who took over the Commonwealth government-in-exile after Quezon died in 1944). Osmeña had criticised MacArthur's poor defence plans, and was a friend of Harold Ickes, who MacArthur hated. On 23 October 1944, in Tacloban, MacArthur summoned Osmeña, and in a brusque ceremony, and speech of no more than three sentences, handed over civilian administration, and got up to go, saying 'Now, Mr. President, my officers and I shall withdraw and leave you to discharge your responsibilities.' But Osmeña was wholly dependent on the Military Administration which controlled all transport, food distribution and money throughout the Philippines. The ceremony was meant to show up Osmeña's dependence on the Governor.[25]

To put his stamp on the Philippines, MacArthur had made sure that executive power was in his hands. MacArthur and his deputy Courtney Whitney agreed that OSS agents from the Southwest Pacific would be barred from the Philippines for fear that they would 'aid leftwing guerrillas'. Even Robert Sherwood's liberal propaganda leaflets were rejected as too inflammatory. In fact MacArthur fought off Washington's attempts to impose any civilian administration. Under the plan he hatched with Whitney

MacArthur could strike down any proposed provincial official, and 'the President of the Philippines should be unavailable, any appointments ... should be made provisionally on his behalf by the Commander-in-Chief'. Since Osmeña was wholly dependent on the US military for his transport, he was often 'unavailable'.[26]

Instead of a civilian administration, MacArthur had his circle of cronies among the foreign business elite. Among MacArthur's staff Courtney Whitney was in William Manchester's account, an 'ultra-conservative Manila corporation lawyer'. Whitney was 'condescending towards all Filipinos except those, who, like himself, had substantial investments in the islands'. US Navy Commander Charles Parsons had bought into the Luzon Stevedoring Company in 1934, having arrived as part of the US administration. Another key player on MacArthur's team was Spanish-born Andres Soriano y Roxas, who had made his fortune on one of the first Coca-Cola franchise businesses, before branching out into San Miguel beer and airlines. Soriano was a supporter and financier of Spanish dictator Franco's Falange party and had been photographed giving the Fascist salute. He was acting Consul General for Franco in the Philippines, until he decided it was more politic to take Filipino citizenship in 1941 (and American citizenship in 1945). When Senator Millard Tyldings tried to introduce a resolution for the immediate recognition of Philippine independence in Congress in 1943 Sorriano, fearful of losing his extensive holdings, successfully lobbied against it.[27]

As an alternative to Osmeña, MacArthur pushed Manuel Roxas – who he felt was more trustworthy, though in fact he had served in Jose Laurel's pro-Japanese administration. MacArthur had Roxas flown over by a specially commissioned plane to meet the Governor in Manila, where he was publicly exonerated for his wartime role. Later, MacArthur endorsed Roxas in the presidential race against Osmeña.

For the Hukbalahap resistance, the writing was on the wall. Frozen out of any post-war settlement, they were vilified as bandits and traitors. From January 1945, local US Commanders started to disarm the Hukbalahap – often at gunpoint, by Military Police. All the time that the Hukbalahap was losing its weapons, the USAFFE forces were being built up. USAFFE commanders realised that the promise of back pay would draw recruits. Ramon Magsaysay's Zambales Military District counted only 1100 troops in early 1945, but in two years it had grown to a force 10,441-strong. As a MacArthur General Staff report had it the Hukbalahap were 'the bitterest foes of our staunchest patriots – a scourge to USAFFE remnants'. Once disarmed, the Huks were at a disadvantage. In February 1945 the disarmed Huk 'Squadron 77' passed through Malolos on their way back to Pampanga. They were seized by men under the command of USAFFE Col. Adonais Maclang. Jailed overnight, the Huk men, over one hundred of them, were taken out into a courtyard and made to dig their own graves, before they were shot and bludgeoned to death. Maclang was arrested, but quickly released: indeed two days later he was made mayor of Malolos by Courtney Whitney's Philippine Civil Affairs Unit.[28] Later that month Huk leaders Luis Taruc and Casto Alejandrino were arrested by the Counter Intelligence Corp, along with other commanders. But MacArthur had acted too soon – 50,000 peasants protested demanding their release, which was granted. Then on 8 April, they were detained again, and taken to the Iwahig Penal Colony.

MacArthur's war against the people who had fought to free the Philippines, the Hukbalahap, was carried on after he left by the President, Roxas. Carrying on a dirty war against the Huk leaders and struggling to disarm the rank-and-file, Roxas only succeeded in galvanising a great insurrection that did not end until 1954.

Korea

Roosevelt at Yalta said to Stalin: 'He had in mind for Korea a trusteeship composed of a Soviet, an American and a Chinese representative. ... He felt that in the case of Korea the period might be from twenty to thirty years.' When the US made clear that Korea was to become a trusteeship, Syngman Rhee, head of the Korean delegation said that Korea was 'the victim of secret diplomacy'.[29]

On 16 December 1945 foreign ministers of Great Britain, the Soviet Union and the US talked about Korea in Moscow. Around that time Lt. General John Hodge wrote a report on Conditions in Korea in which he looked at the potential conflict

Under present conditions with corrective action forthcoming, I would go so far as to recommend we give serious consideration to an agreement with Russia that both the US and Russia withdraw forces from Korea simultaneously and leave Korea to its own devices.

Sadly, Hodge's advice was not taken. The Moscow meeting ended on 27 December with only an agreement that Korea should be put under a four-power trusteeship. Afterwards the USSR agitated for independence, while in practice the two powers divided the country between them along the 38th parallel.[30] When as US Commander John Hodge arrived at Inchon to find a functioning Korean People's Republic, he reinstated the defeated Japanese police and functionaries to displace them.

The Korean People's Republic had been founded on the initiative of Yuh Woon-Hyung. Yuh's Committee for the Preparation of Korean Independence was organised in August 1945 – ironically, at the request of the retreating Japanese – and on 16 Yuh addressed 5000 Koreans, urging unity and no bloodshed. Soon 145 branches of the Committee had been set up, and, with an influx of released prisoners, it was moving in a radical direction.[31]

Yuh Woon-Hyung's Committee for the Preparation of Korean
Independence was sidelined by the Allies

Setting up Headquarters in Seoul the Committee organised its own police force, the ch'iandae, or peace preservation corps, and also a National Preparation Army of Korean Soldiers dismissed from the Japanese Army. The Preparation Committee announced on 28 August that it would establish 'a people's committee elected by a national conference of people's representatives', and on 6 September several hundred met at the Kyŏnggi Girls' High School in Seoul to elect a central People's Committee of 55 members. The two men who would lead the two rival Korean republics, North and South, after the country was divided, Kim Il-Sung and Syngman Rhee, were both elected to the People's Committee, though neither were present. Indeed Syngman Rhee, who was known to be in touch with the US authorities, was appointed Chairman, probably to appease the Americans, though it was a post he never took up.[32]

The Korean People's Republic declaration of 14 September 1945 was that

We are determined to demolish Japanese imperialism, its residual influences, anti-democratic factions, reactionary elements, and any undesirable foreign influence on our state, and to establish our complete autonomy and independence, thereby anticipating the realisation of an authentically democratic state.[33]

According to Yuh Independence

was not something given to us by the Americans or the Soviets. It is something that can be achieved only by gathering together the revolutionary forces within Korea... through our own efforts and our own blood.[34]

The Korean People's Republic filled the gap left between the Japanese and the Allied authorities, and between the American and Soviet rivals. It was ambitious, but untested. The reactionary forces that it identified as collaborationist were already reorganising to meet the challenge.

The 'Korean Democratic Party' was described by a US official at the launch meeting as 'the party of wealth and respectability', and by another US source as 'composed predominantly of large land owners and wealthy businessmen. Many of its leaders, like Chang Tŏk-su had collaborated with the Japanese.[35]

When Commander John Hodge accepted the Japanese surrender on 6 September he refused to acknowledge the Provisional Republic, and instead kept the Japanese officials that had run the colonial administration in place. When that proved too much, he turned to the more reliable reactionaries of the Korean Democratic Party – and Syngman Rhee.

With the end of Japanese rule, Korea's large industrial workforce had the confidence to organise militant trade unions and pushed hard for better wages. Between August 1945 and March 1947 there were 2,388 labour demonstrations involving 600,000 people. Labour disputes married with opposition to the Military Government, and were close to an uprising in autumn 1946 that was brought to a close with the savage repression of the railroad strike of January 1947. Hundreds of left wing labour leaders were 'killed or executed, and thousands were imprisoned'. In March 1947 the US Military Government outlawed the Communist Party. The US created fake, company unions, the Federation of Korean Trade Unions, to take the place of the suppressed labour movement.[36]

It was under these conditions of military and political repression of the opposition that John Foster Dulles called for 'free elections' for Korea in the United Nations, using the Interim Committee to side-step the Soviet veto in the Security Council. The move, rejected by the Soviet military administration in the North, led to separate elections in the South. Of the debate Dulles said that 'the United Nations action on Korea was to be taken as an endorsement of the wider opposition of American foreign policy to communism'. Divided, by the United Nations, Korea was more easily manipulated by its two sponsoring powers, the Soviet Union and the United States.[37]

The Soviets had their excuse to install Kim Il-Sung as premier in the North. In the South Syngman Rhee was reluctant to hold elections, and was reprimanded for the many postponements. To distract attention from its own democratic deficit, and to crank up tension the South Korean administration launched a number of military attacks on border towns in the North in 1949, such as

Wonsan, attacked that June.[38] When Rhee's elections were held, even with the communist opposition outlawed, most elected were independents and not Rhee supporters. Still, the South Korean government's room for manoeuvre was restricted. The Korean Aid Bill passed by the US Congress in February of 1950 carried a clause that said aid would be terminated 'in the event of the formation in the Republic of Korea of a coalition government which includes one or more members of the Communist Party or of the party now in control of the government of North Korea'.[39] In 1950 Kim Il-sung launched an invasion of South Korea starting the conflict that would divide the country to this day, and install, as James Connolly wrote of the partition of Ireland, a 'carnival of reaction on both sides of the border'.

Vietnam

On 2 September 1945 Ho Chi Minh announced the foundation of the Democratic Republic of Vietnam. It is a speech that bears repeating:

> 'All men are created equal. They are endowed by their Creator with certain inalienable rights; among these are Life, Liberty and the pursuit of Happiness.'
>
> This immortal statement was made in the Declaration of Independence of the United States of America in 1776. In a broader sense this means: All the peoples of the earth are equal from birth, all the peoples have a right to be happy and free.
>
> The Declaration of the French Revolution made in 1791 on the Rights of Man and the Citizen also states: 'Also men are born free and with equal rights, and must always remain free and have equal rights.'
>
> Those are inalienable truths.

Ho went on to say

> Nevertheless, for more than eighty years, the French imperialists, abusing the standard of Liberty, Equality, and Fraternity, have violated our Fatherland and oppressed our fellow-citizens. They have acted contrary to the ideals of humanity and justice.[40]

Ho Chi Minh wrote to US President Harry Truman 'Our Vietnam people, as early as 1941, stood by the Allies' side and fought against the Japanese' (16 February 1946). During the war the Viet Minh worked with US Office of Strategic Services and had given US pilots shot down in the war with Japan protection. The OSS had even sent medics to Ho when he was ill.[41]

Ho Chi Minh with advisors from the US Office of Strategic Services

Ho told a representative of the US State Department that 'my people look to the United States as the one nation most likely to be sympathetic to our cause'. A Department of State report was dismissive: 'Perhaps naïvely, and without consideration of the conflicting interests of the "Big" nations themselves, the new government believed that by complying with the conditions of the wartime United Nations conferences it could invoke the benefits of those conferences in favour of its own independence'.[42] The Democratic Republic of Vietnam's government was naïve indeed to imagine that the promises of freedom in the Atlantic and United Nations' Charters would apply to the Great Power's colonial possessions.

Far from honouring Vietnam's independence, the Great Powers invaded. In September 1945 General Douglas Gracey, carrying the title of Commander of Allied Troops in French Indochina, landed at Saigon at the head of the 20th Indian Infantry Division. 'Despite his ceremonious reception by the Vietminh, Gracey immediately ejected the latter's de facto government from the Cochinchina Governor's Palace and installed himself there'.[43] With the Viet Minh on the verge of seizing power Gracey armed and commanded Japanese Prisoners of War as a police force to suppress the rebellion. By October French troops under Leclerc were streaming into Vietnam to take over from Gracey's unconventional force of Japanese and Indians. At the same time Chiang Kai-Shek's anti-Communist Kuomintang Army invaded from the North.[44]

For the French restoration of the Empire in Indochina was essential to French pride. Paris correspondent Frank Giles wrote 'as for General de Gaulle, he seems to have been less concerned with internal developments in Indochina than with the need to uphold French prestige and status'. Even the Parti Communist Français leader Thorez said on 6 March 1946 that he was not keen to see the Tricolour hauled down in Indochina. The French took over, and on 23 November launched a massive assault on Haiphong that left 20,000 dead. In response Viet Minh General Giap led an assault on French forces in Saigon. When the veteran Socialist Léon Blum briefly became French Premier in December 1946 Ho tried to get a message to him, but it was held up by the military. Blum favoured negotiation – but only once order had been restored. Admiral Theirry d'Argenlieu announced in January 1947 that 'it is from now on impossible for us to deal with Ho Chi Minh'. French determination to defend her prestige in Indochina would stoke the most protracted revolutionary war of the Twentieth Century.[45]

Indonesia

The Investigatory Committee for Indonesian Independence (Badan Penyelidikan Kemerdekaan Indonesia, or BPKI) led by Sukarno and Mohammed Hatta was compromised by its closeness to the Japanese, and Sukarno's younger supporters were demanding action. Sukarno also had to face down demands that the movement be Islamic in outlook, which led him to draw up the doctrine of Pancasila – that combined nationalism, social justice and belief in (an unspecified) God. In July 1945 the Japanese War Council – knowing that they were close to collapse – agreed that the Indies should be independent. Indonesia's declaration of independence lacked the poetry of Vietnam's, reading: 'We the people of Indonesia hereby declare Indonesia's independence. Matters concerning the transfer of power and other questions will be executed in an orderly manner and in the shortest possible time.' It was signed, in the name of the Indonesian people, by Sukarno and Hatta at Jakarta, on August 17, 1945 – as the Japanese Army was being stood down after the surrender.[46] According to Mountbatten's report to the South East Asia Command on 15 August 1945:

> Dr. H. J. van Mook, Lieut-Governor-General of the NEI who had come to Kandy on 1st September, had given me no reason to suppose that the reoccupation of Java would present any operational problem beyond that of rounding up the Japanese.[47]

On 12 September General Yamamoto went to the HMS Cumberland to agree local surrender terms after South East Asia Command agreed the terms of the Japanese stand-down with General Itagaki at Singapore. The British cabled 'have just had Yamamoto on board to rub in his responsibilities, which he assures us he fully realizes'. 'Japanese control is undoubtedly deteriorating and new Indonesian nationalist flag is appearing in increasing numbers' they reported. 'Extremists continuing old Japanese-created organisations,' said the British commander, 'are effecting a measure of terrorism and underground movements especially communists are coming to the surface'.[48] The British solution to the challenge of Indonesian nationalism was to use the surrendered Japanese troops as a police force.

Laurens Van Der Post wrote 'I was sent by Lord Mountbatten to the Japanese general commanding the Japanese army in Java to order him to take up arms against the forces of Nationalism he had helped to provoke'. After thinking it over 'he went straight away to order his Chief of Staff to tell his troops to do whatever I wanted', and 'the Japanese fought with us, their old enemies, at places like Bandoeng and Semerang' – against the Indonesian people.[49] The Japanese position was set out by General Nishimura Otoshi, who said that having surrendered they had lost jurisdiction over Indonesia, and should abide by international law. Though Indonesian independence 'comes from the will of the Emperor', the same Emperor has ordered us to stop fighting. Apart from the legal question, the Japanese military plainly identified with the British ambition to restore order, and put their troops at Britain's command. On the other hand, the Japanese had trained a paramilitary Indonesian force of 60,000, and the Indonesian nationalists secured large supplies of guns, ammunition, hand-grenades, vehicles and even 50 tanks from their former masters.[50]

The British intervention in Indonesia caused problems with the colonial power, Holland. The newly liberated Dutch looked forward to restoring control over their most profitable colony. But they were disappointed by Lieutenant General Sir Philip Christiansen's broadcast stating that 'the British have no intention of meddling in Indonesian internal affairs, but only to ensure law and order'. On 19 September 1945 a Dutchman raised the red, white and blue flag of the Netherlands

The Indonesian flag flying over the Hotel Oranje in Surabaya

over the Hotel Oranje in Surabaya, and an Indonesian climbed up to rip off the blue, leaving the red and white flag *Merah Putih* flag of Indonesia flying. Protests and rioting followed.[51]

When they had landed at Batavia, the British troops were faced with slogans that read 'Our government is a government from the people, for the people and by the people', 'What is good for the British Labour Party is good for us too', and 'Hands off Indonesia/Respect our Constitution/Down with Imperialism'.[52] The Japanese forces handed over to the incoming British troops in October and the Seaforth Highlanders soon faced attacks from Indonesian nationalists in Bandung. Protests rang out there and in other centres.

Though reluctant to reinstate their Dutch rivals in the east, the British troops slipped quickly into the role of colonial policemen. Hostility to the Indonesian nationalists came as second nature to Britain's white suprematists, for whom the problem was always the nationalism of the oppressed. Laurens van der Post broadcast on the BBC that Indonesian nationalism was really just anti-European hatred, 'a tragic and abnormal psychology created by yellow fascism in an atmosphere of organised lying and intimidation'.[53]

Brigadier Mallaby's burnt out car after he was killed in Surabaya

Events came to a head in Surabaya in November 1945. A relatively inexperienced Brigadier Mallaby led the 49th Indian Infantry Brigade with the goal of disarming the nationalists. Though Sukarno and Hatta were promising cooperation, local commanders under the militant Bung Tomo were unwilling to hand over their guns. In an argument Mallaby was shot and his car blown up with a hand grenade.

British revenge came on 10 November when Major General Robert Mansergh brought in additional troops and attacked the city with air power and tanks and two cruisers and three destroyers off shore bombarding the city. Mansergh's troops took Surabaya street by street, clearing buildings as they came. Two hundred thousand Indonesians fled the city, and 6,000 were killed in the invasion. British losses were some 600 mostly Indian troops. Indonesians still celebrate 10 November as Heroes Day – and the heroes they have in mind are not Mallaby or Mansergh, but the men and women who fought back against Britain's invasion.

The official British war history records that 'the situation as described to Mountbatten when he was made responsible for the whole of the Netherlands East Indies had been a supreme example of wishful thinking'. 'Instead of willing cooperation by the

Indonesians, there was not only an open threat of war but also a considerable Indonesian force trained and equipped by the Japanese and ready to fight anyone attempting to restore Dutch domination'.[54] At the end of 1946 many of the British troops left, and the Seaforth Highlanders, angered by the role they had been made to play, were heard chanting 'Merdeka!' – 'Independence!' as they marched to the port.[55] Independence, though, would be stymied for another five years, as the British left a Netherlands Indies Civilian Administration in charge of the main urban centres, with Dutch troops taking over from the British.[56]

Chapter Twenty Eight

India uprisen, divided

The suppression of Congress in 1942 and the sapping effect of the British-engineered famine left India traumatised. Congress was for the last two years of the war effectively shackled, directing its attention to welfare activities like the Kasturba Gandhi Memorial Fund.

Without Congress the British had to rely on disparate groups to negotiate for the Indians. Indian Princes were again artificially boosted. The Muslim League, though of real social weight was a lop-sided representative of the Indian people. The British even legalised the Communist Party of India, whose Stalin-inspired support for war production drives recommended it. The Communists characterised Congress as being run by a 'capitalist clique' – but even they were obliged to call for the release of the Congress leaders from jail.[1]

Overshadowing the whole question of a political settlement was the division that Britain had sowed between Mohammad Ali Jinnah's Muslim League and the Congress. In the 1931 census the population of British India included 67 million Muslims or 24.7 per cent, as compared to 178 million Hindus, or 65.5 per cent.[2] Back in March of 1940 Jinnah had given a speech to a crowd of 40,000 Muslim League supporters at Minto Park where he said 'the Musulmans are a nation by any definition'. 'If the British Government are really in earnest and sincere to secure the peace and happiness of the people of this Subcontinent', he had said, then they would have to 'allow the major nations separate homelands, by dividing India into "autonomous national states".' Though Jinnah did not use the word, the crowd called out 'Pakistan! Pakistan!'[3]

In prison, Nehru was in despair at Jinnah's push for a separate state. Reading another Jinnah speech in April 1943 Nehru wrote 'there is no way out as far as I can see except for a real bust-up in India'. Aware of the disaster that partition would be, Gandhi tried again and again to rebuild bridges with Jinnah, writing to the Muslim League leader from his prison cell in May 1943 to ask for a meeting. Churchill, knowing what a threat Indian unity would be for the Empire vetoed the idea of allowing an 'interned person' to talk with anyone for 'the purpose of uniting' to drive the British out.[4]

The detention of Gandhi put Britain in a bad light internationally, with inquiries after his health and liberty coming from Madame Chiang Kai-shek and President Roosevelt's envoy in India William Philip. In 1944 Gandhi was in ill-health and Wavell asked Colonial Minister Leo Amery if he could be released as 'serious difficulties would result if Gandhi died in detention'. A churlish Churchill accused him of faking illness, but he was released on 6 May.[5] Nehru was kept in jail till 15 June 1945.

In August 1944 a Governors' Conference thought that demobilisation at the end of the war would lead to strong pressures for independence. The Viceroy, Archibald Wavell, told the War Cabinet's India Committee that Congress and the Muslim League would have to be drawn into constitutional discussions before hostilities stopped. The British Viceroy's position was that Congress was just another communal party, the Hindu equivalent to the Muslim League, which meant that Britain would not recognise any cross-communal Indian representation. With reason, the Muslim league hoped that their loyal contribution to the war effort, and the heroism of Punjabi soldiers in Burma, would secure them Britain's support against the congress.[6]

The stakes were high for Britain, as Wavell set out to Churchill at the India Committee on 26 March 1945:

The future of India is the problem on which the British Commonwealth and the British reputation will stand or fall in the post-war period ... with a lost and hostile India, we are likely to be reduced in the east to the position of commercial bag-men.[7]

In July 1945 Wavell invited the Congress and the Muslim League to take part in a conference on the future of India and the possibilities of self-rule. Preparatory to the invitation Wavell released the remaining Congress leaders and on 22 June 10,000 came out to welcome them. Under Wavell's plan the Governor General would appoint an executive committee drawn from India's political leaders with an equal balance of Muslims and Hindus. With some internal disagreements, Congress agreed to take part, but Jinnah objected that the Muslim representatives must be nominated by the Muslim League, and in particular to bar any Congress Muslims, as a precondition for taking part in the talks. Even Wavell understood that this was too much, and the conference fell apart. Trying to avoid the obvious conclusion that Jinnah had wrecked the agreement, Wavell publicly took the blame for the failure on himself. For Britain the wider point, though, was to stress that 'the difficulty does not lie as between India and his Majesty's Government, but within India itself', as Colonial Secretary Leo Amery wrote to Wavell on 12 July.[8]

The failure of the Simla conference left India once again in a state of uncertainty, but events would force the British hand. As feared, the end of the war brought new pressures to bear. The end of the war drive robbed the British Raj of the justification for the State of Emergency through which it had ruled. Returning soldiers of the British India Army and of the Indian National Army brought new expectations of a settlement. In particular the Indian National Army, returning for the most part as prisoners facing charges of treason, was a stark challenge to Britain's authority.

One thousand five hundred INA fighters had been captured at Imphal and 17,000 had surrendered in Malaya and Bangkok. Thousands were interrogated in the Red Fort in Delhi. Realising that it was impossible to try them all the British divided them into categories: 'Blacks ... so imbued with enemy propaganda that they remained hostile to the present Government of India and, if released forthwith would constitute a danger to the reliability of the army and to the peace and order of the country'; 'Greys' were those misled, but still influenced by 'enemy propaganda'; 'Whites' were not so. Of the 'Black' group, those who had killed or abused allied troops or citizens were to be court-martialled, the rest to be dismissed without pay. The 'Greys' were to be dismissed with forty days' pay, and the Whites allowed to return to the army.[9]

On 30 June 1945 a train carrying Indian National Army prisoners passed through a Punjabi railway station as crowds were gathering to see Jawaharlal Nehru. The British there were outraged to see the crowd waving pictures of Subhas Chandra Bose.[10] The issue of the Indian National Army prisoners brought all the conflicts of the war in the east back into the public domain. While Britain set out to try the INA fighters, Indians put the whole of the British war to take back its East Asian colonies on trial. On 15 November 1945 India's oldest newspaper, the *Amrita Bazar Patrika* editorialised:

> Never perhaps in the annals of the Indo-British relationship has the government been completely isolated on such questions as the trial of the INA, the use of Indian troops in Indonesia, the surreptitious execution of Indians in Malaya and Singapore, the reimposition of an autocratic rule in Burma and the grave allegations of torture made in the public press, in the Delhi Red Fort and the Lahore Fort. These events have stirred public feeling to its very depths.[11]

The British authorities held elections in October 1945 under a communal system, where seats were reserved for Muslims elected in separate voting lists. The rigged voting system could not disguise the large majority of Indians supporting the Congress which won 91.3 per cent of the vote in the General Constituencies, and was awarded 57 seats when the outcome was announced early in 1946. But the institutionalised communalism of the election did achieve the British aim of dividing India. After years of stirring hostilities between the two communities, the British did manage to drive more Muslims into the hands of the separatist Muslim League. In the Muslim seats the League won 88.6 per cent of the vote and was awarded 30 seats (where its vote had been negligible in the 1937 elections). Sir Stafford Cripps, 'India's friend', told British Prime Minister Clement Attlee that 'we might have to contemplate a division of India into Hindustan and Pakistan as the only solution'.[12] That December, while the elections were taking place Hindu-Muslim riots broke out in Bombay. If Britain could not rule, it could divide.

The threat of partition had become palpably real just as the great mass of Indians were pushing for independence. Protests over the trials of the Indian National Army rose to fever pitch, as Congress took up their cause. In Deshapriya Park in Calcutta 50,000 people rallied for the INA prisoners. In a speech on 16 August 1945 Nehru had called the INA fighters 'misguided patriots' – meaning that, whatever their differences with Congress, they were on the side of right. A popular pamphlet of the time made the point more forcefully, being titled 'Patriots not Traitors'. The popular nationalist paper *The Leader* said that 'the INA men fought for their country's freedom and their countrymen will continue to look on them as national heroes' (13 October 1945) Even the Muslim League gave its support to the prisoners. Only the Communist Party objected, so wedded was it to Britain's war effort. The Communists' paper, *The People's War* worried in its editorial 'in defending victims of British terror, can we ourselves afford to preach ideas and glorify elements whom we were pledged to resist as pro-fascists?' (28 October 1945).[13]

On 5 November 1945 the trials began of Lieutenant Gurbaksh Singh Dhillon, Captain Prem Kumar Saghal and Captain Shah Nawaz Khan for murder or abetment to murder, and of waging war against the King. In their defence the men said that they had committed no treason against the Free India Provisional Government: 'What is on trial before the court is the right to wage war with immunity on the part of a subject race for their liberation'. Nehru offered himself as barrister for the INA leaders who were eventually tried, and defended them saying that their only crime was to have 'loved their country too well'. When Fujiwara was brought to the Red Fort to testify he was welcomed by his old comrades of the INA, and even the Indian Army guards greeted him with the call, 'Jai Hind!' Outside the Red Fort more than a hundred thousand protested - drawing fire from the Army who killed around a hundred. All three men were sentenced to deportation for life, but the sentence was never carried out. Shah Nawaz Khan later became an important figure in Congress; Dhillon lived till 2006 and wrote a memoir of the INA; Saghal married Lakshmi Swaminathan, who had been commander of the INA's women's battalion, in 1947. The other trials were abandoned.[14]

A key problem for Britain was the sympathy that the INA men were getting from the troops of the British-Indian Army, who had just a year before been at war with them. Troops of the Indian Army and the Royal Indian Air Force went to rallies for the INA prisoners wearing their British uniforms. Field Marshall Claude Auchinleck wrote to Wavell on 26 November 1945 that there was a 'growing feeling of sympathy for the INA' in the Indian Army, of which he was Commander-in-Chief. Auchinleck drew up a report 'Appreciation of the Situation in Respect of the So-Called Indian National Army' at the end of October 1945 that concluded that the Royal Indian Air Force was 'one hundred per cent for the INA' while the Indian Army was very sympathetic. Lt General Sir Francis Tuker thought that the INA affair was 'threatening to tumble down the whole edifice of the Indian Army'. 'Nehru's plan is to make use of the INA,' Wavell warned the Viceroy, 'both to train Congress volunteers and as a Congress striking force'. The Indian National Army had failed to free India in the war, but its struggle, like that of the Irish rebels of 1916, had given independence a real meaning and a focal point in the campaign for the INA prisoners.[15]

Events came to a head in February 1946 when the Royal Indian Navy mutinied. On 18 February 1,100 Naval Ratings on the HMS Talwar docked in Bombay came out on strike after being served up rotten food and abused as 'sons of Indian bitches' (and other racial slurs) by Commander King. Joined by their officers the men took down the Union Jack and raised the Indian flag, as well as the colours of the Communist Party of India and the banner of the Muslim League. Their leaders Madan Singh and M.S. Khan were a telegraphist and a signalman respectively, and they used the Navy's own telecommunications to get their message across. By the following day 7000 had joined the strike, including those on shore and at the Castle and Fort Barracks. Naval ratings in Karachi, Madras, Calcutta and Delhi came out in sympathy. They were supported too by units of the Royal Indian Air Force and the Indian Army. Mass demonstrations of civilians on shore supported the Ratings, and collected food, and later there were civilian strikes in solidarity in Bombay and Delhi. Beyond the British Raj, across the Empire Indian Naval Ratings in Cochin China, the Andamans, Bahrain and Aden struck, so that 78 ships and 20,000 men took part in the mutiny. Later there were accusations that the Congress failed to support the strikes, but Madan Singh remembers that they did. The Muslim League by contrast, told the strikers to surrender.[16]

Yet more destructive for the British position was that a mutiny in the Royal Air Force had broken out just before the naval mutiny. British airmen who were angry at the government's failure to repatriate them began a strike in Karachi. The strike spread across India and the Empire, taking in Ceylon and Singapore – 50,000 men took part, and the authorities were reluctant to try the men for mutiny. Wavell cabled Attlee in February about the RAF and the RNI actions: 'I am afraid that example of the Royal Air Force, who got away with what was really a mutiny, has some responsibility for the present situation.'[17]

It was with this level of instability that the British Cabinet undertook a mission to India in March and April of 1946. The Cabinet were trying to square the circle of retaining control over a nation that was determined to be free. Lord Ismay told them that 'from the military point of view it was as nearly vital as anything could be to ensure that India remained in the commonwealth'[18] But as Attlee later admitted the Indian National Army agitation and the naval mutiny meant that the British Raj was finished.[19]

The Congress leaders had been disappointed by their supposed friends in the British Labour Party before, and it was not that encouraging that Stafford Cripps was part of the Cabinet Mission. The Labour Party had trouble accepting that India wanted to be free. 'Bevin, like everyone else hates the idea of our leaving India' he is 'in reality imperialist', said Viceroy Archibald Wavell of the British Foreign Secretary.[20] The Cabinet Mission made two proposals, both of which made communal division the constitutional foundation. The first, in May proposed two autonomous regions, one predominantly Muslim in the North, and the other predominantly Hindu under a central government. This was vetoed by the Muslim League. The Second proposal in June was for partition, which was rejected by Congress. Nehru made it clear that they would rule through the Constituent Assembly, unbound by any agreement. The Viceroy accepted that only Nehru could command the support to be First Minister and left him to try to form a cabinet.

In July the Muslim League Council voted to empower Jinnah to 'resort to Direct Action to achieve Pakistan'. 'Today we have said good-bye to constitutions and constitutional methods', Jinnah announced, naming 16 August 1946 as 'Direct Action' day. When the day came Huseyn Shaheed Suhrawardy, Bengal's Chief Minister and Muslim League member declared a 'public holiday' and all police and other officials were withdrawn from duties. Gangs of Muslims attacked Hindus, and Hindus attacked Muslims. Thousands fled the city, and over the next ten days 10,000 people were murdered in Bengal alone. In October anti-Muslim rioting began in Bihar again leading to an even greater number of deaths. Wavell argued that British forces should withdraw from Hindu India and defend Pakistan. By December Nehru was presiding over an Assembly whose Muslim League members had withdrawn.[21]

Early in 1947, as Lord Louis Mountbatten took over as Britain's last Viceroy in India, Gandhi made a final plea to save India. He told Mountbatten to call on Jinnah to lead a government of all-India – but the Viceroy was not interested in saving India. Mountbatten's goal was to divide India, and he directed all his charm into persuading Nehru to accept the premiership of a truncated state of Hindustan: he refused to pass on Gandhi's offer to Jinnah.[22]

Having fomented the division between the Muslim League – which it had bolstered as a counter to Congress loyal to the war effort – and Congress, Britain stoked up the communal hostilities that would wreck Indian independence. Inter-communal violence was by no means a natural outcome of independence. Rather it was the product of Britain's struggle to retain control by dividing the people against each other. In 1937 just three per cent of the population had voted for the Muslim League while most supported Congress – but that was before Britain's protracted campaign to defeat Congress and to promote the League as a loyal alternative. The Indian Independence Act given the Royal Assent on 18 July 1947 divided the country in two. Inter-communal fighting was severe and 12.5 million people were uprooted, finding that they were on the wrong side of the border, either Hindus in Pakistan or Muslims in India. Estimates of those who died in the fighting that followed range from 500,000 to one million.

Chapter Twenty Nine

The Defeated Powers under Occupation

On the eve of the invasion of Germany Eisenhower was worried that the foreigners forced to work in German factories would revolt. In two radio appeals, on the 5th and 25th of September 1944 he told them first: 'Do not let the Gestapo provoke you into unorganized action' and 'do all in your power to prevent the destruction of communication lines and industrial plants'. Then later: 'The need of the moment is not for revolution, civil war and barricades.'[1] Like Goebbels, Eisenhower feared an uprising by foreign workers for the simple reason that he was about to take Goebbels' place as chief of security in Western Europe.

With the execution of von Stauffenberg and the July plotters Hitler had closed off all avenues for surrender as the Allies made it clear that there would be no armistice, only 'unconditional surrender'. From the invasion of Normandy to the final battle for Berlin the cost in the lives of Allied and German troops was great. American troops met their Soviet counterparts on the Elbe on 25 April 1945. Four days later Hitler killed himself. The Russians beat the Americans in the race to Berlin. No civil authority survived the invasion and the Allies became by the new rulers of Germany. Administration of the conquered Reich was divided between Russian, American, British and later French zones.

Allied instructions to their troops demonised the German people. A paper on the 'German Character' by Brigadier W.E. van Cutsem distributed to all personnel in the British Occupation Zone warned that 'Germans are not divided into good and bad Germans', that 'the sadistic trait is not peculiar to the Nazis' and that 'they exult death rather than life'. The American equivalent 'occupation booklet' told GIs that 'before the German people can learn how to govern themselves' they have to learn that 'their acceptance of the Nazi leadership made their defeat necessary' - not the defeat of the Nazi regime, not the liberation of the German people from the Nazi regime, but the defeat of the German people was needed.[2]

One way the occupying armies dominated the beaten Germans

was to rape them. Rape was endemic. The soldiers of the Red Army raped thousands of German women – which crimes, as we have seen, were later assiduously documented by Federal Government officials seeking to overturn the perception of Germans as aggressors. Though it became a propaganda weapon against the Soviets, the evidence is that rape was indeed widespread. Milovan Djilas remembered Stalin mocking him for raising the issue of Red Army rapes: 'Can't he understand the soldier who has gone through blood and fire and death, if he has fun with a woman or takes some trifle?'[3]

A US Army Intelligence Officer reported that

There is a tendency among the naïve or the malicious to think that only the Russians loot and rape. After battle troops of every country are pretty much the same, and the warriors of Democracy were no more virtuous than the troops of Communism were reported to be.[4]

One GI said

If you are a decent fellow, you demand a lot of love and you get it. If you are a pig, the girl is unlucky, but can't say no anyway.[5]

Upon victory, the army of occupation suffered a severe collapse in discipline. There was, explains John Willoughby 'an epidemic of crime' among American GIs, as there was among their counterparts in the Soviet and British Armies occupying Germany, with 'wanton killing, looting, and threats and assaults on German police and civilians'. In July 1945 the US Infantry payroll was $1 million, but GIs sent home $5 million. The process was called 'liberating', and that cars, furniture, apartments, watches were all fair game. Russian troops were partial to watches. Two American soldiers stole the Hessian Crown Jewels.[6] War correspondent Leonard Mosley wrote that among the British too, it was 'surprising how the looting fever attacked even the staidest members of the Army'.[7] The Allied Command was not in a strong position to prevent looting, because the official Allied policy was to loot the German economy.

While the ordinary G.I. helped themselves to what was left of the ordinary Germans' household goods, the officers of the Occupation Governments lived high on the hog. The Americans had 5008 personnel running the administration, while the British Control Commission had a remarkable 24,785. On 15 August 1946 the British sent the wives of soldiers stationed in Germany to join them with the advice that 'they were representatives of the British Empire'. Since they were to be stationed in homes from which Germans had been evicted 'they should take the greatest care of the houses in which they live, and the contents thereof'. Living in the Germans' few standing homes, the British wives also took advantage of 'domestic help at low rates' – often the former tenants, who would move into an attic or cellar.[8] Theatre critic Hilde Spiel noted that

> The ladies of the Allied occupation, apparently at ease without noticeable consternation at the moral compromise entailed, now lay claim to the amenities – the hairstylists, manicurists, pedicurists, seamstresses, furriers and servants – of the 'high ladies' of the Nazi elite

US diplomat George Kennan was uneasy, too, to find 'the spectacle of this horde of my compatriots and their dependents, camping in luxury amid the ruins of a shattered community'. The American political officers were 'inhabiting the very same sequestered villas that the Gestapo and SS had just abandoned, and enjoying all the same privileges'.[9]

'Demontage'

This programme for eliminating the war-making industries in the Ruhr and in the Saar is looking forward to converting Germany into a country primary agricultural and pastoral in its character.
Morgenthau Plan, September 1944

The Allies' announcement of a plan to 'pastoralise' Germany helped to rally Germany's beleaguered population to the last desperate defense of the country. In September 1945, an American paper to the Allied Control Authority's Directorate of Economics called 'A Minimum German Standard of Living in Relation to the Level of Industry', proposed that industrial and agricultural output should be held down to the level of 1932 - the worst year of the depression in Germany.[10] Though the plan was later amended it did become the basis for the policy of 'demontage', the dismantling of German industry to take East to the Soviet Union – and West to Britain.

Plans were drawn up 'for the total elimination of major shipyards, the equipment of which is to be allocated to reparations or destroyed'. British industries, including Courtaulds, Unilever and ICI, seconded staff to the British Civil Service to take part in the dismantling, so that they could grab machinery and technology (the same thing was done at the end of the First World War).[11] British MP Richard Stokes told the House of Commons in July 1946 that 'the industrialists of this country' had gone to Germany 'like a flock of vultures' to 'pick the remaining flesh from its bones'.[12] In October 1947 the British and US governments listed 682 factories (186 in the American zone and 496 in the British) which were to be dismantled and sent to countries that had suffered German aggression. In the *Manchester Guardian* Stokes and the left wing publisher Victor Gollancz showed that contrary to government claims only a few of

Germans protest against 'demontage' – the dismantling of their industry

these factories were 'war industries' and itemised the plunder of German technical know-how at gun point (29 October 1947).

The British in particular saw doing down Germany in terms of comparative advantage. In August 1950, British High Commissioner Sir Ivone Kirkpatrick issued a press release rubbishing the idea that 'in the matter of dismantling or of restrictions on German industry England has been influenced by the desire to throttle German competition', adding that 'there is no danger that petty considerations such as fear of German competition will influence our policy'. In private, however, the 'petty consideration' of throttling German competition dominated British policy. Lord Cherwell thought that 'it should be possible to reach an agreement with the Russians by which they would take existing German machinery, raw materials and forced labour, while we should take Germany's export markets'. Labour's Herbert Morrison, then Lord President of the Allied Control Council, advised the Prime Minister to 'start shaping the German economy in the way which ... will run the least risk of it developing into an unnecessarily awkward competitor'.[13]

In 1946 the *Times* reported that 'it is reliably estimated here that, food apart, the Russians are taking from the zone as reparations seventy per cent of current production' (27 September). When Russians arrived to carry out the demontage policy and take

A control officer's car overturned in anti-demontage protests

machines from factories there were mass demonstrations.

Under the impact of war and occupation the German economy collapsed. Morgenthau's vision of 'pastoralisation' came close to coming true the Tiergarten was dug over to plant vegetables. With output slashed and Nazi price controls lifted Germany suffered violent inflation at the war's end, leading to a loss of confidence in the currency.

As the economy collapsed, so too did food distribution. The occupying authorities took over the rationing of food. In the House of Commons Richard Stokes laid out the sorry news:

The fat ration in the British zone in Germany today is 1.75 ozs. per week. That is against our 7 ozs. in this country. The sugar ration is 2.25 ozs., as against our 8 ozs. a week. There is difficulty over bread. They have had practically no potatoes. Last week for the first time in six weeks the potato ration was honoured.[14]

Hunger demonstrations in the Ruhr, February 1947

When rations in the British and American Zones of Germany fell below 1100 calories provoking protests, officials explained 'the short answer is that Germany lost the war', while a delegation from the Medical Research Council dismissed complaints about children's rations on the grounds that they 'would have been regarded as satisfactory in England not so very long ago' - in other words, they had brought the problem on themselves.[15]

The Military Tribunals

At the end of the war certain political and military leaders of the defeated powers were tried at International Tribunals in Nuremburg and Tokyo. The men who were hung or imprisoned deserved to pay for what they had done. But the war crimes tribunals themselves were the opposite of justice – they were political expediency masquerading as justice. The impact of the tribunals was to fix in public opinion and in the historical record that the Axis powers were wholly responsible for the war and the perpetrators of war atrocities. That the Allied leaders were not tried for their terrible deeds at Hiroshima, Dresden, Katyn, in India, or for their own role in the colonial land-grabbing, economic blockades and arms race that led to the war, shows that the tribunals had nothing to do with justice.

The trials were not in truth trials at all, but political theatre. Their precedents were the show trials carried on in Stalin's Soviet Union, and, ironically, in Hitler's Germany. Secretary of War Henry Stimson hoped that the tribunals would showcase justice in action and the superiority of the Allied approach over that of the Axis. In fact they made a mockery of every canon of Justice. The defendants were tried for breaking laws that did not exist but were retrospectively manufactured: namely starting wars and the abuse and murder of civilians under military occupation. There is no doubt that these things are wrong. But there simply was no law against starting wars, and certainly every power refused to accept such a limitation on their most sacred right.[16] Also, the legal codes of all the participants, Axis and Allied alike, expressly excluded acts of war from prosecution under the criminal law. As one Quai D'Orsay circular pointed out, the court had to 'operate retroactively,' trying the defendants for actions that were not crimes at the time they were committed. Most obviously, the drawing up of the charge sheets excluded any investigation of the wrongdoing of the Allies. The first tribunal's framework document, the Nuremburg Charter set out in Article One that the court was restricted to 'the trial and punishment of the war criminals of the European Axis' (and Article Three forbade any challenge to that mandate). That is to say that the charges the Allies drew up against the Axis leaders were at the same time an amnesty for their own wrongdoing.

Far from showcasing justice, the War Crimes Tribunals corrupted justice, making justice into little more than a theatrical performance, with its former principles edited out of the script, the ending changed from what was just to what was expedient to the powerful. War Department Lawyer Bernays put it like this: 'not to try these beasts would be to miss the educational and therapeutic opportunity of our generation'.[17] In other words, it was a show trial. The public was to be educated to believe that the war happened because the leaders in Berlin and Tokyo were 'beasts' and the Allies' war was correspondingly just. Each affront to a principle of justice – whether it was retrospective justice, extra-territoriality, or partiality – all sprung from the same source, that this was a show of Might, not Right. It was Victors' Justice.

Should the accused of Nuremburg have been allowed to enjoy a lengthy retirement, then? No. It was quite possible to deal with the deposed dictators and their accomplices without the bogus charade of the War Crimes Tribunal. The partisans who summarily shot Mussolini, and displayed his corpse, had showed the world how to deal with dictators. The execution was an act of war, which, if it means anything means the suspension of ordinary rules of justice. That much was well-known by the Allies, who during the war favoured summary execution as the best way to deal with the Nazi leaders. Churchill was in favour of summary execution, and so was Cordell Hull. A Foreign Office paper of 1942 read that 'there should be no question of such leaders being tried either by national or international tribunals' – rather, as the document sensibly puts it, the 'fate of enemy leaders should be decided as a political question'.[18]

One reason that the Allies were at first against war crimes trials was that they were worried about the precedent. Curtis LeMay thought that if the Allies had lost the war he would have been tried for war crimes, and Winston Churchill wrote to Lord Ismay that the

Nuremburg verdict showed 'that if you get into a war, it is supremely important to win it', because 'you and I would be in a pretty pickle if we had lost'. Perhaps at the front of LeMay's mind was the case of the US airmen shot down over Tokyo in the 'Doolittle Raid' of 1942. The airmen were tried by a Japanese court and accused of crimes against the civilian population. Three of the men were executed. When President Roosevelt heard of the trial and execution, he sent a diplomatic protest through the Embassy in Switzerland to the Japanese authorities against this 'barbarous execution' complaining that the men were members of the armed forces who 'fell into Japanese hands as an incident of warfare'.[19] By the end of the war all of the Allies' qualms about the use of the courts to deal with acts of warfare fell away. They were sure that they were not going to be in the dock, so they looked forward to putting the losers there. In Shanghai in February 1946 the Japanese officers who tried the Doolittle raiders were themselves tried and convicted for the 'war crime' of trying and executing American air force men.

Nuremberg

Goering, Ribbentrop, Borman, Jodl, Speer, von Papen, Streicher and 15 others were tried for Crimes against Peace, and for Crimes against Humanity at Nuremberg. From the outset, many of the law officers taking part had doubts about the legality of what they were doing. Prosecutor Robert Jackson wrote to President Harry Truman in October 1945 pointing out that some of the Allies 'have done or are doing some of the very things that we are prosecuting Germans for'. 'We are accusing the Germans of mistreating prisoners of war' but the French are 'violating the Geneva Convention in the treatment of Prisoners of War'. 'We are prosecuting plunder and our Allies are practising it', Jackson continued. 'We say aggressive war is a crime and one of our allies asserts sovereignty over the Baltic states based on no title except conquest', Jackson added of the Soviet occupation. The British Judge Norman Birkett pointed out that

> One could not for example bring before the court, say, the Soviet Union because of what they did in Finland, or because of what they did in Poland. You could not bring the United States of America, or indeed Britain to judgement for dropping the atomic

bomb on Japan. It does not apply. If it continues only to apply to an enemy, then I think the verdict of history may be against Nuremburg.

The problem of one-sided justice was as Birkett indicated written into the Nuremburg Charter. The attorney for Admiral Doenitz did manage to chip away at the exclusive focus on Axis atrocities by arguing as a part of his defence that the Allies had also sunk ships on site and refused to help enemy seamen as he was accused. The prosecutor David Maxwell-Fyfe protested 'the question whether the United States broke the laws and usages of war is quite irrelevant; as the question before the Court is whether the German High Command broke the laws and usages of war'. Doenitz's defence was one of *tu quoque* ('you too'). In ordinary cases, 'he did it too' is not a defence, but then ordinary cases are not tried under rules that exclude even the possibility that the other person would be tried in his own right. Unfortunately for Maxwell-Fyfe, US Admiral Chester Nimitz made a deposition to the court to the effect that America had indeed set aside ordinary rules of maritime warfare just as callously as the Germans had. The court decided to take that into account when sentencing Doenitz.[20]

The outcome of the Doenitz case put the wartime Allies into a spin as the defence lawyers tried to raise more parallels, such as Britain's planned invasion of Norway in 1940. British lawyers started to look for evidence to rebut the charges, until Prime Minister Attlee insisted 'we are not on trial and we should not put ourselves on the defensive', and withheld documents from the tribunal on British conduct. In March 1946 the Foreign Office's Patrick Dean was glad to report that the judges had decided to reject all evidence of Allied atrocities: 'an important decision' that 'may save much time and embarrassment'. Later he cabled London on another victory: 'all documents on alleged Allied plans to invade Greece and Yugoslavia to block Danube and to bomb Caucasian oil wells were struck out' by the judges.[21]

All through the trial the British prosecuting counsel Airey Neave winced as Russian lawyers mocked his attachment to 'bourgeois legal norms', but this was a case of locking the stable door after the horse had bolted; 'bourgeois legal norms' were abandoned when the

Allies undertook a Moscow-style show trial. The Russian judge Iona Nikitchenko had earned his seat sentencing those old Bolsheviks who stood in Stalin's way, Kamanev and Zinoviev, in the purges of 1935-8. Particularly galling for the young Tory war hero Neave was Count Three, War Crimes Section (C), 'Murder and Ill-Treatment of Prisoners of War', subsection 2, which read: 'In September 1941, 11,000 Polish officers, who were prisoners of war, were murdered in the Katyn Forest, near Smolensk'. This charge had been put on the sheet by the Soviet lawyer Roman Rudenko – though everyone knew that the massacre had been carried out not by the defendant, Herman Goering, but by one of the prosecuting authorities, namely the Soviet Union. The Polish government in exile sent a great dossier of documents to the court, *Facts and Documents Concerning the Polish Prisoners of War Captured in the 1939 Campaign,* to show Soviet culpability. At one point Rudenko introduced a hurried amendment of the numbers killed changing 925 to 11,000. That way the Soviets hoped to enshrine German responsibility for all deaths at Katyn in the legal judgement at Nuremburg. When Goering's lawyers tried to challenge the evidence Rudenko cited the Nuremberg Charter to say that discussion of Allied actions was outside the court's remit. The judges avoided all mention of Katyn in their verdict.[22]

If the Soviet lawyers' charges were a brazen attempt to pin guilt for their own actions onto the defendants, all of prosecuting authorities knew that the trial was a shocking double-standard. Henry Stimson, War Secretary and architect of the trial said in private that he was worried about the use of the atomic bomb because 'I did not want to have the United States get the reputation of outdoing Hitler in atrocities'. US Prosecutor Colonel Telford Taylor admitted that 'it was difficult to contest the judgement that Dresden and Nagasaki were war crimes'. British war historian Basil Liddell Hart thought that a 'weakness in our case' was that the Government had tasked Bomber Command in 1942 with striking at 'the German population': 'Because of its early date, this directive is in some ways more significant that the more discussed use of the atom-bomb to bring about the collapse of the Japanese people's will to resist'.[23]

The point where the prosecuting authorities established the moral high ground over the Nazi accused in the dock was when a film of the terrible atrocities at Dachau and Buchenwald concentration camps was shown. Though the preparation of the charges against the German war leaders put the Crime against Peace to the fore (which is why it was prepared by the American and British prosecutors) historical memory puts more weight on the Crimes against Humanity (prepared by the Russian and French prosecutors). In the prosecution of the war the Allies did not want to use evidence of the slaughter of the Jews into the case against Nazi Germany.[24] But afterwards the pictures of the death camps brought home to the public the full horror of Fascism.

By prosecuting the leading Nazis the Allies were fixing in the public imagination the war guilt of the German people as a whole. In 1946 the Allies denied occupied Germany self-government on the basis of war guilt. Stasi leader Markus Wolf insisted that though 'only a small minority of Germans were actually guilty', 'all Germans who lived willingly under the Nazis bear a responsibility for them' – an attitude which no doubt made it easier for him to keep records on so many of his countrymen.

In the English language, one of the most popular histories of German atrocities was *The Scourge of the Swastika*, by Lord Russell of Liverpool, who had been Deputy Judge Advocate General to the British Army of the Rhine and chief legal advisor to the Nuremberg tribunal. It was a popular and clear setting out of the evidence he had helped to sift at the Nuremberg court. For all that, the *Scourge of the Swastika* was by the time of its publication in 1954, already out of step with the changing British policy towards Germany. When he showed his superiors the draft of the book he was called in to explain himself to the Lord High Chancellor Viscount Simonds. In a letter Simonds thought that the book was untimely because it would 'give support to the opinions of those who are most strongly critical of the policy of giving Germany an opportunity, by rearmament or otherwise, of exerting an interest in world affairs'. British policy had changed. The Germans were no longer the enemy, but allies in the arms race with the Soviet Union. No longer just 'these beasts', the Germans, as Bob Dylan sang sarcastically, 'now, too had God on their side'. Russell, who had helped lay the charges against the German leaders in the Nuremberg tribunal, was now told by the High Chancellor that he was helping to 'stir up hatred of the German people as a whole'. Russell was told that if he published the book, the High Chancellor would 'be obliged to consider' Russell's position. Russell forestalled this threat by resigning. The lesson of the affair was that the Show Trials at Nuremberg were alright for stirring up hatred of the German people in 1945 (the better to rule over them). But those high principles of justice turned out to be nothing more than political expediency, tossed aside when they no longer met British interests.[25]

Much later the Nuremberg Trials would be lauded as a model for how the 'United Nations' should deal with dictators. At the time, though, the Nuremberg process was largely thought of as a failure, and it wound up early when a number of trials collapsed. The trials dragged on and barristers who did not have a jury to perform to read out typed contributions in a dull monotone. The public had lost interest after the executions of the leading Nazis. The second batch of trials was scheduled to begin in 1949 with four German generals Gerd von Runstedt, Erich von Manstein, Field Marshal Walther von Brauschitch and Colonel-General Adolf Strauss in the frame. These generals won the sympathy of military men in the west, who identified more strongly with them, and were also seeking to build up the West German military. Conservative figures like Senator Joseph McCarthy of Wisconsin and Air Marshal Sholto Douglas, military governor of the British Zone, all counselled clemency in the case of the Generals. When three of the generals were judged not to be well enough to stand trial it was a very convenient decision for the Allied authorities who were retreating from prosecution for reasons of political expediency.

DeNazification

Between 1945 and 1949 six million Germans went through the 'denazification' process that ran alongside the more dramatic Nuremberg trials. Every adult had been required to complete a questionnaire outlining their past activities and allegiances. Of these one million were classified as followers, 25 000 offenders and just 2000 major offenders. Historian Mark Mazower judged that 'these purges left intact the same structures of power through which the Germans ruled Europe: local civil servants, police, business organizations and the press'.[26] Allied policy changed from punitive, to ameliorative in the space of a few years. H Stuart Hughes explained the injustice that implied: 'frequently it proved simpler to try the lesser offenders first, since their cases were easier to untangle'. But over time more amnesties were granted before the denazification process ground to a halt in 1949. 'Thus many insignificant people who had been tried earlier received heavy penalties, while some important offenders whose cases had been postponed escaped scot-free'.[27]

Underneath the orderly and quasi-legal process of denazification there was outright police repression. Repression turned out to be a pretty blunt instrument. Britain's Combined Services Detailed Interrogation Centre (CSDIC) ran a secret prison following the British occupation of north-west Germany in 1945 at Bad Nenndorf. Internal investigations revealed that torture was rife at Bad Nenndorf, and that many had died of injuries or of starvation. Some of the prisoners were suspected of being Nazis, but others were identified because they were communists – men in fact who had been persecuted by the Nazis.[28]

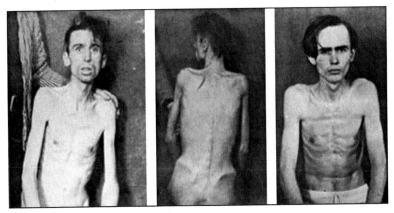

German leftists tortured by the British at the Bad Nenndorf Detention Centre

At the end of the war Americans had seven hundred thousand Germans kept in camps, of whom 56,000 died there. [29] Nuremberg prosecutor Rudenko ran the NKVD Camp No 7, where 60,000 were held at the site of the former Nazi concentration camp at Sachsenhausen – and it is alleged thousands died there. In the summer of 1945 the French government announced that it was putting 220,000 German prisoners of war to work and by the summer of 1946 expected to be employing 1,700,000. [30] The US authorities had transferred 320,000 German prisoners to the French. After the International Red Cross found that these French-held prisoners of war were being ill-treated, the transfers stopped, but in September 1947 France still held 600,000 German prisoners. The British had many prisoners, too. 'We have 40,000 to 50,000 Germans still in concentration camps ... the only right and proper description there is for these institutions', worried Wing Commander Norman Hulbert MP in 1946. In 1954 a review of eighty war-criminal cases under Sir Alexander Maxwell found there were only 25 in which a conviction would have been justified.[31]

Occupying Japan

Unlike the Nazi leadership in Germany, Japan's authorities did surrender to the Allies on 10 August, as announced by Emperor Hirohito by radio broadcast on 15 August 1945. President Harry Truman appointed General Douglas MacArthur as Supreme Commander of the Allied Powers – effectively the ruler of Japan. Six days after the formal surrender on 2 September MacArthur rode into the capital. 'Never in history had a nation and its people been more completely crushed' MacArthur wrote. General George Kenney thought that the Japanese were 'suffering from shell-shock'. [32] To help them run this unfamiliar country, the occupiers had the assistance of the Office of War Information's best anthropologists, sociologists and psychologists, most notably Ruth Benedict. The Japanese, Benedict wrote, are

> both aggressive and unaggressive, both militaristic and aesthetic, both insolent and polite, rigid and adaptable, submissive and resentful of being pushed around, loyal and treacherous, brave and timid, conservative and hospitable to new ways.[33]

...which covered most eventualities. The erudite Ms Benedict also noted of a country that had over fifty years made the transition from a backward feudal society to a modern capitalist superpower, 'Japan has not changed fundamentally since the 1890s'.[34]

MacArthur's power as Supreme Commander was absolute. He

had the power to suspend Hirohito's functions, dissolve the Diet, outlaw political parties, or disqualify any man from public office. When he decided to dismiss all legislators who had belonged to certain militaristic societies Prime Minister Kijūrō Shidehara's cabinet threatened to resign en masse. In that case, said MacArthur, 'Shidehara may be acceptable to the Emperor for reappointment as prime minister, but he will not be acceptable to me'. The resignations were withdrawn. MacArthur's power was not only over the Japanese. US State Department advisor William Sebald suggested MacArthur consult with chiefs of the mission in Tokyo about Korean Developments. 'Why, as a sovereign should I?' he asked. 'President Truman doesn't do so, nor does the King of England or any other head of state'. In the depths of Japan's misery, MacArthur was worshipped as a great hero and benign dictator, much as the Emperor had been adored before.[35]

On the model of Nuremberg, the Allies arranged an International Military Tribunal for the Far East that began sitting in April 1946 under the Australian Judge William Webb, with America's Joe Keenan prosecuting. Twenty eight were charged with crimes against peace and humanity. The accused included the Prime Minister General Hideki Tōjō, Foreign Minister Shigenori Tōgō, the war and naval ministers, the commanders of the Kwantung Army, the Burma expeditionary force, the Shanghai expeditionary force and the Philippines expeditionary force – but not the Emperor Hirohito. In a nod to Asian suffering Judges from India and the Philippines were included. From the outset, Keenan had to face the Elephant in the room:

> We admit that great force and violence, including the Hiroshima bomb, have been employed by the Allies, and we make no more apology for that than does a decent innocent citizen walking home ... and his family employ the use of force to prevent his life from being taken by an outlaw.[36]

Even the judges had difficulty ignoring the evidence of Allied atrocities, since the court sat in the city of Tokyo, devastated by firebombing at the cost of some 150,000 lives. Dutch judge Bernard Röling said 'it was horrible that we went there for the purposes of vindicating the laws of war and yet saw every day how the Allies had violated them dreadfully'.[37]

One of the more obvious cheats in the Tokyo War Crimes tribunal was the fact that the Emperor himself had not been charged. MacArthur, and other US authorities claimed that the Emperor was just a figurehead – a naïve character, preoccupied with his hobby of marine biology, who did not really understand what was going on around him. Inside the court prosecutor Keenan tiptoed around all mention of the Emperor. In private most of the court's officers would have said that this was not true. French prosecutor Oneto wrote that the Emperor 'could not be refused anything', and the British Prosecutor Arthur Comyns Carr wrote in a letter that 'the defendants, if they have done nothing else, have proved the guilt of the Emperor pretty conclusively'.[38] MacArthur understood that his own authority with the Japanese people depended on the way that he had the Emperor in his pocket.

Another problematic aspect of the court's deliberations was a relative lack of evidence of China's suffering under the Japanese occupation. Prince Asaka who had been the commanding officer at Nanking was not charged because of the informal agreement that members of the Royal Family had immunity from prosecution.

The tribunal's weaknesses were thoroughly exposed by the Indian judge Radhabinod Pal. Justice Pal issued a minority judgement, in 1,235 pages detailing the destruction wreaked by the atomic bombardment. He argued that the colonial powers had no right to judge an Asian government and that their war crimes were as bad, if not worse than Japan's:

> In my judgement … it is beyond the competence of any victor nation to go beyond the rules of international law as they exist, give new definitions of crimes and then punish the prisoners for having committed offences according to this new definition. This is really not a norm in abhorrence of the retroactivity of the law: it is something more substantial. To allow any nation to do that will be to allow usurpation of power which international law denies that nation.

Pal continued:

A trial with law thus prescribed will only be a sham employment of legal process for the satisfaction of a thirst for revenge.[39]

As in Nuremberg, the central charge was that of waging aggressive war against peace. However Justice Pal raised an objection. If waging war was in any circumstances a crime, then, he argued, the colonial powers would always dominate the east. 'At any rate in the present state of international relations such a static idea of peace is absolutely untenable', he wrote. The reason was that 'dominated nations of the present day *status quo* cannot be made to submit to an eternal domination in the name of peace'.[40]

From Purge to 'Red Purge'

As with Nuremberg, the Tokyo trials ran in tandem with a proce-dural 'purge' of 'militarist' supporters of Japanese expansion – drawing in some 200,000 people between January 1946 and May 1948 when it was called to a halt. These men were made to stand down from important positions in government and in industry, but unlike the position in Germany, were not detained in large numbers. In the first year of MacArthur's rule as the Supreme Commander of the Allied Powers his administration struck a left-wing note. The General Headquarters 'plan for extending the purge to Japan's financial world was', according to Yoshida Shigeru, postwar Japanese Prime Minister, 'of a most comprehensive nature'. Yoshida added that 'had it been enforced to the letter it would have certainly played havoc with our whole economy'. Indeed there were 'those who referred to this operation as the moral disarmament of Japan' – meaning that it would have wrecked the country as an economic power.[41] In the event, the purge of business was moderated, and later a series of appeal tribunals undid most of the original judge-ments, exonerating 177,000 by 1951.

As well as purging rightists, the Supreme Commander's HQ liberalised trade unions. He also shocked the Japanese leaders by legalising the Communist Party. Prince Konoe told Yoshida Shigeru that 'one of the most serious results to be feared' from the defeat 'was a communist revolution' – though the communists could only muster five per cent of the popular vote. That was a sign of the elite's paranoia about the strength of the communists, but also a fair indication of the prospects of social instability. A perplexed Yoshida tried to see things from the point of view of MacArthur's 'New Deal' inspired advisors: 'the Allied powers considered Japan as a police state in which the rights of man were not recognised and the freedom of citizens was trodden under foot, and the communists were therefore victims of an inhuman regime'. Where the Allies could have got such an idea was something that Yoshida could not imagine. The communists, so impressed by the change in their fortunes called the allied forces the 'army of liberation', though soon they had cause to change their minds.[42]

MacArthur took over responsibility for Japanese society just at the moment the economy was collapsing under the weight of fighting the war and the American bombardment. Hirohito's empire had been cut down by 81 per cent, from 773,781 square miles to 146,690. Eighty per cent of the textile industry was shattered, coal production was one eighth of its peacetime level and 'there were few phones, fewer trains and virtually no power plants'. Inflation was running at 1000 per cent, and production collapsed.[43] By Yoshida's reckoning the 1945 rice harvest was just 77 per cent of what was needed to avoid starvation. Half way through 1946 food rations were either delayed or broken down altogether up and down the country. MacArthur cabled Washington to call for 3,500,000 tons of food. When they quibbled the Supreme Commander replied 'give me bread or give me bullets'. MacArthur managed to get 510,000 tons of rice belonging to the Australian forces in Japan released to avoid an immediate disaster. Food shortages continued to dog Japan under MacArthur's rule: new austerity measures were launched in 1949 and in 1950 the Korean War led to more shortages. Wheat was finally taken off the ration in April 1951.

Food shortages were just one of the problems that were leading to growing disorder in the country. On 19 May 1946 trade unions called a 'food May Day'. There were very large but mostly peaceful demonstrations in Tokyo and other cities calling for larger food rations and higher wages. There were workplace occupations, too, and demonstrators called first for the resignation of the Shidehara government, and then of the Yoshida government that replaced it. Protestors even forced their way into the imperial palace demanding to see Hirohito.[44]

Trade union militancy accelerated and in August 1947 a National Congress of Industrial Organisations was formed with 160,000 members and a radical leadership – a serious rival to the official, company-union General Federation of Labour with some 850,000 members. The new union called a General Strike.[45]

Faced with the challenge of organised labour the Supreme Commander lurched to the right. After the 1946 food protests MacArthur issued a 'Warning against Mob Disorder or Violence' which spoke of a 'growing tendency to mass violence'. MacArthur spoke about 'undisciplined elements' who threatened 'orderly government'. Moreover, if the Japanese government would take no steps to bring 'disorderly minorities' and 'minor elements' under control, then the Supreme Commander would intervene to 'control and remedy such a deplorable situation'. MacArthur likened the trade union leaders to the deposed 'feudalistic and military' leaders. Later that summer MacArthur again attacked 'strikes, walkouts, or other work stoppages which are inimical to the objectives of the occupation.' On the anniversary of the surrender MacArthur warned of a 'conflicting ideology which might negate individual freedom, destroy individual initiative and mock individual dignity'. The Japanese should reject the 'slanted propaganda' of the 'extreme radical left'. When the radical unions threatened the General Strike in January 1947 MacArthur banned it, saying 'I will not permit the use of so deadly a social weapon in the present impoverished and emaciated conditions of Japan'. In July 1948 MacArthur went further with a law that banned general strikes outright and the 'prohibition by law of strikes by government employees'. On 1 June 1949 another new law withdrew the employers' obligation to recognise unions. Later, the Yoshida government following MacArthur's road put in place laws that let the government ban strikes while disputes were settled by a 'Labour Relations Commission'.[46]

As MacArthur and his Japanese cabinet reversed the liberalisation of labour laws, so too did they reverse the political freedoms of their radical critics – first and foremost the Japanese Communist Party. MacArthur's May 1945 statement warned the Japanese people against the alleged 'mass violence tactics of the communists'. In February 1949 MacArthur threatened the suppression of the communist press, and then in April saw in the Organisational

Control Law, which, in the emerging 'Cold War liberal' style, identified the threat of left and right. The law 'prohibited all ultrana-tionalistic and anti-democratic political associations whether of the Right or the Left'. By May 1950 MacArthur said he no longer considered the Japanese Communist Party a 'constitutionally recog-nised political movement' – and around the same time the Communist Party reversed its political position and opposed the US occupation. In June MacArthur's General HQ told the Japanese government to extend the purge to leading communists. On 18 July 1950 the communists' publications were banned and the leaders went underground, after warrants were issued for their arrest under what became known as the 'Red Purge'. Prime Minister Yoshida explained in his memoirs that 'the purge in private enterprises began with the press and radio and was gradually extended to industry in general'. Six hundred communists, sympathisers and other radicals lost jobs in the media, followed by 10,000 industrial workers sacked. With the purge of government employees, teachers, postmen, town hall clerks and others the total victimised came to 22,000 and in 1952 the supervision of radicals was handed over to a Public Safety Investigation Agency under the Subversive Activities Prevention Law.[47]

As the communists fell under the Supreme Commander's dragnet, so too did other 'subversives' – notably Japan's large Korean minority. A General Headquarters staff study on Koreans in Japan thought it best that that they be encouraged to repatriate and their political affiliations monitored with the goal 'to rid Japan of as many Korean communists as possible and prevent their re-entry into Japan', and the ultimate goal, said US Political Advisor to the Supreme Commander was 'reducing the size of this difficult minority group'. Korean ethnic schools in Kobe and Osaka were closed, leading to rioting. Koreans were accused of playing a key role in organised crime, and placed under police scrutiny. Prime Minister Yoshida was glad that the League of Koreans in Japan 'was dissolved and its property confiscated'.[48]

Under the San Francisco Peace Treaty the Allied occupation came to an end on 28 April 1952, by which time Japan had been trans-formed into a US-style Cold War police state. Douglas MacArthur moved on to his controversial role in the Korean War.

Chapter Thirty

From World War to Cold War

As we have seen General Patton wanted to carry on the war by invading the USSR. In the end there was no Allied invasion of the Soviet Union at the end of the war, nor indeed could there have been. The American army, like most, saw a collapse of military discipline at the end of the war that meant they were in no position to invade anywhere. Troops who had been pushed to the limit were ready to go home. America's rise to globalism through the Second World War had been remarkable. The US had moved from being the world's foremost economic power to being the world's foremost geopolitical power as well. The world's pre-eminent power of the nineteenth century, Britain, had been reduced to the status of America's loyal lieutenant. The other challengers to the established order, Germany and Japan, had been defeated. As the new hegemonic power in world relations, the US was still dependent on its allies.

The Allied Military Government of the Occupied Territories was US-led, but still relied on its allies, Britain, the Soviet Union, and more latterly France to exercise authority. In October 1943 the British Conservative politician Quintin Hogg wrote in *Foreign Affairs* about the future of Europe

> The two immediate factors of the situation in Europe after the defeat of Hitler will be the necessity of military occupation and European relief. We—and I mean the United States, the USSR and the British Commonwealth—will not be driven to these acts by vindictiveness or sentimentality but by the sheer logic of events. Some will not like the policy they entail. All will have to accept it.
>
> ...there will be an insistent cry for food. Homeless people will demand houses. War prisoners and foreign workers from German factories will ask care and lodging on their way borne in places which cannot accommodate them. Factories will be closed. Chaos will reign everywhere. The one unifying force will be the

armies of the United Nations. The one sure source of food will be the United Nations Relief Organization. The one instrument of political security will be the authority of the victorious Powers.[1]

The Labour Party journal, the *Tribune,* read Hogg's proposals to mean that the ruling classes want 'the cooperation of British labour in the murder of the infant European revolution'.[2] That proved to be right. As we have seen the Allied Military Governments in Europe, and in the Far East were committed first to disarming the militant partisan movements that had challenged the Axis occupation forces. But the exercise of military government alone was impossible. Very quickly AMGOT found it had to build up local civilian authorities to restore order.

The economic reconstruction of Europe

For the US, the Second World War was an economic spur to recovery, and afterwards conversion of war industries into peacetime laid the basis for the post-war boom. Around $17 billion of government paid-for plant and machinery was sold at distress prices, two thirds of it ended up in the hands of just eighty-seven companies.[3] General Motors, Pan American and Coca Cola were all businesses that transformed American capitalism through war, and into the peace.

Such was the destruction of European industry that its share of the world's manufacturing output was lower than at any time since the early nineteenth century, and even by 1953 it was just 26 per cent of the whole, as against America's 45 per cent.[4] At the war's end, US factories were supplying the world, while Europe was in a state of near collapse. Disorder was a real threat to US hegemony. The challenge of the militant left, its reputation enhanced by participation in the resistance movements, and in mass labour movements, with a call on the geopolitical power of the Soviet Union underlined just how fragile the capitalist order was at the end of the war. To secure the survival of the market system was no easy task. Indeed America's post-war leaders effectively wrote off most of Eastern Europe as a lost cause, when they gave tacit approval to the consolidation of the Soviet Union's 'sphere of influence' in the wreckage of Germany's failed eastern Empire. As George Kennan explained, the idea was to divide 'Europe frankly into spheres of influence – keep ourselves out of the Russian sphere and the Russians out of ours'. [5]

At the end of the First World War, America had retreated from its foray into Europe. Could it do so again? No. US industry was geared up to supply the engines of war. The military Keynesianism of war time was the condition for America's emergence from recession. The great levels of US industrial output depended upon demand from abroad. To keep US output up American policy makers had to redirect their wartime 'Lend Lease' assistance into postwar reconstruction. The means to do that was the European Recovery Program, known as Marshall Aid, (after Army Chief of Staff and then Secretary of State, George Marshall, who announced it in 1947) under which aid and technical assistance was given to Western Europe between 1948 and 1952. These credits helped secure demand for US goods as war industries were converted to civilian goods in what has been called 'Atlantic Fordism'.

It was, according to historian John Gimbel

an economic programme to promote Europe's financial, fiscal and political stability; to stimulate world trade; to expand American markets; to forestall an American depression; to maintain the open-door policy; to create a multilateral trade world which could be dominated by American capitalists.

What is more, it was 'a programme to stop communism, to frustrate socialists and leftists, to attract the Soviet Union's satellites and to contain or roll back the Russians'. [6] Senator Cabot Lodge, thought that 'this Marshall Plan is going to be the biggest damned interference in international affairs that there has ever been in history'. 'It doesn't do any good to say we are not going to interfere', he warned the faint hearts on the Foreign Relations Committee, adding 'I don't think we need to be so sensitive about interfering in the internal affairs of these countries'.[7]

Historian D.S. Painter explains that

US assistance allowed moderate governments to devote massive resources to reconstruction and to expand their countries' exports without imposing politically unacceptable and socially divisive austerity programs that would have been necessary without US aid. US assistance also helped counteract what US leaders saw as a dangerous drift away from free enterprise and toward collectivism. By favoring some policies and opposing others the United States not only influenced how European and Japanese elites defined their own interests but also altered the internal balance of power among the decision-making groups. Thus US aid policies facilitated the ascendancy of centrist parties, such as the Christian Democrats in West Germany and Italy and the more conservative Liberal Democratic Party in Japan.[8]

For the European Recovery Programme to work, America had to reverse the punitive policy of disassembling German industry. Herbert Hoover, as leader of the President's economic mission to Germany and Austria had drafted a report on 18 March 1947, usefully titled 'The Necessary Steps for Promotion of German Exports so as to Relieve American Taxpayers of the Burdens of Relief and for the Economic Recovery of Europe'. Hoover highlighted the fact that Germany was a part of a European division of labour that would not recover without her. After 'demontage' came reconstruction. Major-General Alex Bishop recalled that German technicians would 'set down the new piece of plant on the same seating and screw it on the same bolts that were still sticking up from the ground'. 'Perversely', wrote Patricia Meehan, 'punitive allied policy had given German industry a head start on the road to modernization'.[9] German recovery was indeed central to Western Europe's recovery. Altogether the US paid out $13,365 million to 16 countries under the European Recovery Plan. Between 1947 and 1950 US aid paid for one quarter of Western Europe's imports, and seventy per cent of these came from the US.[10]

The destruction of capital stock through war led to persistent problems of currency devaluation. In Germany the Nazis had financed the war effort by printing money and issuing bonds, increasing the money supply by 800 per cent and Reich Debt by 3000 per cent. Inflation however was kept in check by coercive price and wage controls. At the same time as the money stock increased, output in the Western Occupied Zone had fallen by 60 per cent between 1944 and 1946. In Italy, too, by 1945 industrial output collapsed, to one quarter of what it had been in 1938, while the money supply increased by 50 per cent a year. Both countries suffered violent inflation at the war's end, leading to a complete collapse in confidence in the German Mark, such that nearly a third of all industrial output had to be bartered.[11]

Marshall Aid funded the stabilisation of the Mark. Initially, the occupiers kept the Nazi price and wage controls in place. But in 1948 they introduced a new currency, the Deutsch Mark, issuing DM60 to each person in exchange for RM60. The net effect was a reduction of the money stock by 93.5 per cent as all savings over RM60 were wiped out. They also created an independent Bundesbank, as free from political control as the Federal Reserve, tasked only with defending the currency - an institution that stood in the way of inflationary public spending in Germany, later serving as a model for all Europe. In Italy, too, Finance Minister Einaudi's medicine was harsh. The same problem would dog the sterling area, as production contracted across the Empire, but without the kind of sudden collapse there was in Italy and Germany, there was no decisive currency reform.

Marshall Aid 'primed the pump' of European recovery, with West Germany at its heart. But it did so by consolidating the division between the developed northwest Europe, which would be re-built, and the impoverished eastern and southern Europe, which suffered a corresponding process of disinvestment. To nurture growth in west Europe, capital had to re-trench, to concentrate its resources on reconstruction. This new form of uneven development amplified the traditional advantage northwest Europe enjoyed over the east and south, but this time it was the counter-crisis strategy of reconstruction that raised up the divisions. For the reconstruction funds to be effective, they could not be spread to thinly. Dean Acheson wrote that 'it was easier to offer credits than to find the funds, with lend-lease ending, demobilisation in full swing, Congress cutting appropriations and the domestic economy calling for goods of every sort.'[12]

One measure that reflected the east-west division was the European Customs Union, allowed under 'special circumstances, including the need for economic development or reconstruction'. The need for a customs union arose because the growth engendered by the Marshall Aid would tend to raise prices. But if these buoyant markets were undercut by cheaper goods outside the European Recovery Program area the positive effects would be dissipated. As Jacob Viner explained in 1950, for the United States 'the political and strategic interest in a stable and prosperous and strengthened Western Europe' was more important than 'the market which Western Europe offers for American exports'.[13]

Dividing Germany

Marshall Aid and the German currency reform were focus points for the emerging East-West conflict. As America and her allies put in place reforms that were aimed at stabilising the market society in Western Europe, they were bound to clash with the Soviet adminis-tration in East Germany, as well as the Soviet-backed governments in Eastern Europe. Here, the West's economic policy joined up with its geopolitical policy towards Germany, and its emerging policy towards the Soviet Union.

At Teheran Roosevelt and Churchill argued for a divided Germany. Roosevelt wanted the country carved up into five separate states. Churchill balked at five parts, but agreed that the main thing was 'to keep Germany divided'.[14] That was power politics, and at that time married with a policy of wrecking German industry. With the post-war reversal of the anti-industrial strategy and the commitment to build up German industry, however, there was no reversal of the policy of keeping Germany divided. On the contrary, the Western Allies' new policy cemented the division as it diverged from Soviet goals.

When the administration in the American, British and French zones used Marshall Aid to underwrite the new Deutsche Mark, the Soviet administration in the eastern zone wanted to use the new US-backed Mark as currency for the whole of Germany. On 10 March 1948 the State Department told Lucius Clay, Military Governor of the US Zone that 'the policy of this government is no longer to reach an agreement on currency and financial reform'. As they explained:

> The question arises whether this is desirable from the US stand-point, since quadripartite [i.e. across the four zones] currency reform might enable the Soviets to frustrate further the economic recovery of western Germany.

The important thing was to keep the money in the three western zones, run by the US, Britain and France respectively:

> a quadripartite currency, as opposed to a bizonal or trizonal currency, would deprive us of a very important monetary instrument for achieving effective economic administration of the western zones.[15]

Withholding the new currency from the Soviet zone, Clay had at a stroke effected the division of Germany. At the same time the US faced down Soviet-inspired attempts to promote a political movement for the reunification of Germany, the Volkscongress. There were also attempts to unite the trade unions across Germany which were strongly resisted by the Americans. US Ambassador Walter Bedell Smith said:

> The difficulty under which we labour is that in spite of our announced position, we really do not want or intend to accept German reunification under any terms that the Russians might agree to, even though they seemed to meet most of our requirements.[16]

The official US position was that it was the Soviet Union who was to blame for the division of Germany seemed obviously true when the Soviets built the Berlin Wall dividing the two sectors in 1961. But in 1948 it was the US that enforced the administrative division of Germany, the better to promote the restoration of capitalist stability. 'We soon came to believe that our chief concern should be the future of Europe, and that the reunification of Germany should be subordinate to that', explained Dean Acheson.[17]

Stabilising Europe

Marshall Aid gave the enfeebled and compromised west European elites a breathing space. As John Iatridies and Linda Wrigley argue 'American influence over governmental activity in Western Europe was also instrumental in discouraging revolutionary initiatives and truly radical social reforms.'[18]

In Italy elections set for 1948 put the US State Department into a state of high anxiety. 'If the Communists should win' they announced, there would be no further question of assistance from the United States'. The newly founded Central Intelligence Agency secretly gave $1 million to the centre parties. One month before the election the House Appropriations Committee voted $18.7 million in interim aid, while President Truman sent 29 merchant ships to the Italian government as a 'gesture of friendship and confidence in a democratic Italy'. Then the US gave Italy a further $4.3 million as the first payment on wages due to 60,000 former Italian prisoners of war. On the eve of the election two large shipments of food arrived, one for $8 million worth of grains. On the day the fledgling Christian Democratic Party beat the communists.[19]

The aid filled West German shop windows in 1948, while at the same time the newly unified Western Zone put in place restrictions on left wingers and blocked the all-German trade unions. When the the Hesse Land voted overwhelmingly to nationalise industries it was overruled by Military Governor Lucius Clay.[20]

NATO and the Cold War

In America, there were a rash of labour disputes in 1946 – steel workers and those at General Motors came out, as did the miners on 23rd May.

Truman in a speech written but not delivered vented:

> I am tired of government being flouted, vilified and now I want you men who are my comrades-in-arms, you men who fought battles to save the nation just as I did twenty-five years ago, to come along with me and eliminate the Lewises, the Whitneys, the Johnstons, the Communist Bridges and the Russian senators and representatives ...Let's put transportation and production back to work, hang a few traitors, make our country safe for democracy, tell Russia where to get off.[21]

Traitors were not hung, but the 'atomic spies' Julius and Ethel Rosenberg were sent to the electric chair. Truman attacked the Labour Unions, too, using the war-time legislation to seize control of strike-bound industries: 'In one year he had seized the coal mines twice; he had seized 134 meat packing plants, he had seized twenty-one tugboats; he had seized the facilities of twenty-six oil producing and refining companies; he had seized the Great Lakes Towing Company.'[22]

It was in this frame of mind that President Truman re-motivated US policy globally with his own 'Truman Doctrine' of 12 March 1947:

> I believe it must be the policy of the United States to support free peoples who are resisting attempted subjugation by armed minorities or by outside pressures. I believe that we must assist free peoples to work out their own destinies in their own way.

It was a triumph of hypocrisy. For the sake of 'free peoples ... work[ing] out their own destinies in their own way' the United States would intervene extensively in the internal affairs of other countries, through economic blackmail, clandestine subversion and military intervention. Through Truman's cold war glasses though, the 'armed minorities' and outsiders seeking to pressure and subjugate were not the United States and its allies, but those who opposed them. Popular nationalist or labour-based movements that were unwilling to dance to Washington's tune were characterised as 'communists', whether they were or were not. Identifying all opposition with the authoritarian regimes in the east was a way of parcelling up all America's fears. Anti-communism was a political motivation for US involvement in the wider world. It was remarkably similar to the Axis' appeal for an Anti-Comintern Front and its popular forms of the Anti-Bolshevik League. Now that the Nazis were out of the picture, conservatives in the European governments and in Washington were free to take up the anti-communist cause, rallying the same deep-rooted fears of social change and working class militancy.

The anti-communist crusade, though, was not only being rallied in Washington. West European elites were deeply anxious about their future. Paul Henri Spaak told the Belgian parliament in 1951 that

> The Europe of which we are speaking is a Europe which we have allowed to become grossly mutilated. Poland, Hungary, the

Balkan countries, Eastern German – all these have gone. It is a Europe against which Asia and Africa have risen in revolt. The largest among us [Britain] is at this moment being defied in Iran and Egypt. It is a Europe which for the last five years has been living in fear of the Russians and on the charity of the Americans.[23]

European elite fears' centred on the external threats of the eastern bloc and of third world nationalism, and the anxiety that once again the United States would withdraw from Europe. European statesmen were looking at ways to motivate a continuation of the alliance after the war. No longer Prime Minister, Winston Churchill chose Fulton, Missouri to give a speech outlining the world's coming challenge. Churchill picked up a phrase of Joseph Goebbels to scare his audience about the 'iron curtain descending across Europe'. Taking up the Nazi baton of anti-Communism was audacious, considering that it was Churchill who had proposed the division of Europe into spheres of influence in the West, and in the east to Stalin, at Yalta. But West Europeans, Britain especially, needed an ideological projection of western interests that would keep America in Europe, just as Washington did. As long as America accepted the role of the world's policeman, then Britain could have a role for itself as the willing lieutenant. More, in that Britain had extensive military bases, personnel and experience, it could, if America was willing to pay, continue to punch above its weight.

The military expression of the new Cold War was the North Atlantic Treaty Organisation (NATO). Its first Secretary General was Britain's wartime chief of staff Sir Hastings Ismay. NATO was both a continuation of wartime policy, in that it motivated US involvement in West Europe, but also a transformation, in that the enemy was now the former ally, the Soviet Union, and the ally the former enemy, Germany. More than an Atlantic alliance, NATO was the means by which Germany's sovereignty was restored – but within a subordinate hierarchy. The West German authorities in Bonn were glad to be finally recognised as a sovereign power and therefore willing to accept pointedly disadvantageous terms. Sovereignty was only recognised for West Germany – in other words the Bonn regime had to accept as a fait accompli the division of the country. American and

British bases were sited in Germany, and West Germany was allowed to rearm only within the context of the NATO command structure. The external threat motivated internal discipline among the powers, under US leadership. NATO Secretary General Ismay summed up the triple meaning of NATO with the saying that NATO was there 'to keep the Russians out, the Americans in, and the Germans down'. Keeping the Russians out was ostensible reason for the alliance, its ideological motivation; keeping the Americans in as sponsors of capitalist stabilisation was what West European elites needed; keeping the Germans down was what the US (and Britain) needed from the alliance, the subordination of European rivals in the Great Power game.

The Cold War policy did not just work at the interstate level. It assumed, as Cabot Lodge explained, extensive intervention into the internal affairs of European states. America helped to reconstruct political institutions along lines that corresponded to US ideals.

The allied administration oversaw German reconstruction on the basis that popular sovereignty was a potential danger, and helped create political institutions in the West that introduced many of what America constitutional theorists called 'checks and balances' to limit the 'tyranny of democracy'. 'Germany was explicitly created as a wherhafte Demokratie (defensive democracy), one with structures designed to "protect the Germans from themselves"'.[24] The important structures were the German Constitutional Court, the Presidency, The Bundestag, the Länder and the Bundesbank. The Constitutional Court is part of the judiciary and stands above any elected institution with powers to strike down legislation passed by the Bundestag. 'The German Constitutional Court does serve as a formidable check on governmental action' explains political scientist Lisa Conant.[25] It was the Constitutional Court that outlawed the Communist Party in Germany (1956), and later sanctioned laws against radical civil servants (the Anti-Radical Decree of 1972). The Bundesbank (as it is now called) is also independent. Wilhelm Vocke, first president of what was then known as the Bank Deutscher Länder set out the case in 1948: 'The independence of the Bank and its leadership is an absolute necessity' he said. 'Only when independence is guaranteed on all sides will the central bank be able to earn that asset which is more important than popularity and applause ... trust at home and abroad'.[26] On the model of the American Federal Reserve, the independent Bundesbank would put finance policy outside the reach of politicians and in the hands of economists committed to tight fiscal policy ('trust at home and abroad'). Regional political power is devolved among the Länder. The Presidency is apolitical. The German polity exemplifies Cold War liberalism and its distrust of popular democracy.

Reorganising Europe's Trade Union movement

America's trade union leaders played a special role in US Cold War diplomacy. US Supreme

Court Justice William Douglas told the Congress of Industrial Organisations in 1948, about the 'challenges that should make labor and active participant in international affairs'.

> Labor is peculiarly qualified to bridge a gap that has been growing between the United States and Europe. It is from the lips of Labor that Europe can most readily learn how democracy and freedom can be peacefully achieved in a framework of government.[27]

It might seem surprising that labour leaders should lend themselves to a Cold War anti-communist campaign. But the leaders of both the American Federation of Labor, and of the Congress of Industrial Organisations were steeled in campaigns against communists, and other radical militants in their own unions. For them, the struggle against communism in Europe was just an extension of the struggle against the militants in their own unions. As office holders, they valued orderly relations with management, and identified with those European officials trying to stave of militancy over there. With the support of the AF of L Jay Lovestone had set up a Free Trade Union Committee in 1944 with the goal of fighting communism in trade unions across the world.

In the US administration in Germany, union figures like Sidney Hillman and Jay Lovestone advised Manpower Division on the best way to stop the emergence of a radical labour movement. US administration Labor Relations director Mortimer Wolf had been an attorney at the National Labor Relations Board. Wolf was hostile towards German Socialists who 'elevate immediate social and economic reform in Germany above reparations, and demand treatment of the Germans as a liberated, rather than occupied people'.[28] But Wolf was sidelined accused of being too sympathetic to the communists. Jay Lovestone thought that it was only by building up a union movement in the US Zone that the communists in the Soviet zone could be stopped. The AFL and CIO advisors came up with an interesting way of re-organising the German unions. They chose a relatively strong organisation at the factory floor, but weak integration across industry. Under the 'co-determination' (mitbestimmung) laws workplace representatives were encouraged to sit on management boards. That meant that workers' representatives were focused primarily on the production process, and less on national questions. Wage bargaining would be local rather than national. Co-determination is often seen as a specifically German development, but it was in fact drawn from the US union leaders' experience of organising war production. Under war production, for example, 'when an employer did not produce efficiently, the' International Ladies Garment Workers 'union's engineering department had a right to examine his methods and recommend improvements in the manufacture of garments'.[29] It was Jay Lovestone, who brokered this agreement.

Irving Brown of Lovestone's Free Trade Union Committee landed in Paris in November 1945 and asked for $100,000 funds so that he could help split the Confédération Générale du Travail (CGT), Europe's largest trade union body. Brown used the money to bankroll a right-wing group in the CGT led by Léon Jouhaux and Robert Brotherau. The group called itself Force Ouvrière and was set on fighting for control of the CGT, which Brown thought was unrealistic, but worth supporting all the same because it would lead to a split. Lovestone backed Brown's plan saying that 'France is the number one country in Europe from the point of view of saving the Western labor movement from totalitarian control'.[30] It was Marshall Aid that fomented the split.

On 27 June 1947 Soviet Foreign Minister Vyacheslav Molotov came to Paris to talk to Georges Bidault and Ernest Bevin, his French and British counterparts, about how Marshall Aid might work, the Soviet Union at that time not sure what its policy should be. US

Ambassador to France Caffery made it clear that 'if the Communists get back into the government, France won't get a dollar from America'.[31] Seeing it turned into a crowbar to lever them out of West European ministries, the Moscow communists made it clear that communists worldwide ought to oppose Marshall Aid. It was a self-defeating policy. In 1947 the PCF, rightly, launched strikes against austerity measures – but wrapped them up in a pose of hostility to Marshall Aid that made little sense to most people. The communist delegates on the Confédération Générale du Travail (CGT), National Committee committed the unions to the view that Marshall Aid was 'part of a plan of subjugation of the world by the capitalist American trusts and preparation of a new world war'.[32] French communists struck out the docks that were bringing American food and goods to an impoverished country. This was the strike that was broken with the use of the Corsican mob. It was Irving Brown who struck the deal with the Corsican Pierre Ferri-Pisani, a drug smuggler and friend of mob-leader Antoine Guerini, to terrorise the strikers. The wider public, though, could hardly sympathise with a strike against landing aid in a hungry France. The government fell, the communists lost their seats in the cabinet, and most destructive of all, the trade unions were divided between a pro-communist CGT and a more right wing Force Ouvrière that was launched at a special conference on 18 December 1947. Jouhaux saw Ambassador Caffery the following week and said 'it would be helpful if the Americans did not claim they caused the split from the CGT', hoping to silence Brown's boasts. Caffery cabled Washington saying that the split was 'potentially the most important political event since the liberation of France'. The US State Department sent $28,000 dollars to help, and Caffery sent a truckload of second hand typewriters.[33]

The original 'Third Way' and the myth of the postwar 'Social Revolution'

In 1949 Richard Crossman told parliament that 'we have begun to construct during the last four years the beginning of a permanent democratic socialist system'.[34] The myth that the British labour government, and indeed west European post-war governments had inaugurated a social revolution is built on the argument that, unlike their American counterparts, the Europeans had erected a welfare safety net of socialised medicine, unemployment benefits and nationalised industries.

Even Marxists like Peter Taafe and Tony Mulhearn were taken in by the legend of the wartime radicalisation of the working class. They claimed that 'the revolutionary wave that swept Western Europe at the end of World War II was, if anything greater than that which followed the First World War'. [35] But such radicalisation that did take place was the sporadic collective opposition to the war effort. In the end it was obedience to the war effort, the phoney collectivism of 'we're all in this together' that won out. Militant resistance fighters were persuaded to hand in their weapons to allied Military Policemen, trade union militants were persuaded to put their all into the 'battle for production', and the Forces Parliament in Egypt went into recess to 'take the war to Hitler'. Militant resistance to the militarised war economy was defeated in favour of acquiescence to the Allied War Effort and the post-war reconstruction that followed. The popular opposition handed over its collective power to the authorities.

'Collectivity' came to mean government reforms that were an extension of the Military Industrial Complex in new conditions. The 'Cold War' is often painted as a *deus ex machina* that was somehow brought in from elsewhere to derail the radical spirit of popular frontism. But in truth the ascendance of Cold War conformity and obedience was all predicated on the tutelage that the experience Second World War gave to the populace in submitting to a greater authority.

Though the West European social contract seems to give off a warm and nostalgic glow, seen in retrospect, few understand that the promotion of a kind of tame Socialism was the goal of the US exponents of the Marshall Plan. They called it the Third Way. The idea was to build up moderate socialists as a bulwark against the Communists and the far left. Up to a point, the US was willing for Marshall Aid to be used to promote social programmes where these helped stabilisation (though Britain did not receive Marshall Aid). On the whole, though, the case that the post-war regimes in Europe were all that left wing is hard to sustain. Though the mobilisation of labour in wartime did lead to a greater sense of working class self-confidence that was conditional. The working class had been rallied in a production drive in which it sacrificed all and got little back. As much as they were encouraged by war, the workers were also tutored in obedience to output and production. The end of the war was an anti-climax for most, as it was followed by years of austerity, and fear. According to Pulzer 'what Germans longed for was a return to privacy, family, inner peace and public morality'.[36] As Mark Mazower says, by 1948 'the radicalisation of the war years had vanished'.[37]

How left-wing the post-war reforms were depends on how one sees the expansion of the state into wider social spheres. Socialised education in Britain was less revolutionary than it sounded. Working class children were sent to underperforming Secondary Modern schools, while the Middle Classes were given places at academic Grammar Schools. The nationalised industries in the UK: coal, railways, electricity, gas and the Bank of England were all bankrupt and backward, 'the unprofitable 20 per cent of British industry'. In the new National Health Service it was the consultants whose 'mouths were choked with gold', by Health Secretary Aneurin Bevan, in his push to win support for the scheme, while the nurses stayed among the worst-paid. Former owners were handsomely compensated for the state takeover of their failing companies, and generally sat on the boards of the new nationalised industries. The editor of the Economist, Geoffrey Crowther told an American audience in 1949 that 'the ordinary resident in England, unless he happens to have been a shareholder in any of the expropriated companies, is unable to detect any difference whatever as a result of nationalisation'.[38]

In general the claim that west European society swung to the left after the war is hard to sustain. Indigenous European recovery was funded by holding down consumption, to redirect those resources towards investment. 'The share of personal consumption has generally fallen', while production output continued to rise, recorded the United Nations Department of Economic Affairs.[39] In Britain, the labour movement had been extensively co-opted into making sacrifices for wartime production, and continued to support rationing of consumption goods up till 1949. In France, Mendes-France, inheriting Vichy-level wages argued they should be held down 'until production recovered'.[40]

For German workers, forced labour under the allies anticipated a decade of sacrifice under Erhard, as it built upon the suppression of wages under Hitler. Elmar Altvater argues that: 'the higher level of the rate of exploitation which had been brought about by force was maintained for ten years after the period of fascism', and: 'the "West German economic miracle" was pre-programmed in the course of the "thousand year Reich".'[41] Italian wages, too, were held down right through until the 1960s, largely through the downward pressure of surplus agrarian labour migrating from the south into northern cities, which depressed the domestic market.

Behind the Iron Curtain

Marshall Aid was offered to the East European states but the conditions could never have been acceptable to the Soviet Union, since they stipulated free market insitutions while his allies rested securely on nationalised industries and command economies. In any event the US offer of Marshall Aid to East European countries was propagandistic not sincere. The US set about consolidating market economies and elite political administrations in the west. It was not about to subsidise Soviet-influenced regimes in the east. Without open economies they would not be a market for US exports – even if the supplies of Marshall Aid were large enough to extend across Eastern Europe. As it was the US put most of its funds into West Europe and Japan to kindle the flames of capitalism there. It was unlikely that spreading them any thinner would have the desired effect. As west Europe soaked up all available investment funds, much of the rest of the world, in particular East Europe, Africa and East Asia, was starved of capital.

The eastern bloc was called communist, but these were not the conditions in which to build a new society. The Soviet sphere of influence was defined not by its industrial maturity, as Marx had imagined the basis of socialism would be. Instead the defining feature of the USSR's buffer states was that they were the ruins of Germany's failed Eastern Empire. The prospects of building a New Jerusalem in an area scarred by war, genocide and plunder were close to nil – even if that was what Moscow wanted. In the event, all that Moscow wanted was pliant neighbours, who would honour Stalin.

What would become the Warsaw Pact countries were narrowly based societies run by a military-bureaucratic elite. The elites were modelled on their Soviet sponsor. As we have seen, the nominally independent parties, Peasants Parties, Christian Democrats and others were not really independent at all, but forced to subordinate to the pro-Moscow ruling cliques. Indigenous communist party members were the source for the original leadership. But a great many of these older communists whose background was underground agitating against the powers-that-be were temperamentally unsuited to building orderly regimes. Like their Soviet parent, and at its behest, the local east European communist elites were riven with mistrust and marked by purges and factional conflict. In the Cold War paranoia these ruling cliques were apt to see dissent where there was none, and to find western conspiracies where there were none.

Over the summer of 1948 100,000 were expelled from the Czechoslovak Communist Party, and half a million were reduced from full to candidate membership. Later that year 30,000 members of the Polish Communist Party were expelled. Then between 1949 and 1950 nearly 10,000 were expelled from the Bulgarian Communist Party. 'About two-and-a-half million people were purged in all between 1948 and 1952, and of those between 125,000 and 250,000 were imprisoned.'[42]

Soviet paranoia quickly undid any lingering claims that the USSR had to represent the future. In 1953 hundreds of thousands of East German workers took to the streets in protest at increased work quotas, and added calls for democracy to their demands. They were fired upon and more than fifty were killed, twenty or so in summary executions. Hundreds more were imprisoned. Still, they were disappointed when Winston Churchill failed to speak up for them. Back in Number Ten Downing Street Churchill asked whether the Soviet Union should have allowed 'the eastern zone to collapse into anarchy and revolt', and went on: 'I had the impression that the unrest was handled with remarkable restraint.' Britain's curious indifference is explained in a memo of 22 June 1953 from Selwyn Loyd at the Foreign Office, saying that the allies felt:

a divided Germany is safer at present. But none of us dare say so in public because of the impact on public opinion in Germany.[43]

Churchill was willing to propagandise against the Soviet threat behind the Iron Curtain, but not to see the curtain lifted. US strategy, too, was to 'contain' the Soviet Union, not to overthrow it. That was explained by George Kennan in an anonymous article in Foreign Affairs published in 1947 that became the mainstay of US policy: 'the main element of any United States policy toward the Soviet Union must be a long-term, patient but firm and vigilant containment of Russian expansive tendencies'. That is, they were willing to accommodate the Soviet Union for the simple reason that they did not have the means to rule in Eastern Europe in the USSR's stead.

From World War to Cold War in the Far East

American Senator Joseph McCarthy gave a speech condemning George Marshall for allowing China to fall to Mao's communists, published in 1951 as *America's Retreat From Victory: The Story Of George Catlett Marshall*. The question 'Who lost China?' was the start of a hysterical attack by McCarthy against the Truman administration for being soft on communism. Given the anti-communist intent of the Marshall Plan and Truman's role as architect of the Cold War it was a remarkable attack. For the next four years McCarthy's campaign pushed America's Cold War from being an international strategy into a domestic witch hunt that criminalised dissent in the US and was even turned against the administration officials who had organised America's anti-communist push. McCarthy's challenge, 'who lost China?' was based on a false belief that Chiang Kai-shek's Nationalists were in a position to secure the market in China. McCarthy was right in one respect, though, and that was that it was US policy that laid the basis for the collapse of Chiang's nationalists and the eventual victory of Mao Tse Tung.

Throughout the war US strategy in the Far East was based on getting the Chinese to fight Japan, while America aimed to win the war first in Europe. Promoting Chiang's nationalists had been US policy, but it was undermined by the grotesque corruption of the Nationalist Kuomintang government and its lobbyists in Washington. US doubts about Chiang led some in the Roosevelt administration to talk up the role of the Chinese communists' fight against Japan.

With the conclusion of the European war, the US once again sought to get the Soviet Union to take on some of the burden of fighting, asking Stalin to declare war on Japan, which he did. Soviet troops invaded China from the north, eventually taking Manchuria, the centre of Japanese power. Stalin's view at the time was that Mao's forces were too weak to take China, and he still wanted to build up Chiang as the country's rightful ruler. In Manchuria, the Soviet army's main goal was less to promote the communists than to steal as much of the Japanese industrial machinery as they could get onto rail trucks to Siberia. Throughout the war, Stalin had pushed Mao to work with the nationalists. Mao, on the other hand, hoped that Soviet intervention would tip the balance that would give him the country. Stalin's honest belief that Chiang and Mao could be made to cooperate persuaded the US administration.

With the Japanese surrender, though, Washington got more anxious about Soviet inroads into China. US forces airlifted Chiang's nationalists north to take on the communists, who were ensconcing themselves under the Russian umbrella. Fighting between nationalists and communists became severe, and US president Truman took extraordinary action to save the Kuomintang:

> It was perfectly clear to us that if we told the Japanese to lay down their arms immediately and march to the seaboard, the entire country would be taken over by the Communists. We therefore had to take the unusual step of using the enemy as a garrison until we could airlift Chinese National troops to South China and send marines to guard the seaports.

The Americans transported nearly a half a million Kuomintang troops into Chinese cities, and deployed 50,000 US marines to guard railway lines, coal mines, ports, bridges and other strategic sites. These troops fought with Chinese attacking villages, while US planes strafed and bombed communist forces.[44]

The US and Stalin sought to push the nationalist leadership and the communists to agree a unification of the army and a government under Chiang with communist representatives in the cabinet. Both Chiang and Mao prevaricated, fearing a loss of position. The communists favoured military unification after the formation of the joint government, while Chiang wanted it the other way around, hoping to centralise control over the military forces in the country and reluctant to submit to democratic oversight. Dean Acheson explained that for the Kuomintang the proposals at the Provisional Consultative Conference in 1946 were 'too liberal and opened the way for capture of the government by the Communists; it wished a maximum of power in a minimum of hands'.[45]

In March 1946 George Marshall was sent to China to try to halt the Civil War that had broken out. He visited Mao's Headquarters in Yenan and was impressed by the communist leader. 'I had a long talk with Mao Tse Tung and I was frank to the extreme', Marshall reported to President Truman: 'He showed no resentment and gave me every assurance of cooperation'. By contrast Marshall was impatient with Chiang, and on 31 May demanded that he call off his offensive against communist positions, angry that the nationalists' sneak attacks were calling into question 'the integrity of my position'. All too often 'the Generalissimo appeared to agree' with Marshall, recalled Averell Harriman, 'and then did not fully support the agreement'.[46]

Throughout the war the US had blown hot and cold on the nationalist Kuomintang, hoping that they would take the fight to the Japanese, and serve as a block to the communists, but felt that they were too often let down. They had at various times favoured Mao's communists hoping that they would prove a more militant opposition to the Imperial Army. The effect of their on-off support was itself a disruptive influence. Chiang's nationalists were too dependent on US aid and adopted tactics to entrench their position the better to win it. The communists did at times secure US support, too (some of their peasant-based army was trained up to battlefield standards by US advisors preparatory to unification of the army). US and Soviet sponsorship of rival forces in China aggravated the conflict. 'I began to realise how very weak Chiang was in political terms', wrote US envoy Averell Harriman, adding cynically that 'the best we could hope for, I thought, was a divided China'.[47]

US aid to the Kuomintang was the key problem to the stabilisation of any regime in the country. But as the Americans were aware, the narrow basis of Chiang's support made aid a difficult question. Chiang's alliance of warlords and Merchant Bankers was an untrustworthy regime. Truman wrote to Marshall that 'a China disunited and torn by civil strife could not be considered realistically a proper place for American assistance'. American policy makers worred that, 'the Nationalists' existing resources available for stabilisation and expenditure were not crystal clear, nor were the activities of their host of missions, agents and lobbyists working for a five-hundred-sixty-million-dollar credit toward a three-year program of reconstruction amounting to about two billion dollars.' They 'took a sceptical view of the Nationalist government's probity and competence in managing borrowed funds' and even of 'how much China in its existing state of disorganisation could absorb'. Most of all the Americans were not convinced that a Kuomintang government would be any more likely to follow an 'Open Door' trade policy than would a Communist one. The Marshall mission failed to form a government of Kuomintang and Chinese Communist Party representatives, still less a joint army.[48]

The Kuomintang's accession to power was called 'The Calamity of Victory' by the popular *Ta Kung Pao* newspaper. The Kuomintang 'oppressed the people and sustained itself on the exploitation of the masses by the most barbaric Asiatic methods', wrote the radical Peng Shu-tse. Kuomintang officials were 'indulging in extreme extravagance, whoring wildly and gambling with no restraint', said Chiang himself: 'they brag, swagger and extort and stop at nothing'. 'Besides compulsory extortions' wrote Peng, the regime 'could only resort to issuing paper currency to maintain itself', so that 'the rate of inflation climbed in geometric progression'. The two families at the heart of the administration, the Soongs and the Kungs, explains Jung Chang, 'had access to China's foreign currency at preferential rates, which enabled them to sell US goods in China at a huge profit, causing the largest trade deficit in China's history' and 'this dumping bankrupted swathes of industry and commerce'. The liberal and pro-capitalist China Democratic League of Zhong Lan organised protests against the Kuomintang government. Prime Minister T.V. Soong had to resign and an internal investigation found that Soong and Kung companies had illegally converted more than $380 million. The report was leaked to the Nationalists' newspaper *Central Daily*, which reported the scandal on 29 July 1947. Soong May-ling, Madame Chiang Kai-shek, had her husband pressure the paper to say that they had put the decimal point in the wrong place and the embezzlement only amounted to $3 million.[49]

While the Kuomintang government was in disarray, Chiang Kai-shek sent one of his most trusted generals Hu Tsung-nan with an army of 250,000 to take the communist capital of Yenan. Mao's forces evacuated before he arrived and then harried Hu's army in a series of devastating ambushes – assisted by Hu's confidential secretary, Xiong Xianghui, who was a spy for the communists.[50] Kuomintang histories blame the defeats of 1947-9 on 'red agents' in their army, but the defection of successive Kuomintang generals and military aides showed that the Chiang Kai-shek's army was demoralised by poor leadership, despite its numerically greater size. Chiang's problems mounted with the US decision to cease aid to the Nationalist government. Peng Shu-tse, a leftist, but an opponent of Mao, summed up the impact:

> This final decision of American imperialism came as a death blow to Chiang Kai-shek's regime, which was fuly expressed in the atmosphere of dejection and despair hovering around Chiang's group when news reached China of Truman's victory in the 1948 election and his refusal to aid Chiang.[51]

At the end of 1948 veteran Kuomintang General Fu Tso-yi commanding the army based in Peking decided not to defend the city against Lin Bao's Red Army rather than see the capital destroyed – 'he had lost faith in Chiang's regime'. Nearby Tianjin, the country's third largest city, was also taken with little fighting.[52] Early in 1949 what was left of Chiang's regime and its army fled to the Island of Formosa (modern-day Taiwan). The original inhabitants had been terrorised into acquiescence when America took that colony from the Japanese. Twenty-eight thousand Formosans were killed to make way for Chiang's phoney Chinese government that until 1971 took a permanent seat on the United Nations' Security Council.

The 'loss' of China was in truth the collapse of a corrupt and brutal dictatorship, propped up by the United States for no other purpose than to do the Americans' fighting against the Japanese for them. Mao Tse-tung and the leadership of the Chinese Communist Party were no more interested in liberating the people, who they saw as instruments in a mechanical vision of history to which they were the engineers. If they had an advantage it was that they were largely independent of US help, and so had greater room to manoeuvre. Given the way that successive powers – Britain, Japan, America and the Soviet Union – had treated China as an arena for fighting out their differences, and used the Chinese people as proxy warriors in those conflicts, it was hardly surprising that the regime that did establish itself at the end of that violent era was of a military-bureaucratic character. Even the policy that most offended the western powers, China's supposedly autarkic, protectionist policy was not chosen by Mao, who wanted to trade with the world. World trade in 1949-50, though, was skewed towards America and Western Europe, with the Far East in the doldrums. Mao pleaded with the 'patriotic bourgeoisie' to stay and help build the country, but they preferred the expatriate, 'comprador' life of trading on the margins of East Asia's farming and small handicrafts to the uncertainty of the Chinese mainland. China's peasant communism was simply what filled the vacuum when capitalism failed to develop the country.

In America, though, the 'loss of China', was a traumatic event. For decades China had occupied the public imagination, as a site of protestant missions and more latterly in the headline-grabbing promotion of Soong-ling May, Madame Chiang Kai-shek by her supporters publishing mogul Henry Luce and Republican leader Wendell Willkie. Mao's seizure of power in 1949 convinced the US State Department that fighting communism would be their raison d'être, the crusade that would justify the siting of bases throughout the Pacific for 'Forward Defence', and the sustained interventions in Korea, Malaya, Vietnam, and the subordination of the region to US military control.

Chapter Thirty One

The Intellectuals and the War

Throughout the war intellectuals were torn between participation and withdrawal. Opposition to war was attractive to many though it carried heavy costs. Artists and intellectuals, leftists, democrats and Jews, left Germany in dismay at the country's drift towards war and dictatorship, and indeed from all of central Europe fleeing all kinds of chaos. Of 100,000 who left Nazi Germany for Europe and America, 7,600 had degrees and 1,000 were university teachers.[1] Many ended up in Britain. Already the historian Lewis Namier had come from Poland (as did the anthropologist Bronislaw Malinowski later), the philosopher Wittgenstein from Vienna, and the economist Nicholas Kaldor from Hungary. The German diaspora is vast. Psychologist Hans Eysenk and physicist Klaus Fuchs came from Germany, Karl Popper, the young Frederick Hayek, the art historian Ernst Gombrich and psychoanalyst Melanie Klein from Austria. From Vienna the elderly psychoanalyst Sigmund Freud and the young Eric Hobsbawm, by way of Berlin, came to London. Hobsbawm, alienated from a darkening Germany fixed his loyalties to the Soviet Union, and under the rubric of the 'People's Front' shifted them once more onto Britain. Looking back, Hobsbawm felt affection for 'the old British Empire, run by a country whose modest size protected it against megalomania'.[2] The writers Elias Cannetti and Arthur Koestler ended up in London, too, the latter bringing a striking manuscript denouncing the French capitulation ('The Scum of the Earth'). Some were not so lucky. The radical critic Walter Benjamin was caught by guards at the Spanish border and fearing the concentration camps took his own life. The New Left historian Perry Anderson thought that this white migration was a conservative influence on England, and that homebred intellectuals were put in the shade by these grand thinkers.[3] It would be truer to say, though, that the leftish attitudes of the British – and also the American – intelligentsia tended to give way to a patriotic outlook, albeit one that emphasized the popular character of the war, as those intellectuals began to work for the Allied cause.

The physicists Leo Szilard, Edward Teller and Albert Einstein all came to America from Germany and Hungary. The Frankfurt Institute of Social Research, with the social theorists Theodor Adorno, Max Horkheimer, Herbert Marcuse, Pollock, relocated to Los Angeles, where Bertolt Brecht re-named them the Hollywood Institute of Social Research. 'The lifestyle was formal, with servants', remembered Peter Marcuse,[4] and Brecht wrote a satirical novel 'the story of the Frankfurt Institute' in which 'a rich old man' the Horkheimer character:

> dies disturbed at the poverty in the world. In his will he leaves a large sum of money to set up an institute which will do research on the source of this poverty. Which is, of course, himself.[5]

Adorno and Horkheimer joined many German émigrés of the left, like the Marxists Karl Korsch, Henryk Grossmann and Paul Mattick (who had come earlier than most), and the Social Democratic Party lawyer and social theorist Franz Neumann, with his collaborator Otto Kircheimer. Brecht connected them with the world of literature, Thomas Mann, and of theatre and film, as he met up with the now-established director Fritz Lang, Peter Lorre, who had come from Hungary, and with artists like Georg Grosz. These all grated against one another in the hothouse world of exile politics.

The exiles argued over just what had happened in Germany to let Hitler into power. Adorno, Horkheimer and Pollock worked up a theory that industrial society was bound to lead to dictatorship, as the domination of nature would carry over into the domination of man, showcased in Horkheimer's lectures, collected as *The Eclipse of Reason*, and then later in the influential sociology text *Dialectic of Enlightenment*. Hannah Arendt who came to America in 1941thought along similar lines, as she argued in her book *The Origins of Totalitarianism* (1951). In their own way, each of these theses were drawn from the anti-rational philosophy of Martin Heidegger, except that where he had seen Fordist America and the USSR as the twin exemplars of what he called 'the endless etcetera of indifference', Arendt, Adorno and Horkheimer tweaked the argument and said that, no, it was Nazi Germany that fulfilled the programme of totalitarianism. For Cold War propagandists the identification of

Communism and Fascism under the same label, 'totalitarian' was a great advantage, and a stick to beat off those left-wingers who argued that Fascism arose out of capitalism. Not all of the German exiles were convinced by the totalitarianism thesis. Brecht, pointing to the collapsing Hitler regime, asked Adorno 'what will now become of their economist Pollock, who was expecting a century of Fascism'? Like Brecht, Franz Neumann saw the inner workings of the Nazi state as a terrible mess, not highly rationalised as Adorno and Horkheimer claimed. His thoroughly documented book *Behemoth* (1942) was in danger of overtaking their more speculative theory of the 'totally integrated' and administered society, so they did their best to make sure that it was the official Institute line that won the day. Though *Dialectic of Enlightenment* was heavily promoted in western Sociology departments into the 1980s, today most historians accept that Neumann's was by far the better analysis.[6]

Many of these German exiles took on the cause of their adopted countries and worked to overthrow Fascism from abroad, through the agency of the Allied powers, Britain and America. Amongst the Frankfurt Institute's affiliates Lowenthal worked for the Office of War Information, Neumann, Marcuse and Kircheimer all worked for the Office of Strategic Services (OSS) – an overseas section of the Federal Bureau of Investigations that would later become the Central Intelligence Agency. Years later, when he was a famous radical, Marcuse would be taunted by yet-more-militant leftists who accused him of being a 'CIA stooge' on the basis of his work for the OSS. Those anti-Fascists who worked for the OSS did so in the belief that the American-led military occupation of Germany would be a positive force. Marcuse wrote handbooks on the (presumed) psychology of the Germans as guidance for Officers in Germany. Szilard, Teller and Einstein all contributed to the Manhattan Project that developed the Atomic bomb that was dropped on Hiroshima.

Though many intellectuals fled Germany, many more stayed and the Universities were recruiting grounds for the NSDAP. Scientists like Werner von Braun worked for the Nazi war effort, as did many chemists and engineers. The legal theorist Carl Schmitt did much to theorise the Fuehrer Principal with his doctrine of 'Decisionism'. The existentialist philosopher Martin Heidegger was an enthusiastic

Nazi, taking up the Rectorship of the Freiburg University. Heidegger's students publicly burned books in Freiburg the same week that he was appointed rector. Heidegger made Freiburg a model of Nazi pedagogy. Along with the Nazi salutes Heidegger instituted a 'scholarship camp' in the woods, during summer break, 'SA or SS service uniforms will be worn'.[7] Amongst the discussion topics was nazification of the university. While he was pulling on his jack boots, Heidegger's most promising student Hannah Arendt had fled first to France, where she narrowly avoided deportation back to Germany, and escaped instead to America and worked for the United Nations Relief and Rehabilitation Administration.

Japanese intellectuals were drawn to, and helped to draw up the Pan Asian appeal of the Greater Co-Prosperity Sphere. Think tanks like the Shōwa Research Association gave intellectuals an important role in the framing of Japan's imperial outlook. In June 1933 the leading communists Sano Manabu and Nabeyama Sadachika put out an Apostasy Declaration, where they denounced the Soviet Comintern and instead allied themselves with Japan's imperial mission. The statement framed Japan's cause in the language of militant Marxism, claiming that Japan's

> war with the Chinese nationalists, objectively speaking, has a very progressive meaning. Also under today's international conditions, if Japanese were to fight the United States, that war could turn from both countries' war of imperialism into Japan's war of national liberation.[8]

Many radicals followed their shift. The poet Nguchi Yonejiro defended the war in China to his Indian pen pal Rabindrath Tagore saying that Chiang Kai-shek was a US puppet. Tagore wrote back 'you are building your conception of an Asia that would be raised on a tower of skulls'.[9]

In Italy the idealist philosopher Benedetto Croce supported Mussolini at first but soon distanced himself from the regime. Giovanni Gentile, on the other hand, supported Mussolini throughout, and was called the 'philosopher of Fascism' by the dictator, even taking a government post in the rump republic of Salo. Gentile was killed by partisans in 1944. The Fascists also earned the admiration of the painter Filippo Tommaso Marinetti and his 'Futurist' painters, which included Giacomo Balla, organised as the Novecento Italiano and sponsored by art critic Margherita Sarfatti, who was close to Mussolini. In praising war Marinetti was as good as his word, serving in the Second Italo-Abyssinian War and on the eastern front against the Soviet Union in his late sixties.

American intellectuals also lent their services to the war effort. Many had already been recruited into government service under the Federal Art Project and the Public Works of Art Project, a cultural wing of the Works Progress Administration.[10] The left wing Mexican muralist Diego Rivera got work with the FPA, as did the Abstract Expressionists Ad Reinhardt and Jackson Pollock. Even the militant Marxist Paul Mattick got work writing an economic history of Illinois. As we have seen, the anthropologist Ruth Benedict did work for the Office of War Information analysing the 'Japanese character' and the sociologist Talcott Parsons helped with the psycho-social assessment of the German and Japanese people, preparatory for the post-war occupation.

In Britain many intellectuals made the passage from pacifists to supporters of the people's war. The British civil service went out of its way to recruit new talent during the war, and Secretary to the Labour Ministry Beryl Power accumulated a central register of 80 000 'New Men' to ginger up the gerontocracy.[11] Writers J.B. Priestly and George Orwell worked for the BBC, the latter broadcasting to India, when the censors let him. Orwell rounded on his fellow intellectuals for their lack of patriotism in his 1941 essay 'The Lion and the Unicorn':

> During the past twenty years the negative, fainéant outlook which has been fashionable among English left-wingers, the sniggering of the intellectuals at patriotism and physical courage, the persistent effort to chip away English morale and spread a hedonistic, what-do-I-get-out-of-it attitude to life, has done nothing but harm.

Despite his reaction against left wing critics of war, Orwell's dystopian *Nineteen Eighty-Four*, was a sharp exposure of the oppressive nature of War Socialism in England – right down to the naming of the BBC's own censor's office, room 101, as the regime's torture chamber.

Filmmaker Humphrey Jennings was typical of a certain attitude that the divisions between the intellectuals and the masses were breaking down. 'Some of the damage in London has been pretty heart-breaking', Jennings wrote to his wife in October 1940, 'but what an effect it has had on the people!'

> What warmth – what courage! What determination ... a curious kind of unselfishness is developing ... We have found ourselves on the right side and the right track at last!

It was a feeling that the once-radical poet Spender knew from his work in the Fire Brigade at Cricklewood, which 'fulfilled one of the aspirations which had been a cause of my joining the Communists.' But it was in the service of the British Empire, not World Communism that this needy poet would at last 'get to know the workers'. The psychology at play was not so different from the one that persuaded Martin Heidegger that in signing up for NSDAP he was joining a 'true community of the people'.[12]

British artists worked for the war effort with the support of the Council for the Encouragement of Music and the Arts, set up by J.M. Keynes, which sponsored plays and concerts bringing culture to working class audiences across the country. As the Council's bulletin was pleased to recount 'one of the first *missionary* tours of the Old Vic, by Lewis Casson and Sybil Thorndike, was in the Monmouth mining valleys and it was quickly followed by others in the South and North'.[13] More radical arts groups like the Unity Theatre and the Artists International Association moved from radical pacifism to enthusiastic support for the people's war – with the endorsement of critics like the anarchist Herbert Read and Anthony Blunt (though he was later 'exposed' as a Soviet spy, Blunt's Stalinist boiler-plate writings of the time make it hard to believe that his political affiliations were unknown to the authorities). The conservative critic Cyril Connolly was sceptical about the mission to take art to the people:

> We are becoming a nation of culture-diffusionists. Culture-diffusion is not art. We are not making a true art. The appreci-

ation of art has taken wings, we are at last getting a well-informed inquisitive public. But war-artists are not art, the Brains trust is not art, journalism in not art, the BBC is not art, all the CEMA shows, all the Army Bureau of Current Affairs lectures, all the discussion groups and MOI films and pamphlets will avail nothing if we deny independence, leisure and privacy to the artist himself. We are turning all our writers into commentators until one day there will be nothing left for them to comment on.[14]

Other leftists like the Communist James Klugmann and fellow traveller Basil Davidson took on intelligence work, as did philosopher A.J. Ayer and the future children's writer Roald Dahl, who, along with advertiser David Ogilvy spied on Washington. Ogilvy and sociologist Charles Madge developed the modern science of opinion polling which was used by the Ministry of Information. Analytical philosopher Ludwig Wittgenstein dutifully put higher thoughts aside to work as a dispensary porter at Guy's Hospital. Russian-born political philosopher Isaiah Berlin was First Secretary of the British Embassy in Washington when officials had to make the case for the Empire against American critics by saying that what it withheld in freedom, it more than made up for in welfare – the argument of the 'British Colonial Charter'. Years later Berlin finessed those ideas in his celebrated lecture Two Concept of Liberty (1958), which contrasted negative liberty, by which he meant 'freedom from' restraint, and positive liberty, 'freedom to' achieve goals, which might mean welfare provision. Berlin's biographer Michael Ignatieff explained: '"Two Concepts" was consciously crafted for an era of decolonisation, and its message towards colonial peoples demanding their liberty was highly sceptical' – an argument honed in Washington in the war.[15] Berlin's good work for the Empire earned no points from the anti-Semite Roald Dahl, who nicknamed him 'the white slug'.

In the Soviet Union the heroic days when artists like Aleksandr Rodchenko and Dziga Vertov travelled the country in 'agit-trains' showing constructivist art to the masses were long gone. The experiment of 'ProletCult', which elevated working class art with a violently philistine attack on 'bourgeois' culture had been judged excessive. Instead Soviet writers were drawn into 'Popular Front' work, like the 1934 Soviet Writers' Congress, where the aim was to win foreign intellectuals into sponsoring Soviet 'peace' campaigning. In the war the USSR's cultural life was harshly downgraded in favour of the war effort. Writers like Ilya Ehrenberg and Vassily Grossman were attached to the Red Army as war correspondents. Director Sergei Eisenstein's film Alexander Nevsky of 1938 had been dismissed, but was rehabilitated for its patriotic, anti-German story during the war. Eisenstein made the film Ivan the Terrible in1944 in which many saw parallels with the life of Stalin – flattering in the first part, but leading to suppression of the second. Composer Dmitri Shostakovich who was in Leningrad in the early months of the siege, wrote the first part of his Seventh Symphony there. The symphony caught a mood of pride in Soviet resistance against the Wehrmacht and won Shostakovich not only the Stalin Prize, but also honorary membership of the American Academy of Arts and Letters as well as his portrait, in a fireman's helmet, on the cover of *Time* magazine for 20 July 1942. On 9 August 1942, after the commander of the Soviet artillery carried out an intensive bombardment of German troops to ensure their silence, Leningrad's remaining musicians gathered to play the Seventh, which was relayed by loudspeaker to the people of Leningrad and their tormentors.[16]

Philosopher George Steiner tells this anecdote about the Hungarian Marxist Georg Lukacs, in Moscow during the war, expecting to be taken into custody by the secret police:

he was all packed, in Moscow, ready for when the knock would come on the door, and it came. And he said to his wife very calmly: "Es ist gekommen. It has come. Auf Wiedersehn." The car had drapes, a KGB car, and the airplane was blacked out, of course. He wondered to which camp they were taking him. He said to himself: "Interesting. They still treat me well enough to fly me to the Gador. It was still called Gador, not the Gulag. Then, enormous fences of barbed wire for miles and miles. He walks in, everyone salutes him, they say: 'You are Professor Lukacs. These are the captured German Generals from Stalingrad, the staff of von Paulus. You have been appointed to teach them German history and literature.' He said he almost fainted. He said proudly he was just able to hold on to the suitcase so as not to faint. An hour later he began with a lecture on Heine. In front of von Paulus and the two thousand captured German staff officers, his first lecture was on Heine.[17]

Lukacs, who still bore the scars of a bruising battle with official Communist orthodoxy in the 1920s was careful to toe the line throughout the war.

Collaboration in occupied Europe was an experience that many artists struggled with. The architect Le Corbusier, though, was an enthusiastic supporter of Petain's regime and was appointed to a commission on reconstruction work in 1941.[18] Corbusier worked with the Vichy authorities in Algiers to implement his Plan Obus. The great modernist's utopian projections could not escape the narrow basis of colonial domination. On the contrary, he identified the French mission civilisatrice with modernism:

> The Arab discovered his education, his instructor. He did not bat an eyelid of doubt. With two hands outsretched, leaving all his hopeless deceit behind, he loved, admired, understood the new times and respected France with all his conviction. Architecture and urbanism can be the great educator.[19]

Corbusier's idea was to restructure the North African capital with its higgledy-piggeldy native Casbah subordinated under a large whiplash motorway, and high rise flats. The whole plan was usefully colour-coded to show which populations, Muslims and Europeans, would live in which districts.

Though many French intellectuals collaborated with Vichy, many did not. Albert Camus was active in the Resistance and wrote for the journal Combat.

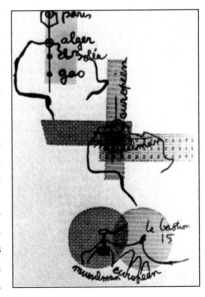

Jean-Paul Sartre worked for the Resistance though a long campaign of slander by the French Communist Party (PCF) sought to undermine his reputation. Claude Morgan, who had been the communist editor of the clandestine *Lettres Francaises* told John Gerassi:

> Sartre was a tremendous guy. He never looked for what could divide, only for what united us all. He was ready to do anything for the Resistance. He was the kind of guy that, once he had decided something, he would go all the way. He faithfully attended all our meetings. ... Most people really liked and everyone respected Sartre - except our chiefs, people like Aragon who kept telling me not to trust him: "Use him but don't trust him," he kept saying.[20]

Sartre himself was more modest. He said that he was a writer who resists, rather than a resistant who writes. He had been among the French troops captured by the Germans early in the war, who were later released. Sartre spent the time studying Heidegger (his guards were happy to give him a fine hardback copy of *Being and Time*) which was scoffed at by the orthodox communists. His real offence in their eyes, though, was that on his release back into France Sartre had been active in a Resistance group Socialism et Liberté he helped set up before the German invasion of the Soviet Union in June 1941. The PCF was only active in the Resistance after June 1941, because from that point they had joined the Allied war effort in line with Soviet policy. Sartre understood the basic limit of the PCF's struggle: 'they did not want power'.[21] Sartre's view was different. He saw the case for fighting against the occupation as an unambiguous call to moral action. In his novel trilogy *The Roads to Freedom* Sartre examined the burden of freedom and the many ways that Frenchmen and women avoided it, in the context of the occupation. His talk 'Is Existentialism a Humanism?' given at the Club Maintenant on 29 October 1945 insisted against all the bad excuses that 'Man is responsible for what he is'. It was at the same time a criticism of the economic determinism of the PCF and the evasions of the collaborators and quietists.

Resistant Hélène Rytmann, smeared as a collaborator by her own comrades in the French Communist Party

Like Sartre, the structuralist philosopher Althusser was also a prisoner of war. He rather liked the loss of liberty. His wife-to-be the sociologist Hélène Rytmann was very active in the Resistance, but that did not stop the PCF from slandering her as a collaborator, when she became too awkward.

Not all intellectuals embraced the war effort. In America the historian Charles Beard, who wrote the influential *Economic Interpretation of the Constitution* opposed the war throughout, and afterwards published a strident attack on Roosevelt's warmongering – though it damaged his career. As we have seen the radical writers Dwight McDonald, A.J. Muste, Irving Howe and CLR James all opposed the war. Folk America, like the communists Woody Guthrie and Paul Robeson, put its shoulder behind the Patriotic Front, while Be Bop floated coolly, disengaged above the conflict. Thelonius Monk's biographer Robin Kelley writes that 'very few black musicians were eager to leave the music scene to fight another white man's war.'[22]

In Britain, the composer Michael Tippet, who wrote the oratorio 'A Child of Our Time' about Herschel Grynszpan, was jailed as a conscientious objector during the war, while the painter Patrick Heron was sent to work in the mines. Novelist Julian Symons' claim to conscientious objection was turned down and he was sent off to fight. The most remarked upon refusals of the war effort were those of the poets W.H. Auden and novelist Christopher Isherwood. Known for their radicalism in the 1930s, both had reacted against the demands of engaged writing. The Marxist motifs of earlier gave way to Anglicanism in the former and Buddhism in the latter. Auden said that he was willing to be called up though that was not likely. Still, both were harshly criticised by Cyril Connolly in *Horizon* for leaving England, and, as we have seen, by Orwell. The accusation was charged because, as most people knew, the ocean liner to America was the rich person's 'evacuation' and widely seen as defeatism. One poet of that generation who worried about the justness of the British cause was Louis Macneice who wrote in his *Autumn Journal* of 1939

> And we who have been brought up to think of "Gallant Belgium"
> As so much blague
> Are now preparing again to essay good through evil
> For the sake of Prague;
> And we must, we suppose, become uncritical, vindictive,
> And must, in order to beat
> The enemy, model ourselves on the enemy,
> A howling radio for our paraclete.

In the event Macneice worked for the war effort at the BBC. Macneice joined Connolly and Stephen Spender writing for Horizon. After the war Spender worked for the British Administration in Germany, where he lauded the Marshall Plan and was rewarded with the editorship of the secretly CIA-funded magazine *Encounter*.[23] Not everyone who was sceptical about the war effort was radical. The Tory novelists Evelyn Waugh (in the Sword of Honour trilogy) and Anthony Powell mocked the seedier compromises and carreerism of the socialist war effort. Painter and novelist Wyndham Lewis parodied the leftish literary scene of the interwar, leading him to write a paean titled *Hitler* in 1931, and spend much of the war in Canada.

The war itself and all its aspects were interpreted artistically and philosophically in many different ways afterwards. The writers Pierre Boulle and J.G. Ballard both fictionalised the European experience of the Japanese invasion of South East Asia. Boulle, who had himself been sentenced to hard labour in the Mekong Delta, recounted the misery of the British prisoners of war of the Japanese in *The Bridge over the River Kwai*, 1952. In *Empire of the Sun* (1984) Ballard, tells the story of the British humiliation in Singapore through the eyes of a boy called Jim, who, like Ballard, is interned by the Japanese. Both authors told the story allegorically, too. Boulle's *Planet of the Apes* (1963) imagines a world where men are slaves to Apes. Allied propaganda of the time often characterised the Japanese as Apes, and the 'reveal' comes when the human visitors first see a hunting party of Apes on horseback. Ballard returned again and again to the image of an unexpected and overwhelming catastrophe, and its impact on human relations, in *The Drowned World* (1962), and *The Wind from Nowhere* (1961), for example. The artist Ronald Searle learnt his skills sketching life in a Japanese prisoner of war camp.

Thanks in part to the GI bill which gave grants to US ex-servicemen to go to college there are many excellent novels of the American experience of war, notably Joseph Heller's absurdist *Catch 22* (1961) which recounts the impossible bureaucracy and casual cruelty of life in the United States Air Force bombing Italy; Kurt Vonnegut's *Slaughterhouse Five* reworks some of the infantryman Vonnegut's life as a prisoner of war in Dresden, as science fiction; Norman Mailer's *The Naked and the Dead* (1948) tells the ordinary marines side of the Pacific War without shying away from the troops brutalisation or racial prejudices.

Frederick Hayek's seminars at the London School of Economics were a meeting place for liberal critics of statism and also logical positivists. Ernst Gombrich and the Austrian Karl Popper took part. Popper later went to New Zealand. In Austria he saw the rise of nationalism as evidence of the delusional power of metaphysical thinking. 'All nationalism or racialism is evil', Popper concluded. He thought the left added to the problem because their Marxism was the 'policy of using violence', which 'gave the police an excuse, in July 1927, to shoot down scores of peaceful and unarmed social democratic workers and bystanders in Vienna'. Popper, whose parents were Jews who had converted to Lutheranism also thought that the 'influx of Jews into the parties of the left contributed to the downfall of those parties' and that 'with so much latent popular anti-Semitism about, the best service which a good socialist could render to his party was not to try to play a role in it'.[24] Though he admired Britain's property relations, Popper was less impressed by popular sovereignty, thinking that 'democracy – even British democracy – was not an institution designed to fight totalitarianism'. In Hayek's seminars Popper read chapters of his later work, the *Poverty of Historicism*, which argues that utopian reform that aims to change society as a whole is doomed to failure. The argument is made more pointed in the two volume work *The Open Society and Its Enemies* where he identifies Hegelian idealism with Fascism ('nearly all the more important ideas of modern totalitarianism are inherited from Hegel') and also Marxism with Fascism, since the Marxists talked of class war and the Fascists waged it.[25]

Along similar lines, Frederick Hayek in his 1944 statement of the case for free markets against statism worried that 'few are ready to recognise that the rise of Fascism and Nazism was not a reaction against the socialist trends of the preceding period, but a necessary outcome of those tendencies'.[26] Hayek advised the Conservative party on their 1945 election campaign and on 4 June 1945 in an election broadcast Churchill argued that 'Socialism is inseparably woven with totalitarianism and the abject worship of the state', and that a Labour government 'would have to fall back on some form of Gestapo'. Not to be outdone in anti-German chauvinism, Labour's Hugh Dalton and Bessie Braddock warned against the Tories' adoption of 'fatal theories of decontrol for its own sake, nurtured by the German theorists recently landed in this country like Professor Friedrich August von Hayek'.[27]

While Logical Positivists saw Fascism incubating in idealism, the idealist R.G. Collingwood claimed that it was those 'realists' who destroyed political theory 'by denying the conception of a "common good," the fundamental idea of all social life, and insisting all "goods" were private'. For Collingwood it was those analytical philosophers who 'for all their profession of a purely scientific detachment from practical affairs, were the propagandists of a coming Fascism'.[28] That was over the top, and a sign that tarring one's opponents as Fascists sheds more heat than light. It would have been truer to say that the analytical philosophy moulded itself rather well to the pragmatic outlook of British policy makers, and then later Cold War liberalism that prevailed in Britain, America and Germany after the war. Collingwood died in 1943, so did not live to see that happen.

After the war

After the war, on July 23, 1945 Heidegger faced the university's denazification tribunal, established under French jurisdiction, whose attitude was 'on the whole, friendly' accepting, against the evidence that Heidegger had 'not been a Nazi since 1934'. One of the crucial components of Heidegger's defence before the denazification tribunal after the war was that, 'he was a secret opponent of National Socialism ever since the Röhm putsch'.[29] With Hannah Arendt's help, Heidegger argued that his philosophical critique of the 'universal rule of the will to power within history, now understood to rule the planet' was aimed at Fascism as well as democracy: 'Today everything stands in this historical reality, no matter whether it is called communism, or fascism, or world democracy.'[30] In this way Heidegger's trying to get out of his ties to the NSDAP led him to much the same ideas about the universal trend to totalitarianism as Arendt, as well as those being argued by Adorno and Horkheimer. Heidegger was 'not all that different from us' Adorno wrote to Heidegger in 1949; later Adorno covered up his intellectual debt to Heidegger when he turned on the master in his polemical book *The Jargon of Authenticity*.[31]

Analysing Heidegger's case to the denazification tribunal, Tom Rockmore, patiently shows that he was not really a critic of Fascism. Heidegger's 'turning away from really existent National Socialism', was really 'towards an ideal form of Nazism'.[32] As Rudiger Safranski rightly notes, Heidegger's objection to official Nazi policy came 'because he was outraged by its concessions to the old bourgeois forces'. Just as Röhm was making the demand for a Second Revolution, Heidegger looked forward to a 'second and more profound awakening'. Unimpressed with the University's exoneration, the French military authorities ordered the tribunal to think again. Ever the petit bourgeois, Heidegger was most concerned to save his library from expropriation and his pension. But Heidegger's books were not burned, and in 1947, his pension – unlike the wages owed Germany's wartime slave labourers – was restored. In March 1949 the tribunal ruled 'Fellow traveller. No punitive measures' and in 1951, his right to teach was restored.[33]

Adorno's Institute for Historical Research was relocated back to Frankfurt, with the help of a grant from US High Commissioner John McCloy and 'the benevolent approval of the Adenauer regime'. The earlier, Marxist terminology was set aside in favour of a more sweeping dismissal of modern society, as 'the sinister, integrated society of today... the open-air prison' where 'everything is one.' Those collaborators who hung onto the Marxist critique of capitalism, like Franz Neumann, Paul Mattick and Henryk Grossman were cold-shouldered. To Lukacs the Institute looked like the 'Grand Hotel Abyss', and many thought that Adorno and his remaining collaborators had become overwhelmed by the defeats the left suffered, raising them up into a great edifice that he and Horkheimer thought was intrinsic to the very character of the human condition. When the student activists of the sixties disrupted Adorno's classes, he called them 'Red Fascists' – while over on the other side of the Atlantic, his old colleague Herbert Marcuse embraced the student revolution.[34]

In the last months of the Third Reich two young men were drafted into military service: Heinrich Böll and Jurgen Habermas. Böll went on to write the Tin Drum about a boy who refuses to grow up to avoid the horrors and moral complicity of the war. Habermas went on to study his doctorate under the anti-war radical Wolfgang Abendroth. But Habermas, studying Lukacs, turned his back on the idea that the working class could be the agent of history, saying Lukacs's collective subject 'wouldn't work'.[35] It was an echo of Heidegger's rejection of Lukacs, that mass man 'is not something like a "universal subject" which a plurality of subjects have hovering above them'.[36] Like Böll, Habermas read the experience of Germany's bid for dominance as a case for modesty and self-limitation.

Chapter Thirty Two

Revising the History of the Second World War

War of the anniversaries

Just as the Second World War came to an end in Europe, the historical record was already open to argument. German Commander Admiral Doenitz ordered General Alfred Jodl to surrender to US military commander Dwight D. Eisenhower one day earlier than the surrender to the Soviets in the east, giving rise to two different 'Victory in Europe' (V.E.) Days, the eighth and ninth of May. Lauding the end of the war has proved to be a hot topic ever since.

On the sixtieth anniversary of the end of the war in Europe, a row blew up just before the Moscow commemorations. American President George Bush seemed to regret the end of the war, and the Russian victory over Fascism: 'For much of Eastern and Central Europe, victory brought the iron rule of another empire'; and this was 'one of the greatest wrongs of history'.[1] And yet the following day George Bush celebrated V.E. Day in Moscow as 'a moment where the world will recognise the great bravery and sacrifice the Russian people made in the defeat of Nazism'.[2] Against any doubters, President Putin insisted on the heroic meaning of V.E. Day, a 'victory of good over evil'. Also present were the German Chancellor, Gerhard Schroeder, French President Jacques Chirac and Japanese Prime Minister Junichiro Koizumi.

Events were also organised in Berlin, which organised a festival of democracy coinciding with the opening of the new Holocaust Museum. President Koehler said that Germany 'looked back with shame and horror' at the war and the holocaust of European Jewry in the Nazi Gas Chambers, conceding that it was impossible for Germany to 'draw a line under its history'. In France President Chirac laid a wreath at the tomb of the Unknown Soldier as jets flew by but in Britain veterans complained that the celebrations were too low key.[3]

The American President's doubts in Moscow echoed the

complaints from national leaders in the former Soviet bloc. In particular, the Baltic States, Lithuania and Estonia boycotted the Moscow Parade after President Putin refused them an apology for occupying them after the war. The Polish editor of *Politikaya*, Adam Kzreminski, objected to the myth of Soviet liberation of the eastern bloc in an article whose title resonated more widely: 'The Second World War is Still Being Fought'. 'The Second World War changed Europe completely, but to this day there is no single European version of it,' wrote Krzeminski, adding 'Time will tell if this clash of national myths will ultimately engender a common European view of the Second World War.'[4] As President Bush's intervention made clear, the dispute over the meaning of the Second World War runs wider than just Europe.

It was Bush's predecessor, President Bill Clinton who first joined the commemoration in Moscow, at the invitation of his Russian counterpart, President Boris Yeltsin on the fiftieth anniversary, though like Chancellor Kohl he did not review the military parade. The decision was criticised by die-hard Conservatives at the time - 'a serious blunder' according to the *National Review:* 'There is only one place the American President should be in Europe on V.E. Day, and that is London, where the British government plans its own commemoration'. 'Snubbing the heirs of Churchill to clink glasses with the heirs of Stalin is an act of truly Rooseveltian foolishness,' they concluded. [5] Britain was not wholly snubbed as John Major records, V.E. Day celebrations in 1995 began in St Paul's Cathedral 'attended by the largest number of world leaders to visit London since the Coronation in 1953', including US Vice President Al Gore. Major flew to Paris that night to attend a lunch with President Mitterand the following day, before going on to Berlin, for a commemorative event with Chancellor Kohl and Boris Yeltsin in Berlin, finally arriving in Moscow for the events there on 9 May.[6]

Previous V.E. Days were marked by open hostility to the formerly Soviet allies. The *New York Times* thought that the thirtieth anniversary of the Victory over Fascism in Moscow in 1975 was 'marked with a lavishly patriotic campaign that bears significant ideological overtones'.[7] Ten years earlier, the *Times* mocked the communist world's 'elaborate campaign to turn the 20th anniversary of Victory in Europe into "Hate West Germany Day"'. 'The Soviet managed anniversary campaign to focus international attention on the evils of Nazism is well along,' they regretted.[8] The previous year, President Lyndon Johnson used the twentieth anniversary of D-Day to berate France for sabotaging Nato.[9] Indeed the strains between former allies were so great that V.E. Day was in danger of being cancelled altogether. French President Giscard D'Estaing had promised as much in 1975, earning praise from West German President Walter Scheel: 'all the inhabitants of the German Federal Republic owe warm thanks to President Giscard D'Estaing for his decision not to commemorate further the defeat of Germany in 1945'.[10]

In 1985, the British Conservative government wanted to abandon the fortieth V.E. Day, Baroness Young explaining: 'any official British international celebration confined to wartime allies could appear at best nostalgic, and at worst anti-German, unbalanced and open to historical distortion by the Soviet Union.'[11] Prime Minister Thatcher, however, had underestimated the popular demand for marking wartime anniversaries - a popular demand that she had done most to crank up - and conceded four days later that 'we should have a national celebration'.[12]

On that day in 1985 Soviet President Mikhail Gorbachev was in Moscow, while US President Ronald Reagan was addressing the European parliament in Strasbourg on the need for his 'Star Wars' defence programme.[13] The speech was overshadowed, however, by an earlier Reagan gaffe, defending himself after being criticised for visiting Kolmeshohe, a German war cemetery at Bitburg, saying that the soldiers buried there 'were victims, just as surely as the victims in the concentration camps'.[14] Taking his bearings from the Cold War rehabilitation of Germany, Reagan was out of step with the growing anti-German sentiment that focussed upon that the Nazi record. The discovery that 49 of the Bitburg dead were from Hitler's Waffen SS shock troops galvanised Jewish and veteran protests.[15]

Though V.E. Day was becoming more problematic, Baroness Young's solution, if not adopted wholesale, was attractive, especially to Britain and the US. The implicit meaning of the British government's 1985 attempt to abandon V.E. Day was not just to save Germany's blushes, if at all, but also to write the Soviet Union out of the victory. What they had in mind was to downgrade V.E. Day in relation to another anniversary, 'D-Day', when American and British troops landed at Normandy, to begin the Western assault on Hitler's Europe, 6 June 1944. The fortieth anniversary of D-Day in 1984 was a grand affair for Britain, America and France, where Ronald Reagan lauded the liberation as well as paying homage to the role of the French resistance. Pointedly absent, of course, were the Germans and the Soviets. Indeed Helmut Kohl said at the time 'There's no reason for a German chancellor to celebrate when others are marking their victory in a battle in which tens of thousands of Germans were killed.'[16]

Even with the exclusion of Germany and Russia, the anniversary of the Normandy landing has sometimes turned into a big row. In 1964 Charles de Gaulle, wartime leader of the Free French, returned to the presidency in 1958, refused to attend, rhetorically asking his advisors 'you want me to go and attend *their* landing, when it was the prelude to a second occupation of the country?'[17] De Gaulle's boycott made it impossible for US President Lyndon Johnson or Prime Minister Harold Wilson to go either; their countries' respective wartime military commanders, Eisenhower and Montgomery, both withdrew. Even in 1984, France's President Mitterand made up for the snub to German Chancellor Kohl by inviting him to a joint commemoration of the First World War battle of Verdun, a better shrine to European cooperation, according to *Le Monde*.[18]

By 1995, Britain's insistent D-Day celebrations were beginning to sound a bit shrill: Special D-Day packs were sent to every school, street parties were arranged with instructions to fry spam fritters, a D-Day beer was brewed, all commissioned by the D-Day Awareness Campaign (run by Tory public relations man Tim Bell), to 'mobilise' the whole nation, said a hopeful John Major. Mobilising the nation behind D-Day, though, also put the veterans in the driving seat, and their demands for a more sombre occasion were immediately accepted, and the spam fritters left in their tins.[19] Meanwhile Chancellor Kohl wrote a memo to his officials about the fiftieth Normandy landing anniversary: 'we don't want to be invited', he wrote adding 'we say nothing else', underlining 'nothing' twice.[20]

By the sixtieth D-Day anniversary in 2004 though, all that had changed, and German Chancellor Gerhard Schroeder happily accepted an invitation from President Jacques Chirac to take part.

'Hugely symbolic,' the chancellor has said of his invitation. 'It means the Second World War is finally over.'[21] Relations between the US and its European allies, having been tested over another invasion, that of Iraq in 2003, were still awkward. The night before the Sixtieth D-Day anniversary, President Bush compared the struggle against Fascism to that against Islamist terrorism. But President Chirac was eager to play down differences, and unlike de Gaulle insisted France 'will never forget those men who made the supreme sacrifice to liberate our soil, our native land'.[22]

One might think that so singular an event as the Second World War ought to be hard fact, not disputed opinion. But as the official commemorations of its successive anniversaries shows, the conflict over the meaning of the Second World War began once the shooting stopped. Two broad trends stand out: first, the differences between Russia and the other allies, America, Britain and France about the post-war settlement made joint commemorations impossible, at least until the collapse of the Soviet Union in 1989, and awkward since; second, American (and British) attitudes to Germany have shifted, having dismissed an undue preoccupation with the Nazi past as 'Soviet propaganda', to themselves dwelling on it. During the Cold War, America rehabilitated the German authorities as junior partners, but when Germany became more powerful in its own right, Americans became more preoccupied with the history of German revanchism, as exemplified in the Nazi era - a change in sentiment that caught out Ronald Reagan at the Bitburg Cemetry. Britain, too, seemed to get a bigger taste for commemorations of victory over Germany, as the event itself receded, and perhaps as German industry outstripped Britain's.

Correspondingly, German attitudes to historical memory changed as the nation became more confident, and German leaders more willing to celebrate the end of the war as the defeat of fascism, than as the defeat of Germany. In that they were helped by a more forgiving attitude from France, as both nation's futures were bound up in the European Union. French discomfort at loss of great power status was perhaps evident in the withdrawal from the 1964 Normandy commemoration, and of all members of the western alliance, France has remained the most critical of the US 'hyperpuissance'. Still, diplomacy is a learning curve, and French Presidents are unlikely to voice their criticisms as loudly as de Gaulle.

V.E. Day was not the end of the Second World War. That came on 15 August 1945 when Japan surrendered, Victory over Japan Day, or V.J. Day. On the tenth anniversary of V.J. Day, American opinion-makers congratulated themselves on 'a remarkable political exper-iment': 'The United States, in a benevolent occupation, undertook to change the whole main currents of Japanese life and thought'.[23] By contrast, Korea's independence from Japan, was 'darkened by strife',[24] and Admiral Nimitz appealed to the nation to be vigilant against 'sneak attacks'.[25] Ten years later Robert Trumbull reported the citizens of a 'resurgent Japan' taking time out to visit an exhibition of 'mementoes of their country's deepest humiliation' in Tokyo.[26] Wartime military leader Masataka Iwata even praised the atomic bombs dropped on Hiroshima and Nagasaki for saving Japanese and American lives by bringing the war to a speedy end.[27] Iwata's view, though, was by no means the general one and the coincidence of the attacks on Hiroshima (6 August) and Nagasaki (9 August) with the surrender have added to the difficulties that the commemoration of V.J. Day represents for the victorious allies. On the 30th anniversary, 1975, it was Japan's new industrial challenge that captured the headlines, as British trade minister Peter Shore appealed to his countrymen to buy domestic goods, and to Japan to restrain exports.[28]

In 1994 the Smithsonian Institute got into trouble for organising an exhibition about the bomber Enola Gay which dropped the atomic bombs on Japan. The exhibition was condemned in a resolution of the Senate, following a campaign by veteran groups. 'If I didn't know better', one member of the internal panel the Smithsonian appointed to review the script fumed, 'I would leave the exhibit with the strong feeling that Americans are bloodthirsty, racist killers'.[29] As the fiftieth anniversary approached President Clinton insisted that 'the United States owed Japan no apology for dropping atomic bombs on Hiroshima and Nagasaki at the end of World War Two'.[30] British Prime Minister John Major declined to invite his Japanese counterpart to the V.J. Day celebrations, though Helmut Kohl was invited to the V.E. Day event two months earlier. The government explained that for V.E. Day 'the theme is reconcili-ation, a celebration of 50 years of peace in Europe and hope for the future', the V.J. Day commemorations 'will have quite a different theme'.[31] As the newspapers saw it: 'there is a huge difference in the way we are treating these once mortal enemies. Rightly so'. Unlike Germany, which 'has done its best to atone' for the war, Japan 'shamefully...has still not found the honour or the honesty to confront its barbaric past'.[32] In 2006 Japanese representatives were once again not invited to the British commemorations at the cenotaph, while only one in fifty British schoolchildren knew what V.J. Day meant.[33] US President George Bush told servicemen and veterans at the Naval Air Station, San Diego that the fight against Japan in the war was the same as the war against Islamist terrorism today: 'Once again, we face determined enemies who follow a ruthless ideology that despises everything America stands for'.[34]

At times it seems that the battle of the anniversaries tells us more about the trajectory of society since the Second World War than it does about the war itself. The striking thing is just how important the war is to the present-day national identities of so many countries. Historian Tony Judt says that 'The Soviet Party-State acquired a new foundation myth: The Great Patriotic War'.[35] More tellingly, Nina Tumarkin explains that the Soviet cult of the Great Patriotic War got more intense years later: Victory Day was made a regular holiday as late as 1965, when ostentatious commemoration started to become part of the Soviet State's appeal to its citizens' loyalty.[36] But then is it not also true that other nations derived renewed authority from their role in the war? For the US the war consolidated Roosevelt's New Deal and established the nation as the custodian of world security; Britain was transformed from laissez faire imperialists to welfare state and head of the Commonwealth; more remarkably (West) Germany was reconstituted as Civil Polity, Japan got its pacifist constitution, Austria became a neutral state - all countries that needed to draw on the post-war settlement to lay out a plausible identity; those countries whose political institutions were compromised, like France, Italy and Yugoslavia drew upon the record of partisan resistance as an alternative source of national pride.

Even the preoccupation with anniversaries itself is something that has got bigger the further we are from the event. People tended to play down the war in the 1950s as they struggled to rebuild their lives. That was especially true of the citizens of the former Axis powers, for whom the past was a source of shame. But that was true, too, of occupied Europe. Even in the victorious nations, the business of reconstruction, and the emerging Cold War kept attention on the present. Oddly, the further from the event the greater weight the historical commemorations of the Second World War seemed to carry. In Britain, America and the USSR, honouring the wartime sacrifice carried a small-c conservative message of obedience to elders that was attractive to authorities, and the message 'people fought to make you free' has been used against radical upstarts ever since. In Germany, reflection on the past had the opposite impact, uncovering the 'collective amnesia' of which the younger generation accused the older. The politicisation of historical memory under-scores the growing interest in wartime anniversaries.

The Official History of the Second World War

From the moment the war ended official efforts to establish the proper and definitive history of the Second World War have been underway. There are official histories of the Second World War published by the governments of America, Britain, the Soviet Union, Australia and New Zealand. The United States of America's Office of the Chief of Army History issued more than 45 publications on the war, under the editorship of Kent Greenfield, the historical office of the air force published seven volumes, and the Navy historical programme produced fourteen volumes. The British history is subdi-vided into military (36 volumes) and civil (29 volumes), foreign policy (5 volumes), intelligence (5 volumes) with many more on medicine, the Royal Air Force and the Special Operations Executive. The first volume was published in 1949, the latest in 2004. The Australian history is 22 volumes, written between 1952 and 1977, the New Zealand history alone runs into fifty volumes. The Chronicle of the Netherlands in the Second World War is 25 Volumes. The Soviet official history is a relatively modest six volumes.[37]

On top of the official histories are the memoirs by leading partic-ipants, Winston Churchill (1948-53), the Roosevelt-Hopkins papers, edited by Robert Sherwin (1948), Cordell Hull (1948), Eisenhower (1948), Erwin Rommel (1950), Montgomery (1949), de Gaulle, Harold Macmillan; the Nazis Goebbels (posthumously, 1948), Schacht (1955) and Speer (1970) all wrote memoirs, which, mostly served to illustrate the wickedness of the Nazis, reinforcing the official version; Stalin discouraged memoirs, saying 'it is still too early',[38] but after his death Marshal Georgii Zhukov (1971) and many others published. As well as the important characters, scores, if not hundreds of lesser figures, like British junior minister Harold Nicholson (1968) and Soviet propagandist Ilya Ehrenberg (1964).

The first draft of history, we can say, is something like the official version, in which the heroism of the allied armies defeats an opponent militarily worthy, but territorially aggrandising, and cruel. The official version tended to restrict the war to its explicitly military dimension, downgrading the civil mobilisation to a strictly supporting role, which is to say insisting on the authorities' monopoly over the conflict. In that way credit for the victory was due to constituted authority in the Allied governments. Similarly, the War Crimes Tribunal and denazification process was restricted for the most part to political leaders, though a vaguer concept of collective guilt was left to hang over the German and Japanese people. It was a view of the war that allowed reconstruction to take place in collaboration with compromised civic leaders in the Axis countries, though it would later be denounced as a cover up. Differences between the Allies are there in the official version but there is in broad terms unanimity over what happened.

Few people today, though, would recognise the official version of 1939-1945 as the definitive account of the Second World War. Today we are surprised that atrocities against the Jews barely featured in the case against Nazi Germany, indeed evidence of them was deliberately played down in official propaganda.[39] People today would be surprised to learn that much of the war in the Far East and North Africa was fought to restore Colonial overlords who had been overthrown. They would struggle to understand that Britain and America both maintained diplomatic relations with Fascist Spain throughout the war and after, and that the US kept its Embassy in Vichy France until April 1942. And today's students of the Second World War are often bemused that the forward march of the Red Army across Eastern Europe was celebrated in Britain and America. We are surprised to learn, in fact, that the war was primarily a war against Germany, and against Japan, not a war against Fascism, a national war, not an ideological one.

The People's War

The most enduring and influential explanation of the Second World War is the one that calls it The People's War. This is the first propagandistic account of the war, and one that was set out during the war itself. According to the People's War thesis, the Allies, Britain, America, and the Soviet Union fought not for national advantage, but for all the peoples of Europe and the Far East, to liberate them from Fascism. The compelling part of the argument lies in the difference between the political structures of the Axis Powers, Germany, Italy and Japan and those of the Allies. Germany and Italy were Fascist dictatorships before the war, Japan ruled by militarists;[40] by contrast the Allies Britain and the United States of America retained parliamentary structures of accountability (and the Soviet Union's claim to be a higher form of democracy was taken more seriously then than it is now). More importantly, the Allies victory led to the restoration of constituent assemblies in the liberated countries of Western Europe, 'People's Democracies' in the east and to the eventual recreation of democratic structures in the occupied Axis countries themselves.

But the British government did not go to war in 1939 to fight fascism. Neville Chamberlain Prime Minister (May 1937-May 1940) had tried to avoid war, but concluded reluctantly that Germany's invasion of Poland threatened British prestige and interests. Radical opinion was unsure at first, but then embraced the national struggle. In doing so, Labour leaders and popular commentators like George Orwell and J.B. Priestley, radicals in the Ministry of Information and the Army Bureau of Current Affairs, imbued the war effort with the character of a People's War. They lent the struggle the character of a social revolution, demanding equality of sacrifice during the war and committing the country to great reforms in the peace to come. Mostly, the government tolerated this radical spin on the war effort as the price of unity. 'Let us go forward, together', was Prime Minster Churchill's slogan.

Soon after Germany invaded Soviet territory on 22 June 1941 Stalin wrote that 'the Soviet Union and Great Britain have become fighting allies in the struggle against Hitlerite Germany'. [41] Asking

Churchill to open a 'Second Front' against Germany in Western Europe Stalin posed the war aims as liberation: ' One should not forget that it is a question of saving millions of lives in the occupied territories of Western Europe and Russia'.[42] That also meant that communist parties across the world reversed their prior opposition to the war to support the Allies. Labour leaders, colonial nationalist leaders, intellectuals, and trade unionists - those who were communist supporters - became proponents of the People's War. Communist ideologue Rajani Palme Dutt lauded an alliance of 'Conservatives, Liberals, Labour, Communists and non-party, who are all united in the common liberation struggle in the cause of national independence and human culture against fascist barbarism'.[43]

America's entry into the war was more gradual, between supporting Britain through the 'Destroyers for Bases' agreement of 2 September 1940 to the formal declaration of war made against it by Germany and Italy on 11 December following the Japanese attack on the US port in Hawaii, Pearl Harbor. Still, President Roosevelt lent the war effort a populist bent in the Atlantic Charter of 12 August 1941, whose sixth clause read: 'after the final destruction of the Nazi tyranny they [America and Britain] hope to see established a peace which will afford to all nations the means of dwelling in safety within their own boundaries, and which will afford assurance that all men in all the lands may live out their lives in freedom from fear and want'.

The 'People's War' is an enduring account, but an ideological one, nonetheless. The persistence of the idea of the People's War is due to the persistence of the institutions that the war itself created. National goverments that participated in the Allied cause have an interest in holding onto the idea that the war was a just war and a popular one. Their prestige is closely tied to their status as victors in the war. The five permanent seats on the United Nations Security Council are still held by the five who fought on the allied side: The United States, Russia (in lieu of the Soviet Union), Britain, France (in lieu of the 'Free French') and China. For half a century the ill-named 'People's Democracies' of Eastern Europe claimed descent from the opposition to Nazi Germany to shore up their own limited legitimacy. Even the governments ruling in the territories of the defeated powers, like Germany and Japan derive their authority from their reconstruction under the sponsoring powers, and so have reinforced the idea that the Allies liberated these countries from their own bad leadership. Not just governments, but political parties, and other civil organisations, draw authority from their argued contribution to the 'People's War'. The socialist and communist parties in Europe all derive their authority from their wartime role as supporters of the Grand Alliance. So too do parties of the centre right, the Christian Democrats in Germany, and Italy, de Gaulle's *Union des Démocrates pour la République,* right through to Silvio Berlusconi's *Forza Italia* lay claim to the legend of opposition to Fascism.[44]

The Second World War and the problem of Historical Revisionism

The official version of the history of the Second World War, and the more politicised 'People's War' legend are profoundly ideological. They are in fact examples of 'Victor's History' – as the Nuremberg and Tokyo War Trials were 'Victor's Justice'. They are ideological because they focus all criticism upon the Axis powers, and suspend judgment on the Allies. In these official versions of the Just War and the People's War, the deaths of millions are justified for the greater good of ridding the war of dictatorship and militarism – even though the outcome of the war was the imposition of militaristic dictatorships over much of eastern Europe, the stabilisation of Fascist dictatorships in Spain and Portugal, the subjugation of millions to military rule in East Asia, and indeed in Germany. In the official version of history the atrocities carried out by the Axis powers come to be the emblematic features of the war, while those carried out by the Allies are dismissed as exceptional episodes, or even justified as the cruelties necessary to bring the war to a speedy conclusion. In the official version only the Axis powers have self-serving interests, while the Allies are motivated by moral exigencies. Racial suprematism and imperialist domination are faults that are never seen in the Allies.

The official version of the Allied War effort is so profoundly ideological that it violently misrepresents almost all aspects of the war. The official version is twisted and stretched to give the most extraordinary explanations of events that are would be quite easy to account for without it. To believe the official version, one must believe that the Atomic bomb saves lives; that the aerial bombardment of Germany was aimed at military targets; that the Nazis killed the Polish officers at Katyn though it was under Soviet rule at the time; that the Allies fought the war to save the Jews; that the Allied invasions of Iraq, Iran, Syria, Poland, Czechoslovakia, Greece, Vietnam, Korea and Indonesia were 'liberations'. The truth creaks and strains under the constraints of the official version of the Second World War, and will keep breaking out, as evidence that there is more than is accounted for in the set texts.

Historians who want to make an impact are drawn to highlight different episodes and events that do not fit the mainstream account. Historians have discovered the truth about aerial bombardment (Jorg Friedrich, and before him, to everyone's dismany, David Irving), about nuclear diplomacy (Gar Alperovitz), about ELAS and the struggle for freedom in Greece (Mark Mazower, and before him Dominque Eudes), about the Indian National Army (Joyce Lebra), about the deportation of Russian prisoners back to the Soviet Union (Nikolai Tolstoy) about the racial prejudices of the war leaders (Andrew Roberts) about the detentions of Japanese in California (Allan Bosworth), and of anti-Nazi Germans on the Isle of Wight (Peter and Leni Gillman). In all of these cases, the public impact of the revelations is heightened because they are unexpected, provoking angry responses from officials, participants and mainstream historians, whose reputations rest on the official version. Though historians engaged in different revisionist accounts have many and varied motives, it should be understood that one thing that drives this constant revision of the historical record is the mismatch between the official version and the truth.

The other main driver of historical revision is the collapse of the post-war settlement that underscored the official version. In one respect, the post-war settlement was immediately re-written, and that is that the western Allies and the Soviet Union fell out. America's policy of rehabilitating the Federal Republic of Germany and Japan as allies in the Cold War led to conflict with the the USSR. So it was that in the 1950s that Soviet commentators and historians emphasized Germany's and Japan's culpability for the war, while mainstream American opinion began to minimise it. From the 1970s, with the rise of Germany and Japan as economic powers, and then again in the 1990s, as the Cold War came to an end and Germany was reunited, attitudes in Washington and London changed. Greater distrust of Germany and Japan made a more receptive audience for histories that emphasized their culpability for the war, the 'collective guilt' of the German and Japanese people, and a greater interest in specific atrocities for which Germany and Japan were responsible.

The end of the Cold War, then, at first brought out a more strident reassertion of the official version of the history of the Second World War. But precisely because it was more strident, and more obviously propagandistic, this re-emphasis only tended to raise more questions. The post-cold war history became a battle of the books, with outraged participants appalled that what they thought of as the established facts opened up for questioning.

Revisionists of the Far Right and 'Holocaust Denial'

The most reported revisionists of the official historical record are those who are motivated by a Far Right political outlook – Neo-Nazis and apologists of the Fascist regimes. Among them, the British historian David Irving is the best known. Drawn to the British Union of Fascists when he was a student in the 1950s, Irving left England to research the Allied bombing campaign, which he wrote up as *The Destruction of Dresden* in 1963, a book that did well critically and in sales, and though it did inflate the numbers killed in the German city it was the first book, post-war to tell the story. It was Irving's knowledge of Nazi source material that persuaded him that the 'Hitler Diaries' were a forgery, which he pointed out to the great embarrassment of historian Hugh Trevor-Roper, who had authenticated them for the *Times* newspaper. Though a talented military historian, Irving's understanding of political events is clouded by anti-Semitism and ostentatious consipiracy theories. Later works, such as *Hitler's War* (in which Hitler is painted as ignorant of the Jewish extermination policy), the *Trail of the Fox* (a biography of Rommel) and Churchill's War were more obviously written with the purpose of making the case for the German war effort, against Britain's.

From the mid-1980s David Irving gave speeches and wrote articles that sought to minimise or deny altogether the extermination of Jews by Germany in the Second World War. Irving, who was already biased in favour of the NSDAP by his political views, abandoned any pretension to historical accuracy and peddled overwrought conspiracy theories to justify his case. He was joining a small band of 'Holocaust Deniers' who had been writing small-print run books for their own select audience of far right readers. Apart from Irving, none of the holocaust deniers ever had much of a reputation as historians. Computer scientist Arthur Butz published *The Hoax of the Twentieth Century* in 1976. Others were drawn to holocaust denial for perverse reasons. Harry Elmer Barnes already had a reputation as an historian and was opposed to the Second World War, but became more aggressively pro-Hitler as he was more isolated, and argued that the holocaust was made up in his self-published 1953 book *Perpetual War for Perpetual Peace*. Paul Rassinier had been sent to a concentration camp, where, as a socialist, he clashed with communists, and in bitterness at the experience dismissed the evidence of the 'Final Solution' as communist propaganda in *The Lie of Ulysses* (1951). Roger Garaudy was disillusioned with the Parti Communiste Français after the invasion of Czechoslovakia and converted to Islam, which he gave a pointedly political slant. Garaudy's *The Founding Myths of Modern Israel* (1996) claims that the evidence of the Holocaust was fabricated.

The revisionist 'historians' of the Far Right are a God-send to the defenders of the official version of the history of the Second World War. These right-wing Holocaust deniers are mostly eccentrics with unattractive opinions, motivated by anti-Semitism, with laughable conspiracy theories to account for the unavoidable evidence of the 'Final Solution'. As long as historical revisionism can be characterised as Far Right Holocaust denial, then the official version is safe. Targeting the Holocaust Deniers, the custodians of the official version of the Second World War paint all attempts at new historical research as a moral outrage, and a threat to the supposedly precarious, postwar civilisation. According Holocaust denial much greater influence than it has, both Germany and France have laws *forbidding* it. Seemingly unmoved by, or simply ignorant of, the problems of making laws against 'thought-crimes' the French courts fined Garaudy and the Austrian authorities even went so far as to imprison David Irving in 2005, giving his claims a much greater impact than he could have achieved any other way. In 1996 Deborah Lipstadt accused Irving of *Denying the Holocaust* in her book of that name, and he sued, on the grounds that there was nothing to deny. Having asked the courts to adjudicate on the matter, Irving is responsible for the uncomfortable position of historical fact being decided by judges. All the same, those historians and lawyers who prepared the briefs against Irving were only too pleased to see the question of the Holocaust removed from historical investigation and made a matter of law. The ostentatious campaign to suppress Holocaust Denial is needlessly defensive. The historical record is safe. The weight of evidence is in no danger of being overturned. The people are quite capable of making their own judgements. The fear that Holocaust Denial will gain any credence is not based on its appeal, but rather on the fears of the defenders of the official version that the great mass of people will embrace Fascism and anti-Semitism at the first opportunity. Most of all, though, the petty persecution of this small band of eccentrics serves as a warning against counter-intuitive research questions, criminalising the re-examination of historical evidence as 'revisionism', or 'denial'. Those who raise awkward questions, as Norman Davies did about Poland, or Norman Finkelstein did about the Israeli use of the history of the Holocaust, risk being accused of 'revisionism', and tarred with the same brush as Irving and Co.

The Meaning of the Holocaust

One reason that eccentrics and conspiracy theorists have been tempted to try to deny that there was a policy of exterminating Jews is that the Holocaust has come to play a defining role in mainstream ideology. Certainly the Holocaust as a motif in political and moral debate has come to play a much greater role. Understandably the Holocaust is important to Israeli leaders and teachers, though in fact Jewish groups tended to play down the Holocaust in the first twenty years after the war.

One anniversary that was not on the official programme for many decades was that of the liberation of the camps. On 17 April 1955, five hundred Jews gathered to remember the anniversary of their liberation from Belsen concentration camp.[45] On the twentieth anniversary, 5000 Germans heard President Heinrich Lubke say that

Germans 'must cleanse themselves of the past', while Jews held a separate commemoration, afterwards.[46] Two thousand and five hundred American Jews also held services in New York to honour victims of the Nazis in the Warsaw Ghetto.[47]

It was only after the 1967 'Six Day war' between Israel and her neighbouring Arab states that the need to redeem the suffering of the Holocaust became a defining theme in Israel's international appeals. Before 1967 the Holocaust was memorialised mostly by left-wing activists and communists. Jewish groups in America had advised that it was unwise to make an issue out of the six million, because that would smack of mixed loyalties, but after 1967 that changed.

In 1975, the New York commemoration had swelled to 5000.[48] Almost 100 million Americans watched NBC's 1978 four-part, 9 ½ hour miniseries Holocaust, 'its answer to ABC's enormously successful Roots'. The Anti-Defamation League distributed ten million copies of its sixteen page tabloid The Record to promote the drama. Jewish organisations worked with the National Council of Churches to promote the drama. The day the series began was designated 'Holocaust Sunday'. The National Conference of Christians and Jews distributed yellow stars to be worn on that day.[49]

In May 1998 the American, British and Swedish governments established the Task Force for International Cooperation on Holocaust Education, Remembrance and Research. They were joined later by Germany, Israel, Poland, the Netherlands, France and Italy. In 2000 British Prime Minister Tony Blair announced the establishment of Holocaust Memorial Day and in 2005 the United Nations designated 27 January as International Holocaust Memorial Day. On the sixtieth anniversary of the liberation of Auschwitz, Israel President Moshe Katsav told heads of state from Europe and North America not only that 'the Germans conducted a genocide industry, a killing factory for the murder of our people', but also that 'the world knew about the destruction of the European Jewry, but remained silent.' Holocaust remembrance passed from a private affair among Jews to an officially recognised expression of guilt that embraced not just Germans but everyone.

Soon after the Washington Holocaust Memorial Museum was opened journalist John Farrell wrote a column asking 'Why do they come?' His answer was that the Holocaust was something like a foundation for modern morality:

> In an era of moral relativity, the Holocaust museum serves as a lodestone. Here there is no rationalisation ... Here is an absolute. And in that absolute of Evil, maybe, the prospect of an absolute Good ... Americans flocking to the Holocaust museum are searching for answers - in the form of moral certainties ...The Holocaust museum offers a basic moral foundation on which to build: a negative surety from which to begin.[50]

But even as the Holocaust is isolated as the one absolute truth in a world of confusion, the meaning of the 'Final Solution' is widely contested. First, the relative importance of the Holocaust in the assessment of the Second World War has increased as time passes. British Prime Minister Tony Blair, interviewed by historian Tristram Hunt on the Sixtieth anniversary of D-Day was trying to rally support for his the invasion of Iraq when he made this argument:

> You go back in the Thirties to the start of the persecution of the Jewish people, the murders and the wholesale plundering of their wealth, and you think well these things were there in 1935, 1934 even and it was only in 1939 they got round to doing something... [they said] this has got to be stopped. (*Observer,* June 6, 2004)

However, Blair's account is a retrospective reconstruction of the Allies' war motives. At the time, the persecution of German Jewry played no part in the decision to go to war, and the specifically Jewish dimension of the Holocaust was played down by the allies even after the camps were opened. The elevation of the extermination of the Jews to the defining atrocity of the Second World War was by no means immediate, but emerged in a complicated interaction between a growing awareness of issues of racial justice, the work of Jewish advocacy groups and US diplomacy towards Europe and the Middle East.

The Holocaust has become a defining issue in contemporary morality, the one incontestable wickedness in an age that struggles to define the boundaries of right and wrong. But it is precisely the ideological weight that is put upon this defining event that distorts historical scholarship. While all are vigilant for any sign of holocaust revisionism, few understand that isolating the Final Solution from the wider conflict that was taking place could itself be a kind of revisionism. But to those who tried to keep the Holocaust within an ethical framework, it appeared that any attempt to explain what happened, to look for any wider cause, was to risk explaining away the personal culpability of its perpetrators.

Commemorating the Holocaust takes us out of historical research into public policy, but at the same time the mood created by the commemorations will tend to inform the research. Here, the singularity of the Nazis' Final Solution for the Jews creates an unfortunate hierarchy of suffering. In 1979 US President Jimmy Carter's Commission on the Holocaust got bogged down in an unseemly debate with the Simon Wiesenthal Centre after Polish and Ukrainian-American lobbies persuaded him that they should be included in Hitler's 'eleven million' victims.[51] This kind of dispute is aggravated by the growing movement to exact reparations from governments and from businesses that profited from the Holocaust, of which the $20 billion dollar class action filed against Swiss Banks in a New York Court is an example.[52]

The politicisation of the history of the Holocaust is extensive, informing the building of Holocaust Museum in Washington (1993) and the memorial in Berlin (2005) as well as the inauguration of the Holocaust Day and laws against Holocaust denial. The impact of the great weight of moral expectation upon historical enquiry is marked. Amazon lists more than 52 000 titles with the word Holocaust, New York Public Library more than 10 000 and the British library 5 870.[53] It is pointed that of all the many atrocities committed in the Second World War, the campaign of extermination against Europe's Jews has been singled out as the exemplar of all suffering. Of course, there is something unique about the Holocaust, its single-mindedness, industrial scale and the grotesque culmination of eugenic policy. But the current reduction of all suffering in the war to the suffering of European Jewry is itself a misrepresentation of what took place.

The Wickedness of the German People

The practicalities of the rehabilitation of Germany as a NATO ally meant an end to denazification in the West. If punishing the Nazis was put on hold that did not mean that restitution to the victims was abandoned. On the contrary: The German Federal Republic paid 100 billion deutschmarks in restitution to victims of the Nazis under the Luxemburg agreement of 1952, and Germany today continues to pay around 1.2 billion each year to around 100 000 surviving pensioners, living in Israel, Germany and elsewhere. Germany also paid 3 billion DM directly to Israel, between 1952 and 1966. Since reunification Germany contributed 1.8 billion DM to restitution funds in Belarus, Poland, the Czech Republic, the Russian Federation and the Ukraine, out of which some compensation has been paid to former slave labourers.

In October 1945, eleven leading German Clergymen made the following declaration in Stuttgart, during a visit by foreign clergy: 'We are especially thankful for this visit, since we realize that we are not only united with our people in a great company of suffering, but also in a solidarity of guilt.' The official position put by Konrad Adenauer is that Germany was liable for the wrongs the Nazis committed in the name of the German people. Since then critics have thought this formula an evasion of the collective guilt of the Germans. Younger, radical Germans criticised their parents' generation for complicity in the holocaust, as did the Red Army Faction terrorists Gudrun Ensslin and Ulrike Meinhof, for whom West Germany was heir to Nazi Germany.[54] Anna Rosmus, whose local history project exposing the Nazi ties of her home town, *Resistance and Persecution — The Case of Passau 1933-1939* (1983) was made into a film, ironically titled *The Nasty Girl*, by Michael Verhoeven in 1990.

Amongst historians Fritz Fischer disturbed the conventional view that Fascism was an exceptional period in Germany's history, by publishing *Germany's Aims in the First World War* in 1961. Though the subject was the *First* World War, the argument was that Germany was not a victim, but the perpetrator, having planned the annexation of Belgium. The meaning, drawn out in later books, like *Hitler Was No Chance Accident* (1992), was that there was continuity in German foreign policy that was expansionist. Fischer revived the idea that Germany had a 'Special Way', argued by conservative historians in the nineteenth century, except that as Fischer told it, Germany was uniquely vicious, rather than uniquely blessed.

Just how radical the theory of 'collective guilt' truly was is open to question. It was, after all the Hitler regime itself that asserted a mythic national community and sought to implicate Germans in the crimes of Nazism; that ideology of common cause was inverted by the occupying powers to justify their presence. In practice, the allies in the western zone used former Nazis because of their familiarity with the machinery of the state; but politically, they let the Germans know that they were all to blame. For West German political leaders 'collective guilt' at least had the advantage of spreading the direct blame for the Holocaust more widely, and of inculcating an attitude of subservience and shame in the population. It was an attitude shared by their opposite numbers among the East German leadership, which shared a secret ambition to de-legitimate popular claims.[55] Though some leaders baulked at the implied loss of authority in the wider world and longed for a normalisation of Germany's record, the more canny understood that reparations and apologies were the way that the country re-established its diplomatic connections and even projected its interests. 'Restitution to Jewish victims became a cornerstone of the newly formed Federal Republic', explains Human Rights professor, Elazar Barkan: 'a moral obligation as well as a pragmatic policy that would facilitate the acceptance of Germany by the world community'.[56]

By the 1980s, with American power waning and the eastern bloc paralysed, the question whether Germany must always be on the defensive was raised. Historians Ernst Nolte and Joachim Fest put the argument that German national identity did not have to be problematic. Joachim Fest argued that the country's exaggerated pacifism was an unwarranted reaction to a past that it should not be so apologetic about, and in its own way left the country still prisoner of the Nazi experience.[57] Ernst Nolte tried to argue that the holocaust was an aberration in German history, a departure that owed its origins to the east, and to Bolshevism, rather than arising out of Germany's inner nature:

Did not the National Socialists, did not Hitler perhaps commit an 'Asiatic' deed only because they regarded themselves and those like them as potential or real victims of an 'Asiatic' deed? Was not the Gulag Archipelago more original than Auschwitz? Was not the 'class murder' of the Bolshevists the logical and factual *prius* of the racial murder of the National Socialists? [58]

This way Nolte shifted the blame for the 'Final Solution' onto the Soviet Union, and, in characterising the extermination as an 'Asiatic deed' appealed to ideas of racial superiority that the Nazis would have recognised. Fest and Nolte's attempts to recover an historical identity that Germans could be proud of stirred a big row in Germany, where more liberal historians were appalled. Beyond Germany's borders, too, the chattering classes latched onto what became known as the Historians' Debate as evidence of German revanchism, highlighting Nolte's evasive account of the holocaust.[59] The right-wing turn in German historiography, though was a case of the dog that did not bark. The end of the debate was not a strident reassertion of the German Way, but more of the guilty self-questioning that Fest reacted against. While the historians' debate was going on Martin Broszat made a plea for a less passionate approach to the history of the Fascist period in German history, which he called 'A plea for the historicization of National Socialism' (1985).

The belief that German people must be uniquely wicked, has gathered more support, as commemoration of the victims of the Holocaust has become more compelling with the passage of time. In his book *Hitler's Willing Executioners* (1996) the Harvard Professor Daniel Goldhagen argued that there was a culture of 'eliminationist anti-Semitism' deeply embedded in German society, of which fascism was just one expression.[60] Goldhagen's thesis was sharply criticised by many historians for its dogmatism, though the ensuing debate created more heat than light, tending to damage the reputations of all involved.[61] Though professional historians were disquieted, Goldhagen's arguments found a wider audience in the United States, but also in Germany itself, where *Hitler's Willing Executioners* topped the best sellers' lists and he was awarded the 1997 Democracy Prize.

Hostility to a perceived rise in German nationalism in other countries grew as Germany's economic and political power grew, most notably within the European Union. Fear of Germany's rise led to a more critical attitude towards German history. From 1972 to 1981 the Secretary General of the United Nations was one Kurt Waldheim. His American sponsors for the position overlooked Waldheim's military career in the Wehrmacht, and the CIA withheld information that Waldheim had been an intelligence officer in the Wehrmacht during the Balkan campaign. Then, in 1985, when Waldheim was running for the Austrian presidency, the World Jewish Congress uncovered his knowledge, as intelligence officer, of a massacre of Jews in Salonika. Though Waldheim was Austrian president, he was barred from entering the United States. Europeans were learning that the historical record that America had snapped shut in the early Cold War could be opened up when it helped put down a pushy rival power.

The collapse of the East German regime and the reunification of Germany provoked British fears. In 1990, the British Cabinet retired to Chequers for a weekend conference on the impending reunification of Germany.[62] Judging by the comments from leading participants, we can guess that the discussion was not a happy one. 'This is all a German racket designed to take over the whole of Europe' Minister Nicholas Ridley told the *Spectator:* 'You might just as well give it to Adolf Hitler, frankly.' (14 July 1990) Nor was Prime Minister Thatcher's judgment much more balanced: 'We've been through the war and we know perfectly well what the Germans are like, and what dictators can do, and how national character doesn't basically change'. On one occasion, Mrs Thatcher grabbed the (Communist dictator) General Jaruzelski 'by the buttons of my jacket and said to me very urgently, "We cannot allow German reunification! You have to protest against it very loudly!"'[63]

In 2002, after two German children were beaten up on a visit to Britain who taunted them as Nazis, the Ambassador Thomas Matussek asked what was being taught in British schools.[64] According to Gordon Marsden MP, head of an advisory group on history teaching the over-emphasis on the Third Reich risks a 'Hitlerisation of history'.[65]

The Origins of the Second World War

In 1961 AJP Taylor published his book *The Origins of the Second World War*, which caused quite an outcry. Taylor's account dismissed the argument of the historians Hugh Trevor Roper and Alan Bullock that Hitler had planned the war from long before his ascent to power. 'Much to my surprise *The Origins of the Second World War* proved to be the most controversial and provocative of all my books'. 'It did not occur to me that anyone would see in it an apology for Hitler or praise for appeasement'. In the 'Second Thoughts' published in the 1963 edition Taylor said 'I make no moral judgement of my own', but only 'to understand what happened and why it happened'.[66] Against the argument that an outline of Hitler's conquest could be found in his speeches, Taylor argued for some perspective:

> Hitler certainly directed his general to prepare for war. But so did the British, and for that matter every other government. It is the job of general staffs to prepare for war.[67]

Hugh Trevor-Roper was outraged, and characterised Taylor's argument 'Hitler was a statesman who merely sought to reassert Germany's "natural weight"', the war was 'not Hitler's fault'. Trevor-Roper saw any surrender of the doctrine that Hitler planned world conquest from the start as too great a concession to doubts about British imperialism. He replied sarcastically that *The Origins of the Second World War's* lesson for the 1950s is clear, caricaturing Taylor: 'Mr Khruschev, we should recognise, has no more ambitions of world conquest than Hitler' and that the proper response to his 'limited aims' is 'unilateral disarmament'.[68] Bullock answering Taylor summed up by saying that 'Hitler and the nation which followed him still bear, not the sole, but the primary responsibility for the war which began in 1939'.[69]

Power Politics

Replying to his critics, Taylor dodged the issue by defending one position he was arguing loudly, and the other only quietly. With some justice, looking back over the debate Taylor wrote 'everyone now agrees that Hitler had no clear-cut plans and instead was a supreme opportunist, taking advantages as they came'. More, Taylor wrote 'the *Origins*, despite its defects, has now become the new orthodoxy'. Taylor says Alan Bullock 'argued in the original version of his *Hitler* that Hitler planned every step towards war and knew exactly what he was doing', but 'when the book went into paperback Alan revised it, now asserting that Hitler had no idea what he was doing and moved from one expedient to another'.[70]

While Taylor laid claim to victory on the argument that Hitler had no blueprint for world domination, he was more guarded about the second argument in the book, which is a restatement of what in international relations theory is known as the 'realist' case. In the 1963 'Second Thoughts' Taylor wrote:

> I have never seen any sense in the question of war guilt or war innocence. In a world of sovereign states, each does the best it can for its own interests; and can be criticized at most for mistakes, not for crimes.[71]

Tim Mason objected to Taylor's argument that by seeing Germany as just another state whose 'foreign policies are determined' by 'raison d'état and the need to respond to international pressures', and because in Taylor's work 'international relations are portrayed as largely autonomous from other spheres of politics', he fails in his declared goal of identifying the causes of the Second World War by leaving out the main one. 'National Socialism was perhaps the profoundest cause of the Seconf World War, but Mr Taylor's book is not informed by any conception of the distinctive character and role of National Socialism in the history of twentieth-century Europe'.[72]

Replying to Mason, Taylor wrote

> He is suggesting, if I understand him aright, that without Hitler and the National Socialist party there would have been no German problem – no unrest, no disputed frontiers, no shadow of a new German domination over Europe.[73]

… a position which to Taylor makes no sense, because the cause of the war is not to be found in the personality of Hitler, or even in the special nature of Fascism, but in the unresolved balance between the Great Powers. On this argument, though, Taylor did not carry the day. Even the celebrated Marxist historian Eric Hobsbawm abandons all pretense to a social scientific analysis of the war, writing dismissively: 'the question of who or what caused the

Second World War can be answered in two words: Adolf Hitler'.[74]

Taylor was of course right to insist that Germany under National Socialism was not qualitatively more belligerent than the other Great Powers. It was not Fascism that led to war, but the unresolved inter-imperialist conflicts among them. Taylor quotes E.H. Carr to underline the point: 'Those who defend the status quo are as responsible for a war as those who attack it'.[75]

But also in 'Second Thoughts' Taylor made it clear that if he was criticising the Allies, it was for not standing up to Germany: 'It was perfectly obvious that Germany would seek to become a great power again; obvious after 1933 that her domination would be of a peculiarly barbaric sort'. In that case 'Why did the victors [of the First World War] not resist her?'[76] To that extent, Taylor was not really willing to stand apart from the case for the British war effort, and his attempts to argue a disinterested, scientific attitude to the causes of the Second World War could not be seen through to its conclusion.

Taylor was of course reaching back to an earlier analysis of international relations undertaken before the Second World War. In the aftermath of the Versailles settlement many people had tried to analyse its weaknesses. Taylor's objection to the 'War Guilt' attached to Germany after the Second World War echoes the many protests against the 'War Guilt' clause in the Versailles settlement, Article 231, which held Germany responsible for the First World War. Two authors in particular made the case against the Versailles Treaty and its blaming of Germany for a war that all the powers had fought: John Maynard Keynes and Edward Hallett Carr. Keynes' short book *The Economic Consequences of the Peace* (1919) which outlined the likely negative effects of reparations, warning that it could only help Lenin 'to destroy the capitalist system'. Keynes polemic against the 'Carthaginian Peace' did much to turn the American public against the Versailles settlement.

E. H. Carr, in his book *International Relations Since the Peace Treaties* (1937), could see that the post-First World War settlement was unstable, not just because of the war guilt clause, or the reparations, but because the buffer states that had been created at the end of the war, carved out of Prussia and the Austro-Hungarian Empire, were fundamentally weak. As Carr explained the end of 1936 saw the world 'divided into two groups, one led by Germany, Italy and Japan, the other by France and the Soviet Union'. But according to Carr 'the rival groups were linked not so much by a common political faith': 'The fundamental division was between those who were in the main satisfied with the existing international distribution of the world's goods and those who were not'.[77] More shockingly, Carr wrote that that 'the war-mongering of the dissatisfied Powers was the "natural, cynical reaction" to the sentimental and dishonest platitudinising of the satisfied Powers on the common interest in peace'.[78]

Carr and Keynes between them were analysts of international relations who wanted to move beyond the atavistic name-calling that characterised the Versailles peace. In their world people were not so naïve as to imagine that one person could start a war, or indeed that one country could. Instead their generation tried to understand the social processes that lay behind the war drive. Carr often talked as if the drive to war was inherent to the history of all nations, but really it is a special feature of capitalist societies, that necessarily take the political form of rival nation states. Keynes, even less willing to look into the abyss than the more cold-blooded Carr, only hoped that the rivalries could be managed by some financial wizardry. After the Second World War scholars fell backwards from the rational approaches of these scholars into a premodern understanding of the war, as Taylor discovered in the outraged reaction to his modestly rational investigation into the causes of the Second World War. Still, the impact of Taylor's book showed that the official version of the Second World War was straining at the seams.

The historians of the New Left

The official version of the Good War was called into question by a younger generation of historians, who were allied to the New Left that grew up outside of the communist and Social Democratic traditions. In particular, opposition to America's war in Vietnam persuaded the New Left historians to ask new questions about the Good War.[79] US militarism might have been tarnished in South East Asia, but the record of the good fight in the Second World War seemed unassailable. The historians of the New Left discovered that there were some gruesome skeletons hidden in Franklin Delano Roosevelt's closet. Todd Gitlin, a leader of the Students for a Democratic Society, whose essay 'Counter-insurgency: myth and reality in Greece' (1967) uncovered the dirty secret that Britain and the US had sided with the pro-Nazi forces to crush the radical partisan forces of ELAS. Gitlin's criticism of western policy during the war was sharpened by his assessment of it afterwards: 'Greece was the Vietnam of the 1940s'.[80] Gitlin's fellow student radical Gabriel Kolko's comprehensive *The Politics of War* (1968) drew together those themes of bad faith amongst the British and American allies, with wider examples of the conservative impulse of the western armies in France, Italy and Greece, drawing on a close reading of the National Security Documents. The linguistics professor Noam Chomsky joined the project of re-examining the good intentions behind American foreign policy during the Vietnam War. Kolko, Gitlin and Chomsky in particular showed that American policy was primarily motivated by a desire to open European and colonial markets to US exports and investment rather than any commitment to freedom.[81] The War Aims turned out to be liberty for US exports, first, whereas political freedom was strictly limited to what could be reconciled with the restoration of the market is Western Europe. Later these researches were bolstered by Kees van der Pijl, in his book *The Making of the Atlantic Ruling Class* (1984) and by the former intelligence officer William Blum. The New Left historians were inspired by the work of William A. Williams, who had served in the Pacific, and in 1959 published *The Tragedy of American Diplomacy*.

The New Left were not allied to the Communist left and so had fewer historical ties to the campaign for the People's War. They were also focused on America's rise to global pre-eminence, of which they were critics, and to cross that bridge meant looking hard at the event that turned the US into the World's policeman, the Second World War. It helped too, in an odd way, that America did not have the same entrenched Social Democratic left that Europe had, since those movements were wedded either to the war effort (in the case of the British Labour Party) or to the post-war reconstruction, as was the German Social Democratic Party. America's footloose leftists had much less commitment to the flag-waving patriotism of the English and French left, and were less neurotic than the Germans. They also had an indigenous tradition of cool, even cynical, criticism to draw upon, in the writings of C. Wright Mills, I.F. Stone, Charles and Mary Beard, Ambrose Bierce and Mark Twain. Marxism was a thin influence in America, but given the way that Marxism had yoked itself to the Great Patriotic War in Europe, that might have been an advantage.

Yalta Betrayal

The post-war settlement did not only come under fire from the left, but also from the right. Many conservatives in America opposed alliance with Britain, let alone the Soviet Union. The alliance with the USSR caused considerable difficulties for the Anglo-American ruling class. Within the alliance, Churchill and Roosevelt never considered Stalin an equal partner - just as he distrusted them. Throughout the war, the clash of Soviet and Western interests was barely concealed.

The pragmatism of the alliance has preoccupied right wing critics ever since. Specifically, the agreement between Stalin and Churchill at Yalta to divide Europe into 'spheres of influence' has been challenged as a betrayal of the peoples of Eastern Europe. A number of populist right-wing tracts, like Felix Wittmer's The Yalta Betrayal (1953), or US ambassador Arthur Bliss Lane's I Saw Poland Betrayed (1948) challenged the official histories and hagiographies.[82] The characterisation of the alliance with Stalin as a betrayal found a resonance among the east European émigrés who were attacking the new 'Soviet Empire' from America and West Europe.

Count Nikolai Tolstoy took up the cause of the 'Cossacks' – actually Russians, Ukrainians, Caucasians and Cossacks – who were forcibly repatriated at the end of the war, of whom many were executed. Tolstoy's campaign to embarrass British ministers was silenced through the libel courts, though historians have since acknowledged that his points were broadly true. Polish émigrés in the West took up the cause of the massacred officers at Katyn, and were supported by the English historian Norman Davies, most fulsomely in his book Warsaw '44.

The course of the Cold War determined the judgement of history. Post-war détente accepted the 'spheres of influence' agreement between Stalin and Churchill as the basis for a realistic, if not a just distribution of power between the USSR and the USA. But the later collapse of the Soviet bloc reinforced the belief that the activist ideal of democratisation was a better guide to diplomacy than the cynical realism that left the eastern bloc dictators in place. The new elites coming to power in Eastern Europe owed an ideological debt to the anti-USSR version of history, and re-wrote their history books accordingly. As we have seen President Bush endorsed the 'Eastern betrayal' assessment on the anniversary of the Victory in Europe. 'V.E. Day marked the end of fascism, but it did not end oppression,' he said in Latvia, on 6 May 2005: 'The agreement at Yalta followed in the unjust tradition of Munich and the Molotov-Ribbentrop Pact.' You do not have to accept George Bush's reading of history wholesale to understand that the Allies' commitment to liberating the peoples of Europe was entirely subordinate to the power politics of the day.

Japanese War Crimes

Up to 1973 Japan paid reparations totalling $1.15 billion, to Burma, the Philippines, Indonesia and South Vietnam. These reparations were, though, coloured by Cold War priorities, so that China and North Vietnam were excluded, which position had the support of the US. In May 1960 the People's Daily argued that with 11-15 million Chinese killed in the war, 60 million made homeless, and $60 billion in damages, the People's Republic ought to be entitled to $50 billion in damages. Later, the PRC abandoned this claim and Foreign Minister Fukuda stated that Japan should apologise to China for the troubles Japanese troops caused in China.[83]

In the 1970s, Japan's rise to economic super-power status provoked a revived interest in Japanese War Crimes. On 23 May 1971 the Conference of the National Federation of Far Eastern Prisoner of War clubs met at Buxton to talk about a planned visit from Emperor Hirohito to London. Philip Toosey told the delegates that on no account should they protest against the Queen's guest, and they reluctantly agreed. The popular British television programme *Tenko*, about European women held in a Japanese prisoner of war camp was indicative a more critical mood.[84]

In the 1970s and 80s a number of accounts of Korean women

forcibly prostituted by the Imperial Japanese Army were published (they were called 'Comfort Women'), leading to calls for a Japanese apology. In 1965 a reconciliation treaty had aimed to close all demands for reparations, but a younger, more liberal and feminist – but also more assertive – generation of Koreans were less willing to forgive and forget, and they were helped by Japanese women like Diet representative Shimizu Sumiko. In 1991 Kim Hak Sun filed a lawsuit in Japan for her suffering as a 'comfort woman' along with a number of other women. They won the case. In 1992 Prime Minister Kiyiichi Miyazawa admitted Japan's guilt and apologised.[85]

By the 1990s the world was in awe of Japan's new status, and President George H. W. Bush's visit in January 1992 asking for economic help was widely seen as shaming (and not just because the President was violently sick at a televised banquet). Corresponding to Japan's move from ally to rival, western criticism of Japan's wartime record increased. Elazar Barkan made the comparison that 'Germany has atoned extensively', but 'Japan has yet to recognize that it was guilty'.[86] British, Dutch and Australian veterans and Prisoners of War protested in Hong Kong, and in Britain, in 1998, when Japanese President Akahito visited.

In 1997 Chinese-American writer Iris Chang published *The Rape of Nanking*, a striking account of Japanese wartime atrocities in the Chinese city in 1937. Chang's book sold 500,000 copies in America, and she was invited to the White House by Hillary Clinton, and also invited to speak on the television shows Good Morning America, Nightline, Newshour with Jim Lehrer, as well as being featured in the *New York Times* and *Readers' Digest* (her first book about a Chinese American persecuted under McCarthyism was less successful in the US). As compelling as the book was, it concentrated on recounting Chinese suffering, and offered little analysis of the Japanese turn towards imperialism, attributing the massacres to the Japanese psyche. It was inspired by the historical genre of holocaust studies. In US media coverage of Chang's book it was reported that the Japanese were wholly ignorant of events in Nanking, though that was not wholly true. Sadly the toll of public interest and condemnation from Japanese conservatives weighed down on Chang, who took her own life towards the end of 2004.

A recurring theme of the debate about Japan's war crimes is the failure to apologise, though in fact successive Prime Ministers have apologised, and these apologies in turn have been taken as evidence of insincerity. Elazar Barkan, for example, thinks that 'the constant repetitions of these formulations transformed them from apologies for the war crimes into failed excuses'.[87] When Prime Minister Tomiichi Muruyama apologised to former Prisoners of War, the *Sun* newspaper claimed expertise in the Japanese language, claiming that the words he used were less than apology. *The Times* announced that the ultimate form of apology was 'hara kiri' – though the newspaper did not say whether just the Prime Minister or perhaps the Japanese people as awhole ought to commit ritual suicide.[88] In all of the discussion of Japanese war crimes the question of whether the Allies ought to apologise for the firebombing and atom bombs on Japanese cities was passed over. Nor was the question ever asked why there were so few Japanese prisoners of war, since the onetime allies would never admit that they had refused to take prisoners, but executed surrendering Japanese troops.

The European Resistance

The official historians of the Allied Powers, Britain and the United States, played down the contribution of the resistance, as a potential challenge to their authority as the new occupying powers in Europe. In Greece the British army waged war against the main resistance army, ELAS, in collaboration with German commanders and the Greek paramilitaries the Nazis had raised. The official British historian of the Special Operations Executive in Europe, M.R.D. Foot made sure to write the resistance movements a secondary role. In Italy, the government sought to control the historical record, sponsoring an official Istituto Nazionale per la storia del Movimento di Liberazione in Italia (INMLI) in 1949 to try to moderate the influence of more radical accounts.[89] The Italian government's efforts to steer the history of the resistance were adopted by authorities across Europe, and in 1958 the first International Conference on the History of the Resistance Movements was held in Liege.

Just as the Cold War served to isolate the left, their wartime record of resistance became more important, and they generated a very different account of the war. In 1953 Roberto Battaglia's *Story of the Italian Resistance,* revealed that the Allied Commander Alexander had encouraged the partisans to fight the Wehrmacht in open combat, only to abandon them to their fate, by postponing the promised autumn 1943 offensive. The record of the Italian resistance was a sore point. Post war Communist leaders tried to rein in the partisan veterans' status in the party in favour of a newer generation of recruits. The record of armed struggle against the state was an important source of self-belief for the left wing terrorist groups that organised in the 1970s.[90]

Among Greeks exiled in France and America, while the Generals ruled in Athens, the wartime record of the resistance army ELAS, and the Allies' betrayal of it, was treasured as a serviceable alternative national idea.[91] These exiles would make up the a new governing class many years later, when the Socialist PASOK government took over from the military authorities, and the history of the resistance and subsequent civil war remained fiercely contested. In Yugoslavia, the post-war government was created out of the partisan movement, which quickly attained the status of a national epic that militated against critical self-reflection. For other East European states, where the resistance was more marginal or divided, the Communist bloc countries struggled to manufacture a myth of resistance out of scant examples.[92]

As the left's star waned in the 1980s, the reputation of the resistance, being the left's central claim to stand for the nation, was itself subject to the harsh light of scrutiny. Accounts of the brutal methods and settling of private grudges that had been only muttered by right wing critics after the war were now said much more stridently. In Italy, the historian and Mussolini biographer Renzo de Felice led a frontal assault on the 'resistance myth'. In Claude Berri's 1990 film *Uranus*, the Communists in the resistance are portrayed as villains, while the collaborators are treated sympathetically. Elsewhere, the disintegration of the Yugoslav state along ethnic lines gave rise to a much more critical examination of Tito's partisans, and much greater scepticism towards their pan-Slav reputation.[93]

Collaboration

Scepticism towards the resistance was more in keeping with the post-heroic age of the 1990s, and so too was a greater interest in collaboration between European elites and the Nazi occupiers. In

1972 Marcel Ophuls' film for German television *The Sorrow and the Pity* packed French picture houses with its remarkable account of the extensive collaboration between the French people and the German occupation (it was not shown on French television until 1981). Ophuls fled Nazi Germany for France in 1933. Before Ophuls' film French wartime memories were an un-reflective mix of overstated resistance heroism and a vague nostalgia for Vichy France. Historians and scholars from America, like Robert Paxton and Stanley Hoffmann disturbed the official account, explaining that collaboration was not imposed upon France, but actively sought. According to Paxton, Marshall Petain's grandiose 'National Revolution was not Hitler's project',[94] it was not, as the *Journel Officiel* reported 'imported into the country by the tanks of the invaders' (13 October 1944). In 1997 the Columbia University historian Paxton was mobbed like a superstar, when he came to give evidence at Vichy official Maurice Papon, who signed the order deporting French Jews to Germany.[95] The trial of Papon, ten years after the trial of the SS Commander Klaus Barbie for war crimes in Lyons underscored the new position of the French government. President Chirac accepted national responsibility for the persecution of the Jews in a speech in 1995. The corrosive impact of the re-examination of the Petainist record had damaged his predecessor, Socialist François Mitterand, who had as a younger man, served as a Vichy functionary.

The hidden record of collaboration was too tempting a scandal for researchers, who scanned all of the governments and institutions of post-war Europe looking for the opportunity for more revelations. Former seminarian John Cornwell wrote the story of Rome's collaboration in *Hitler's Pope* (1999).[96] In 1997 Journalist Tom Bower and Isabel Vincent both published books on economic collaboration between Swiss Banks and the Nazis, to hide funds looted from victims of the Holocaust.

Allied Atrocities

In 1967, Allan Bosworth, a former Naval Public Relations Officer in Japan published *America's Concentration Camps*, telling the story of the wartime internment of Japanese- Americans. It was the first of a welter of books and films that re-cast the internment as a wrong committed by the US government,[97] the launch of a Redress Movement that culminated in a public acknowledgement to that effect by President Ford in 1976. Here was a turning point in the understanding of the Pacific War and a telling moment of self-knowledge in American attitudes towards the Japanese. Amongst historians at least, there is a greater understanding of the racialization of the war against Japan, following the publication of John Dower's *War Without Mercy* in 1986. Knowledge of the suffering at Hiroshima was put before American public in John Hersey's book *Hiroshima* that first appeared as a special in *Time* magazine in 1946. It was not until Gar Alperovitz's book *Atomic Diplomacy* in 1965 that it was first understood that US intelligence knew that Japan was on the verge of surrender, and the case has been resisted ever since.

After the publication of Jorg Friedrich's book, *The Fire*, in Germany in 2002 (Gunter Grass's novel about the Allies' sinking of the refugee ship Wilhelm Gustloff, *Crabwalk* was published in the same year) some German newspapers took the opportunity of a visit by the Queen to Germany to demand that she apologise for the bombing of Dresden and other cities. 'How Josef Goebbels, the original spin doctor must be chuckling', wrote Tony Rennell, author of *Tail-End Charlies: The Last Battles of the Bomber War*: Goebbels' 'clever manipulation of the truth about the Allied bombing of the city of Dresden still has life in it'.[98] The record of Bomber Command had already been raised with the Royal Family when the Queen Mother unveiled a statue of Arthur 'Bomber' Harris in central London in 1992. Anti-war protestors crashed the ceremony and threw red paint over the statue. Later a London jury acquitted them of any crime.

British historians have in the last ten years been more willing to acknowledge that the Allies, too, have blood on their hands. The military historian Max Hastings has written of summary executions in the Normandy landings and other atrocities. Christopher Bayly and Tim Harper have done much to shed light on the colonialist outlook that drove the British war effort in the Far East. Mark Curtis and David French have done much to show that the British re-taking of the colonies was far from a liberation.

Among the Allies, the Soviet Union has been most pointedly exposed for its oppressive record in Eastern Europe – at least it has in western histories and reporting. With the break-up of the Soviet Union, though, and the founding of the Russian-led Commonwealth of Independent States has seen a much more open attitude to historical scholarship. For some, the rehabilitation of the wartime record of the Baltic nationalists who collaborated with Germany is a bridge too far. But on the whole the opening up of the Soviet Union's wartime record to question has been a positive experience.

The malleable history of the Second World War

The first draft of the history of the Second World War was, under-standably, the history from the point of view of the victors. It is not that we have an especial need to hear the version of the vanquished Axis leaders. Rather, the victors' account itself has ideological rigidities of its own. The Allies' cause has been dressed up in lots of clothes - the People's War, the war to liberate Europe, the war against Fascism and Racism. But these different intellectual frameworks arise out of a political coalition mobilised to prosecute the war, one that in its different ways also constructed the peace. The first great breach in the consensus about the meaning of the Second World War came about because of the international breach in that consensus, the Cold War between the former Allies, The USSR on the one hand, and America and Britain on the other. It has suffered since from further tensions within the Western Alliance, and from the fragmentation of the domestic coalition between organised labour, business and the state that was galvanised into supporting the war.

As the postwar consensus depleted, so did the compelling character of the mainstream account of the war lose its definitive character. It was not that the history of the Second World War became less important. On the contrary, it seems to have become more important. But that does not disguise the fact that there are now more and more competing accounts of the war, as different fragments of the wartime coalition lay claim to the mantle of the war, and in doing so harden up competing accounts of the war. More than that, the mismatch between the official version of the war and present-day needs illuminates new aspects of the war, such as the record of Allied atrocities, or the distinctive experience of the war in the colonies. All of this new material deepens our understanding, and at least makes possible a new synthesis of different accounts.

Footnotes

1. The War in the Factories

1. Mark Mazower, Dark Continent, London, Vintage, 2000 p 130
2. Alec Nove, An Economic History of the USSR, 1982, p 279
3. Rajani Palme Dutt, World Politics, London, Left Book Club, 1936, p 15
4. Thomas Fleming, The New Dealers' War, New York, Basic, 2001, p 124
5. Adam Tooze, Wages of Destruction, London, Allen Lane, 2006, p 641
6. Paul Kennedy, Rise and Fall of the Great Powers, London, Fontana, 1988, p 419, 455
7. David Schoenbaum, Hitler's Social Revolution, New York, WW Norton, 1980, p 92
8. Tooze, Wages of Destruction, p 261
9. Andrew Gordon, Evolution of Labor Relations in Japan, Harvard University Asia Centre, 1988, p 258, 268
10. Angus Calder, The People's War, London, Panther, 1971, p 272-3
11. W.B. Sutch, Workers and the War Effort, Wellington, c. 1944, p 46-7
12. Fleming, The New Dealers War, p 248
13. Stephen Kotkin, World War Two and Labour: a lost cause? International Labor and Working-Class History 2000 (58): 181-191, p 186
14. John Barber and Mark Harrison, The Soviet Home Front 1941-1945, Longman, London, 1991 p 61-2
15. Barber and Harrison, The Soviet Home Front, p 164
16. Fleming, The New Dealers' War, p 82
17. Calder, The People's War, p 133, 456
18. W.B. Sutch, Workers and the War Effort, Wellington, c. 1944, p 17
19. Schoenbaum, Hitler's Social Revolution, p 86-8
20. Gabriel Kolko, A Century of War, New York, The New Press, 1994, p 242
21. Edward Tannenbaum, Fascism in Italy, London, Allen Lane, 1972, 120
22. Calder, People's War, 392
23. Nelson Lichtenstein, Labor's War at Home, Cambridge University

Press, 1987, p 96-7; Fleming, The New Dealer's War, p 153

24. Chicago Daily Tribune, 14 December 1940

25. Robert Paxton, Vichy France, Columbia University Press, 1982, p 376

26. Output increases that would later equip the German army, Alan Clinton, Jean Moulin, Plagrave, 2002, p 73

27. Sir John Hammerton, The Second Great War, London, Waverley, Vol II, p 738

28. On 13 December 1939, quoted in Living Marxism, Spring 1940, vol V, no 1, Spring 1940, p 14

29. W.B. Sutch, Workers and the War Effort, Wellington, c. 1944

30. International Communist Correspondence, Vol. III, No 1, January 1937, p 22

31. Schoenbaum, p 97

32. Calder, p 405

33. John Costello, Love, Sex and War, London, Pan, 1986, p 207

34. Gordon, Evolution of Labor Relations in Japan, p 314

35. Harrison and Barber, The Soviet Home Front, 1941-45, London, 1991, p 61, 163

36. Miller and Cornford, American Labor in the Era of World War II, Westport, Praeger, 1995, p 94

37. Morley and Nunn, Arts and the Holocaust, East Renfrewshire, 2005, p 110

38. Robert Black, Fascism in Germany, London, Steyne, 1975, p 989

39. Hugh Rockoff in Harrison, ed., The Economics of World War Two, 1998, p 94

40. Mark Harrison (ed), The Economics of World War Two, Cambridge University Press, 1998, p 14

41. Werner Abelshauser, in Harrison, The Economics of World War Two, 161

42. Calder, 505

43. Kotkin, A Lost Cause?, p 186

44. Barber and Harrison, The Soviet Home Front 1941-45, p 116

45. Barber and Harrison, The Soviet Home Front 1941-45, p 118, quoting expatriate Victor Kravchenko

46. James Bacque, Crimes and Mercies, London, Little, Brown and Company, 1997, p 61

47. Miller and Cornford, American Labor in the Era of WWII, 1995, p 2-

3

48. Costello, Love, Sex and War, p 211
49. Costello, Love, Sex and War, p 197
50. Calder, p 386
51. Costello, p 215
52. Kotkin, A Lost Cause?, p 184
53. Richard Evans, The Coming of the Third Reich, London, Penguin, 2003, p 348, 355-357
54. Alan Milward, The German Economy at War,London, Athlone, 1965
55. Edward R. Tannenbaum, Fascism in Italy, Society and Culture 1922-1945, London, Allen Lane, 1973, p 102, 120, 122, 125
56. Gordon, Labor Relations in Japan, 299; Sanpo revisited, Tetsuji Okazaki, Centre for International Research on the Japanese Economy Discussion Paper, June 2005
57. Presidential Address, July 1940, in Nina Fishman, The British Communist Party and the Trade Unions, 1933-1945, Aldershot, Scolar Press, 1995, p 263
58. Fishman, The British Communist Party and the Trade Unions, p 298 - the speech was written by C.P theoretician Rajani Palme Dutt
59. Art Preis, Labor's Giant Step, New York, Pioneer Press, 1964, p 114-7
60. Preis, Labor's Giant Step, p 131
61. 'Britain's reasons for fighting', New York Times, 8 September 1940
62. Preis, Labour's Giant Step, p 154
63. Hugh Brogan, The Penguin History of the United States of America, Harmondsworth, Penguin, 1985, p 584-6
64. Lichtenstein, Labor's War at Home, 89

2. Rationing

1. Daniel Guerin, Fascism and Big Business, New York, Pathfinder Press, 1983, p 194-5
2. Robert Black, Fascism in Germany, London, Steyne, 1975, p 989
3. Tim Mason, Social Policy in the Third Reich, Oxford, Berg, 1993, p 39
4. David Schoenbaum, Hitler's Social Revolution, New York, WW Norton, 1980, p 98
5. Angus Calder, The People's War, London, Panther, 1971, p 405

6. Andrew Gordon, Evolution of Labor Relations in Japan, Harvard University Asia Centre, 1988, p 285

7. Vera Zamagni, The Economic History of Italy, Oxford University Press, 1997, p 309

8. Vera Zamagni, 'Losing the war', in Harrison, The Economy of World War Two, 179, p 191

9. Robert Paxton Vichy France, New York, Columbia U.P. 1982, p 376

10. Martin Glabermann, Wartime Strikes, Bewick, Detroit, 1980, p 41

11. Nelson Lichtenstein, Labor's War at Home, Cambridge University Press, 1987, p 112-3

12. Hugh Rockoff in Mark Harrison, The Economics of World War Two, p 93

13. Calder, The People's War, p 275

14. Schoenbaum, Hitler's Social Revolution, p 126

15. Adam Tooze, Wages of Destruction, London, Allen Lane, 2006, p 353

16. in Skidelsky, John Maynard Keynes: Fighting for Britain 1937-1946, London, Macmillan, 2001, p 53

17. 16 December 1939, quoted in Living Marxism, Spring 1940, vol V, no 1, p 15

18. 28 November, 1939, quoted in Living Marxism, Spring 1940, vol V, no 1, p 16

19. Angus Calder, The People's War, Panther, 1971, p 445

20. John Carey, reviewing Matthew Sweet's West End Front, The Sunday Times, Culture Section, 30 October 2011, p 47

21. Sir John Hammerton, The Second Great War, Vol II, Amalgamated Press, p 543

22. Quoted in Patricia Cockburn, The Years of the Week, London, Comedia, 1985, p 272, 274

23. Lichtenstein, Labor's War at Home, p 112

24. Calder, The People's War, p 410-11

25. Tooze, Wages of Destruction, p 354

26. Tooze, Wages of Destruction, p 356

27. Calder, The People's War, p 318

28. Tooze, Wages of Destruction, p 361, 541

29. Patricia Meehan, Strange Enemy People, London, Peter Owen, 2001, p 248, 253

30. Tooze, Wages of Destruction, p 542, 366

31. Akira Hara, in Mark Harrison (ed), The Economics of World War Two, Cambridge University Press, 1998, p 255-6

32. Barber and Harrison, The Soviet Home Front, 1941-45, London, Longman, 1991, p 79

33. Fortune, December 1942

34. Schoenbaum, Hitler's Social Revolution, p 105-7

35. Franz Neumann, European Trade Unionism and Politics, New York, 1936, p.42

36. Gordon, Labor Relations in Japan, p 256

37. G. Deborin, Secrets of the Second World War, Moscow, Progress Publishers, 1971, p 130

38. Lichtenstein, Labor's War at Home, p 88

39. Abelshauser, in Harrison, in Mark Harrison (ed) The Economics of World War Two, p 153

40. Calder, The People's War, p 486

41. Stephen Kotkin, World War Two and Labour: a lost cause? International Labor and Working-Class History 2000 (58): 181-191, p 186

42. John Barber and Mark Harrison, The Soviet Home Front. 1941-45, Longman, London, 1991, p 135

43. David Kennedy, Freedom from Fear, Oxford University Press, 1999, p 628

3. Military Industrial Complex

1. Einzig, The Economics of Re-armament, 1934, quoted in R Palme Dutt, World Politics, London, Left Book Club, 1936, p 110-1

2. Keynes, The Means to Prosperity, 1934, quoted in R Palme Dutt, World Politics, London, Left Book Club, p 110

3. 29 July 1935, in R Palme Dutt, World Politics, London, Left Book Club, p 112

4. Alfred Sohn-Rethel, The Economy and Class Structure of German Fascism, London, Free association, 1987, p 81

5. Tooze, Wages of Destruction, London, Allen Lane, 2006, p 571, 109

6. Tooze, Wages of Destruction, London, Allen Lane, 2006, p 340-1

7. Tooze, Wages of Destruction, London, Allen Lane, 2006, p 126

8. Daniel Guerin, Fascism and Big Business, New York, Monad, 1983, p 244

9. Adam Tooze, Wages of Destruction, London, Allen Lane, 2006, p

571

10. Jacques Pauwels, The Myth of the Good War, Toronto, James Lorimer, 2002, p 30-32

11. Adam Tooze, Wages of Destruction, London, Allen Lane, 2006, p 133

12. Jean Monnet, Memoirs, Garden City, Doubleday 1978, p 151

13. Jean Monnet, Memoirs, Garden City, Doubleday 1978, p 135

14. Paul Mattick, Economics, Politics and the Age of Inflation, London, Merlin, 1978, p 139

15. Jacques Pauwels, The Myth of the Good War, Toronto, James Lorimer, 2002, p 54

16. Hugh Brogan, The Penguin History of the United States of America, Harmondsworth, Penguin, 1985, p 584-6

17. David Kennedy, Freedom from Fear, Oxford University Press, 1999, p 621

18. Kolko, Main Currents in American History, New York, Pantheon, 1984, p 310

19. Hugh Brogan, The Penguin History of the United States of America, Harmondsworth, Penguin, 1985, p 585

20. Economist, 22 April 1939

21. Times 11 March 1937, in Skidelsky, Keynes, Vol. III, Lodnon, Macmillan, 2000, p 21

22. Maclaine, Ministry of Morale: Home Front Morale and the Ministry of Information in World War II, London, George Allen and Unwin, 1979, p 149

23. Lizzie Collingham. The Taste of War, London, Allen Lane, 2011, p 68

24. Overy, Why the Allies Won, London, Pimlico, 1995, p 30

25. Mazower, Dark Continent, 159, 210

26. Collingham, The Taste of War, London, Allen Lane, 2011, p 242

27. Thomas Fleming, The New Dealer's War, New York, Basic Books, p 361

28. John Dower, Japan in War and Peace, New York, The New Press, 1993, p 109

29. Robert Black, Fascism in Germany, London Steyne, 1975, Vol II, p 993

30. Mary Beth Norton, Carol Sheriff, David W. Blight, David M. Katzman, A people and a nation: a history of the United States. Since 1865, Cengage Learning, 2009 Volume 2, Chapter 27, p 712

31. Fred Westacott, Shaking the Chains, Tupton, Joe Clark, 2002, p 128

32. Lizzie Collingham, The Taste of War, London, Allen Lane, 2011, p 132

33. Tooze, Wages of Destruction, London, Allen Lane, 2006, p 564-5. Tooze, who points out the change in pricing, argues with the 'story-line' that German industry was protected by 'costs plus', but it is not obvious what real difference the guaranteed profits system makes.

34. Time, July 19, 1943 http://www.time.com/time/magazine/article /0,9171,777836,00.html#ixzz1Rik29RzS

35. Fenner Brockway and Frederic Mullally, Death Pays a Dividend, London, Victor Gollancz, p 124-30

36. Jacques Pauwels, The Myth of the Good War, James Lorimer, Toronto, 2002, p 71

37. David Kennedy, Freedom From Fear, Oxford University Press, 1999, p 622

38. Report of 18 December 1943, quoted in Art Preis, Labour's Giant Step, New York, Pioneer, 1964, p 203

39. Fenner Brockway and Frederic Mullally, Death Pays a Dividend, London, Victor Gollancz, p 120

40. R. Palme Dutt, Britain's Crisis of Empire, London, Lawrence and Wishart, 1949, 43, 45

41. David Kennedy, Freedom From Fear, Oxford University Press, 1999, p 623

42. David Kennedy, Freedom From Fear, Oxford University Press, 1999, 622

43. Keith Middlemas, Politics in Industrial Society, London, Andre Deutsch, 1979, p 259

44. Keith Middlemas, Politics in Industrial Society, London, Andre Deutsch, 1979, p 264

45. Skidelsky, John Maynard Keynes: Fighting for Britain, 1937-1946, London Macmillan, 2000, p 15, 479. £479,529 would be worth £15,205,864, or $23,733,326 in 2011 money

46. Robert Black, Fascism in Germany, Vol II, London, Steyne, 1975, 989-90

47. Tooze, Wages of Destruction, London, Allen Lane, 2006, p 496

48. Tooze, Wages of Destruction, London, Allen Lane, 2006, p 644-7

49. Yoshida Shigeru, Last Meiji Man, Lanham, Rowman and Littlefield,

2007, p 122

4. Dig for Victory

1. Hitler, Mein Kampf, London, Pimlico, 1992, p 263
2. Mein Kampf, p 262
3. The Living Soil, Chapter 1
4. Lobbying for the creation of the Civilian Conservation Corps, see http://www.history.com/this-day-in-history/fdr-creates-civilian-conservation-corps
5. RJB Bosworth, Mussolini's Italy, London, Allen Lane, 2005, p 267
6. Franz-Josef Bruggemeir et al, How Green Were the Nazis, Athens, Ohio University Press, 2005, p 12, 18-21, 32, 34
7. Hitler's 'Second Book', 1928, p 118
8. Hitler's 'Second Book', p 43
9. in Anna Bramwell, Darre, Abbotsbrook, Kensal Press, 1985, p 102
10. Neumann, Behemoth, New York, Harper and Row, 1966, p 349
11. Richard Grunberger, A Social History of the Third Reich, London, Penguin, 1979, p 23; Alfred Sohn-Rethel, The Economy and Class Structure of German Fascism, London, Free Association, 1987, p 57
12. Kleinman, A World of Hope; A World of Fear, 2000, Ohio State University Press, p 104
13. Katie Louchheim, Ed., The Making of the New Deal, Harvard, 1983, p 260
14. Roosevelt to Freeman, September 6, 1932, quoted in The Civilian Conservation Corps and the National Park Service, 1933-1942:An Administrative History, at http://www.cr.nps.gov/history/online_books/ccc/ccc1.htm
15. Alfred Sohn-Rethel, The Economic and Class Structure of German Fascism, London, Free Association, London, 1987, p 74
16. Sohn-Rethel, The Economic and Class Structure of German Fascism, London, Free Association, London, 1987, p 77

5. Trade War

1. Colin Ward, The Awkward Question', Freedom, 17th August 1957 – he might have been quoting John Dryden, for whom, 'War is the Trade of Kings'
2. Fenner Brockway, Will Roosevelt Succeed?, London, Routledge, 1934, p 11

3. Fenner Brockway, Will Roosevelt Succeed?, London, Routledge, 1934, p 12
4. Tooze, The Wages of Destruction, London, Allen Lane, 2006, p 246
5. Tooze, The Wages of Destruction, London, Allen Lane, 2006, p 52
6. Hjalmar Schacht, My First Seventy-Six Years, London, Alan Wingate, 1955, p 328-9
7. Tooze, The Wages of Destruction, London, Allen Lane, 2006, p 86, 88
8. Pauwels, The Myth of the Good War, 2002, p 57
9. Skiedlsky, Keynes Vol III, London, Macmillan, 2000, p 20
10. Jürgen Kaczynski, writing as James Turner, Hitler and the Empire, London, Lawrence and Wishart, 1937, p 36
11. Tooze, The Wages of Destruction, London, Allen Lane, 2006, p 301
12. Tooze, The Wages of Destruction, London, Allen Lane, 2006, p 307
13. Tooze, The Wages of Destruction, London, Allen Lane, 2006, p 308
14. Tooze, The Wages of Destruction, London, Allen Lane, 2006, p 325
15. In Livingston, Moore and Oldfather (eds), Imperial Japan 1800-1945, Random House, New York, 1973, p 372
16. Tooze, The Wages of Destruction, London, Allen Lane, 2006, p 449
17. G. John Ikenberry, Liberal Order and Imperial Ambition, Cambridge, Polity, 2006, p 27
18. Hammerton, The second Great War, Vol I, p 316, 323, 324; Lizzie Collingham, The Taste of War, p 35
19. Churchill, The Grand Alliance, 1950, p 24
20. Overy, Why the Allies Won, London, Pimlico, 1995, p 30
21. BBC Journal, April 1940
22. The Economist, 9 December 1939, quoted in Living Marxism, Spring 1940, vol V no 1, p 16
23. The Wages of Destruction, London, Allen Lane, 2006, p 477
24. Quoted in Kolko, Main Currents in American History, New York, Pantheon, 1984, p 202
25. Quoted in Sylvia Pankhurst, The Truth About the Oil War, Dreadnought Publishers, London, 1922, p 17
26. Quoted in Sylvia Pankhurst, The Truth About the Oil War, Dreadnought Publishers, London, 1922, p 18
27. Tooze, The Wages of Destruction, London, Allen Lane, 2006, p 116
28. Tooze, The Wages of Destruction, London, Allen Lane, 2006, p 116
29. Tooze, The Wages of Destruction, London, Allen Lane, 2006, p 309

30. Tooze, The Wages of Destruction, London, Allen Lane, 2006, p 205

31. Anne Booth Colonial Legacies, U of Hawai'i Press, 2007, p 149

32. W.G. Beasely, Japanese Imperialism, Oxford, Clarendon, 1987, p 223

33. quoted in Acheson, Present and the Creation, New York, Norton, 1969, p 25

34. in Acheson, Present and the Creation, New York, Norton, 1969, p 36-7

35. in Louis, Imperialism at Bay, New York, Oxford University Press, 1978, p 240-1

36. Anthony Sampson, The Seven Sisters, London, Coronet 1975, p 110

37. D.J.M. Tate, The RGA History of the Plantation Industry in the Malay Peninsula, Oxford University Press, 1996, p 346, 337

38. F.P. M. van der Kraajl The Open Door Policy of Liberia, Übersee Museum, Bremen, 1983, p 46, 48

39. S Tillekeratne, Rubber in the Economy of Sri Lanka, Swedish Agency for Reserch Cooperation with Developing Countries, Colombo, 1988, p 17-20

40. quoted in Kees van der Pijl, The Making of the Atlantic Ruling Class, London, Verso, 1984, p 116

41. Dean Acheson, Present at the Creation, New York, Norton, 1969, p 60; Leonard Caruana and Hugh Rockoff, A Wolfram in Sheep's Clothing: Economic Warfare in Spain, 1940-1944, The Journal of Economic History, Vol. 63, No. 1 (Mar., 2003), pp. 100-126

6. Imperialist War

1. Rajani Palme Dutt, World Politics, 1918-1936, London, Left book Club, p 233

2. Captain Norman Macmillan, The Fourth Dimension: Begin Now to Defeat the German Spring Offensive', Flight, 9 January 1941, p 33-4

3. R. J. B. Bosworth, Mussolini's Italy, London, Allen Lane, 2005, p 367-73

4. Unsigned, but probably Paul Mattick, 'Long Live the War' in Living Marxism, Vol V, no 2, Fall, 1940, p 59

5. see Living Marxism, Vol VI, No 1, Fall, 1941, p 34

6. Adolf Hitler Mein Kampf, London, Pimlico, 1992, p 592-5

7. Adolf Hitler, Mein Kampf, London, Pimlico, 1992, p 596, 598

8. Mark Mazower, Hitler's Empire, Nazi Rule in Occupied Europe, London, Penguin, 149

9. Mein Kampf, Pimlico, 601
10. in Mark Mazower, Hitler's Empire, London, Penguin, 2009, p 150
11. R. J. B. Bosworth, Mussolini's Italy, London, Allen Lane, 2005, p 367, 371
12. R. J. B. Bosworth, Mussolini's Italy, London, Allen Lane, 2005, p 383
13. in Louis, Imperialism at Bay, New York, Oxford University Press, 1978, p 14
14. L. S. Amery, 26 August 1942, Louis, Imperialism at Bay, New York, Oxford University Press, 1978, p 33
15. A.J.P Taylor, to William Louis, in Louis, Imperialism at Bay, New York, Oxford University Press, 1978, viii
16. Dutt, World Politics, p 46
17. Richard Vinen, A History in Fragments, London, Abacus, 2002, p 219
18. Sir John Hammerton, The Second Great War, Volume I, London, Waverley, 1947, p 175
19. 'James Turner', Hitler and the Empire, London, Lawrence and Wishart, London 1937, p 37
20. Ian McLaine, Ministry of Morale, London, George Allen an Unwin, 1979, p 223-4
21. in Eri Hotta, Pan Asianism and Japan's War, 1931-1945, London, Palgrave Macmillan, 2007, p 68
22. in Eri Hotta, Pan Asianism and Japan's War, 1931-1945, London, Palgrave Macmillan, 2007, p 183
23. Kolko, Main Currents in Modern American History, New York, Pantheon, 1984, p 201-6
24. in Louis, Imperialism at Bay, New York, Oxford University Press, 1978, p 148
25. Hornbeck, 10 May 1944 – and this was the general tenor. Louis, Imperialism at Bay, New York, Oxford University Press, 1978, p 360
26. R.S. Rose, One of the Forgotten Things: Ggetulio Vargas and Brazilian Social Control 1930-1954, Westport Conn., Greenwood, 2000, pp 79, 93, 95, 99, 98
27. F. P. M. de Kraajl, The Open Door Policy of Liberia, Bremen, Übersee-Museum, 1983, p 47, 50, 51; Kolko, Main Currents in Modern American History, New York, Pantheon, 1984, p 205
28. Mazower, Dark Continent, London, Allen Lane, 1998, p 160
29. Mazower, Inside Hitler's Greece, New Haven, Yale University

Press, 2001, p 24

30. Mazower, Hitler's Empire, London, Penguin, 2011, p 26
31. Furedi, The Soviet Union Demystified, London, Junius, 1987, p 63
32. R. J. B. Bosworth, Mussolini's Italy, London, Allen Lane, 2005, p 383; Lizzie Collingham, The Taste of War, London, Allen Lane, 2011, p 45-6
33. to US State Department adviser Stanley Hornbeck, 25 November 1943 in Louis, Imperialism at Bay, New York, Oxford University Press, 1978, p 31
34. Lizzie Collingham, The Taste of War, London, Allen Lane, 2011, p 121
35. M. Mukerjee, Churchill's Secret War, Basic Books, New York, 2010, p 129
36. Churchill, The Second World War, Book IV: The Hinge of Fate, London, Reprint Society, 1953, p 175; Cain and Hopkins, British Imperialism 1688-2000, London, Pearson, 2002, p 561; Skiedlsky, John Maynard Keynes: Fighting for Britain 1937 – 1946, London, Macmillan, 2000, p 136
37. Lizzie Collingham, Taste of War, London, Allen Lane, 2011, p 140, 133
38. Theodore Friend, The Blue Eyed Enemy, Japan Against the West in Java and Luzon, New Jersey, Princeton University Press, 1988, p 17-18
39. Mazower, Hitler's Empire, London, Penguin, 2011, p 186
40. Ulrich Herbert, Hitler's Foreign Workers, Cambridge University Press, 1997, p 1
41. Johnson, World War Two and the Scramble for Labour in Colonial Zimbabwe, 2000, p 89
42. Johnson, World War Two and the Scramble for Labour in Colonial Zimbabwe, 2000, p 100
43. William G. Clarence-Smith, School of Oriental and African Studies, Commodities of Empire Working Paper No.14 ISSN: 1756-0098, November 2009, p 10
44. Bayley and Harper, Forgotten Armies, London, Penguin, 2005, p 384
45. New York Times, 23 November 2006, 'Of Blood and Rubber...' Larry Rohter
46. John F W Dulles, Vargas of Brazil, University of Texas Press, Austen, 1967, p 238

47. Martin Lowenkopf, Politics in Liberia, Stanford, Hoover Institute Press, 1976, p 44, 78-9; Daniel Lee and Elizabeth Lee, Human Rights and the Ethics of Globalisation, Cambridge University Press, 2010, p 122-3; F. P. M. de Kraajl, The Open Door Policy of Liberia, Bremen, Übersee-Museum, 1983, p 422

48. Stephen Kotkin (2000). World War Two and Labor: A Lost Cause?. International Labor and Working-Class History, 58, p184

49. Bayley and Harper, Forgotten Armies, London, Penguin, 2005, p 403

50. Bayley and Harper, Forgotten Armies, London, Penguin, 2005, p 407

51. Li Narangoa and Robert Cribb (eds) Imperial Japan and National Identities in Asia, London, Routledge Curzon, 2003, p 273

52. Li Narangoa and Robert Cribb (eds) Imperial Japan and National Identities in Asia, London, Routledge Curzon, 2003, p 273

53. Liason Conference Strategy Document, 12 December 1941, quoted in Anne Booth, Colonial Legacies, U of Hawai'i Press, Honolulu, 2007, p 149

54. M Mukerjee, Churchill's Secret War, New York, Basic Books, 2010, p 205; 'Things we forget: the Bengal Famine', Radio 4, 7 January 2008 http://www.open2.net/thingsweforgot/bengalfamine_progr amme.html

55. M Mukerjee, Churchill's Secret War, New York, Basic Books, 2010, p 203

56. Collingwood, Taste of War, London, Allen Lane, 2011, p 35-7; Tooze, Wages of Destruction, London, Allen Lane, 2006, p 479

57. Mazower, Hitler's Empire, London, Penguin, 2011, p 162

58. Mazower, Inside Hitler's Greece, New Haven, Yale, 2001, p 41

59. Bayley and Harper, Forgotten Armies, London, Penguin, 2005, p 405

7. Militarisation of Everyday Life

1. See Brian James 'Pie in the Sky', History Today Volume: 56 Issue: 9 2006; Paul Lashmar, 'The "Few" who saved Britain', Independent, 16 September 2000

2. Richard Grunberger, Social History of the Third Reich, London, Penguin 1979, p 350

3. quoted in Neumann, Behemoth, New York, Harper and Row, 1966,

p 71

4. RJB Bosworth, Mussolini's Italy, London, Allen Lane, 2005, p 475

5. Ilya Ehrenburg, The War 1941-45, London, McGibbon and Kee, 1964, p 123

6. 'The Boy Scouts are Carrying On', Scout Association exhibition; see here: http://www.scoutsrecords.org/exhibitions.php?dil=&icerik= 14&bparent=0&

7. 'Letter from London', Partisan Review, July August, 1941, No 4, p 321

8. Haining, The Spitfire summer: the people's-eye view of the Battle of Britain London, W. H. Allen, 1990, p 34

9. Calder, The People's War, 1971, p 172

10. One Foot in the Past, BBC2, 5 June 1999

11. Fleming, The New Dealer's War, 381

12. Pierre Ayçoberry, The Social History of the Third Reich, 1933-1945, New York, The New Press, 1999, p 59

13. Pierre Ayçoberry, The Social History of the Third Reich, 1933-1945, New York, The New Press, 1999, p 30

14. John Dower, Japan in War and Peace, New York, The New press, p 111

15. Kay Saunders, War on the Home Front, St Lucia, University of Queensland Press, 1993, p 12, 9

16. Orwell, London Letter, Partisan Review, July-August, 1941, no 4, p 320

17. Stammers, Civil Liberties in Britain During the Second World War, London, Croom Helm, 1983, p 27

18. Churchill to Home Secretary, 12 Jan 1941, in The Grand Alliance, p 563

19. House of Commons Debates, 23 July and 30 July 1940

20. Stammers, Civil Liberties in Britain During the Second World War, London, Croom Helm, 1983, p 65

21. Raymond Challinor, The Struggle for Hearts and Minds, Whitley Bay, Bewick Press, 1995, pp 67-73

22. Carissa Honeywell, 'Anarchism and the British Warfare State. The Prosecution of the War Commentary anarchists, 1945', unpublished paper, c. 2011

23. HC Deb 23 May 1940 vol 361 cc288-92

24. Cabinet Minutes, 19 July 1939, p 18; HC Deb 16 October 1941 vol 374

cc1475-6

25. On 14 November 1931, the SPD's Breitschied publicly called on Brüning to use force against the Nazis; On 21 March 1933 the cabinet decree creating special courts to try opponents of the regime is based on a previous decree of 6 October 1931, that the SPD voted for so that Brüning would have powers to take on the NSDAP, Robert Black, Fascism in Germany, London, Steyne, 1975, p 833, 939

26. John D'Emilio, Lost Prophet: The Life and Times of Bayard Rustin, New York, Free Press, 2003, p 73

27. Neil Stammers, Civil Liberties in Britain During the Second World War, p 36

28. Neil Stammers, Civil Liberties in Britain During the Second World War, p 48, 58

29. J. Sakai, Settlers, Chicago, Morningstar Press, 1989, p 96

30. Michael Burleigh, The Third Reich: A New History, London, Pan, 2001, p 208

31. R. J. B. Bosworth, Mussolini's Italy, London, Allen Lane, 2005, p 218

32. Saburō Ienaga, The Pacific War, New York, Pantheon Books, 1978, p 99

33. Stammers, Civil Liberties in Britain During the Second World War, London, Croom Helm, 1983, p 133

34. E.S. Turner, The Phoney War on the Home Front, London, Michael Joseph, 1961, p 224

35. Stammers, Civil Liberties in Britain During the Second World War, London, Croom Helm, 1983, p 141

36. Stammers, Civil Liberties in Britain During the Second World War, London, Croom Helm, 1983, p 96

37. HC Deb 22 January 1941 vol 368 cc185-90

8. Caesarism

1. Christopher Hibbert, Benito Mussolini, London, Reprint Society, 1962, p 61

2. William Manchester, The Arms of Krupp, Boston, Little, Brown and Company, 2003, p 315

3. Paul Johnson, Modern Times,: A History of the World from the 1920 to the 1990s, Orion, 1992, p 110

4. Schmittian decisionism enjoyed a recent revival in Britain, and it is

the basis of Tony Blair's defence of intervention in Iraq was 'I wanted war, it was the right thing to do', Sunday Times, 17 November 2007, and see Chantal Mouffe (ed), The Challenge of Carl Schmitt, Verso, 1999

5. Franz Neumann and Otto Kircheimer, The Rule of Law under Siege, Berkeley, University of California Press, 1996, p 126

6. Neumann, Behemoth, New York, 1966, p124

7. E. Pashukanis, Law and Marxism: A General Theory, London, Pluto Press, 1989, see introduction p 10 for Pashukanis' own fate

8. Quoted in Neal Stammers, Civil Liberties in Britain During the Second World War, London, Croom Helm, 1983, p 27 and 75

9. K.D. Ewing and C. A. Gearty, The struggle for Civil Liberties: Political Freedom and The Rule of Law in Britain, 1914-1945, Oxford, 2000, p.415

10. Quoted in Niall Ferguson, War of the Worlds, London, Allen Lane 2006, p 221

11. Fenner Brockway, Will Roosevelt Succeed, London, Routledge 1934, p 180, 187

12. International Communist Correspondence, Vol. III, No 1, January 1937, p. 3

13. quoted in Mattick, Economics, Politics and the Age of Inflation, London, Merlin, 1978, p 130

14. Fortune, January 1940, p 71, quoted in Living Marxism, Spring 1940, vol V no 1, p 16

15. Fenner Brockway, Will Roosevelt Succeed, London, Routledge 1934, p 237

16. George Rawick, 'Working Class Self-Activity' Radical America, Vol.3 No.2, March-April 1969, pp.23-31, and here: http://www.marxists.org/archive/rawick/1969/xx/self.html

17. Dean Acheson, Present at the Creation, New York, WW Norton, 1969, p 39

18. William Manchester, American Caesar: Douglas MacArthur, 1880-1964, London, Arrow Books, 1979, p 280-281

19. Matthew Cobb, The Resistance, London, Pocket Books, 2009, p 92

20. Matthew Cobb, The Resistance, London, Pocket Books, 2009, p 109

21. Hobson, Imperialism, London, 1938, p xxi

22. Heidegger, An Introduction to Metaphysics, p 45

23. Christopher Hibbert, Mussolini, London, Reprint Society, 1962, p

151, 143, 157

24. Christopher Hibbert, Mussolini, London, Reprint Society, 1962, p 123

25. See Patrick Buchanan, Churchill, Hitler and the Unnecessary War, New York, Crown, 2008, p 255-6

26. John Colville, The Fringes of Power, p 38

27. Quoted in William Louis, Imperialism at Bay, New York, Oxford University Press, 1978, p 357

28. Arno Mayer, Why Did the Heavens Not Darken?, New York, Pantheon, 1990, p 161

29. Christopher Hibbert, Mussolini, London, Reprint Society, 1962, p 140

30. Quoted in Albert Speer, Inside the Third Reich, London, Shere Books, 1941, p 400

31. Jean Barber and Mark Harrison, The Soviet Home Front: 1941-45, London, Longman, 1991, p 110

32. Living Marxism, Vol. VI, No. 1, Fall 1941, p 32

33. Arno Mayer, Why did the Heavens Not Darken? New York, Pantheon, p 279

34. Nicholson Baker, Human Smoke, London, Simon and Schuster, 2008, p 221

9. Race War

1. Quoted in McLaine, Ministry of Morale, London, George Allen and Unwin, 1979, p 137

2. Colin Heaton, German Anti-Partisan Warfare in Europe, Atglen, Schiffer, 2001, p 116-7

3. Quoted in Weitz, Hitler's Diplomat: Joachim von Ribbentrop, London, Weidenfeld and Nicholson, 1992, p 96. Oddly, the law defines Germans as being of several races, but whose blood is compatible.

4. Neumann, Behemoth, New York, 1966: 126

5. Goebbels, Diaries, London, Hamish Hamilton, 1948, p 287

6. in Roy Jenkins, Truman, London, Collins, 1986, p 44

7. 'Discovery of Truman diary reveals attack on Jews', Guardian July 12, 2003

8. Taussig's files on the San Francisco conference, Louis, Imperialism at Bay, New York, Oxford University Press, 1978, p 486-7

9. 14 November 1944, Louis, Imperialism at Bay, New York, Oxford University Press, 1978, p 424

10. Ponting, Churchill, 230

11. 16 Oct 1943 p 257, Harold Macmillan Diaries, the War Years

12. Autobiography, London: Unwin, 1989, p252

13. quoted in Lukacs, Destruction of Reason, London: Merlin, 1980, p609

14. The Future of American Politics NY, Harper and Row, 1951, p28

15. see Wade et al, The Fiery Cross, London: Touchstone, 1987

16. See Kenan Malik, The Meaning of Race, London, Macmillan, 1996, p 112-3

17. New York Times, 20 May 1906 – and here: http://query.nytimes.com/mem/archive-free/pdf?res=F00C16F73A5A12738DDDA90A94DD405B868CF1D3

18. ABC News, May 15, 2005, http://abcnews.go.com/WNT/Health/story?id=708780

19. Greta Jones, Social Hygiene in the Twentieth Century, London, Croom Helm, 1986, p 32

20. Harry H. Laughlin, The Second International Exhibition of Eugenics held September 22 to October 22, 1921, in connection with the Second International Congress of Eugenics in the American Museum of Natural History, New York (Baltimore: William & Wilkins Co., 1923).

21. Ponting, Churchill, London, 1994, p 102

22. Stefan Kühl, The Nazi Connection, Oxford University Press, 1994, p 85

23. Stefan Kühl, The Nazi Connection, Oxford University Press, 1994, p 53-4

24. Robert A. Garson, The Democratic Party and the Politics of Sectionalism Louisiana State University Press, Baton Rouge, 1974 p 75

25. John D'Emilio, Lost Prophet: The Life and Times of Bayard Rustin, New York, Free Press, 2003, p 51

26. Robert A Garson, The Democratic Party and the Politics of Sectionalism Louisiana State University Press, Baton Rouge, 1974, p84

27. Garson, p 26

28. Quoted in Ian McLaine, Ministry of Morale, London, George Allen

and Unwin, 1979, p 141

29. Ian McLaine, Ministry of Morale, London, George Allen and Unwin, 1979, p 142

30. Ian McLaine, Ministry of Morale, London, George Allen and Unwin, 1979, p 144-5

31. Sir Robert Vansittart, The Black Record, London, Hamish Hamilton, 1944, p 16

32. Koch, Stephen. "The Playboy was a Spy", The New York Times, 13 April 2008; The Guardian, Friday 12 April 2002 "Leaders of the banned"

33. Ian McLaine, Ministry of Morale, London, George Allen and Unwin, 1979, p 147

34. Ehrenburg, quoting himself in The War, 1941-45, London, McGibbon and Kee, 1964, p 28-9

35. Marx and Engels on Reactionary Prussianism, Marx Engels Lenin Institute, Moscow, Foreign Languages Publishing House, 1943, p 5 and throughout

36. see Arpad Kardakay, Georg Lukacs, Oxford, Blackwell, 1991, p 421

37. Destruction of Reason, London, Merlin, 1980, p 77, p 50

38. Carolyn Eisenberg, Drawing the Line - The American decision to divide Germany, Cambridge: University Press, 1996, p 24

39. Hippe, Oskar And Red is the Colour of Our Flag, London, Index, 1991, p 275

40. Quoted in Frank Furedi, Silent Race War, London, Pluto, 1998, p 43

41. E.H. Carr, International Relations Between Two World Wars, 1919-1939, London, Macmillan, 1986, p 153

42. 'Capital, Labour and the Colour Bar', Times 14 March 1942 in Louis, Imperialism at Bay, New York, Oxford University Press, 1978, p 138

43. 16 June 1943, Louis, Imperialism at Bay, New York, Oxford University Press, 1978, p 368

44. Quoted in John Dower, War Without Mercy, New York, Pantheon, 1987, p 172

45. See Mick Hume, 'The White Man's Bomb', Living Marxism, August 1995

46. Harry S. Truman, President of the United States of America to Samuel McCrea Cavert, General Secretary of The Churches of Christ in America, 11 August 1945

47. Hitler's Role in the Persecution of the Jews by the Nazi Regime, Irving v. Lipstadt, Defense Documents, 15. Hitler And The Mass Shootings Of Jews During The War Against Russia, 2000 http://www.hdot.org/en/trial/defense/pl1/15

48. Niall Ferguson, The War of the World, London, Allen Lane, 2006, p 443-4

49. Niall Ferguson, The War of the Worlds, London, Allen Lane, p 477

50. Saburō Ienaga, The Pacific War 1939-1945, New York, Random House, 1978, p 170

51. Niall Ferguson, The War of the Worlds, London, Allen Lane, p 265

52. D. Ibarruri, Speeches and Articles, 1936-1938, New York, 1938, p. 130

53. Compton Mackenzie, Eastern Epic, London, Chatto and Windus, 1951, p 1

54. Harold Macmillan, War Diaries: The Mediterranean, 1943-45, London, Macmillan, 1984, p 89

55. David Macey, Franz Fanon: A life, London, Granta, 2000, p 100

56. Todd. Moye, Freedom Flyers: The Tuskeegee Airmen of World War II, New York, Oxford University Press, 2010, 93-5

57. Alan Moorehead, The Desert War, London, Aurum, 2010, p 129

58. in Robert Moeller War Stories, Berkeley, University of California Press, 2001, p 66

10. A Soldier's Life

1. Wolfram Wette, Deborah Lucas Schneider, Wehrmacht: History, Myth, Reality, Harvard University Press, 2007, p 158

2. Allan Bérubé, Coming Out in World War II, New York, Plume, 1991, p 2, 3

3. Catherine Meridale, Ivan's War, London, Faber abnd Faber, 2005, p 71

4. Stephen Welch, 'Harsh but Just', German History Vol. 17 No. 3, 1999, pp360-399

5. John Costello, Love, Sex and War, London, Pan, 1986, p 118

6. Catherine Meridale, Ivan's War, London, Faber and Faber, 2005, p 157

7. John Costello, Love, Sex and War, London, Pan, 1986, p 120

8. James Jones's GI Diaries, quoted in John Costello, Love, Sex and War, London, Pan, 1986, p 119

9. Ian Christie, 'The Colonel Blimp File', Sight and Sound, Winter 1978/9, p 13

10. Alan Moorehead, The Desert War, London, Aurum Press, 2009, p 65

11. Alan Moorehead, The Desert War, London, Aurum Press, 2009, p 439

12. Julie Summers, The Colonel of Tamarkan, London, Simon and Schuster, 2005, p 147

13. Julie Summers, The Colonel of Tamarkan, London, Simon and Schuster, 2005, p 149

14. Catherine Meridale, Ivan's War, London, Faber and Faber, 2005, p 56

15. Catherine Meridale, Ivan's War, London, Faber and Faber, 2005, p 58

16. Anthony Beevor, Stalingrad, London, Penguin, 1999, p 17

17. Samuel W. Mitcham, The Rise of the Wehrmacht, Volume 1, Praeger Security International , 2008, p 588

18. Bischof and Ambrose, Eisenhower and the German Prisoners of War, p 18-20; Japanese prisoners Ulrich Strauss, The Anguish of Surrender, University of Washington Press, 2003, p 49

19. Bill Maudlin, Up Front, Bantam, New York, 1947, p 82

20. quoted in Overy, Russia's War, London, Allen Lane, 1997, p 33

21. in 'The People's Century', BBC TV/WGBH, 1995, episode 10

22. Jon Halliday, A Political History of Japanese Capitalism, New York, Monthly Review Press, 1975, p 145

23. William Manchester, American Caesar, London, Arrow, 1979, p 306

24. Christopher Browning, Origins of the Final Solution, Lincoln, University of Nebraska Press, 2004, p 291

11. Love and War

1. Stephanie Coontz, Marriage, New York, Viking, 2005, p 219

2. In John Costello, Love, Sex and War, London, Pan, 1986, p 215

3. Claudia Koonz, Mothers in the Fatherland, London, Jonathan Cape, 1987, p 185-6

4. RJB Bosworth, Mussolini's Italy, London, Allen Lane, 2005, p 262, 265

5. Roberto Bompiani, Eugenica e stirpe, Roma, L Possi, 1930, p 74, quoted in Eszter Andits, 'Sore on the Nation's Body': Repression of homosexuals under Italian Fascism, MA Thesis, Central European

University History Department, Budapest, Hungary, 2010, p 45

6. Quoted in Claudia Koonz, Mothers in the Fatherland, London, Jonathan Cape, 1987, p 189

7. Claudia Koonz, Mothers in the Fatherland, London, Jonathan Cape, 1987, p 187

8. John Costello, Love, Sex and War, London, Pan 1986, p 215, Claudia Koonz, Mothers in the Fatherland, London, Jonathan Cape, 1987, p 197

9. Stephanie Coontz, Marriage, New York, Viking, 2005, p 221

10. John Costello, Love, Sex and War, London, Pan, 1986, p 229

11. John Costello, Love, Sex and War, London, Pan, 1986, p 214, 211

12. John Costello, Love, Sex and War, London, Pan, 1986, p 195

13. Martin Glaberman, Wartime Strikes, Detroit, Bewick Editions, 1980, p 24

14. John Costello, Love, Sex and War, London, Pan, 1986, p 201

15. AIR-RAID PRECAUTIONS BILL. HC Deb 16 November 1937 vol 329 cc243-307

16. R Titmuss, Problems of Social Policy, HMSO, 1950, p 23

17. Committee on Imperial Defence quoted in R Titmuss, Problems of Social Policy, HMSO, 1950, p 23

18. AIR-RAID PRECAUTIONS BILL. HC Deb 16 November 1937 vol 329 cc243-307

19. John Costello, Love, Sex and War, London, Pan, 1986, p 209

20. John Costello, Love, Sex and War, London, Pan, 1986, p 207

21. John Costello, Love, Sex and War, London, Pan, 1986, p 235

22. John Costello, Love, Sex and War, London, Pan, 1986, p 24

23. Dagmar Hertzog, Sexuality and German Fascism, Bergahn Books, 2005, p 17

24. Quoted in Dagmar Hertzog, Sexuality and German Fascism, Bergahn Books, 2005, p 9; The theory of 'repressive desublimation' – the way that decadent societies broke down taboos and manipulated sexual desire would feature in Marcuse's later work Eros and Civilisation. See Reimut Reiche, Sexuality and Class Struggle, New York, Praeger, 1971, p 45, 48

25. Dagmar Hertzog, Sexuality and German Fascism, Bergahn Books, 2005, p 10

26. John Costello, Love Sex and War, London, Pan, 1986, p 109

27. Chuck Berry, Autobiography, London, Faber and Faber, 1987, p 43

28. Jon Savage, Columbus Day Riot, Guardian, 11 June 2011 http://www.guardian.co.uk/music/2011/jun/11/frank-sinatra-pop-star

29. John Costello, Love, Sex and War, London, Pan, 1986, p 191

30. Kay Saunders, War on the Homefront, St Lucia, University of Queensland Press, 1993, p 90

31. Bara Baldursdottir, 'The Rot Spreads like an Epidemic: Policing Adolescent Sexuality in Iceland During World War II' MA Thesis, University of Maryland Park, 2000, p 26 37

32. Julia Roos, in Dagmar Herzog, Sexuality and German Fascism, Bergahn Books, 2005, p 90

33. Stefan Micheler in Dagmar Herzog, Sexuality and German Fascism, Bergahn Books, 2005, p 106, 109, 113

34. John Costello, Love, Sex and War, London, Pan, 1986, p 161

35. RJB Bosworth, Mussolini's Italy, London, Allen Lane, 2005, p 436; and see Eszter Andits, 'Sore on the Nation's Body': Repression of homosexuals under Italian Fascism, MA Thesis, Central European University History Department, Budapest, Hungary, 2010, p 70

36. Allan Bérubé, Coming Out Under Fire, New York, Plume, 1991, p 217

37. Allan Bérubé, Coming Out Under Fire, New York, Plume, 1991, p 220, 224

38. Allan Bérubé, Coming Out Under Fire, New York, Plume, 1991, p 216-7

39. John Costello, Love, Sex and War, London, Pan, 1986, p 162

40. John Costello, Love, Sex and War, London, Pan, 1986, p 221

41. Stephanie Coontz, Marriage, New York, Viking, 2005, p 222, 223, 224

12. Power Politics

1. Communist International The Second Congress of the Communist International, London: New Park, 1977, p 16

2. E. H. Carr, Twenty Years Crisis, London, Macmillan, 1946, p 83-4

3. R. P. Dutt, World Politics 1918-1936, London: Victor Gollancz, 1936, p 190

4. Even US Under Secretary Dean Acheson concedes that Japan would at least have had to 'move to obtain oil by' overthrowing the Dutch 'through a Japanese-instigated-and-supported Indonesian

revolution' – a course that would have surely been punished by America and Britain, as was the occupation of French Indo-China, Present at the Creation, New York, Norton, 1969, p 37

5. Leon Trotsky, Europe and America, New York, Pathfinder, 1971 (orig. 1924), p 21, 23

6. Christopher Hibbert, Benito Mussolini, London, Reprint Society, 1962, p 152; sir John Hammerton (ed), The Second Great War, Vol II, p 680

7. quoted in Alvin Finkel and Clement Leibovitz, The Chamberlain-Hitler Collusion, London, Merlin Press, 1997, p 12

8. quoted in Alvin Finkel and Clement Leibovitz, The Chamberlain-Hitler Collusion, London, Merlin Press, 1997, p 65

9. Klaus Hildebrand, The Foreign Policy of the Third Reich, London, Batsford, 1973, 92

10. Ponting, Churchill, p 445

11. Finian Cunningham, Historical Notes, Independent, 20 October 1998

12. B.H. Liddell Hart, The German Generals Talk, New York, Quill, 1979, p 135

13. B.H. Liddell Hart, The German Generals Talk, p 136

14. quoted in David Irving, Churchill's War, New York, Avon, 1991, p 391-2

15. Mark Mazower, Hitler's Empire, London, Penguin, 2009, p 341

16. Mark Mazower, Hitler's Empire, p 356, 327

17. Ilya Ehrenburg, Memoirs, 1921-41, New York, Grosset and Dunlap 1966, p 496

18. Lenin, November 1920, in Collected Works 31, p 399

19. Stalin, 'The Social-Democratic Deviation in our party', Report delivered at the Fifteenth all-union conference of the CPSU(B), Nov 1, 1926 in Stalin On the Opposition, Foreign Language Press, Peking 1974

20. Hilger and Meyer, The Incompatible Allies, pp123-4

21. 'Thieves' Kitchen', or 'alliance of robbers' in Julius Katzer's translation of the speech of 15 October 1920, Lenin's Collected Works, 4th English Edition, Progress Publishers, Moscow, 1965, Volume 31, pages 318-333; Stalin in Trotsky, The Revolution Betrayed, New York, Pathfinder,1977 , p 199

22. Robert Black, Fascism in Germany, London, Steyne, 1975, p1035

23. quoted in Churchill, The Second World War III, The Grand Alliance, London, Reprint Society, 1953, p 309

24. Owen Lattimore, Solution in Asia, Boston, Little, Brown and Company, 1945, p 52-3

25. Li Narangoa and Robert Cribb (eds), Imperial Japan and National Identities in Asia, 1895-1945, London, Routledge, 2003, p 154

26. Li Narangoa and Robert Cribb (eds), Imperial Japan and National Identities in Asia, 1895-1945, London, Routledge, 2003, p 162

27. Cabinet Minutes, 19 July 1939, p 4

28. Saburō Ienaga, The Pacific War 1939-1945, New York, Pantheon, 1978, p 140

29. Quoted in Saburō Ienaga, The Pacific War 1939-1945, New York, Pantheon, 1978, p 139

30. Nick Turse and Tom Engelhardt, 'All Bases Covered?' AntiWar, 10 January 2011 http://original.antiwar.com/engelhardt/2011/01/09/all-bases-covered/

31. quoted in Charles Beard, President Roosevelt and the Coming of the War 1941, New Haven, Yale University Press, 1948, p 3

32. Stephen E. Ambrose, Rise To Globalism: American Foreign Policy 1938-1980, Harmondsworth, Penguin, 1981, p 29

33. David Kennedy, Freedom from Fear, Oxford University Press, 1999, p 482

34. These were the merchant fleets that London Mayor Ken Livingstone's father served on – an expression of Anglo-Soviet friendship that greatly impressed his son.

35. H. Stuart Hughes, Gentleman Rebel, New York, Ticknor and Fields, 1990, p 138

36. David Kennedy, Freedom From Fear, Oxford University Press, 1999, p 482

37. 'Joint Board Estimate of United States Overall Production Requirements', 11 September 1941, in Robert Sherwood, Roosevelt and Hopkins, New York, Harper Brothers, 1948, p 417

38. Richard Vinen, A History in Fragments, London, Abacus, 2002, p 222

39. Roosevelt to his son Elliot, in his book As He Saw It, quoted by V Berezhkov, At Stalin's Side, 1994, Birch Lane Press, Secausus, New Jersey, p. 245

40. V Berezhkov, At Stalin's Side, 1994, Birch Lane Press, Secausus,

New Jersey, p. 246

41. Leon Trotsky, Europe and America, 1926, http://www.marxists.org/archive/trotsky/1926/02/europe2.htm

42. David Gerrie, 'War on the Red Empire', Daily Mail, 21 September 2011 http://www.dailymail.co.uk/news/article-2039453/How-America-planned-destroy-BRITAIN-1930-bombing-raids-chemical-weapons.html

43. Skidelsky, John Maynard Keynes: Fighting for Britain, 2000, p xx

44. Skidelsky, John Maynard Keynes: Fighting for Britain, 2000, p 138, 'out of gold and dollars' p 96

45. Skidelsky, John Maynard Keynes: Fighting for Britain, 2000, p 370

46. W. Averell Harriman and Elie Abel, Special Envoy to Churchill and Stalin 1941-1946, New York, Random House, 1975, p 28

47. Skidelsky, John Maynard Keynes: Fighting for Britain, 2000, p 96

48. W. Averell Harriman and Elie Abel, Special Envoy to Churchill and Stalin 1941-1946, New York, Random House, 1975, p 74

49. Skidelsky, John Maynard Keynes: Fighting for Britain, 2000, p 103

50. Louis, Imperialism at Bay, New York, Oxford University Press, 1978, p 24

51. Dean Acheson, Present at the Creation: My Years at the State Department, New York, WW Norton, 1969, p 31-3. Keynes dressed up his support for import controls as modern planning, and rubbished Hull's 'Open Door' as nineteenth century free trade dogma.

52. W. Averell Harriman and Elie Abel, Special Envoy to Churchill and Stalin 1941-1946, New York, Random House, 1975, p 71

53. in Louis, Imperialism at Bay, New York, Oxford University Press, 1978, p 155

54. in Louis, Imperialism at Bay, New York, Oxford University Press, 1978, p129

55. 12 October 1942, in Louis, Imperialism at Bay, New York, Oxford University Press, 1978, p 198

56. Churchill, The Times, 11 November 1942, in Louis, Imperialism at Bay, New York, Oxford University Press, 1978, p 200

57. Times, 21 November 1942, in Louis, Imperialism at Bay, New York, Oxford University Press, 1978, 203

58. Parliamentary Debates, House of Lords, 20 May 1942, c. 1088, in Louis, Imperialism at Bay, New York, Oxford University Press,

1978, 140

59. 28 December 1942, in Louis, Imperialism at Bay, New York, Oxford University Press, 1978, p 209

60. Churchill, talking to a group of American leaders, Louis, Imperialism at Bay, New York, Oxford University Press, 1978, p 16

61. Christopher Eastwood, Colonial Office, minute 21 April 1943, CO 323/1858/9057B, in Louis, Imperialism at Bay, New York, Oxford University Press, 1978, p 247

62. Louis, Imperialism at Bay, New York, Oxford University Press, 1978, p 402

63. Louis, Imperialism at Bay, New York, Oxford University Press, 1978, p 285

64. James Byrnes, Speaking Frankly, New York, 1947, p x

65. Jonathan Fenby, The General, London, Simon and Schuster, 2010, p 42-3

66. Fenby, The General, p 147

67. Ernest Mandel, The Meaning of the Second World War, London, Verso, 1986, p 124

68. Ilya Ehrenburg, Memoirs, The War 1941-45, London, MacGibbon and Kee, 1964, p 128

69. On 17 June 1944 Louis, Imperialism at Bay, New York, Oxford University Press, 1978, p 38

70. Ralph Bunche US State Department, Dependent Areas Division, on the Brazzaville Conference, 6 April 1944, in Louis, Imperialism at Bay, New York, Oxford University Press, 1978, p 45

71. Simon Berthon, Allies at War, New York, Carroll and Graf, 2001, p 109

72. Matthew Cobb, The Resistance, p 139

73. Simon Berthon, Allies at War, New York, Carroll and Graf, 2001, p 168

74. Matthew Cobb, The Resistance, p 147

75. Simon Berthon, Allies at War, New York, Carroll and Graf, 2001, p 76, 78

76. Simon Berthon, Allies at War, New York, Carroll and Graf, 2001, p 54

77. Simon Berthon, Allies at War, New York, Carroll and Graf, 2001, p 147-50

78. Churchill, The Second World War III, The Grand Alliance, London,

Reprint Society, 1953, p 310

79. Jean Barber and Mark Harrison, The Soviet Home Front: 1941-45, London, Longman, 1991, p 35

80. 'Attack Hitler Now!' 1 May 1942, quoted in Sidney Hook, Out of Step, New York, Harper and Row, 1987, p 311

81. Ian Maclaine, Ministry of Morale, London, George Allen and Unwin, 1979, p 201

82. Sherwood, Roosevelt and Hopkins, New York, Harper, 1948, p 697

83. Memorandum on the Teheran talks, in Robert Sherwood, Roosevelt and Hopkins, New York, Harper Brothers, 1948, p 782-3

84. Louis, Imperialism at Bay, New York, Oxford University Press, 1978, p 532

85. Christopher Weeramantry and Nathaniel Berman, 'In The Wake Of Empire', The Grotius Lecture Series, presented at the American Society of International Law's 93rd Annual Meeting in March 1999, http://www.auilr.org/pdf/14/14-6-1.pdf

86. in Kolko, The Politics of War, New York, Pantheon, 1990, p 477-8

87. Louis, Imperialism at Bay, New York, Oxford University Press, 1978, p 552

88. 2 October 1942 in Louis, Imperialism at Bay, New York, Oxford University Press, 1978, p 170

89. Sumner Welles' evidence, US State Department Advisory Committee 10 April 1943, in Louis, Imperialism at Bay, New York, Oxford University Press, 1978, p 237

90. Dean Acheson, Present at the Creation, p 112

91. in Kolko, The Politics of War, New York, Pantheon, 1990, p 276

92. Robert Wilcox, Target Patton: The Plot to Assassinate General George S. Patton, New York, Regnery, 2008, p 112

93. John Willoughby, Remaking the Conquering Heroes: the Postwar American Occupation of Germany, New York, Palgrave, 2001

94. Mazower, Dark Continent: Europe's Twentieth Century, London, Allen Lane, 1998, p 229

95. Skidelsky, John Maynard Keynes: Fighting for Britain, London, Pimlico, 2000, p 242

96. Davidson, Special Operations Europe: Scenes from the anti-Nazi War, Newton Abbot, Readers Union, 1981, p 132

97. Skidelsky, John Maynard Keynes: Fighting For Britain, London, Pimlico, 2000, p 363

98. Robert Litwak, Detente and the Nixon Doctrine: American Foreign Policy and the pursuit of stability, 1969-1976, Cambridge University Press, 1986, p 153

99. Louis, Imperialism at Bay, New York, Oxford University Press, 1978, p 284

100. Averell Harriman, Special Envoy, New York, Random House, 1975, p 356-8

101. Milovan Djilas, Wartime, Wartime, New York, Harcourt Bruce Jovanovich, 1977, p 437

13. A Time of Reaction

1. Sumner Welles, A Time For Decision, New York, Harper Bros, 1944, p 312

2. Mark Mazower, Dark Continent: Europe's Twentieth Century, London, Allen Lane, 1998, p 90

3. Mazower, Dark Continent, p 138

4. International Communist Correspondence, July 1936, Vol.2 No. 8, p 4

5. Mark Mazower, Dark Continent, p 101

6. Clive Ponting, Churchill, London, Sinclair Stevenson, 1994, p 230

7. Serge also accused Kun's Commisars of abandoning Hungary, 'What Everyone Should Know About Repression', http://www.marxists.org/archive/serge/1926/repression/index.htm 2004: 4-4

8. Paul Frölich, Rosa Luxemburg, London, Pluto, 1972 p 297-301

9. Clive Ponting, Churchill, London, Sinclair Stevenson, 1994, p 264

10. Ehrenburg, Memoirs, 1921-41, New York, Grosset and Dunlap, 1966, p 56

11. Nicholas Farrell, Mussolini: A New Life, London, Weidenfield and Nicholson, 2003, p 58

12. William Manchester, American Caesar, Douglas MacArthur, 1880-1964, London, Arrow, 1979, 133-4

13. Mandel, The Meaning of the Second World War, London, Verso, 1986, p 40

14. Daniel Goldhagen, Hitler's Willing Executioners, 1997, p 118-9

15. Robert Black, Fascism in Germany, Volume II, London, Steyne Publications, 1975, p 682

16. Daniel Guerin Fascism and Big Business, New York Monad Press, 1973 (orig. 1936), p 53, 47

17. Victor Farias, Heidegger and Nazism, Philadelphia, Temple University Press, 1989, p 80; Robin Black, Fascism in Germany, Vol. II London, Steyne, 1975, p 609; Franz Neumann, Behemoth, New York, Harper and Row, 1966, p 378

18. Robin Black, Fascism in Germany, Vol II, London, Steyne, 1975, p 808

19. Robin Black, Fascism in Germany, Vol II, p 802-3

20. Henri Michel, The Shadow War, London, Corgi, 1975, p 35

21. quoted in Nicholas Farrell, Mussolini: A New Life, London, Weidenfield and Nicholson, 2003, p 130

22. Clive Ponting, Churchill, London, Sinclair Stevenson, 1994, p 393

23. Ponting, Churchill, p 390

24. Ponting, Churchill, p 394

25. 28 November 1934, in Rajani Palme Dutt, World Politics 1918 – 1936, London, Victor Gollancz, 1936, p 265

26. Keith Middlemas, Politics in Industrial Society, London, Andre Deutsch, 1980, p 236

27. Keith Middlemas, Politics in Industrial Society, p 275

14. Blitzkrieg – The German invasion of Europe

1. Sandhurst trained Fuller worked with Liddell Hart on armoured warfare in the 1930s, but later became a supporter of the British Union of Fascists. On 20 April 1939 Fuller was an honoured guest at Adolf Hitler's 50th birthday parade and watched as 'for three hours a completely mechanised and motorised army roared past the Führer.' Afterwards Hitler asked, 'I hope you were pleased with your children?' Fuller replied, 'Your Excellency, they have grown up so quickly that I no longer recognise them.' In Max Boot. War made new: technology, warfare, and the course of history, 1500 to today, Gotham, 2006, p 224

2. Heinz Guderian, Panzer Leader, 1996, p. 13

3. Victor Madej (ed) The German War Economy: The Motorization Myth, Allentown, Game Publishing Company, 1984 p 3, 121-124; Shimon Naveh of the Israeli Defence Force argued that Liddell Hart had exaggerated his own influence, and Guderian's on the motorization of warfare. Shimon Naveh, In Pursuit of Military Excellence; The Evolution of Operational Theory. London, Frank Cass, 1997

4. Jørgen Hæstrup, Europe Ablaze, Odense University Press, 1978, p

72

5. Henri Michel, The Shadow War: Resistance in Europe, 1939-1945, London, Corgi, 1975, p 38

6. On 5 April 1940, quoted in Gerhard Hirschfeld, Nazi Rule and Dutch Collaboration: The Netherlands under German Occupation 1940-1945, Oxford, Berg, 1988, p 34. The German Marxist Karl Korsch says the same thing: 'the Nazi counter revolution which began in Germany, 1918-1933, is continuing today on an enlarged European scale', 'Prelude to Hitler', Living Marxism, vol V, no 2, Fall 1940, p 14

7. Tony Judt, Postwar: A History of Europe since 1945, London, William Heinemann, 2005, p 39

8. Henri Michel, The Shadow War: Resistance in Europe, 1939-1945, London, Corgi, 1975, p 45

9. Robert Keyserlingk, Austria in World War II: An Anglo American Dilemma, McGill-Queens University Press, Kingston and Montreal, 1988, p 57, 36

10. Gerhard Hirschfeld, Nazi Rule and Dutch Collaboration: The Netherlands under German Occupation 1940-1945, Oxford, Berg, 1988, p 71

11. Gerhard Hirschfeld, Nazi Rule and Dutch Collaboration, p 72, 86

12. Gerhard Hirschfeld, Nazi Rule and Dutch Collaboration, p 77-8

13. Gerhard Hirschfeld, Nazi Rule and Dutch Collaboration, p 185, 198, 206

14. Henri Michel, The Shadow War: Resistance in Europe, 1939-1945, London, Corgi, 1975, p 35

15. Niall Ferguson, War of the World, London, Allen Lane, 2006, p 388

16. Quoted in David Irving, Hitler's War, p 6

17. Sir John Hammerton, The Second Great War, Vol III, London, Amalgamated Press, p 863

18. Niall Ferguson, War of the World, , p 388

19. Interview in Marcel Ophuls, The Sorrow and the Pity, 1969, pt I, 20 minutes in

20. Arthur Koestler, The Scum of the Earth, London, eland, 1991, p 51, 52

21. Robert O. Paxton, Vichy France: Old Guard and New Order 1940-1944, New York Columbia University Press, 1982, p 13, 8

22. James Hayward, Myths and Legends of the Second World War,

Stroud, Sutton, 2004, p 57

23. Paul Johnson, Modern Times : A history of the world from the 1920s to the 1990s, London, Phoenix, 1992, p 366-7

24. quoted in Robert Paxton, Vichy France, 1982, p 136

25. Jonathan Fenby, The General, London, Simon and Schuster, 2010, p 155

26. Marcel Ophuls, The Sorrow and the Pity, 1969, pt I

27. Walther Warlimont, interview in The Sorrow and the Pity, 1969, pt I

28. The Economist, 14 June 1941, in Living Marxism, vol VI, no 1, Fall 1941, p 64-5

29. Quoted in Noam Chomsky, Hegemony or Survival, Metropolitan Books, 2003, p 81

30. Report of the Sub Committee of Patronal Organization, Comite Central Industriel, 31 August 1940, quoted in John Gillingham, Belgian Business and the Nazi New Order, Jan Hondt Foundation, Ghent, 1977, p 167

31. Mark Mazower, Hitler's Empire, London, Penguin, 2009, p 287

32. Henri Michel, The Shadow War: Resistance in Europe, 1939-1945, London, Corgi, 1975, p 28

33. Tooze, The Wages of Destruction, London, Allen Lane, 2006, p 247

34. Mazower, Dark Continent: Europe's Twentieth Century, London, Allen Lane, 1998, p160

35. Living Marxism, vol. VI, no. 1, Fall 1941, p 31

15. Morale Bombing

1. Nicholson Baker, Human Smoke, London Simon and Schuster, 2008, p 134

2. Nicholson Baker, Human Smoke, p 180

3. Nicholson Baker, Human Smoke, p 182

4. Nicholson Baker, Human Smoke, p 185, 199, 213, 216

5. Jorg Friedrich, The Fire, New York Columbia UP, 2006, p 70

6. in James Corum and Wray Johnson, Airpower in Small Wars, University of Kansas, p 65

7. Adam Tooze, Wages of Destruction, London, Allen Lane, 2006, p 510

8. quoted in Vera Brittan, one Voice, London, Continuum, 2005, p 110

9. Harris to Arthur Street in 1944, quoted in McLaine, Ministry of Morale, London, George Allen and Unwin, 1979, p 161-2

10. Jorg Friedrich, The Fire, p 74

11. Jorg Friedrich, The Fire, p 75

12. Jorg Friedrich, the Fire, p 77, 144

13. Jorg Friedrich, the Fire, p 313

14. Jorg Friedrich, the Fire, p 313-5

15. Jorg Friedrich, The Fire, p 81

16. Jorg Friedrich, The Fire, p 82

17. John K Galbraith, A Cloud Over Civilisation, Guardian 15 July 2004, and see Thomas Fleming The New Dealers' War, New York, Basic, 2001, p 529-30

18. Tim Mason, Nazism, Fascism and the Working Class, Cambridge University Press, 1996, p 265

19. Richard Overy, Russia's War, London, Penguin, 1999, p 89

20. Albert Speer, Inside the Third Reich, London, Sphere Books, 1971, p 496-7

21. David Edgerton, The Shock of the Old, London, 2006, Profile Books, p 17

16. The Collapse of the Soviet Empire

1. Erich Wollenberg, The Red Army, London, New Park, 1978, p 123

2. In Robert Low, La Pasionara: The Spanish Firebrand, London, Hutchinson, 1992, p 123

3. Norman Davies, The Past in Poland's Present, Oxford University Press, 2001, pp 56-8

4. Sigurdur Gylfi Magnusson, Finland in the Second World War, London, Reaktion Books, 2010, p 79

5. Sigurdur Gylfi Magnusson, Finland in the Second World War, London, Reaktion Books, 2010, p 69-70

6. Leopold Trepper, The Great Game, London, Sphere, 1979, p 125

7. Tooze, Wages of Destruction, London, Allen Lane, 2006, p 457

8. Leopold Trepper, The Great Game, London, Sphere, 1979, p 127

9. Valentin Berezhkov, At Stalin's Side, Birch Lane Press, 1994, p 54

10. Jean Barber and Mark Harrison, The Soviet Home Front: 1941-45, London, Longman, 1991, p 27

11. Niall Ferguson, The War of the World, London, Allen Lane, 2006, p 435

12. Valentin Berezhkov, At Stalin's Side, Birch Lane Press, 1994, p 56

13. Jean Barber and Mark Harrison, The Soviet Home Front: 1941-45,

London, Longman, 1991, p 54

14. Jean Barber and Mark Harrison, The Soviet Home Front: 1941-45, London, Longman, 1991, p 40-41

15. Lizzie Collingham, Taste of War, London, Allen Lane, 2011, p 187

16. Niall Freguson, War of the World, London, Allen Lane, 2006, p 441

17. Smolensk Declaration in Catherine Andreyev, Andrei Vlasov and the Russian Liberation Movement, Cambridge University Press, 1990 p 207

18. Richard Overy, Russia's War, London, Penguin 1999, p 150, p 130

19. Richard Overy, Russia's War, London, Penguin 1999, p 127, 128

20. Jean Barber and Mark Harrison, The Soviet Home Front: 1941-45, London, Longman, 1991, p 78

21. Jean Barber and Mark Harrison, The Soviet Home Front: 1941-45, London, Longman, 1991, p 87-90

22. Jean Barber and Mark Harrison, The Soviet Home Front: 1941-45, London, Longman, 1991, p 96, 100

23. Jean Barber and Mark Harrison, The Soviet Home Front: 1941-45, London, Longman, 1991, p114-5

24. Richard Overy, Russia's War, London, Penguin, 1999, p 94-5

17. The Arab Revolt

1. 23 May 1941, quoted in Churchill, The Grand Alliance, p 214

2. Excerpted in Marcel Ophuls The Sorrow and the Pity, Part I, around ten minutes in

3. Nicholson Baker, Human Smoke, p 205

4. Howard Sachar, Europe Leaves the Middle East, London, Allen Lane, 1974, p 115, 117

5. Churchill, Their Finest Hour, The Second World War II, London, The Reprint Society, 1953, p 340

6. The Finest Hour, p 343-4

7. Howard Sachar, Europe Leaves the Middle East, London, Allen Lane, 1974, p 123

8. Howard Sachar, Europe Leaves the Middle East, London, Allen Lane, 1974, p 124

9. Gilles Perrault, A Man Apart: The life of Henri Curiel, London, Zed Books, 1987 p 77

10. Howard Sachar, Europe Leaves the Middle East, London, Allen Lane, 1974, p 141

11. Gilles Perrault, A Man Apart: The life of Henri Curiel, London, Zed Books, 1987 p 80

12. Howard Sachar, Europe Leaves the Middle East, London, Allen Lane, 1974, p 226

13. Gilles Perrault, A Man Apart: The life of Henri Curiel, London, Zed Books, 1987 p 82

14. Gilles Perrault, A Man Apart: The life of Henri Curiel, London, Zed Books, 1987 p 85

15. Fieldhouse, Western Imperialism in the Middle East, p 92-5

16. Churchill, World War II, Vol. III: The Grand Alliance, p 207

17. 6 May 1941, in Churchill The Grand Alliance, p 208

18. Sir John Hammerton (ed.) The Second Great War, Volume V, London, Waverley Book Company, p 1676

19. Walid S. Hamdi explains why the document was a forgery in his Rashid 'Ali Al Gailani and the Nationalist Movement in Iraq, Darf Publishers, London, 1987, p 55

20. Sachar, Europe Leaves the Middle East, London, Allen Lane, 1974, p 175

21. Hamdi, Rashid 'Ali Al Gailani and the Nationalist Movement in Iraq, Darf Publishers, London, 1987, p 115

22. Air Ministry Records, 41/30, II, The Siege of Habbaniya

23. The Grand Alliance, p 209-10

24. Hammerton, The Second Great War, Vol V, p 1682

25. Hamdi, Rashid 'Ali Al Gailani and the Nationalist Movement in Iraq, Darf Publishers, London, 1987, p p 170

26. Churchill, The Grand Alliance, 1953, p 265

27. Fenby, The General, 2010, p 172

28. in Howard Sachar, Europe Leaves the Middle East, London, Allen Lane, 1974p 202

29. Robert Lyman Iraq 1941: The Battles for Basra, Habbaniya, Fallujah and Baghdad. Campaign. Oxford, New York: Osprey Publishing 2006. pp. 96

30. Howard Sachar, Europe Leaves the Middle East, London, Allen Lane, 1974, p 206; afterwards, he fled to Germany, and in 1948, took part in the war against Israel

31. Howard Sachar, Europe Leaves the Middle East, London, Allen Lane, 1974, p 214

32. Jonathan Fenby, The General, 2010, p 172

33. Macmillan, War Diaries: The Mediterranean, 1943-45, London, Macmillan, 1984, p 305

34. Jonathan Fenby, The General, 2010, p 173

35. Howard Sachar, Europe Leaves the Middle East, London, Allen Lane, 1974, p 305

36. Howard Sachar, Europe Leaves the Middle East, London, Allen Lane, 1974, p 307

37. 'Levant Situation', Evening Post (New Zealand) 4 Pipiri 1945, p 5

38. Britain's Treachery, France's Revenge by Meir Zamir Haaretz, 1 February 2008 http://www.middleeasttransparent.com/spip.php?article3278

39. Howard Sachar, Europe Leaves the Middle East, London, Allen Lane, 1974, p 157

40. Churchill, The Second World War, Grand Alliance, p 364, 377

41. Howard Sachar, Europe Leaves the Middle East, London, Allen Lane, 1974, p 221

42. F. Eshraghi The Anglo Soviet Occupation of Iran, Middle Eastern Studies, Vol. 20, No. 1 (Jan., 1984), pp. 27-52, p 35

43. The Grand Alliance, p 377

44. The Grand Alliance, p 379

45. The Second Great War, Vol. V, p 1859

46. Answer to History, Stein and Day, 1980, p 67

47. Letters from Tehran, IB Tauris, p 73

48. The Grand Alliance, p 382-3

49. Answer to History, p 67

50. Prime Minister to Stalin, 12 Oct. '41, The Grand Alliance, p 384

51. Hammerton, The Second Great War, Vol V., p 1862

52. Howard Sachar, Europe Leaves the Middle East, London, Allen Lane, 1974, p 225

53. 3 Sept 1941, in Reader Bullard, Letters from Tehran, p 77

54. British Prime Minister to Foreign Secretary, 28 April 1943, Letters from Tehran, p 187, and Letters from Tehran, p 73

55. Answer to History, p 69

56. Mission for My Country, p 77, and see Kamran M Dadkhah 'The Iranian Economy during the Second World War: The Devaluation Controversy.' Middle Eastern Studies April 1, 2001

57. Stephen McFarland, Anatomy of an Iranian Political Crowd: The Tehran Bread Riot of December 1942, International Journal of

Middle East Studies, 17 (1985) pp51-65, p 51, and see Compton Mackenzie Eastern Epic, London, Chatto and Windus, 1951, p 138

58. Mohammad Reza Pahlavi, Mission for My Country, 1961, p 76

59. 18 December 1942, in Letters from Tehran, p 161

60. Letters from Tehran, p 163

61. Mission for My Country, 1961, p 76

62. Paul Carrel, The Foxes of the Desert, London, New English Library 1961, p 198

63. Howard Sachar, Europe Leaves the Middle East, London, Allen Lane, 1974, p 244

64. Louis, Imperialism at Bay, New York, Oxford University Press, 1978, p 50

65. Quoted in Robert Paxton, Vichy France, New York, Columbia University Press, 1982, p 308

66. C Ageron, 'Developments in North Africa in the Second World War' in Ali Mazrui (ed), Africa and the Second World War, Unesco, Benghazi, 1981, p 40

67. Dirk Vandewalle, A History of Modern Libya, Cambridge, 2006, p 36

68. John Wright, Libya: A Modern History, London, Croom Helm, p 46

69. Idris El-Hareir, 'North Africa and the Second World War', in Mazrui (ed) Africa and the Second World War, Unesco, 1981, p 32, 34

70. Alan Moorehead, The Desert War, London, Aurum Press, 2009, p 475-6

71. Monnet, Memoirs, New York, Doubleday, 1978, p 190. The Vichy regime had repealed the Cremieux Decree that gave Algeria's Jews citizenship.

72. Macmillan, War Diaries: The Mediterranean, 1943-45, London, Macmillan, 1984, p 193

73. C Ageron, 'developments in North Africa During the Second World War', in Mazrui (ed) Africa and the Second World War, Unesco, 1981, p 42

74. From the newspaper report in Les Echos de la Soummam, 9 May 1985, quoted in David Macey, Franz Fanon: A life, p 206

75. Tony Cliff, 'The Middle East at the Crossroads', Fourth International, December 1945

18. Collapse of the European Empires in East Asia

1. Eri Hotta, Pan Asianism and Japan's War 1931-1945, London, Palgrave Macmillan, 2007, p 59

2. Amery's speech 27 February 1933, Churchill's 24 February 1933, both quoted in World War – Cold War, Freedom Press, London, 1989, p 87

3. Anne Booth, Colonial Legacies, Honolulu, University of Hawi'i Press, 2007, p 150-1

4. Joyce Lebra, Japanese Trained Armies in South East Asia, New York, Columbia University Press, 1977, 4-8

5. Joyce Chapman Lebra, The Indian National Army and Japan, Singapore, Institute of South East Asian Studies, 2008 (orig. 1971), p 156

6. Joyce Lebra, Japanese Trained Armies in South East Asia, New York, Columbia University Press, 1977, 41

7. Joyce Lebra, Japanese Trained Armies in South East Asia, New York, Columbia University Press, 1977, p 44

8. John Christian, 'Burma', Far Eastern Survey, Vol. 11, No. 3. (Feb. 9, 1942), pp. 40-44.

9. Joyce Lebra, Japanese Trained Armies in South East Asia, New York, Columbia University Press, 1977, p 58

10. Christopher Bayly and Tim Harper, Forgotten Armies, London, Penguin, 2005, p 161-2

11. Christopher Bayly and Tim Harper, Forgotten Armies, London, Penguin, 2005, p 172-3

12. Joyce Lebra, Japanese Trained Armies in South East Asia, New York, Columbia University Press, 1977, 11

13. Joyce Lebra, Japanese Trained Armies in South East Asia, New York, Columbia University Press, 1977, p 45, 41

14. Mark Roehrs and William Renzi, World War II in the Pacific, Armonk, ME Sharpe, 2004, p 191

15. Peter Calvocoressi and Guy Wint, Total War, Vol. II, New York Ballantine Books, 1972, p 181

16. Quoted in Joyce Chapman Lebra, The Indian National Army and Japan, Singapore, Institute of South East Asian Studies, 2008 (orig. 1971), p 34

17. Christopher Bayly and Tim Harper, Forgotten Armies, London, Penguin, 2005, p 163

18. Christopher Bayly and Tim Harper, Forgotten Armies, London, Penguin, 2005, p 142

19. Above, under 'America's War Against Britain', in the chapter on power politics.

20. Christopher Bayly and Tim Harper, Forgotten Armies, London, Penguin, 2005, 143, 146, 149

21. Christopher Bayly and Tim Harper, Forgotten Armies, London, Penguin, 2005, 150

22. See Jose Johnson's diary of the evacuation, BBC 'People's War', http://www.bbc.co.uk/ww2peopleswar/stories/04/a3338804.shtml, and also Sandra Carney's family memoirs, 20 March 2007, http://www.fsmarchives.org/article.php?id=818757, Christopher Bayly and Tim Harper, Forgotten Armies, London, Penguin, 2005, p 180

23. Quoted in Jon Halliday, A Political History of Japanese Capitalism, New York, Monthly Review Press, 1975, p 159

24. Joyce Lebra, The Indian National Army and Japan, Singapore, 2008, p 37-8

25. Joyce Lebra, The Indian National Army and Japan, Singapore, 2008, p 39-74, 64, 75

26. A Journalist, Netaji, Lahore, 1946, p 93-4

27. Joyce Lebra, The Indian National Army and Japan, Singapore, 2008, p 120

28. Anthony Read and David Fisher, The Proudest Day: India's Long Road to Independence, London, Jonathan Cape, 1997, p 343

29. Joyce Lebra, The Indian National Army and Japan, Singapore, 2008, p 186

30. William Manchester, American Caesar, Douglas MacArthur, 1880-1964, London, Arrow, 1979, p 159

31. in Renato and Letizia Constantino, The Philippines: The Continuing Past, The Foundation for Nationalist Studies, Quezon City, 1984, p 45

32. William Manchester, American Caesar, Douglas MacArthur, 1880-1964, London, Arrow, 1979, p 215, 165

33. William Manchester, American Caesar, Douglas MacArthur, 1880-1964, London, Arrow, 1979, p 222-3

34. Renato and Letizia Constantino, The Philippines: The Continuing Past, The Foundation for Nationalist Studies, Quezon City, 1984, p

, 47, 22, 23, 48-50

35. William Manchester, American Caesar, Douglas MacArthur, 1880-1964, London, Arrow, 1979, p 247; James Hamilton Paterson, America's Boy: The Marcoses and the Philippines, London, Granta, 1999, 83

36. William Manchester, American Caesar, Douglas MacArthur, 1880-1964, London, Arrow, 1979, p 263

37. William Manchester, American Caesar, Douglas MacArthur, 1880-1964, London, Arrow, 1979, p 342

38. Anne Booth, Colonial Legacies, Honolulu, University of Hawai'i Press, 2007, p 150-1

39. Joyce Lebra, Japanese Trained Armies in South East Asia, New York, Columbia University Press, 1977, 13

40. Anne Booth, Colonial Legacies, Honolulu, University of Hawi'i Press, 2007, p 153

41. Joyce Lebra, Japanese Trained Armies in South East Asia, New York, Columbia University Press, 1977, 11

42. Christopher Bayly and Tim Harper, Forgotten Armies, London, Penguin, 2005, p 405

19. Quit India

1. Anthony Read and David Fisher, The Proudest Day, London, Jonathan Cape, 1997, p 287

2. Quoted in M. J. Akbar, Nehru: The Making of Modern India, London, Penguin, 1989, p 335

3. Devadas Gandhi, India Unreconciled: A Documentary History of Indian Political Events from the Crisis of August to October 1943, New Delhi, Hindustan Times, 1943 – quoting from the Churchill Papers

4. Madhusree Mukerjee, Churchill's Secret War: The British Empire and the Ravaging of India During World War II, New York, Basic Books, 2010, p xxv

5. Simon Burgess, Stafford Cripps: A Political Life, London, Victor Gollancz, 1999, p 164, 166-7, Akbar, Nehru, London Penguin, 1989, p 335, 338, 339

6. Bertolt Brecht, Journals 1934-1955, London, Methuen, p 227

7. HC Deb 08 October 1942 vol 383 cc1386-460

8. Akbar, Nehru, London, Penguin, 1989, p 339

9.   Devdas Gandhi, A Documentary History of Indian Political Events from the Crisis of August to October 1943, Hindustan Times, New Delhi, 1943; Mukherjee, Churchill's Secret War, p XXX, p 76-7; Akbar, Nehru, London, Penguin, 1989, p 351

10. Madhusree Mukerjee, Churchill's Secret War: The British Empire and the Ravaging of India During World War II, New York, Basic Books, 2010, p 30

11. HC Deb 08 October 1942 vol 383 cc1386-460

12. Madhusree Mukerjee, Churchill's Secret War: The British Empire and the Ravaging of India During World War II, New York, Basic Books, 2010, p 78

13. Madhusree Mukerjee, Churchill's Secret War: The British Empire and the Ravaging of India During World War II, New York, Basic Books, 2010, p 4

14. Niall Ferguson, War of the Worlds, p 413;   Ponting, Churchill, London, Sinclair Stevenson, 1994, p 699; Madhusree Mukerjee, Churchill's Secret War: The British Empire and the Ravaging of India During World War II, New York, Basic Books, 2010, p 34

15. Ponting, Churchill, 700; Skidelsky, Keynes: Fighting for Britain, London, Macmillan, 2000, p 136; Madhusree Mukerjee, Churchill's Secret War: The British Empire and the Ravaging of India During World War II, New York, Basic Books, 2010, p 105

16. Simon Burgess, Stafford Cripps: A Political Life, London, Victor Gollancz, 1999, p 171

17. Madhusree Mukerjee, Churchill's Secret War: The British Empire and the Ravaging of India During World War II, New York, Basic Books, 2010, p 57

18. Madhusree Mukerjee, Churchill's Secret War: The British Empire and the Ravaging of India During World War II, New York, Basic Books, 2010, p 64

19. See Niall Ferguson, War of the Worlds, London, Allen Lane, 2006, p414

20. Madhusree Mukerjee, Churchill's Secret War: The British Empire and the Ravaging of India During World War II, New York, Basic Books, 2010, p 67, 46, 129, 103; Sugata Bose, 'Starvation amidst plenty: the making of famine in Bengal, Honan and Tonkin, 1942-45', Modern Asian Studies, Vol 24, No 4, October 1990

21. Madhusree Mukerjee, Churchill's Secret War: The British Empire

and the Ravaging of India During World War II, New York, Basic Books, 2010, p 210-3

22. Madhusree Mukerjee, Churchill's Secret War: The British Empire and the Ravaging of India During World War II, New York, Basic Books, 2010, p 91-2, 100

23. quoted in The People's War, 14 November 1943

24. Lizzie Collingham (The Taste of War, p 150) gives insufficient weight to this offer, which was indeed genuine.

20. The Revolt against the War

1. Tim Mason, The Workers' Opposition in Nazi Germany, History Workshop Journal # 11, Spring 1981, http://libcom.org/library/workers-opposition-nazi-germany-tim-mason

2. Tim Mason, Nazism, Fascism and the Working Class, Cambridge, University Press, 1996, p 128

3. Goebbels Diaries, London Hamish Hamilton, 1948, p 144-5

4. Ulrich Herbert, Hitler's Foreign Workers, Cambridge, University Press, 1997, p 351-352

5. Hippe, And Red is the Colour of Our Flag, London, Index Books, 1991, chapter eleven

6. Leopold Trepper, The Great Game, London, Sphere, 1979, p 122-3

7. Hippe, And Red is the Colour of Our Flag, London, Index Books, 1991, p 189

8. 1939-1945: The Edelweiss Pirates, http://libcom.org/history/articles/edelweiss-pirates

9. Ian Kershaw, Hitler 1936–1945: Nemesis, p 704

10. Quoted in Ted Morgan, A Covert Life, New York, Random House, 1999, p 133

11. Irving Howe, Smash the Profiteers, New York, Workers Party, 1946, p 4

12. Quoted in Noam Chomsky, American Power and the New Mandarins, Harmonsdworth, Penguin, 1969, p 134

13. See Gregory Sumner, Dwight McDonald and the Politics Circle, Cornell University Press, 1996

14. The Militant, 28 November 1942, and here: http://www.marxists.org/archive/cannon/works/1942/militant.htm

15. Fred Westacott, Shaking the Chains, Old Tupton, Joe Clark, 2002, p 126

16. Raymond Challinor, The Struggle for Hearts and Minds, Whitley Bay, Bewick Press, 1995, p 13

17. HC Deb 21 May 1940 vol 361 cc20-2

18. Fenner Brockway, The Way Out, London, ILP, July 1942, p 7

19. Tim Mason, 'The Turin Strikes of March 1943', in Nazism, Fascism and the Working Class, Cambridge, University Press, 1990, 274-294; Paul Ginsborg, A History of Contemporary Italy, Harmondsworth, Penguin, 1990, p 9-11; Jørgen Hæstrup, Europe Ablaze, Odense University Press, 1978, p 110-111

20. In Nicholas Farrell, Mussolini: A New Life, London, Weidenfeld and Nicholson, 2003, p 374

21. Jørgen Hæstrup, Europe Ablaze, Odense University Press, 1978, p 113-4

22. Matthew Cobb, The Resistance, London, Pocket Books, 2009, p 69-72

23. Jørgen Hæstrup, Europe Ablaze, Odense University Press, 1978, p 119, 124

24. Jørgen Hæstrup, Europe Ablaze, Odense University Press, 1978, p 102-4, 126

25. Jørgen Hæstrup, Europe Ablaze, Odense University Press, 1978, p 128-30

26. Martin Glabermann, Wartime Strikes, Bewick, Michigan, 1980, p 43

27. Martin Glabermann, Wartime Strikes, Bewick, Michigan, 1980, p 42, 44

28. Grace Lee Boggs, Living for Change, Minneapolis, University of Minnesota Press, 1998, p 53

29. Martin Glabermann, Wartime Strikes, Bewick, Michigan, 1980, p 44, 49

30. Martin Glabermann, Wartime Strikes, Bewick, Michigan, 1980, p 82-9

31. Time Magazine, Monday, Nov. 13, 1944 http://www.time.com/time/magazine/article/0,9171,801542,00.html#ixzz1RiKkxOfh

32. Martin Glabermann, Wartime Strikes, Bewick, Michigan, 1980, p 48 49

33. Art Preis, Labour's Giant Step, New York, Pioneer, 1964, p 177

34. Martin Glabermann, Wartime Strikes, Bewick, Michigan, 1980, p 94-6, art Preis, Labor's Giant Step, 1964, p 183, 174-97

35. In Art Preis, Labor's Giant Step, p 192

36. In Art Preis, Labor's Giant Step, p 200
37. in Roy Jenkins, Truman, London, Collins, p 86
38. In Art Preis, Labor's Giant Step, p 205
39. In Margarita Aragon,Brown youth, Black Fashion and a White Riot, London, Goldsmiths University, 2007, p 20
40. Mauricio Mazon, The Zoot Suit Riots, The Spychology of symbolic annihilation, University of Texas, 1984, p 75; Stuart Cosgrove, The Zoot-Suit and Style Warfare, History Workshop Journal. Vol. 18 (Autumn 1984) pp. 77-91, and here: http://invention.smith sonian.org/centerpieces/whole_cloth/u7sf/u7materials/cosgrove.ht ml
41. Rottman, Gordon L., FUBAR: Soldier Slang of World War II, Oxford, Botley , 2007, p 117
42. Mauricio Mazon, The Zoot Suit Riots, The Spychology of symbolic annihilation, University of Texas, 1984, p 26-7
43. Manning Marable, Malcolm X, 2011, London, Allen Lane, p 59
44. Robin D. G. Kelley, 'The Riddle of the Zoot', in Janice Radway et al (eds) American Studies: An Anthology, Oxford, Blackwell, 2009, 284
45. Life, quoted in Alfred Mclung Lee, Norman D Humphrey, Race Riot, Detroit 1943, New York, Octagon Books, 1968, p 89
46. Alfred Mclung Lee, Norman D Humphrey, Race Riot, Detroit 1943, New York, Octagon Books, 1968, p 28, 85
47. Dominic J. Capeci Jr., The Harlem Riots of 1943, Philadelphia, Temple University Press, 1977, p 99-101
48. 'My Friends' A Fireside Chat on the War, New York, 1940, p 6
49. Hansard, 11 June 1942,   http://hansard.millbanksystems.com /commons/1942/jun/11/coal-policy
50. Tom Stephenson and Hugh Brannan, The Miners Case, Independent Labour Party, 1942
51. David John Douglass, The Wheel's Still in Spin, Read'n'Noir, Hastings, 2009, p 46
52. Bevin quoted in 'Chronology', Bulletin of International News, Vol. 21, No. 8, Apr. 15, 1944; and see Tony Dabb, 'Official Secrets', Issue 185 of Socialist Review, April 1995
53. Will Podmore, Reg Birch, London, Bellman Books, 2004, p 11-13
54. Richard Croucher, Engineers at War, London, Merlin Press, 1982, p 218-228

55. Richard Croucher, Engineers at War, London, Merlin Press, 1982, p 239; Sam Bornstein, Al Richardson, War and the International, London, Socialist Platform, 1986, p 117, p 130

56. Greg Dropkin, 'Strikes During Wartime', 23 May 2003 http://www.labournet.net/ukunion/0305/wartime1.html. Northern Ireland was particularly militant during the war, see Boyd Black 'A triumph of Voluntarism?', Labour History Review, Vol. 70, No. 1, April 2005, though ironically that might have been due to the grip of loyalist labour leaders on industry there.

57. K.L Gillion, The Fiji Indians, Challenge to European Dominance, 1920-1946, Canberra, Australian National University 1977, p 180-90; James Heartfield, 'Ancient feud that haunts the cane-fields', Fiji Times, 8 July 2001; James Heartfield, "Fijians paramount?" in Revolution, no. 16, November 2001

58. Jack and Ray Simons, Class and Colour in South Africa 1850-1950, London, International Defence and Aid Fund for Southern Africa, p 555, 547

59. David Johnson, World War II and the Scramble for Labour in Colonial Zimbabwe, Harare, University of Zimbabwe, 2000, p 93

60. Sucheta Mahajan, Independence and Partition, New Delhi, Sage, 2000, p 108

61. Ngo Van, In the Crossfire, Oakland, AK Press, 2010, p 98-99

62. Andrew Gordon, The Evolution of Labor Relations in Japan, Harvard University, 1988, p 302

63. Andrew Gordon, The Evolution of Labor Relations in Japan, Harvard University, 1988, p 313

64. Andrew Gordon, The Evolution of Labor Relations in Japan, Harvard University, 1988, p 317-320

65. Andrew Gordon, The Evolution of Labor Relations in Japan, Harvard University, 1988, p 322

66. John Dower, Japan in War and Peace, New York, The New Press, p 115

67. Richard Kisch, The Days of the Good Soldiers, London, Journeyman, 1985, p 52-3, 56, 69

68. Vice Admiral G. Mezeviris,"Four Decades in the Service of the Royal Hellenic Navy", Athens 1971, http://sites.google.com/site /ccouclelis/mutiny; L.S Stavrianos, 'Mutiny in the Greek Armed Forces, April 1944', American Slavonic and East European Review,

Vol 9, No 4, (Dec 1950) pp 302-11, p 310

69. L.S Stavrianos, 'Mutiny in the Greek Armed Forces, April 1944', American Slavonic and East European Review, Vol 9, No 4, (Dec 1950) pp 302-11, p

70. Gilles Perrault, A Man Apart, London, Zed Books, 1987, p 98-104; and see Constiantine Tsoucalas, The Greek Tragedy, Harmondsworth, Penguin, 1969, p 73

71. Gilles Perrault, A Man Apart, London, Zed Books, 1987, p 105-8; Richard Kisch quotes the Guardian on pages 74-5 of Days of the Good Soldiers, London, Journeyman, 1985

72. Saul David, Mutiny at Salerno: An Injustice Exposed, London, Brassey's, 1995, p 217

73. Noel Crusz, The Cocos Island Mutiny, Fremantle Arts Centre, Fremantle, 2001, p 49

74. Noel Crusz, The Cocos Island Mutiny, Fremantle Arts Centre, Fremantle, 2001, p 132

75. Sanji Gunasekara, 'A daring revolt', Himal Southasian, September 2010, http://www.himalmag.com/component/content/article/289-a-daring-revolt.html

76. Robert L. Allen, The Port Chicago Mutiny, Amistad, New York, 1993, p 43, 33, 55

77. Robert L. Allen, The Port Chicago Mutiny, Amistad, New York, 1993, p 45-6, 71

78. Robert L. Allen, The Port Chicago Mutiny, Amistad, New York, 1993, p 76

79. Ian Kershaw, The Nazi Dictatorship, New York Routledge, 1993, p 164

80. Anthony Beevor, Stalingrad, London, Penguin, 1999, p 47

81. Matthew Cobb, The Resistance, p 210

82. Matthew Cobb, The Resistance, p 211

83. Matthew Cobb, The Resistance, p 211

84. Sabine Reul, 'Hitler's heirs join the resistance', Living Marxism issue 81, July/August 1995

85. Hippe, And Red is the Colour of Our Flag, London, Index Books, 1991, p 189

86. Ulrich Strauss, The Anguish of Surrender, University of Washington Press, 2003, p 49

87. 'The Trotskyist Movement in Great Britain', Cabinet Office, 13 April

1944

88. Croucher, Engineers at War, London, Merlin, 1982, p 239; Sam Bornstein, Al Richardson, War and the International, London, Socialist Platform, 1986, p 118-131

21. The European Resistance

1. Mark Mazower, Dark Continent: Europe's Twentieth Century, London, Allen Lane, 1998, 159; Adam Tooze, The Wages of Destruction, London, Allen Lane, 2006, p 513
2. Eugene Kulischer, quoted in Derek Aldcroft, The European Economy, Longmans, 1978, p 130
3. Mark Harrison (ed) The Economics of World War Two, Cambridge, University Press, 1998, p 143
4. Entry for 2 February 1942, Goebbels, Diaries, London, Hamish Hamilton, 1948, p 29
5. Colin Heaton's précis of Ingr's argument, from German Anti-Partisan Warfare in Germany, Atglen PA, Schiffer Military History, 2001, p 63, citing PRO HS-4/16, Most secret memorandum
6. Basil Davidson, Special Operations Europe, Newton Abbot, Readers Union, 1981, p 86-9
7. Henri Michel, The Shadow War: Resistance in Europe, London, Corgi, 1975, p 50, 51
8. Matthew Cobb, The Resistance, London, Pocket Books, 2010, p 98, 110
9. Matthew Cobb, The Resistance, London, Pocket Books, 2010, p 150, 159
10. Matthew Cobb, The Resistance, London, Pocket Books, 2010, p 117-8, 153
11. Matthew Cobb, The Resistance, London, Pocket Books, 2010, 103, 162, 156
12. Colin Heaton, German Anti-Partisan Warfare in Germany, Atglen PA, Schiffer Military History, 2001, p 45
13. Matthew Cobb, The Resistance, London, Pocket Books, p 173
14. Colin Heaton, German Anti-Partisan Warfare in Germany, Atglen PA, Schiffer Military History, 2001, p 52-3
15. Albert Camus, Between Hell and Reason, Hanover, Wesleyan University Press, 1991, p 41, 58
16. David Mountfield, The Partisans, London, Hamlyn, 1979, p 31-3;

Petr Cornej and Jiri Pokorny, A Brief History of the Czech Lands to 2004, Prague, Práh Press, 2004, p 60-63

17. RJB Bosworth, Mussolini's Italy, London, Allen Lane, 2005, p 491 on hunger and strikes, p 476 on popular disaffection

18. Harold Macmillan, War Diaries: The Mediterranean, 1943-45, London, Macmillan, 1984, p 169

19. RJB Bosworth, Mussolini's Italy, London, Allen Lane, 2005, p 521, 522

20. Mark Mazower, Hitler's Empire, London, Penguin, p 400

21. Farrell, Mussolini, London, Weideneld and Nicolson, 2003, p 413

22. 'CLNs', David Ellwood, Italy 1943-1945, Leicester University Press, 1985, p 157; Paul Ginsborg, A History of Contemporary Italy, Harmondsworth, Penguin, 1990, p 55

23. David Ellwood, Italy 1943-1945, Leicester University Press, 1985, p 157

24. RJB Bosworth, Mussolini's Italy, London, Allen Lane, 2005, p 499, 522

25. Dominique Eudes, The Kapetanios - partisans and civil war in Greece, 1943-1949, New York, Monthly Review 1972, p 10-14

26. Dominique Eudes, The Kapetanios - partisans and civil war in Greece, 1943-1949, New York, Monthly Review 1972, p 33-40

27. Stefanos Sarafis, Greek Resistance Army, London, Merlin Press, 1980, p 426-7; Mark Mazower, Inside Hitler's Greece, New Haven, Yale Nota Bene, 2001, p 155

28. Mark Mazower, Inside Hitler's Greece, New Haven, Yale Nota Bene, 2001, p 178-9

29. Harold Macmillan, War Diaries: The Mediterranean, 1943-45, London, Macmillan, 1984, p 546; Stefanos Sarafis, Greek Resistance Army, London, Merlin Press, 1980, p 427

30. Constantine Tsoucalas, The Greek Tragedy, Harmondsworth, Penguin, 1969, p 67

31. Woodhouse, quoted in Tsoucalas, The Greek Tragedy, Harmondsworth, Penguin, 1969, p 61

32. Mark Mazower, Inside Hitler's Greece, New Haven, Yale Nota Bene, 2001, p 265

33. Stefanos Sarafis, Greek Resistance Army, London, Merlin Press, 1980, p 220, 223, 199

34. Davidson, Special Operations Europe: Scenes from the anti-Nazi

War, Newton Abbot, Readers Union, 1981, p 127

35. Milovan Djilas, Wartime, New York, Harcourt Bruce Jovanovich, 1977, p 443

36. Milovan Djilas, Wartime, New York, Harcourt Bruce Jovanovich, 1977, p 144, 209

37. Djilas, Wartime, New York, Harcourt Bruce Jovanovich, 1977, p 368

38. Quoted in Colin Heaton, German Anti-Partisan Warfare in Germany, Atglen PA, Schiffer Military History, 2001, p 88

39. Davidson, Special Operations Europe: Scenes from the anti-Nazi War, Newton Abbot, Readers Union, 1981, p. 132 – the scene was fictionalised by Evelyn Waugh in, where he has Brigadier Cape say to hero Guy Crouchback: 'Neither you or I are going to make his home in Jugoslavia after the war. How they choose to govern themselves is entirely their business.' Sword of Honour Trilogy, London Penguin, 2001, p 595

40. Quoted in Gregory Sumner, Dwight MacDonald and the politics circle: the challenge of cosmopolitan democracy, Ithaca, Cornell University Press, 1996, p 45

41. Kim Philby, My Silent War, London, Panther, 1973, p 28

22. Partisans of the East

1. Arthur Cottrell, East Asia: From Chinese Predominance to the Rise of the Pacific Rim, London, Pimlico, 2002, p 224

2. Gabriel Kolko, The Politics of War, New York, Pantheon Books, 1990, p 214

3. Jung Chang, Jon Halliday, Mao, London, Jonathan Cape, p 247

4. Niall Ferguson, War of the World, p 483; Jung Chang, Jon Halliday, Mao, London, Jonathan Cape, p 240

5. Arthur Cottrell, East Asia, London, Pimlico, 2002, p 226; and see Stalin's telegram to Mao 22 December 1943, in Jung Chang, Jon Halliday, Mao, London, Jonathan Cape, p 268

6. John Davies' report, New Delhi, 15 January 1944

7. Jung Chang, Jon Halliday, Mao, London, Jonathan Cape, p 210

8. Tony Kennedy, 'South Korea's Take Off', Confrontation 3, London, Junius, Summer 1988

9. Bruce Cumings, The Origins of the Korean War, Vol I, New Jersey, Princeton University Press, 1981, p 77; Hagen Koo, Korean Workers, Ithaca, Cornell University Press, 2001, p 25

10. Bruce Cumings, The Origins of the Korean War, Vol I, New Jersey, Princeton University Press, 1981, p 35-6
11. Christopher Bayly and Tim Harper, Forgotten Armies, London, Penguin, 2005, p 219
12. Chin Peng, My Side of History, Singapore, Media Masters, 2003, 65-6
13. Christopher Bayly and Tim Harper, Forgotten Armies, London, Penguin, 2005, p 265, paraphrasing Holman's memoir of Robert Chrystal, The Green Torture, London, 1962
14. Chin Peng, My Side of History, Singapore, Media Masters, 2003, p 74
15. Jean Lacouture, Ho Chi Minh, Harmondsworth, Penguin, 1967, p 85
16. Jean Lacouture, Ho Chi Minh, Harmondsworth, Penguin, 1967, p 88
17. Ngo Van In the Crossfire, Oakland, AK Press, 2010, p 116-7
18. Jean Lacouture, Ho Chi Minh, Harmondsworth, Penguin, 1967, p 84
19. Jean Lacouture, Ho Chi Minh, Harmondsworth, Penguin, 1967, p 87; Ngo Van In the Crossfire, Oakland, AK Press, 2010, p 120-1
20. Jean Lacouture, Ho Chi Minh, Harmondsworth, Penguin, 1967, p 90
21. Saburō Ienaga, The Pacific War, New York, Pantheon Books, 1978, p 178-9; Gabriel Kolko, Vietnam, London, Unwin Hyman, 1985, 36-7
22. Saburō Ienaga, The Pacific War, New York, Pantheon Books, 1978, p 176
23. Howard Dick, et al, The Emergence of a National Economy, University of Hawaii Press, 2002, p166
24. Theodore Friend, The Blue-Eyed Enemy, Princeton University Press, 1988, p 105
25. Theodore Friend, The Blue-Eyed Enemy, Princeton, University Press, 1988, p 207
26. Saburō Ienaga, The Pacific War, New York, Pantheon Books, 1978, p 177-8
27. Quoted in Renato and Letizia Constantino, The Philippines: The Continuing Past, Foundation for Nationalist Studies, Quezon City, 1984, p 134
28. Renato and Letizia Constantino, The Philippines: The Continuing Past, Foundation for Nationalist Studies, Quezon City, 1984, p 140, 144; Gabriel Kolko, The Politics of War, New York, Pantheon, 1990, p 606
29. Kempetai testimony, reproduced in Theodore Friend, The Blue-

Eyed Enemy, Princeton University Press, 1988, p 209

30. Renato and Letizia Constantino, The Philippines: The Continuing Past, Foundation for Nationalist Studies, Quezon City, 1984, p 147

23. The Collapse of the German Empire in the East

1. Mark Mazower, Hitler's Empire, London, Penguin, 2009, p 145-6, 156

2. Jean Barber and Mark Harrison, The Soviet Home Front: 1941-45, London, Longman, 1991, p 40-41, 104; Arno Mayer, Why Did the Heavens not Darken? New York, Pantheon, 1990, p 283

3. Mark Mazower, Hitler's Empire, p 138

4. in Lizzie Collingham, The Taste of War, London, Allen Lane, 2011, p 191

5. Jean Barber and Mark Harrison, The Soviet Home Front: 1941-45, London, Longman, 1991, p 27

6. Richard Overy, Russia's War, London, Penguin, 1999, p 133

7. Arno Mayer, Why did the Heavens not Darken? New York, Pantheon, 1990, p 340; Richard Overy, Russia's War, London, Penguin, 1999, p 144

8. Degrelle was speaking in 1984, to Colin Heaton, German Anti-Partisan Warfare in Europe, Atglen PA, 2001, p 156; Partisan actions, Richard Overy, Russia's War, London, Penguin, 1999, p 151

9. Arno Mayer, Why Did the Heavens not Darken?, New York, Pantheon, 1990, p 246, 281

10. Arno Mayer, Why Did the Heavens not Darken?, New York, Pantheon, 1990, p 280

11. Richard Overy, Russia's War, London, Penguin, 1999, p 223

12. Richard Overy, Russia's War, London, Penguin, 1999, p 159-60; Arno Mayer, Why Did the Heavens not Darken?, New York, Pantheon, 1990, p 246

13. Donald Gillies, Radical Diplomat: The life of Archibald Clerk Kerr, London, I.B. Tauris, 1999, p 145

14. Pravda, 25 May 1945, in Jean Barber and Mark Harrison, The Soviet Home Front: 1941-45, London, Longman, 1991, p 115

15. Richard Overy, Russia's War, London, Penguin, 1999, p 162

16. When Hitler took on Russia he fought a brutal war that was an orgy of rape and genocide Tony Rennell Daily Mail 23rd June 2011

17. Richard Overy, Russia's War, London, Penguin, 1999, p 169

18. G. Deborin, Secrets of the Second World War, Moscow, Progress
     Publishers, 1971, p 130-1; Zhukov in Richard Overy, Russia's War,
     London, Penguin, 1999, p 194-5, Stalin quote in Averell Harriman
     and Elie Abel, Special Envoy, New York, Random House, 1975, p
     277, and tank corps numbers in Overy, p 191
19. Jean Barber and Mark Harrison, The Soviet Home Front: 1941-45,
     London, Longman, 1991, p 40-41
20. Jean Barber and Mark Harrison, The Soviet Home Front: 1941-45,
     London, Longman, 1991, p 40-41

24. The 'Final Solution'

1.   Arno Mayer, Why Did the Heavens Not Darken?, New York,
     Pantheon, 1990, p 133
2.   Christopher Browning, The Origins of the Final Solution, Lincoln,
     University of Nebraska Press, 2004, p 69-70
3.   Christopher Browning, The Origins of the Final Solution, p 81-9
4.   'Still dripping with the blood of the slaughtered inhabitants of
     Jerusalem, the Christians fell down on their faces at the tomb of the
     Redeemer', Hegel, The Philosophy of History, New York, Cosimo,
     2007, p 392
5.   Arno Mayer, Why Did the Heavens Not Darken?, New York,
     Pantheon, 1990, p 189
6.   Browning, Origins of the Final Solution, Lincoln University of
     Nebraska Press, 2004, p 99
7.   Arno Mayer, Why Did the Heavens Not Darken?, p 265, 268
8.   Arno Mayer, Why Did the Heavens Not Darken?, p 257-8
9.   Arno Mayer, Why Did the Heavens Not Darken?, p 267
10. Arno Mayer, Why Did the Heavens Not Darken?, p 302
11. Arno Mayer, Why Did the Heavens Not Darken?, p 308
12. Arno Mayer, Why Did the Heavens Not Darken?, p 314
13. Mark Mazower, Inside Hitler's Greece, New Haven, Yale Nota Bene,
     2001, p 244, 256
14. Marek Edelman, The Ghetto Fights, London, Bookmarks, 1990, p 29
15. Robert Sherwood, Roosevelt and Hopkins, New York, Harper, 1948,
     p 717
16. Planning Committee Memorandum, 25 July 1941; Tony Kushner,
     'British perceptions of the Final Solution in the Second World War'
     in D Cesarani (ed), The Final Solution, 1994, p 249

17. Lenni Brenner, Zionism in the Age of the Dictators, Lawrence Hill & Co, 1983, Ch. 24

18. In 2004, British Prime Minister Tony Blair said that the Allies only got round to doing something about the persecution of the Jews in 1939. 'They said this has got to be stopped.', quoted in Richard Ingrams, Diary, Observer 16 January 2005 http://www.guardian.co .uk/politics/2004/jun/13/guardiancolumnists

19. Franz Neuman, Behemoth, New York, Harper and Row, 1966, p 552

20. Arno Mayer, Why did the Heavens Not Darken? New York, Pantheon, 1990, p 447

25. The Second Invasion of Europe

1. Sherwood, Roosevelt and Hopkins, New York, Harper, 1948, p 714-5

2. Labour Monthly, February 1941

3. Fenner Brockway, The Way Out, London, ILP, July 1942, p 16, his emphasis

4. Politics, October 1944, quoted in Gregory Sumner, Dwight MacDonald and the politics circle: the challenge of cosmopolitan democracy, Ithaca, Cornell University Press, 1996, 67

5. Bill Moore and George Barnsby, 'The Anti-Fascist People's Front in the Armed Forces', Our History, Communist Party History Series, Pamphlet 81, February 1990, p 11-12

6. Long-time anti-Mafia campaigner Michael Pantaleone's story is repeated in Tim Newark, The Mafia at War, London, Greenhill, 2007 p 158-60, though Newark contests it.

7. Tim Newark, The Mafia at War, London, Greenhill, 2007, p 239-41

8. Tim Newark, The Mafia at War, London, Greenhill, 2007, p 216, 218

9. Harold MacMillan War Diaries: The Mediterranean, 1943-45, London, Macmillan, 1984, p 352

10. Tim Newark, The Mafia at War, London, Greenhill, 2007, p 244-5; David Ellwood, Italy: 1943-1945, Leicester University Press, 1985, p 60, 66

11. Time Magazine (US) 4 Sept 1972, http://www.time.com/time/magazine/article/0,9171,910391,00.html#ixzz1aO1VVw1v

12. Constantine Tsoucalas, Greek Tragedy, Harmondsworth, Penguin, 1969, p 76-7

13. Harold MacMillan War Diaries: The Mediterranean, 1943-45,

London, Macmillan, 1984, p 546

14. Dominique Eudes, The Kapetanios, New York, Monthly Review Press, 1972, p 108; Stefanos Sarafis, The Greek Resistance Army, London, Merlin, 1980, p 226-7; Mark Mazower, Inside Hitler's Greece, New Haven, Yale Nota Bene, 2001, p 329

15. Mark Mazower, Inside Hitler's Greece, New Haven, Yale Nota Bene, 2001, p 233

16. Albert Speer, Inside the Third Reich, London, Sphere, 1971, p 537

17. Constantine Tsoucalas, Greek Tragedy, Harmondsworth, Penguin, 1969, p 85

18. Harold MacMillan War Diaries: The Mediterranean, 1943-45, London, Macmillan, 1984, p 557, writing in October 1944

19. Constantine Tsoucalas, Greek Tragedy, Harmondsworth, Penguin, 1969, p 88

20. Harold MacMillan War Diaries: The Mediterranean, 1943-45, London, Macmillan, 1984, p 599

21. 23 December 1944, Harold MacMillan War Diaries: The Mediterranean, 1943-45, London, Macmillan, 1984, p 614

22. John Iatrides and Linda Wrigley, Greece at the Crossroads, Pennsylvania State University Press, 1995, p 9

23. Dominique Eudes, The Kapetanios, New York, Monthly Review Press, 1972, p 161, 177; Mark Mazower, Inside Hitler's Greece, New Haven, Yale Nota Bene, 2001, p 331

24. Dominique Eudes, The Kapetanios, New York, Monthly Review Press, 1972, p 214, 190

25. Dominique Eudes, The Kapetanios, New York, Monthly Review Press, 1972, p 310

26. See the testimony in Eleni Fourtuni, Greek Women In Resistance, Thelphini Press, New Haven, 1986; there were still 1,359 political prisoners in the camps in 1962 – Polymeris Voglis, Becoming a subject: political prisoners during the Greek Civil War, Bergahn Books, 2002, p 223

27. Battaglia, Story of the Italian Resistance, London, Odhams Press, 1957, p 221-2

28. David Ellwood, Italy: 1943-1945, Leicester University Press, 1985, p 157, 163; Basil Davidson, Special Operations Europe, Newton Abbott, Readers Union, 1981, p 240

29. David Ellwood, Italy 1943-1945, Leicester University Press, 1985, p

163

30. David Ellwood, Italy: 1943-1945, Leicester University Press, 1985, p 40

31. Muriel Grindrod, The Rebuilding of Italy: Politics and Economics, London: Royal Institute of International Affairs 1955, p 9

32. David Ellwood, Italy: 1943-1945, Leicester University Press, 1985, p 160

33. Harold MacMillan War Diaries: The Mediterranean, 1943-45, London, Macmillan, 1984, p 657

34. David Ellwood, Italy: 1943-1945, Leicester University Press, 1985, p 186-7

35. Quoted in David Ellwood, Italy: 1943-1945, Leicester University Press, 1985, p 188

36. Daniele Ganser, Nato's Secret Armies, Abingdon, Frank Cass, 2005, p 64

37. Harold MacMillan War Diaries: The Mediterranean, 1943-45, London, Macmillan, 1984, p 239

38. Joan Barth Urban, Moscow and the Italian Communist Party, London, I B Tauris, 1986, p 171

39. Paul Ginsborg, A History of Contemporary Italy, London, Penguin, 1990, p 48; David Ellwood, Italy: 1943-1945, Leicester University Press, 1985, 83-7

40. Harold MacMillan War Diaries: The Mediterranean, 1943-45, London, Macmillan, 1984, p 396, 23 March 1944

41. David Ellwood, Italy: 1943-1945, Leicester University Press, 1985, p 231-2; OSS report in Tim Newark, The Mafia at War, London, Greenhill, 2007, p 236

42. Tim Newark. The Mafia at War, London, Greenhill, 2007, p 275

43. Isaac Deustcher, Stalin, London, Oxford University Press, 1967, p 506

44. Chester Wilmot, The Struggle for Europe, London, Collins, 1952, p 446

45. Chester Wilmot, The Struggle for Europe, London, Collins, 1952, p 455

46. Chester Wilmot, The Struggle for Europe, London, Collins, 1952, p

47. Frank Furedi, The Silent War, London, Pluto Press, 1998, p 41

48. Averell Harriman and Elie Abel, Special Envoy, New York, Random House, 1975, p 345

49. according to a State Department source David Ellwood, Italy: 1943-1945, Leicester University Press, 1985, p 222

50. Harold MacMillan War Diaries: The Mediterranean, 1943-45, London, Macmillan, 1984, p 401

51. Isaac Deutscher, Stalin, London, Oxford University Press, 1967, p 508

52. Isaac Deutscher, Stalin, London, Oxford University Press, 1967, p 520

53. John Coutouvidis and Jaime Reynolds, Poland 1939-1947, Leicester University Press, 1986, p 83

54. Roy Medvedev, Let History Judge, New York, Vintage, 1973, p 219; John Coutouvidis and Jaime Reynolds, Poland 1939-1947, Leicester University Press, 1986, p 84

55. John Coutouvidis and Jaime Reynolds, Poland 1939-1947, Leicester University Press, 1986, p 85

56. John Coutouvidis and Jaime Reynolds, Poland 1939-1947, Leicester University Press, 1986, p 86-7

57. John Coutouvidis and Jaime Reynolds, Poland 1939-1947, Leicester University Press, 1986, p 88

58. John Coutouvidis and Jaime Reynolds, Poland 1939-1947, Leicester University Press, 1986, p 94, 98

59. John Coutouvidis and Jaime Reynolds, Poland 1939-1947, Leicester University Press, 1986, p 99

60. Norman Davies, Rising '44, London, Macmillan, 2003, p 221-4

61. John Coutouvidis and Jaime Reynolds, Poland 1939-1947, Leicester University Press, 1986, p 100

62. Norman Davies, Rising '44, London, Macmillan, 2003, p 118

63. Interviewed by Ed Vulliamy, 'Brave Old World', Observer Magazine, 4 July 2004, p 25

64. Norman Davies, Uprising '44, London, Macmillan, 2003, p 271

65. Interviewed by Ed Vulliamy, 'Brave Old World', Observer Magazine, 4 July 2004, p 29

66. Averell Harriman and Elie Abel, Special Envoy, New York, Random House, 1975, p 347

67. Norman Davies, Europe at War, London, Pan, 2007, p 188

68. Norman Davies, Rising '44, London, Macmillan, 2003, p 249

69. Averell Harriman and Elie Abel, Special Envoy, New York, Random House, 1975, p 340

70. Averell Harriman and Elie Abel, Special Envoy, New York, Random House, 1975, p 349

71. John Coutouvidis and Jaime Reynolds, Poland 1939-1947, Leicester University Press, 1986, p 100.

72. John Coutouvidis and Jaime Reynolds, Poland 1939-1947, Leicester University Press, 1986, p 103-4; Isaac Deutscher, Stalin, London, Oxford University Press, 1967, p

73. Isaac Deutscher, Stalin, London, Oxford University Press, 1967, p 522

74. Norman Davies, Rising '44, London, Macmillan, 2003, p 457, 572-504

75. Milovan Djilas Wartime, Harcourt Brace, New York, Jovanovich, 1977, p 400

76. Milovan Djilas Wartime, Harcourt Brace, New York, Jovanovich, 1977, p 405, 406-7

77. Milovan Djilas Wartime, Harcourt Brace, New York, Jovanovich, 1977, p 420; The Struggle against the Tito Fascists - Agents of Imperialism: Discussion Outline and Study Guide, Communist Party USA, 1949; James Klugmann, From Trotsky to Tito, London, Lawrence and Wishart, 1951

78. Milovan Djilas Wartime, Harcourt Brace, New York, Jovanovich, 1977, p 436, 390

79. Isaac Deutscher, Stalin, London, Oxford University Press, 1967, p 533

80. Manchester Guardian, 15 December 1945

81. Isaac Deutscher, Stalin, London, Oxford University Press, 1967, p 533

82. Quoted in Chris Harman, Class Struggles in Eastern Europe, http://www.vorhaug.net/politikk/ist/harman/eastern_europe/repression.html

83. Ilya Ehrenburg, Post-war Years 1945-54, London, MacGibbon and Kee, 1966, p 31

84. Milovan Djilas, Wartime, Harcourt Brace, New York, Jovanovich, 1977, p 423

85. Matthew Cobb, The Resistance, London, Pocket Books, 2009, p 245-7

86. Matthew Cobb, The Resistance, London, Pocket Books, 2009, p 247-50

87. Matthew Cobb, The Resistance, London, Pocket Books, 2009, p 251-3

88. Matthew Cobb, The Resistance, London, Pocket Books, 2009, p 255, 257

89. Norman Davies, Europe at War, London, Pan, 2007, p 188

90. Matthew Cobb, The Resistance, London, Pocket Books, 2009, p 262-3

91. Quoted in John Costello, Love, Sex and War, London, Pan Books, 1986, p 143

92. Norman Davies, Europe at War, London, Pan, 2007, p 189; Matthew Cobb, The Resistance, London, Pocket Books, 2009, p267-8

93. Matthew Cobb, The Resistance, London, Pocket Books, 2009, p 276, 279; Frank Giles, The Locust Years, London, Secker and Warburg, 1991, p 11

94. Jørgen Hæstrup, Europe Ablaze, Odense University Press, 1978, p 107

95. John Gillingham, Belgian Business and the Nazi New Order, Jan Hondt Foundation, Ghent, 1977, p 169, 177, 178

96. Tony Judt, Postwar, London, Heinemann, 2005, p 65

97. carried in the Indian Express, 21 August 1943

98. Samuel Hoare, Ambassador on a Special Mission, London, Collins, 1946, p 189

99. Nikolai Tolstoy, Victims of Yalta, London, Hodder and Stoughton, 1977, p 51-2, 75, 88, 103

100. Nikolai Tolstoy, Victims of Yalta, London, Hodder and Stoughton, 1977, p 130, 161-218

101. Stephen Weeks, The Prague Post, 11 November 2004

102. Kirsten Sellars, The Rise and Rise of Human Rights, Stroud, Sutton, 2002: xii

103. Stephen Ambrose, Rise to Globalism, Harmondsworth, Penguin, 1981, p 58

104. Stephen Ambrose, Rise to Globalism, Harmondsworth, Penguin, 1981, p 72

105. John Willoughby, Hail the Conquering Heroes, Palgrave, 2001

106. Eric Hobsbawm, The Age of Extremes, London Michael Joseph, 1994, p 164

107. Alan Clinton, Jean Moulin 1899-1943, Basingstoke, Palgrave, 2002, p 65

108. Mark Mazower, Dark Continent: Europe's Twentieth Century, London, Allen Lane, 1998, p 210; on the Highlanders, see T. M. Devine, Scotland's Empire, London, Penguin, 2004, p 307-12 and p 354-60

26. A war of extermination in the Pacific

1. John W. Dower, War Without Mercy, London, Faber, 1986, p.69; Ben Fenton, 'American troops "murdered Japanese PoWs"', Daily Telegraph, 6 August 2005

2. Dower, War Without Mercy, 1986, p 68

3. Barak Kushner, The Thought War – Japanese Imperial Propaganda, University of Hawaii Press, Honolulu, 2006, p 149

4. Dower, War Without Mercy, p 63

5. 'One War is Enough', Atlantic Monthly, February 1946, pp 48-53, p 49

6. Kim Gravelle, Fiji's Heritage, Nadi, Tiara, 2000, 226; Supplement to the London Gazette, 7 December 1944, p 5616

7. Dower, War Without Mercy, 1986, p 63

8. Bradley A. Thayer, Darwin and international relations: on the evolutionary origins of war and ethnic conflict, University Press of Kentucky, 2004, p 190

9. Mark D Roehrs and William Renzi, World War II in the Pacific, Armonk, M.E. Sharpe, 2004, p 128

10. Roehrs and Renzi, World War II in the Pacific, p 134, 139, 144, 151, 209, 257; Dower, War Without Mercy, p 329

11. Ulrich Strauss, The Anguish of Surrender, University of Washington Press, 2003, p 4

12. Warren Kozack, LeMay, Regnery Publishing, 2009, p 212

13. Roehrs and Renzi, World War II in the Pacific, p 213-5

14. In Mick Hume, 'Hiroshima: the White Man's Bomb', Living Marxism issue 81, July/August 1995

15. Hume, 'Hiroshima: the White Man's Bomb'; Newsweek, 11 November 1963

27. The Second Invasion of East Asia

1. Walden Bello, People and Power in the Pacific, London, Pluto, p 11

2. Quoted in Jon Halliday, A Political History of Japanese Capitalism, New York, Monthly Review Press, 1975, p 159

3. Chin Peng, My Side of History, Singapore, Media Masters, 2003, p 111-112

4. Chin Peng, My Side of History, p 123, 124

5. Chin Peng, My Side of History, p 121; Christopher Bayly and Tim Harper, Forgotten Armies, London, Penguin, 2005, p 55

6. Chin Peng, My Side of History, p 130-1

7. Christopher Bayly and Tim Harper, Forgotten Armies, London, Penguin, 2005, p 451

8. Chin Peng, My Side of History, Singapore, Media Masters, 2003, p 135, 141

9. Chin Peng, My Side of History, p 144-5

10. Chin Peng, My Side of History, p 155-6

11. Chin Peng, My Side of History, p 266; Anne Booth, Colonial Legacies, Honolulu, University of Hawai'i Press, 2007, p 160;

12. Mark Curtis, The Ambiguities of Power, London, Zed Books, 1995, p 57

13. Christopher Bayly and Tim Harper, Forgotten Armies, London, Penguin, 2005, p 429

14. Louis Allen, Burma: the Longest War, London, Phoenix Press, 2000, p 583

15. Louis Allen, Burma, p 584-5

16. Louis Allen, Burma, p 588; Christopher Bayly and Tim Harper, Forgotten Armies, p 442-3

17. Christopher Bayly and Tim Harper, Forgotten Armies, p 443-6

18. Louis Allen, Burma: the Longest War, London, Phoenix Press, 2000, p 588

19. Fergal Keane, 'Save us from our friends', Guardian, 19 July 1997

20. Renato and Letizia Constantino, The Continuing Past, Quezon City, The Foundation for Nationalist Studies, 1984, p 164

21. R & L Constantino, The Continuing Past, p 164-5

22. Gabriel Kolko, The Politics of War, New York, Pantheon, 1990, p 606

23. R & L Constantino, The Continuing Past, p 166

24. Quoted in R & L Constantino, The Continuing Past, p 156

25. R & L Constantino, The Continuing Past, p 171

26. William Manchester, American Caesar, London, Arrow, 1979, p 344; R & L Constantino, The Continuing Past, p 162

27. W Manchester, American Caesar, p 344; R & L Constantino, The Continuing Past, p 159-61

28. William J Pomeroy, The Philippines, International Publishers Co, 1992, p 139; R & L Constantino, The Continuing Past, p 154, 164

29. Foreign Relations: The Conferences at Malta and Yalta, 1945, Washington, Department of State, 1955, p 770 Louis, Imperialism at Bay, New York, Oxford University Press, 1978, p 553

30. Robert K. Schaeffer, Severed States, Rowman & Littlefield,1999, p 73

31. Bruce Cumings, The Origins of the Korean War, Vol. I, New Jersey, Priceton University Press, 1981, p 71-3, 77

32. Bruce Cumings, The Origins of the Korean War, p 84-7

33. Cumings, The Origins of the Korean War, p 88

34. Cumings, The Origins of the Korean War, p 89

35. Cumings, The Origins of the Korean War, 93-6

36. Hagen Koo, Korean Workers, Ithaca, Cornell University Press, 2001, p 26

37. I.F. Stone, Hidden History of the Korean War, Boston, Little, Brown and Co., 1988, p 16

38. John Gittings and Martin Kettle, 'US and S Korea Accused of war atrocities', Guardian, 18 January 2000, p 12

39. Stone, Hidden History of the Korean War, p 18

40. Quoted in Shelton Woods, Vietnam, New York, Hippocrene Books, 2002, p 109-10

41. Woods, Vietnam, p 105

42. Quoted in Gabriel Kolko, the Politics of War, New York, Pantheon, 1990, p 609

43. Ngo Van, In the Crossfire, Oakland AK Press, 2010, p 126

44. Frank Giles, The Locust Years, London, Secker and Warburg, 1991, p 51; Shelton Woods, Vietnam, p 113

45. Frank Giles, The Locust Years, London, p 49, 54

46. Theodore Friend, The Blue Eyed Enemy, Princeton University Press, 1988, p 110, 113

47. Quoted in J. G. A. Parrott, 'Who Killed Brigadier Mallaby?' Indonesia, Vol. 20, (Oct., 1975), pp. 87-111, p 91

48. Friend, The Blue Eyed Enemy, p 215

49. Quoted in Jon Halliday, A Political History of Japanese Capitalism, New York, Monthly Review Press, 1975, p 152

50. Friend, The Blue Eyed Enemy, p 219, 221

51. Friend, The Blue Eyed Enemy, p 217, 222

52. BRITISH TROOPS ARRIVE IN BATAVIA (30/9/1945), film is held by the Imperial War Museum (ID: JFU 385). http://www.colonial film.org.uk/node/2884

53. J.D.F. Jones, The Storyteller: The Many Lives of Laurens Van Der Post, London, Scribner, 2001, p 66

54. Jones, The Storyteller, p 60

55. Jones, The Storyteller, p 70

56. Howard Dick, et al, The Emergence of A National Economy, Allen & Unwin, Crow's Nest, 2002, p 168

28. India Uprisen, Divided

1. Sucheta Mahajan, Independence and Partition, New Delhi, Sage, 2000, p 48

2. R. Palme Dutt, India Today, London, Victor Gollancz, 1940, p 405 – the figures for India as a whole were 239 million Hindus, 68 per cent, and 78 million Muslims, 22 per cent

3. Anthony Read and David Fisher, The Proudest Day, London, Jonathan Cape, 1997, p 294

4. Stanley Wolpert, Nehru: A Tryst with Destiny, Oxford University Press, 1996, p 325, 327

5. Anthony Read and David Fisher, The Proudest Day, London, Jonathan Cape, 1997, p 347; Stanley Wolpert, Nehru: A Tryst with Destiny, Oxford University Press, 1996, p 323

6. Sucheta Mahajan, Independence and Partition, New Delhi, Sage, 2000, p 50, 52, 63; Christopher Bayly and Tim Harper, Forgotten Armies, London, Penguin, 2005, p 448

7. Sucheta Mahajan, Independence and Partition, New Delhi, Sage, 2000, p 52

8. Sucheta Mahajan, Independence and Partition, New Delhi, Sage, 2000, p 63-4

9. Joyce Lebra, The Indian National Army and Japan, Singapore, Institute of South East Asian Studies, 2008, p 200-201

10. Christopher Bayly and Tim Harper, Forgotten Armies, London, Penguin, 2005, p 448

11. Sucheta Mahajan, Independence and Partition, New Delhi, Sage, 2000, p 72

12. Stanley Wolpert, Nehru: A Tryst with Destiny, Oxford University Press, 1996, p 356

13. Sucheta Mahajan, Independence and Partition, New Delhi, Sage, 2000, p 80-85

14. Joyce Lebra, The Indian National Army and Japan, Singapore, Institute of South East Asian Studies, 2008, p 202-9; Stanley Wolpert, Nehru: A Tryst with Destiny, Oxford University Press, 1996, p 355

15. Sucheta Mahajan, Independence and Partition, New Delhi, Sage, 2000, p 87-8; Stanley Wolpert, Nehru: A Tryst with Destiny, Oxford University Press, 1996, p 352

16. 'Witness to History', an interview with Madan Singh, Sunday Tribune (India) 21 March 2004; Sucheta Mahajan, Independence and Partition, New Delhi, Sage, 2000, p 92-5, 99

17. Nicholas Mansergh, ed., The Transfer of Power in India, 1942-47, Volume 6, London, Foreign & Commonwealth Office 1976, p 1055

18. Minute to Prime Minister, 30 August 1946, Sucheta Mahajan, Independence and Partition, New Delhi, Sage, 2000, p 179

19. Dhanjaya Bhat, Sunday Tribune, 12 February 2006

20. On 24 December 1946, M. J. Akbar, Nehru: The Making of Modern India, London, Penguin, 1989, p 366

21. Stanley Wolpert, Nehru: A Tryst with Destiny, Oxford University Press, 1996, p 370, 375, 376, 378

22. Stanley Wolpert, Nehru: A Tryst with Destiny, Oxford University Press, 1996, p 387

29. The defeated powers under occupation

1. Quoted in Ulrich Herbert, Hitler's Foreign Workers, Cambridge, University Press, 1997, 356-8

2. Patricia Meehan, Strange Enemy People, London, Peter Owen, 2001, p 55, Willoughby, 2001: 102

3. Milovan Djilas, Wartime, New York, Harcourt Brace Jovanovich, 1977, p 429

4. Quoted in John Costello, Love, Sex and War, London, Pan Books, 1986, p 144

5. Quoted in John Costello, Love, Sex and War, London, Pan Books, 1986, p 144

6. John Willoughby, Remaking the Conquering Heroes, New York, Palgrave, 2001, p 20

7. Leonard Mosley, Report from Germany, London, Gollancz, 1945, p

45

8. Patricia Meehan, Strange Enemy People, London, Peter Owen, 2001, p 60, 134, 147-8

9. Wolfgang Schivelbusch, In a Cold Crater, Berkeley University of California Press, 1998, p 27-8

10. John Willoughby, Remaking the Conquering Heroes, New York, Palgrave, 2001, p 91

11. Patricia Meehan, A Strange Enemy People, London, Peter Owen, 2001, p 230-1; On the theft of the Haber-Bosch process from BASF at the end of the First World War, see W.J. Reader, Imperial Chemicals Industries, Volume I, Oxford University Press, 1970, p 364

12. HC Deb 29 July 1946 vol 426 column 599

13. Patricia Meehan, A Strange Enemy People, London, Peter Owen, 2001 p 228, 200, 207, 201,

14. HC Deb 29 July 1946 vol 426 column 599

15. Patricia Meehan, A Strange Enemy People, London, Peter Owen, 2001, p 253, 248

16. It was claimed that the Kellogg-Briand Pact of 1928, including a clause outlawing aggression, was a law against starting wars. But it was a treaty, not a law, and was in any event full of comical exceptions (such as Britain's presumed right to defend itself against attacks on its vital interests abroad), and widely ridiculed as utopian and vacuous at the time.

17. Kirsten Sellars, The Rise and Rise of Human Rights, Stroud, Sutton, 2002, p 27

18. Kirsten Sellars, The Rise and Rise of Human Rights, Stroud, Sutton, 2002, p 28

19. United States Communication of April 12, 1943 to the Japanese Government

20. Kirsten Sellars, The Rise and Rise of Human Rights, Stroud, Sutton, 2002, p 31-3

21. Kirsten Sellars, The Rise and Rise of Human Rights, Stroud, Sutton, 2002, p 34

22. Airey Neave, Nuremberg, London, Grafton Books, 1989, especially p 272-3

23. Kirsten Sellars, The Rise and Rise of Human Rights, Stroud, Sutton, 2002, p 35

24. T Kushner, 'British perceptions of the Final Solution in the Second

World War' in D Cesarani (ed), The Final Solution, 1994, p 249; Lenni Brenner, Zionism in the Age of the Dictators, Lawrence Hill & Co, 1983, Chapter 24

25. Kirsten Sellars, The Rise and Rise of Human Rights, Stroud, Sutton, 2002, p 43-4

26. Mazower, Dark Continent: Europe's Twentieth Century, London, Allen Lane 1998, p 211

27. Hughes, Contemporary Europe: A history, Englewood Cliffs: Prentice-Hall, 198, p 404-5

28. Ian Cobain, 'The postwar photographs that British authorities tried to keep hidden', Guardian, 3 April 2006, http://www.guardian.co .uk/politics/2006/apr/03/uk.freedomofinformation

29. Stephen Ambrose, 'Ike and the Disappearing Atrocities' New York Times Book Review, February 24, 1991

30. Times, 18 July 1945

31. Patricia Meehan, A Strange Enemy People, London, Peter Owen, 2001, p 73, 86

32. William Manchester, American Caesar, London, Arrow, 1979, p 424

33. Ruth Benedict, The Chrysanthemum and the Sword: Patterns of Japanese Culture US Office of War Information, 1946 p 2

34. Ruth Benedict, The Chrysanthemum and the Sword: Patterns of Japanese Culture US Office of War Information, 1946 p 213

35. William Manchester, American Caesar, London, Arrow, 1979, p 430

36. Kirsten Sellars, The Rise and Rise of Human Rights, Stroud, Sutton, 2002, p 50

37. Kirsten Sellars, The Rise and Rise of Human Rights, Stroud, Sutton, 2002, p 48

38. Kirsten Sellars, The Rise and Rise of Human Rights, Stroud, Sutton, 2002, p 54-5

39. Kirsten Sellars, The Rise and Rise of Human Rights, Stroud, Sutton, 2002, p 63

40. Kirsten Sellars, The Rise and Rise of Human Rights, Stroud, Sutton, 2002, p 52

41. Yoshida Shigeru, Last Meiji Man, Lanham, Rowman and Littlefield, 2007, p 125, 129

42. Yoshida Shigeru, Last Meiji Man, Lanham, Rowman and Littlefield, 2007, p 184

43. William Manchester, American Caesar, London, Arrow, 1979, 423-4;

Michael Schaller, The American Occupation of Japan, Oxford University Press, 1985, p 49

44. Michael Schaller, The American Occupation of Japan, Oxford University Press, 1985, p 49; Yoshida Shigeru, Last Meiji Man, Lanham, Rowman and Littlefield, 2007, p 168

45. Yoshida Shigeru, Last Meiji Man, Lanham, Rowman and Littlefield, 2007, p 173

46. Michael Schaller, The American Occupation of Japan, Oxford University Press, 1985, p 49-52; Yoshida Shigeru, Last Meiji Man, Lanham, Rowman and Littlefield, 2007, p 177-8

47. Yoshida Shigeru, Last Meiji Man, Lanham, Rowman and Littlefield, 2007, p 185, 189, 193-6; Mark Caprio, Yoneyuki Sugita, Democracy in Occupied Japan, London, Routledge, 2007, p 15

48. Mark Caprio, 'Resident Aliens', in Mark Caprio, Yoneyuki Sugita, Democracy in Occupied Japan, London, Routledge, 2007, p 188-9; Yoshida Shigeru, Last Meiji Man, Lanham, Rowman and Littlefield, 2007, p 190

30. World War to Cold War

1. Quintin Hogg. 'British Policy—A Conservative Forecast' Foreign Affairs October 1943

2. John Adamson, 'Post War Preview',Fourth International, Vol.4 No.10, October 1943, pp.297-300, http://www.marxists.org/history/etol/writers/cochran/1943/10/preview.htm

3. David Kennedy, Freedom from Fear, Oxford University Press, 1999, 622

4. Paul Kennedy, Rise and Fall of the Great Powers, Fontana, 1990, 475

5. Charles S. Maier, The Cold War in Europe: era of a divided continent, Princeton N.J., Markus Wiener, 1996, p 109

6. John Gimbel, Origins of the Marshall Plan, Stanford University Press, 1976, p 1

7. Antony Carew, Labour under the Marshall Plan, Manchester University Press, 1987, p 12

8. in DeConde et al, Encyclopedia of US Foreign Policy, New York, Macmillan, 1978, p. 278

9. Patricia Meehan, A Strange Enemy People, London, Peter Owen, 2001, p 273

10. Derek Aldcroft, The European Economy 1914-2000, London,

Routledge, 2001 p 114; James Wood, European Economic Community, 1975, p 10

11. Geoff Pugh 'Economic reforms in Germany', in T. Lange and J.R. Shackleton (eds) The Political Economy of German Reunification, Oxford, Bergahn 1998; Fratiani and Spinelli, A Monetary History of Italy, Cambridge University Press, 1997, p 160-1

12. Dean Acheson, Present at the Creation, New York, WW Norton, 1969, p 147

13. Charter of the International Trade Organisation, Article Fifteen, Havana, 24 March 1948; Jacob Viner, The Customs Union Issue, New York, Carnegie Endowment for Peace p 133

14. Averell Harriman and Elie Abel, Special Envoy, New York, Random House, 1975, p 281

15. Carolyn Eisenberg, Drawing the Line, Cambridge University Press, 1996, p 382

16. 10 Dec 1947, in Carolyn Eisenberg , Drawing the Line, Cambridge University Press, 1996, p 359

17. Dean Acheson, Present at the Creation, New York, Norton, 1969, p 291

18. John Iatrides and Linda Wrigley, Greece at the Crossroads, Pennsylvania State University Press, 1995, p 4

19. William Blum, Killing Hope, London, Zed Books, 2003, p 30-32

20. Peter Pulzer, German Politics, 1945-1995, Oxford University Press, 1995, p 43

21. Roy Jenkins, Truman, London, Collins, 1986, p 87

22. Robert Donovan, Conflict and Crisis, 1977, New York, W. W. Norton, p 236

23. Spaak, The Continuing Battle: Memoirs of a European, 1936-1966., London, Weidenfeld and Nicolson 1971, p 222

24. Paul Hockenos, Joschka Fischer and the Making of the Berlin Republic, Oxford University Press, 2008, p 40, quoting Ruud Koopmans

25. Maria Cowles et al, Transforming Europe: Europeanisation and domestic change, Ithaca: Cornell University Press 2001, p 103

26. David Marsh, The Bundesbank: The Bank that rules the World, London: William Heinemann, 1992, p 49

27. William O. Douglas, Neither to Right Nor Left, CIO Publications, Washington, 1948, p 4

28. Carolyn Eisenberg, Drawing the Line, Cambridge University Press, 1996, p 156

29. Ted Morgan, A Covert Life, New York, Random House, 1999, p 139

30. Ted Morgan, A Covert Life, New York, Random House, 1999, p 179

31. Ted Morgan, A Covert Life, New York, Random House, 1999, p 181

32. in Val Rogin Lorwin, The French Labour Movement, Oxford University Press, 1954, p 121

33. Ted Morgan, A Covert Life, New York, Random House, 1999, p 180-3

34. Hansard, 28 September 1949, col. 271

35. Peter Taafe and Tony Mulhearn, Liverpool: A City that Dared to Fight, London, Fortress, 1988, p 35

36. Peter Pulzer, German Politics, 1945-1995, Oxford University Press, 1995, p 52

37. Mark Mazower, Dark Victory, London, Allen Lane, 1998, p 237

38. Andrew Davies, Where Did the Forties Go? London Pluto Press, 1984, p 72-3

39. Economic Survey of Europe in 1949, p 21

40. Frances Lynch, France and the International Economy, London, Routledge, 1997, p 75

41. Altvater, Elmar et al, 'On the Analysis of Imperialism in the Metropolitan Countries: the West German Example', London, Bulletin of the Conference of Socialist Economists, Spring 1974, p 6, 7, 9

42. Chris Harman, Revolution and Bureaucracy in Eastern Europe, London, Pluto Press, 1974, p 58

43. Jeevan Vasagar and Beate Steinhorst, 'Churchill betrayed East German rising', Guardian 17 June 2003

44. William Blum, Killing Hope, London, Zed Books, 2003, p 21-2

45. Dean Acheson, Present at the Creation, New York, WW Norton, 1969, p 146

46. Jung Chang and Jon Halliday, Mao, London, Jonathan Cape, 2005, p 306; Averell Harriman and Elie Abe, Special Envoy, New York , Random House, 1975, p 541

47. Averell Harriman and Elie Abe, Special Envoy, New York , Random House, 1975, p 540

48. Dean Acheson, Present at the Creation, New York, WW Norton, 1969, p 147

49. Jung Chang and Jon Halliday, Mao, London, Jonathan Cape, 2005, p 322-3; Peng Shu-tse, The Chinese Communist Party in Power, New York, Monad Press, 1980, p 74-5

50. John Gittings, 'Xiong Xianghui', Guardian obituaries, 26 September 2005

51. Peng Shu-tse, The Chinese Communist Party in Power, New York, Monad Press, 1980, p 77

52. Jung Chang and Jon Halliday, Mao, London, Jonathan Cape, 2005, p 320

31. The Intellectuals and the War

1. Pierre Ayçoberry, The Nazi Question, London, Routledge and Kegan Paul, 1981, p 91

2. Eric Hobsbawm, Interesting Times, London, Abacus, 2002, p 418, and see 55

3. Perry Anderson, 'Components of the National Culture', English Questions, London, Verso, 1992

4. Herbert Marcuse, Technology War, and Facism, London, Routledge, 1998, p x

5. Sadly, the 'Tui Novel' was never completed, this account is from Brecht's Journals, London, Methuen, 1993, p 230

6. Bertolt Brecht, Journals, London, Methuen, 1993, p 287; William Scheuerman, Between the Norm and the Exception, Cambridge, Mass., MIT Press, 1994, p 124

7. Rudiger Safranski, Martin Heidegger, Cambridge Mass., Harvard University Press, 1999, p 262

8. July 1933, in Eri Hotta, Pan Asianism and Japan's War, Palgrave Macmillan 2007, p 147

9. July 1933, in Eri Hotta, Pan Asianism and Japan's War, Palgrave Macmillan 2007, p 154

10. See Graham Barnfield, 'Federal Arts Policy and Political Legitimation', in Nancy Beck Young; William D. Pederson; Byron W. Daynes (eds), Franklin D. Roosevelt and the Shaping of American Political Culture, Armonk, ME Sharpe, 2001

11. Hague and Hennessy, How Adolf Hitler reformed Whitehall. Strathclyde Papers on Government and Politics 41, 1985

12. John Sutherland, Stephen Spender, London, Viking, 2004, p 285; Victor Farias, Heidegger and Nazism Philadelphia, Temple

University, 1989, p 159

13. CEMA Bulletin 41, August 1945, my emphasis

14. Horizon, December 1942, in Robert Hewison, Under Siege: Literary Life in London 1939-45, London, Quartet Books, 1979, p 165

15. Michael Ignatieff, Isaiah Berlin: A life, London Vintage 2000, p 227

16. Laurel Fay, Shostakovich, Oxford University Press, 2000, p 132-3

17. George Steiner, Lukacs after Communism, Eva Corredor (ed) Duke University Press, 1997, p 70

18. Robert Fishman, Urban Utopias in the Twentieth Century: Ebenezer Howard, Frank Lloyd Wright, Le Corbusier, MIT Press, 1982, p 246

19. Zeynep Çelik, 'Le Corbusier, Orientalism, Colonialism', Assemblage No. 17, April 1992, p 66

20. Quoted in Ian Birchall, Sartre against Stalinism, Bergahn, 2004, p 42

21. Quoted in Ian Birchall, Sartre against Stalinism, Bergahn, 2004, p 43; See Hazel Rowley, The Lives and Loves of Simone de Beauvoir and Jean-Paul Sartre, London, Chatto and Windus, 2006, p 119 for Sartre's Heidegger studies in the prisoner-of-war camp

22. Ross Russell, Bird Lives! Da Capo Press, New York, 1996, p 180; Robin Kelley, Thelonius Monk, New York, Free Press, 2009, p 82

23. Frances Stonor Saunders, Who Paid the Piper?, London, Granta, 2000, p 171

24. Karl Popper, Unending Quest, London, Routledge, 1992, p 105, 107. A friend of mine when a student, confused by Popper's arguments, got his number in Switzerland from International Enquiries and rung him up. 'Do people in England still read my book?' asked the surprised, cracked voice at the other end of the line.

25. Karl Popper, The Open Society and its Enemies, Vol II, London, Routledge, 2002, p 67, 112, 180

26. Frederick Hayek, The Road to Serfdom, London, Routledge Classics, 2001, p 4

27. Clive Ponting, Churchill, London, Sinclair Stevenson 1994 p 718; Hugh Dalton, Hansard, HC Deb 14 February 1946 vol 419, col 660

28. R. G. Collingwood, An Autobiography, Oxford, Clarendon Press, 1991, p 49, 167

29. Rudiger Safranski, Martin Heidegger, Cambridge Mass., Harvard University Press, 1999, p 336, 338

30. Tom Rockmore, On Heidegger's Nazism and Philosophy, London, Harvester, 1992, p 94

31. Rudiger Safranski, Martin Heidegger, Cambridge Mass., Harvard University Press, 1999, p 413

32. Tom Rockmore, On Heidegger's Nazism and Philosophy, London, Harvester, 1992, p 299

33. Rudiger Safranski, Martin Heidegger, Cambridge Mass., Harvard University Press, 1999, p 257, 236, 373

34. Frederic Jameson, Aesthetics and Politics, London, Verso, 1979 p 142; Martin Jay, Adorno, London, 1984, p 44-5; Istvan Meszaros, Power of Ideology, London, Harvester, 1989

35. Jurgen Habermas, , Autonomy and Solidarity: Interviews with Jurgen Habermas, Peter Dews (ed.), London, Verso, 1992, p 81

36. Martin Heidegger, Being and Time, Oxford, Basil Blackwell, 1990, p 166

32. Revising the History of the Second World War

1. Riga, 7 May 2005

2. The Scotsman, 9 May 2005

3. Guardian, 9 May 2005

4. Polityka, 23 March, 2005

5. 17 April 1995

6. The Autobiography, 1999, p 530

7. 9 May 1975

8. 28 April 1965

9. 'Johnson implies DeGaulle Perils Alliances Unity', New York Times, 8 May 1965

10. New York Times, 10 May 1975

11. Guardian, 12 January 1985

12. Guardian, 16 January 1985

13. 'A Message from Moscow', Time, 20 May 1985

14. 18 April 1985

15. 'Reagan Joins Kohl in Brief Memorial at Bitburg Graves', New York Times, 6 May 1985

16. Guardian, 4 June 2004

17. Robert Gildea, 'Myth, memory and policy in France since 1945', in Memory and Power in Post-War Europe, edited by Jan Werner Müller, Cambridge University Press, 2002, p. 62

18. 25 September 1985

19. Snatching defeat from the Jaws of Victory', Living Marxism, June

1994

20. Guardian, 4 June 2004

21. Guardian, 4 June 2004

22. Guardian, 7 June 2004

23. New York Times, 14 August 1955

24. New York Times, 15 August 1955

25. New York Times, 14 August 1955

26. New York Times, 15 August 1965

27. New York Times, 14 August 1965

28. New York Times, 15 August 1975

29. Airforce Magazine, November, 1994

30. Reuters, 7 April 1995

31. Downing Street Press Office, 11 January 1995

32. Daily Mail, 6 January 1995

33. Observer, 14 August 2005

34. 'President Commemorates 60th Anniversary of V-J Day' Office of the Press Secretary, The White House, 30 August 2005

35. Post-War, London, William Heinemann, 2005, p.166

36. see Nina Tumarkin, The Living and the Dead: the rise and fall of the cult of World War Two in Russia, New York, 1994, p 104

37. The New Zealand history available on-line at http://www. nzetc.org/tm/scholarly/tei-corpus-WH2.html; L. de Jong, Het Koninkrijk der Nederlanden in de tweede wereldoorlog, 's-Gravenhage, Staatsuitgeverij, 1969-1976; History of the Great Patriotic War of the Soviet Union. 1941-1945. Wilmington, DE: Scholarly Resources, 1984, a US Army translation of Istoriia Velikaia Otechestvennaia Voiny Sovetskogo Soiuza 1941-1945, published by the Soviet Ministry of Defence

38. Tumarkin, p 104

39. Ian McLaine, Ministry of Morale, London, Allen and Unwin, 1979, p.167

40. Tojo's Japan is commonly called 'Fascist', but in the sense that there was no mass Fascist party in Japan, that is not accurate, see Jon Halliday, The Political History of Japanese Capitalism, New York, Monthly Review Press, 1975, p133-40

41. M. Stalin to Prime Minister, 18 July 1941, in Churchill, The Second World War, Vol. III, 1952, p 309

42. Gabriel Kolko, The Politics of War, New York, Pantheon, 1990, p 16

43. Dutt, Britain in the World Front, Lawrence and Wishart, 1942, p. 2

44. See Silvio Berlusconi's speech 'Who we are', 1998, at http://www.forza-italia.it/notizie/int_2815.htm

45. New York Times, 18 April 1955

46. New York Times, 26 April 1965

47. New York Times, 12 April, 1965

48. New York Times, 7 April 1975

49. Peter Novick, The Holocaust and Collective Memory, London, Bloomsbury, 2001, p 209-10

50. Quoted in Peter Novick, The Holocaust and Collective Memory, London, Bloomsbury, 2001, p 234

51. Novick, The Holocaust and Collective Memory, London, 2001, pp 217-9

52. Barkan, The Guilt of Nations, New York, 2000, p 93

53. As at 1 February 2007. Amazon's total includes duplicate editions, and such is the ubiquity of the term, not all books with Holocaust in the title are about the Nazi Holocaust.

54. Stefan Aust, The Baader-Meinhof Group, London, Bodley Head, 1987, p 251, 235

55. Stasi leader Markus Wolf insisted that though 'only a small minority of Germans were actually guilty', 'all Germans who lived willingly under the Nazis bear a responsibility for them', Memoirs of a Spymaster, London, Pimlico, 1998, 251 - an attitude which no doubt made it easier for him to keep records on so many of his countrymen.

56. Elazar Barkan, The Guilt of Nations, New York, Norton, 2000, p 8

57. Ian Buruma, The Wages of Guilt, London, Jonathan Cape, 1994, p25

58. In Roderick Stackelberg, Sally A. Winkle, Nazi Germany Sourcebook: An Anthology of Texts, London, Routledge, 2002, p 417

59. See Ian Buruma, Wages of Guilt, London, Jonathan Cape, 1994

60. Daniel Goldhagen, Hitler's Willing Executioners, London, Abacus, 1997, especially chapter two

61. See Ruth Bettina Burn's "Revising the Holocaust," The Historical Journal, 40.1 (1997); Birn and Norman Finkelstein, A Nation on Trial: the Goldhagen Thesis and Historical Truth, 1998

62. John Major, Autobiography, London, Harper Collins 1999: 175; Timothy Garton Ash, 'The Chequers Affair', New York Review of

Books, Volume 37, Number 14, 27 September 1990

63. Tony Barber, 'The Alf Garnet Version of History' London Independent, 7 October 1996; Guardian, 4 May 2005

64. Guardian, 9 December 2002

65. Observer 18 December 2005; and see Tristram Hunt, 'Conscription of the past', Guardian, 11 June 2005; Guardian 15 February 2005

66. AJP Taylor, A Personal History, London, Coronet, 1984, p 298; AJP Taylor, Origins of the Second World War, Harmondsworth, Penguin, Harmondsworth, 1977, p 7

67. AJP Taylor, Origins of the Second World War, Harmondsworth, Penguin, Harmondsworth, 1977, p 13

68. in E M Robertson, The Origins of the Second World War, London, Macmillan, 1971, p 86, 85, 99

69. in E. M. Robertson, The Origins of the Second World War, London, Macmillan, 1971, p 221

70. AJP Taylor, A Personal History, London, Coronet, 1984, p 299, 300

71. AJP Taylor, Origins of the Second World War, Penguin, Harmondsworth, 1977, p 9

72. in E. M. Robertson, The Origins of the Second World War, London, Macmillan, 1971, p 106

73. in E. M. Robertson, The Origins of the Second World War, London, Macmillan, 1971, p 139

74. Eric Hobsbawm, Age of Extremes, Michael Joseph Ltd, 1994, p 36

75. AJP Taylor, A Personal History, London, Coronet, 1984, p 301

76. AJP Taylor, Origins of the Second World War, Harmondsworth, Penguin, Harmondsworth, 1977, p 9

77. E.H. Carr, International Relations Between the World Wars 1919-1939, London, Macmillan Press, 1986, (Orig. International Relations Since the Peace Treaties, 1937) p 262-3

78. E. H. Carr, Twenty Years Crisis, London, Macmillan, 1946, p 83-4

79. William Appleman Williams Tragedy of American Diplomacy (1959) was the first of the critical New Left histories of the Second World War See Robert Maddox, The New Left and the Origins of the Cold War, Princeton UP, 1973, for a conservative critique of Williams

80. 'Counter-Insurgency...', in David Horowitz (ed) Containment and Revolution, London, Anthony Blond, 1967, p 141

81. Less celebrated today, but an important innovator in this historical

revision of the Second World War, was David Horowitz, whose Free World Colossus (1965), edited collection Containment and Revolution (1967) and Empire and Revolution (1969) took the shine off the western Allies conduct of the World War, looking through the prism of the Cold War, and Vietnam. His subsequent recantation of his radical past to embrace Conservatism has tended to put people off of his researches of the 1960s.

82. It is an alternative account that continues to be rehearsed in such books as Thomas Fleming's The New Dealers' War (2002) and John Flynn's The Roosevelt Myth (1990)

83. Jon Halliday and Gavan MCormack, Japanese Imperialism Today, Harmondsworth, Penguin, 1973, p 21-4

84. Julie Summers, The Colonel of Tamarkan, London, Simon and Schuster, 2005, p 359

85. Elazar Barkan, The Guilt of Nations, New York, Norton, 2000, p 55

86. Elazar Barkan, The Guilt of Nations, New York, Norton, 2000, p 60

87. Elazar Barkan, The Guilt of Nations, New York, Norton, 2000, p 62

88. See Daniel Nassim, 'Still Bashing the Japs', Living Marxism issue 83, October 1995

89. see Charles Delzell, 'The Italian anti-Fascist Resistance in Retrospect: Three Decades of Historiography', Journal of Modern History, 47, March 1975, p 77

90. See Carlo Feltrinelli, Feltrinelli: A Story of Riches, Revolution, and Violent Death, Harcourt. 2002

91. See Andreas Papandreou, Paternalistic Capitalism, 1972, Minneapolis, University of Minnesota, 124-6; Constantine Tsoucalas, The Greek Tragedy, 1969

92. Timothy Snyder, 'Memory over sovereignty and sovereignty over memory: Poland, Lithuania and Ukraine, 1939-1999', in Muller, Memory and Power in Post War Europe, Cambridge University Press, 2002

93. Stevan Pavlowitch, Tito - Yugoslavia's Great Dictator: A Reassessment, Ohio State University, Press, 1992;

94. Robert Paxton, Vichy France: Old Guard and New Order 1940-1944, Columbia University Press, 1982 (orig. 1972), p142

95. Adam Nossiter, The Algeria Hotel: France, Memory and the Second World War, London, Methuen, 2001, p. 10

96. And see Susan Zuccotti's Under His Very Windows: The Vatican

and the Holocaust in Italy, 2000

97. Japanese American Citizens League, The Japanese American Incarceration: A Case for Redress, San Francisco, 1978; Roger Daniels, and Eric Foner. (Eds.) Prisoners Without Trial: Japanese Americans in World War II, Hill & Wang Publishers, 1993; Erica Harth (Ed.), Last Witnesses: Reflections on the Wartime Internment of Japanese Americans, New York: Palgrave Macmillan, 2001; Lawson Fusao Inada, Only What We Could Carry: The Japanese American Internment Experience, Heyday Books, 2000; Alice Yang Murray, What Did the Internment of Japanese Americans Mean? Bedford/St. Martin's, 2000; Jerry Stanley, I Am an American: A True Story of Japanese Internment, Crown Publishing, 1996; Michi Nishiura Weglyn, Years of Infamy: The Untold Story of America's Concentration Camps, Seattle: University of Washington Press, 1996.

98. Tony Rennell, 'Hitler was evil. Our bombs were not', Observer, 31 October 2004

Index

Contemporary culture has eliminated both the concept of the public and the figure of the intellectual. Former public spaces – both physical and cultural – are now either derelict or colonized by advertising. A cretinous anti-intellectualism presides, cheerled by expensively educated hacks in the pay of multinational corporations who reassure their bored readers that there is no need to rouse themselves from their interpassive stupor. The informal censorship internalized and propagated by the cultural workers of late capitalism generates a banal conformity that the propaganda chiefs of Stalinism could only ever have dreamt of imposing. Zer0 Books knows that another kind of discourse – intellectual without being academic, popular without being populist – is not only possible: it is already flourishing, in the regions beyond the striplit malls of so-called mass media and the neurotically bureaucratic halls of the academy. Zer0 is committed to the idea of publishing as a making public of the intellectual. It is convinced that in the unthinking, blandly consensual culture in which we live, critical and engaged theoretical reflection is more important than ever before.